THE HARPERCOLLINS DICTIONARY OF SOCIOLOGY

David Jary and Julia Jary

Series Editor, Eugene Ehrlich

HarperPerennial

A Division of HarperCollins*Publishers*

Please take time to examine these other titles in the
HarperCollins Dictionary series

HarperCollins Dictionary of Art Terms & Techniques
HarperCollins Dictionary of Astronomy & Space Science
HarperCollins Dictionary of Biology
HarperCollins Dictionary of Computer Terms
HarperCollins Dictionary of Economics
HarperCollins Dictionary of Electronics
HarperCollins Dictionary of English Usage
HarperCollins Dictionary of Environmental Science
HarperCollins Dictionary of Mathematics
HarperCollins Dictionary of Music
HarperCollins Dictionary of Sociology
HarperCollins Dictionary of Statistics

Library of Congress Catalog Card Number 91-55446

ISBN 0-06-271543-7
ISBN 0-06-461036-5 (pbk.)

00 01 02 DP/RRD 20 19 18 17 16 15 14 13 12 11

INTRODUCTION

Sociology is not a tidy subject. As the "science of society and social relations," its boundaries are wide and difficult to draw. It overlaps with all other social science disciplines, which, as the general science of society, it must take into account or can even be said to include. Since, in addition, its discourses are also continuous with those of lay society, its subject matter is often controversial and charged by values as well as by disciplinary disputes.

These features and other complexities of the subject are not a weakness of the subject, but are in many ways its strength: the fact that sociology reflects and interacts with real world issues and has no arbitrarily constructed disciplinary closure. However, these complexities do present the compiler of a dictionary of sociology with considerable problems, not least the need to arrive at working criteria of inclusion and exclusion when no one set of criteria is likely to reflect all possible conceptions of the subject. It is important, therefore, to make clear what the criteria have been for this volume. Included are:

(a) major sociological terms and topic areas that have been central in the development of the subject or that are currently important, together with many more minor sociological terms;

(b) entries on other social science disciplines, including key terms from these disciplines where the terms have achieved wide use within sociology;

(c) entries on the most influential sociologists, and entries on major social theorists and philosophers whose influence on the subject has often been on a par with those whose disciplinary links are more explicitly with sociology;

(d) entries on the main research methods used in sociology, including basic statistical terms, together with entries on epistemological and ontological terms and issues that sociology shares with philosophy;

(e) a selection of frequently used "common language" terms in sociology where these are likely to present problems for students.

The breadth of coverage attempted means that the volume includes a greater number of headwords than found in most previous dictionaries of the subject. A further general feature is that, whereas other dictionaries have mostly adopted a discursive approach in communicating the meanings of terms, in this volume a brief definition or definitions immediately follow every headword. This is intended to be useful to the person who wishes to use a dictionary to establish a meaning without having to sort through many paragraphs to arrive at it. This is not to say that the reader will find only short entries in this dictionary. On the contrary, it contains many longer, more encyclopedic entries, but these always begin with initial briefer definitions. It should finally be noted that this dictionary does not set out to be a comprehensive or definitive work of scholarship. For example, it is relatively little concerned with the complex etymologies of terms, or to convey all uses. Rather, its main aim is to function as a study aid.

INTRODUCTION

Using the Dictionary

Entries are arranged in alphabetical order treating all words appearing in the headword as a continuous word—thus, civilizing process precedes civil religion.

Where headwords indicate only a cross reference in small capitals, the location of a definition is usually indicated by the appearance of this headword in italics within the cross-referenced entry.

It should not be assumed that the length of an entry reflects the importance of a term within the subject. This is true of person entries as well as those dealing with individual terms. Material of relevance on a particular entry will often be found in related entries, indicated by small capitals, also used more generally to indicate cross references to key terms defined elsewhere.

Works cited in the text are listed—along with other works of interest—in a general bibliography, which appears at the end of the dictionary, although where the title of the work is given in full in the text, these texts are not always included in the bibliography.

The Contributors

The dictionary is mainly the work of a team of sociologists and social psychologists based at the Department of Sociology at Staffordshire Polytechnic. Outside contributors have also been used where it was felt that this would improve on internal resources.

The general editors, David and Julia Jary, have been assisted by an editorial team of associate editors consisting of Tony Charles, Phil Nicholls, and Alan Sillitoe.

Entries have not been individually signed, since the work is a collective one. The full list of contributors, together with their areas of main contribution, is:

Michael Ball—Anthropology, Interpretive Sociology

Christopher Bryant (University of Salford)—Intellectuals and Intelligentsia

Tony Charles—Industrial Sociology, Sociology of Organizations, New Technology

Rosemary Charles—Strategic Theory

Mike Dent—Industrial Sociology, Sociology of Organizations

Ursula Dobraszczyc—Sociology of Health and Medicine; Mass Media and Mass Culture; Urbanism

David Gatley—Research Methods

Ruth Green—Social Psychology

John Horne—Sociology of Leisure, Sociological Theory

Susie Jacobs (St Mary's College)—Class, Gender

David Jary—General Sociology, Sociological Theory, Philosophy of Science, Methodology, Historical and Comparative Sociology, Religion, Marxism, Class, Political Sociology, Economic Sociology, Higher Education

Julia Jary—Psychology and Social Psychology, Research Methods

Paul Keating (University of Exeter)—Sociological Theory, Historical Sociology, Religion

Derek Longhurst (Dept of Humanities, Staffordshire Polytechnic)—Poststructuralism

Adrian Oldfield (University of Salford)—Political Philosophy

Dianne Phillips (Manchester Polytechnic)—Statistics and Research Methods

John Phillips (Manchester Polytechnic)—Sociological Theory, Philosophy, Language

Jim McAuley (St Mary's College)—Political Sociology

David Newton—Sociology of Education

Phil Nicholls—General and Comparative Sociology, Sociology of Health and Medicine

Steve Outram—Social Policy and Social Welfare, Sociology of the Family, Demography

Martin Parker—Anthropology, Sociological Theory, Philosophy

Alan Roulstone—New Technology

John Shiels—Crime and Deviance, Class and Social Stratification

Alan Sillitoe—Historical and Comparative Sociology, Sociology of Development, Marxism, Socialism and Communism

Gregory Smith (University of Salford)—Interpretive Sociology

Joan Smith—Research Methods

Geof Stanley—Industrial Sociology

Martin Thomas—Social Work, Social Welfare, Family and Marriage

Colin Tipton (University of Surrey)—Marxism, Socialism, Political Sociology

Lorna Warren (University of Salford)—Anthropology

Ruth Waterhouse—Sexuality and Gender, Women's Studies, Feminism, Ethnicity, Urbanism, Culture

Jim Zacune—Ethnicity, Sociology of Higher Education

Acknowledgments

We must also acknowledge the help received from students at Staffordshire Polytechnic; from Andrew Pendleton of the University of Bradford, who read and commented on entries in draft; from Geraldine Nicholls, who assisted with the bibliography and with proofreading; and Jean Wrench and Christine Burton, Secretaries in the Department of Sociology, who assisted with typing and more generally. Finally, we must thank Edwin Moore, our editor at HarperCollins, Ltd., for general assistance, good advice, and considerable patience.

David Jary and Julia Jary

A

abnormal denoting anything deviating from the usual or typical pattern of behavior or social form within a society or group, especially where such deviation can also be viewed as maladjustment, maladaption or DYSFUNCTION (see also FUNCTIONALISM).

Any sociological use of the term faces the problem of determining 'normality'. For example, DURKHEIM made the assumption that the average social form at a particular level of social development was also the functional form. However, whilst conceptions of functional normality and abnormality may be relatively clear in relation to biological organisms, the utility of these concepts in sociology has been widely questioned. With the partial exception of Durkheim and functionalist sociology, sociologists have usually conceptualized individual and social variability and deviation from established patterns of behavior in other ways than in terms of 'normality' and 'abnormality.'

abnormal division of labor see DIVISION OF LABOR.

abortion the artificially induced termination of pregnancy leading to the destruction of the fetus. While abortion, though rarely absent, is officially prohibited in some societies, in many societies, including most modern societies, it is recognized as a legitimate way of terminating unwanted pregnancies. In some modern societies the incidence of recorded abortions approaches that for live births. In recent years, debates about abortion have centered on the rights of mothers as well as the rights of the unborn child. In this way the debate about abortion is also bound up with wider political struggles in modern societies—e.g., ideologies of the New Right, as well as the WOMEN'S LIBERATION MOVEMENT.

absenteeism any absence from work, school, or any social setting in which regular attendance is a normal expectation. Rates of absenteeism are sometimes taken as an indicator of the well-being or otherwise of social organizations.

absentee landowner an owner of agricultural land who lives away from his property and is not directly involved in day-to-day production. Within a PEASANT SOCIETY this form of land ownership can be conducive to the appearance of social and political conflicts between landlords and peasants, as in prerevolutionary France and prerevolutionary China.

absolute poverty that level of poverty defined in terms of the minimum requirements for basic subsistence.

absolutism 1. any political regime in which rulers are unrestrained by custom or the rule of law, and where the exercise of power is arbitrary. **2.** the doctrines justifying such a regime. **3.** the specific state form and related doctrines (for example, divine right of kings) associated with centralizing

European monarchies in the 17th and 18th centuries. **4.** (Marxism) the form of Western European state that precedes the capitalist state.

In reality no ruler possesses absolute power. The conventional view has been that absolute government was a feature of premodern, non-Western states, for example, the Turkish sultanate or Fijian monarchy. However, although arbitrary power and the social mobilization of subject populations (for example, in the building of the pyramids) were a feature of such regimes, the lack of modern technologies of communication and SURVEILLANCE meant that effective power was often severely limited. Historically, Western sociologists and political scientists tended to exaggerate differences between non-European and European constitutional regimes—an aspect of the general ethnocentricism of Western social science, especially in the 19th century.

Western European absolutism was absolutist only in comparison with the feudal monarchies that preceded it and the constitutional monarchies that followed. The Marxist view is that Western European absolutism arose from a balance of power between a traditional landowning aristocracy and a rising bourgeoisie. This enabled monarchs to establish more effective central control, including codified laws, new and more effective standing armies, and more efficient systems of taxation. In practice, restraints on the centralization of political power remained, associated with the continued existence of independently powerful groups and the introduction of new constitutional rights. Debates exist in sociology as to how far absolutism in Europe was an integral element in the rise of Western capitalism, and whether it should be viewed as involving the recasting of feudal aristocratic power (as for ANDERSON, 1974b) or as the onset of modern bourgeois domination (the more conventional Marxist view).

abstracted empiricism a term used by C. Wright MILLS (1959) to refer to those forms of social survey research that involve QUANTITATIVE RESEARCH TECHNIQUES but draw little on the theoretical tradition in sociology and contribute little to sociological understanding. Somewhat unfairly, Mills singled out the work of Paul LAZARSFELD as an exemplar, which he saw as elevating research techniques and the quest for reliability of data at the expense of relevance. See also EMPIRICAL SOCIOLOGY. Compare EMPIRICISM.

accommodation 1. (in race relations) a process in which ethnic groups adjust to each other's existence and coexist without necessarily resolving underlying differences and conflicts. **2.** (more generally, for example, in politics or in domestic life) any individual or group behavior of the above kind. **3.** (as used by the CHICAGO SCHOOL, for example, PARK and Burgess, 1921) a fundamental social process, analogous to biological adaptation, by which societies achieve adjustment to their environments. The vagueness and conservatism of this usage is criticized by Myrdal et al. (1944). **4.** (in PIAGET's theory of child development) one of the mechanisms by which development from one stage to the next is achieved.

accounts the descriptions and justifications offered by social actors for their own conduct, for example, members' rational accounts (see ETHNOMETHODOLOGY) or DEVIANCE DISAVOWALS. While it is a point of principle in forms of sociology such as ethnomethodology or symbolic interactionism to pay close attention to actors' accounts, in other forms of sociology this is not always the case.

acculturation 1. (especially in CULTURAL ANTHROPOLOGY) a process in which contacts between different cultural groups lead to the acquisition of new cultural patterns by one group, or perhaps both groups, with the adoption of all or parts of the other's culture. **2.** any transmission of culture between groups, including transfer between generations, although in this instance the terms ENCULTURATION and SOCIALIZATION are more usual.

accumulation (or expanded or extended reproduction) of capital (Marxism) the process by which capitalism expands by employing labor to create surplus value in order to create new capital, which in turn is used to create further surplus value and further new capital, leading in the long run to a continuous increase in the overall volume of capital.

For Marx, accumulation is the most central imperative and motor of change within a capitalist economy. Unlike Weber, Marx does not see accumulation primarily as a motivational predisposition of capitalists (compare PROTESTANT ETHIC). Rather, it is the essence of capitalism that accumulation must occur, and this is essential for capitalism as a system to survive. Thus any long-term threat to this accumulation is also a threat to capitalism.

acephalous (in SOCIAL ANTHROPOLOGY) (of a society) without formal leadership, for example, with no provision for chief or permanent political authority. See STATELESS SOCIETY.

achieved status any social position gained through personal effort or open competition. As such, achieved status contrasts with ASCRIBED STATUS. See also ACHIEVEMENT, CONTEST AND SPONSORED MOBILITY, PATTERN VARIABLES.

achievement the gaining of social position or social status as the outcome of personal effort in open competition with others, for example, in formal examinations or competition in a market. As such, achievement is contrasted with ascription and ASCRIBED STATUS. See also PATTERN VARIABLES.

While achievement in its widest sense can be seen as a particular feature of modern societies, with an open-class society, for example, one in which careers are open to talents, its opposite, *ascription*, for example, taking over one's father's job, is a feature especially of traditional class-divided societies. However, both modes of allocation of social position and social status will usually exist in any society. One reason for this is that some positions (for example, historically, especially GENDER ROLES) are mainly ascribed, while other positions, for example, where skills or talents required by the society are in short supply, tend to be subject to open competition. Another reason is that there are likely to be ascriptive elements underlying achieved status, for example, the effects of advantages of family background underlying educational achievement. See also FUNCTIONALIST THEORY OF SOCIAL STRATIFICATION, MERITOCRACY, SOCIAL MOBILITY.

achievement motivation a concept, with associated projective tests, introduced by the psychologist D.C. McClelland (1961), that purports to measure individual and cultural differences in the striving for achievement. The concept rests on the hypothesis that the *need for achievement (NAch)* is stimulated by a caring parental relationship, particularly with the mother, which sets high standards of behavior. Achievement motivation is presented as a significant determinant of individual entrepreneurial endeavor and also of different levels of economic development, for example, between developed and underdeveloped societies. This latter assumption is challenged by many sociologists, who regard McClelland as failing to take into account major differences in the social and economic structures of societies apart from achievement motivation.

act *(vb.)* **1.** to carry out or perform any unit or sequence of social behavior. See ACTION. **2.** to play or act out social roles as if on a stage. See DRAMATURGY. *(n.)* **1.** any unit of ACTION or behavior. **2.** the accomplished act rather than the process of social action (Schutz, 1972). See also ACTION.

action 1. any unit or sequence of social activity or behavior, for example, the action of a labor union or government, as well as the action of an individual. **2.** any unit or sequence of individual social activity that is intentional or purposive and involves conscious deliberation rather than merely being the result of a biological reflex.

For Weber, *meaningful social action* consists of any course of action in which subjective meaning guides the action and where this action is oriented toward others. For a symbolic interactionist, such as BLUMER (1969), that actors act, rather than merely react, is a decisive feature of human action (see ACTION THEORY, SYMBOLIC INTERACTIONISM). See also TYPES OF SOCIAL ACTION.

Sociologists are divided as to whether social reality is better explained with reference to individual purposive action (see ACTION THEORY AGENCY, METHODOLOGICAL INDIVIDUALISM, MEANINGFUL UNDERSTANDING AND MEANINGFUL EXPLANATION) or as the outcome of SOCIAL STRUCTURE (see also STRUCTURALISM). There are also those sociologists (see SOCIAL PHENOMENOLOGY, ETHNOMETHODOLOGY, SCHUTZ, GARFINKEL) who argue that action theorists as well as structuralists have failed to show how actors' meanings are actually constituted.

The debate about social action in these terms is one of the most central in modern sociological theory. Various attempts have been made to reconcile action theory and structuralist perspective (see PARSONS, STRUCTURATION THEORY, STRUCTURE AND AGENCY, GIDDENS). While no consensus exists that these attempts are entirely successful, there is an increasing recognition that sociological explanations must include reference to both action and structure (see DOUBLE HERMENEUTIC and DUALITY OF STRUCTURE).

action approach an approach within INDUSTRIAL SOCIOLOGY that stresses the influence of actors' overall orientations to work, including those emanating from beyond the workplace. The approach presents itself as a reaction against those that are more deterministic, including the SOCIOTECHNICAL SYSTEMS APPROACH. See also ORGANIZATION, ORGANIZATION THEORY.

action research a form of research carried out with the aim of inducing changes in social activities (for example, increased participation in cultural events), but with the aim of also studying these changes.

action theory a general orientation to sociological analysis particularly associated with the work of WEBER and the SYMBOLIC INTERACTIONISTS (see also ETHNOMETHODOLOGY). The aim of the approach is the MEANINGFUL UNDERSTANDING AND EXPLANATION of social reality, which is seen as the outcome of purposive social action. See ACT, ACTION, VERSTEHEN, INTERPRETIVE SOCIOLOGY.

While all action theorists regard explanation with reference to actors' meanings (purposes, values, etc.) as an essential first step in sociological explanations, this is seen by some (notably P. WINCH, 1958) as removing all possibility of more general explanations. For most sociologists, including Weber, meaningful explanation and other types of EXPLANATION are complementary forms. See also STRUCTURATION THEORY.

Although it is sometimes suggested that action theory is irredeemably individualistic, this is only so in some cases (for example, METHODOLOGICAL INDIVIDUALISM). That the contrary can be true is illustrated by the work of Weber (especially his comparative studies of European and Asiatic religions). Nevertheless, there remain significant differences between action theory and other more avowedly STRUCTURALIST approaches in sociological theory, for example, in the degree of voluntarism or independent AGENCY seen for social actors.

activism active involvement as a member of a political party, PRESSURE GROUP, or related political organization, for example, a labor union activist. Theories and research concerned with *political activism* suggest that the tendency is for activists generally to be of higher social status, more socially confident and also often better informed than most nonactivists. Levels of political activism obviously also vary according to political circumstances. For example, in times of political crisis many people may be drawn into politics who would not normally be politically active. Some theorists, especially in POLITICAL SCIENCE (for example, LIPSET, 1959), have suggested that in Western societies high levels of political activity and less informed participants in such circumstances may pose a threat to the stability of democracy. More generally in sociology, however, an increasing tendency to participation in politics by members of lower status minority groups (for example, urban social movements) is regarded as a welcome development. See also OPINION LEADER (AND OPINION LEADERSHIP), TWO-STEP FLOW IN MASS COMMUNICATIONS, STABLE DEMOCRACY, SOCIAL MOVEMENTS.

actor see SOCIAL ACTOR.

adaptation the way in which social systems of any kind (for example, a family group, business firm, nation-state) manage or respond to their environment. According to Talcott PARSONS, adaptation is one of four FUNCTIONAL PREREQUISITES that all social systems must satisfy if they are to survive. He argues that in industrial societies the need for adaptation is satisfied through the development of a specialized subsystem, the economy. See also NEOEVOLUTIONISM.

ad hoc hypothesis any hypothesis added to an explanatory theory merely to save that theory from potentially refuting evidence. In Popper's FALSIFICATIONISM, ad hoc hypotheses are regarded as illegitimate. He cites Marx and Freud as examples of social thinkers using hypotheses in this way to protect their theories from refutation.

adolescence the stage in the LIFE COURSE between childhood and adulthood marked by the beginnings of adult sexuality but coming before full adult status or final detachment from the family of origin.

In simple societies the passage from childhood to adulthood is often marked by rites of passage (see RITUAL), or by the provision of young men's (and less often young women's) AGE SETS. However, it is within modern societies, with their distinctive emphasis on YOUTH CULTURE, fostered by the mass media of communication, that adolescence has achieved a particular importance. In these societies, in contrast with more TRADITIONAL SOCIETIES, adolescents must choose their CAREERS and sexual partners as well as their general lifestyle. Thus adolescence, the time of educational choices and entry into work, is also a stage in the life cycle which is associated with individual experimentation in sexual and leisure behavior. It may also be a time for questioning received values, and of rebellion against parental patterns of behavior (see also GENERATION). The search for independence, and the heightened sense of self-awareness and uncertainty about SELF, can also lead to psychological crisis and psychological disturbance. See also YOUTH UNEMPLOYMENT, DELINQUENCY.

Adorno, Theodor (1903–1969), German social philosopher, sociologist, musicologist, and a leading member of the FRANKFURT SCHOOL OF CRITICAL THEORY. His epistemological writings and his critique of modern society and mass culture have been especially influential. Expelled from Germany by the Nazis in 1934, he went first to England and then to the US, where he remained until 1949, when he returned to Germany. In America, Adorno participated in a famous empirical research project, *The Authoritarian Personality* (Adorno et al., 1950), which involved studies of racial prejudice, nationalism, and authoritarianism. In 1959 he became director of the Institute of Social Research, which had returned to Frankfurt from the US.

Adorno wrote more than 20 books on philosophy, music literature, AESTHETICS, social psychology, and sociology. His critique of capitalism particularly focused on the commercialization and perversion of culture by the culture industry. Popular music, for example, produced solely to sell in the marketplace, was standardized and mechanical and served as a social cement for the existing system. Adorno's concern with repressive systems of thought and organization in what he called the "administered world" led him to articulate opposition to traditional epistemological ideas as well as to advocate radical change in society. In his epistemological writings, for example, *Negative Dialectics* (1973), Adorno proposed the dissolution of any theoretical frameworks and conceptual distinctions that threaten to become dogmas, including Marxism. Thus, aspects of his thinking anticipated the later post-empiricist movement in epistemology (compare FEYERABEND). Both EMPIRICISM and POSITIVISM were rejected by Adorno, who regarded them as betraying reason and as no longer leading to enlightenment. Commentators on Adorno's life and work have regarded his stance as increasingly pessimistic and elitist, issues taken up by later representatives of the Frankfurt school, notably HABERMAS. Other important works by Adorno are *Dialectic of Enlightenment* (with Horkheimer) (1960), *Philosophy of Modern Music* (1973), and *The Jargon of Authenticity* (1973). See also BENJAMIN, METHODENSTREIT.

advanced capitalism (Marxism) the hypothetical final stage in the development of capitalism, which is characterized by concentration of ownership and by increased state intervention in the economy. The latter arises from the need to control the effects of increasing economic and social CONTRADICTIONS and increasing tendency to economic crisis. This is seen as culminating in a final crisis and revolution, and a transition to socialism.

advertising the process and the means (press, film, TV, etc.) by which the availability and the qualities of commodities and services are notified to a wider public. Drawing on SEMIOLOGY, Jean BAUDRILLARD (1970) has argued that in modern societies consumption entails the "active manipulation of the sign," so that the sign and the commodity have come together in the production of the "commodity-sign."

It is in such a context that the power of advertising has been a central issue in modern sociology. In a popular sociological exposé, *The Hidden Persuaders* (1957), Vance Packard painted a picture of an armory of psychological and sociological advertising techniques that made these techniques appear all-powerful. In the 1950s, the novelist J.B. Priestley coined the term *admass* to describe the drive to consumption which was fueled by mass advertising in modern societies. Packard also argued that advertising promotes consumption as a solution to personal and political problems. Advertising creates false needs, which are met in a fundamentally unsatisfying way by conspicuous consumption, in the belief that well-being and peace of mind are provided by the purchase of commodities.

Against such views, more conventional paradigms in media research have often argued that barriers to mass communications, for example group opinion, exist which act as a protective screen against any too easy manipulation (see TWO-STEP FLOW IN MASS COMMUNICATIONS). Feminist theories of advertising have taken another line, stressing its frequent sexism, an aspect of its more general recourse to gender, ageist, and racist STEREOTYPES.

aesthetics (philosophy) the study of art and artistic appreciation. Among the topics considered by aesthetics is the extent to which our experience and appreciation of art are similar to or different from our experience and understanding of nature. A further question is whether the inherent qualities of the thing perceived or the contemplative experience itself is decisive in the experience.

In the work of the FRANKFURT SCHOOL OF CRITICAL THEORY (for example, BENJAMIN) or postmodernists (see POSTMODERNISM AND POSTMODERNITY), the focus of aesthetics has been relocated and radically expanded to include, as Lash (1990) puts it, "aesthetic signifiers in the flotsam and jetsam of everyday life." In this, the political nature of the aesthetic is increasingly affirmed and there is a refusal to see art as a separate order of life. This has the effect of making aesthetics more central to the sociology of mass culture. See also SOCIOLOGY OF ART.

affect (*n.*) feeling or emotion. A term used to denote the emotional or feeling side of mental experience, as opposed to the cognitive or thinking aspect. See also AFFECTIVE DISORDERS.

affective disorders disorders of mood or of the emotions. Disorders of the emotions, such as depression or anxiety, are termed "affective disorders."

affective involvement see PATTERN VARIABLES.

affective neutrality PATTERN VARIABLES.

affectual action see TYPES OF SOCIAL ACTION.

affinal (of a kin relationship) arising from a link by marriage, for example, father-in-law/son-in-law is an affinal relationship, whereas the father-son relationship is a relationship of DESCENT. See also KINSHIP.

affirmative action see POSITIVE DISCRIMINATION.

affluent society 1. (GALBRAITH, *The Affluent Society*, 1958) an account of US society in the late 1950s as a society in which basic economic scarcity and insecurity had been substantially conquered, but where private affluence was accompanied by so-called public squalor (for example, producing cars in abundance, but disregarding road improvement and pollution control), and where poor provision was made for the casualties of capitalism. If increasing state expenditure in the 1960s and 1970s led to a departure from this pattern, monetarism and the changing political climate of the late 1970s and the 1980s has again tipped the balance against state provision. Echoes of Galbraith's concerns exist, however, in the importance of environmental issues in modern politics (see GREEN MOVEMENT). **2.** a description of British society, especially in the mid-1950s and early 1960s, in which it was assumed that rising living standards were leading to profound changes in social attitudes, including a decline in traditional working-class support for the Labor Party. See also AFFLUENT WORKER, EMBOURGEOISE-MENT THESIS, CLASS IMAGERY.

affluent worker the new type of affluent manual worker (see AFFLUENT SOCI-ETY), said to be distinguished by new patterns of voting behavior and detachment from traditional working-class loyalties and movement from traditional working-class locations. This EMBOURGEOISEMENT THESIS, however, was challenged in a major study of the CLASS LOCATIONS and CLASS IMAGERY of industrial workers by GOLDTHORPE, LOCKWOOD, et al. (1968a & b, 1969).

age group any social grouping based on age. In some simple societies age groupings (see AGE SETS) have formed a crucial basis of social organization, but age groupings of varying kinds have significance within societies of all types, for example, the over-65s.

ageism any process or expression of ideas in which STEREOTYPING of and/or DISCRIMINATION against people occurs by virtue of age. Ageism applies especially to such actions directed against older people, but the term may also be employed to refer to unreasonable stereotyping or discrimination against anyone where this occurs simply by virtue of age.

agency 1. the power of ACTORS to operate independently of the determining constraints of SOCIAL STRUCTURE. The term is intended to convey the volitional, purposive nature of human activity as opposed to its constrained, determined aspects. Although used in widely different ways, it is especially central in METHODOLOGICAL INDIVIDUALISM, ETHNOMETHODOLOGY, PHE-NOMENOLOGY, and SYMBOLIC INTERACTIONISM. The importance of human intention—possibly also FREE WILL—thus emphasized, places the individual at the center of any analysis and raises issues of moral choice and political capacity. The political problematic is expressed by GOULDNER counterposing "man on his back" with "man fighting back" (1973), but the classic essay is Dawe's (1971) "The Two Sociologies." **2.** any human action, collective or structural as well as individual, that makes a difference in social outcome; thus, for GIDDENS (1984), agency is equivalent to POWER. In this way Giddens opposes any simple polarization of "structure" and "agency." This is related to his view that STRUCTURE must be seen as "enabling" as well as "constraining" (see also STRUCTURE AND AGENCY, DUALITY OF STRUCTURE).

agency and structure see STRUCTURE AND AGENCY.

Age of Enlightenment the period of intellectual ferment leading up to the French Revolution, which was distinguished by a fundamental questioning of traditional modes of thought and social organization, and sought to replace these with an exclusive reliance on human reason in determining social practices. Many thinkers and philosophers were associated with these developments, among them Voltaire (1694–1778), MONTESQUIEU,

Holbach (1723–89), Helvétius (1715–71), Diderot (1719–84), and Rousseau. The movement was not confined to France; it also embraced numerous other thinkers abroad, including members of the so-called Scottish Enlightenment, such as Adam FERGUSON and John Millar, whose work was especially sociological. Despite a common accord on the importance of reason in human affairs, major differences of view existed between thinkers: Voltaire popularized English liberal doctrines of NATURAL RIGHTS; Holbach and Helvétius took these doctrines further and argued for UTILITARIANISM and representative government; and Rousseau's concept of the SOCIAL CONTRACT led to holistic conceptions of state and society realized in the French Revolution. In retrospect, much Enlightenment thought is seen as superficial, lacking an adequate empirical research base, and above all overconfident about human PROGRESS and the ultimate trumph of reason. However, the Enlightenment era signaled a final decisive break between traditional and modern thought, and between traditional and modern forms of social organization. See also COMTE, RATIONALISM.

age sets age-related corporate social groupings, more usually of men, which form an important basis of social organization, especially within segmentary societies. Such age sets create a pattern of social relationships, crosscutting KINSHIP or DESCENT, that perform ceremonial sociopolitical and economic functions, which may include the ownership of property.

aggregate 1. *(n.)* any collection of units or parts, however temporary or fortuitous; thus, the contrast may sometimes be drawn between mere aggregates, with no internal structure or basis for persistence, and GROUPS, COMMUNITIES, etc., which will usually possess clear internal structure, coherence, cohesion, and relative persistence. **2.** *(vb.)* the collecting or assembling of individuals, groups, or institutions to form a whole.

aggregate data analysis any form of analysis that employs available bodies of published or other data (for example, demographic data, suicide statistics as used by DURKHEIM) describing the characteristics of an entire population or similar aggregate of individuals. The attraction of this mode of research is that large quantities of data, including cross-cultural data, are available at little cost. The main disadvantage is that the researcher may have little awareness of how the original data were collected. See also ECOLOGICAL OR WRONG LEVEL FALLACY, OFFICIAL STATISTICS, SECONDARY ANALYSIS, CICOUREL.

aggregate level fallacy see ECOLOGICAL OR WRONG LEVEL FALLACY.

aggregation the process of combining diverse political interests to form a more or less coherent set of policies that can form a political program. In representative democracies, according to Almond (1953), this function is especially undertaken by political parties, whereas the related function of *interest articulation* is carried particularly by interest groups and PRESSURE GROUPS.

aggression a hostile mental attitude or type of action. Aggression is seen in behavior intended to harm another either physically or verbally. In humans, aggressive behavior is generally underlain by emotions such as anger or fear.

This is an area in which ETHOLOGY and PSYCHOANALYSIS as well as sociology have shown great interest, with the result that aggressive behavior can be seen to have three possible situation determinants:

(a) *(Ethology)* in the animal kingdom certain environmental stimuli (releasing mechanisms) may evoke aggression, for example, the presence of another male robin in a robin's territory;

(b) *(Psychoanalysis)* frustration in obtaining one's goals may lead to aggression, not necessarily directed at the source of the frustration. The frustration-aggression theory of prejudice (Adorno et al., 1950) is related to this theory (see FRUSTRATION-AGGRESSION HYPOTHESIS, AUTHORITARIAN PERSONALITY);

(c) aggression may be a learned response, that is, behavior that has been conditioned because it has led to positive results for the individual when displayed in certain situations in the past.

aging the chronological process of growing physically older. However, there is also a social dimension in which chronology is less important than the meanings attached to the process. Different cultural values and social expectations apply according to gender and age group, and therefore there are socially structured variations in the personal experience of aging.

EISENSTADT *(Generation to Generation, 1964)* studied the political role of age groups and argued that age stratification is an important stabilizing influence in societies where (a) two sets of values coexist within the social structure—the particularism of family ties and the universalism of the public division of labor (here age groups act as buffers between the public and the private domain and give members solidarity and support as well as orienting them to the adult world of work), and (b) where the opportunity for the young to have full participation in adult society is blocked by systems of KINSHIP and DESCENT (here the age group becomes the basis for status and also power struggles between the generations).

In demography, the terms *aging society* and *youthful society* are used to indicate the age composition of the population. A youthful society is one in which there is a preponderance of people in young age groups (under 15 years) because of a high birth rate and low life expectancy. An aging society is one in which reductions in the birth rate and greater longevity have resulted in a rising proportion of the population belonging to the older age groups. For example, CENSUS data for Great Britain show that in 1911 men over 65 and women over 60 constituted 6.8% of the population, whereas in 1981 they constituted 17.7%. In the US, AGEISM has become a political issue through the emergence of movements, such as the Gray Panthers, determined to safeguard the citizen rights of older people and counter the negative imagery of old age promoted by the commercialization of youth.

AGRARIAN SOCIETY

The growing proportion of older people in the population and the spread of early retirement have led to age being perceived as a social problem. Older people are subject to negative STEREOTYPING and diminished SOCIAL STATUS. Even academic discourse promotes negative imagery through such terms as "burden of dependency" and "dependency ratio," which refer to the number of economically inactive older people in relation to the number of economically active younger people whose labor provides the services consumed by the older generation. See also YOUTH CULTURE.

agrarian society any form of society, especially traditional societies, primarily based on agricultural production and associated crafts rather than on industrial production. The major preindustrial civilizations, for example, preindustrial Europe, China, and India, were predominantly agrarian societies. Sometimes simpler societies, for example, HUNTER-GATHERERS, which are not based on settled agriculture are referred to as *preagrarian* (see Hall, 1985).

agribusiness 1. agriculture when conducted as a capitalist business enterprise. **2.** economic activities closely related to or directly dependent on agriculture, including the production of producer goods for agriculture (for example, farm machinery and fertilizers) as well as the sale of agricultural produce as food and raw materials.

agricultural revolution 1. the transition from HUNTER-GATHERER to settled agricultural societies, which occurred in the Middle East about 10,000 years ago, bringing about the domestication of animals and the cultivation of crops. Whether, as some theorists suggest, this agricultural revolution was the result of necessity born out of a depletion of naturally occurring supplies of food, the likelihood is that the transition occurred more than once, since patterns of transition that are apparent in the New World show marked differences from those in the Old World. **2.** innovations in agricultural production and organization leading to increased food and other crop production associated with the transition from AGRARIAN to INDUSTRIAL SOCIETY. The example of Europe, and England in particular, is often used as the model. Transformations in agricultural production in the 17th and 18th centuries were associated with increased population, improvements in diet, and growing urbanization. This is seen as one of the factors making possible the INDUSTRIAL REVOLUTION in Europe. Important changes continued throughout the 19th and 20th centuries, with increases in agricultural productivity and a long-term decline in the proportion of the working population engaged in agriculture.

algorithm any method, procedure, or set of instructions for carrying out a task by means of a precisely specified series of steps or sequence of actions, for example, as in long division, the hierarchical sequence of steps in a typical computer program, or the steps in a manufacturing process.

alienation 1. an individual's feelings of estrangement from a situation, group or culture, etc. **2.** a concept used by MARX in his early work in reference to the core relationships of capitalist production and their human and psychological effects. **3.** (following from **2.**) a central term in different interpretations of Marx (see below). **4.** as operationalized for empirical work, the term has its best known use in R. Blauner's (1964) comparison of work conditions and work satisfaction.

In religious and philosophical usage, the term dates back to medieval times and can even be found in the classical philosophy of ancient Greece. Modern sociological usage mainly derives from Marx's critique of Hegel's use of the term in Marx's *Economic and Philosophic Manuscripts* (EPM), written in 1844 but not published until 1932, and not widely known until the 1950s. In it Marx gives several meanings and nuances to the term, but with three central elements: philosophical, psychological, and sociological. Unlike Hegel, who uses alienation to contrast the objectivity of nature with human consciousness, Marx emphasizes the importance of the relationship between human beings (in their social relations of production) and nature for social development, and therefore individual development. The psychological, or social psychological, usage is the one most commonly found in popular and in many sociological accounts. At its simplest, this refers to feelings of unhappiness, lack of involvement, or only instrumental involvement with work and with others. In Marx's explanation these individual manifestations of alienation are a product of social relations. The important aspect of the concept is the sociological one. Within capitalism, workers do not work to express themselves, to develop their interests, or to gain intrinsic satisfaction: work is essentially forced and, in work, people are subjected to the demands and discipline of others, the owners of capital. In addition to this emphasis on the relation of the worker to the act of production, Marx also stresses the importance of the relation of workers to the products they produce. Commodities, the objects workers produce, do not belong to them, but to their employers. In effect, in work, people produce wealth and power for a class that oppresses them. Products do not belong to their producers, they are alien objects.

The philosophical element concerns a particular conception of human nature. Marx portrays human nature not as something fixed or eternal, but as a social product. He writes about alienation, or estrangement from "species being," by which he means those characteristics that are specifically human and distinguish human beings from other animals. These human attributes develop socially, through relations of production, and for Marx they have the potential for unlimited development in a favorable system of social relationships. Simply, Marx sees the process of production as central to human development. It follows that a system based on exploitation, one in which workers are estranged from the act of production and from the products they produce, stultifies and dehumanizes. It alienates human beings from "species being" in the sense that it denies any possibility of the development of human potential or creativity, except for a privileged few. Alienation is thus analyzed in terms of the social structure of capitalism, that is, private property, commodity production, and class relations.

Discovery of the EPM by Western scholars transformed sociological approaches to, and interpretations of, Marx's work. Some accounts have emphasized either a continuity between the humanist preoccupations of the EPM and later, more scientific and less overtly philosophical work, or have argued that the earlier work contains a more satisfactory explanation of the human condition than the later. Others point out that Marx deliberately dropped the term "alienation" in his later work, in part so as to distance himself from other German scholars of the time—the so-called Young Hegelians —but also, some argue, because of a rejection of humanist philosophical values. This interpretation is associated in particular with the work of ALTHUSSER, who argues that a fundamental shift in Marx's approach, an "epistemological break," occurs after 1844. This radical change involves the development of scientific concepts rather than philosophical, humanist, or ideological ones. Opponents of this view argue that Marx's notebooks, published as the *Grundrisse,* show a continuing preoccupation with the concept, and also argue that the concept of "commodity fetishism," which is used in *Das Kapital* Vol.1, is in a direct line of descent from "alienation."

In addition to interpretive disputes, some Marxist or Marx-influenced writers have attempted to use the concept in concert with some themes from Freud's work, in writings on FALSE CONSCIOUSNESS and on the ways in which modern consumer capitalism creates "false needs," which have important consequences for working-class politics (for example, FROMM, 1941; MARCUSE, 1964).

Some sociologists and social psychologists have attempted to use the concept empirically. This operationalization has involved the attempt to divest the concept of its political and evaluative dimensions—in effect to translate it from a distinctively Marxist to a sociological framework. The best-known example of this empirical use is R. Blauner's book *Alienation and Freedom,* in which he uses a redefinition of the concept proposed by a social psychologist, M. Seeman. Seeman argued that alienation could be operationalized in five aspects: powerlessness, meaninglessness, normlessness, isolation, and self-estrangement. Blauner attempted to apply this typology, excluding normlessness, to an analysis of historical changes in the organization of work. He argued that in the shift from traditional craft production (for example, the printing industry) to factory production (for example, cotton mills) and then to mass-production techniques (for example, the auto industry), alienation intensifed and the number of alienating jobs increased. However, for Blauner, the further refinement of technology in process production (for example, chemical works) had the effect of reducing alienation by giving workers enhanced feelings of autonomy, control, understanding, and, generally, work satisfaction. Blauner's thesis has been criticized, especially by Marxist sociologists, on a number of grounds. It has been argued that his evidence is inadequate and his interpretation of data partial and one-sided. His work has also been depicted as psychologistic, focusing solely on inferred *feelings* of workers and ignoring the structural analysis of relations of production central to Marx's conception. As a related criticism, his technological determinism is seen as problematic, as is the attempt to strip the concept of its political, critical connotations.

The debates about the importance of the concept in Marx's work, and its usefulness or otherwise in sociology, have produced many fruitful arguments, but the adequacy of applications of alienation operationally in empirical sociological research has not been demonstrated.

allocative power see POWER.

Allport, Gordon (1887–1967), influential US social psychologist who made important contributions to the development of TRAIT THEORY and the study of ATTITUDES and PREJUDICE. He regarded the SELF as a central aspect of the psychology of the individual, with the self and personality seen as always tending to seek internal coherence. In its concern to establish the dimensions of personality and attitudes, he argued, psychology must be careful not to lose sight of the individual. He suggested that motives possess a "functional autonomy," defying a reduction to behavioristic accounts.

alphabet any set of letters or similar signs used in writing in which each letter represents one or more phonemes. Alphabets were not the earliest basis of writing, having evolved from *hieroglyphs,* or picture writing, as used in ancient Egypt, and *syllabaries,* writing whose units were syllables, as in Mycenae and also later in Egypt. The "convergence" of writing with speech, as Quine (1987) terms it, reached its full extent, however, only with the appearance of the alphabet.

alternative culture see COUNTERCULTURE AND ALTERNATIVE CULTURE.

Althusser, Louis (1918–90), French Marxist social philosopher, and theorist within the French Communist Party, whose theories were especially influential in the aftermath of the student activism of 1968 and in the period of the greatest vogue of structuralist thinking in the 1970s. In particular, Althusser opposed humanist and Hegelian movements within Marxism, proposing instead that Marx's mature work—especially *Das Kapital*, with its emphasis on labor power and class contradictions, etc.—should be seen as a scientific theory on a par with that of Galileo or Darwin. Thus, in *For Marx* (1966) and (with E. Balibar) *Reading Capital* (1970), he rejects all suggestions that the Hegelian concept of ALIENATION can have any place in Marx's mature theory. Drawing on the epistemological ideas of the French philosopher of science Gaston Bachelard (1884–1962)—especially his concept of the *problematique*—Althusser's argument was that an EPISTEMOLOGICAL BREAK exists between Marx's early philsophical (and ideological) work and his later scientific theory. Further key concepts in Althusser's account of Marx's theory are the concepts of OVERDETERMINATION—the idea that major changes in society are complex and multiply determined—and his distinction between the ideological and repressive state apparatuses. Together these concepts are Althusser's way of avoiding a vulgar determinism or "economism," in that they allow, first, that the ideological superstructure is *not* merely a reflection of the economy but also in part conditions the existence of it, and, second, that IDEOLOGY must be seen *not* merely as false consciousness but as an important part of real social relations. Similarly, the Marxian concept of *mode of production* is seen as requiring an interpretation so that it is accepted as involving in each concrete case a complex articulation of economic, political, and ideological practices. It is difficult now to convey the extent of the interest that Althusser's somewhat tortuous conceptions attracted for a time. However, the degree of dogmatism in his Marxism, and the fact that his theory solved few concrete issues and soon ran into self-contradiction, have meant that his star has waned—an eclipse compounded, sadly, by his murder of his wife and his subsequent incarceration.

Althusserian Marxism a structuralist version of Marxism fashionable especially in the 1970s, based on the ideas of Louis ALTHUSSER. Promoted the Marxist English journal the *New Left Review,* Althusser's work influenced many theorists, including Stuart Hall, and Hindess and Hirst (1975). A notable criticism of the approach is E.P. Thompson's *The Poverty of Theory* (1978). In opposing Althusser's dogmatism with humanism, however, Thompson exhibits his own kind of dogmatism in resisting arguments for structural analysis. Previous supporters of Althusserian Marxism now look to sociological theory to provide a recognition of the importance of *both* STRUCTURE AND AGENCY, having failed to find this in Althusser's work. See also STRUCTURALISM.

altruism concern for the welfare of others rather than oneself. Altruistic behavior is therefore the opposite of egoistic behavior. It involves intention to help others when used of human behavior, but the fact that some animal behavior is judged to be altruistic indicates that there are two possible bases to a definition: intentionality, and behavioral effects.

The term "altruism" was coined by COMTE, who saw society evolving toward humanistic values through the influence of POSITIVISM. Rushton and Sorrentino (1981) suggest four possible explanations for altruism:

(a) *genetic inheritance:* this is supported by the animal evidence and by the sociobiologist R. Dawkin's (1976) "selfish gene" theory. It proposes that altruistic behavior toward one's kin (for example, maternal behavior) has the effect of preserving one's genes in common;

(b) *cognitive development:* moral reasoning and the ability to take the role of the other (see G.H. MEAD) increase with age;

(c) *social learning:* SOCIALIZATION involves learning from others by observation and modeling;

(d) *prudential behavior:* helping others is likely to encourage reciprocal action from them (see EXCHANGE THEORY).

This last can be seen as dubiously altruistic, since it is likely to involve the strategic calculation of personal benefit, or mutual benefit, rather than purely altruistic action. In these terms all human action could be interpreted as egoistic, but this would be to lose any distinction between altruistic and egoistic behavior.

Psychologists have proposed a personality trait of altruism, that is, helping behavior is more evident in some people than in others. Altruism toward strangers is particularly influential in the philosophy behind the WELFARE STATE, and is illustrated more specifically in Titmuss's analysis of the British Blood Transfusion Service, in which it is seen as a GIFT EXCHANGE AND GIFT RELATIONSHIP. See also COOPERATIVE ORGANIZATION AND COOPERATIVE MOVEMENT. Compare COMPETITION.

altruistic suicide the form of SUICIDE identified by DURKHEIM (1897) as occurring in highly integrated societies and in certain types of social organization where social integration is similarly strong. Examples of altruistic suicide are the euthanasia of the old and infirm as practiced in some simple societies, or suicides of honor (for example, among the military). See also EGOISTIC SUICIDE, ANOMIC SUICIDE.

amplification of deviance see DEVIANCE AMPLIFICATION.

analogy a comparison made to show a degree of similarity, but not an exact identity, between phenomena. In sociology, analogies are often made between social phenomena and mechanical or organic phenomena. This can be seen in classical forms of sociological functionalism in which societies are often seen as machine-like or, more usually, organism-like entities whose parts interrelate and reinforce each other. Although sometimes useful, and perhaps even indispensable in any science, recourse to analogies is often suspect. Assumptions made or relationships imputed (for example, social needs analogous with animal needs) require separate justification. The use of analogies therefore always involves risks. See MODEL.

analysis of variance (ANOVA) (STATISTICS) a procedure used to test whether differences between the MEANS of several groups are likely to be found in the population from which those groups were drawn. An example might be three groups of people with different educational backgrounds for whom the mean wage level has been calculated. ANOVA provides a way of testing whether the differences between the means are statistically significant by dividing the variability of the observations into two types. One type, called "within group" variability, is the VARIANCE within each group in the SAMPLE. The second type is the variability between the group means ("between groups" variability). If this is large compared with the "within group" variability, it is likely that the population's means are not equal.

The assumptions underlying the use of analysis of variance are:

(a) each group must be a RANDOM SAMPLE from a normal population (see NORMAL DISTRIBUTION);

(b) the variances of the groups in the population are equal.

However, the technique is robust and can be used even if the normality and equal variance assumptions do not hold. The random sample condition is nevertheless essential. See also SIGNIFICANCE TEST.

analytical induction a method of analysis (originally formulated by Lindesmith, 1947), used especially in SYMBOLIC INTERACTIONISM and other forms of qualitative sociology, which involves application of a general hypothesis to successive cases, with progressive modification of the generalization to fit all cases (see Robinson, 1951). The researcher formulates a hypothesis to explain a phenomenon and then attempts to search for a decisive negative case. If one is found, the hypothesis is reformulated to include or disallow it, the process being followed until a degree of certainty can be claimed. The method is seen at work in BECKER's study of marijuana usage (Becker, 1953; see also DRUG USAGE FOR PLEASURE). As with any inductive method, the attempt must always be made to seek out contrary cases, but there is never any clear end point when a generalization can be regarded as final (see INDUCTION). See also GROUNDED THEORY.

analytical philosophy a general term for a type of philosophy based on analytic logic that is hostile to metaphysical speculation. It derives from the English empiricism of LOCKE, HUME, and MILL, through the LOGICAL POSITIVISM of the Vienna Circle and the so-called logical atomism of the early WITTGENSTEIN and Russell. The subsequent development of ORDINARY LANGUAGE PHILOSOPHY is usually also included, but it differs in important ways by focusing on language in use and not only in the abstract. These later variants of analytic philosophy are often called linguistic philosophy. See also SPEECH ACTS.

analytic and synthetic (philosophy) the distinction drawn between two types of statement or propositions:

(a) those that are true by virtue of the meanings of the terms they contain, (for example, "all clergymen are male")—*analytic,* or logically *necessary,* truths;

(b) those that are true or false only by virtue of their empirical content, and not logically implied by the meanings of the terms the statement contains, (for example, the statement that may or may not be true: "50% of clergymen like ice cream")—*synthetic, contingent,* or purely empirical statements.

Often the distinction between the two kinds of statement has been regarded as one that admits of no exceptions. Some philosophers, however, notably Quine, have challenged this assumption, suggesting among other things that the distinction rests on unwarranted assumptions about consistency in the meanings of terms (see also DUHEM-QUINE THESIS).

In practice, in sociology, as in physical science, the production of knowledge involves both the formal definition of concepts, and statements of the logical relation between these, as well as the empirical testing of these relations. Theory and research in sociology move between one and the other, with concepts being restated as the result of empirical evidence, and the framing and interpretation of empirical evidence being altered as the outcome of changes in conceptualizations. It remains important to try to be clear when any additions to knowledge proposed depend mainly on the logical extension of an established conceptual scheme, or when these arise more from new empirical evidence. But that both of these processes can be important in the development of knowledge must be recognized, and a hard-and-fast distinction between the two realms is not one that can be sustained. Compare A PRIORI AND A POSTERIORI, KANT.

ancestor worship varying forms of religious rites and cult activity centered on respect for actual or mythical ancestors. Such rites (found in many types of society and in several parts of the world, for example, West Africa and China) are usually based on membership of a lineage group, CLAN or sib, and are associated with a belief that the ancestral dead can intervene in human social life, and that religious activity can promote the well-being of both the living members of society and the ancestral dead. One suggestion is that ancestor worship reflects the importance of family or communal property within the societies in which it occurs. Another is that it legitimates authority, for example, eldership, within the groups on which it is based, while also unifying these groups against outsiders. In segmentary societies ancestor worship can be an important aspect of the identification of the segments that make up the lineage system. In China, according to WEBER (1951), "the cohesion of the sib undoubtedly rested wholly on the ancestor cult." Since these cults were the only folk cults not managed by the central state, in Weber's view they were also an important aspect of the way in which in China—compared, say, with ancient Egypt—the sib was able to resist the encroachments of patrimonial central power. It is within the context of ancestor worship that a Chinese man without male descendants would often resort to adoption, or his relatives would invent fictitious descendants on his behalf after his death.

ancien regime the prerevolutionary social order in France, which was overthrown by the Revolution of 1789.

ancient society the Greco-Roman epoch in the Marxist periodization of historical development. Within classical Marxism, ancient society is seen as based on a slave mode of production, but more recently, however, the heterogeneity of historically existing modes of production has been emphasized by Marxist sociologists. Nevertheless, the significance of slavery, together with military conquest, remains important in explaining both the expansion and ultimate decline of Greco-Roman society.

Anderson, Perry (1938–), British social theorist and historian. Anderson's earliest writings arose from his association with the *The New Left Review*. Examples of articles from this period are reprinted in *Towards Socialism* (ed. with R. Blackburn, 1965). Wide-ranging theoretical works on developments in Western Marxist theory followed—*Considerations on Western Marxism* (1976) and *In the Tracks of Historical Materialism* (1983); and in *Arguments Within English Marxism* (1980) Anderson reviews the work of the socialist historian Edward Thompson. However, it is Anderson's two major historical works, *Passages from Antiquity* and *Lineages of the Absolutist State,* both published in 1974, which have had by far the most impact. The two works were conceived, on the grand scale, as a dialogue between the historical theories of MARX and WEBER. The argument advanced by Anderson is that "what rendered the unique passage to capitalism possible in Europe was the concatenation of antiquity and feudalism," a thesis he supports by extended comparative analysis of both European and non-European societies. His suggestion is that ABSOLUTISM acts as a filter to modern capitalism only where it is associated with the uniquely Western European lineage. The distinctive feature of Anderson's Marxist historical sociology, besides its impressive range and depth, is the way that it combines Marxism with Weberian perspectives while maintaining a view of social development in which the conception of a transition to socialism in Western societies is retained.

androcentrism the tendency to neglect the female perspective or the female contribution, that is, male bias in cultural ideas and embodied in institutions.

animism the belief that natural phenomena, for example, mountains or plants, are endowed with spirits or life forces and that events in the world are the outcome of the activities of these.

Annales school the group of sociologically inclined French historians associated with the journal *Annales d'histoire economique et sociale,* founded in 1929 by Lucien Febvre and Marc BLOCH. One of the objectives of the group was to bring historical studies and social science closer together. Its links with Marxism have been particularly strong, as have its links with sociology. Distinguished by their opposition to traditional national, political, chronological, and narrative history, members of the school have in particular emphasized the importance of social and economic history and long-term historical trends. As well as breaking with conventional units and methods of analysis in historical studies, the approaches they employed included extensive consideration of geophysical and demographic factors as well as cultural and social structural factors. An example of the work of one of the members of the school is Bloch's *Feudal Society,* which combines comparative analysis and great novelty with scrupulous attention to detail. More recently the work of Fernand BRAUDEL, with its emphasis on writing all-embracing global history, has been especially influential within the social sciences, for example, on the work of Immanuel WALLERSTEIN on the WORLD CAPITALIST SYSTEM. See also HISTORY OF MENTALITIES.

anomic division of labor see ANOMIE, DIVISION OF LABOR.

anomic suicide the form of SUICIDE associated with ANOMIE, that is, with serious disruptions of the social order, such as an unexpected catastrophe or rapid economic growth, or with any similar disturbances in social expectations. Anomic suicide is the third of the three main types of SUICIDE identified by DURKHEIM (*Suicide,* 1897).

anomie or **anomy 1.** ("without norms"—a concept introduced into sociology by DURKHEIM) a condition of society or of personal relation to society in which there exists little consensus or a lack of certainty on values or goals; a loss of effectiveness in the normative and moral framework that regulates collective and individual life. **2.** (a specification by Robert MERTON, 1949, of Durkheim's concept) any social situations, and individual orientations in terms of these, in which a mismatch exists between culturally defined goals and the availability of institutionalized means of achieving these goals (for example, the social conditionss in which organized crime flourished in the US during the depression).

The view of human nature held by Durkheim stands in the tradition of Thomas HOBBES, namely that there is no natural or inbuilt limit to the desires, ambitions, or needs of individuals. For Durkheim, the required limits must be socially produced. Anomie exists, and unhappiness and social disorders result, when society fails to provide a limiting framework of social norms. As Durkheim sees it, anomie is an abnormal social form, resulting from the failure of modern societies to move fully from the MECHANICAL SOLIDARITY characteristic of premodern societies to the ORGANIC SOLIDARITY that would come to typify modern societies.

Durkheim saw anomie as pervasive in modern societies. For example, an *anomic division of labor* existed within these societies since they failed to allocate jobs fairly, that is, according to talents. In more general terms, economic activity in these societies remained essentially unregulated.

In *Suicide* (1897), Durkheim claims to demonstrate a correlation between rates of suicide and anomic social situations, for instance, a correlation between suicide rates and divorce rates. Although anomie can be seen as associated with many social problems, it should be noted that it can

	Adoption of culturally approved means	Acceptance of culturally approved goals
(a) innovation	+	−
(b) ritualism	−	+
(c) retreatism	−	−
(d) rebellion	+ or −	+ or −

Fig. 1. **Anomie.** Merton's typology. See main entry.

also rise from an upward spiraling of social expectations (for example, from new wealth or opportunities) whenever these are not subject to satisfactory social controls, and especially when previously existing social controls are disrupted by rapid change.

As reformulated by Merton, anomie becomes a concept used in the analysis of DEVIANCE. What Merton suggests is that whenever there exists any disjuncture between culturally defined goals and the socially approved means available to individuals or groups, four logically possible responses are available (see Fig. 1.)

(a) innovation, that is, crime or other socially disapproved means to achieve approved goals;

(b) ritualism, that is, going through the motions of pursuing approved means with no prospect or expectation of success;

(c) retreatism, that is, simply opting out;

(d) rebellion, that is, seeking to change the system.

If Durkheim's focus on anomie can be seen as arising from a moral conservatism mixed with a social radicalism, Merton's approach reveals how anomie may be a source of social change as well as a locus of social problems.

anthropocentric viewing humankind as of central importance within the universe.

anthropocentric production systems see HUMAN-CENTERED TECHNOLOGY.

anthropomorphism the attribution of human form or characteristics to natural phenomena, animals, deities, spirits, etc. Anthropomorphism is a central feature of many systems of religion and cosmology, which frequently assert a relationship between human affairs and the natural and supernatural realms.

anticipatory socialization any process in which an individual endeavors to remodel his or her social behavior in the expectation of gaining entry to and acceptability in a higher social status or class than that currently occupied.

antinaturalism any approach to sociological analysis that opposes adoption of a natural-science model (fro example, the formulation of natural laws), regarding this as inappropriate to the study of human social action. Reference to naturalism in this sense must be distinguished from a different usage of the term "naturalism" in sociology to refer to NATURALISTIC RESEARCH METHODS. Here the emphasis is on the study of social action in naturally occurring social settings. In this case, a preference for natural research methods is often associated with opposition to the slavish following of any model drawn from the physical sciences. Thus, naturalism in this second sense is often taken as implying antinaturalism, using naturalism in the first sense.

antinomianism the beliefs held, for example, by the members of some Protestant sects in the 16th and 17th centuries, that, as members of God's elect, they could no longer be guilty of sin. As WEBER (1922) put it, such persons felt themselves certain of salvation, and "no longer bound by any conventional rule of conduct." This belief was interpreted by some believers as permitting them to engage in unorthodox marital practices, including plural marriages, as well as in sexual activity outside marriage, which they justified as bringing others to salvation. Weber's view was that antinomianism is a generally occurring phenomenon, and that the more systematically the "practical psychological character" of a religious faith develops, the greater is the tendency for antinomianism to be the outcome.

antipsychiatry a movement of opposition against both the practice and theory of conventional psychiatry, influential especially in the 1960s and early 1970s. Associated with the work of R.D. LAING (1959) in Great Britain and Thomas SZASZ in the US, antipsychiatry attacks the general concept of mental illness as well as the therapeutic techniques employed in treating this. Both Laing and Szasz were themselves psychotherapists. In Laing's view, mental illness is a concept with little or no scientific foundation; the causation of mental illness is not biological. His suggestion was that the mental and behavioral states so described would be better seen as a meaningful response to the stresses and strains and disrupted communications of family life. Such mental states make sense once the social situation of the person concerned is fully considered. Doctors and the patient's family often collude, Laing proposes, in labeling a person insane. The argument of Szasz was similar in key respects, though different in detail. In *The Myth of Mental Illness* (1961), he pointed out that psychiatrists rarely agreed in diagnosing SCHIZOPHRENIA. It was on this basis that he concluded that schizophrenia is not an illness. The implication of this, according to Szasz, is that patients are people who must be held responsible for their actions and treated accordingly. Both Laing and Szasz regarded the involuntary incarceration of patients in mental hospitals and the use of techniques of treatment such as electroconvulsive therapy, leucotomy, and even tranquilizing drugs, as of uncertain value and repressive, a denial of individual autonomy without good reason. Sociologists who have also exerted an influence on the antipsychiatry movement (although the overall influence of their work is much wider) are FOUCAULT and GOFFMAN—see also MADNESS, TOTAL INSTITUTION, LABELING THEORY.

a posteriori see A PRIORI AND A POSTERIORI.

appearance and reality (especially in Marxism) the distinction drawn between surface social relations—the *appearance*—and the underlying determinants of social *reality,* hidden from view by IDEOLOGY, etc. For example, for Marx, the labor theory of value provides the key to a scientific understanding of the true character of capitalism, that is, its exploitative and contradictory character, rather than the apparent fairness of the capitalist labor contract. In drawing a general distinction between appearance and reality, Marx did not wish to suggest that surface appearances were in any sense wholly unreal, but simply that they disguised more fundamental, ultimately determining relations. The distinction also drawn between *epiphenomena* (surface) and *phenomena* (underlying reality) is another way of saying the same thing. See also REIFICATION.

applied sociology the application of sociological theories, concepts, methods, and findings to problems identified in wider society. For example, sociological ideas have been applied to the practices of SOCIAL WORK, education, INDUSTRIAL RELATIONS, and planning. While sociological ideas and sociological research often lead to a redefinition of social problems (for example, identification of UNANTICIPATED CONSEQUENCES OF SOCIAL ACTION), the extent of the influence of sociological thinking and research is difficult to measure. There has been debate recently (for example, Scott and Shore, 1979) as to why sociological research sometimes fails to gain applications, even though this is intended, and application seems appropriate. The explanation given by Scott and Shore is that applied research is often cast first in terms of "disciplinary concerns" and only second in terms of the realities of the political context of much actual decision making, where political interests often triumph over rational persuasion. See also INDUSTRIAL SOCIOLOGY, SOCIAL POLICY.

a priori and **a posteriori** (literally, what comes before and what comes after) a distinction made between kinds of statements or propositions according to the manner in which we acquire knowledge of their truth; thus, whereas an *a priori* statement is one that can be known to be true or false without reference to experience or empirical evidence (for example, the definition of a square as having four equal sides), the truth of an *a posteriori* statement can be established only by an examination of what is empirically the case. While many rationalist philosophers, most notably in modern times KANT, have argued that some things can, and indeed must, be known a priori, merely from first principles, the opposing view—philosophical EMPIRICISM—holds that our ideas are derived only from experience (see also HUME). More recently the view has been expressed that neither of these positions is satisfactory, that there is no fixed starting point or ultimate grounding in philosophy or knowledge. Compare ANALYTIC AND SYNTHETIC.

a posteriori see A PRIORI AND A POSTERIORI.

arbitration an arrangement, especially in stateless societies, for settling conflicts and disputes between two parties by reference to a third party who acts as arbiter. While the arbiter generally has little or no ability to enforce a judgment, it is frequently the case that the disputants agree in advance to abide by the arbiter's ruling. For example, among the Nuer, the Leopard Skin Chief acts as an arbiter in this way—see EVANS-PRITCHARD (1940), GELLNER (1969).

archaeology 1. the scientific or systematic analysis of the material remains, especially the artifacts, but also the physical remains of human and animal bodies, crops, etc., left by past SOCIETIES and CULTURES, where the aim is to produce an account or reconstruction of these societies or cultures.

Especially important in situations where the societies and cultures in question have left no written records or where these records are few, archaeology may also be practiced in any context in which the study of such remains may complement the written historical record, as recently exemplified by *industrial archaeology*, which studies the relatively recent past as evident in the physical remains left by industrial and extractive processes, modes of transportation, etc. When its focus is on societies and cultures that have left no written record, archaeology is coextensive with the discipline of *prehistory*.

Traditionally distinguished by its use of the method of excavation and careful recording of remains, archaeology nowadays employs many scientific techniques, including aerial photography, computer modeling, radiocarbon dating, and even more precise forms of dating based on the climatic record left in the fossil remains of trees. Since the remains studied are physical remains, modern archaeology often smacks more of science than does sociology itself. However, since its subject matter continues to be cultural and social phenomena, the scientific character of archaeology is not necessarily a sign of its superiority, for archaeology must work hard simply to piece together sufficient data for sociological analysis to begin. Once such sociological analysis is undertaken, the concerns and the problems of archaeology are the same as those of sociology, with the extra difficulty for archaeology that it is usually denied any very direct access to the intended meaning of the social actors involved. Thus archaeology and sociology must be seen as complementary disciplines. There are affinities and continuities, for example, especially between the archaeological study of pre-urban prehistorical societies and modern anthropological study of simple societies. The same kind of division that exists in sociology between comparative and generalizing approaches on the one hand, and the historical or meaningful understanding of unique cultures on the other hand, also exists in archaeology. In fact, a comparable range of competing theoretical perspectives to those found in sociology and anthropology also occurs in archaeology, including, for example, FUNCTIONALIST and EVOLUTIONARY THEORIES, and Marxian approaches. **2.** the approach to the history of ideas employed by Michel FOUCAULT in which, by analogy with archaeology **1,** the origins and specific socioeconomic and cultural context of ideas must be uncovered from the layers of accretions with which through time they have become associated (see Foucault, *Archaeology of Knowledge,* 1972).

archetypes see JUNG.

arena (POLITICAL SOCIOLOGY) any domain of discourse and competition, or of conflict or struggle for political power.

Aron, Raymond (1905–83), French sociologist and influential political commentator with wide interests in sociological theory, strategic studies, and the sociology of industrial societies. His contributions to the discussion of sociological theory include *German Sociology* (1935) and *Main Currents in*

Sociological Theory (1965). In *The Opium of the Intellectuals* (1957) he criticized the tendency of intellectuals to suspend their critical judgments and to be too readily seduced by Marxism. On strategic studies he wrote voluminously, producing important works such as *The Century of Total War* (1951), *Peace and War* (1961), and *Clausewitz, Philosopher of War* (1976). He wrote several books on modern industrial societies, among them *Eighteen Lectures on Industrial Society* (1963) and *Democracy and Totalitarianism* (1965). Closer to TOCQUEVILLE or WEBER than to DURKHEIM or MARX in his approach, in general his work stresses the importance of the political dimension in social life, and the virtues of PLURALISM. The unpredictability he saw in the political and cultural dimensions also meant that he was unimpressed by suggestions that a CONVERGENCE would occur between East and West.

articulation of modes of production (Marxism) a concept in which separate modes of production are seen as coexisting within one society or social formation. The concept was developed particularly within a Marxist critique of DEPENDENCY THEORY to demonstrate links between so-called underdevelopment and development. Especially influential was Wolpe's (1972) analysis of the reserve system in South Africa as a subordinate, precapitalist mode of production based on kinship relations, which provided cheap labor power for the industrialized capitalist economy of South Africa.

There is considerable debate within Marxism. For example, Banji (1977) offered a powerful critique of Wolpe in which he argued that the overall laws of motion of the economy define the social formation, and it is not always necessary that all elements of the capitalist mode be present to define a system as capitalist. The "subordinate modes of production" referred to by articulation theory are not, for Banji, modes of production at all, since they are devoid of their own "laws of motion" and serve to reproduce the capitalist mode of production. Such forms lack the essential ingredient of the ability to reproduce themselves.

asceticism the doctrine and practice of self-denial in which practitioners abstain from worldly comforts and pleasures. Asceticism has been a feature of many world religions, and for some practitioners (for example, the members of some monastic orders) it may involve a fatalistic retreat from most worldly endeavors. Despite this association with fatalism and escape from the world, its challenge to mundane values has also meant that it has often been associated with resistance to political authority and has been instrumental in social change. For example, according to WEBER (1922), Protestant asceticism played a decisive role in the rise of modern western capitalism (see PROTESTANT ETHIC).

ascribed status any social position to which a person is allocated by birth or directly as the outcome of family background, and which cannot readily be altered by individual ACHIEVEMENT. As such, ascribed status contrasts with ACHIEVED STATUS. See also PATTERN VARIABLES.

Asiatic mode of production and **Asiatic society** (Marxism) a mode of production and a type of society in which MARX assumed land was owned either by the state and/or self-sufficient village communities, and in which the historical development evident in European society was absent.

This is the sense in which, according to Marx, Asia has no history. In making these assumptions Marx simply accepted much of the then conventional Western view of Asiatic society as state-dominated, lacking private property in land, and therefore failing to manifest the economic and political development characteristic of European society. Marx also accepted the prevailing, but now largely discredited, view that the distinctive form of Asiatic society could be accounted for by geographical conditions that required widespread public works to build and maintain irrigation systems and flood controls (see also HYDRAULIC SOCIETY).

Today the entire concept of a single basic form of Asiatic mode of production and corresponding form of society is in doubt. This conception has been undermined, first, by empirical research, which fails to support such a picture of Asian society, and, secondly, by the awareness that European thinking has been dominated by a Eurocentric myth of Oriental Society (see Said, 1985). For Marxist theory, the concept of Asiatic society has the added disadvantage of an apparent incompatibility with the general assumption of inherent social progress involved in historical materialism. As Brendan O'Leary (1989) remarks, "The Asiatic mode of production is the Loch Ness Monster of historical materialism, rarely sighted and much believed." It should be noted that Marx referred to the term only once by name.

attempted suicide and **parasuicide** either a genuine attempt at self-destruction which fails, or an attempted SUICIDE which is, in fact, feigned, that is, a *parasuicide*.

The pattern of incidence of attempted suicide is different from true suicide, underlining that these are different phenomena. Usually parasuicide is regarded as a cry for help, with little or no intention to cause self-injury. Nonetheless, the incidence of suicide among those who have previously attempted suicide remains markedly higher than for those with no previously recorded attempt.

attitude a learned and enduring tendency to perceive or act toward persons or situations in a particular way.

The concept of attitude has provoked much consideration and investigation, both by psychologists and sociologists, as it incorporates individual and social aspects. Psychologists emphasize the conditions under which an individual develops attitudes and integrates them as part of the personality. Social psychologists are particularly interested in the way attitudes function within a social setting. Sociologists associate social behaviors with particular social structures and situations, for example, class relations.

There are a variety of definitions of attitude (for example, Allport, 1935;

Haber and Fried, 1975; Rokeach, 1960), Some imply that holding an attitude leads to behaving in a certain way, and others encompass the idea that an attitude may only exist mentally, since overt behavior can be constrained situationally. It is therefore useful to see attitudes as involving three elements:

  (a) a cognitive component—beliefs and ideas.

  (b) an affective component—values and emotions.

  (c) a behavioral component—predisposition to act and actions (Second and Backman, 1964).

  See also ATTITUDE SCALE.

attitude scale/measurement a way of measuring attitudes that relies on the fact that holding an attitude leads to consistency in response to particular persons or situations. An attitude scale therefore presents verbal statements about the attitude object of interest, for example, the presidency or uncontrolled immigration, and the respondent states his or her (degree of) agreement or disagreement with the statement. There are different methods of constructing these scales, dependent on whether they are based on the subjective judgment of many subjects (LIKERT SCALE), on objective judgments of statements by "judges" (Thurstone and Chave, 1929) or on response pattern analysis (GUTTMAN SCALE).

Austro-Marxism an influential group of neo-Marxist theorists, prominent in Austria from the late 19th century until the mid-1930s, whose members included Max Adler, Rudolf Hilferding, Otto Bauer, and Karl Renner. Influenced by NEO-KANTIANISM, one distinctive perspective of the school, articulated especially by Adler, involved an emphasis on socialized humanity, a concept seen as transcendentally given (see also KANT). Perhaps the most famous work by a member of the school is Hilferding's *Finance Capitalism* (1910), in which he described the growth of cartels and monopolies as a new phase of capitalism (*organized capitalism*), ideas that influenced Lenin's thinking on imperialism. Renner's main contribution was to the Marxist SOCIOLOGY OF LAW. Austro-Marxists were also among the earliest Marxist theorists to point to the need for fundamental revisions of Marxist theory to take account of an increasing differentiation of the working class and overall changes in the class structure of advanced societies— for example, Renner's conception of the service class.

autarky or **autarchy** the practice or policy of economic self-sufficiency.

authoritarian personality a person who prefers or believes in a system in which some individuals control while other are controlled. This, therefore, involves dominance and submission, and may be regarded as the obverse of a democratic preference.

  The term *authoritarian personality* was introduced by ADORNO et al. (1950). After studying anti-Semitism, Adorno extended his interest to the negative attitudes to "outgroups" displayed by "ingroup" members. He found that these negative attitudes were only part of a cluster of related attitudes, which could be seen in political, religious, and social behavior, and also within the family setting. Thus, the entire personality is authoritarian: *authoritarianism* is not only expressed under certain eliciting conditions, it is a way of behaving that is a persistent personality characteristic.

Various theories exist as to the conditions that encourage formation of an authoritarian personality, these being closely associated with the formation of PREJUDICE. In particular, having experienced authoritarian treatment, or the frustration of self-expression seem to be conditioning factors. See also FRUSTRATION-AGGRESSION HYPOTHESIS, ETHNOCENTRISM.

autonomous man and **plastic man** a distinction made by Hollis (1977, 1987) between the choosing, rational, self-determining SOCIAL ACTOR, capable of fulfilling goals and expressing his own interests, that is, *autonomous man*, and *plastic man*, who is determined by social structures and biology. Hollis's aim in drawing the distinction is to argue that a model that includes elements of both is required for a satisfactory sociological explanation. As such, his is a more poetic rendering of a widespread modern emphasis in sociology on STRUCTURE AND AGENCY. According to Hollis, while acknowledging that some social outcomes are the direct result of the intended actions of individual actors, an adequate model must also take account of social outcomes that go on behind our backs, including unintended consequences. For Hollis, *Homo sociologicus* should be framed as a role player, guided by norms and influenced by structures, but capable of genuine choice and of trust and morality. See also FREE WILL, RULES AND RULE-FOLLOWING, RATIONAL CHOICE THEORY.

autonomy of sociology the viewpoint, as expressed by DURKHEIM in particular, that sociology must be formulated as a distinctive science, dealing with a level of reality that cannot be explained by reduction to other disciplines such as psychology or biology. Durkheim's view was that society has a reality *sui generis*—that is, of its own kind. See also SOCIAL FACTS AS THINGS, SUICIDE.

avoidance relationship a mode of behavior that involves one person continually avoiding another, usually on the grounds of respect or deference. A common case is when a woman has the duty to avoid meeting her husband's mother. Structural-functionalist anthropologists have explained this pattern as a mechanism that expresses and prevents latent conflict. Later, symbolic anthropologists have classed it as a form of TABOO, which reflects native classification systems.

B

back region any area of social context, in contrast with the FRONT REGION, in which a person is able to relax from the ROLE playing and performance required by the front region. See also DRAMATURGY, GOFFMAN.

band a small group with a simple social structure. This form of social organization is regarded by US evolutionary anthropologists as existing prior to the TRIBE, CHIEFDOM, or the STATE, and is usually associated with hunting and gathering societies. For purposes of definition it is regarded as having no differentiated political institutions and no complex social institutions.

barbarism the stage of development typified by pastoralism and agriculture identified in early theories of social evolution (see EVOLUTIONARY THEORY). MONTESQUIEU was the first to use the term in this way, arguing that the three main stages in social development were (a) hunting or SAVAGERY, (b) herding or barbarism, and (c) CIVILIZATION. Later 19th-century evolutionary thinkers, such as E.B. TYLOR and L.H. MORGAN, also adopted the concept.

Barthes, Roland (1915–80) French social theorist and leading exponent of SEMIOLOGY. Usually associated with the structuralist approach, his work was also influenced by social anthropology and Marxism. His most notable contributions include works on myth, IDEOLOGY, and popular culture. He was an influential figure in cultural studies because of his contribution to semiology and his concentration on the TEXT, rather than its author, as the object of study. He wrote about commonplace events, images, and activities in order to show the prevalence of ideology in areas considered free of political significance, for example, placards advertising wine or margarine. He enlarged on the anthropological definition of myth by describing it as one of the ways in which the norms of a society are endowed with a taken-for-granted status as facts of nature. He regarded myth as a prevalent aspect of culture, composed of sign systems through which we understand and express ourselves. FASHION also can be regarded as a system of meanings, one that differentiates between clothes, stressing the significance of detail and locating the wearer within a constantly changing symbolic order. Barthes argued that cultural forms are essentially ambiguous and are open to different interpretations or readings.

Baudrillard, Jean (1929–) French social theorist who has been influential in POSTMODERNISM. Baudrillard draws particularly on SEMIOLOGY to argue that modern-day consumption in particular entails the active manipulation of signs, so that in modern society the production of the sign and the commodity have come together to produce the *commodity-sign*. An endless reduplication of signs, images, and simulations, launched through the media and elsewhere, in the end effaces all distinction between image and reality. The overproduction of such signs, images, and simulations has the effect of producing a "loss of stable meaning," which is advanced as a characteristic of POSTMODERNISM.

Beauvoir, Simone de (1908–86) French feminist writer, whose main contribution to social theory—in *The Second Sex* (1953)—was an account of PATRIARCHY in which the feminine is seen, in Hegelian terms, as culturally constructed, as other than male. This otherness is explained as arising from the historical cultural fact of the SEXUAL DIVISION OF LABOR, but is in part also determined by women's sexual reproductive capacity, which restricts women's freedom compared with the freedom of men. The only answer she suggests is that women should refrain from marriage and from childbirth and the responsibilities of motherhood.

Becker, Howard S. (1928–) US sociologist whose work within the SYMBOLIC INTERACTIONIST tradition has made an important contribution to the study of student culture, LABELING THEORY, and the SOCIOLOGY OF ART. His most influential works are *Boys in White: Student Culture in a Medical World* (with Blanche Geer, Everett Hughes, and Anselm Strauss, 1961); *Making the Grade* (with Blanche Geer and Everett Hughes, 1968); *Outsiders: Studies in the Sociology of Deviance* (1963); and *Sociological Work* (1970). While focusing on the behavior of individuals in groups and organizations, Becker's treatment of these was uncompromisingly sociological. The responses of individuals, for example to medical treatment, are seen as depending far less "on the individual psychology of patients than on the relations between the healers and the sick. The actions of deviants stem less from their personalities than from the interactions between them, other deviants, and agents of social control." See also DEVIANCE, HIERARCHY OF CREDIBILITY, DRUG TAKING FOR PLEASURE.

belief system the configuration of beliefs that exists in a particular society or culture. The term may be used to refer to the entirety of the knowledge and beliefs within a society, including scientific and technological knowledge. It has more often been used to describe the patterns of religious beliefs and values, and the central principles underlying these, that give distinctiveness and coherence to the modes of thought within a society or culture.

Bell, Daniel (1919–) US essayist and sociologist whose various descriptions of modern society have achieved a wide but contested currency. In *The End of Ideology* (1960), he was among the first to suggest a sharp decline in the relevance of previously dominant class ideologies (see END OF IDEOLOGY THESIS). Later, in *The Coming of Post-Industrial Society* (1973), he advanced the view that modern societies had become not only POSTINDUSTRIAL SOCIETIES but also knowledge-based INFORMATION SOCIETIES, in which science and technology and professional and technical employment were now central. At this stage Bell's main message was one of an optimistic future and a society of declining social conflict. In *The Cultural Contradictions of Capitalism* (1976), however, the tone changes. Now Bell notes the new and unresolved tensions between the three competing "axial principles" of modern society: techno-economic efficiency; universal citizenship, political equality, and entitlements to social welfare; and individual self-expression and hedonistic fulfillment. Thus Bell's sociological analysis of modern society can be said to have captured the changing fortunes and moods of modern society.

Bendix, R. (1916–) German-born US sociologist, known best for his work on the interpretation of Max Weber's sociology (especially *Max Weber: an Intellectual Portrait*, 1960), and for his extensive work in historical and comparative sociology, including *Work and Authority in Industry* (1956), *Social Mobility in Industrial Society* (1959), and *Nation Building and Citizenship* (1964). See also SOCIAL MOBILITY.

Benjamin, Walter (1892–1940) German cultural theorist associated with the FRANKFURT SCHOOL OF CRITICAL THEORY. His work is regarded as particularly important today for its contribution to neo-Marxist theories of AESTHETICS and mass culture. Part of his work constituted a theoretical analysis of the writing of the socialist playwright Berthold Brecht. At odds with ADORNO, who was pessimistic about the critical potential of mass art, Benjamin remained hopeful that a progressive potential would be found. Whereas Adorno retained and even extended an attachment to the classical modernist (and bourgeois) distinction between high culture and other mass cultural forms, Benjamin questioned this distinction. In doing so he embraced many orientations that later became characteristic of POSTMODERNISM.

Bentham, Jeremy (1748–1832) English legal, political, and social theorist and social reformer, and one of the founders of modern philosophical UTILITARIANISM. As a legal theorist, Bentham challenged the adequacy of the COMMON LAW tradition; he was even more critical of conceptions of natural law (see NATURAL RIGHTS AND NATURAL LAW), which he described as "nonsense on stilts." In place of these, Bentham advocated legislation and the general codification of laws, and LEGAL POSITIVISM. His interest in prison reform also led him to suggest designs for the modern prison—see PANOPTICON.

Berger, Peter (1929–) Viennese-born US social theorist and sociologist of religion. In the *Social Construction of Reality* (with Thomas Luckmann, 1966), he provides an account of the role of COMMON-SENSE KNOWLEDGE in the social construction of everyday life and institutions, which he develops from the phenomenological perspective of Alfred SCHUTZ. In his studies of religion, including *The Social Reality of Religion* (1969), he has suggested, controversially, that sociologists should adopt a "methodologically atheist" stance and not seek to discuss whether religion is anything more than a social creation. He has also written an unusual introduction to sociology, *An Invitation to Sociology* (1966), which is a hymn to the pleasures of sociology—"a royal game among academic disciplines," according to Berger—

and is itself a pleasure to read. Rather than presenting a systematic review of the subject, it entices the reader to enter the game with samples of the fare offered on the royal table. See also STRUCTURE AND AGENCY, PHENOMENOLOGICAL SOCIOLOGY.

Bernstein, Basil (1924–) professor in the SOCIOLOGY OF EDUCATION at the Institute of Education, University of London, who is probably known best for his pioneering work in SOCIOLINGUISTICS and his examination of the relationship between social class and children's acquisition and use of language in the context of family and school. His earliest papers, in the 1960s, established the existence of working-class restricted codes and middle-class elaborate codes of formal and public language (see ELABORATE AND RESTRICTED CODES). These language theories, and his empirical research, were widely disseminated in Great Britain and the rest of the world.

Concentration on the sociolinguistic aspects of Bernstein's work has distracted attention from his wider interest in the distribution of power and the principles of social control propounded in his *Class, Codes and Control* vols. 1–3 (1971–7). His approach is essentially structuralist (see STRUCTURALISM), and he draws heavily on the work of DURKHEIM. These aspects are most clearly seen in his work on the organization, transmission, and evaluation of educational knowledge. Education is essentially a form of knowledge code; how it is organized, transmitted, and evaluated reflects the modes of social control. The curriculum is constructed as separate or combined units of knowledge classified in some way (see CLASSIFICATION), where classification refers to the boundary relationships between domains of knowledge. The term is paralleled by the concept of *framing*, which refers to the manner in which educational knowledge is transmitted. Bernstein suggests that empirically the message systems of classification and framing are realized in collection and integrated codes that underpin school curricula and have consequences for order and control. A collection code has strongly classified and bounded domains. Students can select only clearly separated contents in the form of specifically defined subjects, for example, history, geography, chemistry, physics, and biology. An integrated code consists of contents that have an open relationship with each other, for example, social studies and science. Thus the organization of knowledge is mirrored in the educational philosophy embedded in each code and its relationship to the principles of power and control. The collection code implies didactic teaching where facts are inculcated. The integrated code implies a theory of teaching and learning predicated on the self-regulation of individuals or groups of pupils.

It is possible to see how Bernstein has developed his original work on sociolinguistics with a much more sophisticated and thoroughgoing theory of knowledge transmission codes. Essentially, a restricted and collection code are related, and an elaborated and integration code are related. The collection code rests on the principle of restricted choice and limited methods of permitted combinations. The integrated code regulates selection and combination with more degrees of freedom.

bias 1. any situation in which the accuracy, RELIABILITY, VALIDITY, etc. of sociological data or findings are held to be distorted by the limitations of a research method employed, or by a researcher's or a theorist's presuppositions, for example, political or moral beliefs. See also OBJECTIVITY, VALUE FREEDOM AND VALUE NEUTRALITY. **2.** in a more narrowly technical sense, in statistical analysis, a difference between a hypothetical true value of a variable in a population and the value obtained in a particular sample of respondents. See also BIASED SAMPLE.

biased sample a population SAMPLE that is not a true reflection of the parent population (see BIAS 2), that is, not a REPRESENTATIVE SAMPLE.

When the incidence of a certain occurrence or type of behavior in a population is to be investigated, for example, voting intention, it is often impossible to examine the total population, so a sample of this population is taken. For this sample to produce acceptable data, it must be a true representation of the parent population, so it is essential that it be selected in a way that ensures this. If this is not accomplished, bias will result and the information collected will not truly reflect the population being studied. Thus, to select a sample by questioning people in the street will bias it against people who do not walk, do not go shopping, or are at work or school all day. Mail QUESTIONNAIRES attempt to overcome this type of bias, but are likely to be biased against those who do not bother to fill in questionnaires and return them, and against the illiterate. To keep bias to a minimum, if random sampling is not possible, it is necessary to select the sample carefully by matching all relevant parameters of the population, for example, age, class, and residence, and to ensure as high a response rate as possible, probably by personal INTERVIEWING.

biomechanical (or biomedical) model of illness a model of illness based on a conception of the body as a physical system that may break down, become faulty, and need treatment to restore it to good working order. Although there is a good deal of informal health care undertaken outside of medical settings, this model suggests that people normally go to see a doctor when they have a painful or life-threatening condition that cannot be cured by self-medication. It is a model of illness made up of the following elements:

(a) that normally people are either free of symptoms of ill health or are unaware that they are ill;

(b) that illness consists of deviation from a set of biological norms;

(c) that emotional or physical changes that are biological in origin make people aware that something is wrong;

(d) that the initial response to something being wrong is the use of lay remedies such as rest or perhaps a proprietary medicine;

(e) that if the symptoms persist or get worse people will visit the doctor;

(f) that at this point the person is either diagnosed as sick and treated by the doctor, or be told that nothing is wrong;

(g) that the person who has been diagnosed as sick follows a course of treatment prescribed to make the person well, at which point the person is pronounced cured.

Sociologists have challenged this model and distinguished between disease as a biological category and illness as a social category. Disease refers to biological states such as a fractured limb or a tubercular lung; illness refers to both the subjective feeling of being unwell and the social status of sick person. See also SYMPTOM ICEBERG, TRIVIAL CONSULTATION.

black power movement a militant SOCIAL MOVEMENT, originating in the United States in the mid-1960s, which emphasized the role of the white-dominated power structure in subordinating black people. It argued that power had to be taken from whites in order to materially improve the situation of black people. The movement was one of a number of radical responses among black activists to the perceived failure of the civil rights movement to achieve real improvements in the conditions of black people, and its concentration on the segregated, rural, Southern states at the expense of urban ghettos. The black power movement has been particularly associated with the takeover of the Student Nonviolent Coordinating Committee (SNCC) by a group of more radical members, the most prominent being Stokely Carmichael. Two contemporary quotes serve to underline the developments. SNCC (pronounced "Snick"), since its inception in 1960, had been at the forefront of more confrontational and high-profile CIVIL RIGHTS activities, including college sit-ins, Freedom Rides (integrated buses), and voter-registration drives. In a book written just before the emergence of the black power movement, Paul Jacobs and Saul Lindau (1966) wrote: "The weary veterans of harassment, arrest, beatings, and the psychological torture of living in the South have begun to reexamine their objectives at the very time they confront the full and often subtle power of the American economic and political system." In the same year, writing about the emergence of black power, Carmichael wrote: "We had to work for power because this country does not function by morality, love and non-violence, but by power ... integration is a subterfuge to maintain white supremacy" (reprinted in Floyd Barbour, ed., 1969). This shift, drawing on a number of black separatist and black pride themes, castigated the American system as racist and unreformable, and emphasized black autonomy and self-reliance.

Blau, Peter (1918–) US sociologist who first made his reputation as an organization theorist with works such as *The Dynamics of Bureaucracy* (1955) and (with W. Scott) *Formal Organizations: A Comparative Approach* (1962). Subsequently, with O. Duncan, he also contributed an important empirical study on occupational structure, *The American Occupational Structure* (1967). In *Exchange and Power* (1964) he formulated a version of EXCHANGE THEORY in which his goal was to "derive complex from simpler processes without the reductionist fallacy of ignoring emergent properties." For Blau, "social exchange" is the "central principle of social life, and even relationships such as love and friendship can be analyzed as relations of exchange." The institutions of gift exchange in simple societies reveal underlying principles that apply to social exchange in general, for example, "that reciprocated benefactions create social bonds among peers, whereas unreciprocated ones produce differentiation of status." Eager to avoid a merely tautological use of the notion of social exchange, Blau limits its reference to actions contingent on rewarding reactions from others, which would cease where these reactions were not forthcoming.

Bloch, Marc (1886–1944) French medieval historian who taught in Strasbourg and, from 1936, at the Sorbonne in Paris. His influence in sociology is mainly through his important book *Feudal Society,* published in English in 1961, in which he stressed the workings of feudal society as a whole, rather than emphasizing either the political or economic aspects favored by other theorists. He was cofounder (1931) of the *Annales d'histoire économique et sociale* (see ANNALES SCHOOL). He was murdered by the Gestapo in 1944 for his role in the French Resistance.

blue-collar worker an American synonym for a manual worker. The contradistinction involved is with WHITE-COLLAR WORKER.

Blumer, Herbert (1900–1987) US sociologist who was a student and a teacher at the University of Chicago. He is best known as a teacher and writer in the symbolic interactionist tradition deriving from G.H. MEAD. See SYMBOLIC INTERACTIONISM, VARIABLE.

body language communication by gesture, posture, and other nonverbal signs. Argyle (1967 and 1969) and Morris (1978) have both documented detailed observations of human nonverbal communication. Body language may include unintended signs as well as intended communication. In sociology, the appropriate positionings of the body in social ENCOUNTERS have been studied by social theorists, notably GOFFMAN. See also FACE-WORK.

Bogardus scale see SOCIAL DISTANCE.

Booth, Charles James (1840–1916) English businessman, shipowner, and social reformer who recognized the need for systematic and reliable data to support the case for social reform. He was the first person to develop and use the SURVEY METHOD to collect data on poverty and income. His statistical findings were published in *Life and Labour of the People* (1889–91) and *Life and Labour of the People in London* (1891–1903). He was particularly concerned with the aged poor and was influential in the creation of the Old Age Pensions Act, 1908. See also SOCIAL SURVEY, ROWNTREE.

boundary maintenance see SOCIAL SYSTEM.

bounded rationality a model of human action in which choices are seen as limited and imperfect in terms of knowledge of the situation and expected outcomes; action is therefore never completely rational. The concept originated in the work of March and Simon (1985) and Simon (1957a & b) on decision making in organizations. Their work was critical of the model or IDEAL TYPE of perfect rationality presented in economic theories of the firm. In contrast with the assumption of profit maximization in economic theory, March and Simon argued that actual behavior in organizations was *satisficing* rather than optimizing in terms of the achievement of goals. This approach to subjective rationality has been influential in the sociology of organizations (see ORGANIZATION THEORY) because it demonstrated the way in which organizational structure (DIVISION OF LABOR, SOCIALIZATION) and channels of communication limit the range of solutions considered.

Bourdieu, Pierre (1930–) French professor of sociology at the College de France, Paris, who has made significant contributions to general SOCIOLOGICAL THEORY in attempting to find a middle way between action and structure, and is well known for his work in the sociology of CULTURE and for the application of those ideas to the SOCIOLOGY OF EDUCATION (see CULTURAL CAPITAL). He has drawn on the work of a diverse range of theorists, such as MARX, DURKHEIM and WEBER, to develop a distinctive theory of the maintenance of social order. His major works include *Outline of a Theory of Practice* (1977), *The School as a Conservative Force* (1966), and *Reproduction in Education, Society and Culture* (1977). His other influential works include *Distinction* (1984) and *Homo Academicus* (1988). See also HABITUS, STRUCTURE AND AGENCY.

Braudel, Fernand (1902–85) influential French historian, associated with the ANNALES SCHOOL. His best-known work, translated as *The Mediterranean World and the Mediterranean World of the Age of Philip II* (2 vols., 1972–73, originally 1949, expanded in 1966), exemplifies the approach characteristic of members of the school, which is to move beyond conventional political histories by focusing in detail on the material basis of political events, while also tracing their global interconnections. In his analysis of the change in the direction of Spain's foreign policy under Philip II (toward the Atlantic and away from the Mediterranean), demographic and cultural as well as economic data are combined with more conventional political analysis. Braudel was interested in the different pace of social change in different eras and in different areas of social reality. Beneath the short-term events uppermost in conventional histories, there are changes that take centuries or millennia. In these terms, in *Civilization and Capitalism* (tr. 1973–82), Braudel presents an account of the development of the world economy from the Middle Ages to the Industrial Revolution. Critics of Braudel complain that, in de-emphasizing the independent significance of political events, his work may have gone too far in redressing the balance between social and political history. For others, Braudel's work has been inspirational, leading modern comparative sociological historians such as WALLERSTEIN to use it as a model for their own.

Braverman thesis see PROLETARIANIZATION.

bricolage the process of transforming the meaning of objects or symbols through novel uses or unconventional arrangements of unrelated things. The term is used in CULTURAL STUDIES.

Bricolage is a French term and was introduced, in a somewhat different context, by Claude LÉVI-STRAUSS in *The Savage Mind,* and subsequently used by his translators, who could find no suitable English equivalent. He used it to refer to the (*bricoleur's*) practice of creating things out of whatever materials come to hand—the structure and the outcome being more important than the constituent parts, which themselves are changed through the act of creation. See also FASHION.

bureaucracy a type of organization in which administration is based on impersonal, written rules and a hierarchy of offices; there is a clear distinction between the office and its incumbent, and official positions are filled on the basis of formal qualifications. The concept was first systematically defined in Weber's IDEAL TYPE, which provided the frame of reference for much of the sociological research into modern large-scale organizations.

Weber locates the analysis of bureaucracy within a theory of power, DOMINATION, and legitimacy (see LEGITIMATE AUTHORITY) in which modern rational bureaucracy is most closely approximated in "legal-rational forms of domination" (Weber, 1922) dependent on the development of a money economy, the free market, legal codification, and the expansion of administration, particularly in the STATE. Weber's ideal type of bureaucracy involves:

(a) domination based on written rules in a hierarchy of specialized offices;

(b) recruitment based on qualifications;

(c) offices that are impersonal and clearly distinguished from incumbents; they are also segregated from private life and private property.

Consequently, office-holding is a vocation based on expert training, offering a salary with pension and tenure, and a career ladder in which promotion depends on seniority and/or ability.

In its pure form, rational bureaucracy is seen as technically superior to all previous forms of administration, such as patriarchalism and patrimonialism, by virtue of its speed, predictability, precision, and dispassionate treatment of cases without regard to personal considerations. Thus Weber distinguished between rational bureaucracy and earlier forms of bureaucracy in ancient societies, which were based on personal allegiance to the ruler and payment in kind. Modern bureaucracy pervades state administration and all the major institutions in capitalist society, including the military, the church, education, and private enterprise.

Weber's pessimism about the advance of bureaucratic power under capitalism is reflected in his view of bureaucracy as inevitable, even under socialism. The only question becomes "who runs the bureaucratic machine?" (compare IRON LAW OF OLIGARCHY). The conflict between bureaucracy and democracy was a theme running through the works of elite theorists such as MOSCA (1884), as well as the idea of a so-called managerial revolution (Burnham, 1943).

Since Weber, the study of bureaucracy has included a large number of empirical studies and criticisms of the ideal type that form the basis for modern ORGANIZATION THEORY (see also ORGANIZATION). The results of this type of research indicate that actual bureaucracies do not operate in accordance with Weber's ideal type, due to the existence of informal structures and the conflicting interests of subgroups within bureaucracies, and the inflexibility of formal rules that lead to inefficiency. For example, the studies undertaken by MERTON and by Selznick (1966) have become minor classics on the way in which bureaucratic rules may be dysfunctional and give rise to unintended consequences. The rules become ends in themselves rather than means to ends (see GOAL DISPLACEMENT, FUNCTIONALISM). Blau's study of a federal law-enforcement agency (1955) demonstrates that informal practices are more efficient than strict adherence to inflexible formal rules. In addition, formal rules may be used by organizational members to further their own interests in opposition to official goals (Crozier, 1964).

Post-Weber research has generated an interesting literature in its own right, but its significance as a critique of Weber is still a controversial issue (Albrow, 1970; Mouzelis, 1975). There is no doubt that much of the criticism involved misunderstandings about Weber's approach, and reduced Weber's study of the wider social consequences of bureaucracy to a narrow concern with organizational efficiency. Confusion also enters into the evaluation of the ideal type—how it is to be assessed and whether it conceals hypotheses. However, even if the ideal type is vindicated, problems remain with Weber's formulations, namely the absence of any meaningful understanding (a method advocated by Weber) of the actions of subordinates in bureaucracies, and whether alternative ideal types of bureaucracy prove more useful.

busing the transportation by bus of children of a particular group, particularly children of an ethnic group, from one residential area into another residential area of different ethnic mix, with the aim of achieving an ethnic or racial balance in schools. The term had its origin in the United States, and the practice of attempting to achieve such balance by this means has largely been confined to the US.

C

carceral organization any organization, such as the prison system or mental hospitals, in which individuals are confined for punishment or correction and prevented from normal social contact in the wider society. The existence of such specialized institutions of incarceration is held by some to be a particular feature of modern societies (for example, FOUCAULT, 1975). See also TOTAL INSTITUTION OR TOTAL ORGANIZATION, SURVEILLANCE.

career 1. the sequence(s) of professional or occupational positions in the life course of an individual. **2.** (by analogy with **1.**) any individual pattern or progression in a nonoccupational life course, for example, the deviant career of the drug user (BECKER, 1953) or the MORAL CAREER of the mental patient (GOFFMAN, 1964).

Occupational careers may either consist of a sequenced progression in terms of a hierarchy of status and income (as typical of many middle-class careers (see PROFESSIONS), or lack any clear structure or progression, as is more usual for manual workers. Gender differences affecting access to careers has been a recent topic of importance in the sociology of labor markets (for example, Dex, 1985). See LABOR MARKET, DUAL LABOR MARKET 2.

cargo cult a form of MILLENARIAN or millennial movement widespread in Melanesia in the modern colonial era, in which followers of the CULT seek to achieve the delivery of cargoes of Western consumer goods by means of MAGIC and RITUAL, for example, building airstrips and models of planes. Such cults involve the combination of Western and native beliefs in a context of ANOMIE and disruption of the local culture, sometimes by successive waves of colonialism. Based on assumptions in the native religion about the supernatural origins of material resources as well as on inadequate knowledge of the Western culture, when more adequate knowledge became available, these movements have tended to transform into politico-religious movements (see Worsley, *The Trumpet Shall Sound,* 1968).

casework a method of investigation, care, and advice used in social work and some counseling situations. It involves examining current personal problems within the context of the client's personal history. Crucial to this is the keeping of a record of the interactions between the social worker and the client by the social worker in order to illuminate the complex of causes and effects involved in the client's current problems.

caste a form of SOCIAL STRATIFICATION that involves a system of hierarchically ranked, closed, endogamous strata, the membership of which is ascribed, and between which contact is restricted and mobility theoretically impossible. Although it reflects economic inequalities, by virtue of the occupations typically followed by or permitted to members, caste stratification is ultimately rooted in noneconomic criteria. In its purest form, in

Hindu India, the caste principle is religious: castes are ranked in accordance with the degree of ritual purity ascribed to members and to their activities. Some commentators, however, extend the term to cover situations in which divisions are underpinned by racial antipathies, supported perhaps by legal sanctions, as in the cases of South Africa and, until recently, the segregated southern United States (for example, see Dollard's *Caste and Class in a Southern Town*, 1937).

Historically, the most developed form, and some would argue the only true form, of caste stratification has occurred in India in association with Hinduism. More than 3000 years old, the origins of this system are obscure. They probably lie in the twin bases of ethnicity and occupational specialization. India's vast subcontinental area was settled by a variety of ethnic groups, and relations between them were often shaped by conquest and by the fact that they carried specialized occupational skills. The caste system, therefore, appears to have developed out of patterns of military, political, and social subordination; occupational specialization; and ethnic antipathies involving ritual and taboo barriers to contact. From these, the development of the system was guaranteed by two facts: first, the groupings provided suitable units for collectivizing the rulers' arrangements for gathering taxes and tributes; secondly, there existed a powerful priesthood (the *Brahmin*), which was capable of elaborating the taboos into a consistent body of ritual regulations that could be enforced in alliance with the secular rulers.

The system the *brahmins* perfected was founded on five main divisions, four caste groups (*Varna*) and an outcaste group, the *untouchables*. These were and are ranked in a hierarchy of ritual purity derived from the life style and occupations permitted to, and monopolized by, their members; the highest castes are those of the *Brahmins* and the *Khasatriyas*, the latter being the secular and military ruler and landlord caste. Beneath these come the castes of the entrepreneurial middle classes (the *Vaishyas*) and the workers, servants, and slaves (the *Shudras*). Finally, and in strict terms outside the hierarchy, stand the outcastes or untouchables (*Harijans*) who, performing only the most degrading occupational tasks, are considered to be ritually impure. The varna, however, constitute only the broadest divisions within the system. More significant in determining everyday social practices is the subdivision of the varna into several thousand, usually regionally based, individual castes and subcastes, the *Jati* (strictly translated, separate "breeds" and "species"). Each of these jati has its own social rank and body of caste regulations, designed first to maintain the ritual exclusiveness of the group by restricting or prohibiting marriage, COMMEN-SALITY, and social and physical contact across caste boundaries. Secondly, they ritually regulate the occupations and the techniques associated with them that members are allowed to follow. These regulations are supported by temporal and spiritual sanctions derived from the punitive powers of the caste authorities, public opinion, and Hindu theodicy.

CATEGORICAL DISCRIMINATION

Hindu theodicy is associated with a belief in reincarnation. Individuals' caste positions are held to be either a reward or a punishment for their fidelity or lack of it in observing the rules of the castes of their previous incarnations. Since caste rank was congenital and fixed during any one incarnation, the only hope of upward mobility lay in individuals' ability to secure a higher rebirth through the faithful discharge of caste obligations. This provided a powerful incentive for adherence to caste rules, especially since violations were punished in the present incarnation and brought the certainty of a degraded rebirth in the next. In Hindu thinking, two general sets of doctrines underpin this framework of spiritual and social control: *dharma*, the overall order of all things natural and social, including social behavior and social relations proper to a member of a particular caste, and *kharma*, the general doctrine of reincarnation.

WEBER traced the overwhelming traditionalism of the Hindu peoples to these sources. He also argued that the caste system hindered development of capitalism in India for at least three reasons: first, because the divisions of the caste system prevented the urban middle classes from combining to establish the rights of freedom of persons and property on which capitalism is based; secondly, because the multiplicity of special caste laws, framed in the religious interest, pervented emergence of a uniform and universalistic legal system suitable to capitalist development; thirdly, because the ritual stereotyping of occupations and techniques associated with caste hindered the mobility of labor and the application of new technologies.

The reality of caste, however, is different from its theoretical injunctions. One difference of importance is the existence of the process known as *sanskritization*, in which particular jati may succeed in raising their location in the status hierarchy by gradually assuming the behavior and beliefs appropriate to members of a higher caste. In practice, somewhat at odds with Weber's view, the industrial development that has taken place in India since the 1900s has meant that patterns of work behavior have sometimes adjusted to new economic requirements rather than remaining constrained by caste. As a consequence, the relationship between the caste system and economic development must be regarded as more flexible than sometimes assumed. Officially, since independence in 1947, caste divisions no longer receive state backing. In practice, their social significance remains considerable. See also CLASS, SOCIAL CLOSURE; compare ESTATES.

categorical discrimination see DISCRIMINATION.

categorical imperative see KANT, HYPOTHETICAL IMPERATIVE.

category 1. a conceptual class or set. **2.** (philosophy) a fundamental class or kind (for example, Aristotle's 10 classes of all modes of being). **3.** *pl.* KANT'S a priori modes of understanding (for example, "causality" and "substance"), which he believed shaped all our perceptions of the world.

causal modeling a family of techniques of statistical modeling aimed at providing specification and testing of the causal relations underlying correlations between a number of variables. Based on the work of Herbert Simon (1957a), and pioneered in sociology especially by Hubert Blalock (1961), the approach requires the researcher to formulate and test successive theoretical models of the causal relations between variables, seeking a model that best fits the data. Included under the general category of causal modeling are PATH ANALYSIS and LOG-LINEAR ANALYSIS. Causal modeling has been criticized as dependent on initial assumptions that cannot be regarded as fully tested by the data. Technical sophistication may disguise this. Nonetheless causal modeling is important in making possible a more satisfactory exploration of causal relations than is achieved in simpler forms of correlation analysis.

cause, causality, and causal relationship the relationship between two events, such that one brings about the other. Usually, a causal relationship is claimed where:

(a) a spatial and temporal contiguity exists between two events;

(b) one event precedes the other;

(c) the second event appears unlikely to have happened without the first event having occurred.

Where it also appears that a particular type of event always or usually occurs in a particular way, that is, a lawlike relationship, this is usually regarded as further reinforcing a claim that a causal relationship exists. It should be noted, however, that a lawlike association may exist between two events *without* this implying a direct casual relationship, for example, where requirements (b) and (c) remain unsatisfied (that is, CORRELATION rather than causation). A distinction can also be drawn between an immediate cause (for example, striking a match to light a fire) and more underlying explanatory causation (for example, the presence of oxygen in the atmosphere). What this means is that causation usually involves multiple causation. Important ways in which sociologists have sought to identify the relative importance of multiple causes and to distinguish correlation from cause include MULTIVARIATE ANALYSIS and CAUSAL MODELING.

Philosophers, especially recently, have not been happy with the concepts of cause and causality. The concepts are difficult to reconcile with conceptions of logical implications in classical LOGIC. For example, if we refer to an increase in prices caused by increased taxation, the increase in taxation is neither a necessary nor a sufficient condition for an increase in prices. Furthermore, epistemologically, the provisional nature of scientific knowledge always means that claimed causal relationships can never be stated conclusively.

Further issues concerning sociology specifically are: (a) whether the sense in which cause and causation arise in connection with purposive actions is compatible with conceptions of causality in physical science (for example, see WINCH) and (b) whether FUNCTIONAL EXPLANATION is a form of causal analysis. See also EXPLANATION.

census a government-sponsored, universal, and obligatory survey of all individuals in a geographical area. The census is a major source of SECONDARY DATA because:

(a) it offers data on a comprehensive range of topics, many of which are not included in other surveys;

(b) its large size permits the analysis of some topics in great detail;

(c) its size and scope permit the analysis of numerous interrelationships.

With the introduction of punched-card processing and, later, the use of computers, the amount of information that can be collected and processed has been dramatically increased.

A census must be taken in the United States at intervals of not less than ten years.

The census has a number of important applications for the sociologist, including:

(a) studies of SOCIAL STRATIFICATION;

(b) analysis of changing trends reflected in housing, education, work, etc.;

(c) studies of particular groups.

Further, following demand from local authorities, academic researchers, market-research organizations, central government, and other organizations, the United States Census Bureau collects tract data, making it possible to obtain census data on small areas.

The census has also become a fruitful area for historical research and there is a growing interest in time-series research, or cliometrics, in which modern statistical techniques are applied to historical data. See also SOCIAL SURVEY, FAMILY EXPENDITURE SURVEY, GENERAL HOUSEHOLD SURVEY, OFFICIAL STATISTICS, STATISTICS AND STATISTICAL ANALYSIS.

center and periphery a depiction of the division of the world into dominant, mainly industrial, capitalist countries, and others, mainly in the Third World, which are weaker politically and economically. While the terms now have wide usage in sociology and a varied history, they are most commonly associated with WALLERSTEIN and the *world systems* approach. WALLERSTEIN (1974) argued that from the 16th century onward a capitalist world system began to emerge, with England, France, and the Netherlands as the core countries having strong centralized political systems and mercantile economies. As a part of the process, other countries became subordinated to the core and provided cheap labor, most commonly unfree labor in the form of slavery or debt-peonage. These became the periphery countries supplying raw materials, foodstuffs, and luxury goods to merchants from the core who dominated world trade.

Later the concept of *semi-periphery* was introduced by Wallerstein and others to describe countries that in the 20th century have achieved some level of industrialization, are less dominated by the economies of the core, and have achieved some level of political centralization and civic political organization. Most of the southern European countries, some Latin

American countries, for example, Argentina, Brazil, Chile, and some Asian countries, such as South Korea, have been described as semi-peripheral.

While the world systems approach has been criticized for its overreliance on the market as its main analytical focus (Brenner, 1977), the usage is now so widespread that adherence to the original definition should not be assumed when writers use these terms.

Chicago school the pioneering approach to urban sociological research and theory developed at the University of Chicago in the interwar years.

The eminence of Chicago among American universities, and the city's distinctive Midwestern voice in American affairs, has meant that Chicago has been the center of numerous major movements in modern social thought, including philosophical PRAGMATISM and SYMBOLIC INTERACTIONISM, as well as the Chicago school of urban sociology. Founded in 1892, Chicago's Department of Sociology was the first to be established in an American university. Its founder, Albion SMALL, and his successor, Robert PARK, developed an approach to urban social analysis distinguished by careful empirical research and a particular model of urban ecology. Drawing on Darwinian ideas, a model of urban ecological processes was developed that presented urban competition over land and housing as resulting in the spatial organization of cities as a series of concentric rings, each with its own shifting functional focus and also subdivided into distinctive neighborhoods and subcultures (see also URBAN SOCIOLOGY). Chicago has been described as an ideal laboratory for urban social research, and members of the Chicago school were responsible for a stream of classic works in urban sociology, among them Thomas and Znaniecki's *The Polish Peasant in Europe and America* (1917), Park and Burgess's *The City* (1925), Wirth's *The Ghetto* (1928), and Zorbaugh's *The Goldcoast and the Slum* (1929).

chiefdom a form of centralized social organization relying primarily on allegiance and not on formal coercive institutions. US evolutionary anthropologists regard it as existing prior to the STATE and as a development from the TRIBE. Chiefdoms are characterized by the emergence of patterns of social stratification and an economic system based on the redistribution of goods, but the distinction between states and tribes is often tenuous.

child care 1. (generically) any matter associated with the upbringing and welfare of children, both familial and in relation to welfare services. Sociologists have concerned themselves with aspects of both. Studies of child care have included a focus on SOCIALIZATION historically and comparatively across class and cultural groups. Similarly, issues such as nursery provision, the educational system, primary health care, and poverty in relation to children's welfare have all attracted much sociological attention. **2.** (more narrowly) the role of the social worker who has a duty to investigate any situation in which a child's welfare is thought to be at risk as a result of abuse, neglect, desertion, or because a child is offending or is deemed to be beyond control.

chi square (X^2) a statistical test for use with nominal data (see CRITERIA AND LEVELS OF MEASUREMENT). The EXPERIMENTAL HYPOTHESIS predicts how many subjects in each group being tested will fall into certain categories if there are no differences between the groups, and the chi-square test compares the observed frequencies with the expected frequencies. The larger the difference between the observed and expected frequency, the more likely that there is a statistically significant difference between the categories.

church 1. any body of people, social institutions, and associated beliefs and practices constituting a distinctive religious grouping, for example, the Methodist Church. **2.** the Christian church as a whole.

In a more technical sociological sense, as initiated by Troeltsch and by Weber, distinctions are also drawn between the church as any well established religious body and denominations, SECTS, and CULTS, which together with churches can be seen as making up a continuum of types of religious organization (see CHURCH-SECT TYPOLOGY).

church-sect typology a conceptualization of *types of religious organization* initially suggested by Weber and Troeltsch, and extended by Howard Becker (1950) and others, which suggests a continuum, and to some extent also a developmental sequence, of types of religious organizations running from CHURCH through DENOMINATION to SECT and CULT, making up a four-point typology of religious organizations. Sometimes a fifth category is also added, in which the term *Ecclesia* refers to a supranational, formally organized religious organization such as the Roman Catholic Church.

The developmental sequence involved in this typology shows that new cults and sects always tend to appear. Sects in particular can be seen as the dynamic element in religious organization, demanding high commitment from their members and capable of leading to rapid religious and also, in some cases, political and economic change (see PROTESTANT ETHIC). Of course, many sects and cults fail to develop and often wither and disappear. When they survive and grow, however, the tendency in the long run is for them to become more formally organized, more bureaucratic and more hierarchical, and, ultimately, more conservative. In doing so they then pose less of a challenge to, and even become part of, the mainstream of society—the prize, but also the penalty, of success.

While the conceptions involved in the church-sect typology work well enough as ideal types in the discussion of most Western forms of religion, reflecting as they do mainly Christian patterns of religious organization, they are less useful in relation to non-Western religions.

Cicourel, Aaron (1928–) US ethnomethodologist whose influential *Method and Measurement in Sociology* assessed the place of statistical and mathematical work in social science, in the light of the situated, judgmental, and negotiated character of all social categorization. Often taken to be a devastating critique of orthodox sociologies (see MEASUREMENT BY FIAT, OFFICIAL STATISTICS), it in fact left open a wide range of possibilities. In his later work, Cicourel has continued to seek a rapprochement between ETH-NOMETHODOLOGY and other kinds of sociology, as well as continuing to contribute to a wide range of studies of familiar sociological topics, for example DEVIANCE and education, which arise from a rethinking of the place and nature of categorical work in social life.

circulation of elites PARETO's term for the endless cycle of renewal and replacement of ELITES, in which political elites of one type are replaced by another. The tendency Pareto described was for elites with one psychological orientation, *lions* (distinguished by their possession of conservative sentiments conducive to the persistence of aggregates) to alternate with more innovative but more untrustworthy *foxes* (distinguished by their "instinct for combinations"). In this process, Pareto saw no possibility that rule by elites could ever be replaced by more democratic forms of rule. See also RESIDUES AND DERIVATIONS, ELITE THEORY.

citizen rights the rights to which citizens are entitled or to which they may lay claim, especially in modern states.

Following T.H. MARSHALL (1950, 1963), three sets of rights can be identified as significant:

(a) *civil rights*, the right to freedom of expression and access to information, and the right to freedom of association and organization and equality before the law;

(b) *political rights*, the right to vote and to seek political office in free elections;

(c) *social and economic rights*, the right to welfare and social security, and perhaps full employment, but usually stopping well short of the right to share in the management of economic organizations, to break the prerogative of managers to manage and of capitalists to own and direct the use of their capital.

The granting of citizen rights in modern societies in part reflects the fact that, as the result of changed expectations, violence can be used only as a last resort by governments in these societies. Accordingly, populations must be mobilized and culturally and ideologically won over and brought to regard these regimes, at least to some degree, as politically legitimate (see also LEGITIMATE AUTHORITY (OR POLITICAL LEGITIMACY), INCORPORATION, WELFARE STATE). At the same time, however, such rights had also to be won, by political activity and social and class conflict.

Whereas some theorists, such as Marshall, present the expansion of citizen rights as undermining, or at least domesticating and institutionalizing, class conflict, other theorists prefer to emphasize a continuing role for class conflict in preserving such rights, and in seeking to extend these beyond the limits usually placed on them in capitalist societies. See also ENTITLEMENTS, SOCIAL CONTRACT THEORY, DAHRENDORF.

CIVIL INATTENTION

civil inattention the ways in which an individual shows that he or she is aware that others are present without making those others the object of particular attention (GOFFMAN, *Behavior in Public Places*, 1963). For example, the eyes of one person may glance at the other but not directly engage, or may quickly disengage should a more direct engaging seem likely to occur. Civil inattention illustrates the existence of an interaction order and interaction ritual, which Goffman sees as governing the general processes of social interactions (see INTERACTION, INTERACTION RITUAL AND INTERACTION ORDER).

civilization 1. a well-established, complex society. Crucial characteristics of a civilization would include the emergence of towns and cities; an increasingly specialized DIVISION OF LABOR; and the development of trade, manufacture, and commerce, and centers of local and national political and legal administration, systems of communication, literacy, and an ELITE culture of artistic and religious expression. In this sense, the historical worlds of, for example, the Aztecs and Incas, Imperial China, Ancient Greece, and the Roman Empire may all be regarded as examples of civilizations. **2.** a term, in the modern world, that is almost coextensive with CULTURE, signaling the shared standards of political, economic, and social behaviur among different societies, as in Western civilization.

In both cases the material precondition for the emergence of civilization is an economy that has a productivity above subsistence level. It is this point that gives the term its value-positive connotation: *civilization* is usually contrasted favorably with the primitivism, SAVAGERY, or BARBARISM that has been held to prevail when existence is dominated by the need to ensure simple survival. In Thomas HOBBES' terms, life outside civil society is "nasty, brutish and short." Thus, for many 19th century evolutionary theorists the route from primitive to modern societies was a civilizing *process*, which included not only material, but also *moral* advancement.

Needless to say, this view was not only arrogant, but also inaccurate, as World War I, for example, made perfectly clear—the supposedly savage people of simple societies never organized slaughter on such a vast or systematic scale. (It is also worth noting that, ironically, far from their lives being dominated by subsistence-related activities, HUNTER-GATHERERS actually spend more time on nonwork activities than people in advanced industrial societies.) See also EVOLUTIONARY THEORY, MONTESQUIEU.

civilizing process the historical process in which, according to ELIAS (1939), people acquired a greater capacity for controlling their emotions. Elias indicates how in Western societies the pattern of living that came to be regarded as civilized—*structures of affects*—involved profound redefinitions of normal and proper behavior. In a detailed sociogenetic study of manners, social stratification, and state formation, Elias shows how new standards of decorum and repugnance, and new kinds of human beings, came into existence. See also FIGURATION, COURT SOCIETY.

civil religion the quasi-religious beliefs and rituals, for example, salutes to the national flag, parades, coronation ceremonies, or even international sporting events (see Young and Shils, 1953), which can be seen to perform the function of fostering SOCIAL SOLIDARITY and the achievement of POLITICAL LEGITIMACY within a society. The most influential use of the term in sociology was made by DURKHEIM in *The Elementary Forms of Religious Life* (1912). See also FUNCTIONAL(IST) THEORY OF RELIGION.

clan (anthropology) a kinship term that describes a body of people claiming common unilineal descent. This may be matrilineal or patrilineal, but not both. Often clans are distinguished from others by reference to an ancestor who may be nonhuman or mythical (see TOTEMISM).

class 1. the hierarchical distinctions that exist between individuals or groups (for example, occupational groups) within a society. In this general sense class is an alternative general term to SOCIAL STRATIFICATION. The term "social class" is also widely used as a general synonym for "class." **2.** any particular position within a social stratification system or class system, for example, middle class, working class, etc. **3.** (*occupational class*) descriptive classification of the total population into broad occupational classes or socioeconomic status groups, for example, manual and nonmanual classes, as well as more elaborated classification (see OCCUPATIONAL SCALES). **4.** the particular form of open, rather than closed, stratification of class system found within modern industrial societies, in which individual and collective SOCIAL MOBILITY is relatively commonplace (compare CASTE, ESTATE). **5.** (Marxism) the economically determined and inherently conflictual divisions of society based on ownership and nonownership of property, for example, lord and serf in feudal society, bourgeoisie, and PROLETARIAT in capitalist societies, which characterize all large-scale societies and which are held ultimately to determine the destiny of each type of society. Marx also identifies a multiplicity of lesser classes and groupings that influence the outcome of political and social conflicts. **6.** (WEBER, 1922) differences between categories or groups of persons in their typical probabilities of procuring goods, gaining positions in life, and finding inner satisfaction—LIFE CHANCES. Thus, for Weber, class means "all persons in the same class situation," whatever the basis of this and whatever its implications may be for the longer-term destiny of societies (see also CLASS, STATUS, AND PARTY). Weber identified a number of overlapping possible bases of class situation, based on ownership and nonownership of property and also including reference to different kinds of property and the different kinds of income that this yields. In particular, he identifies:

(a) *property classes;*

(b) *commercial classes,* somewhat misleadingly so-called, since these include individuals able to safeguard their position through political or organization activity, for example, professionals or others monopolizing qualifications, as well as entrepreneurs possessing other bases of monopoly;

(c) *social classes*, the totality of such class situations, defined in terms of situations *within which* "individual and generational mobility is easy and typically occurs." The main social classes identified by Weber in this sense are: (i) the working class, (ii) the petty bourgeoisie, (iii) the propertyless intelligentsia and specialists, and (iv) classes privileged by property and education.

Class situations, and the social classes these give rise to, may be positively privileged or negatively privileged, with various middle classes in between. Since mobility among, and the instability of, class positions is considerable, for Weber social class is highly variable, and only sometimes are these the bases of class consciousness or collective action.

The first dictionary use of "class" occurred in the 17th century, in T. Blount's *Glossographia.* Apart from military and school usage, he noted that the term described a "distribution of people according to their several Degrees." The term came into general use in a similar way, as one that described differences of birth, occupation, wealth, ability, property, etc. An overall, but no absolute, distinction can be drawn between those conceptions of class, which set out to be mainly descriptive and those which are more analytical.

Descriptive classificatory approaches: for more on the main descriptive approaches see SOCIAL STRATIFICATION, OCCUPATIONAL SCALES.

Analytical conceptions of class: Marx. Of the analytical approaches to class, the most influential uses in sociology undoubtedly stem from MARX, although he acknowledged that the term had originated earlier, in particular in the work of Enlightenment social theorists and French socialists.

In Marx's own work the term has a number of different applications, but the essential aspects of Marx's general model of social class are clear:

(a) Every society has to produce a surplus to feed, house, and clothe dependent children, the sick and the elderly. Class differences begin when one group of people claim resources that are not consumed for immediate survival as their private property;

(b) Classes therefore are defined in terms of ownership or nonownership of productive property, which makes possible the taking of the surplus. At different times in human history, different forms of property (for example slaves, water, land, capital) have been crucial in shaping social relationships, but all class systems are characterized by two major classes. The most important class relationship as far as Marx was concerned was that found in capitalism, between the bourgeoisie and the proletariat;

(c) The historical importance of classes, for Marx, is that they are intrinsically exploitative: one class, because it takes the surplus produced by another class, exploits and oppresses that class, and therefore conflict is an inevitable product of class relationships. The conflicts associated with class antagonisms are the most important factor in social change: ultimately it is class conflicts, associated with underlying social and economic CONTRADICTIONS, that transform societies;

(d) Marx distinguishes between the objective aspects of class, as set out in (b) above, and the subjective aspects, that is, the fact of membership of a class is not necessarily accompanied by an awareness of membership or a feeling of political identity with the interests of a class. It is only when members of a class realize their common interests and act together to gain them that one can fully talk about a social class.

It should be noted that the above is a theoretical model and, as such, should not be taken as simply descriptive of any historical situation but as indicating the most important structure and processes for understanding social relations and for directing empirical work. In Marx's empirical work he introduced a number of factors into his understanding of social class. In *The 18th Brumaire of Louis Bonaparte* (1852), for example, he discusses the French peasantry of the mid-19th century and he comes close to a formal definition of class that includes variables such as a shared culture and a national political organization.

Major problems arising out of Marx's work have inspired most of the subsequent sociological work on class:

(a) the fact that Marx's account of classes and the role in precapitalist societies was relatively limited leads to questions as to whether class has the centrality of importance in the generation of change in these societies, for example, see CLASS DIVIDED SOCIETY;

(b) the existence and growth of important groups other than the proletariat and the bourgeoisie;

(c) divisions within classes that have often proven as significant politically as divisions between classes (for example, see CONTRADICTORY CLASS LOCATIONS);

(d) the important effect of factors other than social class on people's lives, gender and race in particular;

(e) the fact that CLASS CONSCIOUSNESS in practice has never shown a simple correspondence with Marx's view of objective class situation and, historically, for subordinate classes, has normally been much at variance with objective conditions as defined by Marx.

Analytical conceptions of class: Weber. The most influential alternative theory of class is found in Max WEBER's work. Unlike Marx, Weber emphasized other factors that promoted inequality. In particular he considered status or honor and prestige as a distinct variable. He also emphasized the link between class and opportunity, arguing that a class is a category or group of people who share similar life chances. With Marx, he saw ownership and nonownership as a basic criterion, but Weber stressed divisions within classes (partly based on social STATUS) and empirical changes in class boundaries to a much greater extent than Marx. Examples are

CLASS

Weber's distinction between ownership and commercial classes, and also the way that different skill levels divided the working class in terms of life chances. Here Weber is emphasizing the importance of markets rather than simply ownership or nonownership of property as the basis of inequality, that is, level of skill and demand for skills determining differences in rewards. Weber also differs from Marx in seeing BUREAUCRACY, as well as class, as a fundamental nexus of power in modern societies.

Weber's stress on a variety of factors influencing opportunities and rewards (see also CLASS, STATUS AND PARTY) has made his approach to the analysis of class and social stratification very influential in sociological theory. In British sociology, for example, LOCKWOOD (1958) and later GOLDTHORPE and Lockwood et al. (1968 and 1969) emphasized the importance of taking account of status as well as market situation and work situation (see also MULTIDIMENSIONAL ANALYSIS OF SOCIAL STRATIFICATION, AFFLUENT WORKER). GIDDENS (1981) has taken the emphasis on the market situation of individuals as important in qualifying Marx's view of class and power. Earlier critics of Marx's work also emphasized Weberian themes, notably theorists of MANAGERIAL REVOLUTION, STABLE DEMOCRACY, END OF IDEOLOGY.

Analytical conceptions of class: modern approaches. Most recent approaches have tended to take either Marx or Weber as a starting point. There have been numerious attempts to adapt or refute elements of the classical approaches. Efforts to repair deficiencies in Marx's work, for example, as seen in studies by Poulantzas (1973), Carchedi (1977), and Wright (1978 and 1985), have been widely discussed. A common preoccupation of all these theorists is the problem of CLASS BOUNDARIES, of accounting for the position of the middle classes (see INTERMEDIATE CLASSES AND INTERMEDIATE STRATA) within the Marxist theory of class. They all accept the deficiencies of the orthodox Marxist view of such groups as professionals, managers, and white-collar workers, but they differ in their attempted solutions to the problem posed by the continued existence and role of this group, which the classical Marxian theory assumed in the long run would be assimilated into one or the other of the two main classes in capitalism, or disappear.

Poulantzas follows ALTHUSSER in arguing that there are three relatively autonomous aspects of class relations: economic (PRODUCTIVE versus UNPRODUCTIVE LABOR), political (supervision versus nonsupervision), and ideological (mental versus manual labor); hence, the definition of social classes cannot be purely economic. The direct production of commodities (the economic role) is still seen as the main criterion defining the proletariat, but the situation is complicated by further relations of power. Any worker, productive or not, who occupies a subordinate position in any of the three spheres should be seen as a member of a distinct class: the new petty bourgeosie. Carchedi proposes a variation on this approach. He distinguishes between ownership and functional aspects of the capitalist-labor relation. He argues that as capitalism developed, production became more and more a collective process and, similarly, the function of the capitalist in controlling and organizing the labor force became separated from ownership with the growth of managerial hierarchies. The NEW MIDDLE CLASS exercises the function of capital (control and surveillance) without being part of the class that owns capital. Similarly, Wright (1978) distinguishes between ownership and control, arguing that people who do not own the means of production but have important powers as managers or semiautonomous professionals are in CONTRADICTORY CLASS LOCATIONS. In a later critique (1985), Wright reemphasized ideas of property and exploitation as central to an understanding of class relations. Each of these approaches attempts to overcome the problems the new middle classes pose for Marxian accounts of class by treating power and control of the labor process as in some way independently definitive of class relations. These new approaches, therefore, despite their location within the Marxian tradition and different conceptual frameworks, bear at some points a striking resemblance to aspects of Weber's approach, the difference being that they see their new approach as rehabilitating the Marxian view. The ultimate basis of class, and the fundamental dynamics of society, remain objective economic class interests.

Many other writers have preferred to look more directly to Weber rather than to Marx to develop a more satisfactory theory of class. Among the most influential of these, along with Lockwood and Goldthorpe, has been Parkin (1971; 1974; 1979). Parkin draws on Weber's discussion of SOCIAL CLOSURE, the idea that groups try to monopolize resources and opportunities for their own benefit, and to deny resources and opportunities to others. The key point here is the idea of exclusion of nonmembers. In different societies, criteria of eligibility for membership of dominant classes differ: religion, ethnicity, and gender, for example, are bases for exclusion in different societies. Birth into a particular group is a common criterion, so kinship and descent are crucial, and, in this type of rigid system, privileged groups can maximize closure to their own benefit successfully. Closure in modern societies is not based on descent, but distinct strategies of exclusion are nevertheless employed.

It should be noted that much empirical work on class and social mobility operates with occupational definitions rather than with ones based on property (see SOCIAL STRATIFICATION). Sociological approaches to class have also been much criticized recently for their gender blindness, that is, for being models of inequality relating to males only, and treating women's class positions as dependent on those of their male partners (see GENDER STRATIFICATION, MEDIATED CLASS LOCATIONS).

class boundaries the more or less clearly defined dividing lines held to exist between CLASSES within a society or particular types of society.

CLASS CLEAVAGE

Debates have existed particularly about the boundaries between classes in CAPITALIST SOCIETIES. Such debates have been especially important within Marxism, but also have a more general significance, both theoretically (for example, in relation to assessments of class interests and likely class action, see EMBOURGEOISEMENT, AFFLUENT WORKERS, CLASS IMAGERY, MULTIDIMENSIONAL ANALYSIS OF SOCIAL STRATIFICATION) or, more mundanely, in the construction of classificatory schemata in connection with analysis and accounts of SOCIAL STRATIFICATION and SOCIOECONOMIC STATUS.

Within Marxism and neo-Marxism, debates have centered not only on the location and the implications of the locations of class boundaries, but also on whether the assumption can be maintained that all individual or collective class positions can be located uniquely within particular classes, or whether there exist many class locations that in terms of main classes must be seen as CONTRADICTORY CLASS LOCATIONS. Theoretically and politically, a good deal hinges on decisions on the existence and location of class boundaries, for example, the size, political role, and the center of gravity and leadership of the working class, or the role of INTERMEDIATE CLASSES OR INTERMEDIATE STRATA or the NEW MIDDLE CLASS. Theorists such as Eric Ohlin Wright (1985), for example, argued that groups such as the "middle class within capitalist societies" are "constituted by locations which are simultaneously in the capitalist class and the working class." The implications of this, however, may or may not be seen as indicating a loss of saliency for Marx's basic notions of class.

class cleavage the class-based conflict in Western democracies between competing left- and right-wing political parties. As expressed by Lipset (*Political Parties*, 1960), "in every modern democracy conflict among different groups is expressed through political parties, which basically represent a 'democratic expression of the class struggle.' " For Lipset, such forms of legitimate and domesticated class conflict, which replace earlier, more socially disruptive forms, are a necessary requirement for a stable liberal democracy. Modern stable democracies involve cleavage within CONSENSUS, the existence of a basic agreement on the political rules of the game, and arise from the gradual entry of the lower classes into the political system. See also END-OF-IDEOLOGY THESIS.

Lipset's characterization of class cleavage has come under attack from two directions:

(a) from those who do not accept that the elimination of more traditional forms of class conflict is an inevitable secular tendency in modern Western societies, or that this is a requirement for liberal democracy;

(b) from those who argue that a more fundamental CLASS DEALIGNMENT is occurring, leading to the replacement of class as the main basis of political cleavage (see WORKING CLASS CONSERVATISM).

class consciousness the awareness, among members of a social CLASS, of common interests that are based on their own class situation and are in opposition to the interests of other classes. The term is particularly associated with Marxism, where the concern is often either with the processes fostering development of class consciousness in the PROLETARIAT, or involves discussions as to why such a consciousness has not developed. A basic distinction here is between a *class-in-itself*—the objective basis of class interests—and a *class-for-itself*—the consciousness of these interests. The basic idea is that a set of values and beliefs and a political organization will or should emerge in order to represent and realize the objective interests of a class. In the case of the WORKING CLASS, certain aspects of their work and life situations (exploitation, ALIENATION, periodic mass unemployment, poverty, etc.) are seen as facilitating growing awareness of a common situation and encouraging a collective response. Most Marxists agree, however, that only a limited awareness and set of objectives are arrived at spontaneously. Lenin, for example, in an influential pamphlet (1902) argued that, left to itself, the working class would develop only an economistic consciousness, limited to demands for better pay and conditions within the capitalist system. Lenin, like many Marxists, was interested in the overthrow of capitalism, not in its reform. Thus, he argued that a revolutionary (vanguard) party was necessary to transform TRADE UNION CONSCIOUSNESS into political, revolutionary consciousness and action. This has been a recurrent theme in Marxist writings on the proletariat—the issue of why a revolutionary class consciousness has never developed among the working classes of the most developed capitalist states. In the 1920s and 1930s, for example, LUKACS and GRAMSCI developed different critiques of crude Marxism, emphasizing theoretical and cultural factors that impeded the development of true consciousness or promoted the development of false consciousness.

It might be debated whether the issue of what type of consciousness the working class ought to have is an appropriate area of study. Should sociologists not be concerned with the ideas which are actually held, rather than with those that theorists think would be good for them? (See also FALSE CONSCIOUSNESS.) Thus, there is a substantial literature on CLASS IMAGERY, the actual images of class possessed by social ACTORS, and at the same time sociologists have taken up the issue of the limits and possibilities of the notion of class consciousness in the Marxian sense. This is a theme that also underlies debate on the NEW WORKING CLASS. MANN (1973) argues that one may find awareness of class membership and also group solidarity, but it is rather unlikely that the working class can produce independently an alternative vision of a new society. This type of sociological approach, however, seeks to do more than echo Lenin's 70-year old conclusion. Instead, it attempts to operationalize the concept of working-class consciousness by identifying it as involving four elements:

(a) class identity—the definition of oneself as working class;

(b) class opposition—the definition of an opposed (capitalist) class;

(c) class totality—(a) and (b) taken as together defining the whole society;

(d) an alternative vision of society.

Mann concludes that British workers are usually limited to (a), only occasionally incorporating (b). See also HEGEMONY.

class dealignment the thesis, especially in connection with VOTING BEHAVIOR in Great Britain, that a previous pattern of alignment between POLITICAL ATTITUDES and CLASS is breaking down and is being replaced by more fluid affiliations and more volatile patterns of voting (for example, see Crewe et al., 1977; see also WORKING-CLASS CONSERVATISM, AFFLUENT WORKER, CLASS IMAGERY). The thesis finds some justification in the fact that working-class support for the Labour Party has declined in recent years, while middle-class support for the Labour Party and for parties other than the Conservative Party has increased. Alford (1967) has suggested that the extent of class voting within an electorate can be measured using an *index of class voting* computed as: the percentage of manual workers voting for left parties, minus the percentage of nonmanual workers voting for left parties. Crewe's thesis of class dealignment would appear to rest on a similar conception of class voting and non-class voting. It can be argued, however, that this provides only one baseline for measures of class voting, and not necessarily the most cogent or significant one. Several possibilities can be noted:

(a) taking another baseline (for example, Marxian conceptions of CLASS or sectoral interests, see SECTORAL CLEAVAGES), increasing middle-class support for parties other than the Conservative Party might be seen as reflecting a new recognition of class interests among particular sections of nonmanual workers (see also NEW MIDDLE CLASS, MIDDLE-CLASS RADICALISM);

(b) there is the problem of how to take into account what Wright (1985, 1989) has referred to as MEDIATED CLASS LOCATIONS, especially the influence of a spouse's or partner's employment on the assessment of a voter's class location. In many studies of voting behavior, including those of Butler and Stokes, and Crewe, this influence has not been taken into account; indeed, such studies have mainly used the occupation of the, usually male HEAD OF HOUSEHOLD as their main indicator of class. For this second reason no less than the first, it is obvious that estimates of class or class-deviant voting will vary widely with different definitions of class. See also PARTY IDENTIFICATION, CLASS POLARIZATION.

class-divided society 1. any society in which there exist fundamental class divisions. **2.** (GIDDENS, 1984) any agrarian state in which there is class division, but where this division "is not the main basis of the principle of organization of the society." As such, these forms of society are contrasted directly with modern forms, including the capitalist society, in which class divisions are a main basis of the social organization and the central dynamic of society. In making this distinction, Giddens wished to undermine orthodox Marxist accounts of the dynamic role of class in all societies, that is "the history of all societies as class struggle." See also CLASS, STRATIFICATION, MARX.

class formation the organized collectivities within a class structure; the processes by which these emerge. The distinction between class structure and class formation can be seen as a basic, if often implicit, distinction in class analysis (Wright, 1985). If class structure can be seen as composed of those factors that establish the broad pattern of class interests, class opportunities, life chances, etc. within a society, class formation refers to the actual collectivities, class action, etc. that are generated on the basis of this structure. In classical Marxism, the relationship between class structure and class formation has sometimes been treated as relatively unproblematic. Neo-Marxist and Weberian approaches, on the other hand, have usually regarded the relationship as one requiring empirical exploration, although it is usually agreed the general conditions likely to be conducive to class formations can be identified, for example, the conditions for the existence of CLASS CONSCIOUSNESS.

class identity (usually) a SOCIAL ACTOR's subjective conception of class location (see SUBJECTIVE AND OBJECTIVE CLASS).

classification (SOCIOLOGY OF EDUCATION) the identification of the boundaries between different forms of human knowledge. In the formal educational process this relates to the organization of knowledge into curricula, or the various domains of educational activity. The term is a key concept in BERNSTEIN's theory of knowledge codes.

class imagery the ideas and images of class and class structure, and the distribution of power, held by SOCIAL ACTORS.

There have been many empirical studies of class attitudes and imagery, the great majority of which have been concerned with the manual working class. In the 1950s and 1960s especially, many social commentators, not only sociologists, were interested in exploring the implications of changing life styles, particularly changes in patterns of family and work relationships within traditional working-class communities (see also AFFLUENT SOCIETY, EMBOURGEOISEMENT THESIS, WORKING-CLASS CONSERVATISM). Influential North American and European studies also contributed to the discussion, for example, those of Chinoy (1955) and Popitz et al. (1957). In British sociology, significant studies were carried out by Abrams (1960) and Zweig (1961), but the classic paper was by LOCKWOOD, "The Sources of Variation in Working Class Images of Society" (1966, reprinted together with a number of papers on the theme in Bulmer, 1975).

Lockwood's article drew on a major study of conjugal relationships (Bott, 1957), which included a discussion of social imagery. Bott had concluded that her respondents had two different models of society: a power model (also a "them and us" model), in which society was seen as divided

Ideal type	Social context	Class concepts	Likely party identification
Traditional (proletarian)	Occupational and residential community	Two main classes, them and us; in terms of power and authority	Traditional Labour
Deferential	Small firm; agricultural; older workers; job involvement; status hierarchy	Three (or more) classes; in terms of lifestyle and social background – prestige model	Working-class Conservative
Privatized/ instrumental	Absence of occupational or residential community	Large central and residual classes; in terms of wealth and consumption	Labour support – conditional, but collective instrumentalism and potential militancy

Fig. 2. **Class imagery.** Goldthorpe and Lockwood categories.

into two fairly static, opposing classes (working and middle classes), and a "prestige" model, in which the class structure was seen as composed of a much larger number of groups arranged in a hierarchy of prestige. Bott also suggested that a preference for one or other of these two models could be explained as the outcome of the work and community experiences of people—their primary social experiences. Lockwood drew on these ideas, identifying three types of social consciousness within the working class linked to definite types of work and community structures (see Fig. 2):

(a) the traditional proletarian worker, that is, coal miners, dockworkers, and shipbuilders, having a power model of society, that is, where workers have a strong commitment both to their work and to fellow workers, and live in close, homogeneous communities;

(b) the traditional deferential worker, who recognized the leadership rights of a traditional elite and adopts a prestige hierarchy model of class; these are typically workers in small family firms or in agriculture, in paternalistic employment relations, and in a fixed-status hierarchy in the wider community of the town or village;

(c) the privatized worker, who sees class differences in terms of a money model of society; this group is seen as more home-centered than communally oriented, and more instrumental in its attitudes to work and politics.

Subsequently Lockwood's initial work was extended in a number of empirical studies, especially in the well-known studies of the AFFLUENT WORKER (GOLDTHORPE, LOCKWOOD, et al., 1968a & b, 69).

Although mostly accepting the value of Lockwood's discussion, more recent studies have, in general, revealed a more complex and contradictory picture of working-class class imagery. Notably, the lack of consideration of issues of gender or race by Lockwood has received criticism. Pollart (1981), for example, has shown that the class images of women factory workers are frequently ambivalent, and constantly overlaid by gender roles and the power relations associated with gender divisions. Others have also argued that most conventional studies of class imagery have paid insufficient attention to general structural and theoretical issues relating to class formation and development. Howard Newby, in his study of agricultural workers (1979), has argued, for example, that it is a mistake to see deference as a simple or a single orientation; rather, it is highly variable in form and often a relation of power in which class imagery is not paramount (see also DEFERENCE). For all this, the strength of research on class imagery, in contrast with much of the literature on CLASS CONSCIOUSNESS, is that it attempts to map empirically existing modes of consciousness among the working class.

class-in-itself and **class-for-itself** see CLASS CONSCIOUSNESS.

class location any objective position within the class structure. See CONTRADICTORY CLASS LOCATIONS.

class polarization (Marxism) the tendency for the inherently conflicting interests of the two main classes within capitalism to result in an increasing consciousness of these differences, with the two classes eventually becoming opposing camps. According to Marx, this process comes about as the result of the tendency for the proletariat to experience *immiseration* under capitalism, while at the same time also being thrown together in situations that will encourage collective action, for example, in large factories and towns (see CLASS CONSCIOUSNESS). As part of this polarization, classes that stand in various INTERMEDIATE CLASS locations within capitalism also tend to be drawn into one camp or the other, mostly into the ranks of the proletariat, as tendencies to crisis within capitalism intensify.

It is obvious that Marx's hypothesis has not been borne out, at least in any straightforward way, partly because immiseration has not occurred on the scale Marx expected and also because class interests and the foundations of class consciousness are far more complex than he anticipated (see CLASS IMAGERY). On the other hand, a broadly class-based form of politics has become the norm within most Western liberal democracies (see STABLE DEMOCRACY), despite some suggestions that CLASS DEALIGNMENT had removed this, and although the issue is much complicated by the continued existence of intermediate classes (see also VOTING BEHAVIOR).

Polarization on a world scale between rich and poor nations is a further element of class polarization that can either be handled in terms of Marxian conceptions, or seen as involving a fundamental departure from his schemata (see DEPENDENCY THEORY, WALLERSTEIN). See also UNDERCLASS.

CLASSROOM INTERACTION

classroom interaction a description of the activities of various participants in classroom activity. Interest in the nature of classroom relationships developed with increased research into the way in which educational institutions themselves shape educational outcomes. Using ethnographic techniques (see ETHNOGRAPHY) and concepts derived from SYMBOLIC INTERACTIONISM, researchers analyze the social interactions and values that constitute the social system of the classroom.

class, status, and party three ideal-typical (see IDEAL TYPE), partly competing, partly interrelated, key ways in which, according to WEBER (1922), societies can be seen as hierarchically and politically divided.

We may speak of class, says Weber and his interpreters, when:

(a) a number of people have in common "a specific causal component of their LIFE CHANCES";

(b) this component is determined by economic interests in the possession of goods and opportunities for income within commodity or labor markets.

Thus, class may also be referred to as *market situation*. Classes in this sense need not be communities or collectivities; they merely represent possible, albeit frequent, bases of collective action. In contrast, for Weber, status is normally a matter of actual *groupings* of individuals. As opposed to purely economically determined class situation, *status situation* is any typical component of the life fate of people that is determined by a "specific, positive or negative, social estimation of honour." While status can be linked with class, it need not be, and may also on occasions counteract it.

"Party" refers to political parties. In the circumstances in which these arise—especially, but not only, in modern societies—they may be based on status or class, on both, or on neither. Thus, for Weber, the analysis of class and social stratification could not be reduced to the simple terms sometimes involved in popular versions of Marxism and historical materialism. In Weber's analysis, though class interests may often be the basis of collective political and social action, there is no general tendency for class interests to lead to simple CLASS POLARIZATION or to revolutionary change. Weber's ideas on class, status, and party have been widely influential, for example, see MULTIDIMENSIONAL ANALYSIS OF SOCIAL STRATIFICATION. See also CLASS, SOCIAL STRATIFICATION.

class structure the general pattern of CLASS differences and relations within a society. See also CLASS FORMATION.

clinical sociology a practically oriented approach to sociology, prevalent in North America, in which the aim is professional intervention in social life, especially in making evaluations of, and in seeking solutions to, social problems. Whether the clinical model is an appropriate one for sociologists to adopt, however, is debatable; the term has gained little currency outside North America.

cluster analysis a technique used to identify groups of objects or people that can be shown to be relatively distinct within a data set. The characteristics of people within each cluster can then be explored. In market research, for example, cluster analysis has been used to identify groups of people for whom different marketing approaches would be appropriate.

A rich variety of clustering methods is available. A common method is hierarchical clustering which can work either from bottom up or from top down. In agglomerative hierarchical clustering (that is, bottom up), the process begins with as many clusters as cases. Using a mathematical criterion such as the standardized Euclidean distance, objects or people are successively joined together into clusters. In divisive hierarchical clustering (that is, top down), the process begins with a single cluster containing all cases, which is then broken down into smaller clusters.

The hierarchical structure is often presented in the form of a dendrogram, or tree diagram. There are also several methods available for combining clusters. The simplest is the single link, or nearest neighbor, method. The first two objects to be joined will be those with the smallest distance between them. The next object to join them will be the one with the minimum distance between itself and a case in the cluster. Successive combinations are made using the smallest distance at each stage.

An alternative technique is the complete linkage, or furthest neighbor, approach, in which the distance between two clusters is calculated as the distance between the two furthest cases. Ward's hierarchical clustering (based on within groups sum of squares) and Wishart's mode analysis are two further examples of different approaches.

There are many practical problems involved in the use of cluster analysis. The selection of variables to be included in the analysis, the choice of distance measure, and the criteria for combining cases into clusters are all crucial. Because the selected clustering method can itself impose a certain amount of structure on the data, it is possible for spurious clusters to be obtained. In general, several different methods should be used. (See Anderberg, 1973, and Everitt, 1974, for full discussions of methods.)

cluster sample a method of SAMPLING that selects from groups (*clusters*) existing in the parent population, rather than assembling a RANDOM SAMPLE. This tends to be quicker and cheaper, but may lead to a BIASED SAMPLE if the clusters are not representative of the parent population. For example, polls taken of attitudes toward government policy may be carried out in selected areas of the country thought to be representative, but because of local political dynamics this may not be the case.

cobweb theorem see CYCLE AND CYCLICAL PHENOMENA.

code the differential usage of a system or collection of signs marking differential social memberships. Codes may be conscious or unconscious. The most influential example is BERNSTEIN's notion of differential usages of English, by which fundamental status and class differences are communicated and reproduced (see also ELABORATED AND RESTRICTED CODES). A *restricted code* is used in close communal circumstances, where there is legitimate expectation of shared presuppositions and understandings, and involves speech that is inexplicit, telescoped, and indexical (see INDEXICAL EXPRESSION). An *elaborated code* makes no such presuppositions, is explicit in meaning, and uses full forms of expression and objective standards of reference. Bernstein argues that the English social classes manifest a differential familiarity with each mode of speech, with social and educational implications. Other examples include dress and fashion codes, with identities claimed or refused by items selected, and by the selection of terms, actions, or items used as identification by formal and informal special interest groups, secret societies, sexual minorities, or drug users.

coding the assignment of (generally) numerical codes to specific data in such a way as to allow analysis to be undertaken by means of computer or by hand. The need to code data in a meaningful way is common to much sociological research, whether it is describing a phenomenon or testing a sociological theory.

It is possible to differentiate two basic types of coding–structured and unstructured–depending on the type of data to be analyzed, although the difference between them is blurred. STRUCTURED CODING can generally be used on primary data, that which the researcher collects directly. Unstructured coding is generally used with data collected by the researcher from secondary sources. The main example of the use of structured coding is in QUESTIONNAIRE analysis, and that of unstructured coding in CONTENT ANALYSIS. See also UNSTRUCTURED DATA.

cognitive dissonance the experience of competing, opposing or contradictory thoughts, attitudes or actions leading to a feeling of tension, and the need to achieve consonance. The term was introduced by Festinger (1957). In his definition dissonant cognitions exist when Belief A implies the negation of Belief B. For example, "smoking causes lung cancer" is dissonant with "I smoke." The dissonance can be reduced in a variety of ways, either by adjusting Belief A or Belief B. Belief A could be adjusted by disregarding medical reports that confirm the belief and by paying particular attention to skeptical reports. Belief B can be adjusted by smoking less, or by smoking tobacco of a low carcinogenic type.

cognitive relativism see RELATIVISM.

cohesion see SOCIAL COHESION.

cohort a group of persons possessing a common characteristic, such as being born in the same year or entering school on the same date. The term is usually used in making generalizations derived from quantitative data (see QUANTITATIVE RESEARCH TECHNIQUES).

collective behavior the action or behavior of people in groups and crowds—*crowd behavior*—where, as the result of physical proximity, and the protection and contagion of the group, the action of individuals is out-of-the-ordinary, tends to depart from routine standards of social demeanor, and may be more than usually explosive and unpredictable. In early sociological and social psychological theories of collective behavior (notably in the work of Gustav LeBon, *The Crowd*, 1895), as well as in more recent theories (for example, Smelser, 1962), it is seen as a potential threat to normal social order. As such, the various forms of collective behavior, including such phenomena as demonstrations, riots, and rebellions, sometimes play a significant part in SOCIAL MOVEMENTS and SOCIAL CHANGE.

collective conscience the shared beliefs and associated moral attitudes that operate as a unifying force within a society. As used especially by DURKHEIM, the term particularly refers to simpler societies based on mechanical solidarity, in which DIVISION OF LABOR is not advanced. In more complex societies, according to Durkheim, a shared collective conscience becomes less important, and social solidarity is based on reciprocity rather than likeness (see MECHANICAL AND ORGANIC SOLIDARITY). See also COLLECTIVE REPRESENTATION.

collective consumption any consumption of goods and services whose provision and management, to a degree, cannot be other than collective and which the private sector finds it unprofitable to provide (Castells, 1977). Among such goods and services identified by Castells were public transport, housing, and leisure provision. The term was introduced by Castells in an attempt to achieve a focus on the distinctive features of urban social movements, which he viewed as above all seeking to influence and control the spatially bounded *collective consumption units* provided in the urban context.

Subsequently, the term has been taken up by other political sociologists and political scientists (for example, Dunleavy, 1980) and used in a more general way as the basis of an overall analysis of SECTORAL DIVISIONS that cut across more conventional divisions of class: above all, the distinction between those who, as consumers or workers, are main beneficiaries of collective consumption, and those who are not. Both in Castells' work and in later inquiries, the focus on collective consumption emphasizes the tension between the necessity for collective provision of some goods and services, and the burden on capital this provision represents (see also STATE EXPENDITURES). It is this conflict that is seen as both generating urban social movements and as making sectoral divisions an important dimension of political cleavage in modern capitalist societies.

collective representation the shared—hence social rather than individual—conceptions within a society. The term is DURKHEIM's, who argued that these conceptions must be the fundamental subject matter of sociology. For Durkheim, collective representations must be studied as social facts external to any one individual. See SOCIAL FACTS AS THINGS.

collective unconscious see JUNG.

collectivity any grouping of individuals that cuts across the actor (see SOCIAL ACTOR) as a composite unit (PARSONS, 1951).

Collingwood, Robin (1889–1943) English archaeologist and philosopher known particularly for his ideas on metaphysics and for what he had to say about historical explanation and understanding. Collingwood rejected positivist claims about the unity of knowledge, as well as a naive EMPIRICISM that knowledge of the external world could be obtained in an unfiltered manner from observation. In *An Essay on Metaphysics* (1940) he argued that the intellectual content of any given discipline at a particular stage of its development rested on a priori "absolute presuppositions" specific to each discipline as well as each epoch. Thus, in ways that anticipate aspects of Thomas KUHN's conception of scientific paradigms and scientific revolutions (see NORMAL AND REVOLUTIONARY SCIENCE), he sometimes wrote as if there were no common yardsticks of truth and falsity to which reference could be made in order to judge between different constellations of absolute presuppositions. More often, however, Collingwood wrote that different constellations underlie different modes of knowing. In the work which has exerted the greatest influence on sociology, *The Idea of History* (1946), he distinguished between scientific thinking, concerned with claims to laws established by observation and experiment, and distinctively historical thinking, in which the aim was to question the evidence in order to reveal the specific thought underlying human action. Hence his claim that "all history is the history of thought." Collingwood's ideas, which have some affinities with WITTGENSTEIN's emphasis on distinctive FORMS OF LIFE, have influenced thinking in sociology, particularly as the result of their influence on Peter WINCH.

color bar the systematic or institutionalized restriction on access to resources or social opportunities in which the basis of DISCRIMINATION is determined by socially established criteria of racial origin, especially criteria established by whites and applied to blacks.

coming out a social, psychological, and political process that involves both public and private identification with the designation "lesbian" or "gay." Crucially, the process involves internalization of the label "homosexual" and acceptance of a lesbian or gay life style. The term arose out of the reemergence of radical sexual politics in the context of the wider radicalization of political culture in the 1960s. It was, and continues to be, a key concept within gay and lesbian politics because of the challenge it presents to the negative imagery surrounding homosexuality and the sociopolitical processes that render it invisible. Coming out involves a change in self-image for the individual, which arises from an affirmation of his or her homosexuality. As a political strategy, the process of coming out challenges the normative frameworks surrounding institutionalized heterosexuality.

commensality the act of eating together, literally, sharing the same table; the social sharing of food providing symbolic and social, as well as biological, sustenance. Both domestic and status relations are usually reflected in patterns of commensality, for example, see CASTE. In more general terms, in a sense suggested by LÉVI-STRAUSS, "Food is both good to eat and think."

commercial ethnograhy use of ethnographic techniques to inform design and marketing. As well as the mutual influence of commercial market-research and academic social-survey work, there has been an increasing adoption by commercial firms of qualitative methods of investigating human activity. The most striking is the development of PARTICIPANT OBSERVATION, and a use of the methods of SOCIAL ANTHROPOLOGY as a means of discovering life styles in precise detail in order to tailor the design of products with precision. Investigators, with a cover story, seek to live a life as close to that of the target community as possible. Pioneered by Japanese auto firms in the US, and strikingly successful as a technique, it is ironic that what are usually regarded as soft, or unscientific, social-science methods have, in fact, remarkably powerful commercial applications.

commodity-sign see BAUDRILLARD.

common law a system of law, of which English law is the prime example, based on legal precedents created by judges. Thus, this system directly contrasts with more formally codified systems of civil law, such as those based on Roman law (for example, Scottish law). In common-law systems, however, increasing legislative activity by the STATE has meant that statute law also pays an increasing role within such systems.

commonsense knowledge the knowledge that guides ordinary conduct in everyday life. According to SCHUTZ, common-sense knowledge consists of a huge bundle of understandings acquired through SOCIALIZATION, which resemble recipes for carrying out ordinary actions, such as responding to a greeting or using a telephone. ETHNOMETHODOLOGY studies PRACTICAL REASONING **2.**, which is how this knowledge is *used* in social action.

communication(s) 1. any imparting or exchange of information. Communication may be verbal or nonverbal, intended or unintended (see SEMIOTICS, BODY LANGUAGE). **2.** the message(s) or unit(s) of information communicated. **3.** (*pl.*) the means of communication, for example, mass media of communication.

Human capacity for communication, especially through LANGUAGE, is far more extensive than that of any other animal. The capacity to communicate across time and space has expanded enormously in modern times (see TIME-SPACE DISTANCIATION) with the invention of writing, printing, electronic communications—telegraph, telephone, radio—and media of mass communications, as well as the mechanization of transportation. A reduction of what geographers refer to as the friction of distance has been particularly evident in the present century in the capacity to send messages over long distances at great speed. This has many implications, not least the increased capacity for social control this makes possible for the modern STATE. See also COMMUNICATIVE COMPETENCE.

communicative competence the means, including the rules, by which persons sustain communicative exchanges and interactions with others within a community. The term was coined by Hymes (1966) to focus attention on the skills and knowledge involved in human communication. It reflects the limitations in linguistics of concentration mainly on syntactic competence. Hymes indicates in the formulation of his S.P.E.A.K.I.N.G. acronym some of the elements of social situations which would have to be included: Setting and scene, Participants' Ends, Act sequence, "Key," Instrumentalities, Norms, and Genres. To imagine dealing with these in an integrated set of rules might seem to indicate an impossible ambition, and many critics would question whether a rule formulation is appropriate. However, Hymes' conception points to a vital area of interest, and attempts to model communicative competence will continue to command attention. Without resort to either psychologism or sociologism, HABERMAS, for example, suggests communicative competence implies an ideal speech situation from which post-empiricist conceptions of truth and justice may be derived. Compare SPEECH ACTS, ETHNOMETHODOLOGY.

community (as used by sociologists and geographers) any set of social relationships operating within certain boundaries, locations, or territories. The term has descriptive and prescriptive connotations in both popular and academic usage. It may refer to social relationships that take place within geographically defined areas or NEIGHBORHOODS, or to relationships that are not locally operative but exist at a more abstract, ideological level. For example, the term "lesbian community" may refer to an actual settlement of women (for example, "lesbian ghetto," see E. Ettore, 1978), or it may refer to a collective of women sharing ideas and life styles, but not necessarily residing together in the same spatial area.

It has been suggested that the concept is one of the most difficult and controversial in modern society. Lowe (1986) suggests that it "ranks only with the notion of class in this respect." It is certainly a term that has attracted many different interpretations and been subjected to wide use and abuse.

In popular usage, the term has often been associated with positive connotations, as in the phrases "a sense of community" or "community spirit." It is clear that the term is not only descriptive, but also normative and ideological. Sociological discourse has often reinforced prescriptive usages of the term. Influenced by a tradition of 19th-century romanticism, some sociologists have regarded community as necessarily beneficial to human needs and social interaction. This tradition was particularly strong in the 19th century, but is by no means absent in 20th-century sociological thought.

In the 19th century, the German sociologist TÖNNIES drew a distinction between what he called GEMEINSCHAFT and GESELLSCHAFT. The former denoted community relationships characterized by their intimacy and durability: status was ascribed rather than achieved, and kin relationships took place within a shared territory and were made meaningful by a shared culture. Conversely, *Gesellschaft* gave rise to relationships that were impersonal, fleeting, and contractual. Such relationships were both rational and calculative rather than affective: status was based on merit and was therefore achieved, and *gesellschaftlich* relationships were competitive and often characterized by anonymity and alienation. Tönnies believed that the processes of industrialization and urbanization would give rise to the destruction of *gemeinschaftlich* relationships and that *gesellschaftlich* relationships would consequently flourish. He was concerned by what he took to be the breakdown of traditional society, authority, and community. In Tonnies' work we can see the high value he implicitly placed on the old social order and his ambivalence toward industrialization and urbanization (cf. SIMMEL). It is this romanticized view of traditional society that has given rise to the association of the concept of community with ideas of social support, intimacy, and security. Thus, traditional communities have often been portrayed as close-knit and as facilitating cooperation and mutual aid between members. In contrast, the URBANIZATION process has been identified as destructive of both community and communities. Research by Young and Willmott (1960) and Gans (1962), however, has raised serious doubts about any such simple association between urbanization and loss of community.

Sociologists have usually been less concerned with categorizing and identifying the physical and geographical characteristics of communities than with examining the nature and quality of the social relationships sustained by them. Recent sociology has also been concerned with the analysis of community action and collective resistance to social problems (Castells, 1976).

Whatever the definitional difficulties, all communities, both real and symbolic, exist and operate within boundaries or territories. Boundaries serve to demarcate social membership from nonmembership. Communities may be seen to be inclusive of some people and social groups, but exclusive of others. In some cases, community boundaries are rigidly maintained (for example, some religious communities); in others the boundaries are more fluid and open.

Worsley (1987) has suggested that, despite the difficulties involved in theorizing about community and communities, three broad meanings can be identified within sociological literature. The first he describes as "community as locality." Here the interpretation of the term comes closest to its geographical meaning of a "human settlement within a fixed and bounded local territory." Secondly, he suggests that community has been used to denote a "network of interrelationships" (Stacey, 1969). In this usage, community relationships can be characterized by conflict as well as by mutuality and reciprocity. In the third usage, community can be seen to refer to a particular type of social relationship, one that possesses certain qualities. It infers the existence of a community spirit or community feeling. This usage comes closest to a common-sense usage and does not necessarily imply the existence of a local geographical area or neighborhood. Community remains an important, if controversial, concept in sociology. See CHICAGO SCHOOL, COMMUNITY STUDIES, COMMUNITY CARE.

COMMUNITY CARE

community care the care of individuals within the community as an alternative to institutional or long-term residential care. It has its origins in relation to mental illness and the critique of institutionalization in the 1950s, which led in 1963 to publication of *Health and Welfare: The Development of Community Care*. Since then, the term has been applied to provision for other groups, such as children and older people. In the 1980s, ideas about community care were developed by governments as a means of providing support for a growing number of needy people. This trend was initiated in Great Britain in 1982 with the publication of *Social Workers: Their Roles and Tasks, The Barclay Report*. Although community care has been celebrated as a means of providing an alternative to institutional care—which is seen to lead to dependency—it has been criticized in a number of ways:

(a) its definition is unclear and commentators point to the difficulty of deciding whether community care is dichotomous with institutional care or whether they lie on a continuum of welfare provision;

(b) its lack of definition may mean that community care is little more than caring undertaken by relatives, friends, and neighbors for little or no renumeration;

(c) feminist sociologists, in particular, have argued that community care is euphemistic for the work that women do in the family and in the community, and to promote community care is to reinforce the ideology of women performing the caring role in society;

(d) the sources of funding of community care are often unclear, and some critics have suggested that community care is a strategy for reducing the costs of welfare provision.

A number of empirical studies have demonstrated that most caring is undertaken by women, usually daughters and daughters-in-law. However, the number of male carers increased during the 1980s and some authors have speculated that the proportion of male carers might increase further as more women are encouraged to return to the work force to fill the shortage of labor predicted for the 21st century. On the other hand, historical analyses of women's work demonstrate that women have often been expected to undertake paid work while also caring for others in the family.

A cynical observation about community care, therefore, is that it is a means of providing for the welfare of others at a minimum of government expense. However, community-care programs in countries such as Sweden have demonstrated that community care can be a good means of enabling needy people to live with some independence in the community, although the evidence from these programs shows that effective community care can be more expensive that institutional care.

community politics the political concerns generated by residence in a particular locality or place, and the relationship of residents with the central STATE.

Community politics often arise from local concerns with urban spaces, as workplaces, residences and living areas, and the politics of URBANIZA-

TION. In this sense, the early sociological explanations of community politics can be found in the writings of TÖNNIES (1887) and SIMMEL (1903), both of whom offered a critique of the social and political effects of the transformation of Europe, both seeing the movement from rural to urban living as marked by increasing disengagement from social and political life. Their ideas were developed by Wirth (1938), who argued that certain social and political actions were characteristic of the city. Wirth was a central figure in the CHICAGO SCHOOL, which developed a zonal model of the city. The overall approach became known as urban ecology. Its main assumption was that urban communities are organisms functioning according to laws different from those of the wider society. The approach argues that urbanism and the politics of the community must be seen as a distinct way of life (see URBANISM AS A WAY OF LIFE).

An alternative, classical conceptualization of urban and community politics can be found in works deriving from MARX and WEBER. Here, city residence is seen as a politically defined situation. The experience of urbanization and the aggregation into cities are the exercise of CLASS and POWER and the organization of people, labor, goods, and welfare provision in a specific way. People living in urban communities are therefore brought into direct confrontation with the state and state agencies over scarce resources.

Throughout the 1960s and 1970s, there was a dramatic increase in community groups and community action in the inner cities of the United States and other industrial societies, including Great Britain and France. This was reflected in a growing interest in the political economy of urbanization and community politics by several writers who sought to combine Marxism with a theory of the social production and organization of space. Castells (1977, 1978), for example, was concerned with the "urban problematic": a series of everyday situations, housing, transport, redevelopment, the distribution of ethnic groups, and the provision of shopping and recreation facilities. All of these areas Castells calls a *structured social process*. To understand this process, he suggested, it must be related to the political economy of STATE CAPITALISM AND STATE MONOPOLY CAPITALISM. For Castells, urban politics will develop new directions as contradictions widen between society's productive capacity and its social capacity to use its productive capacity. Because of this, social protest groups involved in community action will increasingly challenge the established order through the urban problematic. Harvey (1973), however, has pointed out that problems commonly regarded as urban are not peculiar to the city but common to society and only made more manifest in urban settings. Within this approach to community politics, local issues, no matter how intensely felt or contested by local community groups, cannot be regarded as either local or urban. See also SECTORAL CLEAVAGES, SOCIAL MOVEMENT.

community power the distribution of POWER within a local community. The works of Floyd Hunter, *Community Power Structure* (1963), and Robert Dahl, *Who Governs?* (1961), are important examples of studies designed to test propositions about local political power. Controversy raged between the exponents of so-called reputational studies of power (asking respondents who they believed held power), and those based on a direct analysis of actual decisions made within local communities. The different approaches have led to markedly different conclusions about community power. While the reputational method tended to discover elites, the decisional approach has more often led to the conclusion that no elite of community power-holders exists. This suggests that the method of research used has played a major part in determining the outcome of the research. Another possibility is that the choice of method of study is also related to the political predispositions of the researchers.

A further difficulty in studies of community power is the issue of how to include *nondecisions,* that is, situations in which a *mobilization of bias* exists (Bachrach and Baratz, 1962), so that key issues never reach the political agenda. For example, in a steel town like Gary, Indiana, studied by Crenson (1971), potential issues such as pollution did not arise as actual issues. See also S. Lukes (1974).

community study the empirical, usually ethnographic, study of the social relations and social structure within a clearly defined locality. Significant American examples of such studies include Lloyd Warner's *Yankee City*. British examples include Dennis et al., *Coal Is Our Life* (1956), a study of a Yorkshire mining community, and Margaret Stacey's *Tradition and Change: a Study of Banbury* (1960), in which the focus was on a changing community, seen by the researchers as the meeting point of two cultures: the traditional local culture and the culture introduced by newcomers. In POLITICAL SCIENCE in America, these studies have been used to provide a unit of manageable size within which to test propositions about the distribution of POWER (see also COMMUNITY POWER).

community work 1. a method of SOCIAL WORK. **2.** a distinct movement aimed at stimulating local programs for development, particularly of education, that arose in colonial societies in the aftermath of World War II. It was originally known as *community development* and defined as "a movement designed to create better living for the whole community, with the active participation and on the initiative of the local community" (HMSO *Community Development, A Handbook,* 1958). Used as a strategy by the British in Africa and by North Americans in Southeast Asia, its aims were contradictory in attempting both to maintain social control and facilitate independence.

In Great Britain in the 1950s, it was seen as an appropriate response, within the context of a WELFARE STATE, to combat growing social tensions in towns and cities.

Some authors suggest that community work has a philosophical aim in attempting to recreate some form of GEMEINSCHAFT within fragmented urban settlements. Although the political values that led to its development may be considered pluralist or consensual, in the 1960s a more radical style developed with the community development projects, whose practices were informed by a structuralist critique (see STRUCTURALISM) of capitalist society. More recently, community work has been criticized for its reliance on the work of women while ignoring the nature and work of women within the community.

comparative method 1. any method that involves examination of similarities and differences between phenomena or classes of phenomena with the aim of: (a) establishing classifications and typologies of social phenomena, and (b) testing hypotheses about causal relations by examining the empirical association and temporal ordering of factors. **2.** any specifically cross-cultural or cross-societal, including historical, comparison of similarities and differences between social phenomena with the above aims (see CROSS-CULTURAL COMPARISON, HUMAN RELATIONS AREA FILES).

Since the comparative method is used in the absence of strict experimentation in sociology, it is also sometimes referred to as the *quasi-experimental method*. See also EXPERIMENTAL METHOD.

An early systematization of the comparative method was provided by J.S. MILL. The three most used of these methods within sociology are outlined

	Antecedents	Outcomes
(a) method of agreement		
empirical case 1	A,b,c	X
empirical case 2	A,d,e	X
empirical case n	A,f,g	X
	A is the only similarly occurring antecedent when X is the outcome ∴ A may be the cause of X	
(b) method of difference		
empirical case 1	A,b,c	X
empirical case 2	b,c	not X
	A is the one difference found between two otherwise identical cases when X occurs ∴ A may be the cause of X	
(c) method of concomitant variations		
over a number of cases	the magnitude of A varies	the magnitude of X varies with the magnitude of A
	∴ A may be the cause of X	

Fig. 3. **Comparative method.** Mill's method.

studies such as DURKHEIM's *Suicide* (1897) and WEBER's *Protestant Ethic and the Spirit of Capitalism* (1904–1905). The method of concomitant variation receives further elaboration and systematization in modern statistical analysis (especially see STATISTICS AND STATISTICAL ANALYSIS, CORRELATION).

Compared with the experimental method proper, the problems that occur when the comparative method is used arise from an inability to manipulate truly independent variables. The main problem is the possible influence of unknown variables that, in the natural settings observed, may affect in unknown ways the variables for which a direct causal or concomitant relation is suggested.

The early use of the comparative method in cross-cultural analysis was in the work of evolutionary sociologists who have often been accused of suspect judgments of similarity and difference, and of studying units out of context.

Generally, the use of the comparative method is not invalidated by such problems, but they do underline the difficulties that can attend the use of the method, especially in its cross-cultural forms.

A more root-and-branch objection to the use of the comparative method in sociology arises from theorists who emphasize the importance of MEANINGFUL UNDERSTANDING AND EXPLANATION, or VERSTEHEN. In extreme cases (for example, WINCH, 1958), no place is seen within sociology for testing general hypotheses of the conventional scientific kind. However, most sociologists reject the RELATIVISM involved in this view and continue to examine general hypotheses.

With implications for both experimental and quasi-exprimental methods, modern philosophical analysis has rejected Mill's view that INDUCTION AND INDUCTIVE LOGIC and the comparative method can provide the conclusive proof possible in deductive LOGIC (see EMPIRICISM, FALSIFICATIONISM). However, this does not undermine the usefulness of the comparative method anymore than it undermines the experimental; it merely points to there being no recipe for establishing causality.

comparative sociology any form of sociology that involves cross-societal or cross-cultural analysis. See also COMPARATIVE METHOD.

competence and performance (linguistics) the distinction between the ability to use language (*competence*) and the actual verbalizations made (*performance*). This distinction is made in psycholinguistics in particular where competence more specifically describes the linguistic knowledge and grammar necessary to understand and speak one's own language, and performance describes the particular utterances that speakers and listeners actually produce and understand. See SOCIOLINGUISTICS.

competition any action in which one person or group vies with one or more other persons or groups to achieve an end, especially where the outcomes sought are scarce and not all can be successful in achieving these ends.

Competition may be direct or indirect; it may or may not be normatively or socially regulated.

In economics the ideal of competition between sellers in a market economy—the hidden hand regulating economic life—has been held to lead to low prices, equality of profits, and the promotion of economic efficiency. In the 19th century, the social benefits of competition were widely stressed by many schools of social theoretists, for example, UTILITARIANISM, SOCIAL DARWINISM, and the sociology of SPENCER. Influenced by economic and biological theories, members of the CHICAGO SCHOOL also made competition central to their accounts of urban ecology. Thus, competition has often been assumed to be a universal and productive element of the human condition.

By contrast, Marxism has viewed competition more as a specific requirement of capitalism, in which the surface appearance of fairness and effectiveness is seen as belied by actual asymmetries of power and by the underlying contradictions and conflicts that competition generates. There also exist many other theories that stress the deleterious social and individual effects of competition in some of its forms, unless regulated or offset by other values (see COOPERATION, ALTRUISM).

The implication of such contrasting views would seem to be that competition is not best seen as a universal drive. Nor is it a phenomenon that should be viewed as wholly positive or wholly negative in its implications. Rather, it should be regarded (as by Weber) as a frequent aspect of social relations, with that of implications requiring individual analysis in each case.

The concept of competition overlaps with CONFLICT. Although the latter concept is more likely to be used to refer to situations that lack institutionalization or normative regulation, or lead to disruptive social tensions, no hard-and-fast distinction exists, as illustrated by the existence of such concepts as institutionalized conflict.

componential analysis a technique, based in phonological linguistics, for analyzing complex elements into their components. In semantics, for example, the meaning of "woman" could be seen as analyzable into "human" + "female," which would be the components. Thus, research in a field of cognitive anthropology may involve assembling the apparently available kinship terms, and then seeking to identify the underlying components or dimensions which, taken together, would yield a particular term. Thus, "aunt" might involve "female" + "one generation older" + "one distance of indirect descent." "Great aunt" would involve two generations, and so on. The ideal would be to account for all variation in the terminology of a field. Similar systems of relation and contrast have also been sought for actions themselves.

Comte, Auguste (1798–1857) French social thinker who coined the term "sociology." Whether Comte should be seen as the founder of sociology is debatable and depends on how one regards precursors to Comte's own sociology (including MONTESQUIEU, SAINT-SIMON, or 18th-century Scottish thinkers), whose thought was certainly sociological although they did not use the term.

Born in the revolutionary era in France, and living through the post-revolutionary turmoil, Comte also witnessed the beginnings of the industrial revolution in that country. Associated with the foundation of modern POSITIVISM and the founder of a social movement dedicated to positive social reform, Comte's goal can be summed up by his own motto: "Order and Progress." A sign of his widespread influence is that today this is still the motto on the flag of Brazil. His objective was to establish a new social science that would both be the basis of understanding society and bring about its radical reform. Always eccentric, and in later life at times considered actually insane, Comte at one stage confidently expected the Pope to resign in his favor. For all this, his contribution to modern social thought has been highly significant.

Comte's approach to sociology drew on the work of Saint-Simon, the no less eccentric social thinker who once employed Comte as his secretary. The idea that society evolved through set stages, with European society as the pinnacle of this development, was current in the period of the French Enlightenment (see AGE OF ENLIGHTENMENT) in which Saint-Simon lived, and to which Comte was heir (see also CONDORCET). Comte's version of this view was his LAW OF THE THREE STAGES of social and intellectual development, a law he advanced as one "as firmly based as any in the sciences." In terms of this, Comte saw society as progressing through Theological and Metaphysical stages, before finally reaching the modern Positive age, an age to be ushered in by Comte's own positivism and sociology. In the Positive stage, an era of reliable knowledge, new rational government, and a Religion of Humanity, Comte expected society to be ruled by industrialists and bankers who would be educated and guided by sociologists. He described the new era as positive to contrast it with the negative, critical revolutionary, and speculative Metaphysical era, the function of which was merely to bring to an end the earlier Theological (and monarchical) one. Parliaments would have no relevance in this new era, and no one would have any rights to stand against the new scientific morality that would be established. Freedom would come from acting in conformity with the requirements of the laws of nature, including those discovered by sociology.

In his general sociological theory Comte distinguished between *statics* and *dynamics*. His statics, which states the requirements for social order, are echoed in later Durkheimian and FUNCTIONALIST sociology. He regarded the family as the social cell, and women's natural place as in the home, and religion is seen as performing essential social functions. His account of *dynamics*, which emphasized the increasing importance of the DIVISION OF LABOR in modern societies, also strongly influenced DURKHEIM.

It is Comte's earlier work, *Cours de philosophie positive* (1830–1842), which today is regarded as his most serious contribution to the subject. His later writings, including *Système de politique positive* (1875–1877), are regarded as more eccentric. The most accessible form in which to read Comte's work today is in collections of extracts such as those by Thompson (1975) and Andreski (1974).

It is easy to poke fun at Comte's sociology, given some of his obvious excesses, but in his lifetime he was highly influential. John Stuart MILL, a notably sober scholar, admired and sponsored his work, and Herbert SPENCER followed in his footsteps in adopting the term "sociology," despite a markedly different view of society. Nor should his modern legacy be dismissed. His emphasis on the importance of both careful observation and comparative and historical study in sociology remains relevant. His conception of a HIERARCHY OF THE SCIENCES, each with their own appropriate approaches to knowledge, shows that he was far from slavish in applying a general model of scientific knowledge to social science. The general view would probably be that Comte nevertheless underestimated the differences between the social sciences and the natural sciences. Thus, there are no strictly Comtean sociologists in modern sociology, although some are prepared to sing his praises (for example, Elias, 1970).

conation mental aspects of doing, as opposed to feeling (affection) and thinking (cognition). The term is now considered out of date and has dropped out of use.

concept the idea or meaning conveyed by a term. The construction of descriptive or explanatory concepts has a central role within any discipline. Given the absence of tightly articulated explanatory theories in sociology, what is usually referred to as SOCIOLOGICAL THEORY is made up of looser articulations of descriptive and explanatory concepts. See also SENSITIZING CONCEPT.

concomitant variation an empirical relationship in which the magnitude of a first variable varies with the magnitude of a second variable (see COMPARATIVE METHOD). The concomitant variation, or CORRELATION, between variables may be used as the test of a CAUSAL RELATIONSHIP between variables. The main causal hypotheses in Durkheim's *Suicide* (1897) were tested using this method.

conditioning a term used in LEARNING THEORY or behaviorism meaning the process of training or changing behavior by association and reinforcement. There are two basic types of conditioning—classical and operant.

Classical conditioning was defined by I. Pavlov (1911) in his research on the salivary reflex in dogs. He observed that if a neutral stimulus (NS) is paired with an unconditioned stimulus (UCS) so that they become associated, then the NS develops the same ability to evoke a response as the UCS. Thus the NS becomes a conditioned stimulus (CS), and the response becomes a conditioned response (CR). This type of conditioning occurs only in involuntary behaviors such as salivation, sweating, heart rate, and other behaviors controlled by the autonomic nervous system, and such a conditioned response may therefore be known as a *conditioned reflex*. Reinforcement is delivered regardless of response, as it precedes it and is typically also the UCS (food in the case of Pavlov's experiment).

Operant or *instrumental conditioning* was defined and extensively researched by B.F. Skinner (1953). It involves training voluntary responses, as the reinforcement is only delivered after the response and is contingent on the response. Learning or conditioning involves development of an association or bond between a stimulus and a response by reinforcing responses when they occur. Because reinforcement follows response, respondent behavior can be manipulated by varying when the reinforcement is given (*schedules of reinforcement*). Learning is more resistant to extinction if the schedule of reinforcement used in training is related to the responses and is unpredictable. An example of this is playing a slot machine. *Extinction* is the fading and disappearance of behavior through nonreinforcement; for example, socially unacceptable behavior should be disregarded and not reinforced. Behavior can be shaped toward a desirable end by the reinforcement of successive approximations to this. In this way, animals can be taught to do tricks that would not be found in their normal repertoire of behavior. Shaping principles underlie much of the control we exert over each other's behavior, especially children's.

Condorcet, Antoine, Marquis de (1743–1749) French aristocrat, philosopher, and social theorist who, in arguing for the discovery of laws of historical development, prefigured the concern of many subsequent thinkers (including COMTE and SAINT-SIMON) in proposing a broad EVOLUTIONARY THEORY. Condorcet's main work was the *Sketch of an Historical Picture of the Progress of the Human Spirit* (1795). This conceptualized the evolutionary development of human society in terms of ten stages. The final stage would be a revolutionary period that would realize the perfection of humanity. This general outlook places Condorcet primarily within the Enlightenment (see AGE OF ENGLIGHTENMENT) and modernist traditions of belief in both progress and in the ability of the intellect to subject the world to rational understanding and control.

Condorcet believed progress to be contingent on universal education and argued strongly for EQUALITY OF OPPORTUNITY. Just as radical were his claims for the emancipation of women, for birth control, for divorce, and for civil marriage. The influence of Condorcet's thought—evolutionary, optimistic, and radical—was widespread and affected many thinkers apart from Comte and Saint-Simon.

conflict the overt struggle between individuals or groups within a society, or between nation states. In any society, conflict may occur between, for example, two or more people, social movements, interest groupings, classes, genders, organizations, political parties, and ethnic, racial, or religious collectivities. Conflict often arises because of competition over access to, or control over, scarce resources or opportunities. This may also apply at the level of relations between states and societies.

Conflict may be institutionalized: peaceful and regulated by sets of rules to which all participants agree, such as procedures of industrial arbitration, or the electoral process of democratic societies; or unregulated, such as the violence deployed by and against terrorist organizations or revolutionary movements.

Institutionalized conflict is often taken as evidence of a healthy democratic process. The PLURALIST view of power regards society as a complex of competing interests, to the extent that democratic rules and institutions allow the articulation and resolution of conflict and prevent any one interest group (like a ruling class) from always prevailing on every issue, so the capacity of the individual citizen to enjoy a free society is enhanced. In short, pluralism argues that a society that gives regulated expression to economic, political, and social conflict is more likely to be and remain free than one that does not. This perspective contrasts with CONSENSUS theories of society, which tend to regard conflict negatively, as a symptom of some defect of social organization, or lack of agreement about the core values of a society (see, for example, Durkheim's discussion of the forced DIVISION OF LABOR, or Talcott Parsons' analysis of family roles or professional/client interaction).

Finally, it is important to see that though all conflict is evidence of an attempt to exercise power, not all examples of the exercise of power involve conflict. Indeed, the power of one agent over another is most effectively exercised when conflict is avoided. See also CONFLICT THEORY.

conflict theory 1. any theory or collection of theories that emphasizes the role of CONFLICT, especially between groups and classes, in human societies. **2.** more particularly, the relatively diffuse collection of theories that in the 1960s were ranged against, and contested the dominance of, Parsonian STRUCTURAL-FUNCTIONALISM and its emphasis on societies as mainly governed by value consensus and the internalization of institutionalized shared values. The main features of such conflict theories were that:

(a) they accused functionalist sociologies of disregarding conflicts of value and interest in human societies, or at best regarded these as a secondary phenomenon;

(b) as an alternative to functionalism, they offered an account of both the integration of society and of social change emphasizing the role of POWER and coercion and the pursuit of economic and political interests in human affairs, as well as the more general role of conflict.

While some versions of conflict theory were Marxist or influenced by Marxism (for example, GOULDNER), others were not, and were advanced on a more eclectic basis. One important approach, for example, was based on the work of SIMMEL (for example, Lewis Coser, 1956) and emphasized the social functions as well as the disruptive effects of conflict. Still others (for example, DAHRENDORF, REX) emphasized the significance of WEBER as well as of Marx in the study of conflict. In a highly influential article ("Social Integration and System Integration," 1964), David LOCKWOOD underlined the importance of an approach in which conflict was more central than in functionalism, when he drew attention once again to the existence of social conflicts and system contradictions, as well as social integration and system integration, as major elements in social life (see also SOCIAL INTEGRATION AND SYSTEM INTEGRATION). In the 1970s and subsequently with the reflourishing of a full range of conflict theories, simple distinctions between functionalism and conflict theory are no longer important, and with this the use of conflict theory in sense **2.** has faded.

conformity behavior controlled by group pressure. Groups have NORMS that group members are expected to abide by in order to maintain the integrity of the group. An individual feels the pressure of the group's expectations and tends to conform to them.

Social psychologists (for example, Allport, 1924; Sherif, 1935; Asch, 1952; Crutchfield, 1955) have investigated the effect of group pressure when the groups are impermanent and the members unknown to each other, as in an experimental situation. The degree of conformity has been found to depend on certain variables, such as the perceived prestige of the group, the amount of ambiguity in the judgments to be made, and the size of the group. These investigators also distinguish two types of conformity:

(a) *internalization*—the group's opinions are believed and internalized;

(b) *compliance*—involving outward agreement but internal disagreement.

connubium (anthropology) the relation between prescribed marital groups. If a certain group of males has either the power or the obligation to marry within a certain group of females, then they have connubium.

consanguinity (anthropology) a kinship term expressing the relationship of DESCENT from a common ancestor. The tie is therefore based on biological facts as opposed to cultural facts (that is, parental or sibling ties, not spouses). In theory, this opposes it to affinal relationships based on marriage, but facts can rarely be classified so clearly. Adoption and fictive kinship constructions complicate the distinction in many societies. *Cognatic* is an alternative term for consanguine.

conscience a person's sense of right and wrong that constrains behavior and causes feelings of guilt if its demands are not met.

These moral strictures are learned through SOCIALIZATION and therefore vary from person to person and culture to culture. The most important influence is that of the parents, who set standards for their child's behavior both by example and by establishing rules, and who enforce the required behavior by a system of rewards and punishments (see CONDITIONING). Parental and societal standards thus become internalized as the conscience.

Freud's theory is particularly specific about the formation of the conscience, which he labels the SUPEREGO. This develops through identification with the parent of the same sex and is essentially the child's idealization of the parent's moral values.

This emphasis on the parental and societal role may be considered limited by those who regard moral judgments as absolute. This view would suggest an innate moral sense and is particularly expressed in religion and mysticism. Compare COLLECTIVE CONSCIENCE.

consciousness the part of the human mind that is aware of a person's self, environment, and mental activity. The conscious mind contains memories, current experience, and thoughts that are available to awareness. The conscious mind in Freud's theory is only a small part of mental life, most of which is hidden in the *unconscious*. See also PRACTICAL CONSCIOUSNESS, STRATIFICATIONAL MODEL OF SOCIAL ACTION AND CONSCIOUSNESS.

consensus the existence within a society, community, or group of a fundamental agreement on basic values. While some sociologists, notably Talcott PARSONS, emphasize the existence of such shared values as the basis of any persisting social order, other sociologists do not, pointing to the frequency with which social systems may be held together by reciprocal interests or by force. See also LEGITIMATE AUTHORITY, NORMATIVE FUNCTIONALISM, SOCIAL INTEGRATION AND SYSTEM INTEGRATION, DOMINANT IDEOLOGY THESIS.

consensus theory of truth see TRUTH.

conservatism 1. any social and political doctrine that seeks to defend the institutions and social values of the existing order. **2.** any relatively stable set of POLITICAL ATTITUDES in support of the *status quo,* that is, policies that seek to sustain or renovate rather than reconstruct the social fabric. As such, conservatism is the opposite of radicalism. **3.** support for the Republican or Conservative Party.

Conservative political ideology in its modern forms first manifested itself as a reaction to the French Revolution. Edmund Burke, in his *Reflections on the French Revolution* (1790), produced a classic statement in defense of the old order. His central argument was that the established social and political institutions should be defended because they existed; they had grown organically. Hence, they were a better guide to action than any theoretical construction, no matter how rational the latter may seem. Burke's ideas have provided a core theme. Conservatism has rarely been based on any *overtly* stated political philosophy, since the danger is that it could be regarded as abstract and ideological.

Another persistent theme of traditional conservatism has been that the social order must be maintained by a leadership composed of ELITES holding key positions of political responsibility. The STATE is seen as playing a central role in guaranteeing the social order, authority, and the maintenance of social hierarchy. Inequalities are seen as necessary elements of society. Conservatives also stress the importance of custom and tradition as prerequisites of a stable social order. MANNHEIM (1953), however, distinguishes between conservatism and static traditionalism. Conservative politics has often involved changes seen as necessary for preservation of the social order: renovation rather than reconstruction of the social fabric. Such notions rest on another central theme in conservative thought, the belief that the mass of people, because of their inherent qualities, including ignorance and selfishness, are unlikely to create a satisfactory social order through their own efforts. See also WORKING-CLASS CONSERVATISM, DEFERENCE, PROPERTY.

conspicuous consumption a term coined by VEBLEN to help define the characteristics of the LEISURE CLASS. Rather than consuming goods or services for their utility, Veblen suggests that some consumption is for show alone, that is, the demonstration of one's social STATUS. This idea has recently been reexamined in the work of Fred Hirsch (1977) on POSITIONAL GOODS, and by BOURDIEU (1984a).

conspiracy theory an element within a belief system in which social consequences, identified as harmful or unwanted, are seen as arising from the activities of groups believed able to influence the operation of power, economic decision-making, etc., in surreptitious ways. Members of successful religious or ethnic minority groups, political extremists, etc. may be identified in such theories, for example, the witch hunt of members of the Communist Party and alleged fellow travelers carried out by Sen. Joseph McCarthy in the United States in the early 1950s, or the so-called Doctors' Plot in the USSR prior to Stalin's death in 1953, in which Jewish doctors were accused of plotting to poison Stalin. Whether or not there are elements of truth in the claims made in such conspiracy theories, it is the exaggerated nature of the claims, and the often slender evidence advanced, that leads conspiracy theories to be regarded as a phenomenon requiring explanation rather than being seen as true. Thus, they might be explained as arising from the believers' powerlessness and structurally precarious situation, and the need for the believers themselves to find some kind of reason for this and some hope of resolution.

constraint any restraining social influence that leads an individual to conform to social NORMS or social expectations. For DURKHEIM, the distinctive SOCIAL FACTS, or sociological phenomena, that sociologists study can be recognized, above all, as "ways of acting ... capable of exercising an external constraint over the individual." Durkheim recognized that such socially constraining forces may also be internalized by individuals, but it was an essential feature of his conception of such constraints that they had an origin external to the individual. Thus Durkheim's use of the term is much wider than the notion of constraint in which the individual who wishes to act one way is made to act in another. As Lukes (1973) points out, Durkheim's use of the term "constraint" suffers at times from considerable ambiguity, failing to distinguish clearly between:

(a) the authority of legal rules, customs, etc. as manifested by the sanctions brought to bear on violators of these;

(b) the necessity of following rules to carry out certain activities successfully (for example, the rules of language);

(c) the causal influence of morphological factors, such as the influence of established channels of communication or transportation on commerce or migration;

(d) psychological compulsions in a crowd or social movement;

(e) cultural determination and the influence of SOCIALIZATION.

However, Durkheim's overall intention is clear: to draw attention to the fact that distinctively *social* reality constrains, and is external to the individual, in each and any of the above senses. See also COLLECTIVE CONSCIENCE, FREE WILL, DETERMINISM.

construct any theoretical or heuristic sociological concept. The use of the term "construct" makes apparent the invented, mentally constructed, heuristic or explanatory purpose of many concepts in sociology. See also IDEAL TYPE.

consumer culture 1. the cultural dominance in modern capitalist societies of an orientation to the marketing and consumption of goods and services. **2.** the status-differentiated and market-segmented culture of modern societies, in which individual tastes not only reflect the social locations (age, gender, occupation, ethnicity, etc.), but also the social values and individual lifestyles of consumers.

Whereas previously, in contrast with economics, sociology has tended to regard consumer culture as manipulative and stage-managed, it is today evident that neither a model of cultural manipulation nor a model of individual consumer sovereignty, as preferred by economists, alone adequately describes the processes involved. As indicated by Featherstone (1990), in modern capitalist consumer societies, consumption:

(a) is continuously encouraged in order for production to occur, and to provide inducement to work;

(b) has become a significant source of status differentiation for all social groups;

(c) is a major source of our pleasures, and our dreams.

All three aspects of consumer culture must be seen as involving complex, and sometimes contradictory, relations. On the one hand, new manipulations of wants undoubtedly occur, for example, as with elements of the fictitious nostalgia and pastiche generated in association with tourism and the new heritage industry. On the other hand—as suggested, for example, by theories of POST-FORDISM—production is increasingly oriented to specialist needs, allowing greater cultural variety and greater individual choice and self-expression. Thus the modern interest in consumer culture has brought cultural questions to the fore and is seeking to move beyond the merely negative evaluation of consumer pleasures associated with many previous theories of mass culture. Compare ADVERTISING, CULTURAL STUDIES.

consumerism those social movements directed at protecting or advancing the rights of consumers. See also CONSUMER MOVEMENT.

consumer movement those organizations that have grown up with the aim of informing and protecting the consumer of goods and services. In the United States, the publication *Consumer Reports* is the prime example.

contemporary history (introduced in the 1950s) the study of contemporary events (events within living memory) using historical methods, including traditional methods such as documentary analysis as well as newer approaches such as oral history. Although the idea of contemporary history may appear paradoxical, and it faces difficulties such as prohibitions in the availability of key documents, contemporary history is a justified and scarcely new approach, in that historians have always studied the recent past.

content analysis a research technique for the objective, quantitative, and systematic study of communication content. It involves charting or counting the incidence, or coincidence, of particular items belonging to a set of (usually) predetermined categories. It has been used, for example, to explore political balance and bias in communication by counting the number of references or time allocation given to political groups. It has also been used to examine the relationships between concepts, as in the case of Hartmann's and Husband's studies of the ways in which English newspapers dealt with issues of race and ethnic relations. They showed that it is possible to identify a language of race, with its own vocabulary of conflict and hate, in reports of ethnic relations. Critics of content analysis challenge the assumption that meanings can be studied quantitatively, arguing that meanings are conveyed by absence as well as presence, and by context rather than frequency. They also challenge the belief that the categories used in content analysis have an objective and value-free reality.

contest and sponsored mobility contrasting modes of SOCIAL MOBILITY via education, identified by R.H. Turner (1960), in which children are either chosen to enter a selective system of secondary education and supported, financially and in other ways, in their passage though this system and ultimately into elite positions: *sponsored mobility;* or must engage in continuous open competition for educational and social advantage: *contest mobility.* Thus, while British grammar schools are an example of sponsored mobility, comprehensive education is intended to produce contest mobility and more continuous EQUALITY OF OPPORTUNITY. In practice, there are likely to be elements of sponsorship within any predominantly contest system.

contextual fallacy see ECOLOGICAL AND WRONG LEVEL FALLACY.

contingency theory an empirical approach within ORGANIZATION THEORY that correlates features of organizational structure with contingent aspects of the environment, technology, etc., and their effect on organizational behavior and performance. Contingency theory thus rejects the classical idea of best organizing principles, and explains variation in organizational form as determined by environmental and technical conditions.

contingent see ANALYTIC AND SYNTHETIC.

contract see SOCIAL CONTRACT THEORY.

contradiction 1. The proposition that something is both the case and not the case at the same time. All argument and theory in science are systematically scrutinized in order to eliminate the presence of contradiction, for any proposition that involves or leads to contradiction is a logically impossible account of the world and may be dismissed a priori. It is important to see that contradiction in this sense involves a purely logical relation between statements. Thus, since to claim that a camel can both pass and not pass through the eye of a needle involves a contradiction of logic, and we know that the situation described cannot be the case. Experiment is redundant. However, to claim simply that a camel can pass through the eye of a needle involves no logical contradiction. It is simply a claim about the world that experimentation with camels has so far shown to be empirically impossible. **2.** *economic and social contradictions*—a key term of Marxist discourse, indicating a tension, opposition, or conflict between two aspects of social structure or processes within a social whole. The contradiction is said to be responsible for the dynamic properties of society. The proposition that all phenomena are composed of opposites is one of the three laws of dialectical materialism. Marx himself was specifically interested in the application of dialectical analysis to the study of history, hence the term *historical materialism*. Here, the notion of contradiction plays a central role in the analysis of social change. Marx argued that in all modes of production, prior to communism, a contradiction eventually develops between the forces of production and the relations of production. Substantively, this contradiction is expressed in, and eventually resolved by, class conflict. Successful revolutionary struggle by the class that represents new relations of production then initiates a new cycle of change.

contradictory class locations non-polarized class locations, that is "class locations within capitalism that are neither exploiters nor exploited" (Wright, 1985. 1989). As such, these are broadly equivalent to the Marxian conception of INTERMEDIATE CLASSES OR INTERMEDIATE STRATA, but these are given greater systematization by Wright, who seeks to provide a theory of potential class alliances on this basis. The chief addition in Wright's analysis, compared with earlier ones, is that he takes into account what he terms "organizational assets" and "skill assets" (for example, educational credentials) as well as more conventional "assets in the means of production." Twelve main class locations are identified in this way (see Fig. 4). Wright examines empirical variations in political attitudes in terms of these schema, although some critics have argued that his approach is over-formalistic and classificatory.

CONTROL

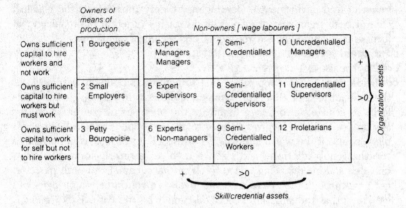

Fig. 4. **Contradictory class locations.** In this figure (from Wright, 1985), the interaction of three categories of "assets" possessed by individuals produces 12 class locations, of which only 1 and 2 do not have contradictory elements. Organizational assets refer to appropriation of surplus "based on hierarchy;" "skills/credential assets" to those deriving from education and training.

control see SOCIAL CONTROL.

control condition see CONTROL GROUP.

control group or **control condition** a group matched with the EXPERIMENTAL GROUP in all aspects except that it is not treated with the INDEPENDENT VARIABLE whose effect is to be studied. A control group is an essential part of EXPERIMENTAL METHOD design since, unless a comparison is made between two groups, one having been subject to the variable and one not, it is difficult to conclude that any change is due to that variable.

conurbation any extended urban area resulting from the fusion of previously independent towns. The term was introduced by Patrick Geddes in *Cities in Evolution* (1915). Related terms are URBAN agglomeration and METROPOLITAN AREA.

convention 1. any existing regularized social practice or accepted rule or usage. For the most part the term is not used in sociology in a sense that departs greatly from everyday usage. **2.** in politics specifically, an established precedent in, or expectation of, procedures in political office, for example, that the parties can hold primary elections. Such expectations or conventions are not promulgated as written laws or formally stated rules, and thus are sometimes a matter of interpretation or dispute. **3.** in the United States, the political assemblies convened to select presidential candidates. **4.** a formal agreement between nation states.

conventionalism 1. (PSYCHOLOGY) an excessive or obsessional adherence to social conventions, sometimes seen as one of the components of, or a manifestation of, an AUTHORITARIAN PERSONALITY. **2.** (philosophy) the view that scientific knowledge is a matter of convention, rather than something that can be given an entirely secure basis resting on the nature of things, or as arising from unchanging methodological rules or procedures. As an epistemological and an ontological view, conventionalism is at odds with EMPIRICISM or REALISM. See also PRAGMATISM, POSITIVISM.

convergence the result of a process in which the structures of different industrial societies come increasingly to resemble each other. The argument for convergence (first explicitly articulated by Kerr et al., 1962) derives its theoretical force from functionalist analysis (see FUNCTIONALISM), that is, that industrialism represents a specific kind of social system whose needs (see FUNCTIONAL PREREQUISITES or FUNCTIONAL IMPERATIVES) must eventually be met, in any society, by similar solutions in terms of social structure. For example, once a society has made a commitment to the science and technology of industrial production, a need arises for an educated, mobile, and diversified labor force. Universal systems of education, with selection for advanced training in specialist skills, are required. At work, managerial hierarchies are needed to coordinate a complex DIVISION OF LABOR. Moreover, in order to maximize the use of available talent and ability, systems of SOCIAL STRATIFICATION need to be open, to allow recruitment from below. Hierarchies of power, prestige, status, and material reward, however, are also necessary, not least to motivate the most talented to acquire the long training needed for the most demanding and important jobs.

The other major features of liberal-democratic, Western industrial and market-oriented societies (such as BUREAUCRACY, URBANIZATION, and the state provision of infrastructure and social services) are derived by similar logic. Value systems, too, it is suggested, will tend to converge. For WEBER, industrialism meant the dominance of instrumental forms of RATIONALITY in organizations, the economy, and science; for Talcott PARSONS, the ROLE relationships of advanced industrial societies need to be structured around the core values (or PATTERN VARIABLES) of achievements, universalism and affective neutrality.

The result of functional analysis is that what is (in this instance the socioeconomic and political structures of the US and similar Western societies) is also necessary and desirable in all other cases. Industrial societies that differ in some way from this pattern must be deviant. This important ideological consequence is taken up below.

Convergence theory is also an example of TECHNOLOGICAL DETERMINISM —the suggestion that forms of technology determine the nature of social organization. Many of the core features around which, it is argued, industrial societies will tend to converge, can readily be seen as consequences of a commitment to science and technology. This suggests that the nature of a society is more influenced by its technological apparatus than by its political values. In fact, it is precisely the way in which convergence theory speaks of the functional requirements of industrialism and the social consequences of technology that makes it (as it was meant to be) a powerful antisocialist manifesto. Convergence theory suggests that inequality is inevitable, that the socialist project is empirically doomed, and that politics, in terms of the class struggle between capital and LABOR, is redundant in the face of opportunities for social mobility, affluence, the dominance of instrumental forms of rationality, and the need for the technically efficient running of the economy. Convergence theory, then, sees an "end of ideology" (see END OF IDEOLOGY THESIS, BELL). Translated, this was always meant to be "a withering away of the relevance of socialism."

Not surprisingly, the idea of convergence had its heyday in the 1950s and 1960s, a period of economic optimism and expansion, combined with cold-war relations between the Soviet bloc and NATO countries. As attitudes began to thaw in 1989–1990, and as Poland, Hungary, Czechoslovakia, Romania, and the USSR begin their programs of liberalizing economic and political reform, convergence theory will probably enjoy revived popularity.

In its strong form, convergence theory remains either an overstatement or a truism. To suggest that present industrial societies show to currently developing societies the image of their own future is to ignore economic relations at the international levels that produce underdevelopment, while to point out that industrial societies need a complex division of labor is true, but trivial. What matters are the values, politics, and cultures that make for comparative differences. For example, both Great Britain and Japan are advanced industrial societies, but the values of the workplace (and of the family, etc.) in the two societies are quite distinct. See also NEOEVOLUTIONISM.

conversation(al) analysis an approach within ETHNOMETHODOLOGY that analyzes naturally occurring forms of talk. The objective is to uncover general principles that govern the organization of talk, for example, the rules governing *turn taking* (how a conversation is managed by its participants, H. Sacks et al., 1974), and the implications of these in specific contexts (for example, Atkinson, 1981). Compare ANALYTICAL PHILOSOPHY, with which conversation analysis has some affinities.

Cooley, Charles (1864–1929) American sociologist best known for his concept of the LOOKING-GLASS SELF. This theory, about the formulation and maintenance of the personality as reflected in the judgments (both real and imagined) of others, was developed by G.H. MEAD and the symbolic interactionists. Cooley was also responsible for making the distinction between the primary and secondary group (see PRIMARY GROUP). In general, his sociology shared the CHICAGO SCHOOL's concern with the relationship between the SELF and the social GROUP. See also SYMBOLIC INTERACTIONISM.

cooling-out process in higher education "the provision of readily available alternative achievements" (for example, transfer from an engineering course to a lower-level course as a technician) (Clark, 1960b). In this process the student does not clearly fail unless he or she wishes to define it so, but instead transfers to some form of more immediate terminal qualification. In alleviating the emotional consequences of failure in this way, the "general result of cooling-out processes is that society can continue to encourage maximum effort without major disturbances from unfulfilled promises and expectations."

cooperation 1. shared action to achieve a desired goal. **2.** voluntary organizations of producers or consumers characterized by collaborative rather than competitive capitalist relations between those involved.

In the general sense **1.** it is something of a paradox that those engaged in mutual conflict, even warfare, must often cooperate, at least to some degree, in order to maintain the conflict. Thus, the widespread existence of cooperation within social organizations and societies does not necessarily answer the question of whether cooperation or competition is the decisive social cement of societies, for example, underlying the DIVISION OF LABOR.

In sense **2.**, the major reference is to the cooperative organizations, and the wider Cooperative Movement dating from the early 19th century in Europe. These derived from the ideas of socialists such as Robert Owen (1771–1858) and the democratic and participatory principles established by the Rochdale Pioneers, who established the first retail cooperative in 1844. As producer organizations, cooperatives have been especially effective in agriculture. In general, in the context of a wider capitalist system, cooperative organizations have tended to suffer from undercapitalization and poor organization.

cooperative organization and **cooperative movement** see COOPERATION.

core and periphery see CENTER AND PERIPHERY.

corporatism 1. as in Spain under Franco and more generally in association with fascism, the state-control of major corporations (for example, labor unions), with the aim of removing or suppressing social conflict, fostering nationalism, etc. **2.** relations between government and key interest groups (see PRESSURE GROUPS), especially big business and TRADE UNIONS, involving:

(a) *intermediation*—bodies standing between the state and the individual citizen negotiate agreements with the government on behalf of their members, for example, agreements on wages and prices;

(b) *incorporation*—the possession of a special status by these organizations so that, in some respects, they become virtual extensions of government, what Middlemas, in *Politics in an Industrial Society,* (1979) calls "governing institutions." Great Britain is often regarded as having moved in a corporatist direction in this second sense in the period 1960 to 1979, a tendency reversed with the election of the Thatcher government in 1979. Modern Austria is sometimes advanced as a more fully developed example of corporatism in sense **2.**, characterized by features lacking in Great

Britain, including wide social agreement on the value of social partnership, compulsory membership in trade unions and employers' organizations, and effective cooperation between capital and labor.

In a more general sense, intermediate organizations, and thus corporatist social structures, were advanced as a solution to modern social ills by DURKHEIM. Corporatism is often regarded as one of the ways in which governments intervene to manage ADVANCED CAPITALISM. However, in many countries corporatism has been undermined by crises of accumulation and a reversal of consensus politics. See HABERMAS; see also SECTORAL CLEAVAGES.

correlation the association between two VARIABLES such that when one changes in magnitude the other one does also, that is, there is a CONCOMITANT VARIATION. Correlation may be positive or negative. Positive correlation describes the situation in which, if one variable increases, so also does the other. Negative correlation describes the situation in which the variables vary inversely, one increasing when the other decreases.

Correlation can be measured by a statistic, the CORRELATION COEFFICIENT, of which there exist several forms. Most of these focus on a linear relationship, in which the variation in one variable is directly proportional to the variation in the other. When presented graphically, for a perfect relationship between variables a straight line can be drawn through all points on the graph. Correlation coefficients are constructed essentially as measures of departure from this straight line. The technique of correlation analysis is mainly used on interval level data (see CRITERIA AND LEVELS OF MEASUREMENT), but tests also exist for other levels of data (see SPEARMAN RANK CORRELATION COEFFICIENT).

Finding a correlation does not imply causation. Spurious relationships can be found between variables so there has to be other evidence to support the inference of one variable influencing the other. It also must be remembered that the apparent association may be caused by a third factor influencing both variables systematically. For situations in which three or more variables are involved, techniques of MULTIVARIATE ANALYSIS exist. See also REGRESSION, CAUSAL MODELING, PATH ANALYSIS.

correlation coefficient a measure of the association between two variables. See CORRELATION, PEARSON PRODUCT MOMENT CORRELATION COEFFICIENT, SPEARMAN RANK CORRELATION COEFFICIENT.

corruption "the abandonment of expected standards of behavior by those in authority for the sake of unsanctioned personal advantage" (Pinto-Duschinsky, 1987). One problem with such a definition is that in many societies corrupt practices, as specified by legal or administrative rules, may often be customary and widely accepted as normal behavior. Such behavior, as in some Third World countries or controlled economies, may be essential for achievement of socially necessary outcomes. Nor is corruption confined to less-developed or state-socialist economies, as scandals such as Watergate demonstrate.

cost-benefit analysis a technique for appraising the total economic costs and benefits—ideally the total social costs and benefits expressed as economic costs—arising from any economic and social activity, especially new projects. Hitherto, the technique has been mainly used to appraise new, large, public projects. But, in an increasingly ecologically conscious era, the proposal now is that many more existing economic and social activities should be subject to full cost-benefit analysis, with many more costs, for example, environmental, also included to a fuller extent than previously. Cost-benefit analysis is far from being a straightforward technique, however, and much depends on the assumptions on which a costing is made. Careful attention has always to be given to the range of external costs and the range of benefits to be included in the calculations, as well as to the basis on which these can be costed. The results usually leave room for controversy.

counseling the process of guiding a person during a stage of life when personal reassessments or decisions have to be made about. As a practice, it is allied to PSYCHOTHERAPY, although less clinical, and more generally associated with normal responses to normal life events, which may nevertheless create STRESS for some people who, therefore, choose to look for help and support. If this cannot be sufficiently provided by family and friends, a counselor may be the choice.

The client-centered or PERSON-CENTERED COUNSELING approach initiated by Carl ROGERS has been very influential in recent decades. This emphasizes the counselor's role in enabling the person to reach greater self-understanding and experience personal growth, and deemphasizes any directive role. Other approaches, such as rational emotive therapy or the cognitive-behavioral approach, are far more directive.

Counselors exist in a wide range of areas of expertise—marriage or career guidance, students' problems, debt management, postoperative counseling, etc. Counseling may be paid or voluntary work. In the past, training has generally been provided by the organization for whom the counselor has chosen to work, and has therefore been specific, for example, courses for career advisers in the public sector; marriage guidance training in the voluntary sector. However, standardization and publicly funded generic courses are being introduced in the late 1980s and early 1990s.

counter culture or **alternative culture** any of the subcultures and *oppositional cultures* in which life styles, beliefs, and values are distinct from those of the main or dominant culture, and which may challenge its central beliefs, ideals, and institutions. Such groups may develop through isolation or threat or around common interests. Since the 1960s there has been a flowering of counter cultural movements, such as the GREEN MOVEMENT, in Western societies.

counterfactual or **counterfactual conditional** a conditional statement, of the form "if a, then b," in which the assertion is that "were a to have occurred, then b would have followed," as in "had the Greeks lost the

Battle of Marathon, then a different historical outcome from the uniquely Western route to modernity would have been the outcome." Since the "antecedent" (the first clause of the statement) in such counterfactual statements is unfulfilled, the empirical assessment of the claim involved in the "consequent" (the second clause) presents some difficulties. The plausibility of such statements depends on the possibility of citing convincing supporting evidence that can justify the conditional statement.

court society the elaboration of etiquette and standards of cultivated manners that occurred in the courts of Western European monarchs in the post-feudal era (Norbert ELIAS,, *Court Society,* 1969, tr. 1983). *Court Society* details the life of the king and his courtiers during the reign of Louis XIV in France. Elias argues that the growth of court society, whereby a warrior nobility was eventually replaced by a courtly nobility, is one instance of a general CIVILIZING PROCESS within European society. Court society is therefore a significant social formation and a major step in the development of the modern world. See also FIGURATION (OR CONFIGURATION), FIGURATIONAL SOCIOLOGY.

covering-law model and deductive nomological explanation a model of scientific EXPLANATION particularly associated with Carl Hempel and Karl POPPER. In this model the defining feature of a scientific explanation is represented as resting on the operation of general scientific laws and initial condition statements (together known as the explanans) which logically entail the phenomenon thus explained (the explanandum). The basic model is as follows:

(a) Laws(s).	
(b) Statements of initial conditions, which point to the applicability of the chosen laws to the case in hand.	} *the explanans*
(c) The phenomenon explained (or predicted as a deduction from above.	} *the explanandum*

The laws involved are *universal conditional statements:* ("For any a, if a, then b"), for example, "All water heated at the pressure existing at sea level boils at 100°C." While the basic model thus identifies science as involving deterministic laws, "probabilistic laws" (asserting "if a, then a certain probability of b") can also be accommodated. An important distinction also made on the basic of the model is between scientific and nonscientific prediction: rather than being unconditional, scientific PREDICTION is conditional on the occurrence of the relevant initial conditions. The model is proposed as providing a unified account of the role of explanation, prediction, and test in science, including a suggested logical symmetry of explanation and prediction (see also FALSIFICATIONISM).

Criticism of the covering-law model has concentrated on its claims to provide a defining model of scientific explanation. It has not generally been accepted that subsumption under empirical covering laws is a sufficient or a necessary condition for scientific explanation. Successful covering laws can be formulated without these being the basis of satisfactory explanation. A suggestion also made is that scientific explanation involves the identification of underlying causal mechanisms that may not depend on empirical covering laws or involve prediction (see REALISM); for example, while Darwinian theory provides an important explanatory account, this is presented in terms of general mechanisms and is not predictive. In sociology in particular it is also clear that important kinds of explanation occur that are neither dependent on covering law nor on general mechanisms (for example, MEANINGFUL UNDERSTANDING AND EXPLANATION). Thus, while the covering-law model may be seen as adequately portraying one form of scientific explanation, there is no widespread acceptance that it provides an adequate overall model of this, or of the range of explanation in general. See also HYPOTHETICO-DEDUCTIVE EXPLANATION AND METHOD, EXPLANATION.

craft apprenticeship the traditional method of learning a craft in many countries, in which the trainee was attached by a legally binding agreement, the indenture, to a master for a specific number of years as an unpaid worker. The goal of an apprentice was to become a master craftsman. However, an intermediate stage existed, that of journeyman, and, in practice, this was often the limit of the achievement of many craft workers. Connected with the earlier medieval system of craft guilds, as well as being a method of passing on the technical skills and trade secrets associated with a particular craft, the system of craft apprenticeship was also a way of controlling entry into a craft (see also LABOR ARISTOCRACY; compare PROFESSION and TRADES UNIONS).

In modern times, with the spread of industrialism and factory production, craft apprenticeship continues to exist, although it is in part transformed. In recent years, however, the association of the system with restrictive practices, and its being regarded in some quarters as a barrier to technical change and the more flexible management of labor, has led to the virtual dismantling of apprenticeship as a general system for the training of skilled craft labor. Its replacement, in Great Britain at least, has been with a system of training based on colleges and ad hoc agencies, and not with a systematic pattern of skills training of the kind that exists in some other countries, for example, West Germany. See also DESKILLING.

credentialism the allocation of persons to social positions, especially occupations, on the basis of specific stated qualifications. Though these qualifications are, in particular, educational ones, this does not necessarily lead to either education for socially relevant need, or improved performance in occupations. There is a high demand for jobs in modern economies, which leads to considerable competition among applicants. The requirement is for educational credentials (certificates, diplomas, degrees), which regulate the flow of manpower. The pursuit of such credentials becomes an end in itself, leading to what Dore (1976) called the *diploma disease*—see also Berg's *The Great Training Robbery* (1970). The form and content of education are of secondary importance. What is of primary significance is the level of qualification attainable. The process is criticized as failing to meet the real needs of industrial societies because it tends to serve mainly as a method of selection in the entry to occupations, rather than providing a preparation for them (see SCREENING AND THE SCREENING HYPOTHESIS). It is also criticized for frustrating many of those who embark on higher education hoping to advance occupationally, since the number of appropriate jobs does not expand to match the expansion in the numbers qualified to fill such posts.

An identical process, although in many ways more insidious in its implications (according to Dore), is the way in which, in Third World countries, credentialism and the attempt to emulate Western systems of secondary and higher education lead to expansion of educational systems in a form inappropriate to the needs of the economies of these societies. For both developed and less-developed economies, however, the counter-argument can be made that the thesis of credentialism undervalues the intrinsic value of extra education, both in employment, in providing specialist as well as general transferable skills, and as a consumption good pursued for its own sake, rather than merely for reasons of gaining employment.

crime an infraction of the criminal law. Scholars have discussed the nature and causes of crime as far back as written history shows. A related issue is that of morality, so until comparatively recently crime was seen as the proper sphere of theological and philosophical comment. In general, sociologists have tended to argue against absolutist conceptions of crime and have opposed psychological and biological explanations of why people commit crimes. Many sociologists have discussed the issue of crime in terms of morality but, unlike the majority of earlier writers, they tended not to use an absolute or universal notion of morality but view moral precepts in particular historical and cultural settings. DURKHEIM, for example, argued that laws changed with changes in social structure; he saw a historical shift from MECHANICAL to ORGANIC SOLIDARITY (from traditional, simple societies to complex, industrial ones) as involving a transformation in social relations that could be understood in moral terms and studied through changes in legal codes. He also argued that a certain level of crime was functional for society; this was indicated by the fact that no known society was free of crime. More significantly, crime served to strengthen morality by uniting the community against the criminal.

While not as absolutist as earlier philosophies, Durkheim's is still a highly generalized discussion of crime. Other sociological traditions have focused on the problem in more specific ways. Examples of this include discussions of the ways in which employment laws change, for example, either to criminalize or legalize strikes, depending on complex balances in the relative powers of employees and employers. There is clearly some merit in this approach of linking the development of criminal law to the interests of particular classes or vested interests, but the more general moral dimension is also clearly important. For example, laws relating to sexuality may have connections with property and inheritance, but they defy analysis in terms of particular class interests. Homosexuality is a case in point. The expression of male homosexual desire was a criminal offense in Great Britain until 1969. The fact that private homosexual acts between consenting adults were decriminalized, following the recommendation of the Wolfenden Report (1967), indicates a change in the conception of the role of criminal law in regulating private conduct. In fact, it signaled that ideas about crime and criminals do not reflect absolute standards, but change over time and differ between cultures. The fact that these legal changes remain controversial, however, and that gay men and women are still marginalized and discriminated against, as MORAL PANICS over AIDS have shown, indicates that the relation between criminal laws and culture is a complex one.

Generally, sociological approaches have tried to explain the relative nature of crime and its causes, as well as the effects of crime on communities and victims. See also CRIMINOLOGY, LABELING THEORY, DEVIANCE.

crime statistics the official statistics recording serious crime, which police forces generally are required to assemble. As with all OFFICIAL STATISTICS, debate exists as to the reliability of these statistics as indicators of the incidence of crime. Plainly such statistics can record only reported crime. Apart from this, numerous biases and sources of inaccuracies exist in the collection of statistics, for example, some categories of crime—white-collar crimes and crimes by women—appear to be systematically underrecorded, the result of police decisions not to prosecute. At the same time, other categories of crime, for example, mugging and drug offenses, which are the subject of public concern, may attract disproportionate police attention. There are also differences over time and between different police forces in the efficiency with which statistics are collected. An alternative source of data on the incidence of crime is *crime surveys* (for example, Jones et al., 1986). In Great Britain, for instance, these indicate that official statistics of crime underestimate the actual incidence of some categories of crime by a factor of five (for vandalism, minor thefts, etc.), with smaller, but still substantial, underrecording occurring for other categories of crime.

criminology a branch of study that has traditionally focused on a number of aspects of the nature and causes of crime and the criminal element in society. It is debatable whether this area of study may be called a discipline in its own right as it has tended rather to focus only on one problem and its ramifications from a variety of disciplinary and epistemological perspectives.

Interest in crime and the infraction of rules is found throughout written history. Morality tales about the effect of lawbreaking are found in ancient Greece and, before that, in pre-Hellenic Babylon in legal codes established about 2000 BC. In modern times, a systematic interest in crime grew with the massive social changes associated with the rise of capitalism in the 18th century. The breakup of traditional societies, the dislocation of forms of social control effective in small-scale and rural societies, and the emergence of new property and class relations, reflected in the political revolutions of the time, all led to a growth of interest in the conditions of social order, and its obverse. Interest in crime was a corollary of this.

In the 18th century, the classical school in law assumed the existence of human rationality and free will, and therefore the rational calculation of the costs and benefits of any action. The implication for criminal policy was to make the cost of infraction greater than the potential benefits. (This model has much in common with more recent deterrent theories.)

Positivist criminology may be seen, in part, as a reaction to the classical tradition, but also as part of the general growth of positivist explanation in the 19th century. Its best-known exponent was Cesare Lombroso, an Italian physician. Lombroso and his followers espoused a biological determinism opposed to the notion of free will. On the basis of measurements of prison inmates and the postmortem examination of some convicts, he argued that criminality was associated with atavism—by which he meant the survival of traits characteristic of a more primitive stage of human evolution. These genetic throwbacks were associated with "the ferocious instincts of primitive humanity and the inferior animals." By the early years of the 20th century Lombroso's work was thoroughly discredited. However, genetic/biological explanations have recurred from time to time, for example, in psychologists' contributions to criminology.

There is a variety of sociological approaches to crime and criminality, most of which are opposed to individualistic and biologistic accounts.

One tendency, incorporating a number of theoretical traditions, is *social pathology*. The basic theme here is that, rather than problems with individuals, it is social problems that cause criminal behavior.

Classical Marxist accounts (for example, by Engels and Bonger) relate crime to inherent features of capitalism, including poverty and the degradation of the working class, and the effects of greed and exploitation in creating a criminogenic culture. This emphasis reemerged in sociology in the 1970s with the growing influence of Marxism on the discipline. In the United States there has been a longstanding interest in the sociological explanation of crime, much of it influenced by the CHICAGO SCHOOL. Early Chicago School authors developed the notion of *cultural transmission*. Studying high-crime areas in Chicago between 1900 and 1925, they argued that in such areas delinquency was a tradition. Delinquent values were transmitted by PEER GROUPS and gangs. Individuals were effectively socialized into delinquency. There is also a well-established interest in the broader explanation of DEVIANCE, for example, in ANOMIE theory and in LABELING THEORY.

These arguments were expanded in DELINQUENT SUBCULTURE and in DIFFERENTIAL ASSOCIATION theories. Attempts have also been made to synthesize these different theoretical tendencies by Cloward and Ohlin (1960) in particular, who brought together cultural transmission and anomie theories. They showed how *structures of opportunity* for legitimate or illegitimate use of resources vary. Cloward and Ohlin identify one section of the lower class as particularly likely to take up the chances available for delinquency: those "seeking higher status within their own cultural milieu" and an alternative to a middle-class lifestyle, an illegal route to affluence within lower-class culture (compare MERTON's use of ANOMIE).

Approaches such as these have been criticized on a number of grounds. For example, that they generally accept the legitimacy of legitimate means and ends and assume that everyone else does likewise. Also the focus has been exclusively on lower working-class males, with little examination of female criminality, white-collar crime, or so-called crimes of the powerful.

In the 1970s, in the United States and Great Britain, sociologists returned to a blend of labeling theory and Marxism, and issues of crime, social class, and capitalism. In Great Britain, work in this style is exemplified by the so-called critical criminology of Taylor, Walton and Young (1973). Radical criminologists were united by a common ethos rather than an agreed theory. They were critical of positivist, functionalist, and labeling approaches, and offered instead a criminology that located the analysis of crime and law in the wider understanding of the capitalist state and social class relations. Thus criminal law, policing, and the prison system were portrayed as aspects of class domination. There is a clear legacy of labeling theory in this approach, but with an emphasis on the labeling of particular acts as deviant, as grounded in the logic and needs of capitalism. The radical perspective has been important in reviving sociological interest in the detailed analysis of aspects of the criminal justice system—policing, courts and sentencing, and prisons.

Further development since the 1970s has been in the growth of feminist contributions to the study of crime and deviance. Apart from the resurgence of the Women's Movement, this interest has owed much to the development of radical criminology, but with an increasing recognition that gender issues cannot simply be incorporated within a class-based perspective. Work on criminal statistics, SUBCULTURES, violence against women, female criminality, sentencing, prisons, and other issues all demonstrated the importance of gender as a specific issue and in informing general theoretical and empirical debates in criminology.

CRITERIA AND LEVELS OF MEASUREMENT

A further development in recent years has been a shift in emphasis from a concern only with offenders, to a concern with the victims of crime.

criteria and levels of measurement the rules that govern the assignment of an appropriate value, code, or score to an observed phenomenon. The most widely used classification is that devised by Stevens (1946, 1951) who identified four levels of measurement—the *nominal, ordinal, interval* and *ratio*—distinguished according to their ordering and distance properties.

In *nominal-level measurement* each value represents a distinct category, and the value is merely a label or name. Values are assigned to the variable without reference to the ordering or distances between categories, in much the same sense that people have given names such as Thomas, Richard, Catherine, and Martha. Thus, nominal level measures lack many of the properties that real numbers possess, and it is not possible to add, subtract, multiply, and divide such variables.

In *ordinal-level measurement* values are arranged in a rank order, such that if "a" is greater than "b," and "b" is greater than "c," then it follows that "a" is also greater than "c," although ordinal-level measurements give no indication of the relative distances between categories. For example, political parties might be arranged on a scale ranking from left-wing to right-wing, and although it is possible to say that in the United States the Democratic Party is more left-wing than the Republican Party, which in turn is more left-wing than the Conservative Party, we do not know what the *relative* distances are between these parties.

Interval-level measurements are an extension of ordinal-level variables, except that the distances between categories are now fixed and equal. The Celsius temperature scale is an example of such a variable in that a change in temperature from say 2° to 3° represents the same magnitude of change as an increase in temperature from 64° to 65°F. However, interval-level scales are purely artificial constructions, and the *zero point* is not inherently determined. Rather, it is defined in terms of an arbitrarily agreed upon definition. In consequence, the zero point, and even negative values on such scales, can represent real values. For example, it is possible to have a temperature of 0°C and temperatures below this value. Because of their artificial and arbitrary nature, interval scales lack the property of proportionateness, and in consequence, for example, 20°C is not twice as hot as 10°C.

Finally, *ratio-level measurements* make use of real numbers, and the distances between categories are fixed, equal, and proportionate (Nachmias and Nachmias, 1976). The zero is now naturally defined and because of this, *ratio comparisons* can now be made. For example, a six-foot-tall man has twice the height of a three-foot-tall boy.

The importance of Stevens' classification is that the statistical tests that may be used are determined by the variable type. Arranging Stevens' variables in order—nominal, ordinal, interval, and ratio—it can be shown that a statistical test applicable to a lower-level variable may also be applied to a higher-level variable. Very few statistical tests may be undertaken on a nominal-level variable, while any statistical test may be applied to a ratio-interval measure. Unfortunately, most variables commonly employed in the social sciences are of a nominal or ordinal nature, and in consequence only a limited number of tests may be applied to them. In the case of ordinal variables, for example, no statistical tests that involve calculating the MEAN are permissible. However, given the more sophisticated tests available, many social scientists prefer to use statistical tests that involve the calculation of the mean and STANDARD DEVIATION, although they are only fully justified with higher-level measurements. Laboriz (1970) and Taylor (1983) have undertaken a series of statistical tests on the validity of this approach and have concluded that it is generally acceptable, provided that the ordinal variables used are not of a dichotomous (see below) or trichotomous nature.

Other social scientists have attempted to elaborate on Stevens' schema. Fixed- and ratio-interval data are often grouped together and called *continuous* data. Finally, *dichotomous* variables (which can take only one of two values, for example, sex) are often treated as a separate level of measurement in their own right because they can be treated as nominal, ordinal, or fixed-interval measures, depending on circumstances. See also MEASUREMENT BY FIAT.

criterion of demarcation (of science) see FALSIFICATIONISM.

critical cultural discourse unrestricted, open discussion of social issues, which offers the potential for undermining ideological justifications of society, establishment of true accounts of social processes, and hence also the potentiality for human emancipation. Contrary to theories of MASS SOCIETY, the increasing importance of educated mass "publics" in modern industrial societies is regarded by some theorists (for example, GOULDNER, HABERMAS) as promoting conditions for such critical discourse, although no guarantees exist that these will be fully realized.

critical rationalism see FALSIFICATION, POPPER.

critical theory see FRANKFURT SCHOOL OF CRITICAL THEORY.

cross-cultural comparison the comparison of a social phenomenon in different societies, and perhaps at different historical times, with the aim of establishing either the common causal basis of shared features, including the existence of any orderly pattern to social evolution, or the unique features of a particular culture or society.

Sociologists have often held sharply contrasting views on the relative importance of these two goals of cross-cultural analysis. Most theorists have recognized the considerable difficulty of defining the units of analysis and of comparing like with like in cross-cultural comparisons. While theorists and researchers taking the first view have been prepared to risk advancing general propositions about the overall form and types of human societies, those taking the second view have used comparisons mainly to highlight differences, usually portraying their use of general concepts merely as aids to comparisons (that is, as heuristic IDEAL TYPES), with their main goal the understanding of particular cultures. See also COMPARATIVE METHOD.

cross-cutting ties the conflicting or potentially conflicting allegiances of individuals, for example, conflict between ethnicity and class, or religion and class. It has been argued that the web of relationships associated with such cross-cutting ties is conducive to social stability, because it inhibits or moderates conflict between groups. Individuals subject to cross-cutting ties tend to be pulled two ways, and so are likely to act to prevent or to limit conflict, for example, presenting both sides of the case. The existence of cross-cutting ties has sometimes been suggested as important in preserving STABLE DEMOCRACY, for example, in counteracting extremes of class consciousness. Compare COGNITIVE DISSONANCE.

cross-sectional study a method of examining a varied population at one point in time in order to gather data about people at different life stages, or in different circumstances. This method contrasts with LONGITUDINAL STUDIES, which investigate groups over a period of time in order to observe the developmental process and the influence of changing circumstances.

The advantage of cross-sectional study is that it is quicker, does not depend on changing resources or research teams, and reduces extraneous variables resulting from the passage of time. The disadvantage is that no account of change can be given.

crowd behavior see COLLECTIVE BEHAVIOR.

cult 1. in both developed and less developed societies, the most informal and often most transient type of religious organization or movement, usually distinguished from other forms of religious organization (see CHURCH-SECT TYPOLOGY) by its deviation from the dominant orthodoxies within the communities in which it operates. Sometimes involving a focus of allegiance to an inspirational or charismatic leader, cults may combine elements from various religions (SYNCRETISM) or, like SECTS, from which cults are not always sharply distinguished, may result from separation from or operate alongside a single more established religion. In preindustrial or transitional societies, cults often coexist with more formally organized religions and perform specialized functions, including magical rites.

Within both underdeveloped and developed societies it is characteristic of cults that they recruit individuals who make a positive choice to become involved. In this, they are unlike more mainstream religious organizations, where recruitment is normally at birth and by family ties. Cults and cult membership are most common in locations of social disadvantage and/or rapid social change and great social fluidity, for example, modern California. See also CARGO CULT. **2.** within the Roman Catholic church, the beliefs and practices associated with a particular physical location, for example, a shrine.

cult of personality the practice in totalitarian regimes in which the leader, for example, Hitler, Stalin, or Mao Zedong, is elevated to a position of total preeminence and presented as the source of all political wisdom, the architect of all worthwhile political and social outcomes, etc. In this process criticism of, and opposition to, the leader is suppressed, and popular political participation reduced to ritualistic celebrations of the life and achievements of the leader.

cultural anthropology (United States) the anthropology of human cultures. It is distinguished from SOCIAL ANTHROPOLOGY in Great Britain by virtue of its focus on the artifacts and practices of particular peoples rather than social structures, although the difference is easily overstated. In practice, this has meant a tendency to stress the material basis of culture, though ideational senses of culture are also important and are represented in cognitive and symbolic anthropology. The two terms are still distinguished, but it is doubtful whether they accurately reflect the current patterns of American and British anthropology.

cultural capital wealth in the form of knowledge or ideas, which legitimate the maintenance of status and power.

As proposed by BOURDIEU in particular, the notion of cultural capital extends the Marxist idea of economic capital. It is suggested that possessors of this form of capital exert considerable power over other groups, using it to gain preferred occupational positions and to legitimate their claims to a greater share of economic capital. Thus a dominant class has the symbols—language, culture, and artifacts—through which it can establish HEGEMONY. Bourdieu argues that the school, through the mechanism of awarding of certificates and diplomas, is a key institution by which the established order is maintained. The language, values, assumptions, and models of success and failure adopted within schools are those of the dominant group. Thus, success in the educational system is largely dictated by the extent to which individuals have absorbed the dominant culture, and by how much cultural capital is shared by the dominant group, thus ideologically legitimating the existing social order.

It is in part as a result of the operation of cultural capital that the working class is often upstaged in the competition for educational and occupational honors. This is because cultural capital not only brings inherent advantages in learning, etc., but it is also possibly a factor leading to an undervaluation of formal qualifications, credentialed skills, etc., and a preference for more loosely defined social characteristics by some employers, for example, a preference for middle-class graduates from elite institutions, even when they possess inferior formal qualifications.

The concept of cultural capital involves a view of the advantages of human capital that differs from the main alternative theory, the HUMAN CAPITAL theory (see also INTELLIGENCE). It is complementary to a further alternative to human capital theory, that is, screening theory, which has some shared features and some differences of emphasis—see SCREENING (AND THE SCREENING HYPOTHESIS). Compare also FUNCTIONALIST THEORY OF SOCIAL STRATIFICATION.

cultural deprivation the lack of appropriate forms of language and knowledge that would ensure success in the educational system. This form of explanation has been used to account for the educational limitations of working-class and ethnic minority children. It was particularly influential in the late 1960s and early 1970s. The Headstart Program in the United States and the Educational Priority Area Project in Great Britain were designed to compensate working-class children for lack of parental interest, the failings of home and neighborhood, and the inadequate provision of appropriate cultural experience.

This *deficit theory* of educational failure has been heavily criticized because it suggests personal inadequacy. Some sociologists believe that the issue is one of cultural difference: the idea that the school incorporates social values and ideas of social knowledge distinct from those held by members of the working class. See also ELABORATED AND RESTRICTED CODES, BASIL BERNSTEIN.

cultural diffusion see DIFFUSION.

cultural evolution see EVOLUTIONARY THEORY and SOCIOCULTURAL EVOLUTION.

cultural hegemony see HEGEMONY.

cultural incorporation see INCORPORATION.

cultural lag the hypothesis that social problems and conflicts are due to the failure of social institutions to keep pace with technological change. This hypothesis is based on the assumption of TECHNOLOGICAL DETERMINISM and is associated with neo-evolutionary theories of social change. The term was first used by Ogburn (1964). See also MODERNIZATION, TECHNOLOGY, FUNCTIONALISM, NEO-EVOLUTIONISM.

cultural materialism (anthropology) an approach, for example, the work of Marvin Harris (1978), which suggests that the appropriate explanations of many aspects of human culture are material factors. In some aspects the approach is like that of MARX, but in Harris's work the determining features of importance are more usually of a demographic or environmental nature. Harris, for example, has proposed ecological/environmental explanations of social practices such as cannibalism, TABOOS, and food prohibitions. See also ENVIRONMENTAL DEPLETION, GEOGRAPHICAL DETERMINISM.

cultural relativism and **linguistic relativism** any doctrine that the concepts and values of one society or cultural area cannot be fully translated into, or fully understood in, other languages, that is, truly universal concepts and values are not available. See also RELATIVISM, FORMS OF LIFE, INCOMMENSURABILITY, TRANSLATION, SAPIR-WHORF HYPOTHESIS.

cultural reproduction the perpetuation of existing cultural forms, values, and ideas. For BOURDIEU, it means reproduction and perpetuation of the culture of the dominant classes to ensure their continued dominance. See also CULTURAL CAPITAL.

cultural studies the distinctive range of interdisciplinary approaches to the study of culture and society, which in sociology has been especially associated with the work in Great Britain of the Center for Contemporary Cultural Studies (CCCS) at the University of Birmingham. Established in 1964 under the Directorship of Richard Hoggart, the Center took its principal inspiration from his influential book *The Uses of Literacy* (1958). The aim was to support and encourage research in the area of contemporary culture and society: cultural forms, institutions and pactices, and their relation to wider patterns of social change. Following the departure of Hoggart to UNESCO in 1968, a sociologist, Stuart Hall, became director, until his move to the Open University in 1979.

The concerns of both the Center and the main sociological strand of cultural studies in Great Britain have been: (a) the social conditioning of cultural production and symbolic forms; (b) the "lived experience" of culture and its shaping by class, age, gender, and ethnic relations; (c) the relationships between economic and political institutions and processes and cultural forms. These include the work of the socialist literary critic, Raymond Williams (especially *Culture and Society*, 1958, and *The Long Revolution*, 1960—see also the entry on "Culture" in *Keywords*, 1976). Influenced by Williams and Hall, Cultural Studies derived many of its concepts from Marxism, but it always avoided reductionism, emphasizing instead the idea that culture is a product of power struggles between different social groups, based on age, gender, and ethnicity, as well as economic divisions (class). For example, in the 1970s a series of *Working Papers in Cultural Studies*, produced by researchers at the CCCS (see Hall and Jefferson, 1976), which focused on youth SUBCULTURES, attracted wide attention (see RESISTANCE THROUGH RITUAL). Later, influenced by the ideas of GRAMSCI and ALTHUSSERIAN MARXISM, members of the Birmingham school explored the cultural implications of *Thatcherism*.

More recently, especially with an increasing centrality of the so-called culture industries within the economy, numerous further areas of focus on cultural forms can also be noticed in addition to those central in the work of the CCCS—see CONSUMER CULTURE, POSTMODERNISM AND POSTMODERNITY, SOCIOLOGY OF ART.

culture the human creation and use of symbols and artifacts. Culture may be taken as constituting the way of life of an entire society, and this will include codes of manners, dress, language, rituals, norms of behavior, and systems of belief. Sociologists stress that human behavior is primarily the result of nurture (social determinants) rather than nature (biological determinants) (see NATURE-NURTURE DEBATE). Indeed, human beings may be distinguished from other animals by their ability to collectively construct and transmit symbolic meanings (see LANGUAGE). Knowledge of a culture is acquired via a complex process that is fundamentally social in origin. Human beings are both acted on by culture and act back, and so generate new cultural forms and meanings. Thus, cultures are characterized by their historical nature, their relativity, and their diversity (see CULTURAL RELATIVISM). They undergo change alongside changes in the economic, social, and political organization of society. Furthermore, human beings initiate cultural transformation out of their unique capacity to be reflexive (see REFLEXIVITY).

It is possible to detect in many societies the belief that culture and nature are in conflict with one another and that culture must seek to conquer nature via the civilization process. Such a view can be found in the natural science traditions of Western societies. It is also a strong element in Freud's theory of culture, in which he sees culture arising out of the repression and sublimation of man's innate drives (EROS and THANATOS). Many cultures, however, regard the relationship not as oppositional but as complementary. Recent feminist theories of culture have suggested that belief systems upholding an antagonistic relationship between nature and culture have proven ecologically dysfunctional. It can be suggested that human beings *are* nature, but that they possess a consciousness of nature (Griffin, 1982).

Human beings not only have the ability to construct cultural forms and are in turn sustained by those forms; they also possess the ability to theorize about culture itself. Implicit in many sociological approaches to the study of culture(s) have been prescriptive ideas on the relative merits of certain ways of life and cultural forms. For example, cultural theorists both within and outside of the discipline have drawn distinctions between high and low cultures, popular culture, folk culture, and mass culture. The concept of mass culture has been used by both radical and conservative critics to express dissatisfaction with the state of contemporary arts, literature, language, and culture generally. Although embracing different political ideologies, both groups have suggested that 20th-century culture has been impoverished and diluted. In the place of an independent, well-informed, and critical public, an unstructured and largely apathetic mass has arisen.

Radical theorists have argued that the threat to the quality of culture comes not from below but from above. Most specifically, it comes from what the FRANKFURT SCHOOL OF CRITICAL THEORY has identified as the "capitalist culture industry." In this view, the capitalist mass media have the ability to manipulate the tastes, wants, and needs of the masses. In contrast, conservative and elitist theorists of culture, such as those put forward by Ortega y Gasset (1930) and T.S. Eliot (1948), identify the threat as coming from the masses themselves. The masses, through what the conservative theorists saw to be their increasing power, would jeopardize culturally creative elites.

In more general terms, sociologists would suggest that it is virtually impossible for any human behavior to reside outside of cultural influences. What initially may appear to be natural features of our lives, for example, sexuality, aging, and death, are all made meaningful by culture and transformed by its influence. Even the consumption of food, so apparently natural, is imbued with cultural meaning and custom.

culture of poverty the way of life developed and reproduced by poor people—an explanation for the existence of poverty in terms of the cultural characteristics of the poor themselves. The term was first used by Oscar Lewis (1961, 1968), who emphasized fatalism as the particular aspect of UNDERCLASS subculture that ensured the inheritance of poverty. Lewis argued that the CYCLE OF DEPRIVATION was self-perpetuating and that children were quickly socialized into the values and attitudes of being poor. Lewis argued that the culture of poverty in underdeveloped societies, typified by a cash economy and high unemployment, inhibited the inculcation of the modern values appropriate for social and economic development. The idea of a culture of poverty has been criticized, notably by Valentine (*Culture and Poverty*, 1968), for its concentration on the familial and local view of poverty, which largely places responsibility for poverty on the individual and the family rather than examining external influences that may preclude social and economic development.

As applied particularly to the Third World, the culture-of-poverty argument can be seen as part of the general debate, which emerged from the work of Talcott PARSONS, about the importance of values in helping or hindering the process of ECONOMIC AND SOCIAL DEVELOPMENT. In this way, so-called backward values, such as fatalism and resignation, were contrasted with the modernizing values of enterprise and achievement visible in affluent capitalist societies (see also ACHIEVEMENT MOTIVATION).

More recent research suggests that people living in the poor shanty towns described by Lewis do not have a fatalistic attitude within a culture of poverty; rather, families and neighbors work together to devise strategies in order to adapt and cope with their changing social and economic circumstances. The impoverished inhabitants of Third World barrios and bidonvilles are far from apathetic. Research has clearly shown (for example, Roberts, 1978; Lomnitz, 1977) how far the qualities of enterprise and inventiveness are needed simply to ensure survival in such adverse circumstances. Typically, family and neighbors develop complicated survival strategies, often involving articulation of many different forms of informal and formal economic activity. Thus, relatively little empirical support has been found for the culture-of-poverty argument. Other explanations are therefore required for Third World poverty.

culture shock the disruption of one's normal social perspectives (own society, subculture, membership groups) as the result of confrontation with an unfamiliar or alien culture. While culture shock can be psychologically unsettling and troublesome to individuals—as when violently removed from their own society or when this has been undermined by outside intervention—it can also be liberating, leading to a new depth of understanding of sociologically significant relationships. It is in this latter context that sociology and anthropology often pride themselves in providing an element of culture shock for new students of their disciplines. See also STRANGER.

custom any established pattern(s) of behavior within a community or society. As in everyday usage, the term refers to regularized social practices, or accepted rules of behavior, which are informally regulated and mark off one cultural group from another. At another level, customary forms of action may be distinguished from rational forms of action (see TYPES OF SOCIAL ACTION), for example, as with TRADITIONAL ACTION, in which there is little consideration of alternative courses of action.

cybernetic hierarchy the notion that social systems, like animal organisms or any complex systems, are governed by a hierarchical network of communications and regulating mechanisms, and that in social systems this means that cultural VALUES and the government play a decisive role in shaping and maintaining the system. It is in this context, for example, that Talcott PARSONS refers to the political subsystem of the social system as involving *goal attainment*.

Parsons sees social life as organized in terms of two interrelated hierarchies (see Fig. 5):

(a) a four-fold hierarchy running from culture, social systems, and personality systems to the biological organism;

(b) a hierarchy within the social system, running from values and norms to collectivities and roles.

See also CYBERNETICS, SOCIAL SYSTEM, STRUCTURAL-FUNCTIONALISM; compare CULTURAL MATERIALISM.

cybernetics "the science of control and communication in the animal and the machine." As coined by Norbert Wiener in the 1940s (see Wiener, 1949), and stimulated by the advent of modern computing, the term was intended to draw attention to common processes at work in systems of all types, whether these be mechanical servomechanisms (for example, a thermostatically controlled central-heating system), biological organisms, or SOCIAL SYSTEMS. The assumption is that all such systems regulate their relation to an external environment by the operation of a *feedback loop*, in which changes in the environment are communicated to the system in a manner that brings about a corresponding adjustment of the system to maintain a steady state, or other state appropriate to the effective functioning or survival of the system (see also CYBERNETIC HIERARCHY). Cybernetics and cybernetic analogies were in vogue in the 1950s and 1960s, but subsequently they have suffered from a reaction against functionalist thinking and SCIENTISM in the social sciences. See also SYSTEMS THEORY, STRUCTURAL-FUNCTIONALISM.

cycle or **cyclical phenomena** any repetitive or recurring social processes in which a sequence of events is followed by a similar sequence on completion. Numerous social processes are accepted as manifesting a cyclical pattern, for example, the life cycle; other suggested cyclical patterns, for example, historical cycles and the CIRCULATION OF ELITES, are more controversial.

Bourdon and Bourricaud (1989) identify an important general category of cyclical phenomena, that is, those that result when "a process, in developing, causes a *negative feedback* to arise, which ends in a reversal of the process." In economics, the well-known *cobweb theorem* has this basis: producers tend to estimate future prices on the basis of current process, so they tend to produce an excess of products they think will be most profitable, and insufficient quantities of goods, which they estimate will be less profitable. This produces, when graphically expressed, a cyclical spider's-web pattern of movements from one equilibrium position to another. A more straightforward example is provided by patterns of vaccination: high levels of vaccination lead to fewer illnesses due to a particular disease, leading to fewer vaccinations and a return of the disease, leading in turn to a renewal of high levels of vaccination. One attraction of conceptualizations of social reality as involving cyclical processes is that these can often be formulated mathematically, although such models rarely manifest themselves in a pure form in social life.

cycle of deprivation an account of the persistence of poverty that stresses the intergenerational transmission of social deprivation, principally through

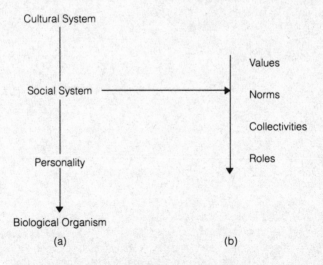

Fig. 5. **Cybernetic hierarchy.** See main entry.

the mechanism of the FAMILY, although individual and community pathology are also implicated. The notion is linked with the so-called culture of
poverty thesis and was given political prominence in Great Britain by Keith
Joseph, Minister for Social Services, in 1972.

The commitment of successive British governments to urban aid programs reflects the concern of community with the supposed cycle of deprivation. Such an approach denies the importance of wider bases of structural inequality, and, as an exclusive basis to social policy, it has now been
discredited.

Various other formulations or models have appeared that are variants of
the cycles of deprivation theme. These alternative explanations acknowledge the significance of structural features such as changes in the occupational structure and unemployment. They also argue that the interrelationship between individuals, families, and communities on the one
hand and wider structural features on the other are much more complex
than Keith Joseph's simplistic version allows.

D

Dahrendorf, Sir Ralph (1928–) German-born sociologist who has spent
much of his working life in Great Britain, including some time as the
Director of the London School of Economics. He is best known for his
influential work *Class and Class Conflict in an Industrial Society* (1959),
in which he proposed a reworking of traditional conceptions of class based
on ownership or nonownership of the means of production, replacing
these with a definition of class in terms of patterns of authority, although
retaining the notion of class conflict. He has also written a number of
comparative works examining citizenship and democracy in modern society, including *Society and Democracy in Germany* (1967) and *The New
Liberty* (1975). He has rejected as Utopian the idea that conflicts of interest based on differences in POWER can ever be removed, but has argued
that the existence of CITIZEN RIGHTS and extension of EQUALITY OF OPPOR-
TUNITY has the potential to reduce and control them.

Darwin, Charles (1809–1882) English naturalist whose theory of natural
selection gave a revolutionary account of the origins of biological diversity.
Darwin's ideas were presented in his *On the Origin of Species* (1859). The
scientific approach he defended, involving the gradual evolution of species
over a massive time scale, has been as influential as its initial reception,
especially by the church, was hostile. Darwin's theories were interpreted
quite wrongly, in fact, as a direct attack on the foundations of ecclesiastical
life, God, the Bible, and the Christian clergy.

Though Darwin is usually given the credit for the evolutionary hypothesis, similar ideas had been advanced by others, such as Erasmus Darwin
(1731–1802)—Charles' grandfather—and Jean-Baptiste LAMARCK
(1744–1829). With this historical foundation, and crucial theoretical contributions from Thomas Malthus (1766–1834) in demography, which suggested competition and conflict as crucial elements of population expansion,
and from Sir Charles Lyell (1797–1875) in geology (the hypothesis that geo-
logical time, and hence the age of the earth, was infinitely greater than had
previously been thought), Darwin's theory of evolution was in reality beg-
ging to be formulated. It is no surprise, then, that Darwin was not alone:
Alfred Russel Wallace (1823–1913) independently and almost concurrently
had come to exactly the same evolutionary conclusions.

Compared with earlier theories of biological change, the decisive contribution of Darwinian theory lay in its specification of the principal mechanism that governed development—natural selection. Darwin argued that
in each generation of any species' offspring there would be some degree of
random mutation and natural variation. Any variation that enhanced the
chances of survival would, over many generations, undergo a process of

positive selection. Quite simply, those offspring lacking the feature would be less likely to survive, less likely to reproduce.

Darwin could give no account of how reproduction ensured, on the one hand, identity, and on the other, variation. This had to await the development of a science of genetics. Nevertheless, his idea that variation, by allowing, for example, some members of a population to compete more successfully in a new or changed environment, could over millennia produce new species, was both simple and compelling. In sum, Darwin's ideas gave a coherent account of how a small number of simple forms could have given rise to a diversity of complex differentiated and specialized species.

The importance of Darwin's ideas for sociology lie in two principal areas: first, the study of SOCIAL CHANGE, with particular reference to the EVOLUTIONARY THEORY of many 19th-century social philosophers, and their intellectual descendants, 20th-century NEO-EVOLUTIONISM and theories of ECONOMIC AND SOCIAL DEVELOPMENT and MODERNIZATION; and, secondly, the social/racial engineering philosophy embraced by the school of SOCIAL DARWINISM.

Dasein (German) man's basic mode of participation in the world: "being-in-the-world"—a central concept in HEIDEGGER'S philosophy. Three main aspects of *Dasein* were distinguished by Heidegger:

(a) "facticity"—what is "given," that is, one's own origins;

(b) "extentiality"—one's "purposive being" and creative potential;

(c) the tendency to deny one's unique potential—a loss of *authenticity*. "Unauthentic" action occurs in modes of being in which action is depersonalized, or regarded as objectivized.

data analysis the examination and processing of information gained from studies, such as surveys or experiments. Social data can be analyzed by a variety of methods, including CROSS TABULATION, statistical tests (see STATISTICS AND STATISTICAL ANALYSIS), and computer programs (for example, see STATISTICAL PACKAGE FOR THE SOCIAL SCIENCES); punch cards were a common method used to collate information before more sophisticated computer analysis became possible. See also RESEARCH METHODS.

data banks or **data archives** repositories for the raw data collected in previous social surveys. Such data, today often made available to users in computer-readable form, may be used to reanalyze data, and used in SECONDARY ANALYSIS, which combines data from several surveys and over time. As well as containing the raw data on many classic studies, data banks usually also have extensive holdings of data on changes over time in public opinion. Data banks can be a source of inexpensive, highly relevant data. The disadvantages of using such data are that a researcher is likely to have less awareness of the limitations of the data than those who originally collected it, and where data from several surveys are combined problems of comparability are likely to arise (see also OFFICIAL STATISTICS). See also HUMAN RELATIONS AREA FILES.

data set a collection of information (observations) made on a group of individuals and relating to certain VARIABLES in which the investigator is interested. Such data may be gained from interviews, surveys, experiments, etc. See also DATA ANALYSIS, RESEARCH METHODS.

debt peonage a coercive form of labor whereby the laborer is tied to an employer or landholder through indebtedness. It was a common method of ensuring a labor supply in AGRARIAN SOCIETIES until the 20th century, although in some areas of the Third World the practice persists illegally. Various forms of indebtedness were found: landowners sometimes paid taxes for the peasantry, requiring their labor services until payment had been made; sometimes laborers became indebted through transportation costs, such as was the case with Chinese immigrants to the United States in the 19th century, when they worked without pay until their transport costs had been deemed to be covered. At its most extreme, individuals were never able to work off the initial or subsequent debt, which may even have been passed on to descendants. In such cases *debt slavery* may be the more appropriate term. See PEASANTS and PEASANT SOCIETY.

decentered self or **decentered subject** a conception of the SELF, or the thinking and acting subject (see SUBJECT AND OBJECT), in which the self is no longer regarded as providing the kind of ultimate grounding for epistemological thinking that is often assumed in traditional forms of philosophy, for example, EMPIRICISM. Particularly associated with STRUCTURALISM and POSTSTRUCTURALISM, the concept of a decentered self derives from a number of sources, especially:

(a) from PSYCHOANALYSIS, the idea that the EGO is not master in its own home and is influenced by the *unconscious;*

(b) from SAUSSURE'S linguistics, the conception that language consists of a system of signs constituted by *différences*, so that the "I" is "only constituted as a sign" by virtue of its differences from "you," "we," "they," etc. and as one element in that system, so that there can be no question of granting it philosophical privilege (GIDDENS, 1987);

(c) from an emphasis on the autonomy of culture, or the TEXT, in which the individual, or the author, exists nowhere.

In this view, rather than a single self, for any individual person there always exist multiple selves or quasi-selves, in which the self exists only as a moment in a *syntagmatic chain*. Whereas in structuralism the decentering of the self leads to the elevation of STRUCTURE as the preeminent basis of accounts of reality, in post-structuralism, neither the self nor structure is regarded as providing any secure basis. See also ALTHUSSER, ALTHUSSERIAN MARXISM, DECONSTRUCTION, DERRIDA, FOUCAULT, LACAN, STRUCTURE AND AGENCY.

deconstruction a POSTSTRUCTURALIST intellectual movement particularly influential in the United States and France since the late 1960s. The term is particularly associated with the work of the French philosopher Jacques

DERRIDA, who has developed powerful critiques, in particular of PHE-NOMENOLOGY, Saussurean linguistics, STRUCTURALISM, and Lacanian psychoanalysis.

Derrida suggests that language is an unstable medium that cannot in any sense carry meaning or TRUTH directly. He has drawn attention to the ways in which Western philosophies have been dependent on metaphor and figurative rhetoric to construct origin, essence, or *binary conceptual systems* (for example, nature/culture, masculine/feminine, rationalism/irrationalism) in which one term is constituted as the privileged norm setting up hierarchies of meaning that are then socially institutionalized. The project of deconstruction is to reveal the ambivalence of all TEXTS, which can only be understood in relation to other texts (*intertextuality*) and not in relation to any literal meaning or normative truth.

By denying that we have any direct access to reality, unmediated by language, Derrida offers a critique of both POSITIVISM and phenomenology. He also traces the extent to which Western linguistics and philosophy have been permeated by *phonocentrism*—the privileged notion of speech as the voice or presence of consciousness—and by *logocentrism*—the belief that the Word of the *transcendental signifier* (for example, God, the World Spirit) may provide a foundation for a whole system of thought. Clearly, for Derrida, any such transcendental origin or essence of meaning is sheer fiction. Further, he argues that social ideologies elevate particular terms (for example, Freedom, Justice, Authority) to the status of the source from which all other meanings are derived. But the problem here is how any such term preexists other meanings through which its meaning is in practice constituted. Thus, any thought system that is dependent on a first principle is, for Derrida, metaphysical.

In Derrida's view, then, LÉVI-STRAUSS consistently privileges a particular ethnocentric view of nature over culture; structuralism, generally, is dependent on the project of constructing general laws based on binary oppositions; LACAN (productively) sees the unconscious in terms of a language, but then falls into the trap of constituting the unconscious as the origin of truth. Further, the relationship between deconstruction and Marxism is a complex one. On the one hand Derrida has pointed to the extent to which Marxist theory has depended on metaphor (for example, base/superstructure) to erect a totalizing account of the world. On the other, he has on occasion declared himself to be a Marxist, arguing that deconstruction is a political practice committed to uncovering false logics upon which social institutions maintain their power. While Derrida has continued to stress this progressive, radical critique, his work has been taken up by literary critics in the United States in particular (the Yale School of Deconstructionists), stripped of its political force, and turned in a direction that focuses on the undecidability of meaning. Derrida himself has indicated the ways in which, ironically, such strategies of deconstruction can ultimately operate in the service of dominant political and economic institutions.

deference 1. an attitude based on the belief that there is a natural order of inferiority and superiority in which the inferior recognize the right of the superior to rule. **2.** an aspect of a power relationship requiring a submissive response from a subordinated actor or group.

Most early work carried out within the framework of definition **1.** was inspired by POLITICAL SCIENCE studies in the tradition of Bagehot, a 19th-century social commentator who, in *The English Constitution,* ascribed the relative stability of British society to its essentially deferential and, hence, elitist character. A number of British voting and attitude studies used the notion of deference, implicitly or explicitly, in discussions of working-class VOTING BEHAVIOR in the 1950s when manual workers' votes had clearly served to maintain Conservative governments in power. In these works, the notion of deference became entangled with those of CONSERVATISM and traditionalism. So a survey might ask whether a respondent thought that a person from a public school was naturally more suited to govern the country than one from a grammar school. If respondents answered "yes," then they were assumed to be deferential (or perhaps they might be assumed to be public school men). Such studies came under criticism on a variety of theoretical and empirical grounds, for example, for the imprecision of the use of the term, for the contradictory notions about the consequences of deference, and for the lack of evidence to sustain the notion. These various critiques both operated within the framework of political-science studies and gradually substituted a more sociological perspective, which recast the notion of deference in terms of social relations rather than of individual attitudes or voting behavior.

The specifically social meaning of definition **2.** might be said to have been recovered, or rediscovered, by British sociologists at the time when studies of working-class consciousness shifted from the study of ATTITUDES, traditionalism, and voting behavior to other ideological and structural concerns such as INCORPORATION and HEGEMONY. This development coincided with a more general growth of interest in issues of SOCIAL CLASS and CLASS CONSCIOUSNESS (for example, M. Bulmer, 1975; see also CLASS IMAGERY). As Newby (1977) argued, the logic of this development was that deference should be seen as a "form of social interaction that occurs in situations involving the exercise of traditional authority." It is in this sense that the concept may be said to have been recovered by sociologists. Sixty years earlier, studies of power in simple horticultural societies had shown how deferential attitudes might be formally built in to relations between, for example, chiefs and others, or young and wise people (for example, see the discussion in G. Lenski, 1966). These studies often indicated that a deferential performance did not necessarily involve a genuine feeling of inferiority due to birth, talent, etc., but did involve conforming to a set of expectations, a ROLE, within a power structure. These expectations might be ideologically legitimated in a number of different ways, but they had the same structural underpinning.

With the rise of feminist theory, deference was considered in gender relations. In this area, as in the critiques of theories of WORKING CLASS CONSERVATISM and deference, both the assumption of natural submissiveness, and the use to which the term had been put, were challenged.

definition a statement or process by which the meaning of a term is conveyed. Ideally, a definition—*definiens*—will be logically equivalent to the word or term being defined—*the definiendum*. However, instead of such strict verbal definitions, *ostensive definitions* may be provided by pointing to examples or by providing general indications of use rather than strict definitions, for example, in indicating the meaning of color terms. Numerous further submeanings of the term "definition" should also be noted, including:

(a) the distinction between descriptive and stipulative definitions, the former stating a meaning that already has currency, the latter a proposed or reformulated statement of meaning;

(b) the distinction between nominal and real definitions, where the intention of the latter is to move beyond a merely conventional statement of meaning to provide a definition of a phenomenon in terms of its underlying or real structural determinants (see CONVENTIONALISM and REALISM). See also ANALYTIC AND SYNTHETIC, OPERATIONALISM.

definition of the situation a social situation as seen in the subjective view of a particular social actor, group, or subculture. While not denying the importance of objective factors in social life, the importance of taking account of the actor's definition of the situation in sociological analysis is summed up in the oft-quoted sociological aphorism: "If one defines a situation as real, then it is real in its consequences" (W.I. Thomas, 1928).

degradation ceremony the communicative work that transforms a person's entire status and identity to something lower (GARFINKEL, 1956). The guilty offender in a court trial, for example, is reduced to a degraded status as murderer or thief. This has implications for the offender's total identity as a human being. According to Garfinkel, the existence of such ceremonies is in dialectical contrast to, and also demonstrates, the "ultimately valued, routine orders of personnel and action" within society. See also DEVIANCE AMPLIFICATION, ETHNOMETHODOLOGY.

delinquency illegal or antisocial acts, typically performed by young males. The emphasis on young males is not necessary in a strict sense, but has been a clear feature in sociological studies of the subject, which have commonly focused on WORKING CLASS youth PEER GROUPS, gangs, or SUBCULTURES, or on aspirations and opportunities for young people.

The first sociologists to study the problem systematically were associated with the CHICAGO SCHOOL. Beginning with the influence of Robert PARK and W.E. Burgess in the 1920s, sociologists at the University of Chicago were encouraged to undertake empirical studies of neighborhoods, gangs, etc., treating the city as a social laboratory. Their lasting influence was in the development of area studies—the most criticized aspect of their work—and in arguments about social disorganization and the importance of subcultures (or cultural transmission). Later US studies presented alternatives to the Chicago approach, or tried to develop themes that had been established by Chicago sociologists.

MERTON, for example, adapted DURKHEIM's notion of ANOMIE to suggest that a disparity between highly valued goals and legitimate opportunities to achieve goals could produce a number of deviant responses (see CRIMINOLOGY). Other researchers, notably A.K. Cohen (1955), developed the concept of subculture in relation to working-class male delinquency. He argued that delinquent subcultures provided an alternative source of status and respect for boys who did not take, or have access to, other solutions, like higher education or a stable adjustment to middle-class values. The values of the delinquent subculture were seen as a reaction to, and an inversion of, middle-class values. Some critics of Cohen pointed out that lower-class culture had its own values that informed and shaped delinquent values. Those most commonly emphasized have been so-called masculinist values of toughness, autonomy, and excitement. The work of Cloward and Ohlin (1960), emphasizing status and opportunities for legitimate and delinquent lifestyles, was an attempt to combine Merton's anomie theory with subculture theory. Critics of US subculture theory have tended to pick out the essentially FUNCTIONALIST assumptions about values, the positivistic, over-deterministic character of the work (see DELINQUENT DRIFT), the fact that females and middle-class youth are almost completely ignored and, finally, the lack of empirical backing for many of the assumptions and arguments of classical subculture theory.

In Britain there has been a long-standing interest in juvenile crime and policy issues. Juveniles were the concern of the people who framed the Probation Act of 1907. Separate provision was made for juveniles in the Criminal Justice System (from 1933), and a number of acts in the 1970s and 1980s have been specifically directed at the problems of crime and treatment of young offenders. This interest has been stimulated by successive MORAL PANICS about YOUTH CULTURES—from teddy boys in the 1950s through a variety of youth subcultures to FOOTBALL HOOLIGANS and so-called lager louts in recent years. Many sociologists have cast doubts on the argument that these phenomena are distinctively new (Pearson, 1983), and others have argued that the mass media of communication have played a significant role in defining working-class youth as a problem and in distorting and exaggerating the nature and significance of the issue (S. Cohen, 1973 and 1981). Even accepting the strength of these arguments, it is clear that juvenile crime and delinquency are serious problems requiring sociological research. CRIME STATISTICS in the 1980s suggest that, automobile offenses apart, for both males and females, offending rates are highest among juveniles. This fact, together with the high visibility of youth problems, which has been encouraged by the mass media, has stimulated a great deal of research by British sociologists. Early work questioned the value of American gang studies for the British case (Downes, 1966). Rather different subculture models have been used, though, and are particularly associated with the Centre for Contemporary Cultural Studies (see CULTURAL STUDIES) at Birmingham University. Other studies have looked at the importance of anti-school cultures (Willis, 1977) and at parental supervision and family life (Wilson & Herbert, 1978). Race has been a separate research area, in which much of the work has focused on the effects of deprivation, on RACISM, POLICING, and political alienation (Beynon and Solomos, 1987; Institute of Race Relations, 1987). Equally important, the issue of gender has been raised in ways that do not simply accept the great discrepancy between male and female delinquency, but attempt to explain the reasons for the much lower involvement of females and for the different treatment that they receive in the justice system (Carlen and Worrall, 1987). There is now a large British literature on different aspects of delinquency, characterized by a diversity of research interests and strategies. See also CRIMINOLOGY, DELINQUENT SUBCULTURE.

delinquent drift the idea that young offenders, who might otherwise respect law-abiding values and people, may drift into DELINQUENCY. The term is particularly associated with US sociologists, David Matza and Gresham Sykes (Matza, 1964; Sykes and Matza, 1957). In arguing against the positivism and determinism of other theories of delinquency influential at the time, Matza suggested that the delinquent was a more active participant in the process of becoming deviant than those theories suggested. The drift into deviance is associated with a weakening of social controls, which the delinquent chooses to enhance by rationalizing or neutralizing normative restraints. The important thing for Sykes and Matza is that the techniques of neutralization allow delinquents to value respectable conduct and retain self-respect, while being deviant themselves. An emphasis on the deviants' explanations of their actions is basic to the nonpositivist stance of such theorists. Matza also elaborates on delinquents' feelings of injustice, which serve to weaken attachment to norms and excuse delinquency (1964). Sykes and Matza describe five techniques of neutralization:

(a) a denial of responsibility: accident, absent-mindedness, etc., are responsible;

(b) the act did not victimize anyone: no one was hurt, so there was no harm done;

(c) someone was victimized: the victim deserved what he got;

(d) condemning those who condemn you: police, judges, newspaper editors—they all have some racket going;

(e) an appeal to higher loyalties: the delinquent act was done to help a relative or friend.

These techniques are important because "neutralization enables drift." Such rationalizations are commonplace in DELINQUENT SUBCULTURE.

delinquent subculture social GROUPS characterized by a commitment to values that are considered, within the dominant value system, to be criminal or antisocial.

The first sociological work in this area was carried out in the tradition of the CHICAGO SCHOOL. The earliest researchers (for example, Shaw, 1930) used the interactionist approaches developed at the University of Chicago by G.H. MEAD and others, in studies of the high-crime, and mainly immigrant (Italian, Polish, Irish, etc.), areas of the inner city. In studying different areas of Chicago, Shaw and McKay (1929) found that much higher recorded rates of truancy and of juvenile delinquency in the relatively impoverished inner city areas, and 80% of recorded delinquency was committed by groups of boys of a similar age. The research interest was thus directed onto the group, rather than on the individual, and the Chicago tradition emphasized SOCIALIZATION and the learning of delinquent values, that is, the cultural transmission of deviant mores. They rejected individualistic explanations of criminality, arguing that the social conditions of the groups concerned encouraged formation of subcultures, and that problems of unemployment and lack of social acceptance (structural dislocations) engendered delinquent subcultures. The groups that took a delinquent path had a distinct set of values that determined status and acceptance attitudes within the subculture. As Cohen (1955), in a classic study drawing on the interactionist approach, put it, "the process whereby they 'get that way' is no different from the process whereby others come to be conforming members of society." This view, then, sees the subculture as a response and solution to the poverty, low status, lack of opportunity, etc., of young people in the inner city. *Status frustration* at school and elsewhere is overcome by status and self-respect achieved within the value system of the delinquent subculture.

Delphi method a method of researching, with the aim of perhaps forecasting, future events. This involves marshaling the views, either by interviews or meetings, of a panel of experts who are thought likely to be well placed to estimate future trends in the field in question. The method is named after the temple of Apollo at Delphi in ancient Greece, famous for its oracle, whose priestesses were renowned for the highly cryptic character of their prophecies. How far experts are always in the best position to provide useful forecasts of events is debatable. Experts by definition having a particular view of the world, may be good at extrapolating trends or tendencies already well established, but they may be less good at spotting insidious change or the unexpected, which an outsider may be better placed to do. See also FUTUROLOGY.

democratic elitism the theory that democratic participation in complex modern societies will inevitably be mainly restricted to participation in periodic elections for political leaders. As such, democratic elitism is another term for PLURAL ELITISM. The theory of democratic elitism has been challenged by those (for example, Bachrach, 1967) who emphasize the possibility of a developmental participation that expands democratic capacities. See also ELITE, ELITE THEORY.

demographic transition the changes in levels of fertility and mortality accompanying INDUSTRIALIZATION that lead one pattern of population equilibrium—characteristic of preindustrial societies—to be replaced by a different equilibrium, characteristic of mature industrial societies.

This transition is held to involve three phases (see Fig. 6):

(a) a preindustrial phase, in which high birth rates are balanced by high death rates, a position of rough equilibrium;

(b) an intermediate phase, in which death rates fall but birth rates remain high, a phase of rapid population growth;

(c) a concluding phase, in which birth rates fall, leading to a new equilibrium.

Explanations usually advanced for this pattern of population change are improvements in public health in phase (b), followed by changes in economic and cultural orientations in phase (c), leading to a reduction in preferred family size.

If this pattern of demographic change can be taken as characterizing the classic historical process of industrialization, the question arising today is whether the pattern is likely to be repeated in newly industrializing societies, or other contemporary societies undergoing MODERNIZATION. In many of these societies rates of population growth and levels of social disruption have been greater than in the middle phase in earlier European patterns of demographic transition. In some societies significant economic

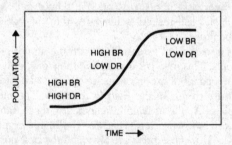

Fig. 6. **Demographic theory of transition.** Changes in rates of fertility and mortality accompanying industrialization in which, after a phase of rapid population increase, a previous pattern of population equilibrium involving high birth rates and high death rates is replaced by a different equilibrium involving low birth rates and low death rates.

growth has been difficult to achieve, and population growth has not been associated with improvements in living standards. It remains to be seen whether a new equilibrium will be established under these different circumstances.

dependency theory a theory of economic, social, and political change that attempts to explain the continuing poverty, deprived social conditions, and political instability of many poor countries in terms of their dominance by rich and powerful countries.

Dependency theory was first developed by economists in Latin America in the 1950s in opposition to the prevailing orthodoxy that Third World countries could achieve MODERNIZATION and INDUSTRIALIZATION by following the examples of the already industrialized world. As it was developed by FRANK (1967b), the theory argues that Third World countries' problems were created by the colonial and trade dominance of Europe and the United States. Their economies were shaped, first, by the needs of the advanced countries for agricultural and mineral goods and, secondly, by the requirement to provide markets for manufactured goods from the North. Any indigenous manufacturing in the Third World was suppressed by a combination of COMPETITION and political coercion. Economic surpluses flowed out of the Third World through the repatriation of any profits, and terms of unequal exchange, whereby prices of Third World exports were comparatively lower than their manufactured imports, were employed. Thus, the Third World contributed to the economic growth and industrialization of Europe and the US, and that process created structures in the Third World that made industrialization there difficult or impossible. The Third World cannot repeat the experiences of the US or Europe because its starting point is different. In Frank's terms, it is underdeveloped, not undeveloped.

The theory was influential in sociology in the 1970s. While often termed neo-Marxist, it came under increasing criticism from Marxist writers. In particular, it has been criticized for concentrating on market rather than production relations. In one of the most rigorous critiques, Taylor (1979) has argued that the central concept of economic surplus is extremely weak. More general criticisms include its relative neglect of the contribution of internal social relations to problems poor countries face, and the increasing diversity of their experiences. In the 1980s, many countries labeled Third World experienced significant processes of industrialization and rapid economic growth, which most dependency analyses would seem to preclude. The main analysis within dependency theory most likely to endure is the work of Cardoso and Faletto (1979). This identifies different forms of dependency over time and space, and incorporates a detailed analysis of the class structure of Latin America. However, as Mouzelis (1988) argues, this too suffers from an overly general analysis, which seems no longer adequate to embrace the diversity of experiences in Africa, Asia, and Latin

America. Roxborough (1984) adds that such overschematized analyses of history can now be improved as social scientific and historical studies become more adequate.

dependent variable the measure of the effect of the INDEPENDENT VARIABLE. Thus, in an experiment, or in data analysis, the independent variable, for example, number of years in school, is manipulated or otherwise controlled, and the effect of this manipulation is seen by the change in the dependent variable, for example, reading proficiency. See also EXPERIMENTAL METHOD.

deprivation the lack of economic and emotional supports generally accepted as basic essentials of human experience. These include income and housing, and parental care—or an adequate substitute—for children. This recognizes that care, shelter, and security are human needs (see also HUMANISTIC PSYCHOLOGY, MASLOW) the possession of which leads to a fuller, more comfortable life experience and allows a more complete development of the individual's potential. See also CYCLE OF DEPRIVATION, RELATIVE DEPRIVATION.

derivations see RESIDUES AND DERIVATIONS.

Derrida, Jacques (1930–) Algerian-born French philosopher whose ideas have influenced sociological thinking in a number of areas, especially the implications for methodology of human LANGUAGE. Derrida is one of a number of philosophers in recent years to argue that philosophers have been simply mistaken in searching for underlying essences or first principles. Derrida's case, drawing critically especially on the ideas of HUSSERL and SAUSSURE, is that language, as a system of internal differences, cannot be the unambiguous carrier of TRUTH in the way assumed by many branches of traditional philosophy and by many social scientists, including LEVI-STRAUSS (see also TEXT, DECONSTRUCTION, DECENTERED SELF). There are affinities, but also some important differences of emphasis, between Derrida's POSTSTRUCTURALIST thinking and postempiricist, anti-epistemological intellectual movements in the United States and Britain (compare KUHN, FEYERABEND).

descent (anthropology) the means by which individuals are allocated to specific ancestral groups. If a society has descent rules, they will specify the basis of the construction of lineages, with all the rights and obligations that go with such membership. Descent may be based on patrilineal, matrilineal, bilateral, or non-unilineal principles, and its discussion was central to postwar British SOCIAL ANTHROPOLOGY.

descent group a group in which all members have a common ancestor.

deskilling a process of job degradation in which work is progressively fragmented and stripped of its complexity, discretionary content, and knowledge base. The most important exposition of this concept is found in Braverman's theory of the labor process based on MARX. Deskilling is seen as a result of capitalist control of the labor process, in which management, using the principles of SCIENTIFIC MANAGEMENT, separates conception from execution and increasingly takes control of the labor process away from workers, leaving them with mundane, repetitive tasks. The argument that SKILL levels fall with the development of capitalism and technology is based on 19th-century craft work as the model for skilled labor. In this theory, deskilling is a major cause of PROLETARIANIZATION in the class structure, reducing both skilled manual and clerical workers to a homogeneous working class.

In sharp contradiction to theories of the labor process, the thesis of POSTINDUSTRIAL SOCIETY posits a general upgrading of skills based on INDUSTRIALIZATION. New technology is seen as creating the need for new skills, multi-skilling (*polyvalency*), and higher levels of qualification and technical expertise to replace the older craft skills of the 19th century. Much of the debate about changing skill levels involves different definitions of skill and different types of evidence. For example, the evidence for skill upgrading has relied on formal job classification and qualifications, whereas evidence for deskilling has analyzed actual skills required in a job.

The deskilling argument has been criticized as deterministic and reliant on a romanticized picture of the craft worker. Comparative research using CONTINGENCY THEORY has found evidence of both job upgrading and deskilling in different industrial sectors and societies, reflecting different managerial strategies, labor markets, and other contingent factors. At the societal level, it is difficult to assess overall changes in skill levels, since economic restructuring may displace skills in old industries and create new skills in expanding sectors. In addition, while certain jobs may be deskilled, workers may not, since they may either be upwardly mobile (for example, male clerical workers), or move into new jobs requiring higher levels of skill. Nevertheless, widespread empirical evidence for deskilling has been found in both the manufacturing and service sectors with mechanization and computerization. See also NEW TECHNOLOGY, FORDISM AND POST-FORDISM, CRAFT APPRENTICESHIP.

determinism 1. the assumption that a hypothetical omniscient observer would be in a position to predict outcomes at a time t + 1, ... t + k, etc., from knowledge at time t. Early classical sociology (for example, COMTE's) can be seen as often adopting such a deterministic view of social structures, so that future social systems could be predicted, at least in principle, from present system states. **2.** the less rigorous assumption that nothing occurs without being caused (see also CAUSE, CAUSALITY AND CAUSAL RELATIONSHIP). However, since in social science, SOCIAL ACTORS may either have uncertain or unstable preferences that may alter social outcomes, a conception of universal causation which *includes* preferences (motives, reasons, etc.) as causes cannot automatically assume predictability, even in principle.

Even in certain areas of the physical sciences, for example, so-called *indeterminism* in quantum mechanics, predictability in principle cannot always be assumed. More straightforwardly, even such superficially simple phenomena as a leaf falling, although predictable in principle, cannot *in practice* be predicted, given the large number of variables involved.

Where social systems are highly structured, and the outcome of any one actor's individual behavior can be shown to have little or no *independent* influence on the macrostructure of a system, relatively *deterministic* structural accounts of social reality may be advanced, for example, Marx's account of the working of competition in so-called perfect markets. On the other hand, where both actors' choices and social outcomes appear behaviorally and structurally undetermined, models that assume a degree of *actual* indeterminism are often proposed, that is, explanatory accounts in sense **2.** rather than in sense **1.** Accounts of this latter sort need not be regarded as unscientific—rather, they can be seen as providing EXPLANATIONS appropriate to the reality. See also FREE WILL, REFLEXIVITY, HISTORICISM, UNANTICIPATED CONSEQUENCES OF SOCIAL ACTION, EVOLUTIONARY THEORY, FUNCTIONALISM. Compare OVERDETERMINACY.

de Tocqueville, Alexis see TOCQUEVILLE.

deurbanization see URBANIZATION.

deviance any social behavior that departs from that regarded as normal or socially acceptable within a society or social context. While deviance includes criminal behavior, its sphere is far wider than this. Furthermore, not all criminal behavior will always be labeled as deviance, for example, minor traffic offenses (see also CRIME, CRIMINOLOGY).

Although there are some recurring elements among the forms of social behavior regarded as deviant within society, for the most part social deviance must be seen as a socially relative phenomenon, in that conceptions of normality and deviance are relative to social context and highly variable between different societies, different subcultures, etc.

As emphasized by Erving GOFFMAN, there is also an important sense in which all social actors are deviant in that no one conforms to all the canons of socially acceptable behavior, none of us entirely fits any social ideal, and we are all sometimes in situations in which we are socially deviant.

A further crucial question is, "What or who within society determines deviance?" As stressed by BECKER (1963), "deviance is not a quality of the act ... but rather a consequence of the application by others of rules and sanctions." Thus, the question of by whom, and how, deviance is labeled becomes crucial to its explanation (see LABELING THEORY).

Two main sociological approaches to the study of deviant behavior can be identified. The first approach includes functionalist accounts of deviance. For example, in the work of DURKHEIM, two complementary usages of the term "deviance" are found. In *The Rules of Sociological Method* (1895), he describes crime as normal, in that it is a universal phenomenon in societies and is functional in that the concepts and ceremonies surrounding crime provide a social reaction to crime and a ritual reaffirmation of social values that strengthen the social order. In *Suicide* (1897), Durkheim focuses on deviance as a social problem arising from abnormal or pathological forms of social solidarity, particularly excessive individualism (egoism) and ANOMIE.

Modern functionalist accounts of crime have largely followed Durkheim's. For example, for Parsons, deviance results from inadequate socialization, while Merton directly builds on Durkheim's concept of anomie.

The second approach has developed, in particular, in opposition to the positivism seen as underlying orthodox criminology and related approaches to the study of deviance. The starting point of such an alternative approach was the LABELING THEORY of Becker and others. This was combined, especially in the work of the Radical Deviance Theorists, for example, Taylor et al. (1973), with a revival of general critical debates about deviance and social control, including Marxian theories of crime. See also PRIMARY AND SECONDARY DEVIANCE, DEVIANCE AMPLIFICATION, NATIONAL DEVIANCY CONFERENCE.

deviance amplification a process in which the extent and seriousness of deviance are distorted and exaggerated, with the effect that social control agencies take a greater interest in the purported existence of the phenomenon and thus uncover, but actually construct, more examples of it, giving the impression that the initial distortion was actually a true representation.

The typical pattern of an amplification spiral is as follows. For whatever reason, some issue is taken up by the mass media of communication—this may be glue sniffing, FOOTBALL HOOLIGANISM, the activities of so-called lager louts, child abuse, or anything else that makes news. The sensationalized representation of the event makes it appear that there is a new and dangerous problem that must be taken seriously. In practice, the problem, however dangerous or socially threatening, will not be new, but some dramatic example will have caught the attention of the media. Their distorted and sensationalized coverage creates a MORAL PANIC, which also leads to increased police action and to more arrests of offenders. The higher arrest rate is seen as a confirmation of the growth of the problem. Judges give exemplary sentences, to show society's disapproval of this supposedly new problem. These sentences make news in themselves and serve to keep the issue public. The police respond to this evidence of public concern with yet more arrests, and so on. In this process, a further dimension of amplification is that those persons newly labeled as deviant become newly conscious of their difference, become part of new deviant networks, and may be driven to defensive action, all of which further rachets the amplification.

Wilkins (1965) made the important point that minorities were the object of this exaggeration and distortion. Other major British studies of amplification have looked at mods and rockers (Cohen, 1971, 1973), muggers (Hall et al., 1978), drug users (J. Young, 1971), and similar groups. The concept has also been used to discuss issues like the criminalization of black communities, the presentation of gay men and women, and the AIDS panic.

More generally it raises the issues of manipulation of public perceptions of minorities, and the powerlessness of minority groups to define their own images or control social reactions to them. See also HIERARCHY OF CREDI-BILITY, BECKER, LABELING THEORY.

deviance disavowal "the refusal of those who are viewed as deviant to con-cur in the verdict" (F. Davis, 1964). The concept is intended to help understanding of ways in which, for example, socially deviant persons, physically handicapped people or criminals, may attempt to structure their interaction with normal, able-bodied, unblemished people so as to mini-mize the effect of their deviancy on these relationships. See also STIGMA.

deviant career the process in which an individual comes to accept a deviant self-identity and, often, to identify with a deviant SUBCULTURE. The con-cept is associated with LABELING THEORY, indicating the fact that people are not born deviant, but only come to consider themselves as such through a process involving SOCIETAL REACTION. See also SECONDARY DEVIANCE, GOFFMANN.

deviant case, (in research methodology) any social phenomenon presented as an exception to what is generally the case, and therefore is of particular utility in *deviant case analysis* in allowing analysis of cause and effect of both the normal and the deviant case.

dharma see CASTE.

dialectic of control the two-way character of power as a form of control in which the less powerful are usually able to exert some control over the more powerful, for example, the personal assistant whom the manager must keep happy if the assistant is to perform his or her duties willingly. The assumption here is that purely alienative forms of power are relatively rare (see TYPES OF COMPLIANCE).

differential association a theory of CRIME developed by Edwin H. Sutherland, in which criminal behavior is viewed as learned behavior resulting from contact with situations in which criminality is defined favor-ably. He argued that this theory could also account for the type of crime engaged in. Thus, in the appropriate contexts, favorable attitudes to tax evasion or petty cheating at work may be learned by people who are other-wise eminently law-abiding and respectable.

Working in the tradition of the CHICAGO SCHOOL, Sutherland was espe-cially interested in street gangs and DELINQUENT SUBCULTURE. However, he intended his theory as a general theory of criminal behavior, its signifi-cance lying in the argument that individuals learn to be criminal in precise-ly the same way that they learn to be law-abiding. He thus rejects accounts of crime that explain it in terms of individual psychopathology. However, there is no acceptance in sociology that differential association explains all aspects or all forms of crime. See also CRIMINOLOGY.

differentiation see SOCIAL DIFFERENTIATION.

diffusion the spread of cultural traits (for example, religious beliefs, technological ideas, and language forms) or social practices from one society or group to another. The concept was first employed by the British anthropologist Edward TYLOR (in *Primitive Culture*, 1871) to explain the presence of nonindigenous cultural traits found within many societies. Such cultural diffusion has occurred on a wide scale throughout human history, so that societies can even be said to exist today as part of a single world society.

In social anthropology, and in sociology more generally, the existence of cultural diffusion is seen as presenting problems, especially for UNILINEAR theories of change that make the assumption that individual societies develop—mainly endogenously—through set stages (see also INTERSOCIETAL SYSTEMS). On the other hand, it should not be assumed that any cultural trait or social institution is compatible with any other, for this would be to assume that individual societies have no internal coherence.

The concept of diffusion has also been linked to the debate that emerged over theories of ECONOMIC AND SOCIAL DEVELOPMENT and MODERNIZATION. Theorists such as Talcott PARSONS (1964a) argued that the diffusion of social institutions (EVOLUTIONARY UNIVERSALS) and cultural values characteristic of Western capitalist democracies was essential if Third World development was to occur. This position was trenchantly criticized by writers from the left, most notably Frank (1969), who pointed out that the diffusion of culture and institutions from Europe to the Third World was centuries old, and rather than producing development, this colonial contact resulted in underdevelopment.

In more mathematical uses of the term, similarities are seen as existing between patterns of social diffusion and those characteristic of epidemiology, for example, the logistical pattern of the spread of a contagious disease—proceeding slowly at first, with small numbers of persons involved, then more rapidly as more become involved and they also involve still others, but then slowing down as there are fewer new people to involve. However, although formal mathematical models of the type used in physical science can be illuminating, these are usually presented as heuristic devices, rather than models that will closely fit patterns of social diffusion likely to be seen as more complex and variable in form than those in the physical realm. One reason for this is that individual human beings and groups often resist change, and diffusion rarely occurs as the outcome of passive imitation (see also TWO-STEP FLOW OF COMMUNICATIONS; OPINION LEADERSHIP).

Dilthey, Wilhelm (1833–1911) German idealist philosopher who argued for a methodological distinction to be made between the natural and the cultural sciences. His major works include *The Life of Schleiermachers* (1870) and *The Construction of the Historical World in the Cultural Sciences* (1910). A NEO-KANTIAN, he argued that while natural science should be practiced in an essentially naturalistic manner, social science should be characterized by EMPATHIC UNDERSTANDING and a psychologistic understanding of cultural phenomena. The only proper way to understand the spirit of the age (ZEITGEIST) is to interpret the world views of its participants. He imported the term HERMENEUTICS from theology to describe this practice, but also used VERSTEHEN (understanding), a term that significantly influenced the thinking of Max WEBER. The two methods have since become distinct, though both are classed as interpretive. Dilthey's historical relativism, his conflation of the SUBJECT AND OBJECT (we are part of what we study) and his psychologistic approach on VERSTEHEN have all been criticized. His view of tests as objectifications of life has been continued in the work of Gadamer. See also IDEALISM, GEISTESWISSEN-SCHAFTEN AND NATURWISSENSCHAFTEN, IDEOGRAPHIC AND NOMOTHETIC.

discourse(s) and **discourse formation** the particular scientific and specialist language(s), and associated ideas and social outcomes that, according to FOUCAULT, must be seen as a major phenomenon of social POWER and not simply a way of describing the world. For example, as the result of medical and scientific discourse(s), conceptions and the social handling of sexuality or MADNESS have changed profoundly in the 20th century from the previous nonscientific view. It is an important aspect of Foucault's conception of discourse(s), that in part at least, social phenomena are constructed from within a discourse, that there are no phenomena outside discourses. See also EPISTEME. Compare PARADIGM.

discrimination the process by which a member or members of a socially defined group is or are treated differently, especially unfairly, because of membership in that group. To be selected for less favorable treatment, a social group may be constructed by reference to such features as race, ethnicity, gender, or religion. A distinction can be drawn between categorical and statistical discrimination. *Categorical discrimination* is the unfavorable treatment of *all* persons socially assigned to a particular social category because the discriminator believes that this discrimination is required by his social group. *Statistical discrimination* refers to less favorable treatment of individuals based on the belief that there is a probability that their membership in a social group leads to their having less desirable characteristics.

discursive consciousness "what actors are able to say, or to give verbal expression to, about social conditions, including especially the conditions of their own action" (GIDDENS, 1984). For Giddens, it is important to notice that such consciousness is not all that actors know, that alongside discursive knowledge there also exists PRACTICAL KNOWLEDGE: what every actor knows, and needs to know, to get around in the social world, but cannot always express. See also STRATIFICATION MODEL OF SOCIAL ACTION AND CONSCIOUSNESS.

disfunction see DYSFUNCTION.

dispersion see MEASURES OF DISPERSION.

dissonance see COGNITIVE DISSONANCE.

division of labor 1. the process whereby productive tasks become separated and more specialized. As used by the early classical economists such as Adam SMITH (1776), the term describes a specialization in workshops and the factory system, and explains the advantages accruing in terms of the increased efficiency and productivity of these new arrangements. In economic theory, the division of labor also gave rise to increased trade and exchange of goods and services based on the law of comparative advantage. In sociology, specialization of productive tasks is seen as incorporating much more than economic efficiency in the narrow sense, and comprises a *technical division of labor* consisting of the subdivision of work tasks, hierarchies of skill, and a structure of power and authority revealed in the relations between management and workers within the company (see SCIENTIFIC MANAGEMENT). **2.** the process of occupational specialization in society as a whole, and the separation of social life into different activities and institutions such as the family, the state and the economy, denoted by the term *social division of labor*. In the writings of evolutionary sociologists such as DURKHEIM or PARSONS, the concept is indistinguishable from SOCIAL DIFFERENTIATION (see also EVOLUTIONARY THEORY). Sociological analysis of occupational specialization may refer to divisions within a society (see CLASS, LOCAL LABOR MARKETS), sectoral patterns of employment (for example, agriculture, manufacturing, and services), and also to the concentration of particular occupations or productive tasks in Third World or advanced capitalist societies respectively (see INTERNATIONAL DIVISION OF LABOR).

The effects of the social and technical divisions of labor figure centrally in theories of social stratification. In recent years, attention has focused not only on class differences but also on ethnic divisions, especially the gendered nature of jobs in the labor market, the separation of the PRIVATE AND PUBLIC SPHERES and the division of labor in the household (see SEXUAL DIVISION OF LABOR, PATRIARCHY, DOMESTIC LABOR, DUAL LABOR MARKET). Thus, it is possible to talk of divisions of labor in the plural to include reproduction as well as production and the relation between commodity and noncommodity production.

DURKHEIM (1893) produced one of the most influential texts on the social division of labor. Developing an evolutionary theory of social change, he contrasts primitive and modern societies. The former are characterized by a low division of labor, a segmentary structure, and a strong collective consciousness, or mechanical solidarity, as the basis of social order; modern societies exhibit a differentiated structure, greater individual consciousness and organic solidarity (increased interdependence between the parts of society). (See MECHANICAL AND ORGANIC SOLIDARITY.) It is the division of labor itself that functions to promote organic solidarity, based both on the awareness of individuality fostered by specialization and the corresponding dependence on others. Thus Durkheim emphasized the social, and hence moral, functions of the division of labor, in opposition to Spencer and UTILITARIANISM, which focused on the individual pursuit of self-interest in a division of labor regulated only by contract. However, Durkheim was aware that organic solidarity was imperfectly realized in modern societies and he therefore postulated *abnormal forms of the division of labor:* the *anomic division of labor* and the *forced division of labor.* The former refers to situations in which the division of labor is not matched by appropriate forms of moral regulation (see ANOMIE), and the latter refers to coercive forms of the division of labor in which class conflict and inherited wealth prevent people from occupying positions appropriate to their natural abilities.

MARX's analysis of the division of labor contrasts markedly with that of Durkheim. Whereas Durkheim saw the solution to anomie as residing in full development of an appropriately regulated division of labor, Marx linked development of the division of labor to emergence of private property, class divisions, exploitation, and ALIENATION. Under capitalism, the division of labor in production-line manufacture involves the progressive separation of mental from manual labor, and the subordination of labor to the requirements of commodity production. Marx traces the development of the division of labor through successive social epochs, involving the separation of towns from the countryside, the state from civil society, and industry from commerce, culminating in the extreme fragmentation of work in capitalist production. At the same time, the contradictory nature of capitalism is apparent in the capacity for increased wealth, and the need for economic cooperation in the division of labor, which prefigures the eventual transcendence of capitalism by socialism. In the *German Ideology*, Marx envisages the abolition of the division of labor under socialism, along with the abolition of classes and private property. However, in his later works, reference is made to the continuation of a "realm of necessity," in which a form of division of labor will continue to exist, but will be one without alienation or forced specialization.

Marx's critical analysis of the division of labor in the production process has been revived in recent years by interest in the labor process, particularly in the work of Braverman (1974). Labor process theory has focused on development of managerial control through the use of scientific management, mechanization and automation, in which labor is increasingly fragmented and deskilled (see DESKILLING).

divorce and **marital separation** the legal or socially sanctioned dissolution of marriage, *divorce*, as distinguished from the severing, temporary or permanent, of a marital relationship, *separation*, which may or may not lead to divorce. Sociological studies of divorce have focused mostly on two issues:

first, the variations in the divorce rate both comparatively and within societies, and secondly, the various social adjustments necessary to the process.

Variations in divorce rates may be accounted for by reference to both individual expectations and to the role of marriage within kin groups. Where expectations are predominantly those of the kin, as in arranged marriages, rates of marital breakdown are likely to be low. Where individual expectations are high, as in most Western societies, there is often an accompanying social acceptance of dissolution in order that those expectations can be fulfilled elsewhere.

Social and personal adjustment to divorce has been studied in great detail both by sociologists and those involved in family counseling work. Divorce, or indeed separation, can have many dimensions, including emotional uncoupling, the negotiation of child-custody and child-care issues, the settling of property and maintenance issues, the realignment of social and community relationships, and the resultant personal adjustments.

domestic labor 1. the numerous, often repetitious tasks, including housework and child care, that serve to maintain the household. In most modern societies, domestic labor is unwaged, privatized, and gendered. Women are primarily responsible for carrying out this servicing role and for ensuring that the physical and emotional needs of the family are met. **2.** (Marxism) the particular forms of work within the household or domestic setting that produce use values rather than exchange values. To conceive of the household or the FAMILY as a mode of production, and to study its characteristics as a socioeconomic entity, involves a revision of the conventional way of viewing the home, which is to see it as an expressive institution, separated from the economics of the marketplace, in which men and women play out their expressive roles. The concept of domestic labor highlights the interconnections between the world of the home (the private domain) and the world of the factory and the office (the public sector) (see also PRIVATE AND PUBLIC SPHERES).

In either sense, domestic labor services the economy in ways hidden by the ideology of the family and private life—it is the sphere of CULTURAL REPRODUCTION and SOCIAL REPRODUCTION in which people are raised and cared for as members of the family and enter into the economy as workers. In the domestic economy, women mainly service men through private personal services that are not classified or remunerated as real work. Despite its importance in the national economy, domestic labor is not usually included in the gross national product, and this is one reason why "Wages for Housework" was a demand made by some postwar women's groups in Britain, who saw domestic labor as an essential aspect of women's oppression. Before the publication of A. Oakley's *The Sociology of Housework* (1974), the SOCIOLOGY OF WORK and the sociology of organizations had ignored this area of life.

A further aspect of domestic labor within the SEXUAL DIVISION OF LABOR is that women experience a double burden of work, since they participate in both wage labor and unwaged domestic labor. Their primary responsibility in the domestic sphere is a key factor exacerbating their exploitation and subordination in the public sector. This primacy was always apparent in history, but since the 19th century in Europe has been accentuated by the *separation of home from work* and the construction of the notion of *housewife:* a married woman whose primary role is to engage in domestic work, with paid work outside the home being secondary. Especially among the English Victorian upper and middle classes, this role became an ideal to which other classes aspired, but could not often achieve because of the economic necessity of having more than one wage or salary coming in to the household. When households were the focus of earned income or of self-provision, women often had important economic roles other than the domestic. Davidoff and Hall (1987), for example, show how male entrepreneurs in Birmingham in the early 19th century depended heavily on the unpaid labor of their wives to establish their businesses. Only later, with expansion of the businesses, development of new premises, and establishment of homes in the new suburbs, did wives cease participating and devote themselves to becoming housewives.

Since the 1970s, attempts to develop a political analysis of housework and child care in capitalist societies have focused on the *domestic labor debate*. This debate arose primarily from the work of S. James (1974) and M. Dalla Costa (1972), who used Italian social capital theory. In doing so they stressed the importance of analying not only the position of the waged worker, but also that of the wageless. Both James and Dalla Costa argued that the wageless should demand wages and that housewives in particular should demand wages for housework. In doing so, the contradictions inherent in advanced capitalism would be intensified. James and Dalla Costa argued that the distinction between PRODUCTIVE AND UNPRODUCTIVE LABOR was politically redundant, and that housework produced surplus value. Their work gave rise to two main Marxist responses, one of which sought to explore the implications of the demand for wages for housework campaign, while the other focused on the surplus value question. The domestic labor debate is concerned with the extent to which Marxist categories can be used to explain the division of labor in the home, and whether the privatization of domestic labor is a necessary feature of capitalism. The debate has played a crucial role in highlighting the dual nature of women's work, and in demonstrating its usefulness to capitalism. A central theme of this debate has been the nature of the relationship of nonwaged members of the working class to waged workers and to the so-called family wage. It fails, however, to explain why it is women, and not men, who have the responsibility for domestic labor. Miles (1986) argues that the debate fails to address a number of important issues. It does not deal with the question of gender domination nor does it explore the ways in which the interests of women and men of the same class may be divergent. By concentrating on what are assumed to be the common interests of working-class women and men, the debate avoids consideration of the part played by male violence in the subordination of women in the home. The debate fails to explore the lack of women's leisure time relative to men's, the position of children, and the role played by men's control over women's sexuality and reproductive power. The domestic labor debate has also failed to address the contribution made by radical feminists in analyzing the relationship between gender and class. Finally, attempts by feminists to examine the virtually universal oppression of women have been characterized as an ahistorical attempt to replace a class analysis of social relations by a gender analysis. It is, however, important to recognize that social class, gender, and race are interactive features within advanced capitalism and indeed within most societies.

dominance (Marxism) the dominant element within a social formation—be this ideology, politics, or the economy—as determined by the particular requirements of the economic base at a point in time (ALTHUSSER, 1966). Althusser wished to draw attention to the internal complexity of social formations, even though these are determined by the economy in the final instance. He contrasted this view with the Hegelian conception of social totality.

dominant ideology thesis (Marxism) the thesis that working-class subordination in capitalist societies is largely the outcome of the cultural dominance achieved by the capitalist ruling class. A strong criticism of the thesis has been mounted by Abercrombie et al. *The Dominant Ideology Thesis* (1980), who argue that proponents of the thesis tend to overestimate the importance of cultural integration in modern societies, and to underestimate the extent to which subordinate groups are capable of generating beliefs and values that run counter to dominant ideologies. In this, the dominant ideology thesis can be seen as a reflection of structural-functionalist theories, which are widely regarded as overemphasizing the importance of shared values. See also RULING CLASS OR DOMINANT CLASS, HEGEMONY, GRAMSCI, IDEOLOGY, REPRESSIVE STATE APPARATUS, INCORPORATION, CONSENSUS, SOCIAL INTEGRATION AND SYSTEM INTEGRATION.

domination 1. in a general sense, the POWER exerted by one person or group over another person or group. **2.** in the more specific sense, used particularly by WEBER (1922) (a translation of the German word *Herrschaft*), the "likelihood that a command within a given organization or society will be obeyed," which is distinguished from power (*Macht*), the capacity of a social actor to impose his or her will on others despite resistance from them (see also LEGITIMATE AUTHORITY).

Weber also distinguishes between domination "by virtue of authority" and economic forms of domination, in which the SOCIAL ACTOR, although formally free and motivated to pursue his or her own goals, is in fact highly constrained to act in one way.

double descent or *bilineal descent* a system of DESCENT in which there are patriclans and matriclans within the same group. They may each be used for different reasons, for example, inheritance of land may be through the male and inheritance of names through the female. A consequence of this is that an individual is a member of both a patrilineal and a matrilineal descent group.

double hermeneutic (GIDDENS, 1984) the assumption that understanding in sociology and social science involves an understanding of social ACTION at two levels:

(a) the understanding of the "meaningful social world as constituted by lay actors";

(b) the "metalanguages invented by sociologists and social scientists to understand and explain social action." See also HERMENEUTICS, ETHNOMETHODOLOGY, VERSTEHEN.

Douglas, Mary (1921–) British social and cultural anthropologist who has made a particular study of RITUAL, symbolism, and TABOO (for example, *Purity and Danger,* 1966; *Natural Symbols,* 1970), much of this study having a special relevance to women's studies. She presents ritual prohibitions, including restrictions on women's activities, as occurring where social phenomena are held to threaten existing classificatory systems.

downward mobility see SOCIAL MOBILITY.

dramaturgy an approach to social analysis, especially associated with Erving GOFFMAN, in which the theater is the basis of an analogy with everyday life. In this analogy, social action is viewed as a performance in which actors both play parts and stage-manage their actions, seeking to control the impressions they convey to others (*impression management*). The aim of actors is to present themselves in a generally favorable light and in ways appropriate to particular roles and social "settings," Goffman's term for the physical trappings that signal particular roles or status. In a related way, SOCIAL ACTORS also cooperate as members of teams seeking to preserve a front while hiding from view the "backstage" of social relations. Since actors will play different roles in different situations, they also on occasion find it necessary to practice *audience segregation,* withholding in a current situation any sign of those other roles they play which, if visible, would threaten the impression being given at the moment, for example, the problems that would arise for a homosexual judge from disclosure of his homosexuality. The model of interaction involved in dramaturgy turns on the inevitability of acting partly on inference. For Goffman, the social order is a precarious accomplishment, always liable to be disrupted by embarrassment and breaches of front.

drug taking for pleasure drug taking, where the aim is merely to gain or enhance gratification. Rather than ascribing some set of deviant impulses or motives that lead to drug abuse, some sociologists (for example, BECKER, "Becoming a Marijuana User," 1953) have been interested in exploring the social mechanisms that lead to drug taking for pleasure. Becker argues that the motivational chain involved in such cases is the reverse of that usually suggested by psychologists: the motivations involved arise, like any other taste, as a socially acquired taste, in which the SOCIAL ACTOR is first introduced to the drug and then learns to enjoy it as a pleasurable sensation. As such, drug takers do not differ psychologically from other social actors; their drug taking can be explained primarily in sociological terms. See also LABELING THEORY.

dualism any doctrine in which the fundamental forms of things, substances, reality, etc. are seen as of two contrasting types, without any possibility of one being reduced to the other, for example:

(a) (philosophy) a distinction between material things and mental ideas;

(b) (SOCIOLOGY) distinctions between nature and nurture (see NATURE-NURTURE DEBATE), or between individual agency and the structural determination of social outcomes.

In philosophy, the alternative to dualism is *monism*, which asserts that things, substances, etc. are all of one basic kind, either material in form or mental. A further position, REALISM, argues that there is only one reality, even if this reality is stratified, that is, contains fundamental differences of type, even if stopping short of dualism.

In current philosophy and sociology, rather than an outright dualism, a frequent position is to recognize the utility of thinking in terms of a *duality* of forms—mind and matter, or structure and agency—in which there exists a dialectical interaction between the two kinds of things, but with no justification for sustaining a claim that there exist any ultimately irreducible kinds, for example, see DUALITY OF STRUCTURE. See also STRUCTURE AND AGENCY.

duality of structure (as formulated by Giddens, 1984) a conception of SOCIAL STRUCTURE as both "the medium and the outcome" of social ACTION. See STRUCTURATION THEORY.

dual labor market the assumption that LABOR MARKETS are systematically divided into two sectors: the *primary* and the *secondary*. The *primary* sector comprises relatively high wage jobs with career prospects, while the jobs within the *secondary* sector lack these characteristics. The rationale for the division was that employers wished to offset the high cost of maintaining a stable, skilled core of workers by employing nonskilled workers to carry out the less central work activities on less favorable terms of employment and for less pay. Alternatively, companies may subcontract the work to small firms operating in a *secondary* labor market in the external environment. Typically, white adult males have enjoyed better access to *primary* sector jobs, while women and members of ethnic minorities have been overrepresented within the *secondary* sector.

Duhem-Quine thesis the view associated with the French philosopher of science Pierre Duhem (1861–1916), and the American logician Willard Quine (1908–) that science consists of a complex network of assumptions, concepts, hypotheses, and theories that are appraised as a whole, with no possibility of individual propositions being appraised in isolation from our entire system of beliefs. See also ANALYTIC AND SYNTHETIC.

Durkheim, Emile (1858–1917), along with MARX and WEBER, one of the triumvirate of major sociologists who did most to establish the shape of the modern subject. Of these three figures, Durkheim above all was quintessentially the sociologist, with his assertions that "society *sui generis*" is the subject matter of sociology, and that "social facts must always be explained by other social facts." In a series of seminal works, Durkheim established many themes and contributed many concepts that continue to be important in modern sociology.

Working within the tradition of POSITIVISM established by SAINT-SIMON and COMTE, but not wishing to refer to his own work as positivism, Durkheim's best-known dictum is "Treat social facts as things." By this he meant that social phenomena exist as an objective realm, are external to individuals, operate by their constraining or coercive influence on individuals, and are general and collective. See also SOCIAL FACTS AS THINGS.

His first major work, *The Division of Labor in Society* (1893), rests on the important distinction he drew between MECHANICAL AND ORGANIC SOLIDARITY. His argument was that while in small-scale societies, with only a limited DIVISION OF LABOR, people were bound together by similarity and a common COLLECTIVE CONSCIENCE, in more complex societies with an advanced division of labor, this division of labor itself acted as the basis of social integration. Two further vital concepts in Durkheim's sociology, which also make their first appearance in *The Division of Labor,* are his suggestion that in modern societies the division of labor is often marred by ANOMIE (that is, is unregulated by society or social values), and that the division of labor is also often forced, which is to say that, as the result of unfairness and inefficiency in the operation of the educational system and in the processes of occupational selection, many people are made to occupy roles for which they are unsuited (see FORCED DIVISION OF LABOR). Durkheim's objective in *The Division of Labor* and subsequently was to establish, both theoretically and practically the conditions for social solidarity in modern societies that would combine individualism and collectivism. He rejected any suggestion (such as SPENCER's) that society could operate effectively on principles of self-interest, without collective norms. On the other hand, he was equally opposed to a strongly centralized state. He suggested instead that the organization of society into occupationally based, intermediate groupings standing between the state and the individual might prove the best way to organize a modern society based on the division of labor. A network of such groups would perhaps be able to place moral restraints on egoism and to regulate the group conflicts that modern societies inevitably generate.

In *The Rules of Sociological Method* (1895), Durkheim laid out his over-all approach to sociological explanation, including his doctrine of "social facts as things." But this work is perhaps equally important for its contribution to the formulation of modern FUNCTIONALISM. Central to Durkheim's functionalism was a distinction between healthy and pathological forms of social organization. As Durkheim puts it, 'It is the function of the average organism that the physiologist studies; and the sociologist does the same." "It would be incomprehensible', he suggests, 'if the most widespread forms of organization were not the most advantageous." Thus, the healthy, or the functional, social form is usually that present in the average at a given level of social development. For modern industrial societies, where the evolution of this type has not yet run its full course, Durkheim recognized that assessment of functionality was more difficult. Here, therefore, one must also seek to establish with some care that the generality of a phenomenon is actually bound up with the "general conditions of collective life" for this social type. As well as establishing the function of a phenomenon, one must also always independently establish its cause.

In *Suicide* (1897), a work seen as a "methodological classic" by some and as greatly flawed by others, Durkheim employed what would now be called the SECONDARY ANALYSIS of existing OFFICIAL STATISTICS, seeking to demonstrate how SUICIDE is a social, and thus a sociological, phenomenon rather than a purely individual one. After first eliminating existing nonsociological explanations—including climatic factors and normal and abnormal psychological factors, such as racial characteristics or insanity—three main types of suicide were identified by Durkheim as corresponding in each case to distinct types of social situations. Thus, *altruistic suicide,* he suggested, was caused by strong mechanical solidarity (for example, the suicide of the old and infirm in simple societies, or suicides of honor in the army); *egoistic suicide,* he suggested, was caused by excessive individuation in modern societies (for example, the higher incidence of suicide among Protestants compared with Jews or Catholics, and among the divorced compared with the married); and *anomic suicide* was said to result when disruptions of normal social expectations occurred (for example, a sudden change in economic circumstances, and as a general tendency in modern societies in their unregulated forms). A fourth type of suicide—*fatalistic suicide*—also occurs where social regulation leaves no scope for autonomous action apart from death, for example, the suicide of the slave. For those who admire it, *Suicide* is both a sophisticated work and a precursor of later forms of MULTIVARIATE ANALYSIS. To its critics, however, it is a work in which Durkheim uses statistics in a manner that imposes MEASUREMENT BY FIAT, with little guarantee that actors' beliefs and values are as he assumed them to be.

In *Elementary Forms of Religious Life* (1912), Durkheim returned to an examination of the nature of the "collective conscience" within simpler societies. This study of religious beliefs and practices in what he took to be their most elementary form, especially Australian aboriginal society, became the basis of much of the modern sociological study of religion (see RELIGION, FUNCTIONALIST THEORY OF RELIGION, SACRED AND PROFANE). The decisive idea in Durkheim's account of religion is that religion functions as a symbolic representation of society in which the beliefs and practices relative to the sacred continually reaffirm communal values. In view of this, one of the tasks of Durkheim's sociology was to discover what have since been called FUNCTIONAL ALTERNATIVES OR FUNCTIONAL EQUIVALENTS to religion in increasingly secular modern societies (see also CIVIL RELIGION).

In addition to these four main works, Durkheim published much else, including numerous essays. Among the most important of these (written with Marcel Mauss) is *Primitive Classification* (1903), in which the basic categories of human thought, including time and space, and number, are seen as reflecting patterns of social organization. For example, classification is seen as reflecting the division of human societies into clans (see also SOCIOLOGY OF KNOWLEDGE). Also of importance are Durkheim's essays on TOTEMISM and on KINSHIP. Along with the ideas contained in *Elementary Forms*, these essays exerted a strong influence on the formation of modern STRUCTURALISM (see also MYTHOLOGIES).

As well as the works published in Durkheim's lifetime, many of his lectures, together with fragments of books left unfinished, were published after his death, including *Moral Education* (1925), *Socialism and Saint-Simon* (1928), and *Professional Ethic and Civic Morals* (1950). As one of the founding fathers of modern sociology, Durkheim was also associated with the journal that attracted around it many celebrated sociologists, anthropologists and historians, among them, Marcel Maus, Maurice Halbwachs and Levy-Bruhl.

On socialism, Durkheim's position was sympathetic but non-Marxist. As pointed out by Gouldner (in the introduction to the English version of *Socialism and Saint-Simon*, 1959), contrary to suggestions that Durkheim was, above all, a conservative, an emphasis on social conflict and social change is an enduring element in his sociology, deriving from Saint-Simon. The possible role Durkheim saw for occupational intermediate groupings in modern societies places him closest to guild socialism. A moral conservative Durkheim may sometimes have been, but he was not a political conservative. Nor was normative integration Durkheim's exclusive focus; relationships of reciprocal interdependence as well as normative integration are recognized as the basis of social order.

Debate surrounds Durkheim's work in general, as to how far it does or does not succeed in satisfactorily combining an emphasis on social structure with individual agency in sociological explanation (see also STRUCTURE

AND AGENCY). For the most part, Durkheim's sociology has been seen as overstating general normative and social structural influences at the expense of individual agency, although it was always Durkheim's intention to leave scope for the latter within his sociology. Durkheim's two main goals were to establish sociology as an autonomous scientific discipline, and to establish the practical requirements for social order in modern societies. In neither of these can Durkheim be regarded as having the last word. What is undeniable is that his influence on modern sociology has been immense, with many modern statements about the subject still being presented as positions either for or against Durkheim.

Two important biographical and critical studies on Durkheim's life and work are by Lukes (1973) and PARSONS (1937).

dyad and **triad** social interactions or relationships comprising two (*dyad*) or three elements (*triad*). As an aspect of his FORMAL SOCIOLOGY, SIMMEL suggested that certain properties of dyads and triads obtain whether the parties to the interaction or relationship are persons, organizations, or nation states, for example, mediation or divide-and-rule is possible within the triad but not the dyad; the peculiar closeness of the two compared with the three. The analysis of dyads and triads provides a particularly clear example of the character of FORMAL SOCIOLOGY, with its emphasis on recurring forms of social interaction.

dysfunction or **disfunction** any social activity seen as making a negative contribution to the maintenance or effective working of a functioning SOCIAL SYSTEM. See FUNCTIONALISM.

E

eclecticism any approach to analysis or research that mixes theoretically disparate perspectives.

ecological fallacy or **wrong level fallacy** the error of inferring that relationships established between two or more variables measured at an AGGREGATE level will also hold at the individual level. Care must be taken to avoid this error in research studies that use areas as the unit of analysis. For example, if an area is found to have a high percentage of unemployment and a high percentage of mental illness, any inference of a causal relationship at the individual level would be invalid. The problem is discussed in Robinson (1951) and Riley (1963).

ecology the study of the interactive relationship between living things and their ENVIRONMENT. The term became popularized in the 1980s due to a growing concern with the fragility of the earth as a living system. A variety of indicators are acknowledged to be warnings that natural systems evolved over millennia are being threatened by the technological developments initiated by the industrial revolution and the resultant population explosion. Such indices include the extinction of many species of plants and animals, the depletion of the ozone layer, global warming and changes in weather patterns, and pollution of large areas of land and water upsetting the natural balance of many smaller systems. See also GREEN MOVEMENT, HOMEOSTASIS, COST-BENEFIT ANALYSIS, ENVIRONMENTAL DEPLETION.

economic and social development any change that results in increased economic productivity and prosperity, and new and more complex forms of SOCIAL STRUCTURE and organization. The study of such development was a central concern of classical sociological theory (see EVOLUTIONARY THEORY, SOCIAL CHANGE). In contemporary work, "economic and social development" is usually used to refer to the specific *process* of industrialization in both its socialist and capitalist forms. Although Barrington Moore's (1967) comparative and historical study continues to be influential, and new studies of changes in the developed capitalist world have attracted attention (see CONVERGENCE, FORDISM AND POST-FORDISM, POSTINDUSTRIAL SOCIETY), much theoretical work is now devoted to current issues and problems of development in the Third World. One, but not the only, characteristic of countries defined as Third World is obviously the level of economic and social development statistically defined in terms of indices such as per-capita income, proportion of population employed as wage labor, etc. See also DEPENDENCY THEORY, NEO-EVOLUTIONISM, MODERNIZATION.

economic sociology the sociological study of the relations between the ECONOMY and other social institutions. Rather than being a specialized area of study within the discipline, the sociological analysis of economic life has been a central concern within many forms of general sociology. It is a central concern, for example, in the work of major classical sociologists such as MARX, WEBER, and DURKHEIM. More specialized areas of sociological inquiry in which economic questions are uppermost include ORGANIZATION THEORY, INDUSTRIAL SOCIOLOGY, SOCIOLOGY OF WORK.

economism (Marxism) any theory or approach that emphasizes the economic determinants of social forms while failing to give adequate consideration to the relative autonomy often possessed by IDEOLOGIES, the STATE, etc., and by human AGENCY.

economy 1. the organized management of human material resources, goods, and services. **2.** the social institutions concerned with the management, production, and distribution of human resources.

It has been suggested that all major sociologies imply an economic form. Both historians and sociologists have distinguished between different forms of society according to the tools that men and women use and the economic power they have at their disposal. In sociology, the most influential models of economic forms and their relation with types of society are those deriving from MARX and WEBER. A central issue running through much sociology is the extent of the determinancy of the economy, or institutional and cultural autonomy of other activities from the economy. See also DIVISION OF LABOR, ECONOMIC AND SOCIAL DEVELOPMENT, ECONOMIC SOCIOLOGY.

ego one of the three elements of the personality in FREUD's theory. The ego is the part of the personality that operates in direct contact with reality, attempting to control the demands of the ID according to the strictures of the SUPEREGO and with awareness of the real world. It therefore operates under the reality principle, in contrast with the id, which operates under the pleasure principle. The id demands immediate gratification by direct means, so the ego's role is to assess whether these demands are realistically possible, and if not, to enforce delay of gratification until expression can be had in a socially appropriate form.

egoistic suicide the form of SUICIDE identified by DURKHEIM (1895) as being associated with excessive egoism, or individualism. As suggested by Durkheim, the incidence of egoistic suicide "varies with the degree of integration of society." For example, the reason why Protestants more frequently commit suicide than Catholics, Durkheim suggests, is that the collective beliefs and practices of the latter involve a stronger integration of the individual within the religious community and far less sanction for individualism.

eidos the general features and characteristics of the ideas and, by extension, the main social institutions and activities, of a particular society. (This relatively uncommon term was introduced by Gregory Bateson, 1936, and also used by Charles Madge, 1964).

Eisenstadt, Shlomo (1923–) Israeli comparative sociologist and comparative historian known for his work on immigrant groups and on MODERNIZA-TION. The work that has attracted most attention is his *The Political System of Empires* (1967), a highly systematic attempt to compare historical, non-tribal, preindustrial political systems and to frame generalizations about the factors influencing the effectiveness or otherwise of this general type of political system. The volume contains nearly 100 pages of tabular compar-isons of particular states in which several measurements are employed to rank systems comparatively on a number of dimensions. The general hypothesis advanced is that to be effective, nontribal, preindustrial political systems must be able to mobilize, and also generate, new, free-floating material and cultural resources, prising these from traditional control, and must mobilize the support of at least some leaders of local lineages. Nevertheless, like most political systems, and in contrast with suggestions made about Oriental despotism, such systems always contain contradictory elements and are inherently unstable.

Eisenstadt is known for his wide interest and academic productivity, ranging from the effects of immigration to the stabilizing effect of age strati-fication on society (see AGING). See also PATRIMONIALISM.

elaborated codes and **restricted codes** specific forms of language and speech derived from particular social contexts, involving different orders of meaning. These two concepts were introduced by BERNSTEIN in his early work and relate to his theory of SOCIALIZATION and the significance of lin-guistic interaction to the acquisition of CULTURAL CAPITAL in confirming social identity.

Bernstein suggests that different forms of socialization point children toward two different modes of speech. One of these controls access to uni-versalistic meanings, the other to particularistic meanings. In a situation where children and hence, subsequently, adults, are likely to use elaborat-ed codes, principles and operations are made explicit, so that hearers can easily and quickly understand the speaker's intentions. In a situation where they are likely to use restricted speech codes, principles are more implicit and context bound, involving specific relationships. Bernstein went on to argue that the working class uses a restricted speech code while the middle class uses both codes. Since the formal educational system transmits class-regulated elaborated codes, the working-class child or student is at a disad-vantage.

These ideas have been developed by Bernstein into a much more sophisticated theory of cultural transmission and its relationship with forms of power and social control in the class structures of society. However, the application of the concepts of elaborated and restricted codes to the speech patterns of middle- and working-class groups, respectively, has not been universally accepted, and considerable skepticism has been expressed about their validity and usefulness since they were first introduced (see Labov, 1972).

electoral sociology the sociological study of elections and voting. This area of sociological study has been a shared enterprise between academic sociologists and behaviorally oriented political scientists. See VOTING BEHAVIOR, PSEPHOLOGY.

Elias, Norbert (1897–1990) German-born sociologist who, after leaving Germany in the Hitler era, first worked in England and later in Ghana, Holland, and Germany. He describes his approach to sociological analysis as FIGURATIONAL SOCIOLOGY, in which changing social configurations, rather than societies, are analyzed as the unintended outcome of the interactions of interdependent individuals (see also FIGURATION). His most important work, *The Civilizing Process* (1939), attracted little attention at the time of its publication in German. However, by the time the English edition appeared (2 vols. in 1978 and 1982), an "Elias school" dedicated to promoting "figurational sociology," had become well established in Holland and England (see P. Gleichman et al., 1977). The theme of *The Civilizing Process* is the relation between European state-formation and changes in individual patterns of behavior and personality, including new forms of morality and individual self-control (see also CIVILIZING PROCESS). *The Court Society* (1969) deals with related themes. The theoretical underpinnings of figurational sociology are outlined in *What Is Sociology?* (1970). There are parallels between Elias's focus on figurations, rather than on individuals or societies as separate entities, and those approaches in modern sociology that emphasize the importance of modes of social analysis and acknowledge the interrelation between STRUCTURE AND AGENCY (see STRUCTURATION THEORY). Other works by Elias include *The Loneliness of the Dying* (1982) and *Involvement and Detachment* (1986).

elite literally the best or most talented members of society (for example, educational elite); however, in sociology the term most usually refers to *political elites*. Here, the assumption of ELITE THEORY has been that a division between elites and masses is an inevitable feature of any complex modern society, and that the aspirations of radical democrats that the people as a whole can rule is mistaken.

elite theory the hypothesis that political elites are inevitable in complex modern societies. In its original form this theory was a sociological response to the relative failure of modern democratic movements, judged by their own highest objectives. Rather than power to the people, the advent of modern democracy brought new bases of elite membership. Associated particularly with the pessimistic view of modern democracy taken by PARETO and, to a lesser extent by MOSCA, elites were seen as an inevitable consequence of psychological differences between elites and MASSES and the organizational requirements of modern societies. See also IRON LAW OF OLIGARCHY, MICHELS. Compare RULING CLASS.

In its more recent form (see DEMOCRATIC ELITISM) elite theory has modified its pessimism about modern democracy. Building on arguments already implicit in the work of theorists such as Mosca and Michels that different bases of elite power have important social consequences, what some theorists (for example, Dahl, 1961) now propose is that a democratic competition between rival representative elites constitutes the best practicable form of modern government. Compare POWER ELITE; see also STABLE DEMOCRACY.

The study of elites and the testing of elite theories has been a notably controversial area. While some researchers (for example, Hunter, 1963) have pursued a reputational approach asking respondents "who holds power," others, including Dahl, have argued only the careful study of actual decisions—the outcomes of the operation of power—can satisfactorily establish who in fact is powerful. Even this, however, is not decisive, for as Bachrach and Baratz (1962) have argued, the study of overt decisions fails to explore the existence of nondecisions (see COMMUNITY POWER), the many circumstances in which the balance of power may be such as to preclude political debate or political contest so that no overt point of decision is actually observable. See also POWER, MASS SOCIETY.

emancipatory theory see HABERMAS.

embourgeoisement or **bourgeoisification** the process of become bourgeois or, more generally, MIDDLE CLASS.

embourgeoisement thesis the argument that the working class in modern capitalism has adopted the life style and political attitudes of the MIDDLE CLASSES. In the case of Britain, for example, this thesis gained currency in the 1950s and 1960s in a number of different spheres. Social commentators, political analysts, and politicians contrasted the condition of the WORKING CLASS before the 1930s in terms of income, housing, employment, health and leisure interests, with its improved situation after 1950. They argued or assumed that the establishment of the WELFARE STATE, relatively full employment, real improvements in living standards, and the mass production of consumer goods had removed material and cultural differences between the classes. They also attributed the success of the Conservative Party throughout the 1950s to these changes, arguing that material and social changes had had a major impact on working-class political consciousness, leading again to an identification with the middle classes (for example, see Rose, 1960). These factors, welfare state, political conservativism, etc., led a number of sociologists to speculate about the END OF IDEOLOGY as a factor in voting and social behavior.

A most interesting effect of the embourgeoisement thesis was its influence on the major political parties and in mass media coverage of politics during the period. Within sociology, some work (for example, in studies of family relations) was thematically consistent with the embourgeoisement argument, but the most influential and most direct response to the thesis, the AFFLUENT WORKER studies, refuted it in terms of workers' attitudes, while earlier work on the extent and distribution of poverty had shown that there were still great numbers of people who did not enjoy a middle-class standard of living. See also CLASS, CLASS CONSCIOUSNESS, CLASS IMAGERY, UNDERCLASS.

emergent properties any properties of a social system or group of which it can be asserted that they cannot be explained simply in terms of their origins or constituent parts, hence the notion that "the whole is greater than the parts." The term is especially identified with functionalist sociologies, such as Durkheim's, which emphasize the AUTONOMY OF SOCIOLOGY from other disciplines (that is, that sociological accounts should not be subject to REDUCTIONISM). The notion of emergent properties has often been criticized. For example, it has been seen as leading to a reified account (see REIFICATION) of social reality, and to a loss of visibility and recognition of the influence of the individual actor. However, the conception of emergent properties need not be associated with the notion that there are *no* links with, or no influence of, underlying levels of reality, but merely that there may be aspects of social reality that cannot be satisfactorily explained reductively. In the physical sciences too, emergent properties play an indispensable role, for example, weather systems in meteorology, where the complexity of reality and the unpredictability of the underlying variables defy a fully reductive account. In an important sense, the existence of separate disciplines in science is testimony to the existence of emergent properties; at the very least emergent properties prove analytically indispensable. The importance of these need not mean the existence of any absolute barriers to attempts at reductionistic analysis, but that these attempts are unlikely ever to be *entirely* successful, and even if successful, will not overturn the utility of emergent properties. Compare HOLISM, METHODOLOGICAL INDIVIDUALISM.

emic and **etic** a distinction originating from linguistics (Pike, 1967), but now widely used in sociology and anthropology, between accounts made from a perspective indigenous or internal to a language or social situation (an *emic* account), and those made from a perspective external to the language or social context, including sociological observers' accounts (*etic* accounts). See also MEANINGFUL UNDERSTANDING, HERMENEUTICS, FORMS OF LIFE.

The original distinction stems from the linguistic terms *phonemic* and *phonetic*. Whereas a phonemic account rests on the speaker's own recognition of patterns of sound, phonetic accounts are based on the observer's model and measurement of these differences.

Emmanuel, Arghiri (1911–) Greek-born, French-based, Marxist economist of development who has sought to integrate aspects of the theory of international trade with Marx's general theory of value.

empathic understanding a form of understanding and explanation achieved by imagining oneself in the role of the social actors whose actions one seeks to understand or explain. Since this form of explanation would appear to rest on a suspect introspective psychology, the method is often dismissed as unscientific (Abel, 1977). Sometimes it is wrongly assumed, as by Abel, that all forms of MEANINGFUL UNDERSTANDING AND EXPLANATION are equally suspect, depending merely on introspection. However, the most widely used forms of interpretive explanation in sociology, for example, in WEBER's work, only impute meanings to actors where the likelihood of such meanings can be confirmed by prevailing social norms and values (see VERSTEHEN). See also EMPATHY.

empathy the feeling of being able to vicariously experience what another person is experiencing. The ability to empathize is crucial in many interpersonal relationships and social settings. If family members do not experience empathy with each other, discord is more likely than if a climate of empathic understanding exists. Close friends, by definition, have an empathic relationship.

Empathy is one of ROGERS' (1951) three conditions for a successful client-counselor relationship, the other two being genuine warmth and unconditional positive regard. Empathy is central to PERSON-CENTERED COUNSELING, since this perspective holds the view that the client's problems can only be understood by the counselor through experiencing the client's phenomenological field. For this, empathy is required.

Empathy is also sometimes seen as the central, although suspect, determinant of techniques of MEANINGFUL UNDERSTANDING AND EXPLANATION widely used in sociology. However, the view that empathy is decisive is challenged (see VERSTEHEN).

empirical sociology any form of sociology that places emphasis on the collection of data. However, the term more specifically refers to forms of sociology using SOCIAL SURVEYS or carefully documented PARTICIPANT OBSERVATION.

Sociology of this latter type has represented a major strand within the discipline as a whole, especially within US sociology (for example, empirical studies of SOCIAL STRATIFICATION, CLASS, VOTING BEHAVIOR). This general approach to sociology has sometimes been criticized as failing to explore important questions of theory (see ABSTRACTED EMPIRICISM) or, in the case of questionnaire-based and statistical research, as involving MEASUREMENT BY FIAT (see ETHNOMETHODOLOGY, OFFICIAL STATISTICS). However, these charges can be countered as far too sweeping, by pointing to the existence of much empirical sociology in which significant theoretical hypotheses are explored (see EMPIRICISM, LAZARSFELD, THEORIES OF THE MIDDLE RANGE).

empiricism 1. (pejorative) the use of empirical methods at the expense of a more adequate theoretical approach (see also ABSTRACTED EMPIRICISM). **2.** the doctrine that all knowledge derives from experience as against a priori categories (the epistemological position of Hume, Locke, the Logical Positivists, etc.). Compare IDEALISM, EPISTEMOLOGY, POSITIVISM. **3.** (especially in Marxism and the recent philosophy of science) the failure to recognize the theory-laden and the socially constructed and reconstructible character of concepts, and thus of facts.

The problems of empiricism in philosophy and the scientific method have long been recognized as the problem of induction: the provisional status of any universal generalization based only on a finite sequence of empirical observations (see INDUCTION AND INDUCTIVE LOGIC).

A further aspect of philosophical empiricism, given the lack of any clear solution to the problem of induction, is that it can lead to skepticism or RELATIVISM, for example, when formulated as a doctrine that we can only have a knowledge of our own sensations, with no necessary relation to a reality beyond this. In this form, empiricism becomes conjoined with IDEALISM, and both can end in skepticism or relativism.

Faced with such difficulties, many philosophers and sociologists have emphasized the importance of concepts, hypotheses, and theories in science and sociology and have asserted a realist, rather than an empiricist, methodology (see REALISM). However, there are problems in the outright assertion of any overall philosophical or methodological position (see METHODOLOGY).

While the importance of empirical methods and empirical knowledge finds wide acceptance within sociology, this does not imply empiricism in the senses specified. See also EMPIRICAL SOCIOLOGY.

employment any activity that one is engaged in for wages or salary. In sociology, there has always been a healthy skepticism about the simple equating of paid employment with work, yet in the wider society the prevailing meaning of the word is just that—so, "an active woman, running a house and bringing up children, is distinguished from a woman who works: that is to say, takes paid employment" (R. Williams, 1976). Sociologists have long been aware that WAGE LABOR, to give its technical name, is only a particular form of work, gaining its centrality and definition from the specific set of productive relations that occurs within capitalist, market-exchange economies. Work, in such societies, is identified with employment, which involves "the sale and purchase of labor power as a commodity in a market, resulting in the direction of activity during 'working hours' by persons who have acquired the right to do so by virtue of the labor contract" (Purcell, 1986). See also PRODUCTIVE AND UNPRODUCTIVE LABOR, SOCIOLOGY OF WORK, PRIVATE AND PUBLIC SPHERES, DOMESTIC LABOR.

encounter any meeting between two or more people in a face-to-face interaction. Everyday life is made up of a series of such interactions, some of them with persons we know well, but many others with people with whom we may have only a fleeting contact. Described by GOFFMAN (1961b, 1967, 1971) as situations of copresence, encounters involve SOCIAL ACTORS in positionings of the body and knowledgeable attention to FACE WORK, creating and preserving the numerous, distinctive kinds of encounter that can be observed. See also INTERACTION, INTERACTION ORDER AND INTERACTION RITUAL.

encounter group see GROUP THERAPY.

enculturation (CULTURAL ANTHROPOLOGY) the informal and formal acquisition of cultural norms and practices. As such, the term is almost synonymous with SOCIALIZATION. Its use reflects the centrality of the concept of CULTURE within cultural anthropology. See also ACCULTURATION.

end-of-ideology thesis the viewpoint, especially prevalent in American political sociology in the late 1950s and early 1960s, that old-style, confrontational left-right ideologies were outmoded and were being replaced in Western democracies by a more consensual, competitive politics. The thesis, propounded for example by Daniel BELL (1960) and Seymour Martin LIPSET (1959), was based on the assumption that fundamental changes had occurred in the character of capitalism, for example, the MANAGERIAL REVOLUTION, and that these changes, accompanied by full working-class participation in liberal democratic politics, had removed any basis for revolutionary political parties. According to Lipset, *political cleavage* between political parties based on labor and those aligned with capital still played a crucial role in Western democracies, but class conflict had been 'omesticated and was no longer a threat to the continuation of the political system or of capitalism (see also STABLE DEMOCRACY). With the upheavals of 1968, and for much of the 1970s and 1980s, the return of a sharp confrontation between labor and capital, new urban and racial unrest, and a renewed polarization of political parties, the end of consensus politics has sometimes seemed a more plausible hypothesis (see LEGITIMATION CRISIS). However, if conflicts remain, the continued absence of an effective socialist alternative to Western capitalist society, especially with the collapse of socialism in Eastern Europe in 1989, has meant that acceptance of social democratic politics is now widespread, even among parties of the left. In this sense, the ideological debate, although not ended, is more restricted than it once was.

endogamy a rule prescribing marriage within a given social group. The group may belong to a lineage, CASTE, CLASS, ethnic affiliation, or other type of social classification. The converse of endogamy is EXOGAMY. Since all marriage systems are both endogamous and exogamous, it is necessary to specify in detail the prescribed and the proscribed groups.

Engels, Friedrich (1820–1895), German socialist. Born into a family engaged in the textile industry in Germany, as a student Engels was influenced by Hegelianism (see HEGEL) and became a socialist. He came to Manchester, England, on family business and, in 1845, published *The Condition of the Working Class in England,* one of the most important contemporary analyses of the emergence of the working class with industrialization, in which he saw the working class as the revolutionary bearer of socialism. He began a long association with MARX in 1845 and, in collaboration with him, published *The Holy Family* in that year, *The German Ideology* in 1845–1846, and *The Communist Manifesto* in 1848. These texts formed the basis of the development of Marx and Engels' political work in the formation of the First International, in which Engels played a key organizational role. In the next two decades, Engels provided financial support for Marx and his family while Marx worked on his major political economy of capitalism, and Engels was important both as a confidant of Marx and as a disseminator of his analyses. He further elaborated the concept of dialectical materialism, and first used the phrase "materialist interpretation of history." He is often seen as promoting a deterministic reading of Marx. After Marx's death, Engels edited to publication the second and third volumes of *Das Kapital,* and was working on the fourth when he died. He was active in setting up the Second International.

In recent years, within sociology and anthropology, his most influential work has been *The Origin of The Family, Private Property and the State,* first published in 1884 (see MATRIARCHY). This is one of the few 19th-century analyses of history to incorporate the position of women and to attempt to understand the basis of gender inequality. It has informed many recent attempts to understand the role of women in history and the bases of their subordination to men in so many known societies. This is despite the empirical weakness of his argument that there was an historical process from matriarchal societies, with women dominant within the family, to partriarchal societies, with the emergence of private property and men exerting control over the marriage and sexuality of women to ensure transmission of property to their heirs. Recent work has further questioned his assumption of a biologically based sexual division of labor. The value of his work lies, however, in the questions he posed about the relationship between socioeconomic and gender relationships (see Sayers et al., eds., 1987).

enterprise culture a set of values, symbols, and practices that include a commitment to profit making, enterprise, innovation, initiative, self-reliance, creativity, and competition. Popular criticism of sociology often refers to its critical stance toward enterprise, profit, and individualism. Sociological research on enterprise culture can be found in studies of ORGANIZATIONAL CULTURE and of the WELFARE STATE and SOCIAL POLICY.

entitlements the rights to social welfare payments and provision that exist in most modern societies for all citizens, but are also the subject of dispute. For example, L. Mead (*Beyond Entitlements,* 1985) has argued that one-sided talk of entitlements has led to the neglect of obligations. All Western capitalist states have experienced problems in sustaining both welfare provision and capital accumulation (see LEGITIMATION CRISIS). On the other hand, there are many who argue that recognition of the rights of all citizens and workers to basic entitlements at a high minimum level (that is, a new SOCIAL CONTRACT) is essential if the modern conception of citizenship and CITIZEN RIGHTS is to be maintained and extended. See also UNDERCLASS.

environment the surroundings or context within which humans, animals, or objects exist or act. The term's meaning is therefore wide and is understood more precisely only within the context in which it is itself used.

Specifically, "environment" is taken to mean, in association with "learning" and "experience," the sum of outside influences on the organism, and is to be distinguished from the inherited potential that is also influential in development and behavior (see NATURE-NURTURE DEBATE).

A quite distinct usage is in relation to the natural world system, which is currently seen as fragile and threatened by the human technology developed since the industrial revolution, and the escalation of population that has resulted from it. This is a prime concern of the GREEN MOVEMENT and ECOLOGY generally.

These two usages by no means cover the many and various ways in which "environment" can be used, but serve to illustrate the diversity of possible uses. See also SYSTEMS THEORY.

environmental depletion the process in which the stocks of available physical and economic resources tend to run down or become degraded as the result of processes such as the *intensification of agriculture,* mining, industrial pollution, physical overcrowding, etc. The idea that the world has reached a situation in which it must pay careful attention to the relative, or even absolute, degradation of the physical and social environment has only recently gained prominence (see GREEN MOVEMENT, POSITIONAL GOODS AND POSITIONALITY). However, some theorists, for example, Marvin Harris (1978), have even suggested that the process has been visible in human societies over a far longer period. According to Harris, Stone-Age peoples may have lived far happier and healthier lives than many of those who have come after them. From his viewpoint of CULTURAL MATERIALISM, Harris also suggests that many of the cultural, political, and socioeconomic transformations undergone by societies in the modern historical era can be explained as the outcome of environmental pressures. These outcomes include the subordination of women, the need for settled agriculture and for state direction, and prohibitions on meat eating in some cultures. However, such claims are obviously far more controversial than the general claim that environmental depletion is not a recent problem and has major implications.

epiphenomena and phenomena see APPEARANCE AND REALITY.

episode any "historically located sequence of change," for example, the origins of PRISTINE STATES, with "a specific opening, trend of events and outcome," but not a part of any necessary sequence of social development (GIDDENS 1981). See also EPISODIC CHARACTERIZATION.

episodic characterization a theoretical orientation towards the study of social change in which change is represented as discontinuous and historically contingent, rather than corresponding to an evolutionary or developmental pattern (see also EPISODE). This approach has been central in the work of a number of prominent historical sociologists, including Michael MANN (1986), Ernest GELLNER, (1964) and Anthony GIDDENS. As expressed by Mann, the thinking behind this view is that while general evolutionary theory may be applied up to, and including, the Neolithic Revolution, "general social evolution ceased (with) the emergence of civilization," when distinctively historical change not subject to laws takes over. In Gellner's phrase, historical change does not fit any simple "world growth story."

Those sociologists who emphasize episodic characterizations usually stand opposed to such doctrines as historical materialism, as well as to EVOLUTIONARY THEORIES, in sociology. However, supporters of these latter positions claim that the materialistic interpretation of history as systematic development, or the statement of evolutionary sequences of change, is not incompatible with a recognition that historical change has relatively accidental, as well as general, features (see Jary, 1991).

episteme any structure of knowledge or, in terms used by FOUCAULT, *discourse formation,* that determines the way in which the world is experienced or seen. As such, there are similarities between the notion of episteme and the concepts of PARADIGM or PROBLEMATIQUE (see also EPISTEMOLOGICAL BREAK).

For Foucault, there are not discrete authors, or subjects, of books or knowledge. Rather, these are the products of anonymous discourses that encompass authors or individual subjects. Nor, for Foucault, is there any possibility of speaking of growth or progress in knowledge, or of truth. Similar questions about objectivity and relativism are raised in connection with Foucault's concept of episteme as are raised about the ideas of KUHN and FEYERABEND, when they refer to the INCOMMENSURABILITY of paradigms.

epistemological break (in science) the revolutionary replacement of one theoretical framework—PARADIGM or PROBLEMATIQUE—by another. In the view of Thomas KUHN or Louis ALTHUSSER, the relations between rival or successive paradigms are always liable to be that of disjuncture and INCOMMENSURABILITY, in which the central concepts and procedures of one paradigm or problematique are unstatable in the language of the other. In Paul FEYERABEND's formulation, different paradigms involve different "worlds" (see also FORMS OF LIFE). In the work of Althusser, the concept of the epistemological break is central to the sharp distinction he draws between the early humanistic writings and the later scientific writings of Marx.

epistemology (from the Greek *episteme,* meaning knowledge) the branch of philosophy concerned with the theory or theories of knowledge, which seek to inform us how we can know the world. Epistemology shares with ONTOLOGY, which is concerned with establishing the kinds of things that exist, the claim to be the bedrock of all philosophical thinking and all knowledge.

An important division in epistemology is that between EMPIRICISM and RATIONALISM or IDEALISM. While empiricists make our direct experience of the world the basis of all knowledge, rationalists and idealists argue that our knowledge of the world is governed by fixed and a priori concepts or CATEGORIES (for example, conceptions of substance and causality) that structure our every thought and argument and therefore our experience or perception of reality (see also KANT).

In most forms of epistemology, the pure thought of the individual thinking ego the philosopher has been taken as providing the route to ultimate understanding of knowledge and the bedrock on which is based the epistemological theory advanced. Recently, however, more sociological forms of epistemology have emerged that have sought to decenter the role played by the traditional individual subject in philosophy (see SUBJECT AND OBJECT, DECENTERED SUBJECT, STRUCTURALISM), emphasizing instead the way in which knowledge is shaped by social structure, FORMS OF LIFE, etc. Thus the way is now open for much of the ground previously occupied by philosophy to be taken over by sociological accounts of knowledge and of science (see SOCIOLOGY OF KNOWLEDGE, SOCIOLOGY OF SCIENCE, KUHN, FEYERABEND).

Since any theory of knowledge must of necessity refer also to itself, it would be wrong to suggest that sociological theories of knowledge can any more avoid the element of circularity that must attend any theory of knowledge than could traditional philosophy. What such a sociological theory can achieve is to dispense with the tendency to dogmatic closure in epistemological thinking of a kind that so often has been apparent in more traditional theories, with their claims to have reached bedrock. Once knowledge, including scientific knowledge, is seen clearly as a socially constructed phenomenon, the expectation of any final doctrines about the nature of knowledge can be seen as misplaced.

epoché the placing in parentheses, or *bracketing*, of any aspects of reality for methodological purposes, for example, the analysis of structure while holding individual agency in parenthesis (see Giddens, 1984). The concept of *epoché* derives from HUSSERL'S PHENOMENOLOGY, where it was intended as a technique for allowing penetration to the underlying grounds of our knowledge by thinking away conventional, including scientific, assumptions. The device has been applied within sociology, particularly by SCHUTZ and, influenced by him, also within ETHNOMETHODOLOGY, with the aim of uncovering the grounds of our everyday social knowledge and SOCIAL COMPETENCE.

equality of opportunity the idea that all persons, regardless of class, age, race, or gender, should have equal rights to compete for and attain sought-after positions in society. In the 20th century, the concept has played an important part in the search to achieve a more just, more equal, and fair distribution of society's wealth and benefits. It has been especially central in debates surrounding education.

Both the sociological literature and wider public debate have focused on two major issues concerning equality of opportunity, in either its narrower or its wider sense: (a) the extent to which it is socially desirable, feasible, and realistic, and (b) the extent to which particular educational innovations aimed at achieving increased equality of educational opportunity have been successful or unsuccessful. On the first count, critics have argued that attempts to engineer equality of outcome conflict with individual freedom. Critics have also argued that educational chances have failed because differences in social background are too pronounced to be removed by educational reforms alone.

Eros the life instinct in FREUD's theory of personality. Eros involves all instincts leading toward survival, so is not synonymous with the sex drive, although this is central to it. Eros is creative, in contrast to its opposite, THANATOS, the death instinct, which is destructive.

essentialism the view that philosophy or science is able to reach and represent absolute TRUTHS, for example, the necessary or essential properties, or essences, of objects. Plato's theory of ideal forms is an example of essentialism.

Today the term is often a pejorative one, used by philosophers who oppose essentialism and emphasize the provisional or conventional nature of knowledge (see also CONVENTIONALISM, NOMINALISM, OPERATIONALISM OR OPERATIONISM, RELATIVISM, POSTEMPIRICISM, DECONSTRUCTION, REALISM).

essentially contested concept a category of general concepts in the social sciences, for example, POWER, the application of which, according to Gallie (1955) and Lukes (1974), is inherently a matter of dispute. The reason given for this is that competing versions of concepts such as power inevitably involve relativity to VALUES. According to this view, hypotheses using concepts such as power can be appraised empirically, but will remain relative to the evaluative framework within which the particular versions of the concepts are couched. There are parallels between this notion and Weber's earlier view that social science propositions are value-relative (see also VALUE FREEDOM AND VALUE NEUTRALITY). See also POWER.

estate (in preindustrial society) a SOCIAL STRATUM within a system of SOCIAL STRATIFICATION, distinguished by a specific set of legally defined rights and duties. The estate system is particularly associated with European, and especially French and German, feudal and postfeudal, so-called ständestaat societies, although there were broadly similar systems in Russia, Japan, and China. Estates might vary from locality to locality, but within their own area they had rigorously ordered boundaries and value systems, and the main divisions are conventionally defined as being between nobility, clergy, and commoners. The rise of gentry, professional, and other groupings might complicate status divisions on a local basis, but the regulation of rights to offices, titles, property, etc., and, less formally, of whom it was appropriate to know and how it was appropriate to know them, was a defining feature of estates.

Estates formed communities in the sense used by Weber, whose conception of STATUS GROUP owes a great deal to his understanding of the historical conformation of estates. The elements of exclusiveness and acceptability, common life chances, and shared culture and experience are found in different historical situations, but the aspects of legal regulation and relatively fixed boundaries define the estate system (compare CASTE).

ethical indifference the doctrine that sociology, in its main research and theorizing, should no more occupy itself centrally with ethical concerns than should the natural sciences. This view has been taken recently, for example, by the ETHNOMETHODOLOGISTS, who have wanted to establish a new focus on careful descriptions of the everyday social competence and social practices of members of society, and to do this free of any distracting requirement to judge these practices. While, in part, this celebration of ethical indifference rests on the aim of advancing the empirical understanding of social action, it also derives from a view that sociology has no special basis on which to make value judgments that are not already possessed by the lay member of society. The social competence possessed by SOCIAL ACTORS is seen as establishing each actor as a moral agent. Compare VALUE FREEDOM AND VALUE NEUTRALITY.

ethics 1. the beliefs and attitudes within a society, culture, or organization that make up its moral values. **2.** the branch of philosophy concerned with how we ought to act in order to be moral. Two predominant schools of thought can be identified: (a) those that emphasize that matters of right and wrong should be decided only by analysis of the consequences of action, for example, UTILITARIANISM, and (b) those that assert that at least some duties are independent of consequences, for example, not telling lies. Generally in the social sciences (a) has had more significance than (b). Other topics in ethics are similar to those that occur in sociology, for example, issues surrounding the FACT-VALUE DISTINCTION and VALUE FREEDOM AND VALUE NEUTRALITY. **3.** a moral code that guides the contact of a group of professional group such as medical doctors or lawyers.

ethnic group a group of people sharing an identity that arises from a collective sense of a distinctive history. Ethnic groups possess their own CULTURE, CUSTOMS, NORMS, beliefs, and traditions. There is usually a common LANGUAGE; boundary maintenance is observed between members; and nonmembers and such groups are traditionally mutually exclusive. Typically, they are transgenerational and biologically self-perpetuating. Not all ethnic groups are endogamous (see ENDOGAMY), however, and membership may be acquired through marriage or other socially approved routes. While socially perceived racial characteristics may be a feature of such groups, ethnic groups are not synonymous with racial groups (see RACE).

The anthropologist Narroll (1964) stressed the importance of shared cultural values and a group awareness of cultural distinctiveness as key elements in ethnic group membership. Barth (1970), in criticism, places emphasis on group organization and the maintenance of ethnic boundaries via ETHNIC MARKERS. Barth argued that cultural traits were a consequence of ethnic group organization, and ethnic boundaries entail a complex pattern of behavior and social relations. The boundaries between ethnic groups are maintained not through isolation, as Narroll argued, but through social processes of exclusion and incorporation; that is, ethnic group members identify themselves in terms of ethnic categories and are in turn recognized as members by outsiders.

The continuity of ethnic units depends on the maintenance of social boundaries. REX (1986) has criticized Barth for his failure to consider conflict between ethnic groups and for his imprecise use of the term "group." Rex also raises the question of whether, immigrants aside, ETHNICITY remains an important means of classification in complex industrial societies. See also ETHNICITY.

ethnicity a shared (whether perceived or actual) racial, linguistic, or national identity of a social group. It is an imprecise term that has given rise to some degree of conceptual confusion. It is often conflated with other terms such as *racial group*.

Ethnicity can incorporate several forms of collective identity, including cultural, religious, national, and subcultural forms. A distinction may be drawn between *cultural ethnicity* and *political ethnicity*. The former refers to a belief in a shared language, religion, or other such cultural values and practices. The latter refers to the political awareness or mobilization of a group on a real or assumed ethnic basis.

Although ethnicity is often used in relation to a group's assumed racial identity, strictly racial attributes (see RACE) are not necessarily, or even usually, a feature of all ethnic groups. Sociologists tend to regard social groups as being identifiable in terms of cultural phenomena such as shared customs, institutions, rituals, and language.

An important distinction can be drawn between groups that have consciously sought to assert their ethnicity, and those that have been designated as ethnic minorities by more powerful groups. In some cases, ethnic characteristics may be exaggerated or created to serve group interests and cohesion. ETHNIC MARKERS, or complex symbolic practices, may be mobilized to accentuate boundaries and divisions between groups, while in some cases the cultural boundaries will be understated in order to maximize INTEGRATION. For example, in contemporary Britain, Pakistani Christian refugees may seek to minimalize group differences, whereas East African Sikhs may attempt to exaggerate ethnic distinctiveness by stringently observing certain types of tradition. Cultural practices may therefore be observed to maximize control separation and boundaries.

As Jeffrey (1979) notes, the Pirzadoe sect in India is an example of a social group employing ritual practices to demarcate cultural boundaries between itself and outsiders. Ethnicity, therefore, implies assumptions concerning membership or exclusion from particular groups. As J. Okley (1975) has suggested in her study of Romany culture, women may function as bearers of collective identity through the observance of certain behaviors, notably the observance of bodily rituals associated with pollution.

In some instances, ethnicity may serve as the basis for minority status. Discriminatory practices against such groups may be legitimated by institutionalized means. As P. Worsley (1985) has noted, ethnic minority status may seriously jeopardize an individual or group's life chances, particularly in relation to health, housing, and employment.

According to C. Peach et al. (1981), British academic concern with the subject of ethnicity increased as a result of black immigration in the post-war period. Thus, despite the presence of immigrants, refugees, and ethnic minorities prior to this period, it was the combination of racial and ethnic distinctiveness that gave rise to both popular and academic interest in the subject. One result of this has been the confusion of the term "ethnic minority" with racial minority, in the British culture. It should also be noted that approaches to social stratification based on economic inequality find it difficult to treat the question of ethnicity adequately. See STATUS CONSISTENCY AND INCONSISTENCY, RACISM.

ethnic marker the means whereby social boundaries between ETHNIC GROUPS are maintained. Territorality, history, LANGUAGE, and SYMBOLS may all serve as ethnic markers emphasizing distinctions between one ethnic group and another. Proscriptions on intermarriage and restrictions on religious worship may also act as ethnic markers. While different ethnic groups may interact for the purpose, for example, of economic activity, ethnic markers ensure the continuity of separate group identity.

ethnocentrism 1. the attitude of prejudice or mistrust toward outsiders that may exist within a social group; a way of perceiving one's own cultural group (in-group) in relation to others (out-groups). The term was introduced by W.G. Sumner (1906) and involves the belief that one's own group is the most important, or is culturally superior to other groups. Thus, one's own culture is considered to be morally and culturally of greater value or significance than that of others, and one becomes distrustful of those defined as outsiders. It also involves an incapacity to acknowledge that cultural differentiation does not imply inferiority of those groups who are ethnically distinct from one's own. **2.** a characteristic of certain personality types. The ethnocentric personality is described by T. Adorno et al. (1950) in *The Authoritarian Personality* (see AUTHORITARIAN PERSONALITY). Initially this study was concerned with the social and psychological aspects of anti-Semitism, but developed into a study of its more general correlates. Adorno et al. were particularly concerned with explaining attitudes toward other out-groups in American society, such as homosexuals and ethnic minorities, and maintained that antagonism toward one out-group (for example, Jews) seldom existed in isolation, but formed part of a constellation of attitudes. They found that ethnocentricism tended to be associated with authoritarianism, dogmatism and rigidity, political and economic conservatism, and an implicit antidemocratic ideology. Thus, hostility toward one out-group (see IN-GROUP AND OUT-GROUP) was often generalized and projected onto other out-groups. The concept of ethnocentric personality serves to link the emergence of ethnic identity to the processes concerned with the formation of intense out-group hostility. The greater the out-group hostility, the greater the sense of in-group identification. There have been criticisms of this approach, and some social psychologists have stressed the need to explore the wider sociocultural factors in the development of ethnocentricism and authoritarianism. See also PREJUDICE, DISCRIMINATION, RACISM OR RACIALISM, ATTITUDE, ATTITUDE SCALES.

ethnography the direct observation of an organization or small society, and the written description produced. Often the method of observation involves PARTICIPANT OBSERVATION. The ethnographic method (sometimes also referred to as *fieldwork*) is a basic method in SOCIAL ANTHROPOLOGY. It is also a method used in some areas of sociology, for example, COMMUNITY STUDIES. Usually researchers gather data by living and working in the society or social setting being researched, seeking to immerse themselves as fully as possible in the activities under observation, but at the same time keeping careful records of these activities.

In anthropology, emphasis on the importance of the ethnographic method was initially associated with the functionalist school, which encoraged analysis of the internal structure and function of single societies rather than historical or comparative studies (see FUNCTIONALISM). However, there is no inherent reason why ethnographic and comparative approaches should not be seen as complementary, or why ethnography should be associated with only one theoretical school.

ethnomethodology the theoretical and specialist approach within sociology, initiated by Harold GARFINKEL, that sets out to uncover the methods (*members' methods*) and social competence that we, as members of social groups, employ in constructing our sense of social reality. Ethnomethodologists claim that mainstream sociologists have failed to study, or even to show any awareness of, members' possession of social competence, treating members merely as "cultural dupes," rather than acknowledging that social reality is created by individuals.

For ethnomethodologists, social reality is always to be seen as the rational accomplishment of individuals. Whereas conventional sociologists, for example, DURKHEIM in *Suicide* (1987) or the symbolic interactionists, are seen as taking actors' capacity to construct meanings merely as an unexamined resource, ethnomethodology makes the methods and TACIT KNOWLEDGE that members possess into a topic for analysis. What ethnomethodologists seek to do is analyze the ACCOUNTS provided by members in particular contexts (hence the extensive use of transcripts of ordinary conversation). In this, there are some similarities and continuities with SYMBOLIC INTERACTION-ISM. Beyond this, however, ethnomethodologists have sought to reveal the more universal recurring *members' methods* involved in social life, for example, organized turn-taking in talk (see also CONVERSATION ANALYSIS).

While ethnomethodology claims to have arrived at universal generalizations, the form of these generalizations, for example, indicating a persistent indexicality (see INDEXICAL EXPRESSION) in members' accounts, suggests that the type of generalizations traditionally sought by sociology are unlikely to be achieved, or at least the claims for them are premature. By the same token, many of the research methods and assumptions about method and measurement in conventional sociology are criticized by ethnomethodologists as involving MEASUREMENT BY FIAT (see A. Cicourel, 1964). See also FIXED-CHOICE QUESTIONNAIRES, AGGREGATE DATA ANALYSIS, OFFICIAL STATISTICS, PRACTICAL REASONING.

ethnosciences (SOCIAL ANTHROPOLOGY) the study of the indigenous bodies of knowledge within a culture area. Thus, *ethnobotany* records local botanical knowledge and plant taxonomies, and *ethnoecology* records local knowledge of ecological factors; while *ethnohistory*, which possess similarities with "history from below" (see HISTORY WORKSHOP JOURNAL), seeks to provide an historical account from the point of view of the society under discussion, using the oral historical record within the community. In general, the prefix *ethno-* used in this context refers to an analysis from the point of view of the folk culture being studied.

The ethnosciences are now seen as having some value in achieving ecologically sensitive forms of development, and forms of development also in tune with local needs. The recovery of lost knowledge that the ethnosciences represent also raises questions about the progressive nature of orthodox science and about RATIONALITY.

ethology 1. a term used by J.S. MILL for the "science of character" that he believed would become the basis of explanations within the moral sciences, using the inverse deductive method. **2.** the science of animal behavior, especially where the findings of this study are intended to be extrapolated to the study of human behavior. Ethology in this sense can be highly controversial, being objected to especially by those sociologists who emphasize the distinctiveness of human consciousness. See also SOCIOBIOLOGY.

etic see EMIC AND ETIC.

eugenics the study of human heredity, founded by Francis Galton (*Hereditary Genius*, 1870), that led Galton and his followers to propose selective policies designed to improve the stock, for example, fiscal and other policies to discourage child-rearing by those intellectually least well endowed. Apart from wider ethical considerations, such policies assume a relationship between heredity and intellectual and cultural characteristics that has not been demonstrated.

Evans-Pritchard, Sir Edward Evan (1902–73) British structural-functionalist social anthropologist. His major works include *Witchcraft, Magic and Oracles Among the Azande* (1937), *The Nuer* (1940), *Kinship and Marriage Among the Nuer* (1951), and *Nuer Religion* (1956). After being trained by MALINOWSKI, Evans-Pritchard undertook ETHNOGRAPHY in the southern Sudan. His writings illustrate both the rationality of apparently pre-logical thought, among the Azande, and the possibility of a peacefully anarchic stateless society, as exemplified by the Nuer. Though he is usually classified as a structural functionalist, his writings stress the affinity of anthropology to history, and not to science. In contrast with his predecessor at Oxford, RAD-CLIFFE-BROWN, he felt it pontless to search for universal laws of social behavior. His particular interest in religion is seen as being a result of his conversion to Catholicism in 1940. That his influence is still so great is probably a result of his focus on humanistic description. He characterized himself as "first an ethnographer and second a social anthropologist."

evolutionary sociology any form of sociology that emphasizes continuities between biological evolution and sociocultural evolution. Notwithstanding the many excesses and oversimplifications of much previous EVOLUTIONARY THEORY in sociology, Runciman (1989), for example, suggests "there is no escape from the recognition that any substantive social theory is and cannot but be evolutionary." What Runciman means by this is that:

(a) while in major part "extra organic," (see also SUPERORGANIC) human social capacities are biologically based;

(b) though no simple pattern of UNILINEAR social development has occurred and prediction is out of the question, as it is also in relation to biological evolution, it remains possible to discuss social evolution in terms of a historical sequence of development (compare EVOLUTIONARY UNIVER-SALS) in which later developments depend on those earlier;

(c) in these circumstances, it makes sense to employ the concept of social "selection" (while at the same time specifying what the "advantage" is) to explain why certain social practices have become established.

Not all sociologists would agree with Runciman's assessment, although many would (see also NEOEVOLUTION, SOCIOCULTURAL EVOLUTION). If few would quarrel with (a) and (b) of Runciman's three points, the main source of disagreement is whether terms such as selection (and related ones such as adaptation), imported from biology, can have any precise content compared with their use in biology (see also FUNCTIONAL(IST) EXPLANATION). Some sociologists, notably GIDDENS and MANN recently, have also rejected any conception of serial history, proposing instead a purely EPISODIC CHAR-ACTERIZATION of social change, presenting this as thus also a rejection of evolutionary and functionalist thinking. Yet, in practice, they too appear to find it difficult to escape evolutionary thinking in something like Runciman's broad terms (see Wright, 1983, Jary, 1991).

Issues often arise especially in the more particular claims for adaptation, functionally effective SOCIAL DIFFERENTIATION, etc. actually made by modern evolutionary sociologists (for example, see MODERNIZATION). A further general issue is whether evaluative conceptions such as PROGRESS have any place in modern evolutionary thinking. Evolutionary theorists are also divided on the issue of whether the general principle of evolution has any implications for the choice between unplanned and gradual evolution (social mutations) or planned development (see HISTORICISM sense **2.**, RATIONALIZATION). Evolutionary sociology in its modern forms has moved a long way from the crude notions of SOCIAL DARWINISM (misapplied biological ANALOGIES, racist theories, and sweeping applications of such notions as the survival of the fittest) advanced in 19th century, but it remains controversial. See also SPENCER, PARSONS.

evolutionary theory 1. the explanation of the origin, development, and diversity of biological species proposed by Charles DARWIN and by Alfred Russel Wallace (1823–1913). **2.** the explanation of SOCIAL CHANGE in terms of Darwinian principles.

Darwin's work influenced many 19th-century social theorists, including MORGAN (1818–81), HOBHOUSE (1864–1919), TYLOR (1832–1917), WARD (1841–1913), and SPENCER (1820–1903). The international ascendancy of Britain's economy and polity during the Victorian age had created a social atmosphere and an intellectual climate that was particularly receptive to ideas of progress and advancement. Darwin's theory, which seemed to establish these trends as features of biological development, was in this sense waiting to be heard. The imperial strength of Britain and the dominance of Western culture could rather crudely be read as nothing more than the outcome of a natural law that always assured the ascendancy of "the best."

Evolutionary theory, then, in the social sphere, saw the newly industrialized countries of the 19th century as representing the most advanced stage of a long-term process of development that had begun with much simpler kinds of society. Contemporary preindustrial, or peasant, or simple hunting and gathering societies could be conceived as living examples of earlier stages of development that the industrial world had left far behind. Evolutionary theory, therefore, typically combined two propositions: first, that evolutionary advancement involved development of complex forms of social organization from simple ones, via the increasing differentiation of social structure (see SOCIAL DIFFERENTIATION) and specialization of function; secondly, that these structural changes involved a parallel process of continuing moral, intellectual, and aesthetic development. Darwin's theory, applied to social development, thus resulted in a distinction between CIVILIZATION and BARBARISM that was especially convenient in an age of imperialism.

The impact of Darwin's ideas on social theory in the 19th century was immense. The politics of social evolutionism could appeal as much to those interested in legitimating the status quo as to those (like MARX) interested in changing it. Yet the receptivity of social theorists to such ideas should have been tempered with caution. Darwin had developed his account of change primarily to explain diversity and adaptation among species in which consciousness, reflexivity, and creativity (or CULTURE) could be ignored as a significant variable. But it was precisely these facts that made human society possible. Ironically, there *was* an evolutionary paradigm available that could take the cultural variable on board. It was not, however, the one elaborated by Darwin, but by his rival theorist, Jean Baptiste LAMARCK (1744–1829), who had argued for the inheritance of *acquired* characteristics in the evolutionary process. Darwin had rejected this, relying instead on the principles of *random* variation and natural selection. Yet it is precisely the capacity of individuals and societies to learn from each other—to acquire culture or copy crucial cultural developments (such as writing, measuring, etc.)—that is distinctive to human social life. Strangely, in pinning its flag to what was destined to be the most successful version of the evolutionary paradigm, Darwinism, social theory largely ignored the thesis that actually had most to offer, that of Lamarck.

By the early decades of the 20th century, evolutionism was falling into disfavor among social scientists. A precipitating cause may have been the catastrophic slaughter and barbarism of World War I, which was hardly an advertisement for a supposedly enlightened Europe that had undergone a civilizing process. More fundamentally, three main difficulties with 19th-century theories of social evolution had by then become increasingly apparent. First, the assumption of unilinearity (see UNILINEAR)—that there was one path of development through which all societies would pass; secondly, an inability to say much about the stages of development intermediate between simple and complex societies, and the processes that produced change; and thirdly, the value-laden proposition that social development involved moral enlightenment, ethnocentrically conceived in European terms.

The second half of the 20th century saw a revival of interest in problems of development as Third World issues began to force themselves onto political agendas. This produced new versions of evolutionary theory (see NEOEVOLUTIONISM, SOCIOCULTURAL EVOLUTION, EVOLUTIONARY UNIVERSAL) and eventually a reopening of critical debate, especially by the underdevelopment school. See also ECONOMIC AND SOCIAL DEVELOPMENT, EVOLUTIONARY SOCIOLOGY.

evolutionary universals as defined by PARSONS (1964a), the developmental steps in social change that "increase the adaptive capacity" of human societies, and without which "further major developmental steps would be blocked." According to Parsons, evolutionary universals are organizational developments that are "hit upon more than once," comparable, say, with the development of vision in the organic world. By adaptation, Parsons means not only adjustment to an environment, but also the ability to cope with an increasingly wide range of environmental factors, including adaptive advantage over other less developed societies. Once the symbol replaces the gene as the main agency of human development, four basic areas of social provision are important:

(a) RELIGION, performing Durkheimian functions;

(b) COMMUNICATION, especially language;

(c) KINSHIP, including the INCEST TABOO and EXOGAMY/ENDOGAMY RULES;

(d) TECHNOLOGY, the primary adaptive relation with the environment.

As the result of these initial changes, bringing economic and organizational functional advantage, the next pair of advantages seen as important by Parsons in breaking out from the primitive stage are:

(e) SOCIAL STRATIFICATION, social prestige and economic advantages attaching to some groups, lineages, etc.;

(f) a differentiated structure providing political and cultural legitimation.

As Parsons puts it, the differentiation of advantage for some groups tends to "converge with the functional need for centralization of responsibility." Stratification releases and centralizes resources for further development, breaking with traditionalism. Literacy, at first the monopoly of only a minority, accentuates stratification and a tendency to primacy of cultural differentiation at this stage. In turn, stratification of all types is itself a source of strain requiring new cultural legitimation.

Five further evolutionary universals, built on the previous ones, follow:

(g) BUREAUCRACY, that is, the Weberian separation of administrative office from kinship and traditionalism;

(h) MONEY and markets, in which money, as "the symbolic medium for resources," increases the mobility of resources, "emancipating these for ascriptive bonds" (see also PATTERN VARIABLES);

(i) a universalistic legal system;

(j) the invention of the "democratic association," especially its application to large-scale societies from the 18th century onward, though with its origins in Greece and Rome and the early Christian church;

(k) science.

Criticisms of Parsons' conception of evolutionary universals are in many ways the usual criticisms of EVOLUTIONARY THEORY in sociology: for example, the lack of any great precision in the use of terms such as "adaptation," and the absence of direct parallels with evolutionary conceptions in biology. It is notable how often in describing his evolutionary universals, Parsons uses such phrases as "probably decisive," "by and large" and "very difficult to pin down." For all this, the general steps identified by Parsons as important in human development are not markedly different from those that were identified by WEBER or by MARX. In other words, what is most at issue is whether there is anything original in Parsons' formulation, and whether such developmental steps are best formulated within a specifically evolutionary frame of reference. See also NEOEVOLUTIONISM, EVOLUTIONARY SOCIOLOGY, SOCIOCULTURAL EVOLUTION.

exchange 1. any social interaction that may have as one aspect an exchange of goods or services, but also serves the purpose of social bonding (see GIFT EXCHANGE AND GIFT RELATIONSHIP). In simple societies there are generalized patterns of exchange of a variety of goods and services, including, for example, ceremonial goods or even marriage partners, in which the givers do not themselves immediately receive directly from those to whom they give. In their various manifestations, these forms of exchange can be seen as not only, or even primarily, economic; rather they reinforce established social relationships, for example, enhancing the prestige of the giver. See also KULA RING. **2.** any social interaction that can be interpreted as involving reciprocal benefits or exchanges, for example, relationships between super-ordinates and subordinates (even master and slave), as well as relationships involving mutual affection and love. See also EXCHANGE THEORY.

exchange theory a theoretical perspective based on SIMMEL'S insight that "all contacts among men rest on the schema of giving and returning the equivalence" (BLAU, 1964). The approach also draws on economics and behavioral psychology, viewing individuals as always seeking to maximize rewards from their interactions with others (see also HOMANS). As a mode of analysis, exchange theory is associated with interesting hypotheses about social behavior, for example, Blau's suggestion that people tend to marry partners able to offer equivalent social assets. Critics of the approach, however, regard it as providing a model that is, at best, capable of presenting only a partial account of human social relations. Limitations of the approach suggested are its tautological assumptions that social relations *always* involve exchange relations; its failure to deal adequately with such phenomena as traditional action or general values, and the great variety of human emotions. See also RECIPROCITY, UTILITARIANISM, RATIONAL CHOICE THEORY, THEORY OF GAMES.

exogamy a rule prescribing marriage outside a given social group. The group may belong to a lineage, CASTE, CLASS, ethnic affiliation, or other social classification. Structural anthropologists have seen this practice as an exchange of women between groups that contributes to social stability. It may, therefore, be enforced by the use of INCEST TABOOS. The converse of exogamy is ENDOGAMY.

experimental group the group that receives the INDEPENDENT VARIABLE in an experiment. Typically, in the EXPERIMENTAL METHOD, the EXPERIMENTAL HYPOTHESIS is tested by treating the experimental group with the independent variable to be investigated, and comparing any resultant effect (measured by the DEPENDENT VARIABLE) with any change observed in the CONTROL GROUP. If a statistically significant difference is found between the dependent measures in experimental and control groups, then the experimental hypothesis is upheld. If there is no statistically significant difference, then the NULL HYPOTHESIS is upheld. An alternative term is *experimental condition*.

experimental hypothesis the statement that there will be a statistically significant difference between the EXPERIMENTAL GROUP and the CONTROL GROUP, and that this difference will have been caused by the INDEPENDENT VARIABLE under investigation.

When an experiment is set up, or observational data are collected, this is done in order to test a hypothesis, or theory, that has been developed from previous work. This is the experimental hypothesis, which states what the expected difference is between the groups if the theory is correct. The converse hypothesis, or NULL HYPOTHESIS, is also conventionally stated— that the predictions from the theory are incorrect. See also DEPENDENT VARIABLE. See also EXPERIMENTAL METHOD.

experimental method the scientific method used to test an EXPERIMENTAL HYPOTHESIS by comparing an EXPERIMENTAL GROUP that has been subjected to an INDEPENDENT VARIABLE, with a CONTROL GROUP that has not. This is the method of choice in PSYCHOLOGY, but sociology has developed diverse methodologies to cope with less controllable data. See COMPARATIVE METHOD, CAUSAL MODELING.

explanation any account in which an occurrence or general phenomenon is made intelligible by identification of its CAUSE, nature, interrelations, etc. In more formal terms, the occurrence or phenomenon explained is the *explanandum,* the explanatory account; the *explanans,* which, in physical science, will usually involve scientific laws, EXPLANATORY THEORIES, etc., but in the social sciences may also involve actors' meanings, reasons, and so on. Thus in sociology, explanation may take any one of a number of forms, which are not necessarily always mutually exclusive:

(a) *causal explanation,* which may embrace various types of explanation, but in its most basic form involves identification of an immediate precipitating cause or causes of a particular occurrence, for example, the cause of a fire identified as the dropping of a cigarette. In their more limited forms, causal explanations usually involve numerous unstated background assumptions about physical laws, etc. (see also CAUSE);

(b) *deductive explanation,* in which an explanandum is deduced, that is, follows logically from established generalizations of general laws (see HYPOTHETIC-DEDUCTIVE EXPLANATION, VERSTEHEN, INTERPRETATIVE SOCIOLOGY, COVERING LAW MODEL AND DEDUCTIVE NOMOLOGICAL EXPLANATION, FORMAL THEORY;

(c) *probabilistic explanation,* in which a specifiable probability (a chance of less than 100% and more than 0%, that is, in probability theory a chance less than 1 and greater than 0) is taken as explaining the occurrence of an event, for example, the appearance of breast cancer in a woman whose mother and sisters have already had the disease. Strictly speaking, rather than explaining a single event probability, explanations relate to the likelihood of a particular distribution of occurrences in an infinite series of events. On their own they are usually seen as unsatisfactory as explanations, at least until further background factors explaining the probabilities are also identified, for example, in the case of breast cancer, the discovery of genetic predispositions, etc.)

(d) *meaningful and purposive explanations,* in which actors' meanings and/or desires, reasons, intentions, purposes, etc. explain an event or a social situation (see MEANINGFUL UNDERSTANDING AND MEANINGFUL EXPLANATION, PURPOSIVE EXPLANATION;

(e) *functional(ist) explanations,* in which the functional requirements of systems explain outcomes (see FUNCTIONAL(IST) EXPLANATION);

(f) *evolutionary or ecological explanations,* which explain the persistence of natural species, types of social system, etc. in terms of their selection by and adaptation to an external environment (see EVOLUTIONARY THEORY);

(g) *teleological explanations* (see also TELEOLOGY), in which purposes, goals, or system end states, rather than antecedent causes, are seen as decisive. Such explanations may be made with reference to human or animal purposes, to the needs and goals of human societies, or to the more arcane operation of processes such as "world spirit" (as for HEGEL) or human destiny. Functional explanation in many of its sociological forms also involves teleological explanation, although in this case recourse to such explanation is not always regarded as incompatible in principle with a reduction to antecendent causes.

explanatory mechanism any scientific account of the causal factors (or causal powers) underlying a general phenomenon, for example, natural selection (in EVOLUTIONARY THEORY), or contradictory modes of modes of production and class conflict (in Marxism). The term has gained in currency recently as a result of the influence within sociology of the scientific realism of Rom Harré (1970 and, with E. Madden, 1975) and Roy Bhaskar (1975, 1979 and 1986), in which the formulation of explanatory mechanisms is presented as the core of scientific EXPLANATION. This account of science and scientific explanation is preferred to those couched in terms of empirical regularities and general laws (for example, the COVERING LAW MODEL) for a number of reasons, above all that laws can be either empirical regularities or universal and transfactual, but not both. The use of the term "explanatory mechanism" both bypasses the problems associated with EMPIRICISM (see also POSITIVISM) and offers a way of recognizing the variety of forms taken by scientific explanatory accounts.

explanatory theory any theory that advances an EXPLANATION of a phenomenon or class of phenomena. Although explanatory theories can take many forms (see also HYPOTHETICO-DEDUCTIVE EXPLANATION AND METHOD, SOCIOLOGICAL THEORY, MEANINGFUL UNDERSTANDING AND EXPLANATION, FUNCTIONAL(IST) EXPLANATION), a general assumption is made that the facts rarely speak for themselves in explaining phenomena.

exploratory data analysis a form of statistical analysis that begins by exploring data rather than testing clearly formulated prior hypotheses.

Exploratory data analysis does as it says: it explores the pattern of the data set under analysis, considering its range, level and outliers, batching it before graphing, and transforming it. The MINITAB computer package, for example, contains these techniques in its subprograms. In either qualitative or quantitative forms, the purpose of exploratory data analysis is to follow parallel procedures in the interrogation of statistics, that is, generating hypotheses through exploring the data before turning to confirmatory statistics to test those hypotheses.

extended family the unit formed both by family members who are in the nuclear family and those who are not but are still considered to be close relatives. While the nuclear family is composed of a couple and their children, the family group is extended when the grandparents, aunts and uncles, cousins, nieces and nephews, or any selection of these are included.

Extended families occur more often in preindustrial societies rather than in industrial societies, where the nuclear family is sometimes seen as more compatible with the needs of modern economies. See also FAMILY, SOCIOLOGY OF THE FAMILY.

extroversion and **introversion** a personality trait (see TRAIT THEORY) characterized, in the case of extroversion, by orientation toward the outside world, sociability, and impulsiveness and, in the case of introversion, by orientation toward the inner world of the self, shyness, and caution. The extroversion-introversion typology was first described by JUNG (1928). It is one of the three central dimensions of personality in the model of personality structure proposed by H. Eysenck (1953), and in this context may be measured using the Eysenck Personality Inventory (E.P.I.). A biological basis for extroversion-introversion in terms of cortical inhibition-excitation has also been postulated (H. Eysenck, 1967).

F

face-work the sequence of interaction in which a potential or actual loss of face is dealt with by those involved in interaction. For GOFFMAN, such sequences are sufficiently standardized to be regarded as ritual, for example, a transgression is noted; the transgressor acknowledges this (for example, "silly me"); this recognition is accepted by other parties to the interaction; the offender registers gratitude for this. In Goffman's work and in related forms of sociology such as ETHNOMETHODOLOGY, the existence of such relatively standardized sequences are seen as a central element in the everyday social order.

factor analysis a MULTIVARIATE statistical technique in which the covariances (or CORRELATIONS) between a large set of observed VARIABLES are explained in terms of a small number of new variables called factors. The ideas originated in the work on correlation by Galton and Spearman and were developed primarily in studies of intelligence. Most applications are found in psychology and sociology.

The technique is variable directed, with no distinction between INDEPENDENT and DEPENDENT VARIABLES in the data set. There are four steps to the analysis. The first is to derive a correlation matrix in which each variable in the data set is correlated with all the other variables. The next step is to extract the factors. The aim of this stage is to determine the minimum number of factors that can account adequately for the observed correlations between the original variables. If the number of factors identified is close to the number of original variables, there is little point to the factor analysis. Sometimes it is difficult to assign a meaningful name to the factors. The purpose of the third (optional) step, rotation, is to find simpler and more easily interpretable factors. If a satisfactory model has been derived, the fourth step is to compute scores for each factor for each case in the data set. The factor scores can then be used in subsequent analyses.

Factor analysis attracts a lot of criticism (Chatfield and Collins, 1980). The observed correlation matrix is generally assumed to have been constructed using product-moment correlations. Hence, the usual assumptions of an interval measurement, normal distributions, and homogeneity of variance are needed. Against this, it is argued, the technique is fairly robust. Another problem is that the different methods of extraction and rotation tend to produce different solutions. Further, although factors may be clearly identified from the analysis, it may be difficult to give them a meaningful interpretation. Despite the need for so many judgmental decisions in its use, factor analysis remains a useful exploratory tool.

factors of production (economics) the different resources that are combined in production: natural resources, labor, and capital. In sociological

analysis and in Marxism emphasis is placed on understanding the socioeconomic relations that production involves.

fact-value distinction the distinction (often associated with HUME and the
Logical Positivists) between factual assertions and moral assertions as two
distinct classes of assertions, and the claim that moral assertions cannot be
derived logically from factual assertions. While some sociologists have
accepted the terms of this distinction (including, significantly, Max
WEBER), other sociologists have refused to accept such a limitation on the
significance of social science on the grounds that, for all practical purposes,
facts and theories both inform and influence values, and to deny this is to
suggest an irrationalism of values that is unwarranted. As GOULDNER (1973)
remarks, "one possible meaning of the term 'objectivity' in social science is
the contribution it might make to a human unity of mankind." See also
VALUE FREEDOM AND VALUE NEUTRALITY, VALUE RELEVANCE, BECKER, HIER-
ARCHY OF CREDIBILITY.

false consciousness any form of CLASS CONSCIOUSNESS, IDEOLOGY, or
social imagery held to be inappropriate to the real or objective class situation or class interests of the actor. The concept, although not used as
such by MARX, is developed from his theory. In particular, it derives from
the argument that ideologies and consciousness generally are products of
social structure and represent real relationships of domination and
oppression. It followed that in time the PROLETARIAT would come to realize its position as an oppressed and exploited class and put that realization to political use through revolutionary struggle.

A major problem facing Marxists has been that a widespread revolutionary consciousness has never emerged among the proletariat. Thus,
after the extension of the vote to nearly all adult males, Engels wrote to
Marx complaining about how the working class had "disgraced itself" by
giving political support to the Liberal Party at election time. In the period up to the 1950s the concept of false consciousness was frequently
referred to in accounting for the failure of a revolutionary working class
to develop.

One persistent theme, established by Lenin, was that, unaided, the proletariat would develop only a reformist, economistic, or trade-union consciousness. It required the organization of a revolutionary vanguard party
to transform the limited awareness of the working class into a truly progressive political consciousness based on the reality of the working-class
situation. Other explanations included the idea that the formation of a revolutionary proletariat was impeded by factors such as nationalism or imperialism, or even that sport and nonpolitical diversions, in effect, sublimated
the revolutionary impulse (see also LEISURE, INCORPORATION).

Theoretically, the concept has also been important in revising central
perspectives within Marxism. Georg LUKACS (1971), for example, writing in
the 1920s, argued for the need for much more attention to be paid to the

issue of consciousness than had been paid by the "vulgar" Marxists who assumed an inevitable move to worldwide revolution. These themes have continued an interest in the study of mass culture, in the work of the FRANKFURT SCHOOL OF CRITICAL THEORY, and more recently in the work of the Birmingham Centre for Contemporary Cultural Studies (see CULTURAL STUDIES).

For sociologists generally, the idea of false consciousness has posed a number of problems. It has been criticized for the elitist implication that "we know what the working class needs better than the working class does." More pertinently, it may be seen to divert attention away from the need to research the actual ideas and consciousness of working-class groups and their social sources. It also requires that one accept the Marxist theory of CLASS and embraces the idea that revolution is a logical necessity and inevitable consequence of social class relations. Although in recent times the notion of false consciousness has tended to fall into disuse, in both Marxism and Marxist sociology the idea of HEGEMONY has replaced it as a popular conceptual tool in the discussion of working-class consciousness (for example in the work of the Birmingham Centre). However, it can be argued that hegemony has at least some of the same drawbacks of the earlier concept. See also IDEOLOGY.

falsificationism the methodological position particularly associated with Karl Popper (1934), based on the notion that while an inductive universal generalization can never be finally verified, given the ever-present possibility of new and potentially refuting evidence, a single nonsupporting occurrence can refute a hypothesis. For example, a single black swan refutes the general hypothesis that "all swans are white." According to this view (and in contrast with LOGICAL POSITIVISM, see also EMPIRICISM), science can be defined in terms of the "falsifiability" rather than the "verifiability" of its theories and hypotheses, and the essential provisionality of scientific knowledge acknowledged. For Popper, the falsifiability of a discipline's propositions is the decisive *criterion of demarcation* between science and nonscience.

A virtue of this realist, rather than empiricist, position is that it recognizes the importance of hypotheses and theories within science, and of changes in scientific knowledge, thus also captures something of the critical spirit of science. Hence, this position is sometimes also referred to as *critical rationalism*.

Although it has attracted some support among social scientists, critics of falsificationism challenge its cogency on a number of counts:

(a) that the facts that are put forward as the basis of the independent test of theories and hypotheses are themselves "theory-laden" experiments, for example, are both constituted *by* and interpreted *using* theories;

(b) in practice, in science, and contrary to the position that can be termed *naive falsificationism,* it turns out that a single refutation is rarely decisive, the rejection and replacement of theories being a matter of a more overall judgment of the cogency and effectiveness of theories;

(c) the attempt (see Lakatos and Musgrave, 1970) to replace naive falsificationism with a *sophisticated falsificationism*, in which an overall judgment is made between *progressive* and *degenerating scientific research programmes* and fails to overcome the problems of falsificationism, for if no single observation is decisive, falsification loses its distinctive position; it no longer provides a clear-cut rule of thumb in the day-to-day procedures of science, or any clear overall demarcation between science and non-science.

As seen by many commentators (for example, see FEYERABEND, 1975), the procedures suggested for science by falsificationists simply fail to fit the past and present activities of science, and if used strictly would be likely to cripple it. See also COVERING LAW MODEL AND DEDUCTIVE NOMOLOGICAL EXPLANATION, HYPOTHETICO-DEDUCTIVE EXPLANATION AND METHOD, SOCIOLOGY OF SCIENCE.

family a group of people related by KINSHIP or similar close ties in which the adults assume responsibility for care and upbringing of their natural or adopted children.

Historically and comparatively, there have been wide variations in the family form. In order to analyze these differing family arrangements, sociologists have used the key notions of the EXTENDED FAMILY and the *nuclear family*. The extended family refers to a group of people, related by kinship, where more than two GENERATIONS of relatives live together or in close proximity, usually forming a single HOUSEHOLD. The nuclear family comprises merely parents (or parent) and dependent children. Sociologists have argued that the nuclear family form has developed as a concomitant of INDUSTRIALIZATION, although there have been suggestions recently that the prior existence of individualistic family structures may have contributed to the rise of industrialism. With the geographical and social mobility normally associated with industrial development, sociologists have argued that the nuclear family has become socially and geographically isolated from wider kin networks, leading to what is known as the *privatized nuclear family*.

There remain wide variations in the forms that extended and nuclear families take, depending on social and cultural NORMS. For example, extended families vary according to kin structures, including polygamous family forms. Similarly, the number of children found in nuclear families differs widely. For example, in the US, the trend has been toward having fewer children; and in China couples are prohibited from having more than one child.

As well as differences between societies, each family goes through a life cycle, and most individuals undergo several changes in family role in the course of their own lifetimes.

Recent changes in patterns of family life in the United States and in many Western societies include:

(a) the increasing importance placed on personal fulfillment, overriding previously more dominant economic considerations;

(b) the increasing percentage of stable reproductive and cohabiting relationships outside conventional marriage patterns;

(c) the increasing incidence of DIVORCE and remarriage;

(d) an increase in the number of single-parent families, especially fatherless families.

A further change in the nuclear family, which may occur as a consequence of an ageing population, is that this might lead to an increase in the number of nuclear families caring for dependent parents (see COMMUNITY CARE). See also SOCIOLOGY OF THE FAMILY, SOCIALIZATION, MARRIAGE, DIVORCE.

fashion modes of behavior or dress "in which the key feature is rapid and continual changing of styles" (E. Wilson, *Adorned in Dreams: Fashion and Modernity,* 1985). Fashion reflects two aspects of modernity:

(a) perpetual change created by ADVERTISING, and fueled by the mass media of communication;

(b) style and choice of clothes, furniture, or similar goods that enable people to exercise an element of control over their immediate social environment and presentation of self and social identity.

D. Hebdige (*Subculture: The Meaning of Style,* 1979) argues that different subcultures make their own style through the creative juxtaposition—*bricolage*—of different clothes or objects. Thus, fashion is subject to the same assessment as other forms of popular culture. It contains elements of both creative expression and manipulation.

fatalistic suicide a form of SUICIDE identified by DURKHEIM (1897) that arises from "oppressive regulation" and from "physical or moral despotism," for example, the suicide of slaves. Thus, Durkheim suggested that this form of suicide could be considered the opposite of ANOMIC SUICIDE.

feminism 1. a holistic theory concerned with the nature of women's global oppression and subordination to men; **2.** a sociopolitical theory and practice that aims to free all women from male supremacy and exploitation; **3.** a social movement encompassing strategic confrontations with the sex-class system; **4.** an ideology that stands in dialectical opposition to all misogynous ideologies and practices.

Feminism has a long history and can, arguably, be traced back to the 15th century (Kelly, 1982), though women's resistance to subordination certainly predates the emergence of feminism as a fully articulated ideology and practice (Rowbotham, 1972). The roots of modern feminist thought are conventionally traced back to the late 18th century and to the works of Mary Wollstonecraft. Since the 19th century there have been numerous manifestations of feminist activity followed by periods of relative invisibility. The first wave of feminism is frequently located between the mid-19th century and the early 20th century. The second wave has been identified with the reemergence of feminism in the late 1960s and has persisted as a social movement into the present. There have, however, been many waves, and Sarah (1982) has criticized the idea of first and second waves as ethnocentric.

Whereas feminism in the late 1960s was concerned with understanding and documenting an oppression believed to be commonly experienced by *all* women, much contemporary feminist writing emphasizes the diversity of women's relationship not only to the male social order but also to each other. It is more accurate, therefore, to talk of feminisms than feminism. Sebestyen (1978) charted over ten political tendencies within feminism, ranging from a liberal, equal rights position to a female supermacist strand. Palmer (1989) listed the following tendencies: academic feminism, cultural feminism, lesbian feminism, liberal feminism, psychoanalytic feminism, political lesbianism, radical feminism, and socialist feminism. Futhermore, black feminism has been concerned with the implicit and explicit racism within feminist thought and has stressed the particular issues concerning the lives of black women (Lorde, 1979). The original four demands of the second wave—equal pay now, equal education and opportunities, free contraception, abortion on demand, and free 24-hour nurseries—have been identified as the primary concerns of white, Western women. Access to food, fuel, and water are the primary needs of many Third World women. Feminism has been identified with white women's culture, and many black women favor the term "womanist" (Walker, 1983). *Ecofeminism* suggests that an end to the oppression of women is bound up with ecological values, and that women should be centrally concerned with ending the exploitation of the ecosystem (Collard, 1988). Ecofeminism has been particularly strong within radical feminism and within the GREEN MOVEMENT.

Case (1988) has followed the convention of distinguishing between two major theoretical divisions within feminism: radical feminism and materialist (socialist) feminism. The former is characterized by the belief that PATRIARCHY is the major and universal cause of women's oppression, and that the power invested in men is the root problem. Radical feminism, the predominant form of feminism in the US, has fostered the notion of an exclusively women's culture, together with a belief in the need to organize separately from men. Materialist (socialist) feminism is critical of the essentialism implicit in radical feminism and the ahistorical approach to patriarchy. Materialist feminism has its roots in Marxism and gives priority to social class as the factor determining the situation of women within capitalism. This approach is therefore concerned with the interaction between the dialectic of class and gender. Not without theoretical problems, Hartmann (1979) has characterized the marriage between Marxism and feminism as an unhappy one. The division between radical feminists, who wish to organize separately from men, and materialist feminists who seek solidarity with supportive men, continues unresolved.

Academic feminism has made an impact on the teaching and research carried out in many academic institutions. WOMEN'S STUDIES courses have been concerned with revising and challenging a wide variety of academic disciplines including sociology, history, and literature. Academic feminism has been concerned to criticize the sex-blind nature of academic knowledge. Within sociology there has been a growing literature on the position of women in society and the development of a specifically feminist research methodology (Stanley and Wise, 1983).

While there is no single ideological position uniting all feminists, most would accept that the subordination of women to men is the result of socioeconomic factors and not the effect of biological determinism. Hence, there is a commonly held belief that major social change culminating in women's liberation is possible. At present, feminism remains a vital and visible social movement, particularly successful in the area of cultural creativity. Despite media references to the Post-Feminist Era, the continuing social inequality of women and its eradication remains at the core of feminism in all its forms. See also MATRIARCHY.

feminist epistemology feminist theories of knowledge that suggest that traditional EPISTEMOLOGY has understated the importance of areas of knowledge that have been uppermost in feminine experience and in women's lives. According to Coward and Ellis (1977), traditional epistemological theory has been either too empiricist or too rationalist. In the view of Stanley and Wise (1983) and Hilary Rose (1986), feminist research methods and a truly feminist epistemology must reflect women's lived experience and place greater emphasis on affectual rationalities.

feminist theory(ies) theories (see also FEMINISM) that, especially with the political and social changes of the 1960s and 1970s, have challenged traditional conceptions of feminity and gender. As Humm (1989) points out, feminist theory "both challenges, and is shaped by the academy and society." It has been, above all, characteristic of the explosion of recent theories, including the work of Kate Millett (1970), Juliet Mitchell (1974), Sheila Rowbottom (1973), and many more, that these theories "describe the historical, psychological, sexual, and racial experiences of women," not just academically but as an indication of "how feminism can be a source of power." Because of this, tensions have existed between feminist theory and sociology, especially given that it has challenged the fact that much sociology has been a sociology of men, stating men's viewpoints. But feminist theory, insofar as it is not always in itself sociology, has contributed to an important reconstruction of sociological perspectives in many areas, including the SOCIOLOGY OF WORK, THE SOCIOLOGY OF THE FAMILY, and the analysis of CLASS and SOCIAL STRATIFICATION.

Ferguson, Adam (1723–1816), philosopher who was a central figure in the Scottish Enlightenment and a practitioner of sociology before Auguste COMTE coined the term. Ferguson, whose work influenced MARX among many others, was particularly interested in the process of historical change, which he understood within a broadly evolutionary framework (see EVOLU-TIONARY THEORY). *An Essay on the History of Civil Society* (1767) discusses the emergence of civilized society from prior states characterized as savage and barbaric, a theme that was to become familiar in the social theories of later thinkers.

For Ferguson, civil society was just that—refined, morally sensitive, and politically sophisticated. Yet the achievement of this condition was not a guarantee of its stability or longevity. What distinguished SAVAGERY from BARBARISM was the institution of private property, and it was the kind of egoistic, individualistic, and self-interested pursuit of wealth that this institution encouraged, progressively embedded as it was in the increasingly complex DIVISION OF LABOR and network of commercial relations characteristic of civil society, that could dissolve the social bonds between the individual and society and lead to the degeneration of civil society into political despotism. Like Emile DURKHEIM after him, Ferguson was acutely aware of the problems of social order posed by economic individualism; like Marx, he understood the alienating (see ALIENATION) effects of a capitalistic division of labor.

fetish 1. (in religious belief or magic) any object in which a spirit is seen as embodied, the worship of such an object being *fetishism* (see also ANIMISM). **2.** (more generally, especially in psychology and PSYCHOANALYSIS) any object of obsessive devotion or interest, especially objects or parts of the body other than those usually regarded as erogenous, for example, articles of clothing and feet.

feud relations of continuing mutual hostility between groups where one group has been wronged by the other (for example, one of its number has been murdered) and retribution is sought. Usually different lineage groups or clans are involved. Feuding relationships occur in situations of kin solidarity, in which an individual can rely on support from relatives. They occur particularly in societies, for example segmentary societies, that lack central political or legal authority, but where the fear of being involved in a feud acts as a major deterrent against wrongdoing. A retaliatory killing may end a feud, but other resolutions, such as the payment of compensation, may also bring it to an end.

feudal mode of production (Marxism) the mode of production that Marx saw as historically preceding capitalism in western Europe, and in which the relations of production were characterized by feudal landlords using political and legal power to extract an economic surplus from an unfree peasantry in the form of *feudal rent*. Marx saw this mode of production as emerging out of ANCIENT SOCIETY and the social forms introduced into western Europe by the Germanic tribes who invaded the Roman Empire. Land was held on condition of providing rent or service to an overlord.

Marx also saw the feudal mode of production as associated with a considerable development of productive forces with the introduction of mills, heavy-wheeled plows, and other innovations that increased agricultural productivity. For Marx, the growth of towns signified a new event in history since, for the first time, the relations of production in the towns differed from those on the land. Thus, unlike previous modes of production, the towns were not a continuation of the countryside, but the two were increasingly in opposition. This dynamic between the social relations of town and countryside, together with the development of trade and manufacturing in the towns, were important elements in Marx's analysis of the dynamic of the feudal mode of production and the TRANSITION FROM FEUDALISM TO CAPITALISM.

Feyerabend, Paul K. (1924–) Austrian-born philosopher of science who has worked in the United States and Britain as well as in Europe. Influenced by Wittgenstein's later philosophy, his main work has involved a repudiation of the FALSIFICATIONISM of Karl POPPER. His best-known works are *Against Method* (1975) and *Science in a Free Society* (1978), in which he rejects the idea of a universal scientific method.

Like Thomas KUHN, between whose work and Feyerabend's there exist many affinities, the account of science that emerges is one that places great emphasis on science as a flesh-and-blood activity, and a socially located one, that cannot be understood in formalistic or simple rationalistic terms. To those scientific rationalists, such as Popper and Imre Lakatos, who claim to have located a universal scientific method, Feyerabend's answer is that the only universal rule in science is that anything goes. One main reason why Feyerabend rejects falsificationism as a universal method is the INCOMMENSURABILITY of scientific terms and the THEORY-RELATIVITY, therefore, of the interpretation of any potentially refuting empirical data. Under these circumstances, Feyerabend's view is that pluralism and a proliferation of theories may often be the best policy, something that is not encouraged by falsificationism. A major part of Feyerabend's objective, especially in his later work, is to debunk the overly rationalist pretensions of modern science, its churchlike status in modern society, and the rule of experts to which this often gives rise. His aim is to return scientific judgments to the public domain, an argument he bases in part on J.S. MILL's *On Liberty*.

The frequent charge that Feyerabend's view of science involves irrationalism is one that his polemical and iconoclastic postures have sometimes tended to encourage. However, Feyerabend is often deliberately deceptive on these matters, preparing traps for dogmatic rationalists to mislead them into more dogmatic expressions of their own position. His own general position, however, is clearly not intended to promote a philosophical relativism, since this is simply another form of philosophical dogmatism. Instead, like Kuhn, Feyerabend wishes to emphasize the way that science and knowledge generally depend on a variety of methods. In this context, while knowledge claims are sometimes relative to a particular scientific paradigm or particular FORMS OF LIFE, as in a simple society, on other occasions more general claims to realism may also be mounted (in Feyerabend, 1981, he talks in these terms of "two argumentative chains"). Feyerabend's point, however, is that there exist no final rules of method and no single identifiable basis of rationality. The rationalists are wrong to suggest otherwise, betraying their own claims to a critical philosophy or to science. There is a similarity between Feyerabend's view and that of Richard Bernstein (1983), who has called for philosophical and sociological thinking on these matters to move "beyond objectivism or relativism" (compare also HABERMAS with whom Feyerabend himself identifies continuities, but also differences).

figuration or **configuration** the nexus of interdependencies between people, the chains of functions, and axes of tensions—both of cooperation and conflict—that can be identified in any social context (ELIAS, 1978). Figuration is the central analytical concept of Norbert Elias's FIGURATIONAL SOCIOLOGY. Elias rejects any model of man as *homo clausus*—the closed or discrete individual. Equally, however, he also rejects purely structuralist forms of explanation. It is the model of the dance or the game that Elias suggests best illustrates the focus he seeks to achieve in social analysis. The "image of the mobile figurations of interdependent people on a dance floor (or playing a sport-game) that makes it easier to imagine states, cities, families and also entire social systems as figurations" (ELIAS, 1939). See also CIVILIZING PROCESS, COURT SOCIETY.

figurational sociology the sociological approach of Norbert ELIAS and those influenced by his writing. The concept of FIGURATION is described by ELIAS (1939, 1970) and further reformulated in works by Goudsblom (1977), Dunning and Sheard (1979), and Mennell (1985). *Eliasian Sociology,* as it is sometimes called, has been more influential in Europe, especially in Holland and Elias's native Germany, than in North America and Britain. In Britain, the chief applications have been in the fields of SOCIOLOGY OF SPORT, SOCIOLOGY OF LEISURE, and CULTURAL STUDIES.

fixed-choice questionnaire a QUESTIONNAIRE in which all or most of the questions are fixed-choice, such that respondents are provided with a range of optional and often precoded answers and are asked to indicate which applies to them. While this type of questionnaire is useful in collecting standardized data, the use of fixed-choice questions is sometimes criticized for wrongly imposing the researcher's meanings (see MEASUREMENT BY FIAT, CICOUREL). See also CODING.

folk devils any stereotypical, socially constructed cultural types identified as socially threatening by other members of society; for example, in the 1960s, high-profile and newsworthy youth subcultures such as mods and rockers.

The folk devil is a cultural type akin to the hero, the villain, or the fool. The term was developed by Cohen (*Folk Devils and Moral Panics,* 1973), who explored the phenomenon of Mods and Rockers and sought to show

how social typing, or labeling, of rule breakers occurs. Such people are labeled as socially deviant and threatening, and all subsequent interpretation of their actions is in terms of the status to which they have been assigned. The study of folk devils and MORAL PANICS belongs to the wider study of the relations between the mass media of communication and the social construction of social problems. See also LABELING THEORY, DEVIANCE, DEVIANCE AMPLIFICATION.

folk society an ideal-typical (see IDEAL TYPE) conception of *primitive* or *simple* society. The term was applied by Redfield (1897–1958) to denote small, isolated groups, characterized and controlled informally by sacred values. Kinship relations predominate, and culture is transmitted orally. The moral order is paramount, resulting in a relatively static society that develops indigenously. Redfield contrasted folk society with its polar opposite, urban society, and conceived of societies as lying on a continuum between the two.

folkways the everyday customs of a social group or community (W. SUMNER, 1906). Folkways are contrasted with MORES, being less strongly sanctioned and less abstractly organized.

football hooliganism in Britain and elsewhere, the violent crowd disorder, and associated football-related disturbances away from football grounds, which first attracted major public and media attention in the 1960s. After initial attempts to explain football violence in terms of the psychological characteristics of the hooligans (Harrington, 1968), more recently a variety of sociological explanations have been suggested:

(a) opposition to the commercialization of football and the growing distance between players and the owners of clubs on the one hand, and ordinary working-class supporters on the other (Taylor, 1971);

(b) rather than true violence, behavior that appears disordered and threatening in fact often has its own rules of disorder and is ritualized (Marsh et al., 1978);

(c) deriving from LABELING THEORY and DEVIANCE AMPLIFICATION (see Cohen, 1973), hooliganism is seen as a media-amplified MORAL PANIC;

(d) since football violence has a long history, increased modern attention to it is a reflection of a civilizing tendency in society that has resulted in a lower societal tolerance of violence of the kind long associated with working-class conceptions of masculinity but now socially unacceptable (Dunning et al., 1988) (see also CIVILIZING PROCESS and (CON)FIGURATIONAL SOCIOLOGY).

Arguably, each of these explanations has some justification.

Fordism and post-Fordism methods of organizing production in advanced industrial societies. Although the fundamental reference point of both concepts is the production process, the terms are often used as a way of conveying associated social and political consequences. Thus, while Henry Ford's great initiative in manufacturing was the mass production of a standardized product at a price that would generate mass consumption, this also implied:

(a) capital-intensive, large-scale plant;

(b) an inflexible production process;

(c) rigid hierarchical and bureaucratic managerial structures;

(d) the use of semiskilled labor performing repetitive and routine tasks, often subject to the discipline of SCIENTIFIC MANAGEMENT;

(e) a tendency toward strong unionization and the vulnerability of production of industrial action;

(f) the protection of national markets.

Though Ford's innovations began in the interwar period with the production of cars, his methods were rapidly employed in other sectors of manufacturing and were increasingly seen as the organizational basis on which the advanced economies could continue to develop and, especially after World War II, prosper. It should also be noted that Fordist ideas of scale, centrality of control, standardization and mass consumption not only influenced the agenda of capitalist production, but also underpinned the nature of Soviet industrialization and the creation and delivery of welfare services in the free-market democracies.

Post-Fordism refers to the new economic possibilities opened up by the rise of microchip technology, computers and robotics in the production, and exchange of information and commodities. In contrast to Fordism, the distinguishing feature of the post-Fordist era is usually held to be the foundation of smaller units of enterprise, catering to segmented markets by the flexible production of specialized goods or services.

Historically, this technological agenda for consumer choice has coincided with the economic individualism of New Right politics, and may be one of the factors involved in the electoral success of this philosophy in a number of the leading economies of the Western world in the 1980s. Associated social and economic changes involved in the post-Fordist transition are:

(a) the decline of old manufacturing and smokestack industries, together with the emergence of the so-called sunrise computer-based enterprises);

(b) more flexible, decentralized forms of the labor process and of work organization;

(c) a reorganized labor market into a skill-flexible core of employees and a time-flexible periphery of low-paid insecure workers performing contract labor;

(d) a consequent decline of the traditional, unionized blue-collar working class, and the preeminence within the occupational structure of white-collar, professional, technical, managerial, and other service-sector employees;

(e) the feminization of many labor processes affected by the new technology;

(f) the promotion of types of consumption around the concept of individually chosen lifestyles, with an emphasis, therefore, on taste, distinctiveness, packaging, and appearance;

(g) the dominance and autonomy of multinational corporations in a global process of capitalist production;

(h) a NEW INTERNATIONAL DIVISION OF LABOR, based on the new flexibility, within which global production can be organized.

The precise dating of Fordism and post-Fordism is impossible. Indeed, debate continues about the utility and content of both concepts, and even about the existence of the transition itself. The least that can be said is that different sectors of national economies are differently affected (for example, the fast-food business continues to expand on classic Fordist principles in the so-called post-Fordist era), and that internationally the implications of post-Fordism are rather obviously different for economies such as that of the United States and that of Bangladesh.

formal and informal structure the distinction between procedures and communications in an organization that are prescribed by written rules, and those that depend more on ad hoc, personal interaction within work groups. The contrast between formal and informal structure or organization emerged from the debate about Weber's IDEAL TYPE of BUREAUCRACY within ORGANIZATION THEORY. Critiques of Weber's ideal type focused on the neglect of informal organization and the ways in which adherence to formal rules can lead to inefficiency and detract from the official goals of an organization. See also GOAL DISPLACEMENT.

The Hawthorne experiments were a famous example of the study of informal norms and expectations in work groups (see HAWTHORNE EFFECT, HUMAN RELATIONS SCHOOL). Studies in organizational sociology have demonstrated the ways in which informal practices bend or circumvent formal rules. From a functionalist perspective, such practices may be seen as conducive to organizational commitment (Katz, 1968), while other studies (for example, Beynon, 1973) emphasize the role of informal work groups as forms of resistance and opposition to the aims of management.

The distinction between formal and informal structure has also been elaborated and operationalized as a key structural variable in organizations. The extent of formalization has been measured empirically in comparisons between organizational types (see CONTINGENCY THEORY). This approach differs markedly from the study of rule negotiation and informal organizational cultures (see ETHNOGRAPHY).

formal and substantive rationality the distinction between the *formal rationality* of, say, economic action, as the "quantitative calculation or accounting that is technically possible and that is actually applied," and *substantive rationality,* which refers to rational social action, which occurs "under some criterion (past, present or potential) of ultimate value"

FORMAL SOCIOLOGY

(WEBER, 1922). Weber, although suspicious of the social implications of too narrow an application of the former (see RATIONALIZATION), nevertheless regarded the latter as so full of ambiguities as to render any possibility of its systematization out of the question, since it involves "an infinite number of possible value scales." It is in this context that Weber is sometimes regarded as an irrationalist. Other sociologists and philosophers (for example, see FRANKFURT SCHOOL OF CRITICAL THEORY, HABERMAS) have taken a different view and argued that improvements in substantive rationality must be a central focus of sociological effort. See also RATIONALITY.

formal sociology a theoretical approach in sociology that focuses attention on the universal recurring social forms that underlie the varying content of social interaction (see FORM AND CONTENT, DYAD AND TRIAD). Georg SIMMEL, whose sociology is most identified with this approach, referred to accounts of these forms as amounting to a "geometry of social life." Following KANT, to indicate that these possess an a priori, or necessary, character as well as an empirical expression, Simmel presented his forms as *synthetic a priori* concepts. Thus, these concepts are different from either conventional a priori concepts (which are purely analytic), or conventional empirical concepts (which are purely synthetic). Among the social forms and other general concepts discussed by Simmel are competition and conflict, SOCIABILITY, and the STRANGER.

Formal sociology differs from all-inclusive macroscopic theories such as FUNCTIONALISM and from merely particularistic MEANINGFUL SOCIOLOGY. While Simmel did not found a school in any strict sense, numerous later influences of his formal sociology can be identified, in the work of Von Weise, the CHICAGO SCHOOL, and GOFFMAN, for example. See also CONFLICT THEORY.

formal theory and formalization of theory the rendering of theoretical propositions relating to a particular phenomenon so that they form a set of logically and deductively interrelated propositions, and in which some of these propositions are seen as *axioms* or *premises,* from which the remainder can be deduced as *theorems.* Zetterberg (1965), for example, sought a *formalization* of Durkheim's *Division of Labor* (1893) in these terms, presenting the following ten propositions:

(a) the greater the division of labor, the greater the consensus;

(b) the greater the solidarity, the greater the number of associates per member;

(c) the greater the number of associates per member, the greater the consensus;

(d) the greater the consensus, the smaller the number of rejections of deviants;

(e) the greater the division of labor, the smaller the number of rejections of deviants;

(f) the greater the number of associates per member, the smaller the number of rejections of deviants;

(g) the greater the division of labor, the greater the solidarity;

(h) the greater the solidarity, the greater the consensus;

(i) the greater the number of associates per member, the greater the division of labor;

(j) the greater the solidarity, the smaller the number of rejections of deviants.

Zetterberg selects propositions (g)-(j) as the axioms from which the remainder can be deduced. While formalizations of this sort can have their uses, particularly in revealing logical weaknesses in the previous nonformal statement of a theory, they are not usually regarded as essential in science or in sociology.

form and content the distinction drawn, especially by SIMMEL, between the universal, recurring (abstract and a priori) *forms* of social interaction (for example, conflict or competition) and the variable *content* given these forms in specific social situations. FORMAL SOCIOLOGY investigates the similarities of form evident in all areas of social life. See also DYAD AND TRIAD, SOCIABILITY.

forms of life the multiplicity of circumscribed language-embedded social practices that, according to WITTGENSTEIN (1953), characterize social life. The socially located and conventional character of all languages is emphasized by Wittgenstein. In this interpretation of the nature and limits of language, all descriptions and accounts, and hence all SOCIAL ACTION are relative to language and to the social contexts in which a particular language is used. In a strict sense, there is nothing that can be said outside the language and context, so translations are problematic.

One consequence of Wittgenstein's view has been to encourage those forms of philosophy and social science that tend toward a relativistic conception of social studies. It also had a seminal influence on the construction of modern linguistic philosophy, which has emphasized the need for analysis of the many particular uses of language (see also SPEECH ACTS).

In sociology, the concept lends support to the notion that the main task of the discipline should be the MEANINGFUL UNDERSTANDING AND EXPLANATION of the distinctive beliefs and practices of particular societies or social movements (see WINCH), and an empathic understanding of historical societies (compare COLLINGWOOD).

Related to the above, the concept has also been important in arguments for a discontinuous view of scientific change. Thus both KUHN's and FEYERABEND's conception of *scientific paradigm*, and associated conceptions such as INCOMMENSURABILITY, draw explicitly on Wittgenstein's notion of forms of life. One of the best ways of describing what a scientific paradigm involves is that it is a form of life. See also TRUTH, RELATIVISM; compare HERMENEUTICS, FUSION OF HORIZONS.

Foucault, Michel (1926–1984) a major figure in the great French philosophical conversation on reason, language, knowledge, and power, whose work was influenced by MARX, FREUD, and NIETZSCHE. Although sometimes referred to as a structuralist (see STRUCTURALISM), he usually rejected this label. He is perhaps best seen as a post-structuralist in the sense that he wished to discover the nonrational scaffolding of reason, but without any commitment to either an underlying order or a finally determinant power in the construction. Working in the "wreckage of history," and enlarging on Nietzsche's linkage of knowledge with power, he sought to locate the varying discursive practices (see DISCOURSE(S) AND DISCOURSE FORMATIONS; EPISTEME) that at different places and times exert power over human bodies. Although he would not have seen himself as a sociologist, Foucault's historical studies of MADNESS, of medical knowledge, imprisonment, and sexuality have been of great interest to sociologists. He challenges the idea that knowledge leads to liberation. Instead, knowledge is seen more often as the basis of new means of social control (see also SURVEILLANCE). Since people are always striving to gain some control over their lives, resistance movements emerge, but there is no guarantee that these will lead to new bases of alienating social power.

frame of reference the basic assumptions delimiting the subject matter of any discipline or approach. For example, PARSONS and Shils (1951) state, "The frame of reference of the theory of action involves actors, a situation of action, and the orientation of the actor to that situation."

Frank, Andre Gunder (1929–) German-born economist who has held professorial posts in development studies and economics at numerous universities in Latin America, Europe, and the United States. While by training an economist, deriving some of his key concepts on ECONOMIC SURPLUS from the Marxist political economist Paul Baran, he is one of the most influential writers within the SOCIOLOGY OF DEVELOPMENT. Frank is best known for his theory of underdevelopment, which had an immediate impact on sociology through his critique, in *Sociology of Development and the Underdevelopment of Sociology* (1967a), of the structural-functionalist theory of development influenced by PARSONS and Almond and Coleman (1960). His best-known substantive work is on Latin America, especially *Capitalism and Underdevelopment in Latin America* (1967b) and the collection of articles in *Latin America: Underdevelopment or Revolution* (1969). In the 1970s and 1980s his work was taken up by the world system theorists, and Frank himself continued to write on global aspects of capitalism and its effects on Third World countries. His later writings, such as *Crisis: in the World Economy* (1980), have been less influential in sociology than his earlier works. See also CENTER AND PERIPHERY, METROPOLIS-SATELLITE, DEPENDENCY THEORY.

Frankfurt school of critical theory a grouping of left-wing thinkers and a style of radical social theory associated with members of the Frankfurt Institute for Social Research, which was founded in 1922 by Felix Weil, a political scientist with a strong commitment to Marxist radicalism. During the Nazi era the institute moved to New York, returning to Frankfurt in 1949. It was disbanded in 1969, but its influence continues, notably, in the recent work of Jürgen HABERMAS. Many leading left-wing theorists were formally associated with the school, including Theodor ADORNO, Walter BENJAMIN, Erich FROMM, Max HORKHEIMER (Director of the Institute 1931–58), Pollart, Neumann, and MARCUSE.

The distinctive approach of the Frankfurt school of critical theory was a type of neo-Marxist and New Left thinking that took issue with both Western POSITIVISM and Marxist SCIENTISM, and was at the same time critical of both Western capitalism and the forms of society created by bolshevik socialism. Among the important contributions made by Frankfurt school theorists have been:

(a) debate on an appropriate non-positivist epistemology for the social sciences;

(b) accounts of the dominant structural and cultural formations of capitalist and socialist societies;

(c) the combination of ideas drawn from Marx and Freud, resulting in radicalization of Freudian theory and provision of Marxism with a fuller theory of personality.

Such features of the work of members of the school were based above all on a recovery of the philosophical thinking of the young Marx and a revision of prevailing, official Soviet interpretations of Marxism that were seen by Frankfurt theorists as economistic and overly determinist.

Despite such shared themes, the work of members of the school does not result in a single unified view. Not only did individual theorists pursue their own distinctive lines of research but, collectively, members of the school continually shifted the terms of their analysis of modern society in response to the massive political and economic changes that have occurred since the institute's formation, including the rise of fascism and the eclipse of revolutionary movements in the West. At first, institute members expected the transformation of competitive capitalism into monopoly capitalism and fascism to lead directly to socialism. Later, the mood of some members of the school, notably Adorno and Horkheimer, became increasingly pessimistic, portraying the working class as ever more manipulated by the new modes of mass culture and as unlikely to develop revolutionary modes of consciousness in the future. Other theorists, especially Marcuse, remained more optimistic, identifying new sources of revolutionary consciousness outside the traditional proletariat, for example, ethnic minorities and students. Whether pessimistic or optimistic about the prospects of revolution, however, all Frankfurt school theorists can be identified as continuing to explore a shared theme: the perversion of the ideals of Enlightenment rationality by a narrow and dehumanizing technical rationality seen as embodied in both Western capitalist and Soviet Marxist forms of social organization, a technical rationality with which positivistic and scientistic forms of social science must be seen as colluding, and which critical theory must seek to combat. Useful accounts of the work of the school are provided by M. Jay *The Dialectical Imagination* (1973) and by D. Held *Introduction to Critical Theory* (1980).

free will the proposition that human beings are able to act according to the dictates of their own will (compare DETERMINISM). Doctrines of free will take a variety of forms, for example:

(a) human beings are morally responsible for their own actions—as in the Protestant world view;

(b) they have the capacity to carry out their own projects, and that to behave as if this were not so is to act in bad faith;

(c) they have a capacity for REFLEXIVITY, which is central to an understanding of both the nature of human action and the social construction of reality, for example, modern forms of symbolic interactionist and interpretive sociology, which emphasize human AGENCY.

Some forms of structural sociology and behavioristic psychology appear to leave no room for free will, being oriented toward discovering causal explanations of social actions and social structures. However, a recognition of actors' reasons and purposes can provide a role in explanations for the choices and decisions they make, as in buying goods or voting. These can alter outcomes, thus having causality, even though wider sociological influences are also involved. Causality in social events therefore need not preclude free will as long as the conception of this is not mystical, that is, does not imply that human action is exempt from ordinary conceptions of physical and social causality.

Equally, however, there is no necessity to use the term "free will" in sociology. Most of what can be stated in terms of free will can be well stated, and is arguably better stated, in terms of choice or decision, without recourse to such a potentially misleading term as free will. Examples might be: in drawing a distinction between situations in which we do not feel under compulsion to act in a certain way, and those where we feel that we have little or no choice; or in drawing attention to social outcomes that might have been different if actors who could have acted differently had done so, and those that appear to have been more structurally determined. See also CAUSE, EXPLANATION, STRUCTURE AND AGENCY, POWER, RATIONAL CHOICE THEORY, METHODOLOGICAL INDIVIDUALISM, UNANTICIPATED CONSEQUENCES OF SOCIAL ACTION.

frequency distribution the number of times each value of a variable occurs in a set of observations.

A frequency distribution is the simplest way of representing sociological observations. It consists of at least two columns: the left-hand one contains the values that a variable may take, and the right-hand one contains the number of times each value occurs. Additional right-hand columns might also be included to show the percentage distribution. In Fig. 7 the numbers of male and female respondents to a questionnaire are shown. See also HISTOGRAM.

Freud, Sigmund (1856–1939) the founding father of PSYCHOANALYSIS and one of the most important figures in the development of PSYCHOLOGY as a discipline. His theory of the structure of the personality, its development and its dynamics, evolved over the course of his life. He influenced many students and colleagues, who often developed aspects of his theory according to their own ideas (for example, see JUNG). This has meant the growth of several psychoanalytic schools that have taken up rather different positions to his own (see NEO-FREUDIANS).

Freud was responsible for the development of a theory of the mind and for a method of treatment for mental illness. His theory of the mind involves the division of mental experience into the conscious and the unconscious, and the structure of the personality into the ID, EGO, and SUPEREGO. He regarded the id as fundamental, containing the inherited biological disposition of the individual, with the ego and superego developing through the formative first five years of life. His theory, therefore, is developmental and describes the process of personality development as part of SOCIALIZATION. This process takes place in stages, and each stage must be worked through satisfactorily for a positive outcome to emerge. If problems are experienced in the correct resolution of a stage, then personality problems occur and cause adult maladjustments. It is then that psychoanalysis may be necessary to uncover the causes within the unconscious, bringing them to consciousness, and so resolving the problem.

Elements of Freud's theory have become accepted psychological concepts—the unconscious and the role of early experience in personality development are particularly important—and the widely used method of talking therapy has developed from his original patient/analyst dialogue. Freud's concepts have also been widely influential in sociology and philosophy, see for example MARCUSE, LACAN, FROMM, NEO-FREUDIANS.

friendship a relationship between persons well known to each other that involves liking and affection and may also involve mutual obligations such as loyalty. In contrast to kinship or other ASCRIBED STATUSES, friendship relationships are difficult to specify with precision since they are, above all, characterized by their fluid and voluntary nature and vary greatly in dura-

Sex	Number	Relative Frequency	Adusted Frequency
Male	2,300	56.1%	60.5%
Female	1,500	36.6%	37.5%
Unknown	300	7.3%	—
Total	4,100	100.0%	100.0%

Fig. 7. **Frequency distribution.** See main entry.

tion and intensity. As stated by Seymour-Smith (1986), "The study of friendship is part of the study of social networks, of RECIPROCITY, and of relationships created by individuals in the social space that is left underter-mined by the system of kin or other obligatory relationships." From the limited amount of research on friendship in modern societies that has been done, it can be suggested that friendship is a significant factor in personal well-being, but that most adults regard themselves as having relatively few close friends (Suttles, 1970). However, there are marked gender differ-ences, women commonly having more close friends than men, and regard-ing these relationships as more central in their lives. Among children, friendship and relations with peers play an important part in the process of SOCIALIZATION. See also PEER GROUP, SOCIOMETRICS.

Fromm, Erich (1900–1980) German-born radical social psychologist and psychoanalytical theorist, and one-time member of the FRANKFURT SCHOOL OF CRITICAL THEORY, who moved to America in 1934. In his best-known book, *Escape from Freedom* (1941), Fromm argued that human beings often lack the psychological resources to cope with individual freedom, suggesting that the rise of fascism could be, at least in part, explained by a longing for a return to the authoritarianism of pre-individualistic society. The solution proposed by Fromm was spontaneous love: the affirmation of others. In *The Sane Society* (1955), he argued that technological growth without altruism would be socially destructive. Fromm wrote many other works reiterating these, his main themes. See also NEO-FREUDIANS.

front region any social context or public locale in which a specific perfor-mance is required of, or produced by, SOCIAL ACTORS, in order to create or preserve a particular impression, for example, the doctor's office or the lec-turer's podium. Compare BACK REGION. See also ROLE, DRAMATURGY, GOFFMAN.

frustration-aggression hypothesis the theory that frustration increases the likelihood of aggressive behavior, and aggressive behavior results from frustration. This involves a circular argument, and original proponents of the theory, in fact, also accepted aggression as an innate drive (see FREUD). A modified version of the theory takes account of the observation that not all aggressive behavior involves frustration and not all frustration results in aggression: behavior is also affected by situational factors and by SOCIALIZA-TION. Nevertheless, the link between frustration and aggression is still accepted.

function 1. *(n.)* the consequence for a social system of a social occurrence, where this occurrence is regarded as making an essential contribution to the working and maintenance of this system. See FUNCTIONALISM, STRUC-TURAL-FUNCTIONALISM, PARSONS, FUNCTIONALIST EXPLANATION, FUNCTION-AL PREREQUISITES, POSTULATE OF FUNCTIONAL INDISPENSABILITY. **2.** *(vb.)* to fulfill a societal requirement for the continuation and effective working of a society, social system, etc.

A distinction is also made between consequences of social action that are *intended* and recognized by the actors involved, and consequences that are *unintended* and unrecognized by the actors involved. See MANIFEST AND LATENT FUNCTIONS, MERTON.

functional alternative or **functional equivalent** any institutional arrangements that fulfil the same FUNCTION, or broadly the same function, in answering the essential needs of a society or social system. Thus, secular CIVIL RELIGIONS (see also SOCIOLOGY OF RELIGION) may perform the same basic functions (for example, in providing social integration) as conventional religions. The conditions for identification of functional equivalents are controversial, however, and may be difficult to satisfy (see FUNCTIONAL(IST) EXPLANATION). See also FUNCTIONALISM, FUNCTIONAL PREREQUISITES OR FUNCTIONAL IMPERATIVES, POSTULATE OF FUNCTIONAL INDISPENSABILITY OR UNIVERSAL FUNCTIONALISM.

functional imperatives see FUNCTIONAL PREREQUISITES.

functional indispensability see POSTULATE OF FUNCTIONAL INDISPENSABILITY.

functionalism theories in sociology and social anthropology that explain social institutions primarily in terms of the FUNCTIONS they perform. To speak of the function of something is to account for a social activity or phenomenon by referring to its consequences for the operation of some other social activity, institution, or society as a whole. Modern functionalists treat societies as wholes or SYSTEMS of interacting and self-regulating parts.

In the 19th century, social thinkers theorized about society in terms of an *organic analogy*. As Herbert SPENCER wrote: "All kinds of creatures are alike insofar as each exhibits cooperation among its components for the benefit of the whole; and this trait, common to them, is a trait common also to societies." The idea of studying social life in terms of social functions was also adopted in early 20th-century British SOCIAL ANTHROPOLOGY. Both RADCLIFFE-BROWN and MALINOWSKI used the concept of function to indicate that society could be conceptualized as made up of *interdependent parts* that operate together to meet different social *needs*.

In the 1950s and early 1960s, structural-functionalism was the dominant theoretical perspective in North American sociology. In the 1950s, the functionalist approach was associated especially with a form of SYSTEMS THEORY (see also STRUCTURAL-FUNCTIONALISM), articulated by Talcott PARSONS at Harvard University. Parsons' theories were widely influential, though there was dissent from other functionalists (see MERTON) and from nonfunctionalists (for example, MILLS). In the 1970s and 1980s, functionalism's star waned, partly as a result of internal theoretical weaknesses, but also from changes in the political climate (see also GOULDNER).

One central area of debate has concerned the nature of FUNCTIONALIST EXPLANATION. A further major area of debate has concerned its treatment of social order, social conflict, and social change. One criticism is that the functionalist perspective neglects the independent agency of individual social actors, in general tending to operate with an oversocialized conception of the human subject (see OVERSOCIALIZED CONCEPTION OF MAN and ETHNOMETHODOLOGY). Social ROLES are seen as essentially prescribed by NORMS and static expectations of behavior, rather than actively taken and recreated through *interaction* with others (compare SYMBOLIC INTERACTIONISM). It has also often been suggested that a functionalist perspective has difficulty in accounting for social conflict and instability.

All these criticisms of functionalism have some substance, but are also an overstatement. Parsons in particular sought to combine an action frame of reference with an emphasis on system and social functions. And, while often concentrating on the conditions of social order, including the functions of SOCIAL CONFLICT, both historically (for example, as for Spencer) as well as in Parson's later work, functionalism has usually also sought to combine the analysis of social order with an EVOLUTIONARY THEORY of social change: a model of increasing SOCIAL DIFFERENTIATION, of increasing functional adaption of society (see also EVOLUTIONARY SOCIOLOGY, EVOLUTIONARY UNIVERSALS). These models of social change have in turn been widely criticized (see MODERNIZATION, DEPENDENCY THEORY), but their existence shows that it is as a *particular* model of change, rather than a theory that entirely neglects change, that functionalism must be discussed.

Despite the many criticisms, both the term "function" and the functionalist perspective retain widespread significance in sociology, for they involve a concern with the crucial issue of the interrelationship of parts to wholes in human society and the relationship between SOCIAL STRUCTURE and human AGENCY, as well as issues of social and social change.

functional(ist) explanation EXPLANATION of the persistence of any feature of a SOCIETY or SOCIAL SYSTEM—and at the same time an explanation for the persistence of the society or social system itself—in which this feature, usually along with others, is seen as making an essential contribution to the maintenance of the society or social system. Thus, perversely, according to some commentators, an aspect of the functionalist explanation is that the consequences of an activity are in part an explanation of its own existence.

Often functional(ist) explanation involves a recourse to *organic analogies*, in which societies or social systems are seen as akin to biological organisms in which specified organs can be identified that fulfill specific system needs. For example, just as the function of the heart is to circulate the blood, the indispensable function of government may be suggested as establishing and implementing policies for society (see also FUNCTIONAL PREREQUISITES OR FUNCTIONAL IMPERATIVES, EVOLUTIONARY SOCIOLOGY). Alternatively, analogies with servomechanical systems may be proposed. See also SYSTEM, SYSTEMS THEORY, CYBERNETICS.

According to Hempel (1959), insofar as it proves an adequate basis for explanation, functional(ist) explanation can be a form of deductive nomo-logical explanation (see COVERING LAW MODEL AND DEDUCTIVE NOMOLOGICAL EXPLANATION), possessing the following characteristics (where "i" stands for any item or trait, within a system "s" at a time "t," and where "c" stands for the conditions or setting in which the system operates):

(a) at a time t, s functions adequately in a setting of kind c, characterized by specific internal and external conditions (statement of initial conditions);

(b) s functions adequately in a setting of kind c only if a certain necessary condition, n, is satisfied (law);

(c) if trait i were present in s then, as an effect, condition n would be satisfied (law);

(d) (hence) at a time t, trait i is present in s (the explanandum).

Criticisms of proposed examples of functional explanation are made by Hempel and others on a number of grounds:

(a) human societies and social systems are different from biological organisms in that they lack precise boundaries, change in form over time, do not exist as clearly demarcated species, are not born and do not die in the clear-cut way in which biological organisms do, and thus do not have clear-cut needs or functional requirements or clearly identified organs fulfilling these. Thus, a major problem exists in specifying the conditions for the survival, efficiency, adjustment, adaptation, etc. of social systems in general, or of types of social systems;

(b) no one has yet provided an adequate overall functionalist and evolutionary account of human societies that identifies the units selected or confirms that institutions have in fact evolved on the basis of such units;

(c) even if broad functional needs can be identified, any number of different items or traits may fulfill the required functions, for example, a system of social welfare in modern societies may be provided by the state, by private insurance, or by political parties or criminal organizations, or any mixture of these (see FUNCTIONAL ALTERNATIVES, MERTON, POSTULATE OF FUNCTIONAL INDISPENSABILITY);

(d) even if it might explain the persistence of a system trait or institution, for example, in terms of its present contribution, functional explanation is no substitute for a historical causal explanation of how an institutional arrangement came into existence, especially where evolutionary accounts are not seen as providing an adequate account;

(e) given the problems outlined in (a), (b), and (c) and also that human social systems are open systems, functional explanation adds nothing to causal or purposive explanations (see Fig. 8) (GIDDENS, 1976b). In particular, the argument can be made against functional explanation, that would-be functional explanations for the persistence of institutions in sociology fail to identify mechanisms that link the suggested functional need with the appearance of its claimed consequences (see also SOCIAL REPRODUCTION).

FUNCTIONAL(IST) EXPLANATION

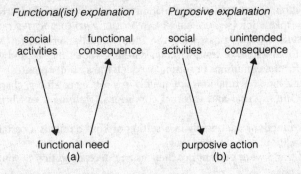

Fig. 8. **Functional(ist) explanation.** In contrast with other kinds of explanation, e.g., purposive explanation (b), functional explanation (a) explains the occurrence of a phenomenon in terms of the functional needs of a system. One argument against functional explanation is that where the "mechanisms" of the system in question remain unclear, reference to "system needs" adds nothing to purposive explanations and will mislead. Unintended consequences may still be acknowledged, but not system needs.

Thus, taking this all into account, for GIDDENS, a so-called latent function, such as that of the Hopi rain dance in providing social integration and a unitary value system for a small society, can be perfectly well restated without loss, as *simply* an unintended outcome. We only mystify the phenomenon by suggesting that functional needs account for this. In such circumstances the concept of function is redundant. We may use the term "function" to refer to the intended purpose of a machine, etc., for example, the function of a ballcock is to regulate the amount of water supplied to a toilet. In the same way, the functions of a political party, where intended functions are involved, may also be properly referred to. But reference to latent functions or to system needs in other terms than with reference to intentions, as in functional explanation of the above type, remains obscure;

(f) in general, one may always define an institution or trait as essential to a particular system, but this risks becoming a tautology, and merely descriptive rather than explanatory, unless some further independent reasons can be given for regarding the relations between the system and the institutions identified as functionally significant.

Notwithstanding such criticisms, and whatever the problems of functional explanation, functional analysis remains a common feature of sociological accounts. The notion that particular societies or social systems have particular *requirements* seems inescapable in sociological analysis (compare Davis, 1948), even if these cannot be precisely pinned down. Whether these requirements should be called functional requirements, risking misleading biological analogies, would seem to be the issue.

functional(ist) theory of religion theoretical accounts of RELIGION that explain its origins, and also its continuation, in terms of the contribution it makes to society (see also FUNCTION, FUNCTIONAL(IST) EXPLANATION). The most influential of these theories by far is DURKHEIM's, and his ideas were further explored by RADCLIFFE-BROWN. MALINOWSKI's theory is also functionalist, and in many ways a broadly functionalist account of religion—albeit with marked variations in emphasis—is behind many of the mainstream sociological accounts of religion on offer. If function is used in a general sense, functional(ist) theories of religion extend from COMTE and the earlier evolutionary sociologists to modern functionalism, and even include Marxism. Though regarding it as eventually dispensable, MARX saw religion as "the opiate of the proletariat," in that it performs social and individual functions.

In its modern form, the functional(ist) theory of religion has two strands: within modern structural-functionalism, and within structuralist theories. There also exist numerous theories and empirical accounts that are presented as counter-theories.

In modern structural-functionalism (especially in the work of PARSONS, the functionalist theory of religion most directly deriving from Durkheim), three main functions of religion are identified that correspond to the three MODES OF MOTIVATIONAL ORIENTATION formulated in Parsonian theory:

(a) provision of a central, ultimately unifying, belief system—the cognitive function of religion;

(b) provision of ceremony and RITUAL, seen as playing a central role in fostering social solidarity—the affective dimension of religion.

(c) enunciation of ethical principles, and along with this bolstering ethical values by positive and negative sanctions—the evaluative aspect of religion;

All of these contribute to the essential role religion is seen as playing in the maintenance of social solidarity (compare Durkheim's similar emphasis—see CIVIL RELIGION). Durkheim's notion that religious beliefs are direct representations of society, however, is dropped.

Structuralist theories of religion have also built upon Durkheim's functionalism, but in a different way from structural functionalism. In these, it is the "sociology of knowledge" aspect of Durkheim's theory, played down by structural-functionalists, which remains more central, for example, accounts of the part played by MYTHOLOGIES in the organization of social activities or of kinship (see LÉVI-STRAUSS).

A counterbalance to either functionalist or structuralist theories, with their emphasis on general outcomes, exists in the many empirical studies of religion that explore the effects of religion in a more ad hoc way, that is, are not tied to any one set of general assumptions.

As a relatively loose general framework involving accounts of the contribution made by religion to society, functionalism retains a wide currency, especially its general injunction to look for latent function (see MANIFEST AND LATENT FUNCTIONS) and UNANTICIPATED CONSEQUENCES OF SOCIAL ACTION. The fact that religion divides as well as unites is *not* necessarily a problem, for this can be accommodated within functionalist theory, since it is the provision of social solidarity by religion that both unites and divides societies. Rather, the main problem is in achieving a *precise* meaning when claiming that religion fulfills functional needs. Once one begins to talk of FUNCTIONAL ALTERNATIVES for conventional religion (for example, civil religion or modern international sport), a functionalist account tends to lose out in arguments involving its most central claim, that religion provides for *universal* human needs, which only religion can answer.

functional(ist) theory of social stratification an account of the origins and persistence of SOCIAL STRATIFICATION in terms of the contribution this makes to human societies. The theory is provided by modern US functionalist sociologists, especially Davis and Moore (1945). For Davis and Moore, social stratification comes into existence as an institutionalized form and persists as the "device by which societies ensure that the most important positions" are "filled by the most qualified persons." Those positions that carry the greatest rewards and the highest rank, are those "that have the greatest importance for society" and also require the "greatest training or talent." Together, those two factors interact to determine the precise form of any system of stratification. As societies evolve, so do their specific requirements for a system of social stratification (for example, from priests to specialists in high tech), but new requirements do not result in the elimination of social stratification.

Criticisms of the functional(ist) theory make a number of main points (especially see Tumin, 1953):

(a) it provides no adequate discussion of the way in which differences in rewards and status arise simply from the operation of POWER. Regarding the correlation between income and education, for example, there are three components that might explain this correlation:

(i) superiority in skills;

(ii) social background and/or social values;

(iii) native abilities. The first of these might conceivably also incorporate the other two, but only if labor markets are fully competitive. The argument against the functionalist theory is that usually labor markets are not fully competitive, with factors such as ascription and CULTURAL CAPITAL often playing a role in the determination of incomes and status;

(b) the assessment of functional needs is also suspect, tending to involve a circular argument that the best rewarded in society are also the most important/scarcest in supply, with no clear independent demonstration of their social indispensability;

(c) no indication is given of why stratification *must* involve differential financial rewards or steep hierarchies of status, rather than more variegated differences in individual prestige, since Davis and Moore themselves suggest that "humor and diversion" and "self-respect and ego expansion" may alone serve to motivate social actors. Thus, the case against the possibility of a far more equal society has not been made by the functional(ist) theory;

(d) no adequate account is taken of the way in which social stratification inhibits participation in education and the achievement of social ends. Davis and Moore do suggest the functional inappropriateness of too great an emphasis on ascription in modern societies. However, they fail to discuss how all systems of social stratification tend to generate such ascriptive elements.

Functionalists seek to reply to such criticisms by arguing, as did DURKHEIM, that anything that becomes established in society is likely to perform essential functions. However, as Durkheim agreed—especially in relation to particular types of society, when the evolution of that societal type is incomplete—an independent argument for functional importance is essential. The argument against the functionalist theory of social structure is that such an independent case has not been forthcoming.

The message is not so much that functional analysis of social stratification is, in principle, impossible, but that this needs to be handled with greater caution. See also FUNCTIONALIST EXPLANATION.

functional prerequisites the provisions that all societies are required to make in order for any society to come into existence or to survive. The identification of functional prerequisites—also known as *functional imperatives*—is controversial.

As formulated by Aberle et al. (1950)—who first defined society as "a group of human beings sharing a self-sufficient system of action that is capable of existing longer than the life span of an individual, the group being recruited at least in part by sexual reproduction of the members"—nine functional prerequisites can be identified:

(a) provision for adequate relationship to the environment and for sexual recruitment;

(b) role differentiation and role assignment;

(c) communication;

(d) shared cognitive organization;

(e) shared articulation of goals;

(f) the normative regulation of means;

(g) the regulation of affective expression;

(h) socialization;

(i) effective control of disruptive forms of behavior.

A different formulation of functional prerequisites is the four-fold set of functional problems identified by PARSONS (1983) (see SUBSYSTEMS MODEL).

Apart from the functionalist bias toward normative integration in all such proposals of functional prerequisites (see OVERSOCIALIZED CONCEP-

TION OF MAN), a general problem in such formulations is in reaching agreement on their exact number and detailed formulation. GIDDENS (1976b), for example, points out that Aberle et al.'s functional prerequisites are either tautologies and follow logically from these authors' initial definition of society, or else they involve assumptions about adaptive capacity that are contentious and arguably misplaced in sociology. Compare also EVOLUTIONARY UNIVERSALS.

fusion of horizons the merging of perspectives that in HERMENEUTICS is seen as an essential feature of the understanding of an unfamiliar TEXT or culture (Gadamer, 1960). For Gadamer, such "understanding is not a matter of forgetting our own horizons of meanings and putting ourselves within that of the alien text or the alien society" (Outhwaite, 1985), therefore not a matter of detachment; instead, it involves a "*rapprochement* between our present world ... and the different world we seek to appraise."

The concept stands opposed to two ideas: (a) that we can expect to understand and explain alien cultures and societies by imposing an external grid, and (b) that we can never hope to understand (or translate) such ideas. Rather truth can be the outcome of such a fusion.

The idea of INTERSUBJECTIVITY as the basis of scientific knowledge or political agreements has a similar basis (compare FEYERABEND, HABERMAS), although the fusion of horizons for Gadamer is far from being the basis for emancipatory knowledge it is for Habermas. However, the similarity indicates that Gadamer's hermeneutics does not necessarily involve the degree of RELATIVISM sometimes suggested.

futurology 1. the purported science of prognosis (Flechtheim, 1965). **2.** any attempt to undertake long-term, large-scale social and economic forecasting. Rather than being defined as a separate science, efforts to illuminate the future are better seen as an aspect of the numerous individual social sciences, with sociology often playing a central role.

According to Daniel BELL (1965, 1973), the varieties of social-science activity that can be involved in statements about the future must be carefully distinguished, including:

(a) academically grounded general speculation;

(b) extrapolation of existing trends or tendencies, or probability generalizations, based on the existing behavior of known populations or natural phenomena;

(c) theoretical general models of the kind associated with Marxism, and developmental social-evolutionary theories of various kinds, including models of exponential growth;

(d) prediction of specific events.

As suggested by POPPER, the distinction must be drawn between prophecy (for example, claims to predict the future made by popular versions of Marxism or evolutionary theory) and scientific prediction, which is always a matter of universal conditional statements and "if, then" in form (see also

HISTORICISM). Apart from our knowledge of what Bell refers to as "structural certainties" (for example, the date of the next US presidential election), exact prediction is rare in the social sciences, given the complexity of the variables involved, including human choice and the fact that most social systems are open systems. The various attempts to chart future possibilities remain valuable, however, as long as the limitations and caveats that must attach to them are not ignored.

G

Galbraith, John K. (1908–), Canadian-born US economist, social commentator, and author of best-selling books, whose analysis of modern capitalist society is at once a critique of modern society and of orthodox academic economics. Galbraith's approach places him in the tradition of *institutional economics*, an approach that emphasizes the study of the real world and historical economic institutions, rather than the creation of abstract economic models, as the best route to an understanding of economic life. Not surprisingly, the significance of his work has not always been accepted by more orthodox economists.

Among his most influential works was *The Affluent Society* (1958). In this, he took the view that modern industrial societies such as that of the United States had moved beyond economic scarcity, but had failed to adjust their economic theory or their economic practice to enable adequate resources to be devoted to public expenditure. Alongside the existence of "private affluence," Galbraith saw "public squalor."

Earlier, in *American Capitalism* (1952), Galbraith had advanced a conception of the modern American economy as governed by countervailing forces, meaning that America was neither a conventional market-driven capitalist economy nor a system directly subject to public control. This same general theme was carried forward in *The New Industrial State* (1967), in which Galbraith identified power in America as being in the hands of a new *technostructure*.

Galbraith's ideas contributed to the climate in which public expenditure increased in the 1960s and 1970s. It might appear that in the 1980s his work began to become outmoded by the shift back to a market economy and new restrictions on public expenditure. Alternatively, his work can be seen as providing a continuing critique of restrictions on public expenditure.

Garfinkel, Harold (1917–), US sociologist and founder of the theoretical and specialist approach of ETHNOMETHODOLOGY.

Influenced especially by SCHUTZ, Garfinkel's contention in *Studies in Ethnomethodology* (1967) is that conventional sociology has neglected the study of the ethnomethods (*members' methods*) possessed by ordinary members of society and used by them in the ordinary conduct of their social lives. Garfinkel claimed to have revealed the existence of these methods by noting the outcome of informal experiments in which, for example, he encouraged his students to act as paying guests in their own homes. According to Garfinkel, what these and similar experiments demonstrate is the existence of "taken-for-granted assumptions" in social interaction and also the indexicality (see INDEXICAL EXPRESSION) of members' ACCOUNTS. Along with the members' creative capacity, this latter feature of members' accounts is seen as invalidating the scientific stance of much conventional sociology. See also DEGRADATION CEREMONY.

gatherings any situations, those "strips" of time and space, in which SOCIAL ACTORS come together in face-to-face interaction (GOFFMAN, 1963). In moving into, or initiating, such contexts of copresence, social actors make themselves available, a process involving mutual monitoring of one another's actions. Gatherings may be either fleeting, including the polite discourse of routine greetings, or longer lasting, in which the paraphernalia in which they are located may be planned and regularized, for example, the fixed timing and formal arrangement of tables and chairs in a seminar. But all gatherings, however trivial they may seem, are implicated in larger social structures and in turn have implications for these social structures.

Geisteswissenschaften and ***Naturwissenschaften*** (German) general terms to refer to the human and social sciences (the sciences of the spirit) and the natural or physical sciences. The German usage, especially by DILTHEY, seems to have derived in part from a translation of John Stuart MILL'S distinction between the moral and the physical sciences. The distinction is now mainly associated with the view that the human and social sciences, since they deal with human meanings and purposes, must be constituted and must operate using different methods than those appropriate to the physical sciences (see MEANINGFUL UNDERSTANDING AND EXPLANATION, VERSTEHEN, HERMENEUTICS, RICKERT, WINDELBAND, WEBER).

Gellner, Ernest (1925–) Czech-born, English social theorist, social philosopher, and social anthropologist whose wide-ranging, often iconoclastic, writings have included critical discussion of analytical philosophy (*Words and Things*, 1959), ethnographic studies (*The Saints of the Atlas*, 1969), studies of psychoanalysis (*The Psychoanalytic Movement*, 1985), studies of nationalism (*Nations and Nationalism*, 1983), studies of Soviet thought (*State and Society in Soviet Thought*, 1988), as well as general studies of social change and historical development (*Plough, Sword and Book*, 1988), and, in addition, numerous articles and books on methodological topics (for example, *Relativism in the Social Sciences*, 1985). Running through all these works is a persistent defense of rationalism, in which changes in knowledge are seen as decisive in social change. Gellner has been especially impatient with approaches within the social sciences deriving from WITTGENSTEIN's second philosophy, which he presents as a "new idealism." See also WINCH, EPISODIC CHARACTERIZATION.

Gemeinschaft and ***Gesellschaft*** the German sociologist TÖNNIES' (1887) twin IDEAL-TYPE concepts referring to contrasting types of social relationship and, by extension, types of society. *Gemeinschaft* (usually translated as "community") refers to relationships that are spontaneous and affective, tend to be related to a person's overall social status, are repeated or long enduring (as in relationships with kin), and occur in a context involving cultural homogeneity. Characteristically, these are the relationships within families and within simpler, small-scale, and premodern societies, including peasant societies. *Gesellschaft* (usually translated as "association") refers to relationships that are individualistic, impersonal, competitive, calculative, and contractual, often employing explicit conceptions of rationality and efficiency. Relationships of this type are characteristic of modern urban industrial societies in which the DIVISION OF LABOR is advanced. For Tönnies, such relationships involved a loss of the naturalness and mutuality of earlier *Gemeinschaft* relationships. See also COMMUNITY.

Tönnies derived aspects of his concept from Henry MAINE's distinction between status and contract. Compare also Max Weber's TYPES OF SOCIAL ACTION and Talcott Parsons' PATTERN VARIABLES.

gender differentiation the process in which biological differences between males and females are assigned social significance and are used as a means of social classification. In most known cultures, anatomical sex is used as a basis for gender differentiation. In some cultures, the biological differences between sexes may be exaggerated and in others minimized. Thus, the biological differences between the sexes cannot be regarded as having inherent or universal meaning.

gender identity the sense of self associated with cultural definitions of masculinity and feminity. Gender identity is not so much acted out as subjectively experienced. It is the psychological internalization of masculine or feminine traits. Gender identity arises out of a complex process of interaction between self and others. The existence of transvestite and transsexual identities indicates that gender does not depend on sex alone, and arises from the construction of gender identities.

gender ideology a system of ideas whereby gender differences and GENDER STRATIFICATION receive social justification, including justification in terms of natural differences or supernatural beliefs. As Oakley (1974) has argued, sociologists have sometimes tended to reproduce the commonsense ideologies surrounding gender differences in an uncritical way.

gender role the social expectations arising from conceptions surrounding gender and the behavioral expression of these, including forms of speech, mannerisms, demeanor, dress, and gesture (see also GENDER IDENTITY). Masculine and feminine ideas are often deemed to be mutually exclusive, and in some societies the role behaviors may be polarized, for example, the equation of passivity with the feminine role, and activity with the masculine role. Prescriptions concerning gender role behavior are particularly apparent in the sexual division of labor in male and female work situations (see also DUAL LABOR MARKET).

gender stratification any process by which gender becomes the basis of SOCIAL STRATIFICATION, in which the perceived differences between the genders become ranked and evaluated in a systematic way. Stratification by gender was often rendered invisible, or misrepresented, by earlier sociologists. Frequently, gender stratification has been subsumed under social class or ethnicity. The importance of gender as a system of stratification, particularly as a system in which feminized persons are ranked and rewarded below masculinized persons, has been mainly stressed by sociologists influenced by feminism (see FEMINISM, FEMINIST THEORY). Feminist sociologists, for example, have employed the concept of PATRIARCHY in conceptualizing and analyzing the present and historical oppression of women.

generalized other the general concept of "other SOCIAL ACTORS" that individuals abstract from the common elements they find in the attitudes and actions of others. According to G.H. MEAD, whose term this is, it is by "taking the role of the generalized other" that the individual internalizes shared values and thus is able to engage in complex cooperative processes.

general systems theory see SYSTEMS THEORY.

generation 1. a body of people who were born in the same period, variously defined. **2.** the period between the birth of such a group and the birth of their children, for demographic purposes usually accepted as 30 years.

MANNHEIM distinguished between generation as location (a *birth cohort*), and generation as actuality, where there is a sense of belonging to a group because of shared experience or feeling, for example, the Sixties Generation, the Vietnam Generation. See also AGE SET, AGE GROUP, AGING, LIFE COURSE.

geographical determinism any analytical viewpoint suggesting that different patterns of human culture and social organization are determined by geographical factors such as climate, terrain, etc. The view has a long ancestry, stretching back to the ancient Greeks. However, although many social theorists, for example, MONTESQUIEU, have strongly emphasized the importance of geography, most see it as one factor influencing social arrangements, not usually a predetermining one. Compare CULTURAL MATERIALISM, WITTFOGEL.

gerontology the study of AGING and of elderly people. It focuses on the societal consequences of a rising proportion of older people in the population, the personal experience of aging—particularly in societies where youthfulness is prized—and the social status of older people. Issues of current sociological debate are the degree to which the problems associated with old age are socially produced through agist ideologies that deny status and resources to older people and result in enforced dependency through retirement and inadequate social services; historically and culturally, comparative studies of the social status of older age groups; the systems of social classification that overlie chronological aging. An emerging issue is the frequent invisibility of age as a theoretical issue for sociology in the same way that gender was until recently. See also OLD AGE.

Gesellschaft see GEMEINSCHAFT AND GESELLSCHAFT.

ghetto a segregated area of a city characterized by common ethnic and cultural characteristics. The term originated in the Middle Ages in Europe to describe areas of cities in which Jews were constrained to live. The term was adopted more generally in sociology by the CHICAGO SCHOOL, and particularly by Wirth (*The Ghetto*, 1928). "Ghetto" has now taken on a meaning that implies not only homogeneity of ethnic and cultural population, but also the concentration of socially disadvantaged and minority groups in the most impoverished inner city areas. The term is often used in emotive, racist, and imprecise ways.

Giddens, Anthony (1938–) British sociologist who, in a prolific career, has established himself, first, as a leading interpreter of classical sociological theory (for example, *Capitalism and Moden Social Theory*, 1971), secondly, as a significant contributor to modern analysis of class and stratification (for example, in *The Class Structure of the Advanced Societies*, 1973), and, thirdly, over the last decade, with his formulation of STRUCTURATION THEORY, as an important general sociological theorist in his own right. In this most recent phase, beginning with *New Rules of Sociological Method* (1976) and *Central Problems of Sociological Theory* (1979), and continuing with *The Constitution of Society* (1984), he developed an account of the interrelation of STRUCTURE AND AGENCY (see also DUALITY OF STRUCTURE) in which primacy is granted to neither. In a continuing series of works, including *A Contemporary Critique of Historical Materialism* (1981) and *The Nation State and Violence* (1985), this conception was then applied to a critique of existing evolutionary and developmental theories, and the provision of an alternative account of social change to replace these. See also LIFE-WORLD, STRATIFICATION MODEL OF SOCIAL ACTION AND CONSCIOUSNESS, POWER, EVOLUTIONARY SOCIOLOGY, TIME-SPACE DISTANCIATION, INTERSOCIETAL SYSTEMS, NATION STATE.

gift exchange or **gift relationship** a reciprocal relationship of exchanging goods and services. Marcel Mauss (1872–1950) wrote a seminal book, *The Gift* (1925), in which he argued that gift giving and taking is one of the bonds that cohere societies. Systems like the KULA RING and POTLATCH provide a system of obligations that comprise a network of presentations that fuse economic, spiritual, and political values into a unified system. These insights were elaborated by the anthropologist LÉVI-STRAUSS into a structural theory of group alliance in which he argues that patterns of giving, receiving, and repaying—as individuals and as as groups—reflect the deepest structures of societies. This was applied, in particular, to the movement of women in and out of a patrilineage.

TITMUSS also used these ideas in his *The Gift Relationship* (1970), a study of blood donors in the United States, Britain, and the USSR. Titmuss argues that the giving of blood in Britain without material reward reflects a sense of community that the other two countries do not have. (In the United States many blood donors—by no means all—are paid for their blood.) The analysis of ALTRUISM in the examination of the British blood donor service made by Titmuss and the idea of the unilateral, anonymous, and voluntary gift has been important in discussions of SOCIAL POLICY.

Ideas of exchange have also been applied to other areas of formal gift giving in industrialized societies (for example, the exchange of birthday presents), but the presence of complex market mechanisms complicates simplistic formulations of exchange.

Ginsberg, Morris (1889–1970) Lithuanian-born sociologist and social philosopher who continued in the footsteps of HOBHOUSE as professor of sociology at the London School of Economics. There, as one of only the small number of British professors of sociology in the interwar years, Ginsberg's teaching and work (including *Essays in Sociology and Social Philosophy*, 1956; *Sociology*, 1934) influenced generations of British sociologists. The relatively ungrounded moralizing tone of much his work now appears outmoded. His work can be seen as the end of a tradition associated with Hobhouse, rather than as pointing in any new directions.

globalization of production the integration of economic activities by units of private capital on a world scale. Globalization is a key element of post-Fordism (see FORDISM AND POST-FORDISM) and resides in the ability of the multinational company or corporation to harmonize, integrate, and make its production flexible. This ability has been enormously enhanced by the new technologies of communication and robotics. Final products can be assembled from many individual units, can be made in a large number of countries, and can be flexibly produced to meet changing demand and to fill individualized market niches. Production thus becomes spatially structured, with multinationals organizing activity internationally in order to take advantage of different wage rates and different levels of unionization, to force employees to compete with each other, and to develop coherent global strategies of accumulation.

goal displacement the process by which means designed to achieve goals become ends in themselves. The concept was first used by MERTON (1949) to explain how the inflexibility of formal rules can lead to individuals' use of tactics of survival that displace the official goals of an organization. Merton's example revealed how government officials tended to act in ways that protected their interests rather than served the public. A classic case study of goal displacement was identified in Selznick's research on the Tennessee Valley Authority (1966), which revealed that democratic ideals of the TVA were subverted by officials in furtherance of their own departmental interests. Although MICHELS (1911) did not use the term, his IRON LAW OF OLIGARCHY was an early example of goal displacement, represented by the conflict between democratic principles and bureaucracy.

The concept of goal displacement belongs to the language of functionalism and implies both the existence of organizational goals and dysfunctional activities. See also MANIFEST AND LATENT FUNCTIONS, BOUNDED RATIONALITY, DYSFUNCTION.

Goffman, Erving (1922–1982) Canadian-born, US sociologist and prolific author who made a unique contribution to the study of face-to-face interaction in everyday life in a number of related areas. In *The Presentation of Self in Everyday Life* (1959), the central perspective is DRAMATURGY, a focus carried forward in *Encounters* (1961) and *Behavior in Public Places* (1963). In *Stigma* (1964) and *Asylums* (1961), the social construction of deviant identities and the actor's management of these are explored. In *Frame Analysis* (1974) and *Forms of Talk* (1981), his attention turned to an examination of the ways in which we define, or *frame,* the world as real, and how framing remains always a precarious accomplishment. Throughout all the stages of Goffman's work, he displayed an unceasing capacity to generate new concepts and conceptual schemas of great ingenuity. An abiding focus of his work was to exhibit social FORMS, those general recurring features of social life that lie beneath the specific content of social life (see also FORM AND CONTENT).

Although standing broadly in the symbolic interactionist tradition, and concentrating attention on face-to-face phenomena, Goffman's interests lay in displaying how even our most minute and apparently insignificant activities are socially structured and surrounded by RITUAL. In his later work, with its focus on the syntax of framing, Goffman moved closer to the analytical concerns of ETHNOMETHODOLOGY and CONVERSATION ANALYSIS.

Goffman's methods of research include PARTICIPANT OBSERVATION and close analysis of various kinds of naturally occurring social documents and happenings, for example, advertising images and radio talk. His validations of his formal conceptual schemas would appear to stem from the persuasive demonstrations of the analytical and explanatory utility of these, which he is able to achieve (a mixture of FORMAL SOCIOLOGY and ANALYTIC INDUCTION). A major element in Goffman's success was his flair as a social observer, which is not easily emulated.

Critics of Goffman's sociology have commented on its so-called demonic detachment, that it is peopled by actors who "lack individual qualities," and that it presents society as a "big con." Nevertheless, even if Goffman's approach may not present people in the round, his sociology has great strengths, not least in its steady production of many SENSITIZING CONCEPTS taken up, to good effect, by other sociologists. See also CAREER, ROLE DISTANCE, STIGMA, ENCOUNTER; INTERACTION, INTERACTION RITUAL AND INTERACTION ORDER; SYMBOLIC INTERACTION, TOTAL INSTITUTION OR TOTAL ORGANIZATION.

Goldthorpe, John (1935–) British sociologist best known for his empirical work on SOCIAL STRATIFICATION, CLASS, and SOCIAL MOBILITY, which includes (with David LOCKWOOD and others) the influential AFFLUENT WORKER studies (Goldthorpe, Lockwood et al., 1968–1969), and the Nuffield College, Oxford, SOCIAL MOBILITY Studies directed by him and published as *Social Mobility and Class Structure in Modern Britain* (1980, revised 1987). The methodological implications, as much as the empirical conclusions, of both sets of studies have been important (see Goldthorpe and Hope, *The Social Grading of Occupations,* 1974) and subject to considerable debate (see Bulmer, 1975; see also MULTIDIMENSIONAL ANALYSIS OF SOCIAL STRATIFICATION, CLASS IMAGERY, OCCUPATIONAL SCALES). Goldthorpe has also made occasional trenchant interventions in debates on sociological theory, on the virtues and vices of ETHNOMETHODOLOGY, on INDUSTRIAL RELATIONS, on class and gender, and on inflation.

Goldthorpe-Llewellyn scale see OCCUPATIONAL SCALES.

Gouldner, Alvin (1920–1980) US sociologist whose contributions to sociological theory were wide-ranging. Although strongly influenced by Marxism, he was not a Marxist in any strict sense. His best-known work, *The Coming Crisis in Western Sociology* (1971), might be seen as a post-mortem on modern STRUCTURAL-FUNCTIONALISM. He had earlier made his name with *Patterns of Industrial Bureaucracy* (1954), which has become a modern classic. In this, he provided an empirical examination of the way in which inefficient administration and industrial conflict may result from the attempt to introduce disciplinary rules that leave little scope for human autonomy. In a number of further works, including *The Two Marxisms* (1980) and *The Future of the Intellectuals and the Rise of the New Class* (1979) (see NEW CLASS, INTELLIGENTSIA), he sought to establish a new route for critical thinking in the social sciences between a seriously flawed FUNCTIONALISM and an unreformed Marxism. Throughout his life, he was always concerned to explore relations of involvement and detachment arising in the social sciences, being critical of those, like WEBER, who argued strongly for detachment (see *For Sociology,* 1973), or who denied the possibility of the goal of an objective grounding for values. In *The Dialectic of Ideology and Technology* (1976), he developed these themes, exploring the implications for public participation of both new thinking in epistemology and changes in communications technology. See also BUREAUCRACY, CRITICAL CULTURAL DISCOURSE, NEW CLASS, VALUE FREEDOM.

Gramsci, Antonio (1891–1937) Italian revolutionary Marxist and political theorist whose concept of HEGEMONY has been influential in modern sociology. Gramsci was born into a poor Sardinian family. In 1911 he won a scholarship to the University of Turin, where he studied linguistics. Because of increasing political commitments he left the university to become a leading socialist journalist and theorist of the Turin factory councils movement of 1919–1920. Gramsci saw direct democracy based on factory councils as destined to replace parliamentary democracy. This would enable the mass of the population to participate directly in making political decisions. In 1924, Gramsci became secretary of the Italian Communist Party. But with the growth of fascism he was arrested in 1926. At his trial the official prosecutor demanded that the judge "stop this brain working for twenty years." Prison did not silence him, but inspired him to write his major theoretical achievement, the *Prison Notebooks*. These cover a wide range of subjects, the common link being the application of Marxism to the problems of Italian history and society. His strategy for change was based on organizing the northern working class and the southern peasantry, and welding a revolutionary alliance between them. See also INTELLECTUALS.

grand theory see MILLS.

gratification the process of satisfying needs or goals, and the state of satisfaction that results from fulfillment of such needs or goals.

green movement a social movement whose prime concern is with ecological issues (see ECOLOGY). While this is broad-based, encompassing concern over environmental pollution, preservation of wildlife and of the traditional countryside, and the control of building development, the movement has a strong political wing that has been a powerful lobby during the 1980s. The Green Party has been most in evidence in West Germany and Holland, emerging significantly in Britain in the late 1980s, with the renaming of the Ecology Party. However, many supporters would regard their allegiance not as conventionally political, but as based on practical issues with which they can be directly involved, through their purchasing habits, their leisure pursuits, or by contributing to conservation bodies.

green revolution the introduction of new species of crops and new techniques leading to greater crop yields. This began in Mexico in the 1950s, and from the mid-1960s new high-yielding varieties of rice and wheat were introduced in many Third World countries. The most noticeable applications were in the Indian subcontinent, where new strains of rice enabled *double-cropping*, eliminating a fallow period in the agricultural cycle. For a while these innovations were seen by many as solving food-supply problems. However, new problems arose, one of the most significant being that the new strains require heavy inputs of fertilizer, pesticides, and machinery. For Third World countries, these can be very expensive imports, and small farmers have been unable to gain access to the credit financing necessary for full advantage to be taken. Generally a process of *increasing* impoverishment of poor farmers has resulted, with increasing income inequalities, a concentration of landholding, and variable increases in food supplies. As Griffin (1979) points out, this was an example of a *technological fix* approach based on assumptions that technical solutions can operate independently of the institutional environment. He sums up by saying, "The story of the green revolution is the story of a revolution that failed." See also INTERMEDIATE TECHNOLOGY.

grounded theory any form of sociological theory that is built up gradually from the careful naturalistic observation of a selected social phenomenon (see also ANALYTICAL INDUCTION). As outlined by Glaser and Strauss in *The Discovery of Grounded Theory* (1968), sociological theorizing of this type contrasts with more abstract general theories of the hypothetico-deductive type (see HYPOTHETICO-DEDUCTIVE EXPLANATION AND METHOD). Compare also THEORIES OF THE MIDDLE RANGE.

group any collectivity or plurality of individuals (people or things) bounded by informal or formal criteria of membership. A *social group* exists when members engage in social interactions involving reciprocal ROLES and integrative ties. Thus, the contrast can be drawn between a social group and a mere *social category,* the latter referring to any category of individuals sharing a socially relevant characteristic (for example, age or sex), but not associated within any bounded pattern of interactions or integrative ties. Any social group, therefore, will have a specified basis of social interaction, though the nature and extent of this will vary greatly between groups. Social groups of various types can be seen as the building blocks from which other types and levels of social organization are built. Alternatively, the term "social group," as for Albion SMALL (1905), is "the most general and colorless term used in sociology to refer to combinations of persons." See also PRIMARY GROUP, GROUP DYNAMICS, REFERENCE GROUP, SOCIAL INTEGRATION AND SYSTEM INTEGRATION, SOCIETY.

group dynamics the processes involved in interaction within social GROUPS. Interest in sociology has focused especially on shifting patterns of tension, conflict, adjustment, and cohesion within groups, as well as on styles of leadership.

The best-known theoretical and experimental approach in the study of group dynamics, and the one with which the term is most associated, is the *field theory* of Kurt Lewin (1951); however, an awareness of the importance of group dynamics in a more general sense is evident in the work of many sociologists and social psychologists, including SIMMEL, MAYO, MORENO, Robert Bales (1950), and PARSONS (see DYAD AND TRIAD, HAWTHORNE EFFECT, SOCIOMETRY, OPINION LEADERS AND OPINION LEADERSHIP, CONFORMITY, GROUP THERAPY).

group therapy the practice of treating psychological disturbance through a face-to-face group process of sharing experiences and emotions and, through this, moving toward greater self-understanding and adjustment. This form of therapy was introduced in the 1930s by J.L. MORENO, who founded psychodrama and sociodrama, and coined the terms. Since the 1940s, Carl ROGERS actively developed the method, particularly in *encounter groups* that aim to provide a developmental experience for people termed "normals." Therapy groups, generally, have a group leader or so-called facilitator, as the composition and the program of a group needs to be carefully planned and controlled for its purpose to be realized in all members. A variety of theoretical approaches may underpin this type of therapy, for example, psychodynamic, Rogerian, or feminist.

guild an association of craft workers, especially in preindustrial societies, formed to provide mutual aid and to control craft standards and entry into the trade (a form of SOCIAL CLOSURE). Compare PROFESSION, TRADES UNION.

Guttman scale, scalogram analysis, or **scalogram method** an ATTITUDE SCALE, named after its designer, Guttman, that first assesses whether the attitude to be studied, for example, racial prejudice, involves a single dimension. If it does, then it will be possible to arrange, hierarchically and ordinally, a series of attitude questions of increasing intensity such that agreement with a given statement implies agreement with statements of lower intensity. That is, they assume that a cutoff point exists within any set of attitude statements such that failure to endorse a particular item means that no item of greater intensity will be endorsed. Respondents' attitudes can then be compared by a simple score, and any individual's response to any item is known from this score. In practice, perfect Guttman scales probably do not exist, and a 10% margin of error is generally considered to be acceptable. Compare LIKERT SCALE.

H

Habermas, Jürgen (1929–) German social theorist and leading living exponent of a style of radical social theorizing originating with the FRANKFURT SCHOOL OF CRITICAL THEORY. The range of Habermas's theorizing is extraordinary. He deals with most of the broad themes developed by earlier critical theorists, including epistemological questions and debate about the fundamental dynamics of advanced capitalist societies. In addition, he had sought to achieve thoroughgoing synthesis of developments in social science and philosophy—including analytical philosophy, philosophy of science, linguistics, political science, and systems theory—that are of relevance in exploring the basis for a rational reconstruction of society on socialist lines.

With the starting point of a critique of the scientization of politics, Habermas has endeavored to reestablish social scientific and political debate as as arena of open discourse. Whereas historically, reason and science had been directed against ignorance and oppression, in Habermas's view in modern societies science and technical rationality now often function as ideologies, preventing the raising of fundamental questions about human ends. In *Knowledge and Human Interests* (1972, German original 1968), Habermas seeks to identify the proper spheres of three forms of scientific knowledge:

(a) *empirical-analytical* inquiry, concerned with establishing causal relations and grounded, above all, in an interest in controlling nature;

(b) *hermeneutic* inquiry, based on MEANINGFUL UNDERSTANDING and arising from the human need for mutual communication;

(c) *critical* and *emancipatory* forms of knowledge, seen as transcending the limits of the other two.

The terms in which Habermas elucidates the character of the third form of knowledge, (c), involve the formulation of a *universal pragmatics,* that is, an account of the normative presuppositions ideally underlying all forms of human communication (Habermas, 1970a & b). All genuine attempts at communication have implicit in them claims to validity (truth, appropriateness, and sincerity). (See also COMMUNICATIVE COMPETENCE.) True rationality can be seen to be achieved only when this emerges from conditions that correspond to an *ideal speech situation,* in which all parties have equal opportunities to engage in dialogue without undue domination by one party, without restriction, and without ideological distortion. This model states the conditions for a critical and truly emancipatory social science. Even if there are difficulties in realizing the model, it establishes a benchmark in terms of which the ideological distortions involved in existing forms of social science can be gauged.

In *Legitimation Crisis* (1975, original German edition 1973), Habermas turned his attention to an examination of tendencies to crisis in advanced capitalist societies. He portrays these societies as characterized by continued economic and class contradictions, and by a new politicization of administrative decisions as a result of increasing state intervention made necessary by economic contradictions, as well as by the new contradictions that these political interventions introduce. A tendency to legitimation crisis is seen as occurring under these circumstances, especially in a situation in which previous bases of legitimacy (for example, DEFERENCE) are not being renewed and where new social orientations (for example, new welfare professionalism) are beginning to act as foreign bodies within capitalism, producing a more critical political culture, potentially challenging to capitalism. Habermas acknowledges that tendencies to crisis in capitalist societies may be successfully managed, and that there are no guarantees that capitalism will be replaced. Nonetheless, he insists that the presence of economic and class contradictions and distorted rationality within capitalist societies are apparent once the procedures of critical theory are brought into play.

Habermas's combination of critical exegesis of the work of others with an elaboration of his own systematic theory has been widely influential. The volume and complexity of his writing mean that it is impossible to indicate all its ramifications in limited space. In addition to the works noted, other main works by Habermas (English translations) include: *Theory and Practice* (1974), *Towards a Rational Society* (1970), *Communication and the Evolution of Society* (1979), and *The Theory of Communicative Competence* (2 vols., 1984 and 1988). A summary and evaluation of Habermas's work is provided by McCarthy (1978) and by R. Bernstein (1976).

habitus "the durably installed generative principles" that produce and reproduce the practices of a class or class fraction (BOURDIEU, 1977, 1984). Centrally, the habitus consists of set of so-called classificatory schemes and ultimate values. These, according to Bourdieu, are more fundamental than consciousness or language, and are the means by which groups succeed, or do not succeed, in imposing ways of seeing favorable to their own interests. While each habitus is set by historical and socially situated conditions, it also allows new forms and actions, but is far from allowing the "creation of unpredictable (or unconditioned) novelty." See also STRUCTURE AND AGENCY.

Hagerstrand, Stig (1916–) Swedish social geographer whose work on spatial diffusion and time-space relations has been influential in sociology (for example, see Giddens, 1984). Hagerstrand's early work was statistical, and involved aggregate data and the use of computer simulations. His later work has been more concerned with analysis of the movements of individuals, but his goal has been to show how aggregate analysis and individual analysis are complementary and can be interrelated. See also AGGREGATE DATA ANALYSIS.

Halsey, A.H. (1923–) British sociologist and Professor of Social and Administrative Studies at Oxford University who has published extensively on SOCIAL STRATIFICATION, SOCIAL MOBILITY, and the SOCIOLOGY OF EDUCATION. The general thrust of his work is best expressed in *Change in British Society* (1978), a summary of his Reith Lectures in the same year. In that book, he is concerned with the extent to which the fundamental values of liberty, fraternity, and equality can be realized in any society, and especially an advanced industrial one. He contrasts Weberian-liberal and Marxist explanations of SOCIAL CHANGE and argues that not all inequality can be accounted for as a consequence of class. Rather, as did WEBER, he sees notions of party and STATUS as essential to an understanding of the complexities of social change, especially the changing distribution of power and advantage through economic, social, and political processes. He concludes that none of the fundamental values identified are realized in Britain, and that there are serious obstacles to them being so. He is nevertheless cautiously optimistic that in Britain the so-called rich traditions of democracy and citizenship offer the sort of basis for fraternity that ultimately transcend the conflicts engendered by class and lead to a new form of social integration. It is a social philosophy that was incorporated into the politics of newly created centrist parties in Britain in the 1980s.

Halsey's contribution to the study of social mobility is *Origins and Destinations* (1980) (with Health and Ridge). Earlier, in the sociology of education, his reader *Education, Economy and Society* (1961) and *Social Class and Educational Opportunity* (1956) (both with Floud and Anderson) were highly influential books that influenced the course of sociological investigation into education for almost two decades. The concerns with equality, inequality of access, and educational achievement in the sociology of education owe their origins to Halsey's early, influential work. The social experiments with comprehensive education, compensatory education, and community education, which spearheaded the drive toward eradication of inequalities within postwar Britain, were the direct result of work inspired by Halsey and his colleagues.

Hawthorne effect a term derived from the Hawthorne investigations (see HUMAN RELATIONS SCHOOL), conducted for the Western Electric Company, in Cicero, Illinois, in which the conduct of experiments produced changes in the behavior of subjects because, first, they knew they were being observed and, secondly, investigators developed friendly relationships with them. In the first instance, the Hawthorne effect made sense of the otherwise puzzling experimental finding of an inverse relationship between illumination (environmental change) and employee output. In the second instance, the attempt to assess the impact of a range of variables on the performance of employees, who were removed from their normal work situation, was rendered problematic, partly because over time investigators adopted a friendly supervisory relationship with the subjects. The difficulty in disentangling the effects of poorly controlled changes on the observed improvement in employee output was controversially resolved in favor of stressing the significance of employee preference for friendly supervision of cohesive and informal work groups. Indeed, this finding became the main platform in the prescriptions of human relations theorists proposed for effective management. In both instances, the Hawthorne effect is associated with the way in which subjects interpret and respond to poorly controlled experimental changes. As the researchers became aware of the need to consider the ways in which employees interpreted their work situation, other techniques of investigation, such as interviews and observation of natural settings, were adopted. Nevertheless, all of the phases in the research program have been subjected to criticism as has the interpretation of the findings (M. Rose, 1988). See also UNANTICIPATED CONSEQUENCES OF SOCIAL ACTION.

head of household traditionally, the senior male of the household (the breadwinner), a tradition that has influenced social research definitions. In government surveys, the head of household has been defined as the man who is the owner or tenant of the house, or the man who lives with the woman who is the owner or tenant of the house. Therefore "female-headed households" are confined to women living alone, or women-headed single-parent households, or women who are the tenant or owner living with older people.

This definition of head of household has consequences for the analysis of household situation: should members of a household be ascribed a social position according to the economic and social status of the, usually male, head of household? The debate on this overlaps with the debate on how social CLASS should be defined. In social surveys social class is measured by such variables as occupation (current job, job grade, responsibility in job), and/or education (years of schooling), and/or housing status. Should these variables be measured for the head of household and that person's social class then be assigned to all other members of the household? Can social class as measured in this way be assigned to other members of the family, for example, the woman he lives with, "his" children, etc.? Alternatively, is social class an individual attribute measured for each adult's own occupational, educational, and housing status? Or, should social class be measured for the household through considering these variables for both male and female adults in the household? Such questions have important repercussions for policy. In the collection of poverty statistics in Britain, for example, it is assumed that resources are shared equitably within the family. If the head of household earns enough, then the entire household is above the poverty line. However, many researchers have challenged this assumption and argued that although in some families resources may be equitably distributed, in others they are not, and women and children may be living below the poverty line in families that appear adequately resourced by government criteria.

Hegel, Georg Wilhelm Fredrich (1770–1831) influential German idealist and post-Kantian philosopher. His major works include *Phenomenology of Mind* (1807), *Philosophy of History* (1817), and *Philosophy of Right* (1821). He believed that the social world was essentially composed of ideas, manifested in the idea of the world (or absolute) spirit (*Geist*). These ideas were to be discovered by a contemplative process of the mind alienating itself from itself. The spirit is illustrated in history by the dialectical movement of ideas through time—a thesis combines with an antithesis to produce a higher synthesis. This historical pattern unfolds with individuals (Napoleon is often cited) as mere pawns in its development. Hegel assumed that it would end with an eternal historical final synthesis and he appears to have believed that the Prussian state constituted such an ending. Despite his frequent evaluation as a philosopher of the right wing, his critique of alienating commercialism crucially influenced the young MARX, who claimed to have rescued Hegel's thought from IDEALISM by placing the dialectic on its feet in the material world. See also IDEALISM.

hegemony 1. the power exercised by one social group over another. **2.** the ideological/cultural domination of one class by another, achieved by engineering consensus through controlling the content of cultural forms and major institutions.

In sense **2.**, the term is derived from the work of GRAMSCI (1971), an Italian Marxist jailed by the fascists in the 1920s. He used the term to criticize the narrowness of approaches that focused only on the repressive potential of the capitalist state. Gramsci argued that the domination of ideas in the major institutions of capitalist society—the Catholic Church, the legal system, the education system, the mass communications media, etc.—promoted acceptance of ideas and beliefs that benefited the RULING CLASS. Gramsci compared civil society to a powerful system of "fortresses and earthworks" standing behind the state. As a result, the problem of cultural hegemony was crucial to understanding the survival of capitalism. Gramsci concluded that before winning power the working class would have to undermine the hegemony of the ruling class by developing its own alternative hegemony. As well as exercising leadership, this required a cultural and ideological struggle in order to create a new socialist "common sense," and thus change the way people think and behave. It followed, therefore, that a subordinate and oppressed class, in addition to organizing to resist physical coercion and repression, had to develop a systematic refutation of ruling ideas. In this sense, of political and theoretical struggle, the idea of hegemony and often the term itself were already established and in common use, for example in the Russian Marxist movements (see Anderson, 1977).

Where Gramsci most influenced later work was in shifting the emphasis from "counter-hegemony" as a political necessity for subordinated groups to hegemony as a factor in stabilizing an existing power structure. In a general sense, there is nothing new in this for sociologists. Weber, for example, writing more than a decade before Gramsci, had emphasized that the crude exercise of force was too unstable a method of guaranteeing continuance of a system. A stable power system also needed a socially accepted principle of legitimation (see LEGITIMATE AUTHORITY). What distinguished Gramsci's contribution, and has influenced sociology in the last two decades, is the encouragement to investigate the ways in which specific institutions operated in the social reproduction of power relations and to examine wider theoretical issues in understanding belief structures, IDEOLOGY, etc. In recent years, there have been many studies that have used it in relation to issues such as working-class youth subcultures, the production of television news, and the development of state education.

Heidegger, Martin (1889–1976) German philosopher and leading contributor to PHENOMENOLOGY and existentialism. His philosophy has influenced modern sociological theory in a number of ways, notably his conception of what is distinctive about human beings: DASEIN, the so-called "analytic of Man's Being"; and, related to this, his conception of TIME. What is distinct about man is a capacity to understand himself, and although not master of his own origin, man has the capacity to undertake authentic actions, that is, actions that do not retreat into anonymity, depersonalized objectivized modes of being, denying Man's distinctive capacities. In *Being and Time* (1929), Heidegger states the authentic self as potentiality for action, an orientation toward the future (becoming), which involves possibilities and requires choice. Heidegger attracted controversy mainly because of his association with fascism, but the fundamentals of his philosophy, having been taken up by other philosophers (for example, SARTRE) and within social science (see STRUCTURE AND AGENCY), show that such an association is not inherent.

herding society any form of society whose main subsistence comes from tending flocks and herds of domesticated animals (see PASTORALISM, NOMADS AND NOMADISM). In practice, subsistence needs are often met by a combination of herding with hunting and gathering and other forms of agriculture. See also HUNTER-GATHERER.

hermeneutics a theory and method of interpreting human action and artifacts. It derives from the term for interpreting biblical texts, a practice that involved detailed attempts to understand the so-called authentic version of the work. DILTHEY used the term (and also VERSTEHEN) to refer to the method of the cultural sciences, that is, the subjects that forge shared understandings between creator and interpreter. MANNHEIM made similar claims and enlarged on the idea that the text could be seen as a document of a particular world view. Gadamer has attempted to validate his "phenomenological hermeneutics" by invoking the idea of the *hermeneutic circle*; that is, we can recognize and generalize a particular view only because we interpret instances of it, but can only understand a particular act or artifact with reference to the world view that produced it. Gadamer argues that this process of validation is always provisional and never complete—our truth can only ever be partial and must be subject to continuing revision. Most recently hermeneutics has been developed by Ricoeur (1981), who has focused on its literary critical insights. He argues that the TEXT is in a key position as a mediator of tradition and uniqueness, and thus stands in a position of potential critique of both the world and the SELF. Similar possibilities have been opened up by HABERMAS with his critical hermeneutics—an attempt to illustrate that any interpretation must take sides in a communication that is distorted by capitalist power relations. Often criticized for its apparent celebration of RELATIVISM and SUBJECTIVITY, hermeneutics remains a position that stimulates central debates within sociology up to the present day. As Habermas points out, two features of hermeneutics have been vital: (a) it reminds the social sciences of problems that arise from symbolic prestructuring of their subject matter, and (b) it undermines objectivist understandings of the natural sciences (compare KUHN, FEYERABEND). See also FUSION OF HORIZONS, DOUBLE HERMENEUTIC.

hidden curriculum a set of values, attitudes, and knowledge frames embodied in the organization and processes of schooling and implicitly conveyed to pupils.

Although all schools have a formal curriculum comprising areas of academic knowledge that pupils are expected to acquire, it is the form of schooling and the messages transmitted as a result of its organization and practices that are more powerful than the content of subjects. It promotes social control and an acceptance of the school's, and hence society's, authority structure.

Sociologists argue that the basic function of schooling is to reproduce society's VALUES and NORMS. Both structural-functionalists and Marxists agree on this, but for quite different reasons. The former argue that it is necessary in order to maintain the stability of the social order in the interest of all (see, for example, Parsons, 1959), whereas Marxists see the basic function of education as the reproduction of the social relations of capitalist economic production, and thus the maintenance of a class order that subordinates the proletariat. It is this latter function that is achieved predominantly through the hidden curriculum (see Bowles and Gintis, 1976).

hierarchy of credibility the notion proposed by BECKER, "Whose side are we on?" (1953) that societies are so organized that those who occupy top positions and positions of authority tend more readily to have their versions of the truth accepted, while the views of those who are underdogs or outsiders often go unrepresented, or are not taken seriously, or are represented only by official accounts. Becker's opinion is that sociologists must side with the underdogs or outsiders if a more adequate overall view of society is to be obtained. The self-conscious pursuit of objectivity and the avoidance of BIAS, or simply undertaking commissioned research for those in authority who can afford to pay, will result in one-sided research.

In siding with the underdog, Becker has been criticized (for example,

GOULDNER, 1973) for making proposals that undermine the attainment of objectivity, and suggesting, like WEBER, that sociology is always relative to values (see also VALUE RELEVANCE). But his position is better seen as indicating that objectivity is not easily achieved in sociology, and that many current practices designed to obtain it may have the opposite effect. See also OBJECTIVITY, VALUE FREEDOM AND VALUE NEUTRALITY, TRUTH, FUSION OF HORIZONS, DEVIANCE, LABELING THEORY, AMPLIFICATION OF DEVIANCE.

hierarchy of the sciences a view of the sciences first propounded by COMTE, in which the different sciences are seen as emerging in a definite sequence, with each science in the hierarchy being dependent on, while also different in character from, and not simply reducible to, those below it (see Fig. 9). Though Comte saw a basic unity between the sciences (see POSITIVISM), sociology, as the "queen of the sciences" heading this hierarchy, is a synthesizing science, more complex than those disciplines below it.

Comte's view of the hierarchical arrangement of the sciences is still accepted in general terms (for example, see Rose, 1973). However, the precise way in which sociology is scientific and the extent of its differentiation from natural science are much disputed.

One reason why sociology can be seen as dependent on but not reducible to other sciences, is the number and complexity of the variables involved. Thus, higher-level concepts and accounts that simplify and summarize the many variables and relationships involved are unavoidable. In biology and in sociology, however, where organisms pursue ends, and human actors are motivated by meanings, entirely new levels of analysis are introduced in which any simple reduction is unlikely to succeed. However, the precise implications of such new levels for sociology are controversial and often different from Comte's.

histogram a diagrammatic representation of a FREQUENCY DISTRIBUTION, consisting of contiguous rectangles displaying interval-level data (see CRITERIA AND LEVELS OF MEASUREMENT) grouped into categories. In a histogram the width of the rectangle is proportional to the class interval under consid-

SOCIOLOGY AND THE MORAL SCIENCES	*INCREASING SPECIFICITY,*
PHYSIOLOGY (BIOLOGY)	*COMPLEXITY,*
CHEMISTRY	*SYNTHESIS*
PHYSICS	
CELESTIAL PHYSICS (ASTRONOMY)	*RELATIVE SIMPLICITY,*
MATHEMATICS	*GENERALITY,*
	ANALYTICAL

Fig. 9. **Hierarchy of the sciences.** According to this view of the sciences, first proposed by Comte (1798–1857), the sciences can be arranged in ascending order of complexity, with sciences higher in the hierarchy dependent, but not only dependent, on those below. Thus, sociology makes assumptions about the physical and biological world, but at the same time also involves an "emergent" level of analysis different from and not reducible to those below.

eration, and the height is the associated frequency. The area of each bar is then proportional to the frequencies for each class interval (see Fig. 10).

historical sociology 1. any sociology focused particularly on the study of past societies or using historical sources. **2.** more particularly, those forms of comparative sociology that focus on historical societies, and on order and change within these societies (see also COMPARATIVE METHOD). Historical sociology in this second sense, after falling out of fashion (see HISTORICISM, EVOLUTIONARY THEORY, SOCIAL CHANGE), has come into vogue again in recent decades as the result of major works by such authors as MOORE and WALLERSTEIN in the United States, and ANDERSON, MANN, and ELIAS in Britain. There is also a sense in which all general theories of social change are historical sociologies. It is in this context that partisans of historical sociology, such as P. Abrams (1982), argue that it forms the central core of traditional sociology, and its importance should be reasserted in modern sociology.

historicism 1. any approach to the understanding of history that emphasizes the uniqueness of each historical epoch, suggesting that each historical situation or period can only be understood in its own terms. Usually historical understanding and explanation are seen as involving only those modes of explanation particularly appropriate to social studies or the human sciences (for example, MEANINGFUL UNDERSTANDING AND EXPLANATION, HERMENEUTICS) and not those forms of explanation (see COVERING LAW MODEL AND DEDUCTIVE NOMOLOGICAL EXPLANATION) widely regarded as uppermost in the physical sciences. See also COLLINGWOOD, DILTHEY, WINDELBAND, IDEOGRAPHIC AND NOMOTHETIC, GEISTESWISSENSCHAFTEN AND WISSENSCHAFTEN. **2.** Karl POPPER's extension of HISTORICISM **1.** to identify *two* distinct kinds of view that imply that explanation in historical and social studies is of a different order than our understanding of the physical world: (a) *non-naturalistic historicism,* as in

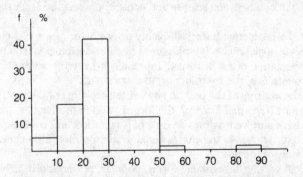

Fig. 10. **Histogram.** A diagrammatic representation (f=frequency) of a frequency distribution, consisting of contiguous rectangles, in which the width of each rectangle is proportional to the class interval under consideration and the area of each rectangle is proportional to the associated frequency.

in HISTORICISM **1.**, and (b) *naturalistic historicism,* in which certain theorists in philosophy and sociology (notably HEGEL, COMTE, and MARX) are seen as guilty of misunderstanding and misrepresenting the true nature of scientific prediction (POPPER, 1957) in claiming to be able to predict historical change. Popper presents both forms of historicism as failing to appreciate the true character of scientific laws and theories, that is, that scientific explanations and predictions are not unlimited and are relative to specific initial conditions. Popper refers to historical predictions (HISTORICISM **2.** (b), for example, Marx's prediction of the collapse of capitalism) as unscientific prophecies. In Popper's view, once the limited nature of scientific laws becomes appreciated, arguments against the relevance of a proper use of scientific laws in historical explanations (non-naturalistic historicism) should also collapse, since reference to scientific laws need not be at oods with a recognition of the existence of elements of relative uniqueness in social situations (see also SITUATIONAL ANALYSIS AND SITUATIONAL LOGIC).

There exist some similarities (and some differences) between Popper's view and WEBER's opposition to historical materialism and the latter's use of both meaningful explanation and IDEAL TYPES in historical sociological analysis. (Both Popper and Weber, for instance, take rational economic models as a benchmark.) Critics of Popper's view, however, accuse him of constructing a straw man of the theorists he opposes, and point out that much of his argument relies on a prior acceptance of his disputed COVERING LAW MODEL of science. This said, while differences in degree and perhaps kind between historical and social reality on the one hand, and physical reality on the other, are widely acknowledged in sociology and conceptions such as HISTORICISM **1.** illuminate these, there is no general acceptance of the view implied in HISTORICISM **1.** that any simple distinction can be drawn between science and nonscience (see also SOCIOLOGY OF SCIENCE).

historicity the distinctive historical quality or character of a social context. This aspect of social reality is emphasized by those sociologists who believe in the importance of an historical approach in bringing authenticity to social accounts. See also HISTORICISM, HERMENEUTICS.

history 1. the entirety of the past. **2.** any written accounts of the past. **3.** the recorded past (*recorded history*); the history of literate societies; societies in which have survived written records of a recorded oral tradition (compare ARCHAEOLOGY). **4.** the professional academic discipline concerned with the study of the past.

Historical writing takes many forms, popular, propagandist, as well as academic. Although in the academic form it is undertaken mainly by *historians,* academic historical writing is not confined to writers located within history as a discipline. Many sociological accounts have as their focus particular historical societies or selected general features of historical societies (see also HISTORICAL SOCIOLOGY). In addition each academic discipline also tends to produce accounts of its own history, for example, the history of science, the history of art, etc.

The relationship between history and sociology as academic disciplines has been uneasy. Whereas for historians the goal has usually been understanding and explanation of specific historical situations, sociologists have more often viewed the findings about particular historical societies as a laboratory for testing more general propositions about society or particular types of society (see also COMPARATIVE METHOD). Such an overall distinction is, however, only partly justified, as is made clear by the presence of meaningful explanatory accounts within sociology (for example, WEBER's *Protestant Ethic and the Spirit of Capitalism,* 1904–1905) and by the frequent recourse to general propositions within academic history (see also MEANINGFUL UNDERSTANDING AND EXPLANATION, HERMENEUTICS).

If, in the 19th century, mutual suspicion between historians and sociologists usually prevailed, a more symbiotic relationship has recently become apparent. In this new and more fruitful relationship, historians are more usually involved in the careful collection and analysis of primary sources, with sociologists, in their consideration of history, often making use of historians' findings as secondary sources in their search for more general patterns and explanations of historical reality. However, such a division of labor is fluid, with role reversals between historians and sociologists not uncommon.

history of mentalities an approach to historical study (as seen, for example, in the work of the French historians Fernand BRAUDEL, 1949, and Emanuel Le Roy Ladurie, 1978) in which the goal is the historical recovery and reconstruction of the ideas, emotions, and mental structures of historical persons, especially the ideas of ordinary persons as well as the great and famous. In the work of Phillipe Aries (1962), the focus is on psychological investigation of the past, that is, on *psychohistory.*

In the work of Braudel, the *mentalities* are the mind sets, paradigms, and points of view embedded in institutions that give coherence to, and make up the totality of, a historical epoch.

Hobbes, Thomas (1588–1679) English philosopher and political theorist responsible for the earliest self-conscious attempt to construct a science of civil society from first principles derived from imagining what man would be like in a state of nature, where all authority, political, moral, and social was lacking. His project was to follow the deductive reasoning of geometry, and his first principles were dictated by a philosophy that was both mechanistic and materialist. Society, like the human beings who are its simplest elements, is a machine. To understand how society works, one must take it apart in imagination, resolve it into its simplest elements, and then recompose it to a healthy functioning according to the laws of motion of these components. Hobbes distinguished between the artificial, made by man, and the natural, found in the physical world. He then claimed that man could only have certain knowledge of what men have created or made. Men could have certain knowledge of geometry because men themselves had created the theorems, propositions, and figures of geometry. A like knowledge was possible of civil society, because men had also created this. The substance of Hobbes' political thinking is contained in *De Cive* (*Concerning the Citizen*) and *Leviathan* (1651). In these, he sought to demonstrate that man's natural condition, in which all authority was lacking and in which he enjoyed a NATURAL RIGHT to everything that would assist his self-preservation, was one of unmitigated strife, in which there was no security for any human purpose. He then argued that since man possessed reason, which was his capacity to know the causes of things, he was able to discover the principles of conduct that he ought prudentially to follow for his security and safety. These principles Hobbes called the "convenient Articles of Peace," under which men agreed to lay down their natural right to everything and submit to absolute and undivided sovereign authority. Hobbes' conclusions here point in a monarchical direction, but he was always careful, when referring to this authority, to use the phrase "one man, or assembly of men." In the times in which he wrote—the English Civil War and its aftermath—it was not prudent to offend either royalist or parliamentary susceptibilities. For commentators such as MacPherson (1962), Hobbes' thinking reflects a bourgeois individualism. For others, it came close to a Kantian view of moral obligation. The question raised by Hobbes—the Hobbesian "problem of order," as PARSONS put it—remains a central question in sociology.

Hobhouse, Leonard Trelawny (1864–1929) British sociologist, and the leading figure in early British sociology, who is primarily remembered today for his contributions to COMPARATIVE SOCIOLOGY and especially to the SOCIOLOGY OF DEVELOPMENT. Hobhouse was a man of rich and varied interests, whose career exemplified a unity of theory and practice. Employment in journalism preceded his appointment to a professorship in sociology at the London School of Economics. Politically, Hobhouse favored the left, although he was well aware of the implications for personal liberty of a state bureaucratic form of socialism. For Hobhouse, a balance had to be struck between market and plan that enhanced individual freedom. His social philosophy is best expressed in his *Elements of Social Justice* (1922), a book that, in its conception of the relation between an economically regulating state and personal freedom, still remains relevant to socialist thought.

Apart from his major contributions to sociology, which included the comparative study *Morals in Evolution* (1906) and the three-volume *Principles of Sociology* (1921–24), Hobhouse wrote on animal and social psychology, logic, epistemology, ethics, and metaphysics as well as on social philosophy. However, the overarching theme of his work was the evolution of mind and society (see EVOLUTIONARY THEORY). For Hobhouse, the evolutionary process could be examined at three logically distinct levels: description, explanation, and evaluation. Social development itself could be estimated in terms of four biologically oriented criteria:

(a) the increasing efficiency with which a society is controlled and directed;

(b) a growing expansion in the scale and complexity of social organization;

(c) an extension of social cooperation in realizing human needs;

(d) the enhanced capacity for human fulfillment.

Hobhouse used historical and comparative evidence to suggest a general association between stages of social development and intellectual advance, manifested in the growth of science and technology, and ethical and religious reflection and art. A final concern was to examine development in terms of ethical standards. Here he employed his theory of *The Rational Good* (1921): development was ethically appropriate to the extent to which it promoted both social harmony and the realization of human capacities and potentialities. Progress was not inevitable, as the outbreak of World War I made clear. Yet, by the 1920s, he was cautiously optimistic that the order, efficiency, and complexity of industrial societies had indeed been shown to be compatible with individual freedom and mutuality, that progress had been achieved, and that this could be advanced still further by the cooperative, self-conscious efforts of nation states. History will probably find his caution more justifiable than his optimism.

holism 1. any form of sociological theory that emphasizes the primacy of social structure, social system, etc. in determining social outcomes, and in sociological explanations. The opposite position is METHODOLOGICAL INDIVIDUALISM. As used by POPPER (1957), the term is mainly a pejorative one. See also SITUATIONAL LOGIC. **2.** in a more neutral sense, the tendency of sociology, in contrast with other more specialized social sciences, to maintain an all-inclusive view of social phenomena.

Homans, George (1910–) US sociologist who, in "Bringing Men Back In" (1964), his Presidential Address to the American Sociological Association, argued that social phenomena can only be explained by reference to the motivations of individual persons. In *The Human Group* (1950), he had earlier argued that "All grander sociologies must be true to the sociology of the group." In *Social Behavior: Its Elementary Forms* (1961), he stated that he had "come to believe that the empirical propositions" in the former work could "most easily be explained by two bodies of empirical general propositions already in existence: behavioral psychology and elementary economics." Along with his fellow American, Peter BLAU, Homans is regarded as one of the main exponents of EXCHANGE THEORY.

homeostasis any process that regulates or maintains a system in a stable state in relation to a changing external environment in which this system operates. The term may be applied to mechanical systems or servomechanisms, to living beings, or to SOCIAL SYSTEMS. Although a central postulate of some sociological theories (especially see FUNCTIONALISM and STRUCTURAL FUNCTIONALISM), the suggestion that social systems act in self-maintaining or self-equilibriating ways remains controversial. See also SYSTEMS THEORY.

homo clausus see FIGURATION.

Hope-Goldthorpe scale see OCCUPATIONAL SCALES.

horizontal division of labor see SEXUAL DIVISION OF LABOR.

Horkheimer, Max (1895–1973) German social theorist and leading member of the FRANKFURT SCHOOL OF CRITICAL THEORY. Beginning in the 1930s, he expounded his own and the Frankfurt school's conception of critical theory in numerous essays and books. Taking as his point of departure the work of the young MARX and also HEGEL, his distinctive viewpoint was that a fundamental transformation of both theory and practice was required if modern civilization was ever to escape from its current alienative and exploitive form. Epistemologically, Horkheimer argued for a repudiation of all absolute doctrines, especially opposing any suggestion that it is ever satisfactory to take social phenomena at face value. Thus both POSITIVISM and EMPIRICISM are rejected. Politically, Horkheimer argued against the assumption that a proletarian revolution would lead to human emancipation. What was required was the establishment of an open-ended conception of reason, capable of informing human values and breaking the link between knowledge and human alienation. Works by Horkheimer include *Eclipse of Reason* (1947), *Critical Theory: Selected Essays* (1972), and (with Theodor ADORNO) *Dialectic of Enlightenment* (1972, original German ed., 1947). See also NEGATION AND NEGATIVITY.

household "a single person or a group of people who have the address as their only or main residence and who either share one meal a day or share living accommodation" (in Britain, the definition offered by The Office of Population Censuses and Surveys). Nonrelated members are problematic in this definition, and sociologists have used two main types of household composition in discussing households:

(a) those based on the familial structure of the household, which identify the number, size, and type of family in that household;

(b) those based on the age and sex structure, which identify the numbers of children, adults and, sometimes, people of pensionable age in the household.

The British CENSUS uses both of these types. The selection of the HEAD OF HOUSEHOLD is left to respondents to choose according to the criterion of "chief economic supporter."

These definitions closely relate household composition to family composition, and new types of social organization, such as apartment sharing, sheltered accommodation for the elderly, and student accommodation, call into question the adequacy of this type of definition. Critics have also queried the usefulness of the *head of household* definition, since it is often assumed that a man is the head of the household regardless of the social position of any women living in the same household. See also HOMELESSNESS.

housewife see DOMESTIC LABOR.

housing see SOCIOLOGY OF HOUSING.

housing class see URBAN SOCIOLOGY.

human capital the productive investment of resources in human beings rather than in plant and machinery. In economics, such investment in human resources is appraised in comparison with levels of economic return from other kinds of investment. Clearly, investment in human capital begins in the family and continues in school and higher education, and is also affected by such inputs as provision for health care.

As a body of economic theory and associated empirical research, *human-capital theory* explains income differentials as, in part at least, a return to human capital, for example, the correlation between the number of years of formal education and earnings is explained in these terms. Thus, the conclusion is often reached by human capital theorists that the returns on education are high. Similarly, poverty is sometimes explained as arising from a lack of human capital.

Challenges to the arguments of human-capital theory arise from a number of different sources, especially that the returns associated with education in fact arise from other sources, that is, education may act merely as a filter, or screen, and native ability and family background actually account for a significant proportion of the correlations between education and earnings (see SCREENING AND SCREENING HYPOTHESIS). Compare FUNCTIONALIST THEORY OF SOCIAL STRATIFICATION. See also CULTURAL CAPITAL.

human-centered technology an approach to technology design and work organization that aims to enhance the skills and abilities of users by according equal priority to human and organizational issues as well as technical design requirements. Also referred to in manufacturing as *anthropocentric production systems,* this approach is in direct contrast to the technical design philosophy, which is based on the engineering assumption that humans are a source of uncertainty and error in production, and are to be eventually replaced by computer-integrated systems in the so-called unmanned factory of the future (see also TECHNOLOGICAL DETERMINISM, NEW TECHNOLOGY). In its ideal-typical form, human-centered technology incorporates design criteria that allow a unity of conception and execution, skill enhancement (particularly the recognition of tacit skills), and a measure of worker control over work processes and technology through participative systems design.

Human-centered technology was at first associated with the work-humanization initiatives of the 1960s and 1970s, such as the Volvo group technology experiments, job enrichment and job enlargement programs, and the SOCIOTECHNICAL SYSTEMS APPROACH (see also QUALITY OF WORKING LIFE, HUMAN RELATIONS SCHOOL). More recently, human-centered technology is seen as a crucial feature of new production systems based on *flexible specialization*. The theory of flexible specialization posits an emerging post-Fordist manufacturing strategy (see FORDISM AND POST-FORDISM) in which multiskilled and functionally flexible craft workers replace the Tayloristic work patterns of mass production. According to the theory of flexible specialization, human-centered technology is both more efficient in management terms, and more humanitarian and democratic in terms of management-worker relations: a nonzero sum worker-management relationship. Although an important corrective to the simplistic logic of DESKILLING implied by labor process theory, critics of human-centered approaches to technology cast doubt on the extent to which they are realized in practice and point to the negative consequences found in case studies, such as increased levels of stress and work intensification. Furthermore, critics of flexible specialization question the extent of genuine worker participation, and note the increase in peripheral workers on part-time or temporary contracts who support core workers enjoying greater job security and better conditions of work (see Wood, 1989).

humanistic movement an influential movement within psychology and sociology that emphasizes the SELF and the power of individuals to realize their human potential. In psychology, these ideas have been developed in particular by MASLOW and ROGERS, who recognized that psychology was overly concerned with the abnormal (see PSYCHOANALYSIS) and the mechanistic. The humanistic school rectifies this imbalance by concerning itself primarily with human values, with understanding through EMPATHY, and with the complexities of the person operating in a unique PHENOMENOLOGICAL field.

human nature the characteristics pertaining to human beings as a natural kind of species. Sociologists are generally agreed that, compared with other animals, the distinctive quality of human nature is its PLASTICITY. Rather than being born with specific INSTINCTS or predispositions, to be developed by maturation or automatically triggered by the environment, the BEHAVIOR of human beings is influenced by CULTURE and SOCIALIZATION. Thus, suggestions that human beings are naturally acquisitive or aggressive can be countered by examples of societies in which acquisition or warfare are absent. Above all, human beings have developed the capacity for REFLEXIVITY, thus introducing the possibility of rational action and rational social development. Against this, however, CIVILIZATION is sometimes seen as a veneer (for example, Freud, *Civilization and its Discontents*), in which the instinctive aspect of human nature keeps breaking through, tending always to limit PROGRESS or rational development.

Human Relations Area Files located at Yale University, this is an ambitious attempt to construct a coded, descriptive data base of comparative

ETHNOGRAPHIC findings about the cultures of the world. The United States anthropologist G.P. Murdock (1987–1985) was central to the enterprise, among the products of which was his *Ethnographic Atlas* (Murdock, 1967).

human relations school an approach that seeks to understand and prescribe for workplace behavior on the basis of the importance of work-group norms, communication, and supervisory skills. This approach originates with the famous Hawthorne studies (see HAWTHORNE EFFECT), which were undertaken at the Western Electric Company in Cicero, Illinois, during the depression of the 1920s and 1930s (Roethlisberger and Dickson, 1939). In asserting the importance of social and informal organization, the researchers rejected the materialist and individualist assumptions of SCIENTIFIC MANAGEMENT. Organizations designed according to scientific management principles simply failed to meet the workers' needs for social anchorage and recognition. While the problems of demonstrating this were reflected in a series of changes in research methods and levels of analysis, the results were interpreted by the researchers to indicate the salience of group norms and styles of leadership for worker behavior. This was taken to indicate the folly of seeking to understand and design organizations regarded as economically rational and individualistic. In contrast, their framework assumed a model of "social man" within a factory conceived as a social system (Eldridge, 1971).

Elton MAYO is sometimes regarded as the founding father who provided the theoretical underpinnings of this approach. Drawing on the Paretian notion of nonlogical action and sentiment (see PARETO), and the Durkheimian notion of ANOMIE, he thought that provision for social anchorage in the workplace could compensate for wider societal disorganization. Human relations techniques in industry could transform managers into brokers of social harmony. Some writers, however, mainly see Mayo as a popularizing publicity officer (M. Rose, 1988).

Subsequent developments within what has become a diverse approach involve, first, some inconclusive attempts to demonstrate the practical merit of human relations supervisory styles and participative approaches to organizational change (Coch and French, 1949). Secondly, others have drawn attention to the need to consider the tasks workers undertake and their implications for interaction. Attention has, for example, been given to the way in which technology influences tasks, work flow, interactions, group formation, and supervisor-worker relationships. This shift to a more inclusive approach begins to question whether attitudes and supervisory styles can be altered independently of restructuring interactions, and therefore of certain features of formal organizations. These shifts in the level of analysis have begun to bridge the gap between the early anti-Taylorian, social-psychological emphasis on informal groups and the need to consider formal organizational arrangements. Similar arguments are to be found among later neo-human relations theorists who developed the model of "self-actualizing man" (MASLOW, 1954; Herzberg, 1968) and among sociotechnical-systems theorists (see SOCIOTECHNICAL SYSTEMS APPROACH).

Several related criticisms of this approach have been made, not least of which is the inadequate conceptualization of CONFLICT. There has been a tendency to locate it within interpersonal relations, this sociopsychological level of analysis drawing attention away from its relationship to structural arrangements and the distribution of resources, both within organizations and in wider society. It has therefore been difficult for the approach to develop an adequate treatment of labor unions. Relatedly, there has been a tendency to end analysis at the factory gates and offer in-plant solutions to problems on the basis of questionable social-psychological assumptions about the social needs of employees (Goldthorpe, 1968). Finally, the focus of much of the research and the definition of problems therein have been seen to reflect an unquestioned value position that not only more clearly reflects the interests of managers than workers but, in the case of the Hawthorne research, generated a selective interpretation of findings derived from poorly designed experiments (Carey, 1967). However, it is important to note that criticism is not universally and equally applicable to writers who are usually located within the human-relations field, but who are not easily classified as a school or movement (M. Rose, 1988).

Hume, David (1711–1776) Scottish Enlightenment philosopher generally regarded as a main influence on modern EMPIRICISM. Hume's examination of deductive and inductive logic led him to see limitations in both, and made him skeptical about the claims of RATIONALISM. His own philosophical position emphasized a knowledge confined to impressions and ideas, in which there could be no certainty about the form of a world beyond these, for example, no basis for claims for causality. Although Hume also wrote at length on historical and social and economic topics, it is the methodological side of his thinking that has been important as an influence on social science (for example, in discussions of the FACT-VALUE DISTINCTION), fostering an empirical emphasis in the study of society.

hunter-gatherer a member of a society that subsists by exploiting nondomestic/wild food resources. This strategy includes the hunting of large and small game animals, fishing, and the collection of various plant foods. A hunter-gatherer typically lives as part of a small camp or BAND made up of kin. The band is generally nomadic, with its movements following the availability of food, and there is a division of labor by age and sex: women collect plant foods, and men hunt. Today, barely 30,000 of the world's population live by hunting and gathering, though it has supported life for 99% of humankind's existence.

Husserl, Edmund (1859–1938) German idealist philosopher and founder of modern PHENOMENOLOGY. His major works include *Ideas for a Pure Phenomenology and Phenomenological Philosophy* (1913) and *The Crisis of the Human Sciences and Transcendental Phenomenology* (1936). In an attempt to found certain knowledge, Husserl followed the method of Cartesian doubt in reducing the objects of investigation to those phenomena we directly perceive, that is, inner mental states. By bracketing off the outside world and concentrating on consciousness, it is possible to avoid unjustifiable ontological claims. While his philosophy has been widely criticized for its subjectivity, it has been hugely influential. SCHUTZ's phenomenological sociology and HEIDEGGER's existentialism are both based on the importance of phenomena as perceived. See also PHENOMENOLOGY, SOCIOLOGICAL PHENOMENOLOGY.

hydraulic society WITTFOGEL's (1955) term for Asiatic society. He suggested that centralized and despotic state power could be explained as the outcome of the dependence of these Asiatic societies on extensive state-directed public works to provide and maintain irrigation and flood-control systems. However, Wittfogel's contention has not survived detailed empirical examination. Not only do many despotic regimes possess no obvious hydraulic basis, many regimes with such a basis are not despotic (for example, see Leach, 1959, Eberhard, 1965; compare Harris, 1978). At the very least, Wittfogel's explanation is vastly overextended.

Wittfogel's more general claim to have entirely undermined MARX's assumptions about the implications of materialism are similarly overstated. His argument that his work also demonstrated (a) that the totalitarianism of Russian as well as Chinese communism could be explained as building on the despotic and hydraulic legacy, and (b) the dependence of any future freedom on a resistance to all encroachments of state power are similarly challengeable. Compare GEOGRAPHICAL DETERMINISM, CULTURAL MATERIALISM.

hypergamy within CASTE, the process in which, on marriage, a woman, but not a man, may be allowed to move into a husband's caste.

hypothesis any proposition advanced for testing or appraisal as a generalization about a phenomenon. See also EXPERIMENTAL HYPOTHESIS, NULL HYPOTHESIS, HYPOTHETICO-DEDUCTIVE EXPLANATION AND METHOD.

hypothetical imperative KANT's term for advice about action that has the form "if you wish to achieve X, do Y." Such advice, based on empirical evidence, is not binding, but optional. Thus it lacks the force of a *categorical imperative,* Kant's term for any moral injunction that can be held to possess a universal force. The basis of such categorical imperatives (for example, "thou shall not kill") is to "act only on the maxim through which you can at the same time will that it should become a universal law."

hypothetico-deductive explanation and method an alternative to INDUCTION based on the idea that HYPOTHESES are essential in science, as both the basis of proposed generalization and their test. In this approach or method, hypotheses and theories are advanced, and generalizations and predictions made, on the basis of deductions from these, with:

(a) successful prediction being taken as a test of the adequacy of the hypothesis and theory;

(b) explanation being seen as achieved once successful predictions have been made.

In its fullest (sometimes also logically formalized) form, hypothetico-deductive explanation and method results in a network of deductively interrelated propositions and theories. The emphasis on the importance of the advancing and the testing of hypotheses, or conjectures, has also meant that the hypothetico-deductive method is often allied with falsification and FALSIFICATIONISM, although not always so. See also COVERING LAW MODEL AND DEDUCTIVE NOMOLOGICAL EXPLANATION, and EXPLANATION. Objections to suggestions that the hypothetico-deductive method is *the* method of science should also be noted (see REALISM).

While a hypothetico-deductive approach to testing and theory, and the construction of formal theories, has been advocated in sociology (see FORMAL THEORY AND FORMALIZATION OF THEORY), it has also been sharply opposed (see GROUNDED THEORY, but compare ANALYTICAL INDUCTION).

I

id one of the three elements of personality in FREUD's theory. It is the basis of personality, containing all the inherited resources, especially the INSTINCTS, and it is from the id that the other two elements, the EGO and the SUPEREGO, develop.

The id is in the unconscious part of the mind, is closely linked to biological processes, and operates under the *pleasure principle,* therefore seeking to gratify the instincts. Freud posits two main instincts—sex and aggression. Sex expresses the life instinct (EROS), and aggression the death instinct (THANATOS).

The desires of the id cannot be met realistically, so the ego develops to ensure that the energies are released in a form acceptable to society. One means of transforming the instinctual energies into acceptable forms is through defense mechanisms.

idealism 1. (philosophy) the doctrine that the world as encountered is in part or whole a construction of IDEAS. **2.** (SOCIOLOGY) the doctrine that sociology must explain primarily by reference to the subjective and conscious intentions of persons (see also MEANINGFUL UNDERSTANDING AND EXPLANATION).

In philosophy, sense **1.** is one of the two basic possibilities that arise in considering the relations between, on one side, mind or subject and, on the other, world or object (see SUBJECT AND OBJECT, EPISTEMOLOGY). For the world to be known by the subject, idealism suggests that there have to be guiding ideas or theories that unavoidably form the world as it is perceived or thought about. It regards its epistemological opposite, EMPIRICISM, as naive in supposing that the world as it really is can form, via the senses, a mind that is initially blank and passive.

Plato's idealism suggested that the objects of the world were in themselves imperfect versions of ideal objects that were their essences. Modern idealism derives from KANT and HEGEL. Kant suggests a two-way relation between mind and world, with the mind contributing universal forms by means of which the substantial and empirical world might be perceived and thought about. For Kant, this carries the implications that the world as it is in itself, unstructured by the mind, is unknowable; and that there is awareness, but not knowledge, of the mind as it is in itself—the "noumenal"—and this is not structured by the forms that permit empirical knowledge, for example, of space, time, and causality. Hegel, rejecting Kant's unknowable "world-in-itself," achieves a fully idealistic reconciliation by regarding mind and subject as essentially social and historical, and simultaneously the world as itself constructed or postulated in the successive categories of mind and subject. He attempted a revision of LOGIC, with the world itself (not simply the mind) conceived as a succession of arguments.

The idea that mind constructs world rather than vice versa is most evident within sense **2.**, in the wide range of sociological theories that see the social world as the outcome of conscious human action, that is, action that necessarily involves thought and ideas on the part of persons. Persons are subjects, essentially knowledgeable about the situations in which they are placed, who intend (see INTENTIONALITY) their actions. The explanation of action necessarily involves reference to those intentions, and normally interprets the meaning of actions by reference to intention, motive, and reason. See also WINCH.

The most significant critique of sense **1.** is that of Marx, who attempts a materialist development of Hegel—Hegel put back on his feet—by which the shape of social history and development is not determined by successive postulations of ideas, that is, the underlying movements of mind in the successions of the spirits of particular ages, but by one range of social forces, particularly economic. For Marx, economic changes underlie all ideological changes. This emphasis on a socioeconomic substructure, he regards as a new form of materialism that nevertheless retains much of Hegel's dialectic notion.

Recent discussion, in attempting to refurbish materialism, has extended Marx's critique to sense **2.** by emphasizing the material aspects of subjectivity, in particular its construction in social location, as opposed to the idealist subject. In doing so, it represents both subject and object, mind and world, as constituted in essentially social and unconscious semiosis, and rooted in social practices.

ideal speech situation see HABERMAS.

ideal type or **pure type** any conceptualization (*idealization*) of a general or particular phenomenon that, for analytical and explanatory purposes, represents this phenomenon only in its abstract or pure (hence idealized) form(s). The foundations of ideal-type analysis in sociology derive from Max WEBER, who was influenced by the use of ideal types in economics.

An element of idealization is a feature of any use of general concepts, whether in science, social science, or everyday life (see also TYPIFICATION). However, there are variations in the extent to which concepts are idealized (compare TYPE, TYPOLOGY).

The most explicit use of abstract and idealized concepts occurs both in the physical sciences (for example, the concept of the perfect vacuum) and the social sciences (for example, in economics, the concept of perfect competition).

In the physical sciences, the use of idealizations allows a more simplified account of phenomena. This makes possible the formulation of high-level universal generalizations (scientific laws), in terms of which real world cases can be analyzed and explained as more complex empirical departures.

Weber's use of ideal types occurred with a somewhat different aim. Most clearly apparent is what Weber did *not* mean by ideal types:

(a) they do not state an ethical ideal;

(b) they do not state an average type;

(c) they do not exhaust reality, that is, they do not correspond exactly to any empirical instances.

What Weber has to say more positively about ideal types is that:

(a) they are mental constructs that are ideal in the logical sense, that is, they state a logical extreme;

(b) they distort and abstract from reality;

(c) they can be used to formulate an abstract model of the general form and the interrelated causes and effects of a complex recurring phenomenon (for example, BUREAUCRACY).

A further requirement is that these concepts must be objectively possible, in that they must approximate to concrete realities and also be subjectively adequate, that is, be understandable in terms of the subjective orientations of a hypothetical individual actor (see also METHODOLOGICAL INDIVIDUALISM).

Weber's main use of ideal-type concepts was to provide clearly stated general concepts (for example, rational or traditional—see TYPES OF ACTION) that in turn can be used to allow the unambiguous statement of historical concepts, formulated as departures from general ideal types. Classification and comparison of phenomena and the appraisal of causal hypotheses are facilitated by this means. For example, while the specific ideal-type concept of the PROTESTANT ETHIC is formulated by Weber as approximating to rational action, and possessing causal significance in the rise of Western capitalism, Catholicism and non-Western religions are formulated as historically specific types of traditional and nonrational action that retard capitalism. Ideal types are used by Weber in *thought experiments* (for example, Weber's estimation that rational capitalism would have originated in Asia as well as in Europe had there been any form of religion in Asia equivalent to Protestantism). Historical concepts formulated as specific departures from ideal types bring a precision that would otherwise be lacking in such comparative analysis.

It is clear from this that Weber's deployment of ideal-type concepts involves him in the use of explicit (or implicit) *type generalizations,* that is, assumptions about the so-called lawlike regularities associated with the occurrence of empirical approximations of ideal-type concepts and models. In this way Weber refers to "typical complexes of meaning" or "established generalizations from experience," such as Gresham's law (that is, "bad money drives out good"). Without assumptions of this kind there could be no appraisal of causal significance in ideal-type analysis.

In contrast with the position in the physical sciences, Weber does not in general envisage that an agreement on ideal-type concepts will emerge in sociology, or that such concepts will become the basis of a system of high-level general laws. At times, he refers to the role of ideal-type concepts as HEURISTIC, as merely aiding the clearer description and analysis of historical cases. Among the reasons for this limit on the scienticity of sociology is the continued presence he sees for multiple perspectives within sociology arising from competing values (see OBJECTIVITY AND NEUTRALITY, FACT AND VALUE). The difficulty that arises from Weber's position is that it renders ideal-type analysis in sociology essentially arbitrary.

Two main responses exist to this problem in Weber's approach. Critics such as PARSONS (1937) argue that whatever differences of degree must be recognized between sociology and physical science, ideal-type analysis can only become coherent by seeking the cumulative development of general concepts and the development of a potentially unitary theory in sociology, avoiding Weber's "type atomism." Other critics (for example, Winch, 1958) argue that ideal-type analysis should be dropped as utterly inappropriate to sociological analysis once this is seen as involving the meaningful understanding of specific cases and not the development of general concepts and general theories.

identity the sense of SELF that develops as the child differentiates from parents and family and takes a place in society.

The NEO-FREUDIAN theorist Erik Erikson has proposed that there is a crisis of identity in adolescence. It is at this stage of development that young persons search for an identity, trying out different friendship groups, different life styles, different career plans. Ideally, by the end of adolescence the identity has stabilized and young persons accept themselves, feeling at ease with this identity.

In Erikson's view, therefore, identity forms as a result of social interaction, and problems with identity occur if an adolescent feels alienated from society through, for example, ethnic differences or unemployment.

ideology 1. any system of ideas underlying and informing social and political action. **2.** more particularly, any system of ideas that justifies or legitimates the subordination of one group by another. **3.** an all-embracing encyclopedic knowledge, capable of breaking down prejudice and of use in social reform. This sense would appear to be the original usage, when the term was coined by Antoine Destutt de Tracy in the period of social optimism in the French Enlightenment (see AGE OF ENLIGHTENMENT). Thus, between sense **3.** and sense **2.** there has occurred a full reversal of meaning. It is senses **1.** and **2.** that are now of prime interest.

In the work of MARX and ENGELS, which has had most influence in the development of the theory of ideology, the term had several connotations. In *The German Ideology,* Marx and Engels emphasized two points. The first was that ideologies presented a picture of the world from the point of view of a RULING CLASS. The second was that this picture was necessarily a distorted one because the interests of the ruling class are, by definition, partial and because they do not represent the interests of humanity in general. In later criticisms and developments, ideology is presented in terms of a social CLASS representing its particular sectional interests as natural and universal (as the national interest, for example).

Many later writers have used the term in something like sense **2.** but in a more general way to refer, for example, to GENDER IDEOLOGY, to race ideologies, and to generational ideologies. Such uses of the term involve the idea that all power relationships include doctrines of justification. For example, in the imperial era the subordination of black people was justified by ideas that emphasized the natural superiority of white people and the enlightenment that imperialism could bring.

One significant challenge to Marx's view is provided by MANNHEIM's SOCIOLOGY OF KNOWLEDGE. Mannheim argued that it was a mistake to see the viewpoint of one class as wrong and another as right. Sociologically, it was more valuable to see *all* belief systems as representing the interests of particular groups, including communist and socialist ideas, along with conservative ones. Mannheim followed Marx's usage in calling ideas that support the powerful ideologies, and ideas that opposed a given system or sought to justify a different one, UTOPIAS.

Modern Marxists have contributed to developments of Marx's theory of ideology, prompted especially by the failure of a revolutionary working class to emerge in Western capitalist societies, a fact that they have sought to explain, at least in part, as the outcome of ideology. Important examples of these approaches include:

(a) the FRANKFURT SCHOOL OF CRITICAL THEORY;

(b) GRAMSCI's account of HEGEMONY, which in turn has also influenced work on the mass media and mass culture;

(c) ALTHUSSER's conception of the ideological state apparatus.

All these theories, however, have attracted criticism for exaggerating the significance of cultural ideas and VALUES in the maintenance of consensus compared with economic and political POWER or everyday routines. See DOMINANT IDEOLOGY THESIS. See also FALSE CONSCIOUSNESS, CLASS IMAGERY.

idiographic and **nomothetic** of divergent orientations to social enquiry (and their associated methods): an *idiographic* focus is on cultural and historical

Discipline	Focus of Study/Method
HISTORY CULTURAL SCIENCES	IDIOGRAPHIC Meaningful reality; empathic method [Dilthey] Unique determinations with respect to values [Rickert; Windelband]
SCIENCE, including SOCIOLOGY in its generalizing modes [Rickert] or excluding it [Dilthey]	NOMOTHETIC Causal law-like explanation

Fig. 11. **Idiographic and nomothetic.** See main entry.

particulars, using methods such as ETHNOGRAPHY and biography; a *nomothetic* focus seeks to establish general laws following an explicitly natural-science model of knowledge. The distinction was first conceptualized in these terms by the German neo-Kantian philosopher WINDELBAND. In the late-19th century METHODENSTREIT, German theorists such as DILTHEY, RICKERT, and Windelband debated the question of which methods best suited particular social sciences, or whether the two methods could be combined (see Fig. 11). These concerns also influenced Max WEBER, who, like many sociologists subsequently sought to combine both methods. See also GEISTESWISSENSCHAFTEN AND NATURWISSENSCHAFTEN, MEANINGFUL UNDERSTANDING AND EXPLANATION, IDEAL-TYPE, VERSTEHEN, HERMENEUTICS, DOUBLE HERMENEUTIC.

idiographic method a method of investigation that is concerned with the individual or unique experience, rather than with generalities. Thus it is the opposite of a NOMOTHETIC approach. See IDIOGRAPHIC and Fig. 12. Compare ETHNOMETHODOLOGY, MEANINGFUL UNDERSTANDING AND EXPLANATION; see DILTHEY, RICKERT.

Illich, Ivan (1926–) Viennese-born libertarian philosopher, social critic, and one-time Catholic priest, currently based in Mexico, whose provocative critique of economic development has attracted much attention. Illich regards so-called economic development as, in reality, leading to the destruction of the *vernacular skills* previously possessed by people in self-sufficient preindustrial economies. According to Illich, people have become increasingly dependent on professionals, experts, and specialists for the satisfaction of many of their fundamental needs—for example, the provision of health services and compulsory schooling. In Illich's terms, the provision of such services have often become *radical monopolies* since, with the destruction of earlier traditions, there is often no longer any alternative but to have recourse to such expert provision, and in many ways the services offered by such experts are debilitating and dehumanizing, leading to passive consumption and dependency. The solutions proposed by Illich are for more democratic, participatory structures that foster human autonomy, for example, instead of compulsory education, access to a choice of educational frameworks; instead of hierarchically controlled specialist services, the establishment of communication networks for the mutual exchange of services. Another of Illich's suggestions is that "high quanta of energy degrade social relations" as much as physical milieu, and that accordingly the bicycle is the mode of transport most compatible with egalitarian participatory principles. While Illich's thinking is utopian and polemical, his combination of a religious romantic conservatism with radical critique has stimulated sociological reflection. Main works by Illich are *Deschooling Society* (1972), *Tools for Conviviality* (1973), *Medical Nemesis: The Expropriation of Health* (1975), and *Shadow-work* (1981). See also HIDDEN CURRICULUM, IATROGENIC DISEASE.

imperative coordination the likelihood that a command within a given organization or society will be obeyed. The term is Timasheff's English translation (also adopted by PARSONS, 1964) of WEBER's concept *Herrschaft*, more usually translated as DOMINATION. As Parsons suggests, *Herrschaft* has no adequate translation in English. Parson and Timasheff were attempting to bring out more clearly the distinction in Weber's work between POWER *(Macht)*—the capacity possessed by a SOCIAL ACTOR to carry out his or her own will despite resistance from others—and *Herrschaft*. Where Weber is more particularly concerned with *legitime Herrschaft*, Parsons uses the term *authority*. See also LEGITIMATE AUTHORITY OR POLITICAL LEGITIMACY.

impression management see DRAMATURGY.

incest taboo the prohibition on sexual relations between certain categories of kin, generally those of close blood relationship. Some form of incest taboo is found in all known societies, although the relationships that the taboo covers vary. Most common are child-parent and sibling relationships. Some societies actively encourage sexual relationships between cousins, whereas in other societies such relationships would be seen as incestuous. Other societies may not prohibit sexual relationships between certain categories, but would prohibit marriage between the same people.

Various explanations have been put forward for the universality of some form of incest taboo. Some have argued that the now known genetic consequences explain this. But not all human groups would have made this link, and cousin marriage preference would probably have not existed if this were the case. LÉVI-STRAUSS argued that it existed to ensure that people marry out of their social group and thus form alliances with other social groups. (However, sexual prohibitions are not the same as marriage rules.) FREUD's explanation rests on the strong attraction of incestuous relations, particularly between son and mother, and the taboo exists to reduce conflict within the nuclear family. The internalization of the taboo is, for Freud, an important part of the psychological development of the individual.

Given the variety of ways in which the taboo is expressed, emphasis on its universality, and hence on universal explanations, is probably misplaced. Greater emphasis on why particular societies designate particular relationships as incestuous and not others may be a more fruitful line of inquiry.

incommensurability 1. a relation between scientific theories in which the propositions and overall content of the theories cannot be directly compared. **2.** a conception of scientific theories holding that all observations are theory-relative (see THEORY REALTIVITY and that there may exist no theory-neutral data language of the kind assumed by inductive, logical positivist or falsificationist conceptions of science. The conception is most associated with Thomas KUHN and Paul FEYERABEND, and it is often assumed to also imply a more general RELATIVISM. However, this is not Feyerabend's view: incommensurability is seen as a possible, not a necessary, relation between theories. If theories cannot always be strictly compared in terms of a theory-neutral data language (or using any unambiguous or unchanging decision rule), the proponents of competing theories can enter into a dialogue with the aim of appreciating each other's view and reaching a decision on this basis. See also TRUTH, POSITIVISM, FALSIFICATIONISM.

incorporation 1. the process in which the occupational and political organizations of the working class are accommodated within the existing order. **2.** the argument that working-class consciousness has been shaped by the values and interests of other, dominant, classes.

The concepts have a place in the arguments about working CLASS CONSCIOUSNESS and CLASS IMAGERY. The first usage, for example, is resonant of the arguments about a separate status group within the working class, especially in the 19th century—the LABOR ARISTOCRACY. The second might be compared to discussions of HEGEMONY. Often the distinction between sense **1.** and sense **2.** is analytical; in practice, organization and consciousness are treated in an integrated, coextensive way.

independent variable the VARIABLE that is experimentally manipulated or otherwise controlled in order to observe its effect. For example, the speed limit may be systematically varied on certain roads and the effect of this measured in terms of road accident statistics. The speed restrictions would be the independent variable, the road accident figures the DEPENDENT VARIABLE. However, in social research it is often not possible to set up experiments to test theories, and observations have to be made from retrospective occurrences. Thus a study may be made, for example, of the effect of age of marriage on family size. In this example, age of marriage would be the independent variable, and family size would be the dependent variable. See also EXPERIMENTAL METHOD.

indeterminism see DETERMINISM.

indexical expression any word or expression that draws its sense only from the immediate context of its use, for example, personal pronouns. *Indexicality* can be seen as a frequent feature of social concepts and many sociological concepts, a feature that means that SOCIAL ACTORS as well as sociologists must often undertake careful interpretive work to determine the meanings prevailing within particular social settings (see also HERMENEUTICS).

For ethnomethodologists, the indexicality of social concepts and social accounts means that the kind of generalized sociological and scientific accounts sought by orthodox sociologists are unattainable. However, elements of indexicality can be seen as a feature of all concepts, including those in physical science (see also INCOMMENSURABILITY, RELATIVISM). While this certainly means that science can no longer reasonably be seen in simple positivist or empiricist terms as directly referring to phenomena, this does not prevent general theories from being advanced. Likewise, elements of indexicality in sociological accounts need not preclude workable general accounts (compare ETHNOMETHODOLOGY).

indicator see SOCIAL INDICATORS.

indigenous group any ethnic group originating and remaining in an area subject to colonization. Native Americans, aboriginals, and Maoris are all examples of ethnic groups that inhabited lands before colonial expansion (in North America, Australia, and New Zealand respectively) and who have retained their distinctive identities. Such groups often appear to go through a sequence of defeat, despair, and regeneration, if they have not been exterminated or their culture completely destroyed by the colonial power. The concept of "indigenous group" is used by the United Nations to obtain lost rights for such groups. A similar term is "native peoples." See also MULTICULTURALISM.

individual level data information collected from individuals by any form of research methodology, for example, INTERVIEWS, observational studies, QUESTIONNAIRES. Individual level data may subsequently be aggregated into groups, for example, households, school classes, or social classes.

induction and **inductive logic** the process in which a general statement, suggesting a regular association between two or more variables, is derived from a series of empirical observations. In contrast with deductive arguments, in which a conclusion follows logically from initial premises (*logical inference*—see LOGIC), no such strict logical necessity exists in connection with induction, even though, following MILL's formulation (see COMPARATIVE METHOD), this is sometimes referred to as *inductive logic*. The reason why no strict necessity exists in connection with inductive statements is that inductive argument depends on generalization from a series of known cases: "A_1 is b, A_2 is b, A_3 is b, etc." to suggest that, therefore, any A *is likely to be* b. The views that scientific statements are only justifiable by further procedural rules such as *falsification* or by realist criteria (see REALISM) arise in this context. See also EMPIRICISM, POPPER.

industrialization the general process by which economies and societies in which agriculture and the production of handicrafts predominate become transformed into economies and societies in which manufacturing and related extractive industries are central. This process occurred first in Britain during the INDUSTRIAL REVOLUTION and was soon repeated in other Western European societies. Profound changes in the social organization of production and distribution are involved, especially a rapid increase in the DIVISION OF LABOR, both between individuals and occupational groups and also between industrialized and nonindustrialized nations, changes that led to a transformation of the techniques and the social organization of agriculture (see AGRICULTURAL REVOLUTION) as well as of extractive and manufacturing industry.

Criteria vary for delineating countries as industrialized or industrializing.

The most commonly used indicators are (a) the percentage of the labor force employed in the industrial and service sectors compared with primary production and (b) manufacturing output as a proportion of gross national product. However, other criteria such as levels of investment (see ECONOMIC TAKEOFF), the extent of URBANIZATION, and levels of literacy may also be used as more general indicators of industrialization and of MODERNIZATION and development. Thus, a country such as New Zealand, which is mainly an exporter of primary products but has a highly modernized agriculture, high literacy, etc., may be regarded as an industrialized country in the most general sense of the term.

The process of industrialization is closely linked with the overall modernization of societies, especially the process of urbanization, the development of science and TECHNOLOGY, and POLITICAL MODERNIZATION. Each of these changes can be viewed as (a) a prerequisite of industrialization, (b) a direct consequence or requirement of it, or (c) both of these.

While similarities exist in the overall pattern of industrialization in the first wave of European industrialized societies, important differences are also evident, for example, in the role played by the state in initiating industrialization, limited in Britain but more extensive in Germany. Differences also exist between countries that were part of the first wave of industrialization and those for which industrialization occurs later. For example, while later entrants can gain advantage by learning from the mistakes of earlier entrants, they often find it difficult to compete with more established industrial economies, thus sometimes restricting new entrants to a relationship of ECONOMIC DEPENDENCY. As well as temporal differences of this sort, important regional differences also exist.

industrial relations the relations between employees and employers, and the study of these relations.

Students of industrial relations have been concerned with the form, basis, and implications of the different ways in which employment relationships have been regulated both within and between societies. Sociology is but one of a variety of disciplines that have contributed to the study of this area. Historically, the study of industrial relations has been either descriptive or prescriptive.

Debate between competing theories led Fox (1965) to distinguish between unitarist and pluralist perspectives. In the unitarist perspective, cooperation is normal and organizational efficiency and rationality reside in managerial prerogative; conflict is seen as irrational and due to communications problems, agitators, etc. Pluralists, in contrast, regard conflicts between legitimate interest groups as normal, but resolvable through mutually advantageous collective bargaining procedures. This approach, exemplifed in the Donovan Commission (1968), underpinned several reforms to British industrial relations in the 1970s, but has been subjected to several criticisms, for example:

(a) that in focusing on the failure of industrial relations institutions to regulate conflict, PLURALISM neglected the inequalities of power and advantage that generate conflict in the first place (Goldthorpe, 1974);

(b) that corporatist or Marxist theories provide a better account of industrial relations (see CORPORATISM).

Thus, theorists have focused on the attempts by successive postwar British governments to deal with industrial relations problems through forms of state intervention that have involved tripartite arrangements (trade unions, employers, and the state). Marxist scholars, however, have remained unimpressed with the attempts to radicalize pluralism (Wood and Elliott, 1977). In the Marxist framework, the employment relationship is characterized by class exploitation and there can be no such thing as a fair wage. Conflict is endemic and employers constantly need to legitimate their control. For some Marxists, therefore, any attempts by employers and labor unions at mutual accommodation are suspect, since the existing unjust arrangements will be preserved. Moreover, pluralist and corporatist views of the state are seen to be naive, since capital is regarded as the main beneficiary of state intervention.

In stressing the need to consider employment relationships within the dynamics of capitalist society, a key feature of which is the way the conflict between capital and labor is expressed in class relationships and state activity, Marxists have produced valuable insights and broadened the study of industrial relations. Nevertheless, this perspective also has its critics. Crouch (1982), for example, suggests that some Marxists underplay the constant choices about goals and means that employees have to make, while attempts to ascribe industrial conflict to class relations is unconvincing. Clearly, the resurgence of forms of unitarism in the 1980s also indicates a continuing debate about the balance of power in industrial relations. In the late 1980s the neoliberalist policies being pursued in Britain, theoretically underpinned by the writings of Hayek and Friedman, are founded on a marked distrust of both corporatist institutions and labor unions, and express the view that many industrial relations problems derive from the excessive use of power by union officials (MacInnes, 1987).

In sum, as with most areas of sociological investigation, the study of industrial relations is marked by theoretical controversy. The above perspectives illustrate the point that perceptions of, and prescriptions for, solutions to industrial relations problems are inextricably linked to particular theories.

Industrial Revolution the massive interrelated economic, technological, and social changes, usually dated *c*. 1760–1850, in which Britain (later, many other countries) became a manufacturing economy based on a new machine technology and the factory system. As a result of these changes Britain also became the first INDUSTRIAL SOCIETY (see INDUSTRIALIZATION).

The decisive features of this industrial revolution were:

(a) increased capitalist control over the labor process and a greatly increased DIVISION OF LABOR and consequent improvements in overall efficiency and productivity in factories and workshops.

(b) the invention of new machinery and the application first of improvements in water power and later steam power, in mining, manufacturing (especially textiles and iron and steel), and transport (roads, canals, railways, and sea).

Once underway, the Industrial Revolution also brought rapid population growth (see DEMOGRAPHIC TRANSITION) and URBANIZATION with attendant social problems, such as urban squalor, ill health, and absence of effective urban administration.

Whether or not in its early stages the Industrial Revolution led to an absolute reduction in the STANDARD OF LIVING is a matter of some dispute (see Ashton, 1954). What is clear is that many categories of workers (for example, handloom weavers) displaced by new machinery and those subject to high levels of unemployment during periods of severe recession suffered greatly, even if, as some commentators suggest, the overall effect of the new industrial society was generally to expand consumption and social welfare. Certainly the increased discipline—the tyranny of the new control over the labor process and of the clock—was a new dimension unwelcome to and resisted by many workers.

The causes of the Industrial Revolution in Britain are complex and much disputed by economic historians. It is agreed, however, that once the revolution was underway it was the capacity of the new industries to provide new products, such as cheap cotton goods and household wares, both at home and overseas, that sustained the impetus to further economic growth and social change. See also ECONOMIC AND SOCIAL DEVELOPMENT.

The onset of the Industrial Revolution in Britain was quickly followed by similar transformations in other European societies and in the United States. Subsequently, a number of these societies were able to outstrip British society and to lead the way in a new period of economic and technological development (including electric power, the new chemicals industry, and radio and telecommunications) sometimes referred to as the *second industrial revolution*.

A further question of importance concerns the link between industrialization and capitalism. While it is clear that the first industrialization was the outcome of the prior appearance of capitalist social relations, it is equally apparent that industrialization was also initiated in SOCIALIST SOCIETIES (see also STATE CAPITALISM AND STATE MONOPOLY CAPITALISM.

industrial society 1. that form of society, or any particular society, in which INDUSTRIALIZATION and MODERNIZATION have occurred.

The general term originates from SAINT-SIMON who chose it to reflect the emerging central role of manufacturing industry in 18th-century Europe, in contrast with the previous PREINDUSTRIAL SOCIETY and AGRARIAN SOCIETY.

As the basic form of modern society, the term "industrial society" covers both CAPITALIST SOCIETIES and SOCIALIST SOCIETIES. The assumption is that all industrial societies share a number of interrelated basic features stemming from the industrialized nature of them, including factory-based production; a declining proportion of the population employed in agriculture; the separation of the household from production; increases in the level of production and improvements in productivity, urbanization, improvements in consumption and social welfare; the provision of mass education; and the achievement of widespread literacy. Among other more disputed general features of industrial societies usually included are the tendency for extended family and kinship relationships to decline as the basis of social organization (see FAMILY, KINSHIP) and for religion to be undermined by secularization. **2.** a disputed model of modern society proposed as an alternative model to either capitalist society or socialist society. In this, more restricted sense of the term, a number of more specific propositions are advanced about modern society:

(a) industrialization rather than capitalism or socialism is the decisive factor shaping modern society.

(b) rather than class conflicts of the dichotomous Marxian kind, CLASS and STATUS divisions occur that simply reflect divisions within the occupational structure of all industrial societies. While these divisions result in a plurality of class and status conflicts (including SECTORAL CLEAVAGES), they occur in a manner that does not routinely undermine the basic effectiveness of continuity of these societies (see also CLASS STRATIFICATION, DAHRENDORF).

(c) there are clear signs of an ultimate CONVERGENCE between capitalist and socialist societies (including domination by a technostructure of managers and technical experts—see also MANAGERIAL REVOLUTION) so that these societies will in the end emerge as neither conventionally capitalist nor conventionally socialist in social and economic form.

industrial sociology the study of work as paid employment, and of industry. The chief concerns of this subdiscipline have been the division of labor, both social and technical (see also OCCUPATIONAL STRUCTURE); the experience of work; and the role and consequences of TECHNOLOGY within industry. In addition, the subject includes the study of industrial bureaucracies and INDUSTRIAL RELATIONS (see Burns, 1962). See also ORGANIZATION THEORY.

Industrial sociology has its roots in the analysis of INDUSTRIALIZATION provided by MARX, WEBER, and DURKHEIM and has involved comparative studies between advanced industrial societies. However, much of industrial sociology has been concentrated on studies of the workplace, with cross-cultural issues dealt with implicitly by reference to North American texts (for example, Blauner, 1964), leaving more explicit comparative analysis to ECO-

NOMIC SOCIOLOGY or COMPARATIVE SOCIOLOGY. In consequence, the subdiscipline has been particularly concerned with the impact of industrialization in terms of the issues raised by worker attitudes and motivation, through a consideration of SCIENTIFIC MANAGEMENT, HUMAN RELATIONS, and ALIENATION and POWER relations *within* industry.

This preoccupation with social relations and worker morale within the factory came under pressure with the development of the postindustrial thesis (see POSTINDUSTRIAL SOCIETY) in the 1960s and the emergence of the service sector as a major employer of labor. More serious criticisms, in terms of their impact on the integrity of the subdiscipline, came in the 1970s, following, first, the rediscovery of the labor process (P. Thompson, 1989) and, secondly, the development of FEMINIST THEORY. The common point of the criticisms was that industrial sociology was too limited in its major focus on factory work. The two critiques, however, differed markedly in their emphases. The labor process critique was more concerned with the political economy and the relationship between, on the one hand, the organization and control of labor and on the other, the appropriation and realization of surplus value. The feminist critique was concerned with extending the domain and discourse to cover the following: the relationship between paid and unpaid work; gender issues; and the relation between work and society. In consequence of these criticisms, the focus of industrial sociology has changed recently from industry to work (see also SOCIOLOGY OF WORK).

informal economy that assortment of paid work that takes place outside the formal structure of paid employment. It is not subject to the normal constraints of registration and taxation, and, generally therefore, is supported by cash payments.

It is now realized that the study of formal employment does not exhaust the scope of the SOCIOLOGY OF WORK. Sociologist Ray Pahl and economist Jonathan Gershuny published a provocative article (1980) in which they put forward the idea that there were in fact three different economies— the formal, the informal, and the household. In the formal economy, the one recognized by governments, people sell their ability to work for wages and salaries; in the informal economy people may work off the books, that is, receive cash but not declare it to the state, or they may do a job for a neighbor or relative that would be repaid in kind; in the household economy the role of women in performing routine cooking, cleaning, and caring in the home is recognized as well as do-it-yourself jobs carried out by both men and women.

Since 1980, conferences have been held, research has flourished, and books and articles have been published on activities outside employment. Fig. 12 summarizes different types of work and economy that have been identified by researchers.

A useful way of clarifying the differences (Pahl, 1984) is to imagine a

Paid	Unpaid
wage-labour formal economy	domestic labour household economy
shadow wage-labour black economy	work outside employment communal economy

Fig. 12. **Informal economy.** Different types of work and economy.

woman ironing a garment at home. She could be ironing the garment before she delivers it to her employer for wages (wage labor in the formal economy). She could be ironing the garment that she proposes to sell to get some extra cash without declaring it to the state (wage labor or self-employment in the informal economy). She may be ironing the garment as a housewife for her husband on whom she is financially dependent (domestic labor in the household economy). Finally, she may be ironing the garment with no expectation of payment for a friend, neighbor, or relative or out of some obligation to the local church, club, or other voluntary organization to which she belongs (work outside of employment in the "communal economy").

Although some research suggests that the informal economy grew during the economic crisis of the 1980s, it is important to keep its size and significance in perspective. In sum, work outside formal employment needs to be studied in relation to that which goes on inside formal employment. Researchers need to consider the *connections* between the two, and examine both how wage-labor relations penetrate unpaid work, and how socially generated ideologies shape patterns of waged work. See also DOMESTIC LABOR, PRIVATE AND PUBLIC SPHERES.

information society see POSTINDUSTRIAL SOCIETY.

information technology (IT) a general term applied to all computer-based technologies of human communication. It can be viewed as a broad subtype of NEW TECHNOLOGY. Office automation is the most widely implemented form of information technology and has had major implications for the organization and experience of clerical work. This development has stimulated much sociological research and commentary on the issues of DESKILLING and PROLETARIANIZATION as well as the feminization of clerical work (Crompton and Jones, 1984). Information technology also underpins the flow of information (that is, information systems) within organizations, and is used as an aid to management in attempts to control and coordinate activities of the enterprise and respond to challenges in their environment. This development has led to interest in the possible impact of information technology on managerial control, particularly whether it concentrates control at the senior levels or, conversely, democratizes it throughout the organization (Lenk, 1982).

INFORMATION TECHNOLOGY (IT)

The sociological interest in information technology extends beyond the issues of office automation and organizational control. There are at least two other related concerns. The first is an evaluation of the claim that information technology has facilitated the evolution of POSTINDUSTRIAL SOCIETY (Lyon, 1988). The second concern is the degree to which information technology is socially shaped rather than technologically determined. Information technology does not develop within a social vacuum, and current developments toward integration and interlinking of computer systems has led to growing concern about confidentiality and the potential misuse of data.

Historically, information technology can be said to have begun with the building of the Colossus computing machines in Britain in 1943, designed to decode the German Enigma code. Parallel to this development was the building of the more general purpose ENIAC (Electronic Numerical Integrator and Calculator) computers in the United States. These early computers were the direct antecedents of the first business computers. The early forms of information technology were based on mainframe computers and batch processing; as a technology limited in its general application to routine numeric activities, it was more a matter of computation of data than the communication of information. With the development and introduction of more powerful interactive (real-time) computer systems and of smaller computers (minis and micros) coupled with the development of off-the-shelf computer programs for word processing, financial spreadsheets, statistics, and similar activities (generally known as software packages), information technology became generally available throughout industry and beyond (extending into peoples' homes and leisure). More recently, similar systems have been developed for the retail sector, known as the Electronic Point of Sale system (EPOS), which can electronically monitor and control all aspects of retailing activities. This is similar in design to library systems, and both use bar coding and light pens to communicate between user and system. This approach to human computer interaction is also being extended to other systems in other types of organizations where objects and people need to be identified, catalogued, and counted, for example, in hospitals. Much research and development within information technology is currently focused on the search for other forms of communicating with computers than the ubiquitous QWERTY keyboard. Bar coding and light pens are one solution applicable to standardized activities. The major research and development interest, however, concerns the development of voice recognition systems. This research is one aspect of a worldwide program of research into the "fifth generation" of computers. It was instigated by the Japanese in the 1970s and swiftly and competitively followed by the Americans, British, and Europeans. While voice recognition is a major interest, it is artificial intelligence (AI) with which the research is principally concerned. AI failed to live up to its early promise, although this has not precluded optimism among many working in this field (for example, Feigenbaum and McCorduck, 1984). While the relative lack of success previously may be partly technological, some observers have argued that the problem is intractable, being essentially philosophical in nature (Weizenbaum, 1984; Searle, 1984).

Another major development is the integration of information and telecommunications technologies. This has occurred following the digitization of telecommunications technology, and permits, for example in the case of fax machines, the instantaneous transmission of facsimiles of documents over distances. Similarly, the development of electronic mail can be used for audio- and teleconferencing. Increasingly, the divide between the information and communications technologies is being eroded, and they are now common technologies of communication.

infrastructure the basic physical structure of a society or an organization, especially the stock of fixed capital equipment in a country, for example, means of transport, schools, and factories.

in-group and out-group twin terms introduced by Graham SUMNER (1906) to refer to insiders in a particular "we" relationship, in contrast with outsiders to the relationship.

inner city an area of urban settlement with high levels of social problems and poverty. The term is sometimes used as a codeword for "minority area" by those who regard the problems of the inner city as problems of minority cultures and not as a concentration of the social problems of capitalist societies. See also ZONE OF TRANSITION, URBAN SOCIOLOGY, URBANISM AS A WAY OF LIFE, URBANIZATION.

inner-directedness see OTHER-DIRECTEDNESS.

institution an established order comprising rule-bound and standardized behavior patterns. The term is widely acknowledged to be used in a variety of ways, and hence often ambiguously. SOCIAL INSTITUTION refers to arrangements involving large numbers of people whose behavior is guided by NORMS and ROLES. In functionalist theory (see FUNCTIONALISM), the concept of institution is linked to that of FUNCTIONAL PREREQUISITES OR FUNCTIONAL IMPERATIVES. MALINOWSKI lists seven social institutions that meet biological and social-psychological NEEDS. GOFFMAN uses the term TOTAL INSTITUTION to refer to bureaucratically organized establishments (see BUREAUCRACY) in which the inmates have little possibility of escape from the norms and roles of the administrative structure. INSTITUTIONALIZATION refers to the process whereby the norms and roles expected in various social settings are developed and learned. Although this often involves an OVERSOCIALIZED CONCEPTION OF MAN, researchers influenced by PHENOMENOLOGICAL SOCIOLOGY stress the creative and adaptive aspects of social life.

institutionalization 1. the process, as well as the outcome of the process, in which social activities become regularized and routinized as stable, social-structural features. See also INSTITUTION. **2.** the process, and the resulting condition, in which SOCIAL ACTORS incarcerated for long periods in TOTAL INSTITUTIONS, such as prisons or mental hospitals, become incapable of, or disabled for, independent social life outside the institution.

instrumental rationality "the subjection of activity to the criterion of effectiveness alone" (GELLNER, 1988). This form of rationality is often regarded as the essence of the process of RATIONALIZATION underlying the transformation from premodern, PREINDUSTRIAL SOCIETIES to modern INDUSTRIAL SOCIETIES. See also TYPES OF SOCIAL ACTION, RATIONALITY.

integration 1. the extent to which an individual experiences a sense of belonging to a social group or collectivity by virtue of sharing its norms, values, beliefs, etc. Integration is a key concept of Emile DURKHEIM's sociology and is one of the two main variables he used in his seminal explanation of variations in rates of SUICIDE. **2.** the extent to which the activity or function of different institutions or subsystems within society complements rather than contradicts the other. For example, the family is integrated within the economic systems of advanced industrial societies to the extent that it sustains and reproduces labor power (but no other commodity), while acting as a unit of consumption (rather than production). **3.** the presence of specific institutions that promote the complementary and coordinated activity of other subsystems of society. The development of institutions of integration of this kind (such as written language or formal legal systems) is one of the FUNCTIONAL PREREQUISITES OR FUNCTIONAL IMPERATIVES of all social systems, and a key to social development in neo-evolutionary theory (see NEO-EVOLUTIONISM).

The use of the concept of integration in all three senses is a characteristic of FUNCTIONALISM, and especially of the work of Talcott PARSONS. *Malintegration* implies a lack or absence of integration or integrative mechanisms. For example, egoistic suicide is a result, for Durkheim, of the malintegration of the individual within the group; economic growth may suffer if the educational system fails to integrate its activity and goals with those of the economy; the important evolutionary advance (see EVOLUTIONARY THEORY) of the separation of power from office represented by the democratic association cannot survive without the supremacy of the integrative mechanism represented by the rule of law. See also SOCIAL SOLIDARITY, MECHANICAL AND ORGANIC SOLIDARITY, SOCIAL INTEGRATION AND SYSTEM INTEGRATION.

intellectuals persons, typically well educated, who engage their intellect in work that they believe to be of cultural importance. In English, "intellectual" as a noun first appeared in the early 19th century, and early usage was often pejorative. Sociological interest largely centers on intellectuals as a distinct social group (see INTELLIGENTSIA). In addition, three episodes in French social thought are worth noting. First, the social scientist SAINT-SIMON introduced the military concept of a vanguard, or *avant-garde,* to social thought in the early 19th century, although his reference was not to intellectuals as such, but rather to scientists, whose positive knowledge would enable them alone successfully to direct the development of France and other industrial societies. Secondly, in 1896, the politician Clemenceau labeled the defenders of Dreyfus as "intellectuals," thus launching its modern usage. The label was promptly adopted as a badge of honor by DURKHEIM and others. Thirdly, the philosopher Julien Benda condemned intellectuals for their readiness to serve particular social and political causes and to betray their true calling—the disinterested pursuit of universal truth and justice—in his *La Trahison des clercs* (1927). Though not a work of sociology, it is a common reference point in sociological discussion. See also HEGEMONY.

intelligence a person's cognitive ability or potential for rational thought and behavior. It is measured by specially constructed INTELLIGENCE TESTS. On the basis of their performance in such tests, children may be allocated to different types of educational provision and experience.

Most of the debate about the nature of intelligence centers on the extent to which it is inherited biologically, or acquired as a result of environmental experience and socialization (see NATURE-NURTURE DEBATE). There are a number of different models of intelligence, each of which has different implications for educational processes. One influential model finds expression in cognitive developmental theories that emphasize the importance of the interaction between inherited potential and environmental experience. This approach is exemplified in the work of PIAGET (1932) and Bruner (1968), both of whom identified stages of mental development, and the type of learning taking place in each. These theorists have exerted considerable influence on the structure of educational provision in recent decades. Other models are based on belief in the infinite plasticity of human behavior, emphasizing differences in group characteristics and achievements, rather than the similarities from which a general theory of learning begins. Both of these approaches, developmental and comparative, have contributed to the growth of theories of intellectual development and models for intelligence testing.

intelligence quotient (IQ) a unit used in the field of INTELLIGENCE measurement and testing as an index of an individual's intelligence relative to a comparable population with respect to age. *IQ* is expressed as a ratio of mental age (as measured by a test) to chronological age, and multiplied by 100 to avoid decimals:

$$IQ = \frac{\text{Mental Age (MA)}}{\text{Chronological Age (CA)}} \times 100$$

The average child at any one chronological age will therefore score 100 on the appropriate set of IQ test items. This was the original IQ measure first used in 1916 in the Stanford-Binet Test.

Modern tests make use of standard scores, which express the individual's distance from the mean in terms of the standard deviation, and assume a normal distribution. In a variant of this, the *deviation IQ,* the mean is 100 and a standard deviation of 15 or 16 is usual.

It is important to note the difference between these measures, since the deviation IQ is not a ratio of mental age to chronological age, and the measured IQs derived from it will depend on the standard deviation used in the test. See also INTELLIGENCE TEST.

intelligence test a variety of items to test the specific mental abilities thought to be significant in general cognitive ability. The items are usually arranged in ascending order of difficulty. The test result identifies a person's IQ (see INTELLIGENCE QUOTIENT).

The development of testing procedures has been based on the assumption that the greater proportion of ability is inherited. Tests are therefore designed to measure innate ability, while controlling for any environmental and cultural factors. There is, however, no agreement on the extent to which it is possible to achieve this aim, and much controversy surrounds the use of such tests. It is difficult to ascertain from the tests whether performance is determined by innate ability or social position, race, or gender. Furthermore, some critics claim that the tests are not culturally neutral, but biased toward the norms and values of dominant groups in society, thus producing results that do not reflect the true ability levels of subordinate groups.

The educational and political significance of intelligence tests can be seen in the reaction to the work of Jensen, who reopened the NATURE-NURTURE DEBATE in 1969. In his paper he was particularly concerned with racial differences in INTELLIGENCE. He distinguished between genetic and environmental aspects of intelligence, concluding that genetic factors account for as much as 80% of intelligence. While acknowledging the poverty of African Americans' environment, Jensen argued that this was an insufficient explanation on its own and therefore could not account for the differences in test performance. The results were suggested as legitimizing the differential educational treatment received in schools by different social groups. Jensen's thesis generated fierce controversy, focusing on the weaknesses of his data as well as the proposed educational implications. (see L. Kamin, *The Science and Politics of I.Q.*)

Within the field of education, progressives have argued that concentration on intelligence testing and the automatic equation of a high IQ score with brightness and achievement have straitjacketed the education system for over half a century. Others have consistently defended the predictive powers of IQ tests. However, the arguments over this issue are now far less strident. There tends to be more agreement that IQ tests are neither wholly neutral nor wholly reliable or valid (see VALIDITY).

intelligentsia 1. a SOCIAL STRATUM of INTELLECTUALS with a self-appointed responsibility for guiding the future welfare and development of the nation. The term is of mid-19th century Polish and Russian origin, and is like CASTE in that some sociologists consider it applicable only to a particular place and time, while others believe it to be more generally extendable. **2.** any constellation of educated, but unpropertied, individuals with some consciousness of its distinctive role either in a national society or in a culture area transcending national boundaries. For example, there have been intelligentsias in this sense in some African societies before and after independence. **3.** intellectuals of any kind, regardless of whether they have any common consciousness or distinctive social position. Thus, according to Geiger (1949), the intelligentsia is composed of the creators and consumers of cultural goods, together with all other possessors of degrees and diplomas. It would seem preferable, however, not to make "intelligentsia" and "intellectuals" synonymous, but rather to reserve intelligentsia for senses **1.** and **2.** Such an approach allows reference to intellectuals in the United States, but not to an intelligentsia.

The first sense of "intelligentsia" arose in the 19th century when Poland was partitioned between Prussia (after 1871, Germany), Russia, and Austria (after 1867, Austria-Hungary). Those few who possessed the school-leaving certificate, the *matura,* and who thus knew their Polish literature and history, considered themselves to be the guardians of the national culture. As such, they supplied the leadership for many opposition movements. Very often they were the sons of pauperized nobility and gentry; they retained gentry values and disdained the borgeois pursuits of trade and industry. Following the restoration of the Polish state in 1918, the intelligentsia played a leading part in the government and administration, but was then decimated in World War II.

Under state socialism, from 1945 to 1989, the Communist Party claimed for itself the leading role in the development of Poland and set out to eliminate all rivals. The classical intelligentsia ceased to exist. According to the official Marxist formula, however, the new Poland had two nonantagonistic *classes*, the workers and the peasants, and the *stratum* of the intelligentsia. Reference to a separate stratum (not class) of the intelligentsia acknowledged that its relation to the means of production was similar to that of the working class, yet aspects of its culture and consciousness continued to set it apart. Entry to the intelligentsia was now defined in terms of completion of higher, rather than secondary, education, and the majority of graduates were now in science and engineering. This led to a distinction between the *creative or cultural intelligentsia,* and the vastly more numerous *technical intelligentsia* whose residual attachment to old intelligentsia values was much less evident. The huge expansion of higher education in itself also made the intelligentsia less of an ELITE. After 1945, the social origins of most new members of the intelligentsia were working class or peasant. However, by the 1960s, Wesolowski and others noted that the now vastly expanded intelligentsia was taking advantage of a selective secondary school system to perpetuate itself from one generation to the next. From 1955, reformist, and from 1968, oppositional, elements of the intelligentsia echoed something of its old role, but it is notable that when Solidarity originated in 1980 it was as a labor union and workers' movement. Even so, there continues to be more social respect for men and women of knowledge in Poland than there is in the United States or Britain.

In Russia, the position of the intelligentsia has been somewhat different. A *déclassé* fraction of the nobility sought to maintain elements of its traditional style of life in an urban setting (thereby guaranteeing its distinction from the bourgeoisie) while leading the nation to its destiny. The latter entailed abolition of tsarism, and the residues of feudalism, by whatever means, and a general commitment to progressive causes. Following the October Revolution in 1917, the creative intelligentsia at first flourished, but Stalin could not countenance its independence and put an end to it. The official Marxist formula of two classes and the stratum of the intelligentsia kept the term alive. That there are today even fewer continuities with the classical intelligentsia than in Poland is, however, hardly surprising given the greater elapse of time since the latter's demise. On the other hand, there have been some similarities between Soviet dissidents and the old reformist and/or oppositional intelligentsia.

In its second sense, the term intelligentsia is consistent with the German word *Intelligenz*. Alfred WEBER orginated the notion of a socially unattached intelligentsia, but it is Mannheim's formulation that is best known: "In every society there are social groups whose special task it is to provide an interpretation of the world for that society. We call these the intelligentsia" (MANNHEIM, 1936). He suggested that they tend either to affiliate voluntarily "with one or other of the various antagonistic classes" or try to fulfill "their mission as the predestined advocate of the intellectual interests of the whole" (Mannheim, 1929). It is arguable, however, that intellectuals felt a common affinity, and monopolized "the right to preach, teach and interpret the world," more in Germany than in most other societies.

There are variants of this second conception of an intelligentsia in Konrád and Szelényi's thesis (1979) of intellectuals on the road to class power in state-socialist societies, and in GOULDNER's thesis (1979) of intellectuals and the rise of the NEW CLASS. Konrád and Szelényi posit that "the transformation of the intelligentsia into a class, principally in the rational-redistributive economies, has indeed meant that in the industrally backward agrarian societies of Eastern Europe the intelligentsia, organized into a government-bureaucratic ruling class, has taken the lead in modernization, replacing a weak borgeoisie incapable of breaking with feudalism." Gouldner argues that in all parts of the emerging world socioeconomic order, humanist intellectuals and the technical intelligentsia constitute a new class that contests the control of economies already exercised either by businessmen or by party leaders.

intentionality 1. the purposiveness of human action. As SCHUTZ and the ETHNOMETHODOLOGISTS underline, intentionality does not, as sometimes suggested, consist only of a series of discrete purposes. It exists also in more tacit forms of actor's knowledgeability, that is, in what GIDDENS (1984) terms PRACTICAL KNOWLEDGE OR PRACTICAL CONSCIOUSNESS, as well as in the DISCURSIVE CONSCIOUSNESS of the actor. See also STRATIFICATION MODEL OF SOCIAL ACTION AND CONSCIOUSNESS. **2.** (philosophy) for HUSSERL and SARTRE, the "reaching out toward an object involved in human consciousness."

interaction (STATISTICS) the compounded effect that two or more INDEPENDENT VARIABLES may have on the DEPENDENT VARIABLE when they act together. In examining the effect of the variables in an experiment, the individual effect of each may not explain the total variation. It is therefore appropriate to use a statistical test such as ANALYSIS OF VARIANCE, which is designed to assess the effect of the interaction between the variables as well as the specific effect of each.

interaction, interaction ritual, and **interaction order** the processes and manner in which social actors relate to each other, especially in face-to-face ENCOUNTERS.

While patterns of interaction have long been studied by social scientists (for example, small groups by social psychologists, or BODY LANGUAGE by psychologists), in such studies the focus on interaction was often largely incidental, with the fundamental, trans-situational structures of interactions being little considered. It is only with the work of Goffman that these structures have begun to be more fully explored. GOFFMAN (1963) defines a social order as the "consequences of any set of moral norms that regulates the way in which persons pursue their objectives." Such moral norms are equivalent to the traffic laws of social interaction. This public order, or *interaction order,* which governs the form and processes, though not the content, of social interaction, stands at the heart of Goffman's sociology (for example, see CIVIL INATTENTION). What Goffman then means by *interaction ritual* is that a ritual cooperation exists, as well as ritual codes, in upholding the enactment of a shared reality, for example, in allowing the actors with whom one interacts to preserve face (see FACE-WORK). As early as 1951, Gregory Batestone suggested the possibility that interaction might be seen as a communication system, with perhaps a syntax. Goffman's work appears to build on these early notions (see Kendon, 1988).

interests the particular social outcomes held to benefit a particular individual or group. Such interests may be those recognized and pursued by the person or group, or they may be identified by others, including social scientists, as underlying or objective interests unrecognized by the persons concerned. Marxism is an example of a theory in which the distinction between apparent interests and underlying, objective interests plays an important role (see FALSE CONSCIOUSNESS).

intermediate classes or intermediate strata (Marxism) in capitalist society, those CLASSES standing intermediate between the capitalist (or bourgeois) class and the PROLETARIAT, and belonging to neither (see Fig. 13). As summarized by Hodges (1961), these class groupings can be seen as consisting of transitional classes of four basic types:

(a) artisans who employ no one and are not themselves employed, who because of this might be seen as lying outside the capitalist system, and so also outside its system of classes;

(b) the PETTY BOURGEOISIE, that is, those relatively small employers who are relatively limited users of capital, and are themselves often politically oppressed under capitalism;

(c) commercial and supervisory intermediate class groups acting on behalf of capitalists, primarily as the realizers rather than producers of surplus value. While their income derives from the proceeds of the exploita-

---

(A) Basic Dichotomous ideal type of classes under capitalism:

BOURGEOIS/CAPITALIST CLASS:	*PROLETARIAT:*
(a) ownership of capital	propertyless — wage earners
(b) 'unproductive' and exploitive – expropriating surplus value	'productive' and exploited – producing 'surplus value' which is expropriated by capitalists
(c) political oppressors	politically oppressed

(B) Trichotomous class pattern: real world patterns of class

BOURGEOIS	INTERMEDIATE CLASSES	PROLETARIAT
	(all those who fall outside the dichotomous model of class)	

i) *artisans* – standing 'outside' capitalism, as neither users of capital nor employed by capitalists

ii) *petty bourgeoisie* – limited use of capital or employment of labour

iii) *commercial and supervisory groups* – 'realisers' of capital on behalf of capitalists, rather than (usually) producers of surplus value

iv) *new middle class* – professional and technical workers

Fig. 13. **Intermediate class or intermediate strata**: the several types of class groupings which under capitalism fall outside the simple Marxist dichotomous model of class and class conflict.

tion of the proletariat, they are themselves often political oppressed and may sometimes be exploited given that they also sometimes produced surplus value;

(d) the NEW MIDDLE CLASS, that is, professional, technical experts who, while partly productive in the sense that they produce surplus value and may themselves be exploited, also receive salaries that in part are the fruits of exploitation. They can also be seen as denied full power under capitalism and thus potentially have interests in the replacement of capitalism, although benefiting from it in part.

In the classical Marxist view, these class locations are seen as likely to be transitional under capitalism, though in different ways. Thus (a) and (b) can be held to consist mainly of a survival from precapitalist patterns of class, and as tending to decline in importance, while (c) and (d) are hypothesized to crystalize into capitalist or proletarian positions, given the tendency for CLASS POLARIZATION to occur in capitalist societies. In the main, this process of crystalization was assumed likely to be in the direction of PROLETARIANIZATION, or at least include an increasing recognition by the members of these classes of interests opposed to capitalism. Subsequent empirical patterns of class locations, CLASS CONSCIOUSNESS, and class action among intermediate groups, however, suggest a complexity of class interests, which has led to a great variety of neo-Marxist and non-Marxist accounts and theories of class within capitalist societies and the place of intermediate class groupings within these.

intermediate group or **secondary group** any group that can be seen as occupying an intermediate position between central state institutions and PRIMARY GROUPS such as the family or other face-to-face groupings. The number and variety of such intermediate and secondary groups are sometimes suggested as providing an important counterbalance to tendencies toward MASS SOCIETY in modern industrial societies.

intermediate societies societies of size and complexity intermediate between simple societies and modern industrial societies, and intermediate in developmental sequence.

intermediate technology production techniques that avoid the NEW TECHNOLOGY and capital-intensive nature of Western production systems, but are an improvement on indigenous methods. The use of intermediate technology is increasingly proposed as appropriate technology for some Third World countries that lack the infrastructure to adopt advanced technology satisfactorily and may not benefit economically or socially from export-oriented capitalist production (see also DEPENDENCY THEORY, GREEN REVOLUTION).

Following E.F. Schumacher's (1973) prescription that "small is beautiful," local programs for irrigation, conservation, organic farming, etc., using indigenous skills and locally available resorces, have been encouraged, enabling the population to exert more control over their lives. Such programs are also proposed as "ecologically friendly," avoiding the ENVI-

RONMENTAL DEPLETION that may result from inappropriate enterprise, and as providing a preferred basis for long-term development. (Such development is increasingly proposed as ecologically appropriate for more advanced societies.) See also ETHNOSCIENCES, MULTICULTURALISM.

internal colonialism the incorporation of culturally distinct groups by a dominant group into one national identity, centralized political rule, and a national economy. In many analyses the process has similarities with external colonialism, whereby one state subordinates another. In contemporary literature on this subject there are two main areas where the concept is at the center of analysis. One is in Latin American scholarship, where the term has been used to analyze the relationship between Europeanized social groups and indigenous groups (often called Indians) with different languages, beliefs, and ways of life. Stavenhagen (1975) argues that internal colonialism emerged in Latin American countries with independence from Spain and Portugal in the 19th century and with the development of capitalist economies. Indian communities lost their lands, were made to work for strangers, were integrated into a monetary economy, and incorporated into national political structures. This led to a form of ethnic stratification that, in Stavenhagen's analysis, operates alongside changing social class relationships.

In Europe and the United States, the concept has been used to discuss ethnic and race relations and the emergence of nationalist movements within established nation states. The term gained currency with the civil rights and black power movements in the US in the 1960s, when comparisons were drawn between the position of African Americans and the situation in Africa, where European colonialism was giving way to independent states. Hechter (1975) produced one of the most influential academic formulations of the concept and, by using it to analyze national development in Britain, widened the debate. Hechter used aspects of world systems analysis to argue that internal colonialism involves subordination of peripheral cultural groups by core dominant groups partly as a result of the uneven industrialization of territories. Those groups in the most advanced regions achieve dominance over those groups in the less advanced. Later this may lead to the emergence of nationalist movements in those regions, as was the case in some European countries and Canada in the late 1960s.

internalization the acceptance and incorporation of the standards or beliefs of other persons, or of society, by the individual. Internalization is a basic concept in FREUD's theory of personality development. The child's conscience (SUPEREGO) is formed by internalizing society's MORES, as represented by the parents' personal values and standards. As illustrated by this psychodynamic usage, crucial to the more general usage is total acceptance of beliefs and values. In contrast, some expressed attitudes or behaviors may be based on social pressures, such as CONFORMITY, and involve *compliance* rather than internalization.

interpretation a method that stresses the importance of understanding intentional human action. Semantically, any account is an interpretation. What distinguishes the interpretive paradigm from other movements is the recognition that any statement about the social world is necessarily relative to any other. It inevitably sets itself against the notion of the Durkheimian social fact by asserting that facts are always produced by specific people in certain circumstances for explicit reasons. There is little agreement on detail, since interpretive sociologists cover a wide range of epistemological positions. The extreme subjectivist or relativist wing (HERMENEUTICS) takes the position that no single interpretation can predominate over another. SCHUTZ's phenomenological sociology occupies a fairly central position within the paradigm in attempting a systematic study of the intersubjective nature of social life. On the other hand, WEBER considered understanding (VERSTEHEN) to be a method of elucidating the motivations for action, not experience of action, that did not prevent the sociologist from making generalizations from the data (see also IDEAL-TYPES). ETHNOMETHODOLOGY is often classed as an INTERPRETIVE SOCIOLOGY, but this can only be partially valid, since it gains much of its intellectual heritage from American EMPIRICISM. In sum, while there is a general commitment to EMPATHY and understanding the actor's point of view, the research that flows from interpretation is so varied as to be difficult to categorize as a school, possibly because the meaning of interpretation is itself subject to interpretation.

interpretive (or interpretative) sociology a variety of forms of sociology (including SYMBOLIC INTERACTIONISM, SOCIOLOGICAL PHENOMENOLOGY, and the approach of WEBER) united by an emphasis on the necessity of sociologists to understand or interpret actors' meanings (see also INTERPRETATION, MEANINGFUL UNDERSTANDING AND EXPLANATION, VERSTEHEN, HERMENEUTICS, DOUBLE HERMENEUTIC). In this argument all social reality is pre-interpreted, in that it only has form as (and is constituted by) the outcome of SOCIAL ACTORS' beliefs and interpretations. Thus it is, or ought to be, a truism that no form of sociology can proceed without at least a preliminary grasp of actors' meanings. DURKHEIM's suggestion, in *Rules,* that we can proceed to the objective study of social facts without any reference to actors' purposes is wrong or misleading.

On a charitable reading, what Durkheim wanted to suggest was that sociology, if it genuinely wished to be a science, could not rest content merely with the social accounts contained in actors' meanings. Even here, however, most forms of sociology that refer to themselves as interpretive part company with Durkheim, arguing that the pre-interpreted reality with which sociologists deal precludes a positivistic approach, especially given that the actions of social actors can change meanings and are not only the outcome of received meanings.

Among the various forms of sociology that adopt this stance, some (for example, the proposals of WINCH) suggest that an understanding of actors' meanings can alone suffice in providing descriptions *and* explanations of social action. More usually, however, the argument is that the meaningful character of social reality and sociological explanation restricts, but does not eliminate, the possibility of accounts of social reality that move beyond actors' meanings. For example, for Weber, IDEAL TYPES play an important role in the formulation and testing of historical hypotheses; in a not dissimilar way, within SYMBOLIC INTERACTIONISM, general SENSITIZING CONCEPTS play an important role in the analysis of particular cases; and in GOFFMAN's sociology the generation of general conceptual frameworks is central. In all such approaches—though there are many disagreements—the aim is to achieve a nonpositivistic formulation of social science that does not violate the premises that actors' meanings must always be understood and that actors' social competence and actors' choice preclude deterministic "lawlike accounts" of social reality. Whether wider structural, or even scientifically causal, forms of sociological analysis can also ultimately be constructed on an interpretive basis, raises a further set of questions that have received a variety of answers (for example, compare PARSONS' functionalism or the STRUCTURATION THEORY OF GIDDENS). (See also STRUCTURE AND AGENCY.)

intersocietal systems any social arrangements or social systems that "cut across whatever dividing lines exist between SOCIETIES or societal totalities," (GIDDENS, 1984). The claim of Giddens is that sociologists have often failed to take into account the importance of intersocietal systems. According to MANN (1986), sociologists have often conceived of society as "an unproblematic, unitary totality," and as the "total unit of analysis," when in fact this concept applies at best only to modern NATION STATES. Usually, historically, societies lacked such clear boundaries. Moreover, given the interdependence of modern nation states as part of a worldwide economic and NATION-STATE SYSTEM, modern nation states cannot be properly understood as isolated social systems. See also TIME-SPACE DISTANCIATION.

intersubjectivity shared experiences between people; agreements on knowledge, etc. The existence of intersubjectivity, since it need make no claims to OBJECTIVISM, counteracts such doctrines as SOLIPSISM, RELATIVISM, and INCOMMENSURABILITY, all of which suggest barriers to working agreements on knowledge. See also LIFE-WORLD.

intertextuality see DECONSTRUCTION.

intervening variable a VARIABLE that mediates the effect of an INDEPENDENT VARIABLE on a DEPENDENT VARIABLE. This may be an internal mechanism whose existence is hypothesized from the effects it is observed to have (for example, the effect of the organism that intervenes between the S [stimulus] and R [response] in behavioristic psychology), or another external explanatory variable (for example, social class has an observed effect on morbidity, but this is mediated by income, diet, housing, etc.).

interview a method of collecting social data at the INDIVIDUAL LEVEL. This

face-to-face method ensures a higher RESPONSE RATE than POSTAL QUES-
TIONNAIRES, but can introduce INTERVIEWER BIAS by the effect different
interviewers have on the quality, VALIDITY, and RELIABILITY of the data so
collected.

Interviews may be *structured*, with the interviewer asking set questions
and the respondents' replies being immediately categorized. This format
enables easy analysis and less possibility of interviewer bias, but the data will
not be as rich as that elicited by an unstructured design (and may be subject
to problems such as MEASUREMENT BY FIAT—see also CICOUREL). Unstructured interviews are desirable when the initial exploration of an area is
being made, and hypotheses for further investigation are being generated, or
when the depth of the data required is more important than ease of analysis.
See QUALITATIVE RESEARCH and QUANTITATIVE RESEARCH TECHNIQUES.

interviewer bias the BIAS that may be introduced into social-research findings when the social background (for example, social class, ethnic background, or gender) of an interviewer affects the response made at an
interview. For example, as well as a mistrust or lack of rapport between an
interviewer and an interviewee, there may exist *over-rapport*, in which an
interviewer relates to the interviewee as if certain responses can be taken
for granted, thus distorting outcomes.

iron law of oligarchy the tendency for political organizations (POLITICAL
PARTIES and TRADE UNIONS) to become oligarchic, however much they may
seek internal democracy. "He who says organization, says oligarchy," said
MICHELS, who first formulated this law in his book *Political Parties* in 1911.
Michels' suggestion was that once parties move beyond the fluid participatory structures that often accompany their formation, they inevitably
become more bureaucratic and more centrally controlled, falling under the
domination of a professional leadership. In this process the original goals
of the organization may also be replaced by more narrowly instrumental
goals, including a concern for the maintenance of the organization (see also
GOAL DISPLACEMENT). Three sets of factors were identified by Michels as
central in this process:

(a) *technical factors,* that is, the need to maintain an effective fighting
machine, but when this happens the machine develops its own vested
interests and is able to control agenda and communications, manage internal opposition, etc.

(b) *psychological characteristics of leaders,* that is, that they may be gift-
ed orators, relish the psychic rewards of leadership, come to share the
motivations and interests of a wider political elite, and thus tend to cling to
power at all costs.

(c) *psychological characteristics of the mass,* that is, that the rank and
file members of political organizations tend to be apathetic, are willing to
be led, are readily swayed by mass oratory, and venerate the leadership.

Critics of Michel's "iron law" point out that the tendency to oligarchy in political organizations is highly variable. For example, it may be a feature of labor unions more than of political parties. The extent of oligarchy is also affected by the characteristics of the membership and by the constitutional context in which the organizations in question operate (for example, see LIPSET, 1960, and MacKenzie, 1963).

Nevertheless, Michels' work has exerted a strong influence on the study of political parties and labor union democracy. See also ELITE THEORY.

irrationalism see RATIONALISM.

J

Jakobson, Roman (1896–1982) Russian-born, post-Saussurean theorist in linguistics and formalistic literary studies who had a major influence on the development of modern theoretical linguistics and STRUCTURAL-ISM. In the analysis of literature and poetry, his approach was innovative, employing a structural analysis in which form was separated from content. A founder member of the so-called Prague school of linguistics, his main technical contribution to linguistics was in the study of *phonology* (the sound systems of LANGUAGE), in which sounds were analyzed to reveal a comparatively simple set of binary oppositions underlying human speech. More generally, in the analysis of languages and human sign systems (see also SEMIOTICS), he suggested the existence of "structural invariants" and that the apparent differences between cultures were merely surface features. Driven from Europe by Nazism, it was as a European cultural theorist in the New World that he had his widest influence. Among those profoundly influenced by his thinking were LÉVI-STRAUSS and Chomsky, who were his associates in New York. His emphasis on linguistic universals presented a contrast with the more culturally relativist view of language propounded by American anthropologists such as Boas and Sapir (see SAPIR-WHORF HYPOTHESIS). In his linguistic theories, the use of psychology was also different from the prevailing American view in the 1940s and 1950s. While pioneering American theorists of linguistics, such as Leonard Bloomfield, were wedded to a behavioristic view, Jakobson's emphasis was philosophically rationalist, with its emphasis on innate cognitive structures that were universal, rather than on an acquisition of language seen as arising primarily from interactions with the social environment and from stimulus and response. Especially as the result of Chomsky's success, it is Jakobson's rationalistic formalism that on the whole has triumphed in linguistics. But this formalism, and its associated concentration on language as universal structures, while it discounted behavioristic accounts, also contained limitations, for example, the lack of any very adequate treatment of SEMANTICS and the contextuality of language, or of linguistic and social creativity and agency. These overstatements and' omissions were also to become weaknesses of structuralism as this emerged as a modern movement, partly as a result of Jakobson's influence. See also STRUCTURE AND AGENCY, PRAGMATICS, POSTSTRUCTURALISM.

jati see CASTE.

Jim Crow Laws the name applied to laws in the Southern states, which enforced SEGREGATION of white and black persons in transport, education, marriage, leisure facilities, and so on. These laws were common in the

South from 1883 to 1954 despite the emancipation of slaves in 1865. All over the South, "whites only" and "blacks only" signs were a visible reminder of the inferior status of African Americans. The Supreme Court ruled in 1896 *(Plessey v. Ferguson)* that so-called separate but equal facilities for blacks and whites were legal. Until 1954, when the Supreme Court reversed its view *(Brown v. Board of Education)*, separate, but very inferior and unequal, provision was the order of the day in the South.

job redesign an approach to the design of work that seeks to offset the negative social and psychological implications of directly supervised, simple, and routine tasks through the provision of wider tasks, increased autonomy, and feedback on performance. See also QUALITY OF WORKING LIFE, SOCIOTECHNICAL SYSTEMS APPROACH.

There have been several approaches to job design that, operating at different levels, have sought to offset the negative aspects of SCIENTIFIC MANAGEMENT. The first level at which job redesign operates involves adjusting the horizontal division of labor. *Job rotation* seeks to increase the variety of work an employee does by providing for mobility between specialized jobs. *Job enlargement* combines two or more previously specialized activities within one job. Critics of job redesign at this level point out that employees are unlikely to be satisfied by jobs that deny them opportunity to exercise judgment and discretion. Little is to be gained by piling one boring job on top of another. Hence, proponents of *job enrichment* suggest that there is a need to reconstitute the vertical division of labor so that some traditionally managerial tasks, such as deciding on work methods, are built into the jobs of workers. Sociotechnical systems theory, which stresses the need to consider more than individual responsibility and judgment, can be seen to be compatible with the extension of job enrichment to tasks more technologically interdependent (Child, 1985). For example, self-regulating, multiskilled work groups reduce the need for direct supervision and enhance the judgment, discretion, and skill requirements of employees.

joint conjugal role relationship a division of labor within a household that involves sharing of household tasks between partners. The term was first used by Elizabeth Bott (1957), who suggested that such relationships were most often found in communities with high geographical and social mobility. The fragmentation of family and kin relationships consequent on such conditions is said to have disrupted the traditional pattern of the SEGREGATED CONJUGAL ROLE RELATIONSHIP and led to men becoming more involved in the home. An increase in working women, unemployed men, and the existence of new social values are suggested as contributing to the increasing interchangeability of gender roles late in the 20th century. Despite the suggestion that such families are more egalitarian, there is much evidence that the existence of gender segregation in household tasks is highly persistent. See also DOMESTIC LABOR, SEXUAL DIVISION OF LABOR.

joking relationship the anthropological term for ritualized insulting behavior. RADCLIFFE-BROWN is credited with identifying widespread patterns of insult and stealing practiced on the mother's brother by the sister's son. He interpreted this as a means of releasing the tensions inherent in certain social structural arrangements. Mother-in-law jokes are often seen as an example of the same phenomenon.

Jung, Carl Gustav (1875-1961) born in Switzerland and medically trained, he became a psychiatrist and admirer of FREUD. However, in *The Psychology of the Unconscious* (1912), his personal development away from PSYCHOANALYSIS was evident, and he distanced himself from Freud, his subsequent work being known as analytic psychology. He traveled widely, observing African cultures and the Indians of the Americas and of the East, and making various European visits.

Jung's extensive knowledge of the religions, mythology, philosophy, and symbolism of many cultures became incorporated into his theory of the *collective unconscious*. To him, the deepest levels of the unconscious contain inherited universal *archetypes*—ideas or symbols common to all cultures, which are made manifest in dreams, myths, and stories. Jungian psychology tends toward the mystical, which perhaps explains its popularity in recent years. His therapeutic method involved assisting patients to contact the healing powers within themselves, in the collective unconscious.

His more specific influence on psychology and analysis includes his introduction of the terms INTROVERSION and EXTROVERSION to describe personality characteristics; the Word Association Test; and the notion of personality *complexes* that comprise associated emotions or ideas and are revealed through word association or dream interpretation.

jurisprudence legal and sociological theories that seek to situate the body of laws and legal institutions in an overall social context. Thus, jurisprudence to some extent overlaps with the SOCIOLOGY OF LAW.

Historically, it is possible to identify the following subdivisions of jurisprudence:

(a) *legal positivism,* for example, Kelsen's conception of law as an objectively stable, hierarchical system of norms, or Hart's view of law as resting on basic norms. This view of law has been seen as in tune with traditional legal professionalism, and viewed by its practitioners as involving theories requiring little input from social science. Jeremy BENTHAM's application of utilitarianism to legal reform can also be seen as a form of legal positivism.

(b) *natural law theories,* (see NATURAL RIGHTS AND NATURAL LAW), theories that were a main target of the legal positivists.

(c) *historical and evolutionary theories,* for example, MAINE's theories and Savigny's account of laws as reflecting the custom or *Volkgeist* of a nation or people.

(d) *conflict theories,* theories that emphasize the conflicts of interest underlying the formation and social control functions of legal systems, for example, Roscoe Pound's pluralism.

(e) *legal realism,* American approaches influenced by PRAGMATISM, which emphasized the social basis and fluid, living character of law.

All the above approaches have exerted an influence on the sociology of law, but a recent resurgence of sociolegal studies has owed much to a new vein of empirical sociological studies of legal systems and the operation of the law.

justice 1. the general principle that individuals should receive what they deserve. The definition, a commonsense definition, has also received many philosophical formulations, including those of classical philosophers from Aristotle to KANT. More recently, the ideas of the United States philosopher John Rawls (*A Theory of Justice,* 1971) have been highly influential. **2.** *legal justice,* sometimes called "corrective justice," the application of the law, and the administration of the legal institutions, which in modern societies are mainly operated by trained legal professionals. Here conceptions of formal or procedural fairness are uppermost, that is, the operation of the law according to prescribed principles or due process (the rule of law). **3.** *social justice,* general conceptions of social fairness, which may or may not be at odds with conceptions of individual justice or with conceptions of justice in sense **2.** Competing conceptions of social justice also exist. For example, Utilitarian conceptions of justice, which emphasize an assessment of collective benefit as the overriding consideration, are at odds with conceptions that emphasize a balance of individual and collective rights.

While influenced by philosophical conceptions, sociologists have generally attempted to avoid the abstractions and definitional debates that have characterized philosophical works on justice. The major location of sociological work has been in discussions of political and civil rights and particularly welfare and social policy. The central focus has been on distributive justice, that is, the substantive allocation of benefits, rather than merely formal or procedural conceptions of justice.

It is as an example of a philosophical approach that combines formal and substantive concerns that Rawls's discussion has attracted particular attention. Defining justice as "fairness," Rawls asks what people would be likely to regard as fair in a hypothetical "original position" in which a "veil of ignorance" prevents them from having knowledge of their own possession of social characteristics. Rawls's suggestion is that inequalities are acceptable only if they leave all people better off. Thus, Rawls also supports state interference. A contrary view (for example, Robert Nozick's (1974) elegant defense of the "minimalist state") is that justice consists in the recognition and protection of individual rights, including PROPERTY rights.

Although the differences between conceptions of justice may appear sharp, and often overlaid with ideology, empirical resolutions should not be ruled out. For example, theories as apparently divergent as those of Rawls, Nozick, or Hayek (1944) all involve arguments about the aggregate and the distribution of economic benefit that potentially at least are empirically resolvable, however difficult this may be to achieve in practice (compare ESSENTIALLY CONTESTED CONCEPT, HABERMAS). One route, for example, that taken by Barrington MOORE (1972, 1978) is to focus on injustice, his assumption being that agreements on this will be more easily reached.

K

Kant, Immanuel (1724–1804) preeminent German philosopher, whose major works include *Critique of Pure Reason* (1781), *Critique of Practical Reason* (1788), and *Critique of Judgment* (1790). He argued that our minds structure our experience of the world; we can never know the things-in-themselves (*dinge-an-sich*), only the things-as-they-seem; never noumena, only phenomena (see also RATIONALISM). He went on to suggest that certain CATEGORIES (particularly substance and causality) may not be in the world-as-it-is, but conditions of our knowing it at all. These "pure percepts of the understanding" were "synthetic A PRIORI" truths, because without them it would be impossible to make any sense of the world. Kant's critical philosophy, described by him as a "Copernican revolution in philosophy," saved knowledge from skepticism, but only by jettisoning traditional claims to absolute knowledge.

As a social and moral philosopher Kant is best known for (a) his concept of the person in which determinism in the phenomenal realm is not seen as incompatible with freedom to act, and (b) his concept of *categorical imperative*—a method to guide free human action—which can be paraphrased as "act as if your actions should be taken as indicative of a general law of behavior" or "think what would happen if everyone did this."

Kant's immense influence has a number of sources: (a) it can be seen to result from his attempt to straddle EMPIRICISM and IDEALISM, (b) his distinction between phenomenal and noumenal realms and his concept of the person provide a basis for numerous distinctions between natural and social science (see NEO-KANTIAN, RICKERT, WINDELBAND, WEBER).

kharma see CASTE.

kibbutz (*pl.* kibbutzim) small socialistic agricultural communities (of between 50 and 1000 or more members) established in modern Israel, with the aim, among other things, of producing an alternative to the conventional FAMILY. The objective has been to achieve social equality between men and women by making both child-rearing and work a collective responsibility, although links between children and their biological parents remain strong. Assessments of kibbutzim (see Bettelheim, 1969) suggest that they have been more successful in child-rearing than in achieving an overall equalization in the DIVISION OF LABOR and relations between the sexes.

kinship (anthropology) the social relationships and lineage groups characterized by, and bound together through, a system of well-defined customs, rights, and obligations. Kin relationships may derive from descent or may be established through affinity. In so-called simple societies, the most important STATUSES are those defined predominantly in terms of kinship and, consequently, anthropologists have directed a great deal of attention to the structure and meaning attached both to kinship and to kinship nomenclature. Many early anthropologists (for example, MORGAN, 1870) contended that a link could be established between types of kinship nomenclature systems and the stage of evolutionary development reached by a particular society. More recently, anthropological studies have cast doubt on this approach.

In sociology, kinship has been given less priority as, in the main, modern industrialized societies are not so influenced by kinship systems. Sociologists have tended to focus attention on the functions, role, and structure of the FAMILY rather than on wider kin networks. D. Gittens has questioned the existence of any one identifiable FAMILY form and has suggested that sociologists should be concerned with families rather than with the family. Feminist sociologists have noted the important role played by women in maintaining and sustaining kin networks. Women are identified as "kin keepers."

Studies of kinship are concerned with the structure of relationships within the domestic domain and the way these relate to socioeconomic and political spheres. Kinship is considered by many theorists to constitute the primary bond between people, and the one most resistant to change. The anthropologist Meyer Fortes (1969) maintained that ties of kinship are particularly binding, creating (for the most part) inescapable claims and obligations. In general terms, students of kinship systems are concerned with three main areas:

(a) modes of DESCENT and inheritance;
(b) forms of MARRIAGE and the associated rules of residence;
(c) the regulation of sexuality through INCEST TABOOS.

While kinship systems appear to be a universal feature of social organization, Goody, among others, has stressed that major differences exist between societies in terms of specific kinship characteristics. Goody notes that major differences exist between societies in terms of inheritance systems. In Eurasian societies, diverging inheritance is common. This is a form of bilateral inheritance in which property goes to children of both sexes. Such a system is largely absent in Africa. Inheritance may occur *inter vivos* at marriage, as in the dowry system, or on the death of the property holder—*mortis causa*. Goody also notes that in many Eurasian societies women inherit male property, although there are various restrictions on the type of property and the amount. For instance, under Salic law women cannot inherit land, and under Muslim law they are restricted to half the property. In some Eurasian societies women do not inherit property on the death of the holder, but on marriage, in the form of a dowry. Dowry systems vary, being either direct or indirect, as in the case of bridewealth. In Africa, dowry systems tend to occur only in those societies, either Muslim or Christian, that have come under the influence of

Mediterranean law and custom.

Where this influence is absent, property transferred at marriage takes the form of bridewealth. In this case, the property tends to be transferred between the male kin of the groom and that of the bride. Goody suggests that African societies are largely characterized by what he calls "homogeneous inheritance." In this case, a man's property is transferred exclusively to members of his own clan or lineage. The property passes down to members of the same sex irrespective of the system of descent.

Much of the work on kinship is concerned with the structure of descent systems and forms of marriage. The major types of descent are patrilineal, matrilineal, double descent, and bilateral descent. Goody notes that the existence of different descent systems does not necessarily coincide with major economic differences between societies. G.P. Murdock (1949) regarded the institution of marriage as a universal feature of society. He contended that marriage exists "when the economic and sexual functions are united into one relationship." Murdock believed that marriage necessarily involved residential cohabitation and provided the basis for the NUCLEAR FAMILY. He has been challenged by numerous theorists, for example, Goody (1971). Furthermore, marriage is not necessarily characterized by the union of heterosexual partners. The Nuer, Cheyenne, and the Azande all endorsed homosexual marriage under certain circumstances. So-called ghost marriages were practiced among the Nuer and in traditional Chinese society.

In many societies the choice of marriage partner is prescribed or proscribed by law. *Endogamous marriage* prescribes that marriage shall take place within certain specified groups. *Exogamous marriage* only permits marriage outside specified groups.

In most societies social and/or legal norms prescribe the number of spouses allowed to any one woman or man. In general, marriage systems are either *polygamous* or *monogamous*. Group marriage is virtually unknown. Polygamous marriage takes two major forms: *polygyny*, in which a man is permitted to have more than one wife, and *polyandry*, in which a woman is permitted to have more than one husband. Polyandry is a relatively rare phenomenon. Monogamy, where the individual is allowed only one spouse, is the most common form of marriage. The work of LÉVI-STRAUSS (1949) suggests that a system of exchange forms the basis to the rules of marriage.

All human societies formulate rules to govern and restrict sexual relations between certain kinds of relatives. An incestuous relationship is one that violates these taboos. While INCEST TABOOS discouraging sexual relations among those defined as primary relatives are virtually universal, the precise nature of these taboos varies from culture to culture. One of the consequences of incest taboos is that conjugal families cannot be independent or self-sufficient in the selection of sexual partners.

Marriage usually requires that one or both of the couple be relocated. Kinship rules of residence vary. In *patrilocal* systems the bride is normally expected to move to or near the parental home of the groom. This is the most common form of residence. *Matrilocal* residence requires that the groom move to or near the parental home of the bride. *Neolocal* residence requires that the couple establish a domicile separate from either parental home; *avunculocal* residence, that the couple establish a home in or near the dwelling of the groom's maternal uncle. *Bilocal* residence allows establishment of a home with either parent.

The way people refer to their relatives can provide information about other aspects of culture and social organization. It is important to distinguish between kinship positions (kin types) and kin terms. For instance, in British society it is possible to refer to any elderly person as mother or father (kin term), but this does not mean that they occupy a kinship position. Similarly, religious and political organizations both use kinship terms (sister, brother) without implying kinship positions. Despite cross-cultural variations, the number of different kinship nomenclature systems is limited. See also EXTENDED FAMILY.

Kuhn, Thomas (1922–) United States historian of science whose sociological accounts of science have done much to undermine conventional, abstract, general philosophical accounts such as EMPIRICISM and FALSIFICATIONISM. In Kuhn's view there is no universal scientific method in terms of which the achievements of science can be presented in an abstract general form (see also FEYERABEND).

Kuhn's central thesis is that science can only be properly understood as a historically and socially located product. In understanding a particular scientific approach, the historian of science must learn to apply its central concepts in the same way as a scientist working within a particular tradition applies those concepts. This being so, the study of science becomes no different from the study of any other group or community studied by the sociologist or anthropologist. Kuhn specifically notes the affinities between his own methods and HERMENEUTICS and MEANINGFUL UNDERSTANDING AND EXPLANATION, and between his own central concept of *scientific paradigm* and the Wittgensteinian notion of FORMS OF LIFE.

In his most influential work, *The Structure of Scientific Revolutions* (1962), Kuhn advances a general account of science in which he sees it as undergoing periods of revolutionary change in which previously established notions are overturned. Central to this account is Kuhn's claim that the upheavals are such (for example, the INCOMMENSURABILITY of the scientific concepts that reign supreme before and after) that conventional notions of cumulative scientific progress cannot be sustained (see NORMAL AND REVOLUTIONARY SCIENCE).

Critics of Kuhn reject the tendency to philosophical RELATIVISM involved in such an account of science. In the view of one critic, science becomes no different from mob psychology. However, a rejection of conventional philosophical accounts of scientific rationalism and an advocacy of historical, sociological, and psychological accounts of science need not imply support for a doctrine of outright philosophical relativism. It must be said, however, that Kuhn himself has been ambiguous on these issues.

Ku Klux Klan a secret racist organization founded in the southern United States in 1865 to promote and uphold so-called white supremacy. It was the most virulent white racist organization in the United States and had international links. The Ku Klux Klan (KKK or Klan) was devoted to maintaining the alleged superiority of white Anglo-Saxon Protestants.

This highly secretive underground organization was responsible for lynching, killing, bombing, and intimidating blacks and other groups throughout the last 125 years. The KKK manifesto states: "Our main and fundamental objective is the maintenance of the supremacy of the white race.... History and physiology teach us that we belong to a race which nature has endowed with an evident superiority over all other races...."

It is best known for its members wearing white robes and hoods as they publicly terrorize their victims. However, the KKK engages in less violent, if covert, political activity, and while it is impossible to be accurate about the extent of its membership, at times estimated to be over one million, the influence of the Klan until quite recently was still considerable.

kula ring a system of reciprocal exchange found in the Melanesian Islands. It was described by MALINOWSKI in his *Argonauts of the Western Pacific* (1922). Within the Trobriand Islands, certain groups of tribes on specific islands continually exchange ritual objects. Necklaces circulate in one direction around the ring, and armshells in the other. Malinowski saw the long journeys and extensive ceremonials required in order to service the practice as functionally necessary to ensure the stability of this group of communities. Integrative patterns of status and prestige are produced, which are often compared to those produced by the POTLATCH system of the Canadian Northwest. The emphasis on the importance of exchange is paralleled in the theories of M. Mauss and LÉVI-STRAUSS. See also EXCHANGE THEORY.

kurtosis see MEASURES OF DISPERSION.

L

labeling theory an analysis of the social processes involved in the social attribution (labeling) of positive or (more commonly) negative characteristics to acts, individuals, or groups. This approach has been particularly influential in the sociology of deviance. It developed within the interactionist perspective (see SYMBOLIC INTERACTIONISM) and is sometimes also referred to as SOCIETAL REACTION theory.

The classic statement of labeling theory is by H.S. BECKER (1963) in which he pursued insights developed by earlier theorists such as Tannenbaum (1938) and Lemert (1951), and argued that acts are not naturally good or bad: normality and deviance are socially defined (see also DRUG TAKING FOR PLEASURE). In Becker's famous formula, "Deviance is *not* a quality of the act a person commits but rather a consequence of the application by others of rules and sanctions to an 'offender'." This may seem no more than a sociological application of truisms like "give a dog a bad name" or "throw enough mud and it will stick." What takes the labeling approach beyond common sense or cliché is the way in which the symbolic interactionist approach is drawn on to explore the effects of negative labels on individuals' self-conceptions, especially the development of deviant identity, DEVIANT CAREER, and deviant subcultures. Examples are the way in which societal reaction—the condemnation and criminalization of specific types of social acts by judges, media, police, etc.—can be shown to lead social actors to alter their individual identities, and to adopt the values of deviant subcultures that the labeling process itself helps to create (see also DEVIANCE AMPLIFICATION, MORAL PANICS, FOLK DEVILS).

The labeling approach gained great currency in the 1960s and 1970s and constitutes a movement away from positivist approaches in the study of deviance. The antipositivist aspect is found especially in the fact that unlike many previous approaches, normality and deviance were not seen as unproblematic but as issues to be studied in their own right. An important outcome of the labeling approach has been its establishment of a distinctive interactionist approach to SOCIAL PROBLEMS. Issues that researchers have studied in these terms have included the social construction and regulation of mental illness (for example, see ANTIPSYCHIATRY), the effects of labeling in classrooms, and gender labels. Since interactionist approaches not only raised the question, "Who gets labelled?" but also "Who labels?" and why ostensibly the same acts, when committed by people from different social backgrounds are responded to by labelers (for example, the police or courts) in different ways, Marxists and conflict theorists have also developed an interest in labeling theory.

Labeling theory has been criticized on numerous grounds, for example, for presenting an overly deterministic account of the effects of labeling, for ignoring the element of moral choice by actors, and for romanticizing deviance and ignoring victims. Also, the approach largely ignores preexisting individual psychological predispositions which may, in part, explain individual deviance, offering accounts that are complementary to those provided by labeling theory. Finally, there exist many forms of criminal or deviant behavior that cannot be explained by the reaction of social control agencies, for example, CRIMES such as embezzlement or gay social identity.

labor aristocracy a group (or groups) within the WORKING CLASS in Victorian Englang seen as holding a privileged position either economically or socially, or both.

Most of the writings on the labor aristocracy concentrate on whether such a category of workers actually existed, and if so, what were its essential features and its role in segmenting the Engliash working class.

Several writers (for example, Crossick, 1978; Hobsbawm, 1968) have identified a fraction of the working class, roughly those identified with the apprenticed trades, who were separate in several ways from other segments of the working class and from the middle class. This distinctiveness included high stable earnings, a low rate of marriage into other class groups, distinctive nonwork and leisure pastimes and social values, and a strong belief in trade unionism and in voluntary cooperative action.

One criticism of this, however, is that it does not consider fully the politics of the workplace or the process whereby the labor aristocracy was created. This question has been addressed by several further studies (Foster, 1974; Steadman-Jones, 1975; Gray, 1975). One question concerns the political role of the labor aristocracy. Foster claims the labor aristocracy greatly weakened working class opposition to capitalism, identifying the working class as a conduit for the transmission of so-called bourgeois values. Gray introduces a sophisticated notion of HEGEMONY, acknowledging a labor aristocracy with some level of autonomy, but recognizing that any ensuing struggles must remain locked within a framework of subordination.

The labor aristocracy can be usefully conceived as a temporary product of a particular phase of the development of British capitalism. From the mid-19th century onward, their experience had more in common with the rest of the working class than as an autonomous grouping.

labor market the economic relations between the buyers (employers) and sellers (workers) of labor power. In classical economics the assumption is that the supply of labor would be determined by its price (that is, wage levels). Alternative economic models point to the existence of relatively autonomous, that is noncompeting, *internal* labor markets within firms that could not be explained by the classical model and referred to as the *Balkanization* of labor markets by Clark Kerr (1954). These *internal* (firm specific) markets are connected to the *external* labor markets through recruitment mechanisms (criteria for selection), referred to as *ports of entry,* which explicitly emphasize educational qualifications, technical merit, and experience, but also implicitly include criteria premised on tradition, geographic location, and even prejudice.

Sociologists became particularly interested in labor market analysis in the early 1970s in their attempts to better explain the variations of employment experience between different social categories, in particular women, ethnic groups, and the young. This was initially attempted by reference to the *dual* labor market model, which comprises two sectors: *primary* and *secondary.* This model was, again, initially developed by economists, notably Doeringer and Piore (1971), who postulated that employers pay high wages and offer good career prospects only insofar as necessary to ensure that they retain a stable group of *primary* sector workers, that is, those with the necessary skills and commitment to ensure that the firm can remain competitive by adapting to any technological changes necessary. It is for this reason, it is argued, that primary sector jobs are to be found in the larger corporations, for it is they that invest most in maintaining their dominance of a market through application of technological innovation. The policy of maintaining a core of *primary* sector workers is expensive, however, and in order for it to be viable, other groups of workers have to accept lower wages and poor, or less good, conditions of employment that characterize *secondary* sector jobs. In this *secondary* sector, employers can tolerate much higher rates of labor turnover because the tasks performed are generally viewed as less skilled and less crucial to the production process. This *secondary* sector may be included within the company or be located within the smaller firms that typically carry out work on a subcontractual basis for the larger companies. In this way the general model offers an explanation as to why adult white males have tended to be recruited to the better paid and secure jobs within the economy, while others, including women, blacks, and other ethnic groups as well as young adults have tended to be allocated to the poorly paid, insecure, and low status jobs.

While, in general terms, the *dual market* model can account for some of the variability in labor market conditions, it has been found to be limited in its explanatory power. This is in part because it is based on a technologically deterministic assumption that companies pursue labor market policies solely in order to maintain their economic dominance through the application of technology (Rubery, 1978). It is also the case that the model fails to explain why the social groups associated with the two parts of the dual labor market are as they are, for example, why women tend to get *secondary* sector jobs. In adopting labor market forms of analysis, sociologists have attempted to overcome these limitations, notably by development of the concept of *segmentation,* and identification of *local* labor markets (see LOCAL LABOR MARKET). Both developments emphasize the sociohistorical patterns that underpin labor market behavior and the integral interconnections between work and nonwork institutions, for example, the family.

labor migration the movement of people, either within a country or between countries, to fill vacant jobs. Sociologists have argued that labor migration is an important feature of economic development. There is a pull of migrants to a country or region where there are job vacancies and a shortage of labor, and there is a push of migrants away from countries or regions with high unemployment or underemployment. One consequence of this process is the continued underdevelopment of countries or regions that provide the source of migrant workers. The Treaty of Rome and its subsequent amendments provide for the free movement of labor within the European Economic Community. See also MIGRATION, LABOR MARKET.

labor power 1. a general term for those employed within an organization. **2.** (Marxism) the capacity to work that is bought and employed by capitalists and from which the capitalist extracts surplus value. The distinction made by MARX between labor and labor power is important in Marx's economics and his theory of capitalism and the capitalist mode of production (See ALTHUSSER and Balibar, 1968, Hodgson, 1982). Unlike labor, labor power can be traded in a market and is an object of possession. Under capitalism, the hiring of labor power involves an agreement by the worker to submit to the employer's authority for a set period of time. The employer then has freedom to use as he wishes this labor power and the surplus product created. It is this labor power that is the source of surplus value.

Lacan, Jacques (1901–1981) French psychoanalyst whose work is particularly associated with STRUCTURALISM and involved a reinterpretation of the work of FREUD using concepts derived from structural linguistics. Freud's view of the SELF as both an entity created in particular circumstances and as inherently split in its creation can be opposed to humanist claims for the unity, integrity, and creative power of the subject. Departing from an early commitment to humanist PHENOMENOLOGY, Lacan was influenced by structural linguistics, with its revelation of unknown orders underlying the transparency of consciousness. A semiotic rereading of Freud provides a comparable set of structures, with the realms of cognition and consciousness as the product of an underlying transformation of desire. The conscious subject is a semiotic product involved in DISCOURSES it does not control and which cannot readily be brought to consciousness. The location of the self in social (including gender) positions, preserves and creates spaces for semiotic work and play that evade all fixity. Lacan's contribution has been strikingly influential, for example, in feminist thinking on the creation of gender identity. Lacan's early writings are assembled in *Ecrits* (1977). See also DECENTERED SELF AND DECENTERED SUBJECT.

Laing, Ronald David (1927–1989) Scottish psychiatrist and critic of orthodox psychiatry. His radical critique (see ANTIPSYCHIATRY) grew from varied experience and interests. His initial clinical experience was with psychotic (see PSYCHOSIS) long-stay patients in a large mental hospital, and he subsequently undertook psychoanalytic (see PSYCHOANALYSIS) work with neurotic patients and their families at the Tavistock Clinic in London. He became interested in existentialism and the phenomenological experience of the person. He developed the view that mental illness must be understood as individual experience within a social context, particularly the family context, as perceived by the individual. In his view, mental illness may be seen as a valid response to this phenomenological experience, and treatment can be effected by understanding this and assisting the mentally ill person to grow through it. His own practical application of the theory can be seen in Kingsley Hall, the therapeutic community he established and worked in.

Laing developed his ideas during the 1950s and 1960s, publishing *The Divided Self* (1959), about the schizophrenic experience, *The Self and Others* (1961) and *Sanity, Madness and the Family,* with Esterson (1964), both concerned with family dynamics, and *The Politics of Experience and the Bird of Paradise* (1967). His radical views on mental illness and its treatment and his refusal to label people as sane or insane, but as making different responses to different phenomenological experience, have had significant influence on the orthodox view, substantially humanizing it. However, with the perspective of a quarter of a century, his ideas are not regarded as being of central theoretical importance in the treatment of schizophrenia, but only as offering a useful perspective in some cases. The importance of family dynamics in the etiology of mental illness generally, and in its treatment, is recognized in the development of family therapy.

Lamarck, Jean (1744–1829) French biologist remembered for his now discredited theory that traits acquired by an organism during its lifetime are inheritable. This theory was contested principally by Charles DARWIN (1809–1882), who suggested the now widely accepted theory of organic evolution by random variation and natural selection.

Lamarck's connection with the 20th century and with political theory lies in the preference the Soviet state under Joseph Stalin gave to Lamarckian rather than Darwinian principles. The project of creating a new socialist state and a new socialist person meant that any theory of development and change that suggested the inheritability (and thus, by implication, the perfectibility) of acquired characteristics would find favor. Michusin (1855–1935), a Russian horticulturalist, was among the first to earn the praise of the Soviet government for attempting to prove Lamarckian principles. The infamous biologist and agronomist Lysenko (1898–1976) continued Michusin's project. With Stalin's support, Lysenko imposed theoretical uniformity on the scientific community as director of the Institute of Genetics of the Academy of Sciences of the USSR (1940–1965) and as president of the All-Union Academy of Agricultural Sciences. Lysenko's baleful influence on Soviet science was not dislodged until the mid-1960s. See also EVOLUTIONARY THEORY.

LAND

land 1. territory valued for its natural resources or its potential for human use for cultivation, living space, or natural beauty. **2.** the territory with which a particular people identify: "This land is our land."

In economics, land is generally viewed as a FACTOR OF PRODUCTION. Sociologists and anthropologists have been mainly interested in the social relations involved in LAND TENURE and land use. In STATELESS SOCIETIES and AGRARIAN SOCIETIES there are a variety of forms of land ownership with communal or corporate group ownership in the former and various forms of state and private ownership in the latter. However, often in these societies issues of *land ownership* may be secondary, or the concept itself may be the issue—who has rights of use of the land (*usufruct*) and rights to the products of the land.

Different forms of land tenure and land use are often considered important by social scientists in distinguishing between different forms of society: for example, the holding of land on condition of providing service to a superior is characteristic of feudalism, as opposed to the notion of private ownership characteristic of capitalism. In capitalist societies, however, land is often not just another factor of production equivalent to others. Thus, zoning may prevent certain uses of land in certain regions, as with the designation of National Parks in the United States, and most societies have planning regulations governing the use of land. More recently, the rise of environmental pressure groups has led to calls for limitations on land use, for example, to control deforestation or the use of nitrate fertilizers.

land tenure the rights involved in holding land, whether this involves ownership, renting, or communal forms. The most common forms in contemporary industrial societies are *freehold*, involving ownership, and *leasehold*, involving some form of renting.

language 1. a system of symbolic communication, that is vocal (and written) signs, which arguably distinguishes human beings from all other species. Language is rule-governed and primarily comprises a plurality of arbitrary conventional signs. These signs will have a common significance for all members of a linguistic group. **2.** the "crucial signifying practice in and through which the human subject is constructed and becomes a social being" (W. Mulford, 1983). **3.** the most important, but not the only sign system of human society—some of which may also be referred to as language—compare BODY LANGUAGE).

Language is the means whereby subjectivity is stabilized and crystallized (including knowledge and science, and the stretching of societies across time and space; see TIME-SPACE DISTANCIATION). Language also exists as an objective institution independent of any individual user. In common with all aspects of human culture, language can be seen to be historical and subject to change. Currently there are between three and five thousand active languages and a large number of nonactive languages.

Often sociologists and social psychologists have been less concerned with the syntactic structure and related formal properties of language than with the relationship between language, ideology, knowledge, and the social nature of verbal interaction. Social psychologists have tended to concentrate on the last named, whereas sociologists have tended to explore the relationship between language and nonlinguistic structural arrangements such as class and gender. The work of Basil BERNSTEIN (1971/7), however, has shown that different forms of social relation generate different forms of linguistic code. Bernstein has suggested that, within the context of schooling, lower-working-class children may be disadvantaged due to their utilization of a restricted linguistic code (see ELABORATED AND RESTRICTED CODES).

A distinction has been made by Scott (1977) and Turiel (1983) between linguistic competence and social communicative competence. They have suggested that communicative skill depends on an individual's ability to combine both these aspects of competence. Linguistic competence refers to the individual's command of vocabulary and grammatical rules. Social communicative competence refers to the degree to which the *encoder* (person sending the message) is responsive to the social and linguistic characteristics of the *decoder* (audience). Recently it has been suggested that social competence and linguistic competence must be seen as highly linked, for example, that SEMANTICS can only be formulated in terms of PRAGMATICS, that is, language usage is to be understood contextually.

Sociologists and social psychologists (as well as philosophers—see FORMS OF LIFE, LANGUAGE GAMES, SPEECH ACTS, WITTGENSTEIN) have become increasingly interested in examining the complex and socially determined rules governing linguistic action. For example, verbal interaction is characterized by rules relating to the structuring of conversation and to TURN-TAKING. Ethnomethodologists have been particularly concerned with the unstated rules governing communicative interaction (see H. GARFINKEL, 1967, H. Sacks et al, 1974).

Other general areas of interest concern linguistic relativity. The nature of the relationship between language and our perception and understanding of the world has been approached from many perspectives, one of the most influential being the work of the linguists Benjamin Lee Whorf and Edward Sapir. The SAPIR-WHORF HYPOTHESIS contends that the kind of language someone uses determines the nature of that person's thinking about the world. It has been suggested by other theorists that language does not have this determining function and that language itself is in fact largely determined by experience.

A further growing field of investigation is the relationship between gender and language. Writers such as D. Spender (1980) have argued that language is man-made, while M. Daly (1981) has shown the androcentric or phallocentric nature of language. In its stead she argues for the necessity of gynocentric language. Underlying these different approaches is the assumption that the oppression of women is both revealed in and sustained by language and the process of language interaction. While such approaches are not new (see, for example, Herschberger, 1948; Merriam, 1964), the second wave of feminism has given impetus to the development of such critiques and forms of analysis.

Last but not least, language has been increasingly employed as a model for social relations in general, especially resting on the structural, rule-governed character of both. In STRUCTURALISM (see also LÉVI-STRAUSS, LACAN) social relations are not simply *like* language, they are a language; thus a further implication of this is that individual actions (in the same way as particular utterances) can be viewed as structural outcomes (see also DE-CENTERED SELF). For critics of structuralism, however, it loses touch with the creative power of the subject, evident not least in relation to language use, which involves a creative grasping of rules that are interpreted and also sometimes transformed. Since, in view of the increasing recognition of the dependence of syntax on context, structural linguistics is no longer widely seen as providing an adequate model *even* of language, it is not surprising that it should fail to provide one for society. See also SOCIOLINGUISTICS, SEMIOTICS.

language games the conception of LANGUAGE as akin to an assemblage of different games, like chess, football, children's play, and so on, each governed by a different set of rules and located in a different FORM OF LIFE, and with only very general family resemblances in common (WITTGENSTEIN, 1953). According to Wittgenstein, we cannot generalize usefully about language, but must simply notice that language use follows from the rules and practices that operate in particular kinds of use (for example, jokes, greetings, story telling, as well as science and philosophy) and particular social contexts. As with many games, a further feature of languages viewed as rule-following activities is that, while rules are followed, they are never followed slavishly but always interpreted. This is a further dimension of the apparently relativistic and inherently non-universalizing character of language as portrayed in Wittgenstein's second philosophy variously interpreted by later philosophers and sociologists. See also RULES AND RULE-FOLLOWING, INCOMMENSURABILITY, KUHN, FEYARABEND).

langue and **parole** (linguistics) the distinction between LANGUAGE as a communal resource, a socially established system of linguistic units and rules (*langue*), and as actually produced speech (*parole*). Introduced by SAUSSURE, the distinction is an important not only in theoretical linguistics, but also for its influence in the formation of the more diffuse body of ideas in social science known as STRUCTURALISM.

In his own work Saussure regarded the understanding of *langue* as the paramount concern of theoretical linguistics. The significance of this is that it places an emphasis on the internal structural relations of language, even though language is constantly changed as the result of *parole,* that is, by language use. In structuralism more generally, it is the same emphasis on structural explanations, sometimes to the exclusion of the individual subject or AGENCY, that is uppermost and defines the approach, but is also much criticized for its onesidedness.

latent function see MANIFEST AND LATENT FUNCTIONS.

law see SOCIOLOGY OF LAW.

Law of the Three Stages a proposed historical sociological law formulated by COMTE in which knowledge and the general form of society are seen as moving through three stages:

(a) knowledge permeated by "Theological" conceptions and a society dominated by priests and by monarchy;

(b) "Metaphysical" speculative knowledge, associated with a negative era of social criticism and political upheaval and revolution;

(c) the modern era of "Positive" scientific knowledge (see POSITIVISM) in which Comte expected that social reorganization guided by scientific knowledge would occur, and including the application of a scientific sociology.

Sociologists do not disagree with Comte that a growth in the importance of scientific knowledge is an important general feature of modern societies. There is much disagreement, however, over how far it is appropriate to regard sociology as an applied science on a par with the natural sciences. Whether or not they accept the goal of scientific laws in sociology, there is general agreement that Comte's formulation of the Law of Three Stages lacks the precision (or perhaps even the correct testable or falsifiable form—see HISTORICISM) to gain acceptance as a truly lawlike statement.

Lazarsfeld, Paul (1901–1976) Austrian-born, later US-based social researcher and sociologist, who made an outstanding contribution to the development of survey research and techniques of quantitative data analysis in sociology. After early research in Austria on class and unemployment, he emigrated to the US in 1933, working first on research into the mass media, before moving to Columbia University, where he set up what was to become one of the leading centers for empirical sociological research, the Bureau of Applied Social Research. Among the most famous of the studies with which he was associated were those on voting behavior, including *The People's Choice* (1944), with Berelson and Gaudet, and *Voting* (1954), with Berelson and McPhee. Criticism of his work, for example from C. Wright MILLS, that it amounted only to ABSTRACTED EMPIRICISM, is unfair, as it was Lazarsfeld who can claim to have first established the systematic SOCIAL SURVEY as an analytical sociological tool rather than merely a means of collecting facts or opinions. His systematization of methods of HYPOTHESIS testing using cross-tabulations remains central in sociology. He also contributed much to the development of research methods in other areas, including the construction of indicators, and his contributions to MATHEMATICAL SOCIOLOGY were instrumental in helping to establish this as a distinctive subsection of sociological endeavor. He himself claimed that his research goal was always to seek THEORIES OF THE MIDDLE RANGE. The continuing influence of a number of his theories in mass communications research (see OPINION LEADER and the TWO-STEP FLOW IN MASS COMMUNICATIONS) is testimony to this.

leadership the abilities, qualities, and behavior associated with the ROLE of group leader. This role may be conferred on individuals on the basis of personal characteristics and experience, or through tradition and/or position occupied. However, contingency approaches to leadership have led to awareness that effective leaders are not so simply by virtue of specific characteristics or behavior. Rather, different styles of leadership (for example, task-oriented v. relationship-oriented) are required by different situations. See also GROUP, GROUP DYNAMICS, LEGITIMATE AUTHORITY (OR POLITICAL LEGITIMACY), OPINION LEADER.

left-right continuum the division between radical or left-wing POLITICAL PARTIES and orientations on the one hand, and conservative or right-wing political parties and orientations on the other, originally so-called because of the arrangement of seating in the two sides of the French National Assembly. Subsequently, the terms have persisted as general terms referring to the spectrum of political orientations, despite the obvious oversimplifications involved in any assumption that political issues and political parties can be arranged on a single continuum. One reason why confining political analysis merely to a left-right division is an oversimplification is that other dimensions, such as the liberal-authoritarian dimension crosscut the left-right dimension. See Fig. 14. See also AUTHORITARIANISM, POLITICAL ATTITUDES.

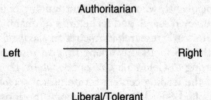

Fig. 14. **Left-right continuum.** The existence of a left-right continuum in politics is widely acknowledged, but a crosscutting dimension also exists which crosscuts this.

legal positivism a form of legal theory in which the law is seen as capable of being expressed in formal and objective terms as a hierarchical system of general principles (see JURISPRUDENCE).

legitimate authority or **political legitimacy** any form of political rule in which the rulers successfully uphold a claim that they govern by right in accord with law, tradition, or similar basis.

WEBER identified three pure types of legitimate authority:

(a) *legal-rational authority*, resting on a belief in the legality of enacted rules and those achieving authority under these rules, for example, elected representatives or civil servants.

(b) *traditional authority*, resting on an established belief in the sanctity of tradition and the acceptance of those chosen to rule in accordance with the customs and practices within this tradition, for example, kings, queens, or religious dignitaries.

(c) *charismatic authority*, resting on the devotion to an exceptional individual or leader and on the normative rules ordained by this individual, for example, a prophet or warlord.

The last of these provides the dynamic or revolutionary element in Weber's overall account of political legitimacy. In the long run, however, for example after the death or departure of the exceptional teacher or leader, there occurs a *routinization of charisma*, and a reversion to traditional, or legal-rational, forms of authority. See also BUREAUCRACY, STATE, POWER, NATION-STATE, HOBBES, LEGITIMATION CRISIS.

legitimation the manner and the process in which a STATE or POLITICAL SYSTEM receives justification. See LEGITIMATE AUTHORITY, LEGITIMATION CRISIS.

legitimation crisis the tendency of modern political systems, which depend on consent for their maintenance of political authority, to meet major problems amounting to a crisis in doing so. Such problems are seen as arising especially from contradictions and conflicts between the logic of capitalist accumulation and escalating demands for social welfare, as well as demands for increased participation and social equality.

From a neo-Marxist point of view, in *Legitimation Crisis* (1975) HABERMAS identified three main crisis tendencies in capitalist societies:

(a) *economic crisis*, arising from fact that the state acting as the unconscious "executive organ of the law or value" acts as the planning agent of united monopoly capital;

(b) *rationality crisis*, the "destruction of administrative rationality" that occurs through (i) the opposing interests of individual capitalists (for example, between monopoly and nonmonopoly forms of capitalism) and (ii) the production—necessary for continued existence of the system—of structures foreign to the system, such as welfare provision, including new types of welfare workers with new values;

(c) *legitimation and motivation crises* arising from the politicization of administrative interventions that results from the above, and from the erosion of previously important traditions (for example, deference) and the overloading of the existing political and economic system "through universalistic value-systems ('new' needs)."

Habermas's suggestion was that the state in the future may prove unable to manage the tensions between competing values that such tendencies involve, especially in a context encouraging a new emphasis on rational critical discourse. In most Western states over the last decade, however, the tendencies to crisis have been handled by rolling back the WELFARE STATE, by refashioning justifications for the market economy, by programs of privatization, etc.

leisure 1. the time free from work and routine domestic responsibilities and available for use in recuperation, relaxation, hobbies, recreation, and cultural and artistic pursuits. **2.** the activities actually occupying such free time.

Theorists of leisure have generally either stressed the individual freedom involved in leisure, compared with work or family responsibilities, or they have emphasized the illusion of this freedom, identifying the constraints on free choice arising from domestic responsibilities (especially on women's leisure) and the way in which leisure is shaped by the constraints arising from consumer culture and capitalist society.

Sociological interest in leisure grew in the 1980s, made more urgent by the increase in unemployment. The sociology of leisure first developed out of INDUSTRIAL SOCIOLOGY in the 1950s during the era of affluence that also spawned theories of POSTINDUSTRIAL SOCIETY. Dubin (1955) even argued that leisure was replacing work as a central life interest. Subsequent research focused on exploration of the relationship between work and leisure (see Parker, 1971, Roberts, 1970). This demonstrated the continued centrality of work and a complex pattern of work-leisure relations.

More recently an interest in leisure research has also emerged from two critical theoretical traditions: Marxist structuralism and radical cultural studies. Unlike earlier Marxist and critical analysis of leisure, which tended to view leisure in modern society as largely constrained by capitalism, these new approaches view leisure as a contested sphere, characterized by increasing resistance to its commodification and standardization (see Hall and Jefferson, 1976, Gruneau, 1983). See also CULTURAL STUDIES, RESISTANCE THROUGH RITUAL.

"Leisure," derived from the latin *licere*, shares a common root with "license." It thus contains within itself the dualism of freedom and control, individual agency and constraint, with which modern sociological theorists have been concerned. See also PLAY, SOCIABILITY.

leisure class a term coined by VEBLEN (*The Theory of the Leisure Class,* 1899) to refer to a particular stratum of the upper classes in the United States in the latter half of the 19th century. Veblen was critical of the *nouveaux riches,* who expressed disdain for all forms of manual and productive labor and sustained their own status position through acts of CONSPICUOUS CONSUMPTION and abstention from work.

leisure society any society in which work is losing its former centrality. Since the 19th century, various commentators have used "leisure society" with little precision or consistency of meaning. In the second half of the 20th century it has been used by writers in conjunction with other terms such as POSTINDUSTRIAL SOCIETY, suggesting that fewer average hours of paid employment leads to a greater concern for leisure in such societies. Leisure, it is argued, comes to take on the centrality that paid employment had in the past. The notion of the leisure society is highly contested, however. The basic idea that fewer hours are spent working in modern industrial society than in the past is contestable on a number of counts, and both historical and comparative evidence suggest LEISURE was a central part of life in preindustrial societies.

Le Play, Fréderic (1806–1882) French mining engineer and professor of metallurgy, and later an independent scholar and researcher, whose studies in sociology and involvement in industrial management and in public life (for example, in organizing major international exhibitions) led to his making a wide-ranging contribution to the early development of empirical sociology. In particular, he used data gathered in pioneering interviews to provide accounts of working class family life and domestic economy (for example, *Les Ouvriers Européens,* 1985). He regarded the family as the fundamental social unit, and its health and stability as an indicator of the overall state of society. He also proposed a more general classification of types of family, seeing the modern family as increasingly corresponding to an unstable type, the outcome of unregulated urban and industrial change, poor housing, and women's industrial work. A conservative politically, Le Play emphasized the importance of traditional values, including original sin. This led him to emphasize the importance of establishing the social facts about the interrelation of society's interdependent parts, even if his own prejudgments often colored his work.

lesbianism 1. a sexual categorization referring to female homosexuality. In this usage, sexual behavior and sexual identification are taken as the primary factors denoted by the term. **2.** (feminist usage) homoerotic desire between women, or more widely a specifically female experience involving the social, emotional, and erotic bonding of women. In this usage lesbianism is seen as primarily a political category, placing less importance on the issue of genital sexuality and more on woman-identified experience.

Political lesbianism stresses that lesbianism is "far more than a sexual preference; it is a political stance," (Abbott and Love, 1972). Nestle (1981) challenges this approach for its misrepresentation of lesbian history and for its implicit desexualization of lesbian culture. Rich (1980) has suggested that lesbianism should, however, be regarded as one of the primary forms of resistance against compulsory heterosexuality. In this context, Rich (1980) has distinguished between *lesbian existence* and the *lesbian continuum*. The former refers to conscious lesbian identification, the latter to a broad range of woman-identified experience or sisterhood. In both, Rich places less emphasis on sexual desire as the primary criterion for identification with lesbianism, and more on women's active, political resistance to heterosexual privilege.

Lesbianism is subjected to both social and legal control in many contemporary societies. In Britain, lesbianism is not subject to criminalization except in the armed forces. Lesbians, however, tend to be subject to control via the civil courts, particularly in custody cases involving children of lesbian mothers. The history of lesbianism and its regulation via law and custom are different from the history and regulation pertaining to male homosexuality, and has been the subject of both misrepresentation and invisibility.

Lévi-Strauss, Claude (1908–) Belgian-born, French social anthropologist, who is usually seen as an intellectual descendant of DURKHEIM and Mauss, although also strongly influenced by MARX, FREUD, and JAKOBSON. A major figure in modern STRUCTURALISM, Lévi-Strauss claimed that Marx and Freud advanced the structuralist method of analysis by seeking to comprehend surface reality through reference to a deeper structural level. The central concerns in Lévi-Strauss's work are primitive classification and the study of KINSHIP and MYTHOLOGIES in TRIBAL SOCIETIES. His major translated works include *Structural Anthropology* (1963), *The Elementary Structures of Kinship* (1969), *The Savage Mind* (1969), *Totemism* (1963), and *Mythologies* (4 vols.) (1969–78). The distinctive feature of his work is the attempt to discover universal rules that underlie everyday activities and customs. Culture is held to embody principles that mirror essential features of the human mind, "binary classificatory systems." The influence of linguistics, particularly phonology, led Lévi-Strauss to formulate the main task of anthropology as the discovery of semiotic, and hence cognitive, structures deeply underlying the surfaces of social activity. It is in these terms that he locates neat systems of contrastive classes underlying marriage systems and beneath myths. Such structures are layered, and the same structures can underlie different surface patterns in different societies, so that one may illuminate another. It is the deepest layers that Lévi-Strauss sees as cognitive, and which permit reconstruction of universals of the human mind. Although the layers of structure are systematic and ordered, they are not directly available to the consciousness that is constituted by them: they are unconscious structures of consciousness, reconstructable in scientific logics. The existence of these logical systems have been challenged by recent thinkers, for example, poststructuralists, who insist on the fragmentary, open, evasive and sliding character of semiotic underpinnings. But, in their critique of rational consciousness, and their decentering of the subject, they continue the critique of the transparency of action, communication, institutions, and history that sociology owes to Lévi-Strauss.

life chances the material advantages or disadvantages (for example, material rewards and social and cultural opportunities or lack of opportunities) that a typical member of a group or class can expect within a particular society. Originally a Weberian conception, and especially associated with WEBER's analysis of class and status, the concept has also been employed by DAHREN-

DORF (1979). Its focus is on inequality. Perhaps the most poignant of life chances is unequal distribution of health care and associated inequality in life expectancy.

life course the process of personal change from infancy through to old age and death, brought about as a result of the interaction between biographical events and societal events. The term is preferred by many over *life cycle* because, in recognizing that people do not experience their lives strictly in terms of chronology, it focuses on sociohistorical processes as both the result of human action and as a background to personal biography.

Life cycle may be regarded as the process of change and development of a person, an institution or an entity and is therefore similar in meaning to "life course." However, because it suggests a continuous and renewable process, as in "the cycle of the season," it has connotations of inevitability, similarity, and determinism, which may be considered inappropriate to an understanding of how human lives are experienced at the level of individual personal relationships and in the context of the social and historical forces that influence lives. Both terms are used interchangeably, but current preference is for "life course" for the reasons given.

Sociological and psychological concern with the life course has grown in recent years. One of the first theorists to propose that development does not end when adulthood is reached, and who described eight successive stages of psychosocial development, was Erik Erikson (1963). Other classic authors include Charlotte Bühler (1953), whose work, like Erikson's, particularly illustrates the nativist approach, emphasizing the common process underlying the human life course (this being closest to the definition of *life cycle*). Other authors (for example, Dohrenwend and Dohrenwend, 1974) have emphasized the effect of different experiences, that is, the contrast between lives rather than their similarities (this being closest to the definition of *life course*).

life history and life history method a sociological historical or psychological account of a single person, which may be produced from face-to-face interviews or from letters or documents.

life-world *(Lebenswelt)* the natural attitude involved in everyday conceptions of reality, which includes "not only the 'nature' experienced ... but also the social world" (Schutz and Luckmann, *The Structures of the Life-World*, 1973).

Whereas HUSSERL's PHENOMENOLOGY bracketed the life-world, for SCHUTZ it was the major task of SOCIAL PHENOMENOLOGY to uncover the basis of this natural habitat of social life (of actors' social competence), with its central problem of human understanding. For Schutz it is the taken-for-granted, routine character of the life-world that is most striking (for example, in contrast with science). The "stocks of knowledge" (what everybody knows—see also MUTUAL KNOWLEDGE) and the interpretive schemes employed by social actors in bringing off everyday action, as made apparent by Schutz, become the subject matter of ETHNOMETHODOLOGY. Schutz's thinking has also influenced GIDDENS' formulation of STRUCTURATION THEORY. See also PRACTICAL CONSCIOUSNESS.

Likert scale a technique for measuring the strength of a person's ATTITUDE or predisposition toward a person, object, idea, phenomenon, etc. (Likert, 1932). Likert scales assumed that attitudes lie on a simple, dichotomous continuum running from one extreme position through neutral to the other extreme, for example, capitalism/communism, religion/atheism.

Likert scales are subjective in nature, insofar as they are based on the replies given by individuals to a battery of questions. In constructing such scales a sample of respondents from the target population are presented with a large number of statements thought to have a bearing on the subject. For example, to construct a scale to measure the strength of religious belief, respondents may be presented with statements such as: "We can be almost certain that human beings evolved from lower animals"; "Every woman has the right to terminate an unwanted pregnancy if she so wishes"; "The miracles in the Bible happened just as they are described there." Respondents are asked to indicate to what extent they agree or disagree with each statement, using a three-, five-, or seven-point scale. A five-point scale is generally considered to be best. The replies given to each question are then coded (see CODING) so that a high score indicates a strong disposition toward the subject under consideration, and a low score indicates its polar opposite. Finally, the Likert scale is constructed using those items whose scores correlate most closely with the overall scores, that is, the scale has internal consistency and each item has predictability. This final form of the scale can then be administered to the population for whom it is intended.

The main problem with constructing Likert scales is that of ensuring that the individual items included in the scale tap one dimension only. In measuring religious attitudes, as discussed above, for example, people's opinions about abortion are determined by many factors, of which the individual's religious persuasion is only one. Various statistical techniques, such as FACTOR ANALYSIS, have been devised that enable researchers to calculate the internal consistency of their scales. See also ATTITUDE SCALE AND MEASUREMENT, GUTTMAN SCALE.

lions and foxes see CIRCULATION OF ELITES.

Lipset, Seymour M. (1922–) leading US political sociologist who, after his early work on radicalism, and on democracy and oligarchy in labor unions (*Union Democracy*, 1956), has become best known for a number of influential general works on the social bases of liberal democracy and nondemocracy, including *Political Man* (1960), *The First New Nation* (1963), and *Party Systems and Voter Alignments* (with S. Rokkan, 1967). See also END-OF-IDEOLOGY THESIS, IRON LAW OF OLIGARCHY, SOCIAL MOBILITY.

local labor market the market for jobs within a particular locale. At this level of analysis, specifics relating to the role of the family, social networks, and employers within the local milieu all play their part in developing and sustaining the work expectations, attitudes, and behavior of individuals and groups. These can vary greatly between localities and influence the ways individuals, groups, and employers respond to external LABOR MARKET pressures, for example, economic recession (Ashton et al., 1987). Studies of local labor markets add to our understanding of the dynamics of labor markets, in particular *segmentalism* and emphasize the importance of local sociohistorical and cultural patterning of these relations.

Locke, John (1632–1704) English philosopher and political theorist, whose major political writing, the *Two Treatises of Government* (1690), was occasioned by his belief that the Stuart monarchs were seeking to restore ABSOLUTISM. In the *First Treatise,* he was concerned with demolishing arguments about the patriarchal origins of political authority. Man's duty to God, under natural law, is to use his peculiarly human qualities—reason and free will. Political authority, properly so called, is limited to securing the conditions under which people can pursue these purposes (see NATURAL RIGHTS AND NATURAL LAW). This means that their property must be protected, and by "property" Locke meant the "lives, liberties, and estates" of people. Political authority is thus instituted by men in the *state of nature,* through contract, for their greater security; it is exercised according to trust, is sustained by an implicit contract, and consent can be withdrawn if that authority either proves incompetent or, as Locke thought likely, it oversteps the boundaries of the trust. Since civil government is entrusted to men who ultimately cannot be trusted, a right of popular resistance to political authority remains always in reserve as a deterrent to incipient absolutist and despotic pretensions. In putting forward a SOCIAL CONTRACT THEORY and limited constitutional government, Locke was to have a far greater influence on the American colonies and their post-independence constitutions, than he has ever had on the British political system. He was also an early proponent of the labor theory of value, in that he argued that men legitimately appropriated land from the common stock by mixing their labor with it. In EPISTEMOLOGY, Locke also laid the foundations of modern EMPIRICISM. He denied that men had innate knowledge, and he rejected the rationalism of Descartes. In the *Essay on Human Understanding* (1690), he argued that all knowledge is derived from experience, either directly through the senses or through reflection. Man could have intuitive knowledge of their own existence and of mathematical truths, but his knowledge of the external world was conjectural and probabilistic. Locke's doctrine of the mind as a *tabula rasa,* a blank slate, indicates the extent of his empiricism. And his interest in children's learning and the acquisition of ideas meant that aspects of his thinking also contributed to philosophical psychology. The SELF, for example, for Locke arises as a set of ideas and actions for which the individual takes responsibility. Like HOBBES, Locke's central doctrines are individualistic, more so than Hobbes', and his proposals for civil society are for intellectual freedom and checks and balances.

Lockwood, David (1929–) British sociologist who has worked mainly at the London School of Economics and the University of Essex, and whose main concern has been with the study of CLASS and SOCIAL STRATIFICATION, especially his studies of the so-called black-coated worker (1958) and the AFFLUENT WORKER (Lockwood, 1966; Goldthorpe, Lockwood et al., 1988–1989). See also MULTIDIMENSIONAL ANALYSIS OF SOCIAL STRATIFICATION, CLASS IMAGERY.

In addition to his contributions to studies of class and stratification, he has made important interventions in central debates on SOCIOLOGICAL THEORY, notably his critiques of Talcott PARSONS and STRUCTURAL FUNCTIONALISM (see "Some Remarks on the Social System," 1956, and "Social Integration and System Integration," 1964)—see also SOCIAL INTEGRATION AND SYSTEM INTEGRATION.

logic the branch of philosophy concerned with analysis of the universal and context-free (A PRIORI) principles of sound reasoning and valid inference by which conclusions may be drawn from initial premises. These general principles are formal in that they are abstract in character and are usually also capable of being expressed in symbolic notation. An early formulation of logic, which held sway until modern times, was Aristotle's systematization of the basis of the syllogism (also known as *propositional logic*). This was added to in the 19th century by highly technical forms of logic, increasingly linked with mathematics.

logical action and **non-logical action** see PARETO, RESIDUES AND DERIVATIONS.

logical positivism the philosophical doctrine of a group of philosophers, including R. Carnap (1891–1970) and O. Neurath (1882–1945), known collectively as the *Vienna Circle*. See POSITIVISM.

log linear analysis a technique of statistical analysis commonly used on cross-tabulations of data. It transforms nonlinear models into linear models by the use of logarithms. This is necessary because social data are often nominal or ordinal and therefore do not meet the assumptions needed by many statistical techniques (see CRITERIA AND LEVELS OF MEASUREMENT). It is a CAUSAL MODELING device, involving setting up models to test against the data, successively adjusting the model till the best fit is found.

logocentrism see DECONSTRUCTION.

longitudinal study an investigation involving making observations of the same group at sequential time intervals. Thus, a longitudinal study of a COHORT of children may be made to assess, for example, the effect of social class on school achievement. Longitudinal studies are not only appropriate for studying human development or change, but may also be used to observe change over time within organizations.

The advantage of longitudinal studies compared with CROSS-SECTIONAL

STUDIES is that the causal factor involved in a sequence of changes can be directly explored using data collected before and after changes (for example, analysis of the effect of changes in the school curriculum). The main disadvantages are the greater expense of repeated study, the possible HAWTHORNE EFFECT of repeated studies and the influence of other changes that may be occurring concurrently (for example, changes in the school curriculum may take place at the same time as changes in the resourcing of educational services). Compare PANEL STUDY.

looking-glass self the conception of the social self as arising reflectively as the outcome of the reaction to the opinion of others. This term was coined by Charles COOLEY, but the general idea is one that he shared with William James and SYMBOLIC INTERACTIONISM.

Lukács, George (1885–1971) widely influential Hungarian Marxist, philosopher, and literary theorist. The young Lukács attended the Universities of Budapest, Berlin, and Heidelberg where he studied under George SIMMEL and Max WEBER. At the end of the First World War he joined the Communist Party and became Deputy Commissar for Education in the short-lived 1919 Hungarian Soviet Republic. His literary writings, which attempted to develop a Marxist theory of AESTHETICS, established him as a theorist of international distinction. The best-known book by Lukács, *History and Class Consciousness* (1923), covered several major themes, including the importance of HEGEL for the interpretation of Marx; Marx's theory of ALIENATION; and the relationship between ideology, class consciousness, and revolution. In ways that later influenced members of the Western European New Left and members of the FRANKFURT SCHOOL OF CRITICAL THEORY, Lukács argued against scientistic interpretations of Marxism, emphasizing the importance of historical PRAXIS. In some tension with this view, however, he also gave strong support to Leninist conceptions of the supremacy of the Communist Party. In 1930 Lukács moved to the Soviet Union, where he remained until 1945, when he was appointed Professor of Aesthetics and Philosophy at the University of Budapest. He was always a controversial figure, accused by his critics of condoning Stalinism. Nevertheless, during the Hungarian popular uprising of 1956 he was appointed Minister of Culture in Imre Nagy's government. Other major works by Lukács include *Theory of the Novel* (1920), *The Historical Novel* (1937), *The Young Hegel* (1948), *The Meaning of Contemporary Realism* (1963), *On Aesthetics* (1963), and *Solzhenitsyn* (1969).

lumpenproletariat literally, the "proletariat of rags," from the German *lumpen* meaning "rag." MARX and ENGELS were two of the first 19th-century writers to recognize the existence of a class drawn from all classes, living on the margins of society, not in regular employment, and gaining their subsistence mainly from crime. According to Marx, the composition of the Parisian lumpenproletariat in the mid-19th century included vagabonds, discharged soldiers and jailbirds, escaped galley slaves, swindlers, pickpockets, tricksters, gamblers, pimps, brothel-keepers, ragpickers, and beggars. These groups were sharply differentiated from the industrial working class by politics and by being outside the normal social relations of wage labor. Marx and Engels distrusted the lumpenproletariat, because it did not make an obvious contribution to the struggle of the working class for socialism. They therefore considered the lumpenproletariat were "the dangerous class," "the social scum" whose parasitic ways of life prepared them for becoming bribed agents of reactionary elements in the ruling class. They threatened to lead workers into arbitrary violence, and their highest forms of political activity were mob agitation and street fighting. These were primitive forms of political action, according to Marx and Engels, who maintained that where large scale capitalist production exists, modern revolution demands the mass seizure and control of the means of production by the working class.

Dissenting from the Marxist view, the African socialist Fanon, in *The Wretched of the Earth* (1967), stressed that the lumpenproletariat or "classless idlers" living in the shanty towns of Third World societies could play an important role in revolutionary struggles.

M

macrosociology the level of sociological analysis concerned with the analysis of whole societies, social structures at large, and social systems (compare MICROSOCIOLOGY). While the terms "macrosociology" and "microsociology" are used in sociology, the distinction is not as well established or as central as the related distinction between micro- and macro- in economics.

madness mental derangement ("insanity") that disrupts the normal social functioning of an individual, leading to strange and unpredictable behavior. In modern medical or psychiatric DISCOURSE, madness is conceptualized and treated either as one of a number of physically grounded medical conditions (hence also treatable by drugs) or as a clinically identifiable personality disorder (see also PSYCHOSIS). In the sociological literature, it is more likely to be analyzed as an example of the wider phenomenon of social LABELING and SOCIAL CONTROL. For FOUCAULT, for instance, modern ways of handling madness must be analyzed in modern societies as an aspect of the wider phenomena of social POWER and SURVEILLANCE, and social exclusion. Thus for sociological purposes there can be no question of any simple acceptance of the scientific labels attached by so-called experts. In other societies and at other times, the kinds of behavior now usually labeled "insane" would be more variously labeled, for example, as shamanism, witchcraft, etc., and the social treatment of these would be similarly variable. In order to capture the social character of madness, there must be analysis of the social basis and social implications of madness. Medical and associated psychiatric conceptions will be part of this analysis, but can have no automatic priority in their own terms. See also LAING, SZASZ.

magic the attempt to activate supernatural or spiritual agencies in order to attain a specific outcome by ritualized means. Magic is not always readily distinguished from religious activity (see RELIGION), and in operation is often associated with it. However, an activity is usually identified as magic by its more instrumental, often more immediate, concern with the achievement of specific ends. In functionalist terms (see MALINOWSKI, 1948), magic is employed in situations in which effective technologies to achieve the desired end are lacking. Thus, the social function of magic is to allay anxieties and fulfill the need to do something, and it can be cathartic.

In its broadest sense, magic is not only a feature of so-called primitive societies, but is also operative in modern societies, for example, confidence in various pseudosciences, such as astrology, and in the survival of superstition. The interpenetration of true technologies and ritualized magical activity can be seen as a pervasive feature of social activity, present even in modern medicine. In all discussion of magic there is the difficulty that, since the distinction between empirical science and nonscience is never a straightforward matter, the distinction between technology and magic is correspondingly blurred. It is the case that many of the users of magic do not operate with a sharp distinction between the natural and the supernatural. Thus, magic is often an observer's concept rather than one shared by participants.

Maine, Henry James Sumner (1822–1888) social philosopher and jurist best remembered for his *Ancient Law* (1861), which approaches the problem of social development in terms of the way in which legal systems evolved (see EVOLUTIONARY THEORY). The basic elements of Maine's understanding of SOCIAL CHANGE involve the development or evolution of societies based on kinship; family relationships; communal ownership; relations of status and political despotism to those based on territory, citizenship, private property, relations of contract, and liberty. Maine's point was that legal terms could only be fully understood within a framework of social change.

The status/contract dichotomy was a variant of many attempts to conceptualize the evolutionary distinction between traditional and modern society. Related formulations have come from SPENCER (MILITANT AND INDUSTRIAL SOCIETY), DURKHEIM (MECHANICAL AND ORGANIC SOLIDARITY), TÖNNIES (GEMEINSCHAFT AND GESELLSCHAFT), Robert M. MacIver (COMMUNITY AND ASSOCIATION), and Robert Redfield.

Malinowski, Bronislaw Kaspar (1884–1942) Polish functionalist anthropologist. His major works include *Argonauts of the Western Pacific,* (1922), *Sex and Repression in Savage Society,* (1927), and *The Sexual Life of Savages* (1929). He is best known for stressing the importance of ETHNOGRAPHY, or detailed participant observation, in anthropology. His use of a detailed ethnographic diary is notable in this regard. Working in New Guinea and the Trobriand Islands (see KULA RING) he was able to provide detailed monographs on all aspects of the culture of these peoples. Together with RADCLIFFE-BROWN he shaped British structural-functionalist (see STRUCTURAL FUNCTIONALISM) anthropology while teaching at the London School of Economics from 1927 to 1938. His focus on the functional needs of a sociocultural system did not prevent him from attempting to put psychoanalytic theories into practice in many of his works.

managerial revolution the growth in the number and professionalization of managers who do not own the companies they control. The idea of the separation of management from the ownership of business organizations, sometimes expressed as the *divorce between ownership and control,* is seen to rest largely on the progressive diffusion of shareholding at the same time as organizations increase in size and become more technically complex. It is suggested that, as shareholding becomes both fragmented and absentee, and as the premium placed on professional, technical, and administrative expertise increases, the professionalization of management fosters emergence of a relatively homogeneous stratum of managers who both acquire effective control of organizations and have an orientation to both employees and wider society that is different from that of traditional capitalists. However, even when this thesis is accepted, there is debate about whether managers act either in their own distinct interest (Burnham, 1942) or with a broader social conscience, guided by professional values (Berle and Means, 1933). In any event the implications for developments in both stratification and capitalism are profound. One theorist, for example, suggests that new authority relationships replace the traditional conflict of interests between employers and employees (DAHRENDORF, 1959). See also POSTCAPITALISM, POSTINDUSTRIALISM.

The thesis, however, has not gone unquestioned. Subsequent attempts to evaluate it involve more sophisticated analyses of patterns of shareholding (Zeitlin, 1974; Barratt-Brown, 1968), the stability and means of recruitment to executive positions (Stanworth and Giddens, 1974), the values and ideologies of managers (Nichols, 1969), "decision-making in process" (Pahl and Winkler, 1974), and corporate networks (Scott, 1979). While these studies have their limitation, collectively they suggest that the managerial revolution thesis was premature. Some researchers have pointed to the similarity between owners and managers in their values, objectives, and social origin and have drawn attention to the way these similarities are upheld through connections and social activities (Nichols, 1969; Stanworth and Giddens, 1975; Whitley, 1974). It has also been suggested that theorists who have based their arguments on analyses of shareholding concentration have done so on the basis of questionable methodology. In the approach adopted by Berle and Means, for example, both made dubious assumptions about the level of shareholding diffusion required for managerial control and encouraged the analysis of companies considered in isolation from others (Barratt-Brown, 1968; Zeitlin, 1974). Attempts to avoid such pitfalls have revealed a more complex and variable relationship between shareholding concentration and ownership control. Hence the particular constellation of investment patterns within and between companies will influence whether or not top executives, who may collectively muster but a small percentage of total shares, can and do in fact control. Some theorists suggest, therefore, that while many shareholders are separated from company control, ownership is not. This is reinforced by findings that reveal the persistence, in some instances, and in particular sectors, of personal and family ownership and control of large corporations. While the growth of both institutional investment in, and financial loans to, companies complicates the ownership-control relationship, they do not eliminate it. Indeed, given the tendency for these to go hand in hand with interlocking directorships, questions are raised about the progressive fragmentation of shareholding, the extent and implications of ties between institutional worlds, and the independence of managers (Hill, 1981).

Attempts to answer these questions are also significant for the broader analysis of the UPPER CLASS. In this respect, while the distinctions made between entrepreneurial, internal, and finance capitalists reveal subtle changes, for example, in the intergenerational bases of CLASS composition, they do not preclude the persistence of a cohesive upper class that, aided by a network of interlocking directorships, has not relinquished significant control of capital to a "managerial technostructure" Galbraith, 1979, Scott, 1979.

The debate has not been helped by the failure to clarify what is meant by both management and control. It has been suggested that, minimally, it is necessary to distinguish between the allocative control exercised by top management, concerning decisions over corporate goals and the distribution of resources, and the operational control exercised by lower managers who are involved in day-to-day operations and have their own sectional interests (Pahl and Winkler, 1974). Whatever the merit of such refinement, the extent of management choice and the significance of internal divisions remain contentious issues. Some theorists, for example, argue that a key weakness of the managerial revolution thesis is the tendency to neglect the nature of the economic system in which management takes place. In particular, economic competition is seen to both constrain and unify management objectives through an enforced attention to a balanced attainment of growth and shareholder earnings. It has become clear, however, that in order to understand the types of management expertise represented in company decisions, be they allocative or operational, or boardroom positions, other historical and contextual factors need to be considered. In the United States, for example, personnel managers appear to be less significant than accountants and lawyers.

The managerial revolution thesis is clearly an important topic that is central to debates arising from attempts to theorize about contemporary society through concepts such as capitalism, POSTCAPITALISM, and POSTINDUSTRIALISM.

manifest functions and **latent functions** the distinction between those functions of a social system that are intended and/or overtly recognized by the participants in that social system, *manifest functions*, and those functions that are hidden and remain unacknowledged by participants, *latent functions*. For example, in the most influential discussion of the distinction, by MERTON, the rain dances of the Hopi indians, although intended to have the effect of bringing rain, in fact can be seen as having the function of increasing social integration. See also FUNCTIONALISM, UNANTICIPATED CONSEQUENCES AND UNINTENDED CONSEQUENCES (OF SOCIAL ACTION).

Mann, Michael (1942–) British historical sociologist and analyst of SOCIAL STRATIFICATION, whose book *The Sources of Social Power* (1986, volume one of a planned three-volume work) has attracted critical acclaim from historians as well as sociologists. Having previously written incisively on contemporary political culture and class (for example, *Consciousness and Action in the Western Working Class*, 1973), Mann turned his attention to historical analysis with the aim of bringing about a total reorientation in the treatment of POWER and SOCIAL CHANGE in sociology. The distinctive focus of Mann's approach to POWER is his insistence that it has four principal sources: economic, ideological, military, and political, with none of these alone being decisive, and with no simple evolutionary or developmental pattern of social change (see also EPISODIC CHARACTERIZATION). The range and acuity of his account of the development and operation of power from neolithic times, through the civilization of the Near East, the classical age, and medieval Europe, to 1760 (his conclusion of volume one) are remarkable.

Mannheim, Karl (1887–1947) Hungarian-born sociologist who was an enforced emigrant to England in 1933, and whose most important contributions to sociology were in the SOCIOLOGY OF KNOWLEDGE and in his writings on political issues of the day, including education and planning. In his main work, *Ideology and Utopia* (1929), he systematizes distinctions between IDEOLOGY and UTOPIA as different kinds of belief system, the first performing the function of justification and preservation of a system, the second oriented to its change. More generally, in his SOCIOLOGY OF KNOWLEDGE, he argued that the main forms of knowledge are conditioned in various ways by the needs of social groups, although, contrary to MARX, not simply by class interests. He suggested that one way in which knowledge might escape RELATIVISM was if INTELLECTUALS adopted a free-floating or nonaligned position. See also INTELLIGENTSIA.

Marcuse, Herbert (1898–1979) widely influential German philosopher and social theorist. Marcuse studied philosophy at the Universities of Berlin and Freiburg (at the latter with the leading German philosophers HUSSERL and HEIDEGGER). He became a member of the Institute of Social Research (later referred to as the FRANKFURT SCHOOL OF CRITICAL THEORY) in 1933 and emigrated, with other members, to the United States following the Nazi rise to power. Marcuse continued his association with the Institute, which had moved to Columbia University. Between 1942 and 1950 he worked as a researcher for the US government. Subsequently he held posts at leading American universities before becoming an honorary professor at the Free University of Berlin.

Marcuse's wide-ranging interests covered all the current debates of his time: art and revolution, PHENOMENOLOGY, existentialism and the legacy of classical German philosophy, the nature of technological change, transformation in the capitalist mode of production, the rise of psychoanalysis, the nature of the individual and the problems of socialism, and Marxism and the critical theory of society. Pippin et al. (eds.) (1988) have suggested that what gave unity to all these concerns was Marcuse's commitment to the task of developing critical theory in light of deficiencies of classical Marxism.

MARGINALITY

In his *Soviet Marxism* (1958) he argued that Marxism in the Soviet Union had lost its function as the ideology of revolution and instead had become the ideological prop of the *status quo*. In his diagnosis of capitalist societies, Marcuse thought that the pressures of consumerism had led to total incorporation of the working class into the existing system. As a result, rather than looking to the workers as the revolutionary vanguard, Marcuse in *One-Dimensional Man* (1964) put his faith in an alliance between radical intellectuals and "the outcasts and outsiders, the exploited and persecuted of other races and other colors, the unemployed and the unemployables." In May 1968 his vision of a "nonrepressive civilization" and total human emancipation inspired student radicals of the international New Left movement. His major writings include *Reason and Revolution: Hegel and the Rise of Social Theory* (1941); *Eros and Civilization: a Philosophical Inquiry into Freud* (1955); *Soviet Marxism: a Critical Analysis* (1958); *One-Dimensional Man: Studies in the Ideology of Advanced Industrial Society* (1964); *An Essay on Liberation* (1969); and *Counterrevolution and Revolt* (1972).

marginality the state of being part insider and part outsider to a social group. The term was perhaps first used by PARK (1928) to refer to the so-called cultural hybrid who shares "the life and traditions of two distinct groups." Park focused particularly on migrants, stressing the disorienting effects of marginality. However, the concept can obviously be used to refer to many types of *social marginality*, for example, the marginality of the parvenu, the stigmatized, etc. See also STRANGER.

market situation those aspects of the position of an individual or group within SOCIAL STRATIFICATION that are determined by market forces. It is one of three general dimensions of stratification seen as important by LOCKWOOD (1958 and 1966) and GOLDTHORPE and Lockwood (1968–1969). For Marx, ownership or nonownership of the means of production was ultimately decisive in determining a person's overall class position. In Lockwood and Goldthorpe's analysis, strongly influenced by WEBER (see CLASS; CLASS, STATUS AND PARTY), three related dimensions of social stratification must always be taken into account: work situation, STATUS SITUATION and market situation. See also MULTIDIMENSIONAL ANALYSIS OF SOCIAL STRATIFICATION.

marriage a socially acknowledged and sometimes legally ratified union between an adult male and an adult female. Some preindustrial societies recognize polygamy, either *polygyny* in which a man may be married to more than one woman or, much more rarely, *polyandry*, in which a woman may be married to more than one man. MONOGAMY, however, is by far the most common form of marriage, even in societies where polygamy is permitted. See also KINSHIP, SOCIOLOGY OF THE FAMILY.

In preindustrial societies marriage has been regulated by kin relationships and has for the most part reflected kin interests. Expectations would be to either marry within the group, thus ENDOGAMY, or in other societies the opposite, EXOGAMY. Within industrial societies personal choice is more prominent, with the idea of *romantic love*, or affective individualism, having great influence. Choice of marital partner, however, would appear to operate generally within a narrow social range.

Another marital form increasingly found in industrial societies is *cohabitation*, in which a male and female live together in a sexual relationship without marrying, although often as a prelude to marriage. On a much smaller scale there are also gay (both LESBIAN and HOMOSEXUAL) marriages and communal arrangements.

The sociological study of marriage in industrial societies currently has a number of preoccupations, including:

(a) marriage rates–the number of adults who are married as a proportion of the adult population. This is a figure that seems to be influenced by a range of factors, including age at marriage, changes in fertility, longevity, migration, wars, and broad economic circumstances, including the changing patterns in employment of married women;

(b) the distribution of power within the marital relationship. The evidence is that this may be changing slowly. Across all social classes, however, the evidence is that economic and locational decisions are still made by men. The SYMMETRICAL FAMILY remains exceptional;

(c) the so-called discovery of violence within marriage. This has led to a substantial body of research revealing widespread abuse of women within marriage in many societies and in all social classes (see WIFE BATTERING). Such studies have provided part of the feminist critique of the institutions of marriage and family;

(d) the factors affecting remarriage. Within industrial societies, remarriage is increasing among the divorced and the widowed. This phenomenon has led to recognition of a new familial form, namely the *reconstituted family* (or stepfamily), involving the coming together of partners who bring with them the offspring of earlier relationships. Despite the growth in the divorce rate, remarriage in most industrial societies is increasingly popular, giving rise to the notion of *serial monogamy*.

Marshall, Thomas H. (1893–1981) British sociologist who trained first as a historian, and whose discussion of citizenship and CITIZEN RIGHTS, *Citizenship and Class* (1950), remains the starting point of most modern discussions of the subject. Marshall was interested in exploring the implications of an expansion of citizenship rights and welfare rights for class relations and, likewise, the implications of a continuation of class divisions and a capitalist economy for citizenship: a clash between democracy and egalitarianism in the civil and political realm and nondemocracy and inequality in the economic realm. Commentators have sometimes regarded Marshall as overly sanguine in his judgment of the benefits flowing from the expansion of citizenship in modern Western societies. More recently, especially with the advent of Thatcherism in Britain, his emphasis on the importance of citizen and welfare rights in establishing social fairness and in contributing to the maintenance of political legitimacy in these societies has increasingly been regarded as sound. His many essays on these topics and on the importance of an historical perspective in the understanding of modern society are collected in *Sociology at the Crossroads* (1963).

Marx, Karl (1818–1883) German philosopher, economist and revolutionary. He was born in Trier in the Rhineland and educated at the universities of Bonn and Berlin, where he studied philosophy and law. At Berlin he came under the influence of HEGEL's philosophy and associated with a group of radical democrats who were trying to fashion the critical side of that philosophy to attack the Prussian state. This association cost Marx a post in the state-dominated university system. Thus began a career as an independent scholar, journalist, and political activist that he pursued in the Rhineland, in travels throughout Europe from 1843, and thereafter in London, where he settled from 1849. In 1864 he participated in the establishment of the International Working Men's Association (the First International). The main works by Marx (sometimes written in association with ENGELS) include *Poverty of Philosophy* (1847); *Communist Manifesto* (1848); *Grundisse* (written 1857–1858, first published only in 1939–1941), *A Contribution to the Critique of Political Economy* (1859); *Das Kapital* (volume 1, published in 1867, with volumes 2 and 3 published only after Marx's death).

Conventionally Marx's thought is held to derive from three main sources:

(a) French socialist thought, not least that of SAINT-SIMON, with whose work Marx was familiar before his university studies;

(b) Hegel's philosophy, the principles of which Marx modified but never entirely disavowed;

(c) English political economy, on which Marx built but also went beyond. Experience of social conditions gained in his travels, and contact with radical and communist groups and individuals, notably Engels, with whom he formed a lifelong friendship and intellectual partnership from 1846, also played a part in Marx's transformation from radical democrat to communist revolutionary.

Marx's overall intellectual project encompassed several objectives. Briefly, he sought:

(a) to understand and explain the human condition as he found it in capitalist society;

(b) to lay bare the dynamic of that society and to lift the veil on its inner working and impact on human relations;

(c) to obtain a theoretical grasp in order to achieve adequate understanding of the mechanisms at work in the overall process of historical change in which capitalism was but a phase.

These projects were realized, albeit imperfectly, in Marx's philosophical, economic, and political writings. These were not in any strict sense sociological, and Marx did not claim that they were. Nevertheless, his thought has had a profound impact on the development of sociology: it has provided the point of departure for a wide-ranging tradition of scholarship and research, and has stimulated productive critical reactions from non-Marxist scholars.

Marx's efforts were informed by the belief that it was necessary not only to study society, but to change it. He had no hesitation, therefore, in making social science subserve the ends of the social liberation he sought. Essentially he saw the human condition under capitalism as being characterized by ALIENATION, a condition in which human beings were estranged from their world, and from their work, products, fellow creatures, and themselves.

Alienation was an early preoccupation of Marx; it did not figure much in his later work, which was concerned to provide an analysis of the inner workings of the capitalist economy framed against the background of a theory of history known as the "materialist conception of history." The theory is so called because it rests on the view that the economy is a primary influence on the formation and development of social structures, and on the ideas that people hold about themselves and their societies. Before people can philosophize, play politics, create art, etc., they must produce economic necessities. To do this they must enter into social relations of production. According to Marx, economic relations constitute the base of society on which is erected the superstructure of noneconomic institutions, the nature and scope of which are substantially determined by the base. It is because of this argument that critics have sometimes regarded Marx as simply an economic determinist. However, while occasionally ambiguous, Marx and Engels usually insisted that noneconomic institutions, that is, the state, religion, etc., were capable of playing a relatively autonomous role in social development. Nevertheless, in the last analysis, it is the productive relationships into which people enter that exercise the decisive influence. This is because the relations of production become CLASS relations, and because class relations are the constitutive bases of both social structure and social change.

Class was thus fundamental to Marx's analysis, though strangely he never provided a definitive definition of the concept. Clearly it is an economic category; classes are formed by groups of people who share a common interest by virtue of the fact that they stand together in a common relationship to the means of production. Classes can only form when the productive activity of a society yields a surplus above the subsistence needs of its members. A dominant group can then wrest ownership of, and control over, the means of production, and constitute itself as a RULING CLASS OR DOMINANT CLASS. This class appropriates to its own use the surplus produced by the rest of society, the members of which are rendered a subordinate class, forced to put its labor at the disposal of the possessing group. Marx referred to the process of surplus extraction as *exploitation*. Exploitation is basic to all forms of class society, though it takes different forms.

Marx's theory speaks of different types of modes of production. These were conceived of as a developmental sequence, since each one marked an advance in humanity's productive capacity and hence its mastery over nature. Marx thus postulated a *primitive communist* (classless) society that was replaced by a series of class societies resting successively on slavery, feudalism, and capitalism. The motor of change was held to be class conflict generated by constant development of the forces of production. In each mode of production the relations of production were maintained by the dominant class, because they were best fitted to the forces of production at their level of development within that mode. Within each mode, however, the forces of production were developed in novel ways that gave rise to new class formations, class conflict, and revolution. Conflict arose because the relations of production maintained by the dominant class tended to strangle the novel development, provoking the rising class associated with new development to overthrow the old system and replace it with a new one. Thus, concretely, the feudal relations of production (the lord-serf relationship) acted as a brake on the capitalism that was developing within the womb of feudal society. Capitalists, therefore, had to overthrow the feudal relationships and replace them with a new set of relations between themselves, as the dominant class, and the propertyless PROLETARIAT, as the subordinate class.

In his economic writings Marx sought to expose the inner workings of the capitalist system. His analysis convinced him that the system was riven with contradictions that were bound to bring it down; for technical economic reasons, he held that capitalists would suffer from a declining rate of profit, and that the system would be subject to periodic crises of *overproduction*. Its ultimate downfall, however, seemed guaranteed by the antagonism that resulted from the conflict of interests between the working-class proletariat and the capitalist bourgeoisie.

Although Marx was aware of the existence of INTERMEDIATE CLASSES in capitalist society, his analysis convinced him that society was increasingly polarizing into two great hostile classes, the bourgeoisie and the proletariat. This antagonism resulted from an objective conflict of interest between the two groups: the bourgeoisie exploited the proletariat by paying less than the value of their labor, and through their private ownership of the means of production, frustrated the collective, social interest in the rational development of the productive forces at the disposal of society. Once the working class became conscious of these facts, Marx predicted that it would act to overthrow capitalist society and establish a new form of *classless society*.

The importance of human consciousness needs to be emphasized within Marx's analysis. Revolutions did not happen automatically, and classes must become conscious of their interests before they can play their historic roles in the process of moving society forward. Marx held that consciousness developed as a reflection of the material conditions of existence to which classes were subject, though he recognized that ruling classes were capable of obstructing development of consciousness in subordinate classes. The class that dominated economically also dominated in other spheres of life. It was the dominant input into the state, politics, religion, etc. Thus, it could also generate an IDEOLOGY, inducing a FALSE CONSCIOUSNESS that blinded the subordinate class to the true nature of the social relationships in which they were involved. Nevertheless, Marx predicted the eventual victory of the proletariat in a revolution that would usher in a new era of human freedom.

That Marx's ideas should have been such a major factor in the Russian Revolution of 1917, in conditions he had not predicted, is a commentary on the power his ideas have exerted but is equally an indication of their weaknesses.

Marx's social and economic analysis inspired generations of political activists, social critics, and social scientists. Like Marx, they have emphasized that bourgeois social science and social thought are often confined to appearances and neither penetrate nor illuminate the true reality underpinning capitalist economic and social relationships. After Marx's death, especially in Soviet Marxism, aspects of Marx's ideas were taken to reveal the "laws of motion of capitalist societies." Within Western Europe, the failure of the working class to combat fascism led politically committed Marxists (for example, the FRANKFURT SCHOOL OF CRITICAL THEORY) to reappraise the working-class role in politics. More recently, Marxists have continued to differ fundamentally in their interpretations of Marx's thought. Some, such as ALTHUSSER, reject the philosophical, Hegel-influenced humanistic concerns of the early writings and insist that only the later writings with their scientific analyses of capitalist society are important. Others, for example E.P. Thompson (1978), dispute this, stressing both Marx's humanism and the continuities in Marx's work.

Marx's output has also attracted much opposition and trenchant criticism. His economic writings and his evaluation of capitalist society have been widely challenged. His class analysis has been attacked on the grounds that it did not take sufficiently into account the rise of new middle-class groups, or affluence (see Parkin, 1979). This also suggests that his theory of social change and revolution is wrong. Marxists have responded by pointing out that Marx never set a time scale for revolution, that the real worth of his analysis is in revealing the underlying mechanisms that sustain capitalism, but make its future uncertain. The resultant body of analysis shows that, notwithstanding criticism, the Marxist tradition remains influential and, to many and in many areas of sociology and social science, still a powerful method of analysis.

Marxist sociology approaches within academic sociology that utilize Marxism. These grew in importance particularly in the 1960s in Europe and the United States as a reaction to the perceived dominance of STRUCTURAL FUNCTIONALISM and the political conservation of established sociology. In the 20th century, the intellectual development of Marxism had taken place mainly outside academic institutions and was of limited direct influence in the social sciences. In the 1960s, there was wider questioning of the consensus models of society and of the presumed evolutionary nature of social change. Marxist sociology developed not just around conflict models of society and revolutionary models of social change (see CONFLICT THEORY), but also around methodological challenges. The assumed value neutrality of orthodox social science was seen to be undermined by its privileged position within society and its practioners' roles as advisers to large organizations and governments: "The professional eyes of the sociologists are on the down people, and the professional palm of the sociologist is stretched toward the up people," (Nicolaus, 1972).

For some critics, the logic of this argument meant that Marxist sociology was a contradiction in terms: the academic pursuit of abstract knowledge divorced from the class struggle could only hinder socialist political ends. Others argued that Marxist academics had a political role through counteracting bourgeois ideology within academic institutions and influencing future generations of students. The predominant approach, however, has been to utilize Marxist theory to develop a more adequate social science and to make that knowledge available to political groups.

During the 1970s and 1980s, Marxist work had a wide influence within, first, sociology and historical studies, and then the other social sciences and literary studies. Often the debates were taken up in an eclectic fashion, so that the widespread use of Marxian concepts and ideas no longer necessarily reflected a political commitment to socialism or any identification of the user as a Marxist. See also AUSTRO-MARXISM, ANDERSON.

Maslow, Abraham (1908–1970) American psychologist and member of the HUMANISTIC MOVEMENT in psychology, who developed a theory of motivation that was based on a *hierarchy of needs* (*Motivation and Personality*, 1954). He proposed that human needs can be categorized as: physiological, safety, love and belonging, esteem, and self-actualization. Higher needs cannot become important to the individual until lower needs have been satisfied. In *Toward a Psychology of Being* (1962) Maslow discussed how the uniqueness of the individual can be developed toward fulfillment, or *self-actualization*. This involves the achieving of potential, the fulfilling of *being needs* (which are distinguished from the *deficiency needs* of the lower levels of his hierarchy). To define his concept of self-actualization, Maslow studied the lives and personalities of people he considered to be self-actualized. He suggested that such people have greater acceptance of self and others, greater identification with humanity generally, and higher levels of creativity and heightened perception, particularly of the natural world. Heightened awareness leads to *peak experiences* during which the individual feels at one with the world. Maslow's ideas have been taken up by a number of social philosophers and sociologists.

mass production the production of long runs of standardized products for a mass market. This so-called Fordist form of production was associated with a well-developed division of labor and a tendency to routinization of the labor process. Subsequently, under post-Fordism, with the introduction of computer technology and more flexible modes of production, mass production is being replaced (see FORDISM AND POST-FORDISM).

mass society a model of society that pessimistically depicts the social transformation brought about by modernization, for example, urbanization, the democratization of politics, and the growth of mass communications and popular education, as involving a process in which individuals become:

(a) increasingly detached from previous social groupings, that is, a process of social fragmentation and atomization;

(b) increasingly open to commercial and political manipulation by centralized ELITES.

This process, in which people are increasingly treated en masse, is also referred to as the *massification* of society.

Diversity in the intellectual and political orientations of writers using the concept has resulted in a variety of theoretical meanings. However, general themes are a decline in social VALUES and COMMUNITY, a lack of moral core, and growing levels of social alienation. Because relationships between people are weakened, the suggestion is that they become vulnerable to manipulative forces, to proposed simplistic solutions to problems, and to lowest common denominator forms of *mass culture*, forms of culture produced, sold, and consumed in the same way as any other commodities for the masses. Theorists on the right, for example, T.S. Eliot (1948) have generally emphasized the threat to elite forms of high culture presented by mass culture, and a loss of the social continuities associated with rule by traditional elites. While also echoing some of these themes, theorists on the left (for example, members of the FRANKFURT SCHOOL OF CRITICAL THEORY) have focused instead on the new opportunities for political manipulation of the masses by right-wing forces (for example, *fascism*) and the general seductiveness of commercial forms of mass culture in incorporating the working class within *capitalism*. More generally, in a now classical modern discussion C. Wright MILLS contrasts modern forms of mass society with a situation in which multiple publics once existed, as follows:

(a) "far fewer people express opinions than receive them";

(b) channels of opinion are relatively few and centrally controlled;

(c) the autonomy social actors once possessed in the formation of opinion is increasingly lost.

The heyday of the concept of mass society was in the period immediately before and after World War II. Subsequent research and theorizing have tended to suggest that the concept was too sweeping. Thus, although it was influential in the early years of mass communications research, this research has resulted in studies that have demonstrated that the audience for the mass media is not an undifferentiated mass, that the manipulative power of the media is relatively limited and that the growth of popular culture did not occur at the expense of art or community. Similarly, research into forms of political behavior and political participation in modern Western democratic societies has revealed no overall tendency to mass society.

material culture 1. "those aspects of CULTURE that govern the production and use of artifacts" (DOUGLAS, 1964). **2.** the material products or artifacts actually produced by societies.

Debate about the reference of the term has focused on whether the objects or the ideas and social arrangements associated with the objects should be central. However, the study of material culture is bound to be concerned with the artifacts produced by a society, especially including its implements for collecting and hunting food and cultivation of plants, its modes of transportation, its means of housing and clothing, its techniques of food preparation and cooking, its art, and its magical and religious paraphernalia. An important part of sociology and social anthropology, the study of material culture is even more central in ARCHAEOLOGY, given that it has little to study but artifacts. See also CULTURAL MATERIALISM.

mathematical sociology the use of mathematical procedures and mathematical models in sociology. The rationale for most mathematical sociology, as stated by James Coleman in *Introduction to Mathematical Sociology* (1964), is that: "Mathematics provides a battery of languages, which when carefully fitted to a set of ideas, can lend these ideas great power." Mathematical sociologists usually do not operate with the expectation that high level, mathematically expressed general laws will be established in sociology. Rather they have made more limited claims that mathematics can be employed to good effect in illuminating areas of social life.

Examples of mathematical approaches that have enjoyed some influence in sociology are:

(a) the THEORY OF GAMES, deriving from the work of Herbert Simon and others;

(b) probabilistic *stochastic process models,* for example, Markov chains, used in modeling population processes and social mobility (see Coleman, 1964);

(c) CAUSAL MODELING, arising especially from the work of Blalock (1961);

(d) applications of finite (nonquantitative) mathematical models, as in Harrison White's analysis of the formal properties of kinship structures (*Anatomy of Kinship* 1953);

(e) applications of mathematical *graph theory* in the analysis of social networks (see P. Doreian, *Mathematics in the Study of Social Relations*, 1970).

The boundaries between mathematical sociology and STATISTICS AND STATISTICAL ANALYSIS are not easily drawn, but one distinction is that, while statistical analysis uses relatively standardized procedures, making standardized assumptions about the character of data, mathematical sociology uses a wider array of mathematical procedures and is more likely to involve construction of theoretical models intended to achieve a more direct, more purpose-built, modeling of the area of social reality under analysis.

matriarchy any social organization based on female POWER. The literal meaning refers to the rule of the mother as head of the family, and can therefore be contrasted with the term PATRIARCHY, referring to the rule of the father.

The term is subject to much dispute both within the discipline of sociology and within feminist theory. Historically, the term was adopted by a number of 19th-century anthropologists and social theorists concerned with the origins of social organization and the family. Bachofen (1861) argued that the original family structure was matriarchal. In 1865 McLennan published *Primitive Marriage*, in which he claimed that the origins of social organization were characterized by a matriarchal structure. ENGELS, influenced by the work of Lewis Henry MORGAN, wrote *The Origin of the Family, Private Property and the State* (1884), in which he argued that the primitive matriarchal clan predated patriarchy. Engels believed that the overthrow of "mother right" led to the defeat of the female sex and culminated in the institution of the patriarchal family. Both women and children were thereby subordinated to the power and control of adult men. Thence arose the monogamous family unit based on supremacy of the man. The main purpose of this unit was to produce heirs of undisputed paternity. Such accounts of the origins of social organization were disputed by writers such as Henry MAINE (*Ancient Law*, 1861), who argued that the original form of social organization was a corporate family group ruled over by a despotic patriarch. Such debates have assumed fresh impetus with the rise of feminist anthropology and feminist sociology. Much interest has been directed at the work of Engels as providing a possible explanation of the roots of female oppression.

Debates continue as to whether matriarchal societies ever existed. Radical FEMINISM has focused more attention on this issue than have other strands of feminist thought. Radical feminists argue that such societies did exist, but patriarchal history has erased knowledge of them. The Greek island of Lesbos, 600 BC, is taken as an indication of the existence of a matriarchal era.

Within contemporary feminist thought, wider meanings of the term denote female supremacy, female-focused or female oriented societies, and women-centered culture.

Mayo, Elton (1880–1949) a prominent figure within the HUMAN RELATIONS SCHOOL who was associated with and wrote about the HAWTHORNE EFFECT. This association, and the interpretations he made of the Hawthorne experiments, made him an influential figure within the human relations tradition. Echoing DURKHEIM, he felt that scientific and technical developments had outstripped the social skills and social arrangements of man, one consequence of which was widespread ANOMIE. This was evident, for example, in the spontaneous organization of informal groupings within industry, as revealed by the Hawthorne research. Mayo consequently advocated development of social skills for managers who would provide for, communicate with, and sensitively lead small work groups in industry, since these would provide social anchorage and meaning for otherwise anomic workers. In this way hope was held out for the ability of industry to provide for a satisfying and cooperative venture in an otherwise debilitating and individualistic society.

His ideas have, to varying and debated degrees, influenced both managerial practice and ideology and subsequent social and psychological research in industry (Mayo, 1949; Bendix, 1974; Rose, 1988).

Mead, George Herbert (1863–1931) US Pragmatist philosopher, sociologist, and social psychologist based at the University of Chicago, whose approach to sociology is today most identified with SYMBOLIC INTERACTIONISM. Mead termed his approach to sociology and social psychology *social behaviorism* to distinguish it from the more orthodox psychological behaviorism of Watson. Influenced especially by his fellow Pragmatist philosopher John Dewey and by Charles COOLEY, Mead's sociology and psychology emphasized the conscious mind and the self-awareness and self-regulation of SOCIAL ACTORS. In Mead's view, the SELF emerges from social interaction in which human beings, in "taking the role of the other," internalize the attitudes of real and imagined others. Drawing on Cooley's concept of the LOOKING-GLASS SELF, he postulated that the "I" (myself as I am) is involved in a continual interaction with the "Me" (myself as others see me). The Me represents the attitudes of the social group, the GENERALIZED OTHER, and through role-taking in play and "imaginative rehearsal" of interaction we internalize the group's values as our own. By continually reflecting on ourselves as others see us we become competent in the production and display of social symbols. Human nature is seen by Mead as part of evolution and nature, but the importance of language and symbolic communication as an aspect of this evolution is such as to free human action from natural determinism. Mead can be seen to represent the epitome of CHICAGO SCHOOL sociology in his attempt to articulate the relationship between the self and society. Herbert BLUMER took over Mead's lectures on his death, refined his social theory, and coined the term SYM-BOLIC INTERACTIONISM. Mead's main works, collected essays and lectures, all published after his death, are *Mind, Self and Society* (1932), *The Philosophy of the Act* (1938), and *The Philosophy of the Present* (1959). See also PRAGMATISM.

meaningful sociology any form of sociology premised on the assumption (a) that social actors above all inhabit a universe of social meanings; (b) that SOCIAL ACTION is *meaningful action*, and (c) that social occurrences must be explained primarily as the outcome of actors' meanings, that is, the beliefs, motives, purposes, reasons, etc. that lead to ACTIONS. The term is commonly applied to WEBER'S ACTION THEORY but can equally apply to related approaches such as SYMBOLIC INTERACTIONISM. See also MEANING-FUL UNDERSTANDING AND EXPLANATION, INTERPRETIVE SOCIOLOGY, VERSTE-HEN.

meaningful understanding and explanation the comprehension of SOCIAL ACTORS' meanings (that is, their beliefs, motives, purposes, reasons, etc. in any social context) that at one and the same time automatically con-stitute an explanation of their ACTIONS and of the social occurrences to which these give rise. See also VERSTEHEN, MEANINGFUL SOCIOLOGY, WEBER, WINCH, PURPOSIVE EXPLANATION, EMPATHY, INTERPRETATION, INTERPRETIVE SOCIOLOGY.

measurement by fiat measurement (for example, indirect indicators of a phenomenon) where "we have only a prescientific or commonsense con-cept that on a priori grounds seems to be important but which we do not know how to measure directly" and, with some degree of arbitrariness, we impose a measure (W. Torgerson, *Theory and Method of Scaling,* 1958). CICOUREL (1964) has criticized such imposing of equivalence classes with-out theoretical or empirical justification—a viewpoint influential in the establishment of ETHNOMETHODOLOGY.

measures of central tendency the different ways of conceptualizing the central or middle position of a group of observations, numbers, etc. There are three measures of central tendency: the *mode,* the *median,* and the *mean.* The *mode* is the value that occurs most often. The *median* is the value that occupies the central position, having as many values below as above it. The *mean* (more commonly called the *average*) is found by adding together each individual value and dividing by the number of cases, or observations. An example will illustrate the differences between these terms. A set of nine observations gives the following set of values: 1 2 2 2 3 5 6 11 22.

In this example, the mode is 2, as it occurs most often; the median is 3, as it occupies the central position; and the mean is 6, being equal to the sum of the observation (54) divided by the number of cases (9).

Sometimes a set of observations will yield a *bimodal distribution*—where two different values occur most often. Also, if there is an even number of observations there is no central value to represent the median. In this case the median may be taken to lie midway between the two centrally placed values.

Where there are many values in the distribution, the approximate value of the median can be calculated by *interpolation*. The data are first grouped into a set number of bands, and the median is taken as lying within the middle group, its value being calculated mathematically by estimating its position from the percentage of cases lying in the lower and higher bands.

The choice of which measure of central tendency to employ is determined by two factors: the level of measurement (see CRITERIA AND LEVELS OF MEASUREMENT) being employed and the amount of dispersion in the set of observations. Where a nominal-level measure is being employed, only the mode should be calculated. For example, if numerical values have been assigned to different types of accommodation, then the mode will show which is the most popular type of accommodation, but both the mean and the median would be meaningless. The median is best used with ordinal-level measures, where the relative distances between categories is unknown (although it should be said that many social scientists do use the mean when dealing with ordinal-level variables because of the large number of statistical tests that can then be undertaken). Finally, the mean is generally the best statistic to use with interval level measures, except in those instances in which there are a number of extreme values that *skew* the distribution. For example, the mean incomes of a group of respondents may be skewed because of the inclusion in the sample of a few high-income earners. In such instances the median is often a better statistic to employ. Another instance in which the median might be calculated is where data have been grouped and the highest category is open-ended. For example, income might have been grouped in such way that all earning over $100,000 a year are grouped together and there is no upper limit to the amount that people in the category earn. In such a case the mean cannot be calculated, but the value of the median can be estimated by the process of *interpolation* mentioned above. See also MEASURES OF DISPERSON.

measures of dispersion the different ways of calculating the extent to which a set of observations, numbers, etc. are clustered together around a central point. Measures of dispersion are closely related to MEASURES OF CENTRAL TENDENCY. There are six measures: the *range, variance, standard deviation, standard error, skew,* and *kurtosis*.

The *range* is the simplest measure of dispersion; it relates to the actual spread of values and is equal to the maximum less the minimum value.

The *variance* is a measure of the dispersion of a set of values from the mean, and should only be used with interval-level measures. It measures the extent to which individual values are clustered around the mean. It is calculated by averaging the squared deviations from the mean, and in so doing it takes into account both negative values and the existence of unduly low and unduly high values. A low variance suggests that there is a high degree of homogeneity in the value, and high variance is an indication of a low degree of homogeneity.

The *standard deviation* is the square root of the variance. It is used in preference to the variance because it is easier to interpret, having a value in the range of the values from which it is derived. In the example given, with a mean of 6, the variance is 45.5, a number that is more than twice the largest number in the sequence, while the standard deviation is 6.74, a figure that is easier to comprehend: 1 2 2 2 3 5 6 11 22.

The *standard error* is an estimation of the extent to which the mean of a given set of scores drawn from a sample differs from the true mean score of the whole population. Again, it should only be used with interval-level measures.

The *skew* attempts to estimate the extent to which a set of measures deviates from the symmetry of a curve of normal distribution, whether to the left or the right. Where measures tend to be located to the right of the curve, its value is negative; conversely, where measures are located to its left, its value will be positive.

The *kurtosis* show the extent to which the curve of a set of observations is flatter or more peaked than the normal distribution, whose kurtosis is zero. A peaked (narrower) distribution has a positive value and a flatter curve has a negative value.

mechanical and organic solidarity the distinction drawn by Emile DURKHEIM (1893) between two types of SOCIAL SOLIDARITY: *mechanical solidarity*, based on the similarity between individuals, the form of solidarity predominant in simple and less advanced societies, and *organic solidarity*, based on the DIVISION OF LABOR, and complementarities between individuals, the form of solidarity ideally occurring in modern advanced societies. Durkheim formulated the distinction between the two types of solidarity by identifying the demographic and morphological features basic to each type, the typical forms of law and formal features and content of the *conscience collective* that ought to be associated with each type (see Fig. 15). The reality, Durkheim argued, was that in modern societies organic solidarity was as yet imperfectly realized. See also INTEGRATION.

mediated class locations dimensions of individual locations within the class structure that arise from people's kinship networks and family structures, rather than from a direct relation to the process of production (that is, personal occupations or personal ownership of productive assets). The term was proposed by Wright (1989), but the importance of such locations in influencing class orientation and political behavior has long been evident (for example, GOLDTHORPE and LOCKWOOD, 1969a).

medicalization 1. (in a medical context) the extension of medical authority into areas where lay and common-sense understandings and procedures

	Mechanical Solidarity	Organic Solidarity
	based on resemblances (predominant in less advanced societies)	based on division of labour (predominant in more advanced societies)
(1) Morphological (structural) basis	Segmental type (first clan-based, later territorial) Little interdependence (social bonds relatively weak) Relatively low volume of population Relatively low material and normal density	Organized type (fusion of markets and growth of cities) Much interdependence (social bonds relatively strong) Relatively high volume of population Relatively high material and moral density
(2) Type of norms (typified by law)	Rules with repressive sanctions Prevalence of penal law	Rules with restitutive sanctions Prevalence of cooperative law (civil, commercial, procedural, administrative and constitutional law)
(3) (a) Formal features of *conscience collective*	High volume High intensity High determinateness Collective authority absolute	Low volume Low intensity Low determinateness More room for individual initiative and reflexion
(3) (b) Content of *conscience collective*	Highly religious Transcendental (superior to human interests and beyond discussion) Attaching supreme value to society and interests of society as a whole Concrete and specific	Increasingly secular Human-orientated (concerned with human interests and open to discussion) Attaching supreme value to individual dignity, equality of opportunity, work ethic and social justice Abstract and general

Fig. 15. **Mechanical and organic solidarity.** A summary of Durkheim's ideal types (from Lukes, 1973).

once predominated, for example, childbirth, where a medical frame of reference devalues the woman's perspective by stressing active management by professionals in order to minimize risk to mother and child at the same time as evaluating the success of the outcome by, mainly, technical criteria. **2.** (more generally) the tendency to view undesirable conduct as illness requiring medical intervention, thus extending the realm of medical judgments into political, moral, and social domains.

The concept has been criticized for presenting medicine as a unitary institution, for presenting lay and medical frames of reference as mutually exclusive, and for stressing the social control dimension of medicine without acknowledging the social value of medical work. It is regarded as a valuable concept because it focuses on issues of professional power and ideological domination. See also SOCIOLOGY OF HEALTH AND MEDICINE.

meritocracy a form of society in which educational and social success is the outcome of ability (measured by IQ) and individual effort. The notion, given prominence by Michael Young (*The Rise of the Meritocracy*, 1958), figured prominently in the work of Fabian socialists, who did much to promote it as a guiding principle to legitimate the changes proposed to reorganize education in Britain along comprehensive lines. Meritocracy emphasizes equality of competition rather than equality of outcome, assuming that positions in an occupational hierarchy will be obtained as a result of achievement on merit against universal, objective criteria, rather than on ascribed criteria of age, gender, race, or inherited wealth. No person of quality, competence, or appropriate character would be denied the opportunity to achieve a commensurate social status. Essential to meritocracy is the belief that only a limited pool of talent exists among a nation's children and that it is an important function of the education system to see that such talent is not wasted but is developed and fostered.

The principle of meritocracy is by no means universally accepted. Young himself was ambivalent about some of its consequences, for example, a denuding of working-class culture and leadership. Major criticisms have also come from those who argue that genuine equality can only be achieved by strategies designed to produce greater equality as an end product of the system rather than at its starting point. In any event, those advocating the meritocratic view have to resolve the recurring difficulty of devising objective measures of ability, see also INTELLIGENCE.

Merton, Robert (1910–) leading US sociologist, who was a student of PARSONS and became an influential voice of functionalist sociology in his own right. He was a colleague of LAZARSFELD'S, as associate director of the Bureau of Applied Research at Columbia University, and in his work Merton has tried to bridge the divide between the abstract theory of Parsons and the empirical survey work that typified much of modern American sociology. Merton's called his alternative to these THEORIES OF THE MIDDLE RANGE, which connected with and organized empirical data, and conducted empirical research to test theory. His most influential general work is a collection of essays, *Social Theory and Social Structure* (1949, subsequently enlarged and revised). It contains a number of seminal essays, including "Manifest and Latent Functions" (see also MANIFEST AND LATENT FUNCTION, UNANTICIPATED CONSEQUENCES (OF SOCIAL ACTION), POSTULATE OF FUNCTIONAL INDISPENSABILITY) and "Social Structure and Anomie" (see ANOMIE, CRIME, DEVIANCE). In these essays, and in a succession of further essays and books, he lived up to his claims for middle-range theory by both providing critiques and codifications of theoretical approaches (most notably FUNCTIONALISM), and applications of these approaches in empirical analysis. Of his own empirical work, the most significant are perhaps his contributions to the study of BUREAUCRACY, the SOCIOLOGY OF SCIENCE, and SOCIOLOGY OF MASS COMMUNICATIONS, as well as to ROLE THEORY and the analysis of RELATIVE DEPRIVATION and REFERENCE GROUPS. The following jointly authored and edited books are among his more important: *Mass Persuasion* (1946), *Continuities in Social Research* (1950), *A Reader in Bureaucracy* (1952), and *The Student Physician* (1957). Although all of these have been influential, his doctoral dissertation on science, *Science, Technology and Society in Seventeenth Century England,* was particularly so. First published in 1938, it built on WEBER's thesis on the relationships between Protestantism and capitalism, and was the work that made his reputation. Merton's hypothesis was that the growth of scientific activity in the 17th century was closely related to social forces, including Puritan religion, a perspective that led to a sea change in the historical and sociological analysis of science. Subsequently, Merton also wrote important essays on science as a social institution and on modes of organization and competition in scientific work (see *The Sociology of Science,* 1979). Although in recent years Merton's commitment to functionalism and a natural science model of sociological theories has been extensively criticized (for example, GIDDENS, 1977), the importance of is wide-ranging contribution to sociology is undoubted.

Methodenstreit methodological dispute between NEO-KANTIANS and naturalists in late 19th-century Germany. The former asserted that the natural and cultural sciences were different in kind and therefore needed different methodologies, the latter that the same methodology would do for both. The methods of HERMENEUTICS and VERSTEHEN became theoretically articulated during this period (see also IDIOGRAPHIC AND NOMOTHETIC). Running to some extent in parallel with these disputes, there were also disputes between the historical and the neoclassical school in economics, and debates about the role of VALUE JUDGMENTS and issues of value freedom (see VALUE FREEDOM AND VALUE NEUTRALITY; see also WEBER). The term *methodenstreit* has also been applied to the dispute between POPPER and ADORNO (among others) in Germany in the 1960s. Popper presented a falsificationist model (see FALSIFICATIONISM) of politically neutral social science, which was hotly contested by critical theorists (see FRANKFURT SCHOOL OF CRITICAL THEORY).

methodological bracketing see EPOCHE.

methodological individualism theoretical positions holding that adequate sociological accounts necessarily involve reference to persons, their interpretations of their circumstances, and the reasons and motives for the actions they take. WEBER and POPPER both propose specifications by which all social categories, like "capitalism" or "the state," should be explicated by reference to real or abstract (idealized) individuals or persons.

Methodological individualism comes in at least two broad versions. The first proposes that all sociological explanations must begin and end in reference to individuals in the sense outlined. To this, the standard objection is that individuals usually owe the relevant features, for example, of psychological disposition, to their cultures and their historical circumstances, so the proposed termination is sociologically nonsensical.

A milder, more plausible, version of methodological individualism is simply logical: all social terms can be redefined without loss (although with growth in complications) in terms of persons, their characteristics, and their relationships; that is, all individual terms will presuppose social relationships reflecting the social constitution and positioning of the individual person. This version is characterized by Lukes (1977) as true but relatively innocuous; that is, it rules out very little. It does, however, imply the following. It is extremely tempting to argue for a change in level between sociology and psychology: the first concerned with social relations, the second with individuals. So-called logical methodological individualism rules out this idea: there is only one level. The individual is inherently social, embodying social relationships; the social necessarily involves individuals and their powers, including the relations they enter into. See also SITUATIONAL LOGIC AND SITUATIONAL ANALYSIS, HOLISM, STRATEGIC INTERACTION. Compare STRUCTURALISM, STRUCTURE AND ACTION.

methodology 1. the philosophical evaluation of investigative techniques within a discipline; a concern with the conceptual, theoretical, and research aspects of knowledge. **2.** the techniques and strategies employed within a discipline to manipulate data and acquire knowledge. Used in this narrow sense, methodology refers to the RESEARCH METHODS used by an investigator and does not question the validity or appropriateness of undertaking research.

Used in sense **1.**, methodology is an aspect of the EPISTEMOLOGICAL concern with the scientific status of sociology. Methodology was a central concern of Durkheim, Marx, and Weber, who all attempted to demonstrate that they had developed a distinctive approach to the study of society and therefore to knowledge. By demonstrating the validity of new investigative techniques, they contributed to the development of sociology as a distinctive discipline.

In sociology, a central aspect of methodology **1.** has been a comparison between sociology and the natural sciences. Natural science is often associated with the EXPERIMENTAL METHOD whereby one variable (the INDEPENDENT VARIABLE) is manipulated in a carefully controlled way. If consistent results are obtained, the scientist may draw conclusions about the cause and effects involved, or conclude that a previously made HYPOTHESIS is confirmed or denied. Since the experimental method is usually inapplicable in the social sciences, sociologists have developed new techniques to achieve a degree of VALIDITY that corresponds to that of the natural sciences. DURKHEIM, for example, advocated the use of the COMPARATIVE METHOD, although this entails attempting to control a large number of variables. Alternatively, sociologists have sought to develop methods that do not seek to emulate the natural science goal of scientific laws, but are more appropriate to the nature of social reality.

Michels, Robert (1876–1936) German sociologist and political scientist, remembered best for his book *Political Parties* (1911), in which he formulated the tendency for an IRON LAW OF OLIGARCHY to operate in formal democratic political organizations. The work arose from Michels' disillusionment with the leadership of the German Social Democratic Party (SPD). A tension existed between Michels' critical indictment of the class betrayal and reformism of the leadership of the German SPD and his suggestion that such a betrayal was perhaps inevitable, given the operation of the iron law of oligarchy. In his later work, Michels' position achieved greater coherence, and he was one of a number of theorists (including his friend Max WEBER) to advance a theory of the social benefits of limited representative democracy. This theory can be seen as the forerunner of the modern theory of STABLE DEMOCRACY. See also ELITE THEORY.

microsociology the level of sociological analysis in which the focus is on face-to-face interactions in everyday life and on behavior in groups, etc. (see SYMBOLIC INTERACTIONISM, ETHNOMETHODOLOGY). While often concerned with understanding individual meanings (see MEANINGFUL UNDERSTANDING AND EXPLANATION), microsociology does not confine itself to particular forms of explanatory accounts. Compare MACROSOCIOLOGY.

middle class(es) the nonmanual occupational groups(s) that are located between the UPPER and the WORKING CLASSES.

The term "middle" itself reflects a widely perceived common-sense conception of a status hierarchy in which nonmanual work is accorded greater prestige than manual work, but is recognized as socially inferior to groups with major property or political interests. The presence of a large middle class in capitalist societies has been a subject of interest for a number of reasons. Important changes in occupational structure, involving a large increase in nonmanual occupations, have forced reexamination of the concept of social CLASS, particularly with reference to the social and political role of the middle class(es).

Until the 19th century, there existed few relatively specialized occupational roles of the kind that now exist, for example, accountancy, teaching, and nursing. This is not to say that middle-class roles in banking and government, and in the traditional PROFESSIONS did not exist. However, in both industry and government, especially over the past 100 years, there has occurred as enormous expansion of nonmanual occupations, while the number of manual workers has shrunk (see Fig. 16).

The growth of nonmanual occupations and the persistence of small businesses and the professions pose theoretical problems for some traditional

		1911	1921	1931	1951	1971
1	Professional					
	A Higher	1.00	1.01	1.14	1.93	3.29
	B Lower	3.05	3.52	4.46	4.70	7.78
2	Employers and managers					
	A Employers	6.71	6.82	6.70	4.97	4.22
	B Managers	3.43	3.64	3.66	5.53	8.21
3	Clerical workers	4.84	6.72	6.97	10.68	13.90
4	Foremen	1.29	1.44	1.54	2.62	3.87
5–7	Manual workers	79.67	76.85	76.53	69.58	58.23

Fig. 16. **Middle class.** The figure indicates the increasing middle-class proportion of the gainfully employed population of the UK in the period 1911–71 (percentages). (Adapted from Routh, 1980.)

approaches to CLASS and SOCIAL STRATIFICATION. Until recently, Marxist theory especially had no well-developed analysis of the nature and significance of the middle classes. The problems are compounded by the great diversity of nonmanual work that ranges from routine clerical work to relatively powerful managerial and professional roles, with the owners of independent small businesses in between. This has led to radically different ideas of where to locate the middle classes within the class structure. It has been argued, for instance, that a process of PROLETARIANIZATION has reduced the status, pay, and working conditions of clerical workers to those of the manual working class. Others (for example, Ehrenreich and Ehrenreich, 1979) have argued that the professional-managerial class is a new and distinct class in its own right, while still others (for example, Poulantzas, 1975) see the development of a NEW PETTY BOURGEOISIE (see also CONTRADICTORY CLASS LOCATIONS).

Such differences in theoretical perspective reflect the diverse and ambiguous character of the middle class(es). It has often been argued, for instance, that nonmanual occupations are distinguished by relatively higher pay, better working conditions, more opportunities for promotion, etc. than manual occupations. This argument cannot be sustained for women working in routine clerical jobs or behind department store counters; their WORK and MARKET SITUATION are quite different from those of higher middle-class occupations. On the other hand, routine white collar workers do, on average, often work fewer hours per week than manual workers, and commonly enjoy greater security of income, and greater job security. The further one moves up the status hierarchy, the greater become the advantages of higher pay, career prospects, and various benefits (for example, company cars, low interest loans, or health insurance). The marked differences that exist within the middle class(es) mean that debates about their class situation and the implication of this for CLASS CONSCIOUSNESS will continue to be held in sociology. See also MULTIDIMENSIONAL ANALYSIS OF SOCIAL STRATIFICATION, CLASS IMAGERY, SOCIAL MOBILITY.

middle-class radicalism forms of political radicalism, including left-wing voting, by people from nonmanual backgrounds. Parkin (1968) employed the term to refer to members of the Campaign for Nuclear Disarmament (CND) in Britain. Middle-class radicalism is of interest in much the same way as WORKING-CLASS CONSERVATISM as a form of *class-deviant political action,* that is, activity contrary to prevailing or expected class norms. Two distinct locations of types of middle-class class-deviant political activity in Britain can be identified:

(a) the *lower middle class left*, left-wing voting and action by those marginal to the middle class, for example, routine manual workers, and

(b) the *upper middle class left*, forms of left-wing political activity particularly associated with membership of the caring professions and public sector employment (Jary, 1978). See also VOTING BEHAVIOR.

militant and industrial societies Herbert SPENCER's evolutionary distinction between two types of society in England: the earlier form of society based on "compulsory cooperation," *militant society,* and the newer type of society into which militant societies transform, *industrial society,* based on "voluntary cooperation" (see Fig. 17). Spencer's conception of modern industrial society reflected this view that contemporary English society represented the highest stage of evolution. His typology formulates an idealized distinction. Spencer recognized that many societies had not reached his second stage. He was also acutely aware that modern societies displayed many signs of reverting to the militant form. However, he retained his belief that the industrial type was the most evolved form, and one that individuals and governments ought to seek to achieve.

military *(n.)* the armed forces of a STATE; *(adj.)* pertaining to the armed forces or to WARFARE. The Austrian sociologist Ludwig Gumplowitz (1838–1909) argued that military conquest was the origin both of the state and SOCIAL STRATIFICATION. Whether or not this view is accepted—it usually is regarded as far too simple—it is clear that the military plays a crucial role in the maintenance of state power once this is established. Despite this, until recently sociological study of the military and of warfare has occupied only a relatively marginalized place within mainstream sociology. This neglect has been challenged recently by a number of theorists (for example, MANN, 1983 and 1988). The argument is that in a world threatened with extinction by the military might of two superpowers, and with militarism today a more pervasive feature than in earlier societies, the study of warfare and the military ought to be more central.

Mill, John Stuart (1806–73) English philosopher and leading 19th-century exponent of liberalism, who also took a keen interest in developments in social science and sociology; for example, he sponsored COMTE's work. Apart from his own wide-ranging philosophical and more general work

Characteristic	Militant Society	Industrial Society
Dominant function or activity	Corporate defensive & offensive activity for preservation and aggrandizement	Peaceful, mutual rendering of individual services
Principle of social coordination	Compulsory cooperation; regimentation by enforcement of orders; both positive and negative regulation of activity.	Voluntary cooperation; regulation by contract and principles of justice; only negative regulation of activity.
Relations between state and individual	Individuals exist for benefit of state; restraints on liberty property, and mobility.	State exists for benefit of individuals; freedom; few restraints on property and mobility.
Relations between state and other organizations	All organizations public; private organizations excluded.	Private organizations encouraged.
Structure of state	Centralized	Decentralized
Structure of social stratification	Fixity of rank, occupation, and locality; inheritance of positions	Plasticity and openness of rank, occupation, and locality; movement between positions
Type of economic activity	Economic autonomy and self-sufficiency; little external trade; protectionism	Loss of economic autonomy; interdependence via peaceful trade; free trade.
Valued social and personal characteristics	Patriotism; courage; reverence; loyalty; obedience; faith in authority; discipline	Independence; respect for others; resistance to coercion; individual initiative; truthfulness; kindness.

Fig. 17. **Militant and industrial societies.** Spencer's contrasts between militant and industrial societies. This table (from Smelser, 1968) is derived from Herbert Spencer, *The Principles of Sociology*, 1987.

(including *Utilitarianism*, 1861a, *Representative Government*, 1861b, and *Principles of Political Economy*, 1848), Mill's own contribution to social science was made especially in *A System of Logic* (1843). In this he provided a formal analysis of the main methods of INDUCTION AND INDUCTIVE LOGIC, which he advanced as the basis of empirical research and the scientific method in social science as well as natural science (see COMPARATIVE METHOD). Making the assumption of a "uniformity of nature," Mill sought to combat traditional philosophical skepticism; however, he cannot be seen to have solved this problem. Influenced by de TOCQUEVILLE, in *On Liberty* (1859) Mill argued against all forms of censorship and for a toleration of different viewpoints, one reason for this being that the development of knowledge required such openness—a viewpoint that can be interpreted as an argument against any fixed method (see FEYERABEND, TRUTH). Another reason was the importance of living life as one chooses, of allowing experiments in living that do not threaten others. In *The Subjection of Women* (1869) he made a case against gender inequality. His contribution to UTILITARIANISM, the extension of the work of his father, James Mill (1773–1836), and his godfather, Jeremy BENTHAM, is also of sociological interest. Mill followed their views in making judgments of right and wrong a matter of the "pleasure principle," the degree to which particular actions or social arrangements increase, or do not increase, overall happiness. However, he differed from them in insisting that a distinction should be drawn between higher and lower forms of pleasure.

millenarianism and millennial movement a type of religious, often also politico-religious, movement based on a belief in the imminence of a radical sociopolitical transformation by supernatural intervention, for example, that the Messiah will return, bringing a new millennium—one thousand years—hence the general term. In medieval and early modern Europe, millennial movements were movements mainly of the of the disadvantaged and the dispossessed (see Cohn, 1957). This pattern is repeated elsewhere, for example, the North American Indian Ghost Dancers or in the related phenomenon of CARGO CULTS. All such movements can be seen as prepolitical responses to cultural disruption, which in time may give rise to non-millenarian forms of political movement. Equally however, many modern forms of political movement have been interpreted as involving elements of millenarianism in that they promise root-and-branch social and economic transformations for which there exists no immediate feasible means.

Mills, C. Wright (1916–62) US sociologist and prominent critic of the two orthodoxies of American sociology in the 1950s: Parsonian functionalism and social survey research. The former he castigated as vacuous *grand theory* and the latter as ABSTRACTED EMPIRICISM. In Mills' eyes these forms of sociology had ceased to raise truly significant questions about society. In his own sociology he sought to relate private ills to public issues. He was critical above all of the "intellectual default" that he believed existed in modern sociology and modern society, that is, the failure to intervene effectively in history.

As editor and translator (with Hans Gerth) of selections from Max Weber (*From Max Weber: Essays in Sociology*, 1946), Mills argued for a sociological method grounded in historical understanding. Influenced also by SYMBOLIC INTERACTIONISM, in *Character and Social Structure* (1953) he also advocated a sociology that would interrelate character structure with social structure. *The Sociological Imagination* (1959) provides the most general summary statement of Mills' overall approach and attitudes.

Of his more substantive studies, two in particular attracted wide attention: *White Collar* (1951) and *The Power Elite* (1956). In the first of these Mills charted the declining importance and loss of public role of the old independent middle class, whom he saw as being increasingly replaced by a new middle class, made up of bureaucratized office workers, salesmen, and the like. These were "cheerful robots," according to Mills, with little control over their own lives. In *Power Elite*, Mills' more general thesis was that power in modern America was becoming more concentrated. Characteristically, three interrelated and overlapping groups of pivotal powerholders were identified by Mills: corporation chieftains, military warlords, and political bosses, all of whom Mills suggested could be comfortably accommodated in a medium-sized suburban movie theater (see also ELITE THEORY). Although by their occupation of the commanding heights of American society, the members of this power elite have the potential to given a moral direction to society; in practice, according to Mills, their actions were often such as to constitute a "higher immorality," for example, a drift to World War III.

Critics of Mills' work have concentrated on two aspects: first, its relatively speculative empirical base and its populist tone, and secondly, its failure to relate systematically to other general theories of modern society, including PLURAL ELITISM and modern Marxism. However, Mills was an important and provocative voice in postwar American sociology, contributing to the development of a more critical stance.

Minitab (STATISTICS) a much-used software package in Britain for performing statistical analysis. Developed initially to help in the teaching of statistics, Minitab is fully interactive and based on the idea of entering numerical information in a worksheet of rows and columns, rather like a spreadsheet. Frequently updated, Minitab now has programs that enable it to handle many complex MULTIVARIATE ANALYSES and time series analyses. Unlike many standard packages, Minitab is particularly strong in techniques associated with *exploratory data analysis (EDA)*. For the analysis of survey data the package contains a wide range of statistical techniques and graphs; its one drawback is that labeling facilities are limited. Available in both mainframe and microcomputer versions, Minitab is regarded as one of the most user-friendly statistical programs.

mode see MEASURES OF CENTRAL TENDENCY.

model 1. any representation of one phenomenon by another, for example, ANALOGY or metaphor. **2.** any formal (that is, mathematical or logically formal) representation of a set of relationships. **3.** a physical or a pictorial or diagrammatic representation (including maps) of a set of relationships. **4.** computer models, which can enable the simulation of real-world processes.

MODERNIZATION

In a final, looser sense, any abstract general concept (for example, IDEAL TYPE or THEORY may sometimes be referred to as a model.

Models vary in the degree to which they are regarded as approximating reality (their degree of *isomorphism* with the reality). Their functions also vary, and may be heuristic as well as explanatory, including:

(a) the proposal of new hypotheses for exploration by suggesting comparisons between unfamiliar phenomena and those better known or better explained (for example, between cultural and biological evolution);

(b) the simplification of complex reality for analytical purposes by the provision of an unambiguous general concept (Weber's ideal type of BUREAUCRACY) or to highlight fundamental explanatory causal mechanisms in isolation from complicating factors;

(c) comparisons between the so-called ideal model and the real world (as in both Marx's and Weber's models, or the THEORY OF GAMES), intended to increase awareness of real-world processes. Ultimately no clear-cut distinction exists between the terms "model" and "theory," since both imply some simplification of reality, necessary in order to achieve generality.

modernization 1. the overall societal process, including INDUSTRIALIZATION, by which previously agrarian historical and contemporary societies become developed. The overall contrast usually drawn is between premodern and modernized societies. The term includes a wider range of social processes than industrialization (see also POLITICAL MODERNIZATION). **2.** the more particular model of societal development, suggested especially by US functionalist sociologists in the 1950s and 1960s, in which the decisive factor in modernization is the overcoming and replacement of traditional values and patterns of motivation hostile to social change and economic growth. In more general terms, structural-functionalist theories also emphasize the process of SOCIAL DIFFERENTIATION involved in modernization, including political PLURALISM (see also TRADITIONAL SOCIETIES, ACHIEVEMENT MOTIVATION).

While modernization **1.** is an open-ended concept, modernization **2.** has been widely criticized as a Western-centered approach. This criticism has been directed at the use of the concept (in the 1950s and 1960s) by the STRUCTURAL-FUNCTIONALIST theorists, influenced by the work of PARSONS, to examine the prospects of development in Third World societies.

While there are important differences between authors, the main tenets of the structural-functionalist theory are:

(a) modern society is contrasted with TRADITIONAL SOCIETY that is seen as hindering economic development;

(b) change occurs through evolutionary stages that are broadly similar for all societies;

(c) Third World countries need agents to help them break out of tradition;

(d) such agents for changes may either come from within the society, such as modernizing elites, or may come from outside, for example, with the injection of capital or education models;

(e) dual economies and dual societies may exist in contemporary Third World countries. Some regions persist in traditional forms, while others, especially urban areas, experience modernization;

(f) both the preferred and likely outcome are societies similar to those in Western Europe and the United States. In this last respect authors share similar assumptions to CONVERGENCE theorists.

The criticisms came primarily from DEPENDENCY THEORY and underdevelopment theorists in the late 1960s and subsequently. The main critical points were:

(a) modernization theory concentrated on internal social processes, thus ignoring the effects of colonialism and neocolonialism on the structure of Third World societies;

(b) the contrast between modern and traditional was both oversimplified and erroneous. FRANK argued that existing Third World societies were not in any sense traditional because they had been changed by centuries of contact with northern countries. The obstacles to change were a creation of this contact;

(c) these were not dual societies because often the so-called traditional sectors were an integral part of the national economy;

(d) the evolutionary approach imposed a Western model of development and denied the possibility of novel forms of society emerging in the Third World;

(e) behind modernization theory were both political and ideological concerns. Many of the main theorists were from the United States, involved in governmental advisory roles and explicity committed to the curtailment of socialism or communism in the Third World. This was particularly seen in the 1960s, when the Alliance for Progress in Latin America was instituted in response to the Cuban Revolution of 1959 and adopted many of the suggested policies and aims deriving from modernization theory. See also EVOLUTIONARY THEORY, NEOEVOLUTIONISM, SOCIOLOGY OF DEVELOPMENT, SOCIAL CHANGE.

modes of motivational orientation three forms or modes of *motivational orientation,* identified by Parsons and Shils (1951):

(a) *cognitive,* that is, the perception of objects in terms of their characteristics and potential consequences;

(b) *cathectic,* that is, the perception of objects in terms of the emotional needs of the actor;

(c) *evaluative,* in which the actor allocates his energy among the ends and attempts to optimize outcomes.

All three modes of orientation can be involved in any instance of social action, but equally particular instances or types of social action can be characterized by primarily involving one rather than the others.

money any commodity or token generally acceptable as a medium of exchange, and in terms of which other goods and services may be priced. Originally, the physical material used as money usually had an inherent usefulness as well as being a symbolic medium (for example, gold). In modern societies money takes many forms, including paper and also machine-held records.

Absent in barter economies, in which goods are exchanged directly, money can be seen as an important human invention (see also EVOLUTIONARY UNIVERSAL). As a "symbolic medium for resources" (Parsons, 1963), money underlines the generalized instrumentality of resources as against their more particular uses. Money, together with the development of MARKETS for resources, is immensely significant historically, for the following reasons:

(a) as a store of purchasing power or value;

(b) as a unit of account or record; as a measurement of the relative value of goods and services whether or not these are actually to be sold;

(c) as *money capital*, the money used to finance production;

(d) as a source of credit.

For MARX in particular, and for the classical economists generally, money played an indispensable role in the rise of capitalism and the capitalist mode of production. However, a number of its characteristics were also recognized as bringing problems. These arise from the storage and hoarding of money, and from situations in which goods cannot be sold for money, or credit obtained—one reason for economic crises. For Marx, such crises have less to do with the characteristics of money as such than with the character of capitalism.

In a classic work, *The Philosophy of Money*, SIMMEL points to the fact that the transition to a money economy has far-reaching consequences beyond its role in the development of the economy. Not least, there is the general impetus it gave to rational calculation and a rationalistic world outlook, including scientific measurement. A further consequence was an increase in impersonal social relationships.

In the work of Parsons, analogies between the concept of money and the concept of POWER are also suggested. Thus, political power can be seen as a generalized resource that can be used in many ways.

monoculture in agricultural practice, the concentration of one crop in a given area. This is generally associated with the growth of commercial agriculture and of cash cropping, and can be contrasted with mixed farming more characteristic of agriculturalists growing for their own consumption. While monoculture may have benefits for some crops, there may also be disadvantages: certain forms of mixed cropping may control pests and preserve the fertility of the soil, whereas monoculture is generally associated with increased use of pesticides and artificial fertilizers. For this reason monoculture is generally associated with large-scale organizations, such as plantations, which can mobilize the resources for the necessary inputs and manage the marketing of the crop. Even then, problems for Third World countries resulting from monoculture arise from dependence on a few crops for export earnings that are vulnerable to changes in world prices and demand over which Third World countries may have little control. See also AGRIBUSINESS.

monogamy a MARRIAGE rule permitting only one partner to either sex. It may include prohibitions on remarriage, but where it does not the terms *serial monogamy* or *serial polygamy* are sometimes used.

monotheism the belief in the doctrine that there is only one god; religious belief systems based on this doctrine. Of the major world religions, only Judaism, Christianity, and Islam are monotheistic, and they share a common root. According to Lenski and Lenski (1970), although rare in hunter-gatherer and horticultural societies, conceptions of a supreme being become widespread in agrarian societies. Monotheism and a belief personal ethical God, however, appear only in the Near East. PARSONS regards the appearance of monotheism as a decisive developmental step encouraging the development of ethical universalism. WEBER's account of the Jewish conception of the jealous God, Yahweh—"Thou shalt have no other gods but me" and the notion of the "chosen people"—is that these conceptions were a response to the vulnerability of the tribes of Israel to foreign domination, problems explained by the PROPHETS as a supreme God punishing his people for worshipping false gods.

Montesquieu, Baron Charles de (1689–1755) French aristocrat and early sociological thinker, chiefly remembered for the massive social investigations comprising the *Spirit of the Laws* (1748). Educated in natural history, physiology, and law, Montesquieu first came to the attention of the Parisian social elite with the publication of his *Persian Letters* (1721), which examined familiar French customs from the point of view of the cultural outsider.

Spirit of the Laws, however, is a more massive and seriously sociological study. It consists of 31 books, written over a period of 20 years, examining different forms of government, environmental influences on social structure, culture, trade, population, religion, and law.

Montesquieu's conception of the precondition of political liberty, which he valued, was a form of PLURALISM; that is, freedom depended on a balance of power distributed among various groups or institutions. He was among the first to examine the legal apparatus of society in its social context and is thus regarded as a founding figure in the SOCIOLOGY OF LAW. Montesquieu is also remembered for his advocacy of EMPIRICISM, and his early delineation of Asiatic despotism (see ASIATIC MODE OF PRODUCTION AND ASIATIC SOCIETY).

Moore, Barrington (1913–) US sociologist and social historian, whose most influential work, *Social Origins of Dictatorship and Democracy* (1966), did much to rejuvenate comparative historical sociology after an era dominated by overly generalized functionalist and evolutionary accounts of social change. In his earlier works, *Soviet Politics—The Dilemma of Power: The Role of Ideas in Social Change* (1950) and *Terror and Progress USSR* (1954), Moore had himself used functionalist modes of analysis in suggesting that the functional requirements associated with the necessity to industrialize had placed a limit on attempts to realize a socialist society. In *Social Origins of Dictatorship and Democracy,* however, rather than working with the idea of a single set of functional requirements for modernization, Moore's argument is that three distinctive historical routes to the modern world can be identified:

(a) a democratic, and capitalist, route—"revolution from below"—based on commercialized agriculture and the powerful emergence of bourgeois interests (England, France, United States);

(b) a route leading ultimately to fascism—"revolution from above"—in which the bourgeois impetus was far weaker, and modernization involved recourse to labor-repressive modes of work organization in agriculture by a traditional ruling group backed by strong political controls (Germany, Japan);

(c) a route leading to communist revolution, in which neither the commercialization of agriculture nor a recourse to labor-repressive techniques by traditional ruling groups proved effective in the face of peasant solidarity (Russia, China).

Not all Moore's conclusions about these three routes have found universal acceptance (see Smith, 1983). Rather, it is the subtlety of his sifting of historical data while addressing general questions that has impressed many sociologists and has done much to stimulate the postfunctionalist flowering of historical sociology evident in recent years. Barrington Moore's own subsequent work has failed to reach the heights achieved in *Social Origins.* It is of interest, however, that in *The Causes of Human Misery* (1978), an exercise in seeking conclusions on moral questions, he makes the suggestion that while social science is in a position to identify social evils, it is far less able to identify the basis of the good society. See also JUSTICE.

moral career the identifiable sequences in a labeling process in which a person's identity (particularly deviant identity) and moral status are progressively changed. For example, the moral career of the mental patient (GOFFMAN, *Stigma* 1963), in which the patient is first sane, then a patient, and finally a former patient. In this process the entire biography of a person may be reinterpreted in the light of the moral evaluations progressively imposed. Compare DEGRADATION CEREMONY.

moral crusade a SOCIAL MOVEMENT, for example, Mary Whitehouse's National Viewers' and Listeners' Association in England, in which members seek to mobilize support for the reassertion and enforcement of legal and social sanctions in defense of what are seen as fundamental moral values.

Often, but not exclusively, these movements attract members with strong religious affiliations. In some sociological accounts, the suggestion is that they tend to attract members with particular personality needs, for example, AUTHORITARIAN PERSONALITY, but there is no indication that this applies generally to membership. See also MORAL ENTREPRENEURS, PRESSURE GROUP.

moral entrepreneurs those members of society with the power to create or enforce rules (H. BECKER, *Outsiders: Studies in the Sociology of Deviance*, 1963). For Becker, for whom DEVIANCE represents "publicly labeled wrongdoing," someone must call the public's attention to such wrongdoings. Deviance is the product of enterprise in the sense that there are (a) those who act to get rules made and (b) those who apply the rules once a rule has come into existence, so that offenders created by the abstract rules can be identified, apprehended, and convicted. Becker's interest is in reversing the emphasis of most social scientific research, which concerns itself with the people who break rules. Instead, he suggests "We must see deviance ... as a consequence of a process of interaction between people, some of whom, in the service of their own interests, make and enforce rules that catch others who, in the service of their own interests, have committed acts that are labeled deviant." See also LABELING THEORY, MORAL CRUSADE.

moral panic an exaggerated, media-amplified social reaction to initially relatively minor acts of social DEVIANCE, for example, social disturbances associated with mods and rockers (S. Cohen, *Folk Devils and Moral Panics*, 1972). Such an overreaction by media, police, courts, governments, and members of the public in labeling and drawing attention, far from leading to an elimination of this behavior, tends to amplify it. It does so by constructing role models for others to follow or by identifying as instances of the designated behavior examples of unruly or unsocial behavior that might otherwise attract little attention. Some theorists also suggest that moral panics are encouraged by governments as useful in mobilizing political support by creating a common threat (see Hall et al., *Policing the Crisis*, 1978). See also DEVIANCE AMPLIFICATION, LABELING THEORY.

moral relativism see RELATIVISM.

moral statistics social data collected, for example, in France in the 19th century (preceding the development of sociology as a discipline), and seen to be indicative of social pathology, such as suicide, crime, illegitimacy, and divorce. The concern for the collection of social data influenced social reformers in Britain, notably Edwin Chadwick (1800–1890). See also SOCIAL REFORM, OFFICIAL STATISTICS.

Moreno, Jacob (1890–1974) Austrian-born, US psychologist who developed early forms of PSYCHOTHERAPY—*psychodrama* and *sociodrama*—that involve role-playing to act out troublesome emotions and relationships. Psychodrama may take place only between the person and therapist, or in groups when several or all members of the group may role-play. The more usual term for group role-playing is *sociodrama* (see also GROUP THERAPY). Moreno also developed the technique of SOCIOMETRY.

mores the accepted and strongly prescribed forms of behavior within any society or community (W.G. Sumner, 1906). Mores are contrasted by SUMNER with FOLKWAYS in that the latter, though socially sanctioned, are less fundamental, less abstract in organization, and folkways transgressions are less severely punished than those of mores.

Morgan, Lewis Henry (1818–1881) American ethnologist and anthropologist whose principal influence on sociology and on Marxism can be traced to his materialistic theory of social evolution (see EVOLUTIONARY THEORY) presented in *Ancient Society* (1877).

Morgan's first venture into ETHNOGRAPHY was a detailed study of the Iroquois, the results of which were not published until 1891, after his death. Struck by the distinctive mode of relative classification, Morgan hypothesized that a search for similar systems abroad might establish the geographical origins of Native Americans. This led to a massive research effort. The result, which Morgan held to prove the Asiatic origin of the tribes, appeared in 1871 in *Systems of Consanguinity and Affinity of the Human Family*.

Morgan's analysis of KINSHIP terminology suggested an evolutionary process, with family relationships developing through early promiscuity to so-called civilized monogamy. Later, Morgan was to give the hypothesis of a general process of social evolution more systematic attention. This resulted in his most famous work, *Ancient Society* (1877). Two approaches to SOCIAL CHANGE were explored: IDEALISM and materialism. According to the former, social institutions developed as a reflection of changing and accumulating human ideas; according to the latter, human CULTURE evolved to the extent that people were able to exert increasing control over nature. In this way human society moved through three basic stages: SAVAGERY, BARBARISM, and CIVILIZATION.

Morgan drew on a wide range of ethnographic data in pursuing these ideas, ranging from material on Australian aborigines to the societies of Ancient Greece and Rome. His idea of the evolutionary role of increasing control over the material reproduction of life resonated strongly with the materialist conception of history being developed by Marx and Engels. For Morgan the history of property and the evolution of culture were inextricably linked. Moreover, the property-centeredness of modern societies stood in the way of advance to a social order of greater justice. Small wonder that *Ancient Society* became a classic text in the foundation of Marxist thought. Marx himself planned a text on Morgan, though this was never written. Engels, in *The Origin of the Family, Private Property and the State* (1884), explicitly recognized Morgan's independent formulation of historical materialism.

Morgan remains one of the founding figures in anthropology, and together with E.B. TYLOR and Herbert SPENCER, stands out as one of the great systematic evolutionary theorists of the 19th century.

Mosca, Gaetano (1858–1941) Italian political scientist and politician who, along with PARETO and MICHELS, is usually identified as one of the originators of ELITE THEORY. In Mosca's view, society always consisted of two classes of individuals: the rulers and the ruled. Like Pareto, with whom he continually contested the priority in formulating elite theory, Mosca regarded many of the justifications (*political formulae*) that surround rule as merely a veneer of rationalizations underpinning and preserving political power. He acknowledged that a distinction existed between political systems that were guided by liberal principles (that is, they have an elected leadership) and those that were autocratic. What he denied was that such an arrangement, including provision for recruitment of new entrants to the political elite, meant government by the people or majority rule. By the same token, although classes could be represented in government, there could be no question of rule by an entire class—least of all a so-called classless society, in the way suggested by Marx. Mosca's best-known work *Elementi di scienza politica* (1896), variously revised in successive editions was translated as *The Ruling Class* in 1939. It is a mistake to regard Mosca as an advocate of autocracy; rather, his own preference was for particular forms of representative democracy. His theory can be seen as the forerunner of the influential modern theory of DEMOCRATIC ELITISM, with its celebration of representative elites and its scaling down of what it regards as the unrealistic expectations associated with conceptions of participatory democracy and Marxism.

multiculturalism the acknowledgment and promotion of cultural pluralism as a feature of many societies. In opposition to the tendency in modern societies to cultural unification and universalization, multiculturalism celebrates and seeks to protect cultural variety, for example, minority languages. At the same time it focuses on the often unequal relationship of minority to mainstream cultures. After decades of persecution, the prospects of indigenous or immigrant cultures are now helped somewhat by the support they receive from international public opinion and the international community, for example, the United Nations.

multidimensional analysis of social stratification any approach to the analysis of SOCIAL STRATIFICATION and CLASS that emphasizes the importance of a plurality of factors in determining the overall SOCIOECONOMIC STATUS or CLASS LOCATION of a person or particular category of persons. Often such a view is seen as stemming from WEBER's as against MARX's approach to the analysis of social stratification and class (see CLASS, STATUS AND PARTY). Among the most influential formulation in these terms is David LOCKWOOD's analysis of the class location of black-coated workers, in which he proposes three separate dimensions: MARKET SITUATION, work situation, and STATUS SITUATION. The importance of multiple dimensions to stratification, and the significance of these in influencing CLASS CONSCIOUS-NESS, were also central in the AFFLUENT WORKER studies, in which Lockwood and John GOLDTHORPE were the main researchers. More recently, the idea of sectoral interests that cut across more conventional class locations has been advanced. (See SECTORAL CLEAVAGES).

While multiple dimensions of social stratification may be seen as undermining more unitary conceptions of class, especially Marxist conceptions, the argument is not decisive. Examples of Marxian forms of analysis that involve multidimensional analysis include those emphasizing CONTRADIC-TORY CLASS LOCATIONS (see also INTERMEDIATE CLASSES OR INTERMEDIATE STRATA). The crucial difference between Marxian and non-Marxian theories lies more in what the implications of a multidimensional analysis are ultimately seen to be, for example, whether or not analysis is conducted in terms of an assumption that objective economic interests determine class relations and class conflict in the long run. See also STATUS CONSISTENCY AND INCONSISTENCY.

multivariate analysis the analysis of data collected on several different VARIABLES. For example, in a study of housing provision, data may be collected on age, income, and family size (the *variables*) of the population being studied. In analyzing the data the effect of each of these variables can be examined, as well as the interaction between them.

Many multivariate techniques are available, but most aim to simplify the data in some way in order to clarify relationships between variables. The choice of method depends on the nature of the data, the type of problem, and the objectives of the analysis. FACTOR ANALYSIS and principal component analysis are exploratory and are used to find new underlying variables. *Cluster analysis* seeks to find natural groupings of objects of individuals. Other techniques, for example, multiple REGRESSION ANALYSIS, aim to explain the variation in one variable by means of the variation in two or more independent variables. MANOVA (multivariate analysis of variance), an extension of univariate ANALYSIS OF VARIANCE, is used when there are multiple dependent variables, as in the example above. An example of multivariate techniques for analyzing categorical data is LOG LINEAR ANALYSIS.

multiversity Clark KERR's (1982) conception of a multicentered and multifunctional higher education institution, containing within it a variety of levels and kinds of provision: elite and mass, nonvocational and vocational, etc. Kerr envisaged such institutions as replacing the more unified traditional university.

mutual knowledge the knowledge of how to go on in different forms of social life "shared by lay actors and sociological observers" and providing the necessary preconditions "for gaining access to valid descriptions of social activity" (GIDDENS, 1984). See also DOUBLE HERMENEUTIC, POSTULATE OF ADEQUACY.

myths and mythologies religious or sacred folk tales, whose content concerns the origins or creation of the world, gods, a particular people or society, etc. Sometimes these stories, which have a particular importance in preliterate societies as part of an oral tradition are acted out in RITUALS.

Mythologies have been of interest to anthropologists:

(a) as a source of quasi-historical data about societies that have no written record;

(b) as a coded indication of the central values of a society;

(c) as a heavily symbolic metaphorical expression of perennial psychic and social tensions, for example, the Oedipus myth;

(d) as revealing, via the logics of myths, the universal structures of the human mind (for example, the work of LÉVI-STRAUSS). It is the last of these that has recently attracted most interest and has generated much debate.

In Lévi-Strauss's structuralist approach, recurring universal *binary oppositions* are identified in myths, for example, opposition between nature and culture, male and female, friendship and hostility. Lévi-Strauss quotes Mauss: "Men communicate by symbols ... but they can only have those symbols and communicate by them because they have the same instincts." Lévi-Strauss regards the function of myths as providing justifications for the particular combination of all possible binary oppositions that have been actually adopted in a particular society. However, Lévi-Strauss is more interested in the complex transformations of mythologies across time and across cultures, as in the analysis of particular societies, in the way in which myths structure reality, and in what this reveals about "primitive universal logic." The main objection to Lévi-Strauss's structuralist analysis of mythologies is that it is not clear how one can move beyond possible interpretations of the universal logics of myths when many of these interpretations seem arbitrary and leave open other possible interpretations (see Leach, 1970).

N

naive falsificationism see FALSIFICATIONISM.

National Deviancy Conference a group of British sociologists prominent in the late 1960s and the 1970s interested in reconstituting traditional *criminology* and the sociology of DEVIANCE. One of the founding members of the NDC (Cohen, 1981) summarized its interests as including four main themes:

(a) to emphasize the sociological dimension of criminology and integrate it into mainstream sociological interests;

(b) to extend the insights of LABELING THEORY and SOCIETAL REACTION theory in a more structurally and politically aware way;

(c) to emphasize the importance of the deviants' own understandings and meanings;

(d) to recognize the political character of defining and studying crime and deviance.

As Cohen argues, the ineptly named NDC was important as a vehicle for developing new approaches to deviancy (sometimes known as *radical deviancy theory*), and laying the basis, for instance, for *critical criminology* and later victimology studies and for radical approaches in social work theory and practice (see RADICAL SOCIAL WORK). The emphasis on critical and political issues was very much of its time and, as external political realities changed and internal theoretical divergences were developed, the NDC fragmented, although its influence is evident in the development and greatly increased status of criminological and deviancy issues within sociology.

National Health Service (NHS) the system of health care provided for all citizens by the British government.

In 1948, after more than a century of public health reform, and in the centenary year of the first Public Health Act, the National Health Service was established. It occupies a unique position in British society because (a) it has the largest client group for social welfare, since it provides care for people at all stages of the LIFE COURSE, and (b) more than any other welfare institution established as a result of the Beveridge Report of 1942, the NHS embodies the welfare principle—care as a social service rather than a market commodity. It is the subject of political debate because of New Right theories about the state and the responsibilities of individuals, and it is the subject of academic discussions concerning the power of the medical profession and the nature of illness and health in Britain.

The NHS was set up to provide a fully comprehensive service of curative and preventive medicine for physical and mental illness. The service was to be free at the point of treatment in accordance with the patient's medically defined needs. The means-test principle of eligibility was abolished and the service was funded centrally from insurance and taxation. Its architects believed that the NHS would mop up the pool of ill health and that full employment would combine with the other agencies of the welfare state to lead to higher standards of health and a long-term fall in demand for health services.

This has not happened. Rising costs, changes in health expectations, changes in the pattern of disease, demographic change, and the persistence of class-related illness have resulted in high levels of demand. The balance of supply favors the acute, hospital, interventionist sector at the expense of the community, disability, geriatric sector. Garner (1979) refers to this as the "no hope, no power paradigm." These Cinderella patients have no power themselves and no powerful medical interests working on their behalf. Their conditions require care rather than cure. In a profession where success is associated with high-technology medicine, conditions that hold out little hope of scientific advance or breakthrough are unattractive to ambitious doctors.

The development of the medical profession in Britain is inseparable from the history of the NHS, since it guarantees the medical monopoly and has secured a number of professional rights:

(a) the right to contract out of the NHS for private medicine;

(b) independence from some aspects of the NHS management structure for teaching hospitals;

(c) the right of individual practitioners to prescribe whatever treatment they consider appropriate (clinical autonomy);

(d) systems of payment and administration that confirm the status differentials between hospital doctors and general practitioners, specialists and the rest of the medical profession.

In the early 1990s the NHS is undergoing reform, acknowledging the increasing demands on its finite resorces. Market criteria are being applied, provoking considerable resistance since these apparently contradict the principles under which the NHS was inaugurated.

nation-state the modern form of STATE, possessing clearly defined borders, in which the boundaries of state and society tend to be coextensive; that is, the territorial claims of the state typically correspond with cultural, linguistic, and ethnic divisions. As such, these modern forms of states contrast with the most successful earlier state forms (for example, preindustrial empires), which usually lacked the administrative or other resources to impose such cultural integration.

As GIDDENS (1985) puts it, a decisive feature of modern nation-states is that they are "bordered power containers" enclosing far greater administrative intensity than traditional states. Furthermore, these modern states have also existed as part of a NATION-STATE SYSTEM of similarly constituted states, in that: (a) WARFARE and the preparation for war played a fundamental constitutive role, and (b) in providing a model, paved the way for all subsequent modern nation-states, for example, in Asia and Africa. In recent years, sociologists have tended to place a new emphasis on the role of the state in transforming the traditional world, often granting political institutions greater autonomy from, and sometimes even primacy over, economic institutions.

nation-state system the territorial division of the modern world into a network of national political communities, or NATION-STATES, replacing the previous pattern of simple societies and imperial systems. This worldwide contemporary system of nation-states (which originally derives from the Western European state system that grew up in connection with ABSOLUTISM) has a number of decisive implications, above all, the crucial role of WARFARE, or its threat, in shaping the modern world.

naturalistic research methods approaches to social research that emphasize the importance of the study of social life in naturally occurring settings. See also SYMBOLIC INTERACTIONISM.

natural law see NATURAL RIGHTS AND NATURAL LAW.

natural rights and natural law 1. (moral and political philosophy) originally, the doctrine that the principles of correct conduct could be discovered by a process of rational inquiry into the nature of Man as God made him. For a political theorist such as John LOCKE, the laws of nature were the commands of God. From natural law, men derive rights to the means they need in order to perform these duties. **2.** the entitlements advanced as attaching to all human beings by virtue of their common humanity. While, in this second sense, *natural rights* may still be advanced as the foundation of normative theory, they are nowadays usually detached from their original religious basis, although conceptions that these rights are or should be self-evident, and that they provide a standard for all evaluations of political and legal rights, remain a powerful force in political discourse.

The connection between natural law as the commands of God and natural rights was a strong element in the United States Declaration of Independence. Thereafter, the language of rights became steadily divorced from its natural-law setting, and from the French Revolution onward took off into the realm of the so-called rights of man. The 20th century has added an array of economic and social rights to the original ones (see CITIZEN RIGHTS), but it is now relatively uncommon to meet the terms "natural rights" and "natural law" in their original usage, and these have virtually disappeared from everyday political discourse.

nature-nurture debate the debate surrounding the question of the extent to which behavior is the result of hereditary or innate influences (nature), or is determined by environment and learning (nurture). Assessing the relative contributions of each is extremely difficult, since both interact continually throughout development. Historically, each side of the debate has had its support, *nativists* believing in hereditary determination, and *empiricists* in the dominance of the environment.

Naturwissenschaften see GEISTESWISSENSCHAFTEN AND NATURWISSENSCHAFTEN.

need(s) 1. the basic requirements necessary to sustain human life. "Needs" are defined differently according to the use made: MASLOW (1954) suggested a *hierarchy of needs* from the basic physiological needs for food, safety, and shelter to psychological needs of belonging, approval, love, and finally the need for self-actualization. Only the physiological needs are essential for sustaining life and, according to Maslow, must be fulfilled before higher needs can be met. Some sociologists have argued that the existence of human needs indicates that universal FUNCTIONAL PREREQUISITES for the survival of any society can be identified. Both conceptions of need involve a systems model (see SYSTEMS THEORY) of man and society. **2.** any socially acquired individual drive (*personality need*), for example, ACHIEVEMENT MOTIVATION. **3.** a distinction may also be drawn between *basic needs* and *felt needs*. In economics, the term *wants* is used to refer both to psychological and social "felt needs" and to the goods that stimulate these.

While many sociologists have registered their dissatisfaction with NEEDS **1.**—arguing that human needs are not universal but socially formed—conceptions of human needs have not been confined to psychologists or functionalist sociologists. Frankfurt School neo-Marxist sociologists (for example, MARCUSE) have referred to the "false needs" created by capitalist societies, thus implying human needs. Conceptions of absolute and relative poverty also depend on conceptions of physiological and social needs. However, generally the term "need(s)" has not been applied with great precision in sociology.

negantropy see SYSTEMS THEORY.

negation 1. (LOGIC) a proposition that is the denial of another and is true only if the other is false. **2.** (Marxism) a phase or moment in a dialectical process that negates a previous one, leading ultimately to a resolution ("negation of the negation"). In the work of members of the FRANKFURT SCHOOL OF CRITICAL THEORY, especially ADORNO's *Negative Dialectics* (1973), *negativity* was expressed as an opposition to all fixed categories and to the "administered world" to which both orthodox Marxism and POSITIVISM were seen to lead.

negative feedback see SYSTEMS THEORY.

negotiated order an influential idea in studies of organizations that sees social order as the emergent product of processes of negotiation between persons and groups (for example, conferring, bargaining, making arrangements, compromising, reaching agreements). Social order is not fixed and immutable but is open to revision and reorganization through these processes. See also ORGANIZATION THEORY.

negritude a cultural and political movement started in the 1930s to encourage the development of pride and dignity in the heritage of black peoples by rediscovering ancient African values and modes of thought. The movement was originally concerned with an artistic and cultural critique of

Western societies, but was broadened into a more political program under the influence of Leopold Senghor, poet and president of Senegal. Negritude was an attempt to raise the consciousness of blacks throughout the world.

neo-evolutionism a school of theory emerging in the middle of the 20th century that attempted to revive the explanation of SOCIAL CHANGE according to evolutionary principles (see DARWIN, EVOLUTIONARY THEORY).

Neo-evolutionism probably received its most theoretically complex expression in the work of PARSONS (1964, 1966, 1971). The key texts here represent a systematic attempt to show that FUNCTIONALISM could produce an adequate account of social change, and that neo-evolutionary theory could overcome the deficiencies of its forerunners. Nineteenth-century evolutionism has been compromised by three principal problems: its unidirectional assumptions (see UNILINEAR), an inability to specify adequately the intermediate stages of development between simple and complex societies, and a moralistic and ethnocentric view of progress.

The problem of unilinearity is dealt with in the neo-evolutionary approach by drawing a distinction between the *general* evolutionary process, conceived in terms of crucial cultural, institutional, or structural breakthroughs (such as language, writing, legal systems, money, markets, bureaucracy, and stratification) achieved in different societies at different times, and the concrete evolution of any *specific* society. The development of these breakthroughs (or EVOLUTIONARY UNIVERSALS, as Parsons calls them) play a critical part in his approach, for so-called universals enhance SOCIAL DIFFERENTIATION (see also FUNCTIONAL PREREQUISITES AND FUNCTIONAL IMPERATIVES) and so the "general adaptive capacity of society." Given that evolutionary universals may be borrowed by, or diffused from, one society to another, the specific evolutionary path of any concrete society will not necessarily follow the general evolutionary pattern.

These concepts also enable Parsons to confront the issue of how to characterize intermediate stages of social development. Simply, this is achieved by using the degree of structural differentiation achieved, and kinds of integrative (see INTEGRATION AND MALINTEGRATION) solutions adopted. In effect, this is equivalent to the number and kinds of evolutionary universals that have been incorporated. Parsons identifies five distinct stages in the general evolutionary process, each of which is exemplified by historical or existing societies. The final stage—that of advanced industrialism—is the terminus of the evolutionary process, and the future therefore of all currently existing societies that have not yet achieved industrialization.

The solution to the final problem—that of obtaining a value-free definition of evolutionary advance—should now be apparent. In Parsons' scheme, notions of progress are reduced to the empirically specifiable concept of "general adaptive capacity." Other neo-evolutionary theorists, for example, the anthropologists Sahlins and Service (1960), share the Parsonian tactic of using empirically identifiable criteria. Rather than relying on a concept such as "evolutionary universal," however, they suggest that evolutionary advance can be measured in terms of the efficiency with which societies are able to exploit energy resources, which in turn are related to enhanced autonomy from environmental factors, and the ability to displace and replace less advanced societies.

Parsons (1964) is specific that neo-evolutionary theory has substantive implications for development policy in the Third World. It is on this issue that most of the deficiencies of the approach have come to light. A.G. FRANK's (1969) famous polemic points out that what neo-evolutionary theory such as that of Parsons, or an economic version such as that proposed by Walt Rostow (1960), lacks is the perception of an historical connection between development and underdevelopment, that is, the development of the First World led to and continues to sustain the underdevelopment of the Third World. The Third World has continued to face problems of development despite centuries-long exposure to the diffusion of Western evolutionary universals, and to the values of achievement and universalism that underpin the patterns of role relationships in successful industrialized societies.

It is also doubtful whether Parsons actually succeeded or even meant to succeed in producing a value-free theory of social change. Development is still conceived in Western terms. This is apparent in terms of the implications that neo-evolutionary theory was meant to have for Third World governments interested in development, and even more so in terms of its implications for the developed communist world. One of the crucial evolutionary universals for Parsons is "democratic association," which is held to separate POWER from bureaucratic office. Industrial societies lacking this political complex, like the USSR, are then held to be deviant or pathological examples of development. In this way, Parsonian theory can easily supply theoretical justification for democratic powers to intervene in Third World affairs where communist movements threaten to take control of the state.

Further important critical contributions may be found in GELLNER (1964), POPPER (1957), and BENDIX (1970). See also EVOLUTIONARY SOCIOLOGY.

neo-Freudians followers of FREUD who have modified his theory, often elaborating and clarifying its concepts and developing it further according to their own experience as analysts.

These theorists emphasize social and cultural influences on the personality and deemphasize the role of biological factors. They regard some parts of his theory, for example, the emphasis on the role of the instincts and particularly of sex as central, as outdated, and they generally find no evidence for the Oedipus complex or the implied inferiority of women except as manifestations of cultural forces. Neurosis is seen as the outcome of problematic interpersonal relationships, and a healthy personality also as a social product.

Among the most influential neo-Freudians are Erich FROMM, Erik Erikson, Carl JUNG, Karen Horney, Harry Stack Sullivan, Alfred Adler, and David Rapaport. Though they can all be regarded as HUMANISTIC, their theories are personally distinctive, and the above generalities are found in different forms in their personal reworkings of Freudian theory.

neo-Kantian applied to German social philosophical movements of the late 19th and early 20th centuries that attempted to return to KANT, acknowledging (a) an objective (or intersubjective) phenomenal realm (natural science), and (b) the social realm, a realm of human ACTION and values. During the METHODENSTREIT of the 1890s, RICKERT and WINDELBAND were particularly influential in reintroducing the idea that mind and mental CATEGORIES shape our perceptions of the world, and in stressing a distinction between the historical and cultural sciences—concerned with unique determinations—and the natural sciences, and insisted that the former required a method that recognized the specificity and value-related nature of their subject matter. They suggested that any attempt to analyze and describe the social world is thus bound to simplify either by imposing general categories or by interpreting reality in relation to its relevance for values. This way of thinking influenced both SIMMEL and WEBER. See also IDIOGRAPHIC AND NOMOTHETIC.

neo-Machiavellians a term sometimes applied to the group of political sociologists and political theorists, especially PARETO, MOSCA, and MICHELS, who in a way analogous to that of Niccolo Machiavelli prided themselves on their realistic analysis of political power, for example, emphasis on the role of elites. See also ELITE, ELITE THEORY.

neo-Marxist denoting any recent theorists and theories that draw on Marx's thinking, or on the Marxist tradition, while at the same time revising and reorienting this, for example, SARTRE's existentialist Marxism or HABERMAS's critical theory.

network theory the doctrine in the philosophy of science associated with Duhem (1861–1916) and Mary Hesse (1980), that scientific statements cannot be appraised in isolation from the overall framework of concepts and theories in which they are stated.

neutralization of deviance the rationalizations of their own actions by which deviants (see DEVIANCE) minimize or justify their deviant acts. See DELINQUENT DRIFT.

new class the concept, first formulated by the Yugoslavian dissident writer Milovan Djilas in 1957, that Eastern European societies had not succeeded in overthrowing class rule and were in fact dominated by a new dominant class of party bureaucrats.

More recently GOULDNER (1979) has generalized the notion, suggesting that despite Marx's assumptions that the underclass in any revolution *never* comes to power, nor do underclasses seem likely to do so in future. Gouldner identifies five theories of the forms in which the *new class* appears within modern societies:

(a) a new class of "benign democrats" and managers, for example, the theories of GALBRAITH, BELL, and of Berle and Means (1932);

(b) the new class as a "master class," which is simply a further "moment in a long-continuing circulation of historical elites," and still exploitive (for example, Bakunin's view);

(c) the new class as "old class ally," in which the new class is seen as "dedicated professionals" who uplift the old moneyed class to a new "collectivity-oriented" view (for example, PARSONS);

(d) the new class as the "servants of power," in which the moneyed or capitalist class retains power much as it always did (for example Zeitlin, 1977);

(e) the new class as a "flawed universal class" (Gouldner's own view); that the new class remains self-seeking and out to control its own work situation, but is "the best card that history has presently given us to play."

Gouldner suggests that the new class in this fifth sense is growing and is more powerful and independent than suggested by Chomsky but less powerful than suggested by Galbraith.

new deviancy theory a radical approach to the study of DEVIANCE that has presented itself as an alternative to positivist approaches, which suggested that one could scientifically establish biological, physiological, psychological, or social determinants of deviance, and that a scientific approach necessitates an objective and nonpolitical stance. Against such deterministic perspectives, new deviancy theory emphasized an interactionist approach that took as central the understanding of the *meanings* of deviant actors and the social construction of deviance. The common starting point for practitioners of new deviancy theory was LABELING, emphasizing SOCIETAL REACTION rather than human nature as a determinant of deviancy. Emerging in the late 1960s and early 1970s, new deviancy theory argued that it was crucial to understand the political implications of deviance, and that the political stance of the researcher should be made explicit. The predominant politics of new deviancy theory were libertarian and hence antiauthority. Typically theorists took the side of the deviant against various forces of reaction: the family, the police, courts, prisons, and the state. This political stance had several consequences. One was an emphasis on the damaging effects of social control—an interest in prisons, for example, that emphasized the brutalizing effects of incarceration and the fact that imprisonment did not deter offenders. Other typical areas of interest were the users of so-called soft drugs (Young, 1971), and studies debunking popular myths about young hooligans (Cohen, 1971) among others. As Young later acknowledged, they tended to take easy topics and frequently ignored the devastating effects of crime, for example, on women, black people, and the working class. For all this, new deviancy theory has been highly influential in developing later criminological approaches. These developments are summarized in Young (1988), and for a selection of papers showing a different line of development see Cohen (1988). See also NATIONAL DEVIANCY CONFERENCE.

new international division of labor (NIDL) the change in the world economy whereby some manufacturing processes are located in the Third World. Frobel et al. (1980) offer the most systematic analysis of this process, arguing that changes in communication and transport in the 1970s, combined with slowdowns of growth and profitability in the most advanced capitalist industrial countries, have made profitable the location of manufacturing in the Third World. Most commonly, assembly processes in textiles and electrical goods were moved by transnational companies to countries that had cheap and politically repressed labor forces. The factories typically were located in free trade zones without tariff or other barriers on imports or exports. Nearly all the production was exported, giving rise to the term *world market factories* and to export-oriented industrialization. Changes in production processes, telecommunications, and transport meant that large firms could use skilled and technical labor for some processes in advanced countries, and untrained, low-paid labor for routine processes elsewhere. Any product could be assembled from components produced in several different countries.

While the term has come into more general usage to account for the emergence of manufacturing processes in poor countries, the analysis provided by Frobel et al. is only partial. As Jenkins (1984 and 1986) has cogently argued, the industrialization process in the Third World is more complex and varied. Thus, little of the Latin American manufacturing capacity is located in world market factories or free trade zones, and much of the Southeast Asian industrialization is locally owned and covers a wider range of processes than routine assembly. But it remains true that some of the poorer and smaller Third World countries may only have this type of manufacturing. Recent changes may be leading to reversal of this process, for example, computerization of textile production favors relocation back to industrialized countries.

new middle class see CONTRADICTORY CLASS LOCATIONS.

new petty bourgeoisie categories of supervisory and mental workers (for example, many office workers) who, according to neo-Marxist theorists such as Poulantazas (1975), should be placed outside the working class (even though they sometimes produce surplus value) but also should not be seen as part of the traditional bourgeoisie, since they do not own or control the means of production. In Poulantazas' view such workers are usually hostile to the working class and, like the traditional petty bourgeoisie, remain caught between labor and capital. See also INTERMEDIATE CLASSES, CONTRADICTORY CLASS LOCATIONS.

new technology any form of technology that is more advanced or automated relative to that which preceded it in a given social context. The term is normally used to refer to information and communications technologies based on microelectronics. "New technology" entered the vocabulary of sociology in the early 1970s. The term is used loosely, often left undefined, or assumed to include the various applications of microelectronics. Other new technologies, such as biotechnology or the technologies of light, have so far received little attention from sociologists.

Developments in information technology have been heralded by some writers as a major qualitative advance in technology, comparable to mechanization and worthy of the labels "information society" and "second industrial revolution" (BELL, 1980). Studies of technology in the 1960s generally divided technical change into three broad stages: craft production, mechanization, and automation (see TECHNOLOGY), but recent research had adopted more complex classifications to describe more accurately the changes involved with information technology. In manufacturing, three broad stages of automation have been identified (Coombs, 1985):

(a) primary mechanization, the transformation of raw materials into products;

(b) secondary mechanization, the mechanization of transfer of materials between machines, for example, the assembly line;

(c) tertiary mechanization, the use of information technology to control and program the operations of transformation and transfer in the overall production process.

Information technology therefore involves a considerable advance in process technology (the way things are done) that is more significant than developments in product technology (what is produced). The implications of process technology for work and employment have been examined in studies of economic growth and innovation and, in sociology, in research into unemployment and the INFORMAL ECONOMY (Pahl and Gershuny, 1979). In the service sector the introduction of information technology has involved similar developments in process technology, in which new computer and communications applications have automated the collection, processing, and retrieval of information. (See the glossary at the end of this entry.)

Sociological research into new technology has included its relationship to changes in occupational structure and unemployment and, in the workplace, changes in the nature of work and work organization. Research on the consequences of the introduction of new technology for overall employment levels is inconclusive. Automation eliminates many routine jobs in both manufacturing and services; at the same time, jobs requiring new skills are created, such as computer programming and highly skilled maintenance and technician jobs. The consequences for employment and the future of work are difficult to estimate on balance, because the assumed effect of new technology cannot be separated from managerial employment strategies and other causes of changes in employment, such as the international division of labor, economic recession, and the market for goods and services. Sociologists have also been concerned with changes in the pattern of employment and the labor market—for example, the possible polarization of the work force into a minority of "technology winners," who are highly skilled and enjoy secure employment, and those who are "technology losers" in the sense that their jobs are either deskilled or displaced altogether. These changes in the occupational structure also reveal inequalities based on class, gender, and race. See also DUAL LABOR MARKET.

These optimistic and pessimistic scenarios for new technology and work are also found in the research on changes in the quality of work. One line of argument develops the earlier work of Woodward (1970), Blauner (1964), and BELL (1980) (see TECHNOLOGY), to argue that new technology permits an increase in skill levels and more participative work organization. In contrast, labor process theory has analyzed the use of new technology for managerial control of the labor force and DESKILLING. Recent research (Piore and Sabel, 1984) into new technology in manufacturing has suggested that new forms of automation (CNC machines and FMS) permit the possibility of *flexible specialization*—multiskilled, "high-trust" work—in contrast to Fordism and Taylorism as predominant features of earlier production systems geared to mass production. However, the evidence for these emerging new work forms is limited and confined to sectors such as machining (see also FORDISM AND POST-FORDISM, SCIENTIFIC MANAGEMENT).

Applied sociological research on new technology has generally been critical of TECHNOLOGICAL DETERMINISM and supportive of programs for human-centered technology.

The following glossary of new technology abbreviations outlines some of the major applications in manufacturing and services.

AMT (Automatic Teller Machines), used in commercial banking.

CAD (Computer-Aided Design), the use of interactive computer graphics, simulation, and design calculation to replace drawing boards.

CAM (Computer-Aided Manufacture), a number of applications that, in combination, lead to a workerless factory (in theory but not in practice). (Included in CAM are several of the more specific terms listed here.)

CAPM (Computer-Aided Production Management), which extends computerization to stock and inventory control.

CIM (Computer-Integrated Manufacture), the integration of CAD, CNC, FMS, etc. into an automated factory.

CNC (Computer Numerical Control), machine tools controlled by their own programmable computer.

EDP (Electronic Data Processing).

EFT (Electronic Funds Transfer), used in banking for instant transfer of funds (cashless).

EPOS (Electronic Point of Sale Machines), gradually being introduced in retailing for transactions by "intelligent" plastic cards.

FMS (Flexible Manufacturing Systems), used in the machine tool industry, and consisting of groups of CNC machines, a transfer system, and a computer to control the sequencing of operations. Flexibility here refers to an automated machining process that is capable of producing a range of parts. This type of automation can be applied to small-batch production in contrast with earlier forms of mass production automation.

MIS (Management Information Systems), computerized information systems for management decision-making and accounting.

NC (Numerical Control), a means of programmed metal-cutting using punched tape, now superseded by the newer technology of CNC.

Robots, machines capable of preprogrammed sequences of action. At present, these are used for relatively simple tasks such as spot-welding or "pick-and-place" in the automobile industry.

new working class a stratum within the WORKING CLASS that is seen as distinguished from the traditional working class, first, by the fact that its members work as technicians in new forms of technologically based industry and, secondly, by a greater labor union militancy, directed at issues of power and control rather than purely economic issues.

This use of the term was originated by the French writer Serge Mallet in 1963 and was adopted in different ways by other French authors, notably Alain Toraine and Andre Gorz (see Mallet, 1975; Gorz, 1967; Toraine, 1971). The argument in some ways recalls that of Blauner (1964). Both Mallet and Blauner saw recent developments in the application of technology to work as having important consequences, but their conclusions are radically different. Blauner saw modern process industry as producing worker satisfaction and harmonious workplace relations. Mallet argued that, compared with the old working class, the work situation of workers in the new automated industries would inevitably produce demands for workers' control that would spread throughout industry and lead to a revolution in capitalist production relations. The nature of automated work, together with the need to maximize efficiency and productivity, would produce a group of workers who were relatively highly trained, autonomous, and highly integrated into the enterprise. These factors of community, knowledge, and power (all encouraged by management in the interests of the enterprise) would facilitate the growth of confidence and demands "to acquire control of the enterprise by and for the workers—and thus to a new political awareness ..." (Mallet, 1975, p. 105).

Mallet's original argument has been criticized and undermined by subsequent empirical studies. Studies of British automated companies by Nichols and Armstrong (1976) and Nichols and Beynon (1977), for example, showed that donkey work was still common and that the new working class remained a minority even in highly automated plants. These studies also suggested that work organization and management strategies were still successful in dividing workers and preventing development of political organization. Similarly, in the best known test of the new working class thesis, Gallie (1978) studied three oil refineries, one in Britain and two in France, finding that technology did not have the effect claimed either by Blauner or by Mallet. Instead, distinct national differences existed between the work forces existed, indicating that wider cultural factors were more important than technology, and no significant amount of support for workers' control was found either in Britain or France. See also AFFLUENT WORKER, ALIENATION, EMBOURGEOISEMENT.

Nietzsche, Friedrich (1844–1900) German thinker of the late 19th century who expressed the sharpest and most alarming doubts about the rationalism, humanism, and scientism that had become the prevailing belief in the West, about the "plausibility of the world." By this he means a world of circumscribed possibilities and outcomes, framed by a single objective truth, prescribing essentially limited forms of human practice and endeavor. He regarded such assumptions as removing responsibility for actions, and as leading to a MASS SOCIETY of mediocrity, hypocrisy, and failure. He challenges objectivity by revealing the desire for power behind claims to knowledge, and by showing the impossibility, as well as the poverty, of a rationalist ethic. To both he opposes the open horizons of art, and of a striving for an excellence and superiority beyond the possible, with a necessary competition and elitism. The supposed political implications of this, including spurious links claimed by National Socialism, made him a favorite target, often unread, for liberals of all persuasions. Nevertheless, his ideas have influenced many sociological writers, notably WEBER and FOUCAULT.

nomads and **nomadism** any people or society, for example, the desert Bedouin of North Africa, distinguished by impermanence of place of residence, and who move from place to place in search of food or pasture. As such, *nomadism* may refer to HUNTER-GATHERER societies as well as to PASTORALISM.

nomenklatura (in the USSR and the remaining state socialist Eastern European countries) **1.** lists of names held by committees of the Communist Party from which are selected candidates for vacancies in state, party, or social organizations, such as labor unions. **2.** people holding positions as in **1.** or on the nomination lists, and in particular those involved in the highest organizations in the countries, and who have been identified by many observers as the rulers of these countries (Voslensky, 1984). Until the late 1980s in the USSR, the existence of such practices was not publicly acknowledged, but under the impetus of glasnost and perestroika, not only were they openly discussed, they were strongly criticized. After the political changes in 1989, this has gone even further in East Europe, and in countries where the Communist Party has been removed from power, such as in Czechoslovakia, the system has broken down. See also STATE SOCIALIST SOCIETIES.

nominalism (philosophy) the doctrine that universal concepts, which define general classes of things (for example, redness, roundness), cannot be conceived of as having real existence in the way that individual things exist (compare ESSENTIALISM).

nomothetic see IDIOGRAPHIC AND NOMOTHETIC.

nondecisions see POWER, COMMUNITY POWER.

nonliterate society a society in which the population do not have access to a system of writing. While it is often regarded as being an evolutionary stage prior to civilization, this view takes no account of the possible complexity of oral traditions. Lengthy myths and systems of genealogy can be preserved by word of mouth, but the possibility of information being disseminated by texts and not individuals undoubtedly contributes to substantial cultural change. It is also important to note that there have been situations in which the minority do have access to writing but the majority do not, thus creating a privileged class of scribes with the power to define versions of the status quo for the nonliterate.

nonparametric statistics statistical methods used for analysis of ordinal and categorical level sample data that do not require assumptions about the shape of the population distribution from which the samples have been drawn. Such statistics are often referred to as "distribution-free statistics." In contrast to PARAMETRIC STATISTICS, assumptions underlying the use of the methods are lenient, and the formulae involved are simple and easy to use. Examples are the runs tests, the signs test, and Cramer's V. Although such measures are popular in sociology, they have the disadvantages that they waste information if interval data are degraded into categorical data, and that the tests are not as powerful as parametric tests (see also SIGNIFICANCE TEST). Against this, they are often more robust, that is, they give the same results despite the violation of assumptions. Hence, if the assumptions of a parametric test are not met, the use of an equivalent nonparametric test will still be valid.

nonresponse a problem in the social sciences caused by people not completing QUESTIONNAIRES, refusing to be interviewed, etc. Nonresponse is a common problem in sociological research, especially in those instances where a POSTAL QUESTIONNAIRE is being used, where a RESPONSE RATE of above 50% is generally considered to be good.

In order to discuss ways of increasing the response rate, it is necessary to consider briefly why people do not return questionnaires. Some people have died or moved before the questionnaires are sent out; others simply refuse to complete questionnaires. Apart from people who have moved, died, etc., probably the main reasons why questionnaires are not returned are forgetfulness and inertia. This problem can be minimized in a number of ways. In constructing the questionnaire, care should be taken in writing and listing the questions to make the questionnaire as simple and easy to complete as possible. In the covering letter, the purposes of the study should be explained and assurances given concerning the confidentiality of the data. A few days after sending the questionnaires, a reminder card should be distributed, and second and even third copies of the questionnaire may be sent to nonrespondents. A shortened version of the questionnaire, asking key questions only, may be sent, or the short questionnaire may be administered by telephone.

A number of techniques exist to calculate the extent to which nonrespondents might differ from respondents. Depending on the data source, the data known about nonrespondents can be coded (see CODING) for analysis and comparison with respondents. For example, a study of young people using addresses obtained from careers offices may make it possible to construct a picture of nonrespondents that includes data on gender, age, examination results, employment status, etc. Also, replies can be weighted on the basis that respondents who reply to the final reminder have more in common with those who replied earlier. It may also be possible to estimate some characteristics of the total population by using alternative data sources (for example, other questionnaire studies, and CENSUS material) and then the data can be weighted accordingly.

nonstructural social mobility see SOCIAL MOBILITY.

norm a standard or rule regulating behavior in a social setting. The idea that social life as an ordered and continuing process is dependent on shared expectations and obligations is commonly found in sociological approaches, although some place more emphasis on it than others. For DURKHEIM, society was theorized as a moral order. This perspective was influential in the development of modern FUNCTIONALISM, particularly in the work of PARSONS, in which the concept of NORMATIVE ORDER is the central element of the SOCIAL SYSTEM. Here the idea of norms is related to SOCIALIZATION and ROLES. These prescriptions operate at every level of society, from individuals' actions in daily life, for example, in table manners or classroom behavior, to the formulation of legal systems in advanced societies. The concept of norms also implies that of SOCIAL CONTROL, that is, positive or negative means of ensuring conformity and applying sanctions to deviant behavior (see DEVIANCE).

Other sociological approaches deal with the issue of social order in rather different ways. In some, RULES are emphasized rather than norms, while in others there is a greater emphasis on POWER and coercion.

normal distribution a continuous distribution of a random VARIABLE with its means, median, and mode equal (see MEASURES OF CENTRAL TENDENCY). Thus the normal curve is symmetrical and bell-shaped as in Fig. 18. See also PROBABILITY.

PARAMETRIC STATISTICS assume that the parent population has a normal distribution. In reality, a normal distribution is only approximated, and this is regarded as acceptable to fulfill this requirement of a parametric test.

normal science and **revolutionary science** the important distinction, drawn by KUHN (1962), between periods of stability of concepts and assumptions in science, and periods of upheaval and rapid change. Contrary to the view that all science is characterized by bold attempts to falsify theories (see FALSIFICATIONISM), Kuhn sees *normal science* as usually involved in puzzle-solving that accepts and works entirely within the assumptions of a particular scientific paradigm. Only when an established paradigm fails to generate new puzzles or is beset by major anomalies do exceptional scientists turn to *revolutionary science*, in that new paradigms are created. Examples of such revolutionary shifts cited by Kuhn are the Copernican and Newtonian revolutions, Dalton's new system in chemistry, and the work of Einstein. In periods of normal science, scientific work is characterized by psychological and social conformity and group solidarity. Scientific revolutions "are like political revolutions" and must struggle to overcome such conformity, and when these occur "there is no standard higher than the standard of the relevant community" (Kuhn, 1977).

normative relating to, or based on, NORMS.

normative functionalism those forms of FUNCTIONALISM that emphasize the importance of the part played by VALUES and value CONSENSUS in the overall INTEGRATION of societies. The charge is often made that these forms of functionalism give disproportionate weight to the importance of values and *normative integration* (including the internalization of values) in producing social integration. The STRUCTURAL-FUNCTIONALISM of Talcott PARSONS is often held to be a prime example. See also SOCIAL INTEGRATION AND SYSTEM INTEGRATION, OVERSOCIALIZED CONCEPTION OF MAN; compare DOMINANT IDEOLOGY THESIS.

normative integration see NORMATIVE FUNCTIONALISM.

normative order a system of rules and standards appropriate to a given social situation. In the work of PARSONS, a normative order is said to comprise two elements: VALUES and NORMS. Norms are rules that are specific to a given social situation, for example, a meeting or a Christmas party. Thus, they are seen as regulating action and relations within a group or system. Values are also moral and regulatory, but they have a wider significance inasmuch as they go beyond a specific situation and are seen as informing norms in different contexts and thus as serving to connect different systems. In Parsonian terms, therefore, the value aspect of the norma-

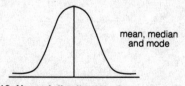

Fig. 18. **Normal distribution.** See main entry.

tive order is crucial in ensuring pattern maintenance (see SUBSYSTEMS MODEL).

normative theory any theory that seeks to establish the VALUES or norms that best fit the overall needs or requirements of society, either societies in general or particular societies, and that would be morally justified. For those who see the aim of modern social science as descriptive and explanatory and not prescriptive, such a goal for social science or sociology is not acceptable. Hence, in these circumstances "normative theory" can be a pejorative term. For others, however, the aim of appraising and establishing values is an important goal, perhaps the most important goal, of the social sciences. See also FACT-VALUE DISTINCTION, VALUE JUDGMENT, VALUE RELEVANCE, VALUE FREEDOM AND VALUE NEUTRALITY, FRANKFURT SCHOOL OF CRITICAL THEORY, POLITICAL SCIENCE.

noumena and phenomena see RATIONALISM.

nuclear family see FAMILY.

null hypothesis a working hypothesis that states there will be no statistically significant difference between the EXPERIMENTAL GROUP and the CONTROL GROUP.

When an experiment is set up, or observational data have been collected, the effort is designed to test a HYPOTHESIS, or theory, that has been developed from previous work. This is the EXPERIMENTAL HYPOTHESIS, and it states what the expected difference is between the groups if the theory is correct. The converse hypothesis is also conventionally stated: this is the null hypothesis—that predictions from the theory are incorrect and there is no difference between the groups in the VARIABLE investigated. See also INDEPENDENT VARIABLE, DEPENDENT VARIABLE.

O

objective 1. (philosophy) existing or held to exist independently of our perceptions, for example, being a material object. **2.** freedom from distorting subjective (personal or emotional) bias. See also OBJECTIVITY, OBJECTIVISM, VALUE FREEDOM AND VALUE NEUTRALITY.

objective class see SUBJECTIVE AND OBJECTIVE CLASS.

objectivism the view that it is possible to provide objective representations and accounts of the external physical and social world, that is, representations that capture these worlds accurately and reliably, without the importation of bias, or the coloring of the view by one's own preferences and prejudices. It is now generally acknowledged that any simple doctrine by which we directly represent the world oversimplifies the degree to which we are able to achieve OBJECTIVITY. A rejection of objectivism, however, need not mean the outright endorsement of its opposite, RELATIVISM. A third argument, which finds much support in modern sociology and philosophy (see Bernstein, 1983), is that we should seek in our epistemological thinking to move "beyond objectivism and relativism," since neither of these can be sustained as a general argument. See also EPISTEMOLOGY, FEYERABEND, KUHN, VALUE FREEDOM AND VALUE NEUTRALITY.

objectivity 1. accounts of the external world held to represent the world as it exists independently of our conceptions. **2.** knowledge claimed to meet criteria of VALIDITY and RELIABILITY and held to be free from BIAS. Most disciplines establish working criteria of objectivity in sense **2.** However, they usually fall well short of providing more than conventional, working answers to the question of what constitutes objectivity in sense **1.**

Problems arise as to whether objectivity is an attainable goal even for the physical sciences. Currently the philosophers' answer is that in any strict sense it is not, since our view of reality is mediated by our finite cognitive abilities and by the ever-changing theories and concepts that always structure our view of reality (see THEORY-RELATIVE, INCOMMENSURABILITY). Thus, claims to knowledge are today more likely to be presented in terms of INTERSUBJECTIVITY and provisional agreements (compare REALISM).

For the social sciences there exist additional difficulties in conception **1.**, in that social reality does *not* exist independently of our collective conceptions of it. However, it can be seen as existing independently of any individual conceptions of it and to this degree as existing objectively. Thus, there seems no reason why social science should not aspire to objectivity, at least in sense **1.**, always accepting that this must *include* objective accounts of what social actors hold subjectively in constituting and reproducing their social worlds. That objective accounts may be difficult to

achieve, must be recognized. What is *not* acceptable is any dogmatic assertion of objective forms of measurements (for example, fixed-choice questionnaires insensitive to nuances of meaning) on the assumption that such
methods constitute the only way in which social science can be rendered
truly scientific (see MEASUREMENT BY FIAT, CICOUREL, OFFICIAL STATISTICS;
compare SOCIAL FACTS AS THINGS). See also EPISTEMOLOGY, TRUTH, ONTOL-
OGY, IDEALISM, POSITIVISM, EMPIRICISM, RELATIVISM.

objectivity and neutrality see VALUE FREEDOM AND VALUE NEUTRALITY.

occupational class see CLASS and OCCUPATIONAL SCALES.

occupational scales measures of the prestige status, social standing,
and/or social class position of different occupations. Mainly used in the
study of SOCIAL STRATIFICATION and SOCIAL MOBILITY, occupational scales
are constructed in one of four ways—the intuitive, relational, constructed,
and reputational—all of which are based on the premise that it is possible
to arrange occupations hierarchically through similarities of market and
status situation. In intuitive approaches, researchers rank occupations on
the basis of the researchers' subjective assessments of the social standing of
the occupations in the community. In relational approaches, occupations
are ranked on the assumption that people mix with others of broadly similar social standing to themselves. In constructed approaches, a number of
different factors, such as income and levels of education, are used to rank
occupations. In the reputational approach a group of people chosen at random are asked to rank occupations according to their perceived standing in
the community, and the social ranking of each occupation is then calculated on the basis of the replies.

Probably the occupational scale most widely used in Britain, for example, is the *Registrar General's Classification*, devised using the intuitive
approach for the 1911 CENSUS and extensively modified for use in subsequent censuses. To use this schema, details are needed of each individual's
precise job title, employment status (self-employed/employer/employee),
industry of employment, and educational qualifications. In its original form
this had five SOCIAL CLASSES:

Class I (senior professionals): doctors, lawyers, accountants, etc.;

Class II (intermediate occupations): teachers, nurses, and managers;

Class III: all people in skilled occupations, both white collar and blue
collar;

Class IV: semiskilled workers, such as agricultural workers and machine
operators;

Class V: laborers and others in unskilled occupations.

In 1961, Class III was subdivided into Class IIIN (white collar workers
such as clerks and shop assistants), and Class IIIM (manual workers such
as underground workers in mines, welders, and carpenters).

The main advantage of using the Registrar General's classification is that
a detailed list of occupational titles is regularly produced, giving each occu-

pation a number determined by its social class position, industry, and employment status. These codes can then be combined to form the six social classes. In 1961 the Registrar General introduced a new form of coding in which occupations are assigned to 17 socioeconomic groups, which can be further combined to form an alternative schema:

Class 1: professionals;

Class 2: employers and managers;

Class 3: intermediate and junior nonmanual;

Class 4: skilled manual, foremen, and self-employed;

Class 5: semiskilled and personal service;

Class 6: unskilled manual.

Further changes were introduced into the Registrar General's schema in 1981 in which occupations are coded in such a way as to make the schema comparable with the International Standard Classification of Occupations.

Historical data, such as those obtained from the 19th century census enumeration books, cannot be coded using the Registrar General's classification because of the amount of detail necessary. However, Armstrong (1972) demonstrates how the 1951 classification can be adapted for use by historical sociologists.

One of the problems with the Registrar General's Occupational Scale is that, since it was constructed using the intuitive approach, it cannot easily be used to test sociological theories. For example, it cannot be used to identify the bourgeoisie and petty bourgeoisie. One attempt to overcome this problem has been made by GOLDTHORPE and Llewellyn (1977), who devised their own social class schema based on the work of Hope and GOLDTHORPE (1974). The *Hope-Goldthorpe Scale* was constructed using the reputational approach, and occupations need to be precoded according to the full Registrar General's 1971 classification. Occupations are then combined into 36 distinct hierarchically arranged groups with similar levels of "social desirability" and separate categories for employers, managers, professionals, the self-employed, technical, white-collar, agricultural, supervisory, and manual workers. These categories are recombined by Goldthorpe and Llewellyn into seven social classes. Class I, high-grade professionals, managers, administrators, and large proprietors; Class II, lower grade professionals and managers, and higher grade technicians; Class III, routine nonmanual workers; Class IV, small proprietors and the self-employed; Class V, lower grade technicians and supervisors of manual workers; Class VI, skilled manual workers; and Class VII, semiskilled and unskilled manual workers. The Hope-Goldthorpe schema was devised to study the occupations and social class positions of men, so its use in studies of women's employment has been questioned.

occupational structure the DIVISION OF LABOR within the economy, and by extension also society, largely in sectoral and status terms. Sectorally, the division of occupations has been classified into primary, secondary, and tertiary sectors, a schema commonly used by sociologists studying INDUSTRIALIZATION and POSTINDUSTRIAL SOCIETY. In status terms the concept centrally informs the study of socioeconomic categories (CLASSES) for, in Parkin's (1971) classic statement, "The backbone of the class structure ... of modern Western society, is the occupational order." Probably the best known and most used schema (in Britain) has been developed by GOLDTHORPE et al. (1980), derived from the earlier Hope-Goldthorpe Scales (see OCCUPATIONAL SCALES) for the analysis of SOCIAL MOBILITY. The concept has historically been blind to the involvement of women in the work force, tending to focus on the occupations of adult males only (Walby, 1986).

occupational transition see SOCIAL MOBILITY.

official statistics any data collected and published by government departments. Such data have varied reliability and utility. Although many of these data can be highly valuable to the sociologist, for example, those presented in the CENSUS, major debates exist concerning the limitations of official statistics (for example, CRIME STATISTICS). The way in which statistics are collected, for example, as a by-product of the work of administrative agencies, sometimes by a large number of untrained recorders, can lead to major inconsistencies, unreliability, and uncertainties about the meaning and worth of data. Also, statistics may have positive or negative implications for the agencies and individuals that collect them, which can affect what is recorded. Finally, statistics are always collected for some purpose, which will usually be different from that of the sociological researcher; above all, they are the result of a process of categorization and the attachment of numbers, which involves inherent difficulties of the kind identified particularly by ethnomethodologists (see CICOUREL, 1964). A classic example of the issues that can arise is the debate concerning DURKHEIM's use of SUICIDE statistics (see Douglas, 1967). See also MEASUREMENT BY FIAT.

old age the last part of the individual LIFE COURSE, associated with declining faculties, low social worth, and detachment from previous social commitments. It is a social construct rather than a biological stage, since its onset and significance vary historically and culturally. See also AGING, GERONTOLOGY.

oligarchy see IRON LAW OF OLIGARCHY.

one-party system, one party-state, or **one-party rule** a political system and state in which a single political party rules and opposition political parties are not permitted or are precluded from rule. As well as being a feature until recently of eastern European socialist and communist states and of other systems based on Marxism, one-party systems have also been introduced by rulers in developing societies, in which the existence of ethnic and tribal divisions (rather than modern class divisions) are claimed to provide an unsuitable basis for two-party or multiparty democracies (compare STABLE DEMOCRACY).

ontology the branch of philosophy (and *metaphysics*) concerned with establishing the nature of the fundamental kinds of things that exist in the world, for example, "Do minds exist?" Examples of philosophical ontological theory are Plato's theory of forms, or recently, scientific realism, which asks, "What kinds of things are presupposed by scientific theories?"

Ontological arguments are also an explicit (or implicit) feature of sociological theory itself, for example, DURKHEIM's conception of "social facts," WEBER's (or the SYMBOLIC INTERACTIONIST's) emphasis on individual actors, or MARX's materialism and emphasis on modes and relations in production.

One argument (HUME's view) is that ontological inquiries are bound to be inconclusive or are even pointless. Against this, the clarification of underlying assumptions is often important. Undoubtedly, debate in sociology since COMTE, much of it broadly ontological in nature, has done much to clarify the nature, while also underlining the very great complexity, of "social kinds" (social action, social structures, etc.). However, it has done so not as a separate realm of inquiry, but as an inherent part of sociological inquiry properly conducted. Philosophy can inform these discussions, but it is no longer regarded as the kind of *final* arbiter it was once assumed to be. The expectation must be that ontologies will change as knowledge and individual sciences and modes of study change (compare EPISTEMOLOGY, KUHN, FEYERABEND).

open-ended question a type of question in a QUESTIONNAIRE in which the respondent's choice of answer is not prestructured but is left entirely free. Analysis of open-ended questions is obviously less straightforward than for FIXED-CHOICE QUESTIONS, which can be precoded. However, open-ended questions have the advantage of *not* imposing a frame of reference on respondents (see MEASUREMENT BY FIAT). For this reason they may be preferred to fixed-choice questions in some contexts and by some researchers (for example, as an adjunct to PARTICIPANT OBSERVATION or in the early exploratory stages of research), and can be used alongside fixed-choice questions as appropriate. See also SOCIAL SURVEY.

open society Karl POPPER's conception of a "free society," in which all forms of knowledge and all social policies can be openly criticized. He regards it as the only form of society compatible with his falsificationist and critical rationalist epistemology (see also FALSIFICATIONISM, HISTORICISM sense **2.**). However, Popper's conception has been criticized (for example, by FEYERABEND) as open only in an elitist way and involving a "guided exchange" between competing views, where all the parties to an open debate are required to accept falsificationism. In this, Feyerabend finds Popper's concept less open and less acceptable than the conception of a liberal society found in J.S. MILL's *On Liberty* (1859).

operant conditioning see CONDITIONING.

operationalism or **operationism** the philosophical doctrine that defines scientific concepts entirely in terms of the working (that is, operational) procedures with which they are associated. In the form proposed by the physicist P.W. Bridgman (1927), the doctrine, though intended to be empiricist (for example, to exclude all reference in science to "unobservables"), in fact appears as a radical form of CONVENTIONALISM. In social science, an example of operationalism is the statement that "intelligence is what intelligence tests measure." Seen thus, the limitations of operationalism are obvious: science in all its forms would be condemned to having no rational way of judging between concepts in terms of realism, for example, between different measures of intelligence. Operationalism should be distinguished from OPERATIONALIZATION, which need not depend on operationalism.

operationalization the process of defining a concept empirically so that it can be measured, and repeated observations can be made that are RELIABLE and VALID. Thus, intelligence can be defined as what INTELLIGENCE TESTS measure (though this is not recommended), and social class can be defined in terms of occupation, income, and life style. The danger, as with any attempt at QUANTIFICATION, is that much information implicit in the original concept is lost by a categorization that tends to oversimplify, so the operationalization may not be valid. Selection of relevant measures to be included in the quantification also introduces the possibility of BIAS. See also OPERATIONALISM.

operationism see OPERATIONALISM.

opinion leaders the minority of individuals in any area of social life who influence the ideas of others. LAZARSFELD et al. (1944) introduced this term in connection with their account of VOTING BEHAVIOR and a TWO-STEP FLOW OF MASS COMMUNICATIONS.

oral tradition the aspects of a society's CULTURE that are passed on by word of mouth. Some societies (see NONLITERATE SOCIETY) may rely solely on this method of documenting their history and GENEALOGY through song, poetry, and narrative. In literate societies the oral tradition usually plays an increasingly marginal role in culture transmission and may often stand in opposition to the dominant forms of representation. While anthropologists have long been interested in folklore and storytelling, sociologists and social historians are now also using this method to document the histories of groups (for example, women, ethnic minorities, and the working class) who have not previously been focused on in the written tradition.

ordinal level measurement see CRITERIA AND LEVELS OF MEASUREMENT.

ordinary language philosophy a detailed analysis of language in use. Also referred to as *linguistic philosophy* (or *analysis*), and *Oxford philosophy*, the term applies to a group of Oxford philosophers (Austin, Moore, and Ryle) influenced by the philosophy of WITTGENSTEIN. The aim of this ordinary language philosophy is to analyze natural language as a flexible rule-governed practice. This approach contrasts with that of the logical positivists (see LOGICAL POSITIVISM), who wished to rid language of metaphysics by reducing it to an "object language" capable of rigorous logical investigation. Ordinary language philosophers prefer to dissolve rather than solve problems, demonstrating that puzzlement often occurs only when metaphysics is used. Their own image of it is as a form of philosophy dispelling linguistic confusions, a view reflected in the title of Austin's *How to Do Things with Words* (1962).

Approaches in sociology that emphasize the importance of everyday language and talk (for example, ETHNOMETHODOLOGY and CONVERSATION ANALYSIS), have been influenced by ordinary language philosophy (see also SPEECH ACTS).

organic analogy see FUNCTION; see also ANALOGY.

organic solidarity see MECHANICAL AND ORGANIC SOLIDARITY.

organization 1. a type of collectivity established to pursue specific aims or goals, characterized by a formal structure of rules, authority relations, a division of labor, and limited membership or admission. The term is used mainly to refer to large-scale or complex organizations, which pervade all aspects of social life in modern society, for example, business enterprises, schools, hospitals, churches, prisons, the military, political parties, and labor unions. Such organizations involve patterns of social relationships that differ from other social groups such as the family, peer groups, and neighborhoods, which are largely spontaneous, unplanned, or informal (compare PRIMARY GROUP). Forms of association in organizations tend to occupy only a segment of a person's life (with the notable exception of TOTAL ORGANIZATIONS). **2.** any purposeful arrangement of social activity or set of activities (compare SOCIAL STRUCTURE). Organization in this sense implies active control over human relations for specific ends, for example, work organization to specify allocation and coordination of tasks, patterns of authority, forms of recruitment, and employment relationships.

Organization and BUREAUCRACY are frequently treated as synonymous, inappropriately, since although all modern bureaucracies are organizations, not all organizations are bureaucracies. WEBER, for example, was careful to distinguish organization (*Verband*) from bureaucracy, since the former could include patterns of domination other than the legal-rational type characteristic of modern bureaucracy.

The fundamental problem in defining organization **1.** concerns the specification of organizational goals. To state that organizations have goals either reifies the collective concept of organization or assumes that the goals of an organization are identical to those defined by the power holders at the apex of the organization (see FUNCTIONALISM). Clearly, organizations as such have no goals. Rather, groups and individuals within organizations may hold a variety of different and competing goals. Organizational controllers may attempt to establish overarching goals for the organization through selection, training, rewards, and punishments, and the perpetuation of an "organization culture," but the nature and extent of compliance by subordinates and the degree of cooperation and conflict within an organization can only be established by empirical research. This issue is reflected in the distinction between *formal* and *informal organization*. The former refers to the official hierarchy and lines of authority, with their spans of control, as first described by formal theorists of organization and scientific management; the latter refers to the ways in which official rules are negotiated or subverted through informal practices of subordinates, as in the early Hawthorne experiments. See HUMAN RELATIONS SCHOOL.

There is, in fact, no generally accepted definition of organization; its meaning varies in terms of the different theoretical approaches to organization in the literature (see ORGANIZATION THEORY).

organizational culture the particular configuration of norms, values, beliefs, and ways of behaving that characterize the manner in which groups and individuals collaborate within organizations.

Organizational culture became a prominent concern within American and British management schools in the 1980s as a result of three main factors:

(a) the challenge of Japanese competition;

(b) concern over the economic recovery of industry;

(c) the apparent failure of previously attempted solutions to organizational inefficiencies based on alternative forms of organizational design, for example, matrix structures. See also ORGANIZATION.

This concern has been principally a prescriptive one, exemplified in the works of the American authors Deal and Kennedy (1982) and in Britain by Handy's four-part cultural schema (1984). One has to look elsewhere for sociologically informed analyses. Currently, the main writer on the subject who adopts such an approach is Pettigrew (1973), although Morgan's treatment of the subject (1986) is also relevant. Both authors point out the role of managerial power and control in the shaping of organizational culture.

Deal and Kennedy's (1982) analysis is prescriptive in intent and sets out to identify the rites and rituals of corporate life that constitute corporate cultures and the authors argue that business success relies on what they refer to as "strong culture." Successful corporations have "values and beliefs to pass along—not just products" (ibid.). The authors describe organizational culture as possessing five elements: (i) business environment, (ii) values, (iii) heroes, (iv) rituals, and (v) cultural network (that is, informal communications). This model does have the merit of specifying what the dimensions of organizational culture are believed to be. Its main limitation is its assumption that organizational cultures need to be of a particular kind if the organization is to be successful. This conclusion results from a preparedness to overgeneralize from research on a sample of powerful corporations. Such conclusions may be less applicable for organizations operating in different markets, with different technologies, and employing fewer highly qualified employees (see CONTINGENCY THEORY).

Handy (1985) offers a more complex model, which is able to distinguish between different cultural forms and organizational types. This model is based on an earlier one designed to distinguish between organizational ideologies. Handy's view of organizational culture is, in general terms, similar to that of Deal and Kennedy (1982) in that organizational culture is "... founded and built over the years by the dominant groups in an organization" (ibid.). Handy, however, differs from Deal and Kennedy in arguing that there are four main types of culture, not just "strong" and "weak" cultures. The Handy schema lists *power, role, task*, and *person* cultures as viable alternatives, each of which can be an effective culture within the appropriate context (1985).

There is, however, more to organizational culture than managerial prescriptions and manipulation. Pettigrew has argued that organizational cultures relate also to the language, ideology, and beliefs as well as the dominant symbols, rituals, and myths of work organizations. Moreover, organizational culture is also part of a wider political and cultural system within which values and interests are often subject to negotiation and bargaining. This means that organizational culture is neither homogeneous nor wholly constructed by senior management. For a sociologically grounded analysis, it would be necessary to look to INTERPRETIVE SOCIOLOGY and in particular the ACTION APPROACH (Burrell and Morgan, 1979; Silverman, 1970).

organizational sociology see ORGANIZATION THEORY.

organization theory 1. the sociological and multidisciplinary analysis of organizational structure and the dynamics of social relationships in organizations. Topics studied are formal and informal structures of control, task allocation, decision-making, management and professionals in organizations, innovation, technology, and organizational change. Major contributing disciplines, apart from sociology, include psychology, economics, management science, and administrative theory. The psychological emphasis on individual behavior is concerned with the study of motivation and reward, leadership and decision-making. This is frequently referred to under the title *Organization Theory and Behavior.* Inputs from management science and administrative theory have tended to stress the relationship between organizational design and behavior and the efficiency and effectiveness of organization arrangements. Organization theory is a subject normally found in the curriculum of most business and management courses. **2.** an alternative term for the specialist area, *Sociology of Organizations* or *Organizational Sociology.* Its subject content is often indistinguishable from the applied field of organization theory. Nevertheless, the subdiscipline can be identified by the use of perspectives and discussion of issues closer to mainstream academic sociology and derived particularly from Weber's ideal type of bureaucracy. There is also a focus on all types of organization, including nonprofit organizations, such as schools, hospitals, prisons, and mental institutions in an attempt to arrive at a general theory of organizations (for example, PARSONS, 1956), develop typologies of organizations, and explain similarities and differences in organizational structure. In practice, the boundaries between the multidisciplinary study of organization theory and the sociology of organizations are difficult to discern, since writers in these fields often publish in the same journals (for example, *Administrative Science Quarterly*), and many organizational issues (such as managerial strategy, decision-making, and innovation) draw upon a multidisciplinary framework. Since the 1970s much sociological writing on organizations has adopted a more critical stance toward managerially defined applied issues and problems in organizations, such as worker motivation and efficiency, in an attempt to reestablish the study of organizations in historical context and in relation to the wider society, to include, for example, studies of the way in which class and gender inequalities are reproduced in organizational contexts, for example, Clegg and Dunkerley (1970).

Weber's ideal type of bureaucracy provided the point of departure for the postwar development of a sociology of organizations. GOULDNER's (1955a) distinction between punishment-centered and representative bureaucracy and Burns and Stalker's (1961) comparison of mechanistic and organic forms of organization have been particularly influential for later research. Gouldner demonstrated how bureaucratic rules can be resisted and suggested that bureaucratization can take different forms with varying levels of participation by its members. The contrast between mechanistic and organic organization was used by Burns and Stalker to suggest that different organizational structures are appropriate, depending on the degree of stability or uncertainty in the environment. Mechanistic structures are bureaucratic, hierarchical, and rigid in contrast to organic structures, which are flexible, decentralized, and more able to cope with innovation and rapidly changing environments. Comparison between organizations was further elaborated in the attempt to develop general organization typologies based on, for example, the criterion of "Who benefits?" (BLAU, 1955) and on TYPES OF COMPLIANCE (Etzioni, 1961).

The subsequent development of organization theory reflects both the various theoretical approaches in sociology as a whole and the influence of managerial perspectives, particularly SCIENTIFIC MANAGEMENT and the HUMAN RELATIONS SCHOOL. FUNCTIONALISM has exerted a powerful influence on organizational theory either explicitly, as in the concept of the organization as a system (see SYSTEMS THEORY), or implicitly via assumptions about organizational survival and adaptation to the environment. Organizations have been conceptualized as "open systems" with an emphasis on "input-output" exchanges between the organization and its environment. In similar vein, the Tavistock Institute in England (Trist et al., 1963) has used the concept of "sociotechnical system" (see SOCIOTECHNICAL SYSTEMS APPROACH) to describe the interaction between technical production requirements and social system needs and to demonstrate that a variety of forms of work organization are compatible with given types of technology allowing a degree of organizational choice.

Contingency theory (Pugh et al., 1968; Lawrence and Lorsch, 1967) has synthesized many of these findings, drawing on the work of Burns and Stalker on the impact of the environment, and Woodward's (1970) comparison of organizational structures in relation to levels of technological complexity in the production process (see TECHNOLOGY). Contingency theory uses an empirical, survey approach to establish correlations between contextual variables (size, technology, and environment), structural aspects of the organization (degree of formalization, standardization, and centralization) and their effect on performance. This approach has been embraced by management theorists because of its potential in relating organizational design to performance, and the implication that earlier prescriptions from Scientific Management for organizational blueprints or "one best way" are inaccurate. Interestingly, contingency approaches have been criticized by management theorists with the renewed emphasis on universal principles, such as the need for a power organizational culture (Peters and Waterman, 1982) in response to the success of Japanese managerial methods (Ouchi, 1981). In sociology, contingency theory has been heavily criticized for different reasons, namely: its deterministic assumptions, empiricism, and the weakness of the correlations established. The neglect of power relations by contingency theorists has been stressed by Child (1985), who proposes a *strategic contingency* approach to organizations that concentrates on the role of managerial choice in actively shaping organizational structures in response to contingencies. Contingent factors, such as the environment, are, in turn, not treated as independent variables but are partly chosen or controlled by powerful organizations (multinationals, for example). The study of power relations and decision-making in organizations has been influenced by Simon's (1957a & b) concept of BOUNDED RATIONALITY and includes the analysis of organizational "micropolitics" (Perrow, 1979).

Interactionist contributions to organization theory have emphasized the socially constructed nature of organizational arrangements as "negotiated orders" and the precariousness of organizational rules (Silverman, 1970) as a corrective to the top-down systems view of organizational life. Perspectives derived from SYMBOLIC INTERACTIONISM have informed an expanding area of current research into organizational cultures using ETHNOGRAPHIC methods.

ostensive definition see DEFINITION.

other-directedness an attitudinal orientation or personality type in which a person's sense of social identity depends on the approval of others. In the twofold schema proposed by RIESMAN (1950), other-directedness is contrasted with *inner-directedness,* in which a person's behavior and sense of social identity is mainly governed by internalized standards and con-science. Riesman's suggestion was that modern societies like the United States, dominated by mass consumption, were increasingly moving toward other-direction and an anxiety-riven conformity; a fear of not fitting in (other-direction), rather than a deeper sense of guilt or shame (inner-direction).

out-group see IN-GROUP AND OUT-GROUP.

overdetermination 1. for FREUD, the process in which a condensation of a number of complex thoughts gives rise to a single image, as in recurring dreams. **2.** by analogy with the above, the combined outcome of the multiple contradictions existing in the different areas of a social formation at any given time, in which, according to Louis ALTHUSSER (1969), each contradiction is "inseparable from the total structure of the social body" and is determined by and in turn also determines this total structure. The existence of such overdetermination is seen as accounting for such phenomena as uneven development, since complex overdeterminations mean that no social formation develops simply.

oversocialized conception of Man the charge (for example, by Dennis Wrong, 1960) that functionalist theory, including the work of DURKHEIM and PARSONS, in answering the Hobbesian question of what "makes possible an enduring society" has tended to overstate the "internalization of values." Likewise, Marxian sociology is also seen as often taking an "overintegrated view of society" in answering the question of how "complex societies manage and regulate and restrain … conflicts between groups." See also SOCIAL INTEGRATION AND SYSTEM INTEGRATION.

Oxford philosophy see ORDINARY LANGUAGE PHILOSOPHY.

P

panel study a technique for investigating change over time in the attitudes or opinions of a SAMPLE of people. This is a form of LONGITUDINAL STUDY, but is usually distinguished as being of shorter duration or more focused. It involves questioning the same sample at (regular) intervals to observe trends of opinion, for example, voting intention and party preference before, during, and after an election. As with any longitudinal study, this method may have advantage compared with CROSS-SECTIONAL STUDIES, since the sample members remain constant, and change can be monitored using data gathered before and after it. Against this, some respondents may be lost through death, removal, or lack of interest, and those that remain may become atypical through the experience of being panel members (compare HAWTHORNE EFFECT).

panopticon a design for British PRISONS that was intended to allow guards to oversee every aspect of the inmates' lives. As such, the panopticon has often been regarded as symptomatic of a new emphasis on SURVEILLANCE and SOCIAL CONTROL in modern societies (see also FOUCAULT).

Invented by the English UTILITARIAN philosopher Jeremy BENTHAM in the early 19th century, the panopticon was intended as a new, rational prison design, geared to personal reform as well as confinement and punishment. The idea did not only relate to the structure of the building, but involved a complete philosophy of imprisonment, incorporating ideological and organizational features as well as architectural ones. These included a strictly organized day, based around the reformatory influences of hard work and prayer, based on a single-cell system so as to avoid the moral contagion of association with other criminals. The physical design was intended to make constant observation and control possible. In many respects this idea broke sharply with previous conceptions of imprisonment and may be seen as part of a rationalization and rethinking of the role of imprisonment. It was linked to new ideas about the value of work: indeed, many writers have argued that there was an integral connection in Britain between the developing factory system and the regulation of the poor through the Poor Law and the reorganized prison system, although the early expressions of this theory are sometimes considered overstated. What is clear is that the panopticon may be seen in a context of major revision in the ideology of punishment and correction. It influenced a number of prison projects in Britain, the United States, and elsewhere. See also CRIMINOLOGY.

paradigm any example or representative instance of a concept or a theoretical approach, for example, MERTON's (1949) summary exemplifying discussion of the strengths and pitfalls of functional analysis in sociology. In some branches of philosophy a "paradigm case" is seen as providing an "ostensive definition" of a concept.

parametric statistics inferential statistics that assume that the population from which the SAMPLE has been drawn has a particular form, that is, they involve hypotheses about population parameters. These assumptions are generally that the populations involved have a NORMAL DISTRIBUTION, that they have equal variances (see MEASURES OF DISPERSION), and that the data are at interval level (see CRITERIA AND LEVELS OF MEASUREMENT). Examples are the PEARSON PRODUCT MOMENT CORRELATION COEFFICIENT, multiple regression, and analysis of variance. Such procedures use all available information, and tests are more powerful than nonparametric tests. In sociology, the problem of data that are not normally distributed in the population frequently arises. A transformation of scale, a reliance on the robustness of the technique, or a move to a nonparametric equivalent are the available solutions. Compare NONPARAMETRIC STATISTICS.

parasuicide see ATTEMPTED SUICIDE AND PARASUICIDE.

Pareto, Vilfredo (1848–1923) French-born, Italian engineer and social scientist who turned to sociology in later life. In social science, he sought to apply the principles of mechanical systems in equilibrium with social systems, an approach that influenced Talcott PARSONS. He is best known in sociology for his work on political ELITES.

His first recognition in social science was as an economist, in which subject he is still remembered for his ideas on the distribution of income (see PARETO OPTIMALITY). Disillusioned with liberal politics and believing that political economy could not ignore psychological and sociological factors, the major focus of his sociological analysis was on social differentiation as an enduring feature of social and political life, including a distinction between elites and masses.

Critical of SPENCER's evolutionism as well as MARX's socialism, Pareto made the "unequal distribution of capacities" the bedrock of sociological theory. He accepted neither liberal nor Marxian conceptions of social progress. Rather he saw history as involving the endless CIRCULATION OF ELITES. According to Pareto, "a political system in which the 'people' expresses its will (supposing it had one, which is arguable) without cliques, intrigues, lobbies and factions, exists only as a pious wish of theorists. It is not observable in the past or present either in the West or anywhere else."

As Pareto conceived of it, much of social life was governed by the operation of underlying nonrational psychological forces (see RESIDUES AND DERIVATIONS). These, he believed, had been ignored by most previous theorists, and had been given a proper scientific analysis only by him. Above all he distinguished between nonlogical and logical forms of action (see LOGICAL AND NONLOGICAL ACTION). Previous theorists had simply underestimated the extent of the former, while overestimating the movement from nonrationality to rationality in human societies. Equilibrium in societies is seen by Pareto as something that can only be understood as the outcome of the complex interplay of sentiments and interests.

Pareto's major sociological work, *Trattoto di sociologia generale*, first published in Italy in 1916 (and translated as *The Mind and Society*, 1936) is a rambling treatise of very great length, in which, despite great pretensions to a new scientific rigor, his ideas are illustrated rather than systematically tested. While his contribution to ELITE THEORY and his conception of "social system" influenced many (including Mussolini), no one now accepts the detail of his sociological thinking.

Pareto optimality a theoretical condition of the economy in which the distribution of economic welfare cannot be improved for any one individual without reducing the welfare of one or more other individuals. Thus a "Pareto improvement" occurs when a reallocation of resources renders one or more persons better off. In any situation where more than one optimum is possible, Pareto optimality cannot be established.

pariah 1. in India, a member of a low CASTE or "untouchable" group, thus subject to ritual and social exclusion. **2.** by analogy, any social outcast, or stigmatized individual or group.

Park, Robert (1864–1944) influential US sociologist and Professor of Sociology at the University of Chicago. As well as writing, with Ernest Burgess, a major general textbook on sociology (*Introduction to the Science of Society*), he is best remembered for his contributions to URBAN SOCIOLOGY and to the study of race relations. Park studied under William James and also under WINDELBAND and SIMMEL. His general sociology was eclectic, combining insights drawn from a variety of American and European sources. Along with other members of the CHICAGO SCHOOL, he influenced research methods and attached a new importance to empirical studies in sociology, especially studies based on PARTICIPANT OBSERVATION.

Parsons, Talcott (1902–1979) American sociologist, who was arguably the most influential American sociologist of the 20th century, and the leading modern exponent of FUNCTIONALISM. Because his concerns ranged so widely, it is difficult to summarize even Parsons' main ideas briefly.

Among his earliest work was a translation of Max WEBER's *The Protestant Ethic and the Spirit of Capitalism*, which did much to introduce Weber's work to US sociologists. His first major volume in his own right, *The Structure of Social Action* (1937), involved an assessment of the theoretical legacy of PARETO, DURKHEIM, and Weber—as usual in Parson's work, Marx was a conspicuous omission. All three of these thinkers were presented as attempting to provide a solution to what Parsons called "the problem of social order": why is it that society is not characterized by a Hobbesian war of all against all?

In this first stage of his thinking, Parsons saw himself as working within an *"action frame of reference,"* viewing social action as "voluntaristic." All three of his chosen theorists were presented as contributing to the repudiation of a merely "positivistic theory of social action." Based on their work, he saw himself as working toward achievement of a single, coherent, analytical sociological theory of voluntaristic social action. This involved repudiation of all theories that represented social action merely as an automatic response to external stimuli, or sought to account for social order simply in terms of "coercion" or "self interest."

For Parsons, in *The Structure of Social Action* and subsequently, the answer to the "Hobbesian question" was that social action is engendered, although not simply determined, by shared NORMS and VALUES. These ideas were developed in the direction of functionalism and SYSTEMS THEORY, especially in *The Social System* (1951), and *Towards a General Theory of Action* (1951), the latter written with Edward Shils. Three main aspects of Parsons' thinking in this period can be identified:

(a) the notion of FUNCTIONAL PREREQUISITES of society;

(b) a conception of social order that presents societies as internally interrelated and self-sustaining SOCIAL SYSTEMS, operating in an external environment;

(c) the general theory of action systems, developed from the work of Robert Bales (for example, *Working Papers in the Theory of Action*, Parsons, Bales, and Shils, 1953)—see SUBSYSTEMS MODEL.

In a final phase of his work, Parsons also added to these a neo-evolutionary model of social development (see EVOLUTIONARY UNIVERSALS, NEO-EVOLUTIONARY THEORY). All these elements of Parsons' work were enormously influential at the time. Parsons' books became virtual bibles for a generation of functionalist sociologists. However, an increasing emphasis on the primacy of norms and values in his work, allied with his systems perspective (see CYBERNETIC HIERARCHY), also led to much criticism. For example, as well as the many general criticisms increasingly directed at functionalism and evolutionary theory (see FUNCTIONALIST EXPLANATION), the suspicion grew that Parsons' thinking involved an OVERSOCIALIZED CONCEPTION OF MAN and fostered conservatism. The result of this was that in the 1970s and 80s, when the general dominance of functionalism within US sociology also declined, interest in Parsons' work waned, but it has enjoyed a minor revival of late.

As well as his contributions to general theory, some of Parsons' briefer, more empirical applications of his theory have also been significant and can be said to have stood the test of time rather better than his overall functionalist framework, for example, essays on the SICK ROLE, on POWER, on education, and on racial integration. In these Parsons displays a sharp analytical flair in the application of general conceptions to particular cases. Research inspired by the Parsonian conceptual legacy has also been extensive, especially research based on his conception of PATTERN VARIABLES. At its peak, Parsons' influence on American sociology was immense. In

Britain his role as a *bête noir* has tended to overshadow his considerable contribution to questions of how to theorize about society. See also SOCIAL INTEGRATION AND SYSTEM INTEGRATION, MILLS, MERTON, THEORIES OF THE MIDDLE RANGE, GOULDNER.

participant observation a method of social research in which the researcher becomes a participant in a naturally occurring social activity. Supporters of the method contrast it favorably with other research methods such as EXPERIMENTAL METHODS or FIXED-CHOICE QUESTIONNAIRES, which are seen as introducing artificiality into social observation and investigation.

In participant observation, data are collected informally in the course of a researcher's interactions in normal social life. However, the accurate recording of data and systematically focused intensive INTERVIEWS of key informants are normally an essential feature of the approach, and these are often also supplemented by documentary evidence.

While some participant observers have been content to write up their findings in the form of descriptive ETHNOGRAPHIES, claims to greater generalization may also be advanced (see ANALYTICAL INDUCTION). Participant observation is seen to good effect in the work of Erving GOFFMAN on asylums and of Howard BECKER on marijuana use.

The generalizability of research findings need not be a problem for participant observation, but problems do arise in:

(a) the labor-intensive character and the expense of the method, given that lengthy periods of observation are usually required;

(b) the difficulty of minimizing and controlling the social researcher's influence on the social processes observed;

(c) ethical as well as methodological dilemmas in entering and leaving the field, including the problem of whether to reveal that one is engaged in social research.

Whatever the problems of participant observation, it remains an invaluable method of sociological research, which is perhaps best seen as complementary to other approaches rather than as an outright alternative to them (see RESEARCH METHODS). Participant observation is an especially useful method where the social action being researched is deviant or covert. Participant observation can be described as a "discovery-based approach" as well as a means of testing propositions.

particularism the orientation of any culture or human grouping in which the values and criteria used in evaluating actions are internal to the group, without any reference to values or criteria that apply to human beings universally. Thus, many traditional cultures are seen as particularistic, while modern societies have increasingly tended to be dominated by universalistic criteria, by *universalism*. See also PATTERN VARIABLES.

party identification a voter's enduring link with a political party (Budge, 1976). Butler and Stokes (1969) in Britain seek to establish a respondent's party identification, asking the question: "Generally speaking do you usually think of yorself as Conservative, Labor, or Liberal?" Some early students of VOTING BEHAVIOR assumed that voters might operate like individual consumers, with voting a matter of personal preference and voters likely to be readily persuaded to change sides. Subsequent studies of party identification have generally shown that this is not so, that in a majority of cases voters possess a party identification to which they return even if in a particular election, or when polled in advance of an election, their stated voting intention may sometimes differ from this. The increased volatility of voting behavior in recent years (see also CLASS DEALIGNMENT) may have reduced the numbers of people who possess a persistent party identification (and also its strength), but it remains the case that individual voting behavior has a continuity over elections. See also PARTY IMAGE.

party image the positive or negative conceptions of policies, programs, and leaders that a political party has established within an electorate. The term was first used, early in the 20th century, by the English political scientist Graham WALLAS. Influenced by sociological theorists of collective and mass behavior, he suggested that the mind of the electorate is rather like a "slow photographic plate," influenced by generalized past perceptions, and ATTITUDES and evaluations built up over a long period rather than guided by rational appraisal of the policies of competing parties. Subsequently the term became widely used in studies of VOTING BEHAVIOR. It has also been much employed by those consciously seeking to transform the political image of particular political parties, for example, by political advertising.

pastoralism and pastoral society a mode of subsistence economy and social organization, as among the Nuer of southern Sudan, in which the main livelihood is gained by tending flocks and herds of domesticated animals by moving on a regular basis or wandering with them in search of pasture. It has been suggested that pastoralism tends to be associated with egalitarianism and independence of mind (Spooner, 1973), but also with patriarchy. Whatever the truth of this, pastoralism and NOMADIC herding societies have historically been a frequent source of threat to more settled and more urban forms of society, and sometimes have been seen as a source of renewal within these as, for example, by the classical Arab social theorist Khaldun. See also AGRARIAN SOCIETY.

paternalism a system by which a government or organization deals with its subjects or employees by deploying an authoritarian family model of relationships, that is, the directive but benevolent father dealing with a child. In such a relationship, the more powerful seeks to legitimate social, economic, and political inequality by claiming that domination is in the best interests of the oppressed. The dominated are said to be childlike, that is, immature and unable to look after their own affairs, so the government or organization must act *in loco parentis* (in the place of parents).

Paternalism is used widely as a legitimating ideology in preindustrial societies, in colonial regimes, and in personal relationships. Examples would include PATRON-CLIENT RELATIONSHIPS, the so-called civilizing mission of European powers in Africa, master-slave relationships in chattel slavery, and some teacher-student relationships.

path analysis a statistical method using REGRESSION to quantify relationships between VARIABLES. A causal model is generated, depicted by a *path diagram* that shows how the variables are assumed to affect or be affected by each other. The observed data are compared with this model and if they are compatible it can be concluded that the causal effects may be as depicted in the model; it is not proof that the paths of causation are correct. See also CAUSAL MODELING.

patriarchy 1. a form of social organization in which a male (the *patriarch*) acts as head of the family/household, holding power over females and children, for example, in Roman society. **2.** any system whereby men achieve and maintain social, cultural, and economic dominance over females and younger males. The term may refer to a pattern of organization within the family and households, etc., or within a whole society.

Although historically sociologists have mainly used the term descriptively, more recent use by feminist sociologists has emphasized mainly its negative features. Analysis in sociology has been concerned with the origins and implications of patriarchy. Although biological differences between men and women, for example, physical strength in warfare, have sometimes been seen as the basis of patriarchy, the cultural and social sources of patriarchy, and its variations in form and importance, are equally striking.

Within FEMINIST THEORY, use of the term "patriarchy" has lead to the politicization of discussion of gender relations, enabling gender relations to be understood as predicated on inequalities of power.

patrimonialism any form of political domination or political authority based on personal and bureaucratic power exerted by a royal household (WEBER, 1922). As such, "patrimonialism" is a relatively broad term, not referring to any particular type of political system. The crucial contrast between patrimonialism and other types of political power is that (a) this power is formally arbitrary, and (b) its administration is under direct control of the ruler. This means it involves the employment of retainers or slaves, mercenaries and conscripts, who themselves possess no independent basis of power, that is, are *not* members of traditional landed aristocracy.

The limitation of patrimonialism, according to Weber, is that it was inherently unstable, tending to be subject to political upheavals, which arose from the emergence of rival centers of power. Since historically patrimonial systems were usually replaced by further patrimonial systems, their existence is seen as a barrier to any sustained economic and social transformation. See EISENSTADT.

patron-client relationship any continuing relationship, often contractual, in which a powerful or influential person provides rewards and services to humbler and weaker persons in return for loyalty and support, and perhaps also including reciprocal exchange of some services. Such relationships are found especially in simple or traditional societies; similar relationships may also exist between states.

The concept may cover personalized relationships and include instances in which both coercion and consent are involved. It has been of particular importance in understanding relationships of the peasantry (see PEASANTS) with other groups in society, such as landlords or politicians. Usually the patron provides favors, services, or protection in return for loyalty, political support, and perhaps economic control. This relationship may extend outside the peasantry to a style of national politics in which electoral support is gained through fostering patron-client relationships, with a politician either giving or promising favors. Thus, a system of *clientelism* may be one way of incorporating a wide population into national politics. Mouzelis (1986) discusses this and contrasts it with *populism* as a form of political incorporation in parts of Latin America and the Balkans.

pattern variables the four (sometimes five) basic "pattern-alternatives of value orientation" for individuals and cultures, according to PARSONS. In this formulation, cultures are seen as organizing action, and actors as faced with implicit choices in relationships, in terms of four dichotomous alternative modes of orientation to "social objects," including other actors:

(a) *affective involvement/affective neutrality*: orientation by the actor to immediate gratifications *or* the absence of such immediate gratification, for example, eating a meal or watching a football game compared with work that does not engage one's emotions;

(b) *ascription/achievement* (also referred to as the *quality/performance* distinction): judgments about "social objects," including actors according to their membership or not of specified social categories *as against* judgments made in terms of more general criteria that apply to the actual performance of actors. For example, in most societies gender is ascribed, while success at football or in a musical career involves achievement;

(c) *particularism/universalism*: the choice of whether to treat a "social object" in accordance with its standing in some particular relationship independently of general norms, *or* to treat it in accordance with "a general norm covering all the objects in a category," for example, a mother's relationship with her child may sometimes be particularistic but at other times involve universalistic criteria (appraising school performance, for example);

(d) *diffuseness/specificity*: social relationships involving an across-the-board personal involvement, for example, the mother-child relationship and family relationships in general, *or* relationships that have only a specified and limited purpose, for example, a bus driver collecting fares.

	Achievement (what actors do)	Ascription (who actors are)
Universalism (general principles)	MODERN US	GERMANY IN THE LATE 19TH CENTURY
Particularism (particular values rather than general principles)	ANCIENT CHINA	COLONIAL SPANISH AMERICA

Fig.19. **Pattern variables.** A location of examples of contrasting types of society in terms of their dominant cultural values, expressed in terms of Talcott Parsons' pattern variables.

A fifth variable, *collectivity-orientation/self-orientation,* originally proposed by Parsons, was subsequently dropped as being of a different order from the other four.

Parsons' conceptions of pattern variables was presented by him as deriving from previous characterizations of types of society such as TONNIES' distinction between GEMEINSCHAFT AND GESELLSCHAFT. He saw his pattern variables as providing an exhaustive general statement of the fundamental dilemmas perennially facing all actors and involved in all social organization. Accordingly, it was also possible to locate particular societies in terms of the schema (see Fig. 19).

While the vocabulary provided by the pattern variables has been widely used in both sociology theory and empirical research, Parsons' suggestion that these variables can be regarded as a formal derivation from his overall general theory of social systems is no longer convincing.

Pearson product moment correlation coefficient (r) a CORRELATION coefficient for use with continuous variables (interval or ratio scales) with a NORMAL DISTRIBUTION. A theoretical justification for the measure is that r^2 is the proportion of the variance in one of the variables that can be predicted from the other.

peasants "small agricultural producers, who, with the help of simple equipment and the labor of their families, produce mostly for their own consumption, direct or indirect, and for the fulfillment of obligations to holders of political and economic power," (Shanin, 1988).

Until the 1960s, the peasantry were largely ignored in sociology as having no significant role to play in history. This was despite the now recognized point that peasants have existed for most of recorded history and in many parts of the world. From the 1960s the publication of key works, such as Wolf (1966) and Barrington MOORE (1967), began to change this perception, introducing to sociology perspectives developed in anthropology and political economy. The role of the peasantry in the Vietnam War and the growth of peasant political activity in Latin America and Asia raised questions about the assumed passivity of the peasantry. Within Marxist work, partly under the influence of Maoism and events in China around the 1949 Revolution and subsequently, there emerged the question of whether the peasantry in the Third World represented the revolutionary force of socialism. This was especially so in the light of analyses that saw the proletariat of the advanced capitalist world incorporated as a labor aristocracy into the dominant capitalist world. There is now a major area of interdisciplinary peasant studies, but one of the most important debates is still over whether a distinctive category of peasantry can be identified both conceptually and empirically. Shanin presents one of the strongest and most influential defenses of the concept. Drawing on all strands contributing to peasant studies in this century, he argues that there are four main interrelated characteristics of the peasantry (Shanin, 1982; Shanin (ed.), 1988, Introduction);

(a) The family farm is the major economic unit around which production, labor, and consumption are organized.

(b) Land husbandry is the main activity, combined with minimal specialization and family training for tasks.

(c) There is a particular peasant way of life based on the local village community that covers most areas of social life and culture and that distinguishes it from urban life and from those of other social groups.

(d) Peasants are politically, economically, and socially subordinated to nonpeasant groups against whom they have devised various methods of resistance, rebellion, or revolt.

There are two further subsidiary facets:

(e) A specific social dynamic involving a cyclical change over generations that irons out inequalities over time via land division and the rise and fall of the availability of family labor.

(f) Especially in the contemporary world, a common pattern of structural change, drawing peasants into market relationships, often through the influence of outside bodies such as AGRIBUSINESS, and incorporation into national politics. The precise outcome of these common changes is not predetermined.

According to circumstances, the peasantry may survive, they may migrate because of declining opportunities on the land, they may combine wage labor in urban or rural areas with some elements of land husbandry, becoming worker-peasants, or they may become totally reliant on wage labor without land, becoming a rural PROLETARIAT or some combination of these.

Further, two general distinctions are usually made between peasants and other farmers. The first contrast is with TRIBAL peoples. Post (1972) distinguishes peasants as having:

(a) group or individual rather than communal land ownership;

(b) a social division of labor that is not exclusively based on kinship;

(c) an involvement in market relationships even though the extent of this will vary;

(d) political hierarchies that are not exclusively based on kinship and with a state structure to which they are subordinated;

(e) a culture that is not as homogeneous as that of tribal peoples. Peasant culture coexists with cultures of other groups in the same society.

The second contrast is with small capitalist family-farmers, who may rely predominantly on family labor but who may also employ wage labor; who buy seeds, fertilizer, livestock, and so on, and sell most of the output rather than using it for the family's own consumption. Thus, both inputs and outputs are COMMODITIES.

Peasants can be most clearly distinguished in AGRARIAN SOCIETIES. A key issue is what effect the emergence of capitalism has on the peasantry. For some authors this raises the issue of *differentiation of the peasantry*, which may increase with the development of capitalism. Following Lenin, one distinction is between rich peasants who have more land than they need for their own consumption and either rent it out or employ others to work it, middle peasants who conform to the definition of peasant used here, and poor peasants who do not have enough land to supply their own needs and may have to sell their labor for an income. A graphic definition of a poor peasant is given by a Malaysian who said he "had to shit on someone else's land" (Scott, 1985). An important debate has been whether, with the development of capitalism, rich peasants become capitalist farmers, poor peasants become PROLETARIANS, and middle peasants become one or the other.

Neglected in peasant studies until the 1980s has been the question of gender. In the past the structure of the peasant household was treated unproblematically, but now it is increasingly recognized that PATRIARCHAL relationships are central. Thus, women are frequently subordinated in many ways and carry a heavy burden of work. The division of labor between men and women varied in time and place but was rigid. Peasant women have limited public identity, and in extreme cases, such as China before the 20th century, scarcely counted as human beings.

There are several strong arguments that the concept of "peasant" has no place in social-scientific analysis. Polly Hill (1986), drawing on her work in Africa and Asia, argues that there are such variations over time and place of the ways in which rural farmers make a living and organize their social life, that only a small proportion of people fit usual definitions of the peasantry: an individual over a lifetime may engage in trade, wage labor, small-plot farming, trucking, or employing others. Conceptually, others have argued that the term "peasant" has vague implications: one cannot read off from the definitions of "peasant" implications for understanding the wider society, economy, or politics in the same way that one can for other concepts. Finally, there is debate over whether the central importance attached to the peasant HOUSEHOLD in Shanin's and other formulations are appropriate. This focus is derived from the work of the Soviet economist Chayanov (see Thorner et al., 1966). However, given the extent of inter-household activities, the importance of the village in many peasant communities, and the influence of nonpeasant groups on the peasants, it remains open to question whether the dynamics of peasant life are best approached with the household as the main unit of analysis. Some of these arguments are persuasive and still inform the current debates.

peasant society small-scale social organization in which PEASANTS predominate with features distinctive from other social groupings. While sometimes the term is used to refer to a large SOCIETY in which peasants are the majority, most uses would limit the term to a narrower meaning approximating that of COMMUNITY. Peasants live in various societies, mainly AGRARIAN SOCIETIES, within which there are other social groups, so that it is not possible to characterize the entire society by referring to one of those groups. Within a village or region, however, peasant social relationships may dominate. Characteristically, these may be centered around kin and family ties, the importance of access to land, a distrust of outsiders, and a cyclical view of time. An area of debate is whether such commonalities can be easily distinguished, considering the wide range of locations it has been claimed that peasants have occupied for most of human history.

In any peasant community there will be people who are not analytically defined as peasants. These may be traders, truckers, moneylenders, laborers without land, or craftspeople, who may command a similar income to peasants and who may have close social and economic links to peasants. People who are analytically defined as "peasants" will often engage in some of these activities for part of their time. In the modern world in particular, there will also be people who may be more economically and socially distant from the peasantry. Most importantly, these will be state functionaries, representatives of national or foreign corporations selling anything from tractors to pharmaceuticals, and there may be independent professionals: lawyers, physicians, etc. Some of these may be identified as *brokers*, who mediate between the peasant village and the wider society. The larger the village, the more likely that these will be present, and even villages without them will have strong links with provincial towns where these nonpeasant groups are located. Thus, while definitions of the peasantry sometimes rest on the functioning of the household, it is essential to see how this is firmly integrated into a wider social, political and economic network.

peer group a GROUP of individuals of equal status. The term is most generally applied to children and adolescents, who experience a different influence on their SOCIALIZATION by interacting in groups of their own age, as compared with the hierarchical family experience. See also YOUTH CULTURE.

penology the systematic study of punishment, particularly imprisonment. The term was coined in the 19th century along with the reorganization of the prison system and at a time of much debate about the purposes of imprisonment. In part, the introduction of the term reflected a positivistic belief that a scientific solution could be found to many human problems. See also FOUCAULT, PANOPTICON.

periphery see CENTER AND PERIPHERY.

personal construct theory a psychological theory that aims to provide a complete and formal explanation of the whole person by reference to the person's possession, use, and development of a unique personal construct system made up of numbers of interrelated bipolar constructs (for example, good-bad). The most frequently used method for eliciting and measuring constructs, *the repertory grid technique,* involves the generation of constructs through identification of similarities and differences between triads of elements (for example, people known to the individual). Personal construct theory's deliberately precise formulation (a fundamental postulate and 11 elaborative corollaries) by its originator, George Kelly, (Kelly, 1955), has been usefully and simply characterized as presenting a view of the "person as scientist." Thus, constructs and construct systems are used to construe—make sense of—and predict or anticipate events in the individual's social and nonsocial environment; failure in prediction leads to construct modification or abandonment. The process of construing events can be seen to have major theoretical relevance in areas such as social perception, social interaction (which is guided by construing social events), and personality (individual differences in construct systems). Applications of personal construct theory include a distinctive psychotherapy, and analyses of problem behaviors such as stuttering, obesity, alcoholism, and schizophrenia.

person-centered counseling the approach to COUNSELING pioneered by Carl ROGERS in the 1930s and 1940s, and that regards the client/person as the essential focus of the therapeutic relationship. This may seem to go without saying, but Rogers' insight was that PSYCHOANALYSIS and other theoretical approaches *impose* a diagnosis and treatment on the client. He suggested that the client best understands the client's problem and ultimately it is from within that change or healing has to come. The counselor, then, is seen as a facilitator, is nondirective, and responds to the client with genuineness, empathy, and unconditional positive regard (Rogers' three core conditions). Only through understanding the client's phenomenological experience can the counselor be effective in helping the client to resolve the clinet's problems and take the right decisions for the future, and it is through experiencing this relationship with the counselor that the client is enabled to take self-responsibility.

petty bourgeoisie or *petite bourgeoisie* the class of small capitalist business owners. Some theorists also include self-employed artisans, middle

and small peasantry, and other smallholding farmers. The term has its origins in MARX's work. He distinguished between the social and economic situation of big and small businesses and argued that the logic of competition
and successive economic crises is to encourage the growth of monopolistic
big business (and CLASS POLARIZATION and PROLETARIANIZATION of the
petty bourgeoisie). In practice, despite the insecurity and instability of
small business ownership (only about 20% survive for more than five years,
see Fidler, 1981), the rate of establishment of new small or independent
concerns remains very high and may have been encouraged by high unemployment and recession. Empirical studies of the petty bourgeoisie suggest
that their social and political attitudes can be characterized as individualistic and independent-minded, mistrustful of large organizations, and generally conservative and antisocialist (Bechhofer et al., 1974). The support of
members of the petty bourgeoisie is usually considered significant in the
rise of European fascism in the 1920s and 1930s in Germany (see Franz
Neumann, 1942). More generally, they are found disproportionately
among the supporters of right-wing and extreme right-wing political movements, for example, McCarthyism in the United States (see BELL, 1964).

A recent theoretical redevelopment of the concept occurs in Poulantzas
(1973). He has proposed that the nonmanual MIDDLE CLASSES can be best
conceptualized as a NEW PETTY BOURGEOISIE on the grounds that they are
not members of the bourgeoisie, since they do not own the means of production, but nor can they (contrary to the PROLETARIANIZATION thesis) be
members of the working class. Their role as assistants of capital and their
ideological identification with capitalist interests make it more appropriate
to see them as identified with the old petty bourgeoisie. In many ways,
however, this theory is better seen in the context of the debate about the
NEW MIDDLE CLASS than the traditional conception of the petty bourgeoisie
(see CONTRADICTORY CLASS LOCATIONS).

phenomenalism the empiricist doctrine (for example, advanced by J.S.
MILL) that things "are permanent possibilities of sensations." Thus, phenomenalism is not to be confused with PHENOMENOLOGY. DURKHEIM was
influenced by phenomenalism.

phenomenological sociology sociological approaches deriving especially
from the work of Alfred SCHUTZ (see also SOCIAL PHENOMENOLOGY, PHE-
NOMENOLOGY). The clearest contemporary expression of phenomenological
sociology is BERGER and Luckmann's *The Social Construction of Reality*
(1967). This influential text on the SOCIOLOGY OF KNOWLEDGE argues that
all knowledge is socially constructed and oriented toward particular practical problems. Facts can therefore never be neutral but are always reflec-
tive of why they are required. This stress on commonsense knowledge has
influenced CONVERSATION ANALYSIS, ETHNOMETHODOLOGY, modern
HERMENEUTICS, and varieties of detailed ethnographic PARTICIPANT OBSER-
VATION, though the common strand is less a common method than an aver-

sion to POSITIVISM, which is characterized by use of QUANTITATIVE RESEARCH TECHNIQUES.

phenomenology 1. "the descriptive study of experiences"—a phenomenon being anything perceived by our senses. For example, the term was used by HEGEL in his *Phenomenology of Mind*, 1807; compare also KANT). **2.** more recently, a philosophical approach particularly associated with Edmund HUSSERL, in which philosophy is seen to rest fundamentally on the introspective examination of one's own intellectual processes in experiencing phenomena. A central doctrine of phenomenologists is that of the INTENTIONALITY of perception—we cannot simply be conscious, but must be conscious of something. In Husserl's *a priori* rather than empirical method, all incidental aspects of the mental processes under inspection—all that is not *directly* presented to the individual consciousness, for example, extraneous conceptions—are *bracketed* (literally held in parentheses) to permit the systematic scrutiny of "logical essences." Thus, "phenomenological reduction" is aimed at revealing the a priori essences of thought divested of the inconsistencies of perception.

Albeit with considerable variations in focus, phenomenology has exerted a major influence on sociology and social analysis. Other philosophers and sociologists who have adopted phenomenological methods include the EXISTENTIALIST philosopher Martin HEIDEGGER, existentialist Marxists (for example, SARTRE and Merleau-Ponty), and Alfred SCHUTZ. Schutz's SOCIAL PHENOMENOLOGY involves a critical appropriation of Husserl's approach, but an application of this to the study of the assumptions involved in, and the constitution of, everyday social knowledge—a focus on the LIFE WORLD bracketed in Husserl's original method. Applications of a phenomenological approach are also seen in the so-called radical psychiatry of LAING and Cooper.

The term also continues in wider use to refer to any investigation of how things are experienced, for example, the experience of works of art or architecture. Compare PHENOMENALISM. See also ETHNOMETHODOLOGY.

Piaget, Jean (1896–1980) Swiss development psychologist, particularly significant for his stage theory of cognitive development.

Piaget's background was in zoology, and he retained a strong biological, NATIVIST orientation, emphasizing the innate specification for development through a serial process of learning, each stage being the necessary foundation for the next. This was not to deny the importance of the environment, which he saw as an essential aspect of this process, though later theorists, such as Jerome Bruner, have tended to give environmental experience more weight than did Piaget. The four developmental stages were termed the *sensorimotor*, the *pre-operational*, the *concrete operational*, and the *formal operational*. Through the processes of assimilation and accommodation, the child gradually develops from sensing and responding at birth, to the capacity for abstract, hypothetico-deductive thought in the early teens.

Piaget has been criticized for his nativist emphasis, the rigidity of the stage theory, and for his methodology. His work was undoubtedly pioneering, stimulating much research that has supported the main tenets, but also indicated that the boundaries between stages should be regarded as fuzzy, and has also shown that the way in which children are assessed affects their responses, and therefore their stage categorization.

piecemeal social engineering the limited form of economic and social planning suggested by Karl POPPER as all that is justified by social science knowledge. Popper's claim arises from his falsificationist epistemology (see FALSIFICATIONISM) and his view that knowledge—and hence social life—is inherently unpredictable (see HISTORICISM, sense **2**). He also argues that parallels can be drawn with biological evolution, that, as well as being unpredictable, social evolution best proceeds by small steps. See also EVOLUTIONARY SOCIOLOGY.

pillarization (from the Dutch, *verzuiling*) a stable vertical division of society in which patterns of political organization, including labor unions and political parties, are determined by religious or linguistic affiliations that substantially override or cut across horizontal class divisions (compare SOCIAL STRATIFICATION). In Holland, where separate Calvinist, Catholic, and secular organizations exist in many spheres of life, this pattern of social organization has become highly institutionalized, the basis of a segmented integration and shared political power. Elsewhere, however, for example, the Lebanon and Northern Ireland, pillarization has often been associated with instability and the failure of power sharing.

pilot study a small-scale version of a planned experiment or observation, used to test the logistics and design of it. Thus, a questionnaire schedule may be piloted on a small sample of the proposed SAMPLE population to see if any of the questions present particular problems of interpretation, or lead to ambiguous responses that would be difficult to interpret as data. If the design works without problems, then the main experiment can go ahead, but if problems have come to light these can be rectified first. It is also possible that a pilot study will suggest valuable extensions to the study, or restrictions of aspects that are unlikely to be helpful in the investigation.

plasticity the quality of being modifiable. In sociology and psychology this term is generally used to describe flexibility or malleability of human BEHAVIOR, since it is accepted that this results not only from inherited factors, but is also subject to environmental and cultural influences (see CULTURE, NATURE-NURTURE DEBATE). Thus the process of SOCIALIZATION is all-important in producing human behavior.

plastic man see AUTONOMOUS MAN AND PLASTIC MAN.

play any activity that is voluntary, gives pleasure, and has no goal other than enjoyment.

Play is considered by psychologists to be a necessary part of development. Various theories have suggested why this should be. Early theories include the anticipatory theory (Gross, 1901), the surplus energy theory (SPENCER, 1881), and the recapitulatory theory (Hall, 1908). These all suggested that play was an essential activity in the young, but seemed to disregard fun. Currently there is recognition of the fun aspect, which indicates that a certain attitude of mind is involved in play activity.

Play is regarded as valuable for physical development, for learning skills and social behavior, and for personality development, (see Millar, 1968, for full discussion).

Play therapy is used as a technique for understanding young children's psychological problems and helping to resolve them.

Sociological interest in play has developed around two concerns: the role of play in the SOCIALIZATION of SELF, and the increasing attention paid to the role of pleasure in the formation of IDENTITY in the late 20th century. See also LEISURE.

plural elitism the doctrine that power in modern liberal democratic states is shared between a multiplicity of competing ELITES (for example, Dahl, 1967). Plural elite theorists acknowledge that in complex modern industrial societies, elites will inevitably dominate. In this they are at one with classical ELITE THEORY. Modern plural elite theory differs from classical elite theory, however, in two key respects:

(a) in accepting that elites in modern liberal democratic societies are representative elites—thus, while the people may not rule, the people's elites do;

(b) in asserting that in modern liberal democracies, power is either shared between multiple elites or these elites compete openly and continuously for political power without any one group achieving a lasting dominance over the others. It is in these terms that modern elite theory distinguishes between democracies and nondemocracies.

Critics of plural elitist theory (for example, *The Theory of Democratic Elitism*, Bachrach, 1967) object first to what they see as its tendency to understate systematic biases in the actual distribution of power in modern societies (see also NONDECISION, MOBILIZATION OF BIAS) and, secondly, to the restricted conception of political participation and individual development with which a democratic elitism is associated. In responding to these criticisms, plural elite theorists point to the greater realism of their own view of democracy compared with traditional models, further insisting that the distinctions between democracies and nondemocracies captured by their models reflect key differences between actual political systems.

pluralism the situation within a state or social organization in which power is shared or held to be shared among a multiplicity of groups and organizations. The original use of the term was in association with opposition to the Hegelian conception of the unitary state. In a socialist conception of pluralism, *Guild Socialism*, the dispersal of economic and political power to occupational groups was proposed as an ideal. However, the most important use of the term in modern sociology and political science is the suggestion that modern Western liberal democracies are pluralistic polities, in which a plurality of groups and/or elites either share power or continuously compete for power (see also PLURAL ELITISM).

pluralistic ignorance the situation in GROUPS where individuals believe that the group members know or understand something that they do not know, but in fact each member is in this ignorant position and holding this belief about the rest of the group.

plural society any society in which there exists a formal division into distinct racial, linguistic, or religious groupings. Such distinctions may be horizontal (see also SOCIAL STRATIFICATION) or vertical (see PILLARIZATION).

political anthropology that part of social anthropology that focuses on the study of the political processes and institutions in SIMPLE SOCIETIES. As well as being a particular focus within social anthropology, the study of the politics of simpler societies is also an essential part of POLITICAL SOCIOLOGY.

A distinguishing feature of the political systems of simpler societies is that they do not always exist as a differentiated set of relatively specialized, explicitly political, institutions as they do in modern state societies (see SEGMENTARY SOCIETY, STATELESS SOCIETY).

political culture the norms, beliefs, and values within a political system. It is usually assumed that a particular political culture is built up as the result of a long historical development and that its distinctive character exerts a profound influence on the form and effectiveness, or otherwise, of the political system with which it is associated. The term is most associated with the systems approach within political analysis, which was in vogue in the 1950s and 1960s in the United States (for example, G. Almond and S. Verba, *The Civic Culture*, 1965). The approach has been of most value in stimulating cross-cultural comparative research on political cultures, for example, Almond's distinction between "participatory," "subject" and "parochial" political orientations within political cultures. One central assumption of political-culture theorists is that the particular *civic culture* underlying liberal democracies such as the US and Britain, a mixture of participatory orientations tempered by political DEFERENCE, has been both a cause and effect of the greater political stability and effectiveness of these systems compared with other systems. From a different theoretical perspective, however, political culture can also be seen as involving cultural and ideological HEGEMONY. In this context, rather than being a sign of political effectiveness, the role of political culture may be viewed as a conservative force preventing a social transition to more favorable social and political arrangements, (see also CULTURE, POLITICAL SOCIALIZATION).

political mobilization the aggregation and deployment of people and resources by the STATE (for example, see EISENSTADT).

political modernization the process, usually seen as crucially affected by economic modernization, in which traditional or colonial forms of political organization and state forms are replaced by Western state forms, including modern political parties.

Identification of the socioeconomic requirements for political modernization to succeed (education, the creation of appropriate POLITICAL CULTURE) was a central topic in the 1950s and 1960s in forms of POLITICAL SCIENCE and POLITICAL SOCIOLOGY influenced by SYSTEMS THEORY and STRUCTURAL-FUNCTIONALISM. Theories of political modernization of this type (for example, D. Apter, *The Politics of Modernization,* 1965) usually adhered to a model of social development that saw Western European patterns of liberal democracy as the most rational and appropriate form of political development for non-European societies to pursue (see also STABLE DEMOCRACY). Understandably, such a Western-centered conception of political modernization was widely criticized. Thus the term is now used in a more open-ended way, to refer to the process of political modernization whatever its form.

political science the science (or study) of politics and government.

One of the oldest of systematic studies, political science has manifested great ambivalence on how, and whether, to present itself as a science. Political scientists generally have divided into two (albeit often overlapping) schools of thought:

(a) those who describe and compare patterns of government and politics, drawing on the work of philosophers, historians, constitutional theorists, public administrators, etc., as well as collecting their own material, without any pretensions that political studies can ever be a science in any natural science, or even social science, sense of the term;

(b) those who have wanted to bring political studies into far closer relation with the more avowedly scientific social sciences, such as sociology, economics, and social psychology, (for example, see POLITICAL SYSTEM).

political socialization the process in any society in which occur the acquisition and internalization of political norms, values, and beliefs; the acquisition of POLITICAL CULTURE.

The study of political socialization, including child socialization, has been particularly important in those branches of political science and political sociology that have emphasized the role of political culture in the stability of political systems. Research into child political socialization faces significant problems. While a direct empirical study of the place of political ideas in child socialization has sometimes been possible, much research has of necessity had to rely on less reliable data based on adult recall of child socialization or on documentary evidence. See also AUTHORITARIAN PERSONALITY.

political sociology the branch of sociology concerned with the study of politics or the political subsystems of society. Although a branch of sociology, political sociology also exists as a distinct approach within POLITICAL SCIENCE. In comparison with orthodox political science, both political sociology and the political sociological approach within political science insist that the investigation of political institutions must be treated as fully implicated in society, not as a system that can be understood in isolation. The following main areas of study within political sociology can be identified:

(a) the general nature and functions of the STATE and the political system (or subsystem);

(b) the nature of political parties, PRESSURE GROUPS, and political organizations and political movements of all kinds;

(c) empirical study of patterns of individual political participation and political behavior, including nonparticipation, for example, empirical research on VOTING BEHAVIOR;

(d) comparative research on the types of political system and the relative effectiveness and stability or instability of these;

(e) particular and general analysis of the relations between states, including WARFARE, and the location of states within the world system;

(f) running through all the above areas, perhaps something that political sociology has been most identified with is the study of political ELITES and MASSES and the extent to which modern societies can be said to be dominated by a RULING CLASS (see MOSCA, PARETO, MARX). See also POWER, POLITICAL ANTHROPOLOGY.

The study of political phenomena has a long ancestry. Aristotle's *Politics* is often regarded as in many ways a work of political sociology. The same is true of the works of Niccolo Machiavelli, HOBBES, MONTESQUIEU, and many other political writers whose works anticipate aspects of the approach of modern political sociology.

polyarchy literally, the rule of the many. In its widest usage in political science and sociology, the term refers to any political system in which power is dispersed; thus, its antonym is totalitarianism. As such polyarchy may take many forms, it is not synonymous only with liberal democracy, although it is sometimes used as if it were, for example by Dahl (1956, 1985). In sociology and in political science especially, a generic association is often seen between the existence of polyarchy and the rise of the modern NATION STATE. However, this is a relationship that has often been interrupted, and it ignores the existence of societies prior to the emergence of nation states, in which power was relatively dispersed.

Popper, Karl (1902–) Austrian-born philosopher of science who has worked since 1945 at the London School of Economics and is renowned for his advocacy over many years of FALSIFICATIONISM and critical rationalism.

It was in his *Logic of Scientific Discovery* (1959–Ger. 1934) that Popper first claimed to have "solved the problem of empiricism" (see also EMPIRICISM, INDUCTION AND INDUCTIVE LOGIC), proposing a criterion of science based on the falsifiability rather than the verifiability of hypotheses (compare POSITIVISM). In taking this view Popper has also been a leading advocate of the COVERING LAW MODEL of science, which is an integral part of his falsification view.

Although at first Popper's focus mainly concerned physical science, subsequently he extended the scope of his philosophy to include social science, notably in *The Poverty of Historicism* (1957) and *The Open Society and Its Enemies* (1945). In the first of these Popper attacked forms of historical social theory that claim a special status for the social sciences as historical sciences but in doing so either overstate the possibilities of scientific laws or see no possibility of these (see HISTORICISM). Both forms of theory are seen by Popper as failing to appreciate the true character of laws and theories in science and social science, that is, that these involve limited, not unconditional, predictions.

In *The Open Society and Its Enemies,* Popper continued his critique of historicism, focusing particularly on Hegel and Marx, whose historicism, he suggested, makes them "enemies of the open society." The OPEN SOCIETY is Popper's formulation of his preferred kind of society, one in which individuals can aspire to change history and in which the future as a whole is recognized as inherently unpredictable. This form of society is the only one compatible with the kind of scientific laws that Popper believes are possible in the social sciences, laws that are couched in terms of situational logic (see SITUATIONAL ANALYSIS AND SITUATIONAL LOGIC) and METHODOLOGICAL INDIVIDUALISM and make only limited predictions.

A similar reliance on this general epistemological view is also apparent in Popper's conception that PIECEMEAL SOCIAL ENGINEERING, rather than any utopian scheme, represents the only form of social planning that can be justified by social science.

In the exposition and elaboration of his views, Popper has drawn latterly on EVOLUTIONARY THEORY, arguing that, as in the biological world, knowledge and societies advance by gradual steps involving "hopeful conjectures," which are sometimes successful but are unpredictable overall (see also EVOLUTIONARY SOCIOLOGY).

Although Popper presents his philosophy as "anti-Positivist," it remains broadly within the empiricist and positivist tradition with its claims for an absolute foundation for science and a unity of social and physical science.

In recent years Popper's position on science and social science has been subject to a number of damaging critiques, notably:

(a) critiques of both the falsificationist and the covering law model (see FEYERABEND, KUHN).

(b) critiques of methodological individualism.

(c) suggestions that part of the undoubted wide appeal of Popper's philosophy is ideological.

population pyramid a two-dimensional graph used to display the age and gender structure of a population. See Fig. 20.

positional goods and **positionality** any commodity or situation where supply is inherently limited, either as the result of physical or social scarcity

POSITIONAL GOODS

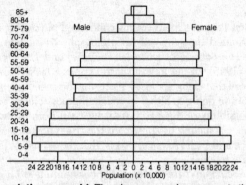

Fig. 20. **Population pyramid.** The above example represents the age structure of Scotland in 1976.

(for example, environmentally pleasing residential areas or holiday resorts, major works of art, top jobs). The satisfactions obtained from such goods or situations derive in part from scarcity and social exclusiveness, as well as from the intrinsic satisfactions. The deficiencies in the supply of such goods cannot be overcome by normal economic growth.

In *Social Limits of Growth* (1977), Hirsch suggests that as societies become richer, many of the extra goods, services, and facilities sought by consumers cannot be acquired or used by all, without spoiling them for each other: "What each of us can achieve, all cannot." Thus, as pointed out by Mishan (1967): "The tourist in search of something different, inevitably erodes and destroys that difference by his enjoyment of it." According to Hirsch, "Our existing concept of economic output is appropriate only for truly private goods, having no element of interdependence between consumption by different individuals." Many of the environmental issues— problems of congestion, pollution, etc.—that increasingly arise in modern industrial societies, involve positionality in Hirsch's sense. The need for a distributional morality to support a limit to growth is emphasized by Hirsch. This view contrasts with the technocratic optimism usually associated with economists' theories of economic growth. See also PUBLIC GOODS.

positional jobs any sought-after job where the supply is inherently limited, for example, all so-called top jobs. According to Hirsch (1979) the spiraling quest for educational achievement in modern industrial societies is a phenomenon of positionality. More and more people compete for best-paid, high-status occupational positions. However, since the supply of such jobs is inherently limited, and at best increases less rapidly than the expansion of higher education, the result of this is an escalation of the formal qualifications required without any corresponding return to most individuals or to society. See also CREDENTIALISM.

positive discrimination social policies encouraging favorable treatment of socially disadvantaged minority groups, especially in employment, education, and housing. These policies aim to reverse historical trends of DIS-CRIMINATION and to create EQUALITY OF OPPORTUNITY. The term is roughly synonymous with *affirmative action* and *reverse discrimination*.

In the United States, where affirmative action programs have been in operation since the 1964 Civil Rights Act, these policies have created considerable controversy and litigation. In defending the concept of positive discrimination, President Lyndon Johnson said: "You do not take a person who, for years, has been hobbled by chains and liberate him, bring him up to the starting line of a race and then say, 'you are free to compete with all the others,' and still justly believe that you have been completely fair."

The arguments of those opposed to positive discrimination can be represented by the views of Glazer (1975), who argues that affirmative action "has meant that we abandon the first principle of a liberal society, that the individual's interests and good and welfare are the test of a good society, for now we attach benefits and penalties to individuals simply on the basis of their race, color, and national origins."

Despite calls for programs of positive discrimination in Britain, it remains illegal under existing Sex Discrimination and Race Relations Acts.

positivism 1. the doctrine formulated by COMTE asserting that the only true knowledge is scientific knowledge, that is, knowledge that describes and explains the coexistence and succession of observable phenomena, including both physical and social phenomena. Comte's positivism had two dimensions: (a) methodological (as above) and (b) social and political, in which positive knowledge of social phenomena was expected to permit a new scientifically grounded intervention in politics and social affairs that would transform social life. **2.** (*Logical Positivism*) the philosophical viewpoint of a group of philosophers in the 1920s and 1930s known collectively as the Vienna Circle, whose ideas were in part based on Comte but presented as giving Comte's positivism a more secure logical basis. The central doctrine of the Vienna Circle, the *Verification Principle,* states that the only valid knowledge is knowledge that is verified by sensory experience. More strictly, the expectation was that scientific knowledge would ultimately find formulation in logically interrelated general propositions, grounded in statements about "basic facts" stated in a strictly formulated "sense datum" language. Some but not all members of the Vienna Circle also embraced Comte's project to extend the methods of the physical sciences to social science. **3.** any sociological approach that operates on the general assumption that the methods of physical science (for example, measurement, search for general laws, etc.) can be carried over into the social sciences. **4.** (pejoratively) any sociological approach seen as falsely seeking to ape the methodology of the physical sciences.

In choosing the term "positivism," Comte conveyed his intention to repudiate all reliance on earlier religious or speculative metaphysical bases of knowledge (see LAW OF THREE STAGES). However, Comte regarded scientific knowledge as "relative knowledge," not absolute. Absolute knowledge was and always would be unavailable. Comte's social and political program envisaged a new consensus on social issues and a reorganization of society on lines suggested by the new science of sociology. A role would exist for sociologists in government and in education, and in establishing a new "Religion of Humanity."

Since it was the work of a school rather than an individual, the methodological position of Logical Positivism is more varied than that of Comte, and in crucial respects at odds with his view. In the realm of ethics, for example, Logical Positivists were often associated with a doctrine that draws a sharp distinction between facts (which are verifiable) and values (which are not). While most philosophers associated with Logical Positivism maintained that science, including social science, could be expected to provide increasingly reliable knowledge, enabling achievement of preferred goals, they did not usually accept that science can decide questions of value, "ought" questions rather than "is" statements (see also FACT-VALUE DISTINCTION).

Neither the details of Comte's methodological principles nor his social and political programs find strong support among modern sociologists. Nor has the attempt of the logical positivists to achieve a stricter logical formulation of positivism and science proved durable.

Methodologically, a central problem of positivism arises from the so-called "problem of empiricism": the lack of any conclusive basis for verification in inductive logic (see INDUCTION AND INDUCTIVE, LOGIC, EMPIRICISM). A further telling criticism, the so-called "paradox of positivism," is that the Verification Principle is itself unverifiable.

In recent years, new approaches in the philosophy and history of science have shed doubt on the idea of a single philosophical basis to science. Positivism can be criticized for betraying its own conception of scientific knowledge as relative knowledge and as dogmatizing about scientific method. See also FALSIFICATIONISM.

If the above difficulties apply to Positivism in relation to physical science, further problems arise in relation to sociology specifically. The fact is that sociological positivism has not been successful in achieving either the expected unification of sociological knowledge, or a consensus on schemes for social and political reconstruction. For some sociologists, the failure of positivism points to the necessity to pursue sociology in other than conventionally scientific terms. See MEANINGFUL SOCIOLOGY, VERSTEHEN.

postal questionnaire or **mail questionnaire** a QUESTIONNAIRE that is mailed or posted to respondents. See also RESPONSE RATE.

postempiricism the repudiation of the idea that science and knowledge can be grounded in entirely theory-neutral observations of the kind suggested by EMPIRICISM and POSITIVISM. Postempiricism involves an acceptance of accounts of science such as those proposed by KUHN and FEYERABEND. This need not imply that science or knowledge is an irrational or relativistic enterprise. However, it does mean that scientists and social scientists cannot escape the need to argue the reasons why one theory should be accepted and another rejected, that there exist no simple grounds for knowledge claims.

post-Fordism see FORDISM AND POST-FORDISM.

postindustrial society a conception of late 20th century society that highlights the declining dependence of the societies on manufacturing industry, the rise of new service industries, and a new emphasis on the role of knowledge in production, consumption, and leisure.

As formulated by Daniel Bell in *The Coming of Post-Industrial Society* (1974), modern societies, such as the United States and many European societies, are seen as increasingly *information societies,* that is, societies centered on knowledge and the production of new knowledge. An indication of this is the increased importance of higher education within these societies. According to Bell, knowledge is becoming the key source of innovation and the basis of social organization in these societies. This being so, new knowledge-based professional and occupational groups are also seen as increasingly achieving dominance within the class structures of these societies.

In this view, postindustrial societies may also be seen as a species of *postcapitalist society*, in which the owners of capital have conceded power to professional managers (compare MANAGERIAL REVOLUTION; see also CONVERGENCE). Although it finds some support, Bell's concept has also been widely criticized as failing to demonstrate that the undoubted increase in the importance of knowledge in modern societies actually does lead to a shift of economic power to a new class, especially to a new noncapitalist class.

In more general terms, there is relatively little acceptance that modern societies have moved beyond industrialism in any of the senses suggested. For example, if primary and manufacturing industry may seem to have declined in importance, this is deceptive, since much service production is production for manufacturing industry. Similarly, according to many commentators, the society of affluence and abundant LEISURE, often suggested as part of the idea of postindustrialism, remains a long way off (see also LEISURE SOCIETY).

postmodernism and **postmodernity** a cultural and ideological configuration variously defined, with different aspects of the general phenomenon emphasized by different theorists, postmodernity is seen as involving an end of the dominance of an overarching belief in scientific rationality and a unitary theory of PROGRESS, the replacement of empiricist theories of representation and TRUTH, and increased emphasis on the importance of the unconscious, on free-floating signs and images, and a plurality of view-points. Associated also with the idea of a postindustrial age (compare POSTINDUSTRIAL SOCIETY), theorists such as BAUDRILLARD (1983) and Lyotard (1984) make central to postmodernity a shift from a "productive" to a "reproductive" social order, in which simulations and models—and more generally, signs—increasingly constitute the world, so that any distinction between the appearance and the "real" is lost. Lyotard, for example, speaks especially of the replacement of any *grand narrative* by more local "accounts" of reality as distinctive of postmodernism and postmodernity. Baudrillard talks of the "triumph of signifying culture." Capturing the new orientation characteristic of postmodernism, compared with portrayals of modernity as an era or a definite period, the advent of postmodernity is often presented as a "mood" or "state of mind" (see Featherstone, 1988). If modernism as a movement in literature and the arts is also distinguished by its rejection of an emphasis on representation, postmodernism carries this movement a stage further. Another feature of postmodernism seen by some theorists is that the boundaries between "high" and "low" culture tend to be broken down, for example, motion pictures, jazz, and rock music (see Lash, 1990). According to many theorists, postmodernist cultural movements, which often overlap with new political tendencies and social movements in contemporary society, are particularly associated with the increasing importance of new class fractions, for example, "expressive professions" within the service class (see Lash and Urry, 1987). See also FORMS OF LIFE, DECENTERED SELF (OR SUBJECT), INCOMMENSURABILITY, STRUCTURALISM, DECONSTRUCTION.

poststructuralism see STRUCTURALISM, DECONSTRUCTION.

postulate of adequacy 1. the doctrine, especially in SOCIAL PHENOMENOLOGY, that sociological accounts and explanations must be understandable to the social actor(s) involved in the social situations described or explained (see SCHUTZ, 1972). **2.** the doctrine, particularly in WEBER, that sociological explanations must be adequate at the level of meaning (see also MEANINGFUL UNDERSTANDING AND EXPLANATION), but they must also possess *causal adequacy*. This means that there must be indication that the events described are grounded empirically, including a grounding in empirical regularities, that is, some probability that they would inevitably occur.

Not all sociologists accept Schutz's or even Weber's view, arguing instead that actors' understandings are frequently incoherent and may be properly explained away or supplanted by sociological explanations, for example, as merely surface meanings explicable in terms of underlying, perhaps unconscious, meanings (see PSYCHOANALYSIS) or as FALSE CONSCIOUSNESS resulting from IDEOLOGY, or explicable without any reference to meanings (as in BEHAVIORISM). In any of these cases, social outcomes may be seen as the UNANTICIPATED CONSEQUENCES OF SOCIAL ACTION.

GIDDENS' (1976a) response to this, in some ways a refinement of both Schutz's and Weber's views, is that while sociological accounts should always start from actors' meanings, they must often move beyond these, although they must never ignore or discount the actors' concepts. The view also exists that even complex decodings and supplantings of actors' meanings by sociological accounts can be fed back to the actors involved for acceptance and for action (as intended, for example, in FREUD's psychoanalysis or in HABERMAS's proposals, which are based on Freud and Marx, for an emancipatory social science). See also DOUBLE HERMENEUTIC.

postulate of functional indispensability or universal functionalism the doctrine in some forms of FUNCTIONALISM (see also FUNCTION) that "in every type of civilization, every custom, material object, idea and belief fulfills some vital function" (MALINOWSKI, 1926) and that "no cultural forms survive unless they constitute responses that are adjustive or adaptive in some way" (Kluckhohn, *Navaho Witchcraft*, 1944)—both of these quoted in Merton (1949). DURKHEIM (1897), though more cautious, nevertheless also made the assumption that the "average form" in any type of society was likely to be functional for the type.

Robert MERTON in particular, in his famous "codification of functional analysis" (Merton, 1949), challenged what he termed this "postulate of universal functionalism," which he defined as holding "that all standardized cultural forms have positive functions." The alleged "indispensability of religion," for example (see also FUNCTIONALIST THEORY OF RELIGION), is wrongly seen as based on the assumption "that it is through 'worship' and 'supernatural prescriptions' *alone* that the necessary minimum 'control over human conduct' and 'integration in terms of sentiments and beliefs' can be achieved." In challenging this view, Merton asserts that "the same function may be diversely fulfilled by alternative items." See FUNCTIONAL ALTERNATIVE, CIVIL RELIGION. See also FUNCTIONAL(IST) EXPLANATION.

potlatch a ritualized ceremony for the exchange of gifts and thereby the establishment of social standing and honor. It is found among various peoples of the northwest coast of North America. In its extreme form, potlatch could involve the symbolic public destruction of large quantities of goods, a practice that European colonizers banned. See also GIFT EXCHANGE AND GIFT RELATIONSHIP, KULA RING.

poverty trap the situation in which a slight increase in earnings leads to an individual or family being worse off overall as a consequence of losing entitlement to other benefits. People on low incomes in Britain, for example, may be eligible not only for social security support but may also make lower income tax and National Insurance (NI) contributions. A slight increase in their earnings may lead to loss of social security entitlement and put them in a position where they have to pay higher income tax and NI contributions; the slight increase in earnings may be considerably less than the extra amount they have to pay in NI and income tax contributions and their loss of social security support. The existence of a poverty trap is seen to be inevitable where there is a system of means-tested social security benefits.

A similar situation exists where single mothers may be considered to be in a poverty trap insofar as a woman in a reasonably well-paid job may have that income jeopardized by the need to pay for child care. By taking a part-time job or giving up paid work altogether, she may be able to look after her child or children but is likely to lose any occupational benefits, including a pension, as well as her career prospects.

power 1. the "transformational capacity" possessed by human beings, that is, "the capacity to intervene in a given set of events so as in some way to alter them" (GIDDENS, 1985). **2.** "the probability that one actor within a social relationship will be in a position to carry out his own will despite resistance" (WEBER, 1922). **3.** the reproductive or the transformational capacity possessed by social structures, which may be seen as existing independently of the wills of individual actors, for example, the power of market forces under capitalism.

Although power, especially in sense **2.** and sense **3.**, is often seen in negative terms, as involving coercion and conflicts of interest, all three senses of "power" can also be seen in more positive terms, as "enabling." Power relationships may involve both interdependence and conflict. For PARSONS (1963), for example, power is the capacity to achieve social and general societal objectives, and as such can be seen as analogous to MONEY, that is, it is the basis of a generalized capacity to attain goals.

As Giddens expresses it, power must be recognized as a primary concept in sociological analysis. It is potentially an aspect of all relationships, but one that he suggests has to be broken down into its various components before it can be used effectively in sociological analysis. A major distinction made by Giddens is between two types of resources involved in power, neither of which has primacy:

(a) control over material resources, that is, economic or *allocative resources;*

(b) *authoritative resources,* including LEGITIMATE AUTHORITY but also numerous other expressions of *authoritative power,* for example, SURVEILLANCE.

A further important distinction made by students of power (for example, Bachrach and Baratz, 1962, and Lukes, 1974), is between the power visible in overt *decisions* and that involved in *nondecisions,* that is, situations in which power is the outcome of a *mobilization of bias* within communities, the passive acceptance of established institutionalized power in which potential issues never reach the political arena.

Within structures or organizations we may also talk of the scope or intensity of the power or control that superordinates exert over subordinates. But control is never total. A DIALECTIC OF CONTROL can be said always to exist in that no agent (even a slave or child, or the inmates of a prison or an asylum) is ever totally powerless in a relationship, given that the active compliance of the subordinates is usually essential if a power relationship is not to become onerous for both parties to the relationship. Even when the balance of power between participants is unequal, there usually will be some reciprocities in power relationships (see also TOTAL INSTITUTION, VIOLENCE).

While power is an aspect of all areas of society and all institutions (for example, in families, churches, groups, and organizations of all types), in modern societies the major concentrations are the power of (a) NATION STATES and (b) capitalism. The first rests on the maintenance of LEGITIMATE AUTHORITY, but is ultimately grounded in physical violence. The second, in contrast to political power, is in its pure form quintessentially nonpolitical, and the major modern manifestation of allocative resources in modern society. However, in modern Western societies, capitalism also plays a central role in the maintenance of political legitimacy, in view of its effectiveness and widespread acceptability compared with other economic systems, although some commentators regard this as involving ideological and CULTURAL INCORPORATION, contrary to long-term interests (compare LEGITIMATION CRISIS).

Studies of the distribution as well as the implications of power in modern society have occupied a central place in POLITICAL SOCIOLOGY), with its focus on ELITES and RULING CLASSES, on parties and PRESSURE GROUPS, and on political and economic powerholders of all kinds. For Harold Laswell, for example, political sociology is about "Who gets what, when and how."

While some theorists such as C. Wright MILLS have suggested that modern societies are dominated by a narrow POWER ELITE, others including Robert Dahl and Seymour LIPSET strongly contest this view, seeing the situation as one involving PLURAL ELITES grounded in participant political cultures (see also STABLE DEMOCRACY). In an important study, followed by a seminal debate, Dahl sought to ground his viewpoint in empirical studies of community politics. However, his conclusions remain contested, being opposed particularly by those who point to his failure to take into account nondecisions in reaching his conclusion that no one person or group is in a position to dominate (see also COMMUNITY POWER). A third main viewpoint is provided by Marxist theorists, who argue either that an overt capitalist ruling class exists or, more usually, a more diffused structural power, seen as arising from capitalism's general allocative power, backed by control over what ALTHUSSER refers to as the *ideological state apparatus* or else by a more diffuse HEGEMONY.

One thing evident from all such debates is that issues arise in the conceptualization and study of power that are not readily resolved, so much so that doubts have been raised (for example, by Lukes, 1974) as to whether power is not an ESSENTIALLY CONTESTED CONCEPT, by which Lukes means that the value issues surrounding it can never be resolved in empirical terms, or indeed ever satisfactorily resolved. There are similarities between Lukes' position and Max WEBER's (see VALUE RELEVANCE).

It can be argued, however, that both views are needlessly restrictive. The complexities and the contested character of the concept of power can be acknowledged. But rather than singling out notoriously difficult concepts such as power as having a special status, sociological inquiry might be better served by recognition of the way in which many concepts in sociology tend to carry value loadings, leaving open the question of whether this makes them irresolvably contested. This would be closer to the viewpoint of Gallie (1955), the originator of the notion of "contested concepts."

Lukes is also cautious in the support he gives to any concept of structural power. This raises a final point about power: its overlap with both the concept of agency and the concept of structure, suggesting that Lukes' dismissal of structural power is too sweeping. Although there are problems in the use of either of these concepts in isolation, recently their use as a paired set has been held to offer greater prospect of a resolution of the problems that have attended use of either alone (see STRUCTURE AND AGENCY).

power elite the inner circle of power-holders in modern American society, according to C. Wright MILLS (1956). As portrayed by Mills, this elite group was composed of three loosely interlocking groups who had come to occupy pivotal positions of power in modern American society: heads of industry, military leaders, and leading politicians. Mills insisted that these three groups constituted a power elite rather than a RULING CLASS (in the Marxian sense), in that the basis of their power is not simply economic. Instead, the relative unity possessed by the power elite is seen as arising from their shared cultural and psychological orientations, and often also their shared social origins.

The further main theory of modern political elites is PLURAL ELITISM, in which multiple elites are held to exist but not seen to act as a unified group.

practical knowledge or **practical consciousness** (especially in SOCIAL PHENOMENOLOGY and ETHNOMETHODOLOGY) "what any social actor knows" in relation to his or her own action and social situation, but cannot necessarily express. Thus, practical knowledge is often TACIT KNOWLEDGE, involving either a general or a specific social competence.

practical reasoning 1. thought directed to, and having outcomes in, social activity. This usage originates in philosophy, where it is contrasted with theoretical reasoning, considered as describing the world and its contents. Practical reasoning, by contrast, either emanates directly in action or brings an immediate pressure to bear on it. It thus subsumes: considerations of the "self" realizing and maximizing its goods, "prudence," and considerations that restrict or encourage action or restraint from action in relation to others, that is, "morality." The most dramatic claims to a special status for practical reason derive from Aristotle's proposal of a *practical* *syllogism,* separate from theoretical syllogisms, in which an action itself (not a description or specification of an action) is held to follow logically from precedent premises, often summarized as a desire and a belief. The effect is to render action itself logical, and this is held by some to be the source of the meanings of action. Such logical connection is then held (for example, Von Wright, 1971) to mark the fundamental difference between the explanation of human activity and the explanation of natural events (see also MEANINGFUL UNDERSTANDING AND EXPLANATION). **2.** mundane, or everyday, thought in social situations. This ethnomethodological usage takes practical reasoning to be the central feature of routine social organization, and hence the subject matter of serious empirical sociology (see ETHNOMETHODOLOGY).

pragmatics the subdivision of linguistics concerned with the use of language in context. Pragmatics seeks to describe the systematic variation in the selection and production of linguistic items arising from the social environment. It is thus the most complex proposed level of language study, and the one about which fundamental disagreements exist. It is not settled whether it can be a systematic study, perhaps focusing on permissible or favored sequences of speech and action in systematically represented contexts, or whether it is a catchall category for all those aspects of meaning, largely particular, that fall outside SEMANTICS. Influential approaches include SPEECH ACT theory, which, following Austin and Searle, seeks to specify the rules for bringing about actions in speech (for example, promising) and ethnomethodological CONVERSATION ANALYSIS which, with its detailed evidence of preferred sequences, can make a serious claim to being the first successful empirical pragmatics.

pragmatism a philosophical approach that embraces the work of a number of US philosophers, including C.S. Peirce (1839–1914), William James (1842–1910), and John Dewey. Its central doctrine is that the meaning, and ultimately the TRUTH, of a concept or proposition relates merely to its practical effects. Thus, for Peirce, scientific hypotheses should be judged by the testable deductions they permit, as well as by their simplicity, capacity to cope with new evidence, etc. For William James, ideas become true only insofar as they help us to interrelate our experiences. In at least some of their forms, CONVENTIONALISM and *instrumentalism* are doctrines related to pragmatism: in all three, scientific laws and theories tend to be seen as principles that guide our actions, rather than as literal descriptions of the world. Similarities also exist with modern philosophical notions that all theories are "underdetermined" by evidence, and that criteria other than "empirical fit" are involved in or decisions about theories.

praxis (Marxism) purposive action, including political action, to alter the material and social world, including humanity itself. As a central general concept within Marxism, praxis draws attention to the socially constructed nature of economic and social institutions and the possibility of changing these—people's capacity for freedom, which cannot be achieved entirely at the individual level. Praxis can be given more specific meanings, for example, "revolutionary praxis," but its main use is as a general concept capable of receiving a variety of emphases, for example, in some uses (within Marxism) a tension may exist between praxis and necessity.

prejudice any opinion or ATTITUDE that is unjustified by the facts. The term tends to have a negative connotation both because a prejudiced person's opinions are unfounded and often not formed through first-hand experience, but also the attitudes described are usually negative in relation to the object they are held about. However, one can hold a positive but prejudiced attitude.

Prejudice has been related to personality type (see AUTHORITARIAN PERSONALITY), and also to group membership. As with all attitudes, prejudices are the result of social learning within families and other social groups where opportunities for modeling and strong pressures toward conformity exist. See also STEREOTYPE, ETHNOCENTRISM.

pressure group (POLITICAL SCIENCE) any organized association of persons with the aim of influencing the policies and actions of governments or changing public opinion. In contrast with political parties, pressure groups do not seek to become the government, although in some cases organizations that begin as pressure groups may become political parties. The term *interest group* is mainly used interchangeably with pressure group.

A distinction can be drawn between:

(a) groups that succeed, if only for a time, in establishing a continuing direct relationship with government, for example, the National Farmers' Union and the American Medical Association;

(b) *attitudinal* or *promotional groups* (for example, the National Rifle Association), which mostly attempt to influence governments more indirectly by seeking to alter the general climate of public opinion.

Groups in the former category are usually based on a clearly defined economic interest. Their ability to establish a continuing direct relationship with government appears to depend on (i) the claim to represent a significant proportion of potentially eligible membership and (ii) advantages that arise for government as well as the interest group from a sustained cooperative relationship (see Eckstein (1960)).

The existence of a multiplicity of pressure groups of varying types is often regarded as an important indicator of the extent of political pluralism within a society. This may be so, but should not disguise the fact that significant differences exist in the capacity of individuals to engage in, or find representation in, effective pressure group activity. See also PLURALISM, CORPORATISM, SOCIAL MOVEMENTS.

primary deviance the initial act of rule-breaking. Lemert (1961) used the term "primary deviance" rather than DEVIANCE, but the latter is now in more common use. It has to be understood in relation to SECONDARY

DEVIANCE.

primary group a small group, such as the family, friends, or colleagues at work. COOLEY (1909) classified groups into primary and *secondary groups*. The former have their own norms of conduct and involve much face-to-face interaction, while the latter are large and rarely involve direct interaction with all the members (for example, a labor union or a political party).

primary sector the sector of the economy, including agriculture and mining, concerned with production and extraction of raw materials.

primitive society the least internally differentiated, and earliest, form(s) of human societies. As one of a number of terms (for example, SIMPLE SOCIETY or SAVAGERY) used to refer to such societies, the use of "primitive society" suggests an elementary or basic level of technological and social organizational complexity. Theorists such as Levy-Bruhl (1923) have also proposed prelogical forms of *primitive mentality* associated with such levels of technological and social organization.

Notwithstanding the sympathetic and nonjudgmental way that the term "primitive society" has often been employed, its pejorative connotations have tended to lead to the use of alternative terms, such as simple society, TRIBAL SOCIETY, and NONLITERATE SOCIETY. However, these alternatives cannot escape derogatory overtones entirely. These arise from the basic cultural assumptions of modern societies in which modern society is seen as a superior form. The only solution is to continue to work toward accounts of premodern societies that do not automatically adopt such assumptions but explore the qualities of these forms of society in an open-ended way. See also EVOLUTIONARY THEORY.

primogeniture 1. the condition of being the firstborn child. **2.** the right of succession or inheritance of the firstborn child. Inheritance systems vary between societies and are extremely important for the transmission and hence accumulation of property. Many Northern European societies practice primogeniture, and this may be associated with greater accumulation of wealth and property than where these are dispersed among several members of a family. In particular, primogeniture prevents landholdings from being divided into ever smaller plots. In many societies, the first born usually means the firstborn male.

prisoners' dilemma a paradigm case in the THEORY OF GAMES, in which two prisoners, against whom there is some evidence of a crime but not enough to convict and who cannot communicate with each other, are each promised a light sentence if one of them confesses and the other, who would then be given a severe sentence, does not. If both confess, they are promised a moderate sentence, but if neither confesses then both will receive a light sentence. The case this illustrates is the nonzero-sum game (see ZERO-SUM GAME), since there is no single rational outcome. If neither confesses, both gain more than if both confess, but by not confessing they risk the most severe of the three possible penalties that will be imposed if only one confesses. Like all such hypothetical examples in game theory, the suggestion is that such models illuminate situations in the real world— even if they do not exactly match them.

pristine states or **primal states** the first STATES, believed to have arisen in the Middle East and perhaps also in North India, from which all subsequent states, *secondary states*, are assumed to have developed, as both a defensive reaction to, and modeled on, the first states. Fried (1967), Carneiro (1970), and Harris (1978) for example, make warfare a major factor in the origins of the first states. However, since warfare existed long before the existence of states, the decisive factors accounting for the rise of states were:

(a) the much closer proximity—or impaction—of adjacent peoples in river valley societies (for example, Mesopotamia before 3000 BC; Peru, first century AD; and Mesoamerica, AD 300) that had undergone the AGRICULTURAL REVOLUTION but were confined by natural barriers;

(b) the far greater competition for resources that occurred in these societies when, relative to population expansion, there may have been a depletion of resources. Under conditions of food shortages and an escalation of conflicts between societies, a new coordination of populations is hypothesized as leading to an increasing incidence of warfare and the origin of states. The process involved subordination of defeated groups within ever larger groupings, and also incorporation of others who preferred to pay taxes and tribute rather than engage in warfare or flee beyond the reach of states.

private and public spheres a dichotomous model of social relations that posits the separation between the domestic sphere of the family and that of socialized labor (wage work) and political activity. This model finds expression both commonsensically in phrases such as "a woman's place is in the home" and within the social sciences (see Elshtain, 1981). It has been common practice for historians and social scientists to argue that industrialization and urbanization effected a separation between home and work, the personal and the political. This separation was gendered, with the domestic sphere being associated with women and children, the public sphere with adult males. The domestic ideal of separate domains for men and women was particularly promoted in the 19th century by the emergent middle classes and was given expression in 19th-century social policy and legislation. However, the splitting of the domestic from the economic and political spheres was, and continues to be, more ideological than empirical. It also serves as an example of the dualism found in much Western thought.

The work of Davidoff (1979) and Summers (1979) has questioned the historical existence of the dichotomy. Davidoff argues that the division between public and private spheres cannot be taken as given, even in the 19th century. She argues that the existence of domestic service, the taking in of lodgers, homework and the performance of a wide variety of subsidiary household tasks for payment indicates that the economy cannot be located solely outside the home. Summers documents the ways in which both middle and upper class women continually renegotiated the divisions between private and public in pursuit of their philanthropic work.

Siltanen and Stanworth (1984) also challenged the immutability of the boundaries between the spheres, criticizing both political and industrial sociology for taking the dichotomy for granted. Industrial sociology has operated according to the principle of the "job model for men" and the "gender model for women" (for example, Blauner 1964). Men are defined in terms of their relationship to work and the economy, women in terms of their relationship to the family. Men's class position is therefore determined mainly by their place in the occupational structure, women's by their position in the family. Political sociology has often located both women and the private sphere outside of politics. Political sociologists have characterized women as either apolitical or more conservative than men (for example, see Dowse and Hughes, 1972). A "male-stream" view of women's engagement with politics and economics has been fostered, rendering their involvement invisible or subject to misrepresentation.

The resurgence of feminism in the late 1960s was responsible for stressing the political nature of personal life, particularly in the areas of domestic labor, child care, sexuality, and male violence against women. Thus, the definition of what constituted "the political" was widened to incorporate the private sphere. Siltanen and Stanworth argue, however, that feminists have been less successful in challenging the dichotomy as a whole. For them the relationship *between* the spheres is a matter for political analysis, which must take account of the fluid nature of the spheres and reject a tendency to depict them as fixed. They argue that just as politics is not the prerogative of the public sphere, so the personal sphere enters into and influences the public sphere. Neither sphere is the exclusive domain of one gender. Men's involvement in the public sphere is influenced by their position in the domestic sphere, and, historically, women have occupied space in the public realm, and continue to do so. Furthermore, the state continues to engage with the private sphere, regulating and reconstructing it.

private property see PROPERTY.

privatization 1. the sale or transfer of nationalized, publicly owned industries into private ownership and control. In Britain this process is particularly associated with the economic and social theories of Thatcherism. The sale of shares in British Telecom, British Petroleum, British Gas, British Airways, and other companies is one aspect of this. In other areas the sale of council houses, and proposed changes in the WELFARE STATE, particularly in the funding of health and education, are comparable. This tendency is mirrored, to a lesser extent, in the United States. **2.** retreat of the individual from participation in political and PUBLIC activities. **3.** a process in which traditional, working-class communal lifestyles are said to have been replaced by more family and home-centered lifestyles, away from the older working class housing and in relatively new housing estates. Sense **3.** is particularly associated with the AFFLUENT WORKER study of GOLDTHORPE, LOCKWOOD et al. (1968–1969). The focus of interest in this work is the hypothesis that significant changes in attitudes are associated with privatization. In particular, the breakdown of class loyalties, an "instrumentalist" orientation to work, a new concern with living standards and status, a more pragmatic political orientation (rather than an automatic support for the Labor Party), greater job mobility, and, generally, more individualistic attitudes. The Affluent Worker study is undoubtedly a classic of British sociological research. Drawing on a number of themes that were popular in the 1950s and 1960s, it has been a source for theoretical and empirical work in the areas of working class structure, CLASS CONSCIOUSNESS, and CLASS IMAGERY. Critics have indicated the oversimplification of Lockwood and Goldthorpe's categories, questioning their empirical usefulness in circumstances in which nontraditional class locations are associated with instrumentality and increased political militancy. Critics have also noted the lack of consideration given to factors other than social CLASS in the work: race, gender, religion, and age, for example, may all affect attitudes (see Rose, 1988). As part of the reorientation of British sociology in the study of social class and class consciousness, though, this study of changing aspects of social class structure and consciousness remains of central importance.

probability (STATISTICS) a number ranging from 0 (impossible) to 1 (certain) that indicates how likely it is that a specific outcome will occur in the long run. *Probability theory* is concerned with setting up rules for manipulating probabilities and calculating the probabilities of complex events. It predicts how random variables are likely to behave and provides a numerical estimate of that prediction. In sociology, it is particularly important for sampling procedures and statistical inference.

A *probability sample* is another name for a RANDOM SAMPLE, that is, a sample selected in such a way that all units in the population have a known chance of selection. The advantage of using random (probability) samples in sociological research is that probability theory enables an estimate to be made of the amount of sampling error when sample results are generalized to the population. See SAMPLE AND SAMPLING.

Statistical inference deals with two related problems, the estimation of unknown population parameters and the testing of hypotheses from sample data. From sample data, summary descriptive statistics are obtained, for example, the sample mean or the sample proportion. The Central Limit Theorem states that if random large samples of equal size are repeatedly drawn from any population, sample statistics such as the mean will have a normal (Gaussian) distribution. One property of this distribution is that there is a constant proportion of probabilities lying within a specified distance from the mean. It is this characteristic that allows statistical inferences from random sample statistics to populations. Calculating a sample mean does not allow a certain statement of what the population mean is, but with the knowledge of the sampling distribution, an estimate of it can be made with a specific level of confidence, for example, a probability of 0.95 (95%), or 0.99 (99%).

A SIGNIFICANCE TEST tests the probability of an observed result in sample data occurring by chance. Knowledge of the theoretical frequency distributions allows a probability value to be attached to the test statistic and if this is sufficiently low, for example, $p = < 0.05$ or $p = < 0.01$, the NULL HYPOTHESIS is rejected (see SIGNIFICANCE TESTS). Both tests of significance and confidence levels are based on the laws of probability.

probability sample see PROBABILITY.

probability theory see PROBABILITY.

problematique or **problematic** the system of questions and concepts that makes up any particular science (ALTHUSSER and Balibar, 1968). This concept plays a broadly equivalent role within the work of Louis Althusser to the concept of PARADIGM in the work of Thomas KUHN or the concept of EPISTEME in the work of FOUCAULT. As for Kuhn, in Althusser's view new scientific problematiques involve a revolutionary EPISTEMOLOGICAL BREAK with previous ways of thinking. Thus, Althusser argues that Marxism as a scientific problematique was born only after Marx's break with Hegelian ideas in 1845. Thereafter, Marx operated within an implicit problematique, which later scientific Marxists developed.

problem of demarcation the problem(s) surrounding the identification of science, especially proposals for a single *criterion of demarcation of science,* such as FALSIFICATIONISM (see also POSITIVISM).

problem of order see SOCIAL ORDER.

productive labor and **unproductive labor** (Marxism) contrasting forms of labor within capitalism and the capitalist mode of production that arise as an implication of acceptance of the labor theory of value. While *productive labor* refers to those forms of labor that create surplus value, *unproductive labor* refers to those forms of labor that do not do so. Only those forms of labor that in a fully socialized economy would be necessary are regarded as socially necessary labor. All other forms of labor, which may be necessary within a capitalist economy for the realization of surplus value rather than its creation (for example, bank clerks) or for the ideological justification of capitalism (for example, some forms of intellectual labor), are held not to constitute forms of productive labor. If the labor theory of value is challenged, such Marxist conceptions of unproductive and unproductive labor lose much of their cogency. See also CONTRADICTORY CLASS LOCATIONS.

profession any MIDDLE CLASS occupational group characterized by claims to a high level of technical and intellectual expertise, autonomy in recruitment and discipline, and, in Britain, a commitment to public service. The traditional professions are law, medicine, the ministry, and the armed forces, but both the term and its application are still debated. Among the reasons for this are the rise of new areas of technical knowledge and specialization and the everyday use of the term to refer to any and all occupations, or to distinguish between individuals who have exactly the same expertise by some nontechnical standard (for example, money, social class). In the sociological literature, the debates have tended to concern problems of definition and the most significant features of professions.

Until the 1970s, there was a tendency in sociological work to discuss professions in their own terms and thus to reflect a functionalist ideology of expert public service as the main criterion for professional status. An early contribution (Flexner, 1915) exemplifies this. Flexner emphasized the intellectual, nonmanual character of professions that necessitated long, specialized training in knowledge and techniques, their strong internal organization to deal with communication and discipline, and their practical orientation, which was seen as altruistic—motivated by public service rather than personal profit.

Most sociological work until recently echoed these themes, emphasizing the high status that followed from these characteristics. Later functionalists continued to debate the nature of professions, emphasizing different elements but broadly agreeing on the essential points. Talcott PARSONS (1964a) took the argument further. He started with the familiar features of esoteric knowledge and altruism but added that by virtue of expertise and knowledge, the professional has authority over the lay person and that the characteristics of professionalism were a distinct and increasingly important feature of modern institutions. The implication that professionalization was occurring on an important scale has been a theme in much of the work on professions but has not always been developed in the same terms used by Parsons or other functionalists. Whereas functionalists tended to emphasize the value to society and the high prestige and selflessness of professions, other approaches have emphasized power and self-interest. One might say that where the view from the professions emphasized the advantages of professionalism to the community, later critical approaches stressed the advantages to the professionals themselves. One of the earliest of these analyses was by Hughes (1952), who argued that professions did not simply operate to the benefit of clients, their organization and practices also protected and benefited the practitioners. In particular, the claim to authoritative knowledge means that only the professionals can judge whether work has been done properly, and the professional organization can serve to defend the practitioner rather than the client. This critical view has been typical of more recent approaches. Johnson (1972) developed the argument on the relationship between client and practitioner, emphasizing the power professionals have to define the needs and treatment of their clients and to resolve any disputes in their own favor. Parry and Parry (1976) studied the medical profession and argued that the producer-consumer relationship is a less important consideration than the wish to establish a monopoly of practice—to get rid of rival medical approaches. The claim to unique competence, legally supported, is the basic strategy of professionalization. Self-regulation and control of recruitment are essential parts of the process. The advantages of professional (monopoly) status are to guarantee high material rewards, exclude outside judgment of performance, and give guaranteed security of tenure to those allowed to practice.

This argument sees professionalization as a self-interested strategy and, in that sense, breaks down many of the distinctions that were formerly made between middle class and working class occupations. Skilled manual workers, for example, also have attempted to control recruitment by apprenticeships and to protect members' security by labor unionism and restrictive job definitions whereby permissibility to do particular jobs was strictly limited to a craft member. Manual workers, due to factors such as technological change and market situation in periods of high unemployment, have been less successful than professions in maintaining their monopoly privileges, but there are signs that the traditional professions are under pressure in their claims to monopoly and autonomy. The increasing popularity and success of alternative medicine, for example, and proposed changes in the legal profession in Britain, including the weakening of solicitors' effective monopoly on conveyancing and barristers' monopoly on higher court representation, are cases in point. These changes, though, have not diminished the popularity of professionalization as a strategy of SOCIAL MOBILITY, because material and prestige rewards are still apparent.

professionalization the process whereby an occupation succeeds in claiming the status, and therefore the rewards and privileges, of a PROFESSION.

progress 1. a movement toward a desired objective; a development or advance that is favorably regarded. **2.** the result of social development, involving the enhancement of scientific and technological knowledge, economic productivity, and the complexity of social organization.

Two main viewpoints in sociology on the idea of progress can be noticed:

(a) theories that embrace the concept in identifying the main historical route taken by progress—20th-century theories such as Parsons' conception of EVOLUTIONARY UNIVERSALS, and 19th-century theories (see EVOLUTIONARY THEORY);

(b) theories, especially since the end of the 19th century and the early 20th century, that for a variety of reasons reject the idea of progress.

The concept of progress lay at the core of early sociological thinking and is especially evident in the work of the discipline's founding trinity. For MARX, progress lay in the development of the forces of production and their eventual use, after revolutionary struggle, in the satisfaction of human need rather than private accumulation; for WEBER, somewhat more ambivalently, it lay in the RATIONALIZATION of economic, organizational, legal, and scientific life; and for DURKHEIM in the enhanced possibilities for individual freedom in forms of organic solidarity (see MECHANICAL AND ORGANIC SOLIDARITY).

Much earlier 19th-century EVOLUTIONARY THEORY, however, had tended to see development as also involving a civilizing process, that is, a transition from simple SAVAGERY and barbarism to the so-called enlightenment achieved by the European ruling, capitalist, and Christian classes. NEOEVO-LUTIONISM attempted to avoid this problem of value-laden definitions of progress by speaking of an increase in the "general adaptive capacity of society" or the "all-round capability of culture" (M. Sahlins and E. Service, 1960).

A continuing characteristic of advanced and especially capitalist industrial societies is the rapidity of technological progress, with particular reference to the new technologies. The impacts of these developments on economic and social life are a continuing source of debate and are intimately connected with contemporary theories of SOCIAL CHANGE. See also MODERNIZATION, FORDISM AND POST-FORDISM, POSTINDUSTRIAL SOCIETY.

The alternative, more pessimistic, view of progress includes:

(a) pessimism, especially associated with conservative thinking, for example, from NEO-MACHIAVELLIAN political theorists (for example, PARETO, MICHELS) and NIETZSCHE, over the implications of "mass democracy," MASS SOCIETY, etc.;

(b) pessimism associated with concrete political events, especially the end of the long peace of the 19th century (which had led earlier theorists, for example, SPENCER, to believe this would usher in a new, pacific age), including World War I, the rise of fascism in the interwar years culminating in World War II, and the threat of nuclear holocaust of the postwar era of cold war. Added to this, there have arisen concerns about new threats to the environment, and questions have been raised about the sustainability of current patterns of economic growth.

The 20th century retreat from POSITIVISM and EMPIRICISM, and the undermining of most forms of philosophical ESSENTIALISM, have been a further dimension questioning any simple assumptions about progress (see POSTMODERNISM, DECONSTRUCTION).

progressive and degenerating scientific research programs see FALSIFICATIONISM.

projective test an indirect test of personality in which individuals are assumed to reveal their personality traits by projecting them onto the deliberately ambiguous stimuli responded to. Examples include the RORSCHACH INKBLOT TEST (Rorschach, 1921) and the Thematic Apperception Test (TAT) (Murray, 1943).

proletarianization 1. (Marxism) the process whereby intermediate groups and classes (see INTERMEDIATE GROUPS) are reduced, by an inevitable logic of monopolization and capitalization, to the level of wage laborers. **2.** in more recent sociology, the process in which the work situation of some middle-class workers becomes increasingly comparable to that of the manual working class, with consequent implications for labor union and political attitudes.

In the latter, more common sociological meaning, the focus has usually been on routine WHITE-COLLAR and office workers. One of the first extensive discussions of office work in this context was that of David LOCKWOOD (1958), who concluded that tendencies to proletarianization were offset by differences in the STATUS and work situation of these workers compared with manual workers. The argument was later taken up, notably in the work of Harry Braverman (1974), who suggested that the logic of capitalist development was to deskill and routinize work wherever possible, whether by introduction of new technology or by reorganization of work, broadly on the principle of SCIENTIFIC MANAGEMENT. The outcome of these changes in the labor process was to degrade work and make redundant previous status differentials. Braverman's thesis, however, has been the subject of extensive debate. His work has been criticized, among other things, for oversimplifying the degree of deskilling, neglecting the development of new occupational groups with new and high-level skills, and ignoring the extent to which workers are able to resist management pressures. Also, continuing Lockwood's theme, while it is the case that the lower sectors of white-collar and MIDDLE CLASS occupations are comparable to manual work in some terms, for example, pay and autonomy, important differences remain in working conditions and, for some white-collar workers, job security, sick pay, and promotion prospects. Routh (1980), for instance, showed that about 80% of male white-collar workers who started in routine office work were promoted during their working lives. This is not the situation for women, who constitute about 70% of routine office workers and have far fewer opportunities for upward mobility (Crompton and Jones, 1984) (see also CONTRADICTORY CLASS LOCATIONS). The situation is also complicated by the ways in which gender expectations affect market and work situations. See also CLASS, SOCIAL STRATIFICATION, SOCIAL MOBILITY, MULTIDIMENSIONAL ANALYSIS OF SOCIAL STRATIFICATION, CLASS POLARIZATION, CLASS IMAGERY.

proletariat 1. (Marxism) the class of propertyless laborers who live by selling their LABOR POWER to capitalists in exchange for wages. The condition for employment is held to be exploitative, in that in creating value workers increase the wealth and power of the bourgeoisie against their own interests. Thus, in this perspective, the proletariat is conceptualized in an antagonistic relation to the bourgeoisie and is, inevitably, exploited and oppressed. **2.** more generally, in sociology, the WORKING CLASS. See also PROLETARIANIZATION, CLASS.

property the rights of possession or ownership recognized within a society.

PROPERTY

Such possessions may be individually or collectively owned (including corporate as well as communal or state ownership), and include rights to LAND and housing, means of production and capital, and sometimes other human beings. Wide variations exist in the rights recognized within different societies, and these differences are often regarded as fundamental in determining overall differences between societies. In their widest sense, rights of property include rights to alienate (to sell, will, etc.) but often may be limited to rights of control and rights to benefit from use. Historically—for example, in many simple societies and preindustrial agrarian societies—absolute rights of *private property* have been comparatively rare. Conceptions of absolute rights of private property existed for a time in ANCIENT SOCIETY, but achieve a decisive importance only in CAPITALIST SOCIETIES. Even then, however, restrictions have usually remained.

Justifications of forms of property are an important part of the ideological legitimation that occurs in most societies, not least justifications of private property, notwithstanding that one of the justifications for private property has been the argument that it is a natural form (see LOCKE, SMITH). Among important justifications for it have been the idea, especially influential in the period preceding modern capitalism, that individuals have a right to the fruits of their own labor. Arguments for unlimited rights to private property have been countered by an emphasis on the social character of all production, the concept of social needs, and conceptions of social JUSTICE and ideals of equality. On the other hand the recognition of individual property rights has been emphasized as a significant source of limitations on STATE power, the development of civil society, and the appearance of modern CITIZEN RIGHTS.

Sociological assessment of differences in, and consequences of differences between, societies in property rights is usually considered by sociologists to require more than regard merely to legal categories of property. An assessment of effective ownership and control, and the inequalities in wealth and income, life chances, etc. related to these, is also essential. See also PUBLIC OWNERSHIP.

prophet any "individual bearer of charisma" (for example, as demonstrated by ecstatic powers or MAGIC) who by virtue of his or her mission, "proclaims a religious doctrine or divine commandment" (WEBER, 1922). For Weber, it is the "personal call" and personal revelation of the prophet that distinguishes him or her from the *priest*, who has authority only as the "servant of a sacred tradition." Weber also notes that prophets have usually come from outside the priesthood.

A further significant distinction in Weber's discussion is that between *ethical prophecy*, in which the prophet proclaims God's will (for example, Muhammad), and *exemplary prophecy*, where the prophet demonstrates by personal example the way to personal salvation (for example, Buddha). According to Weber, the latter is characteristic of the Far East and the former appears initially in the Near East and is associated with the appearance of conceptions of a personal, transcendental, ethical God only in this region. See also MONOTHEISM.

prostitution 1. (common usage) a practice involving sexual services for payment or other reward. **2.** (legalistic usage) a sex-specific offense; although in England and Wales prostitution has technically been regarded as behavior open to both women and men, in practice only women have been legally defined as common prostitutes and only women are prosecuted for the offenses of loitering and soliciting related to prostitution. Legalistic definitions of prostitution, however, are culturally and historically relative. Prostitution is not always subject to criminalization and in some cultures the practice may be regarded as a sacred rite. In societies where prostitution and related behaviors are criminalized, it is typically the prostitute rather than the client whose behavior is regulated, reflecting double standards of sexual morality. **3.** (extralegal usage) an economic contract intrinsically equal to the practice of a man and woman contracting marriage primarily for economic reasons (see ENGELS, 1884). Such attempts to go beyond the legal definitions of prostitution have been influential in feminist theory. Marx drew parallels between the economic prostitution of the worker arnd that of the prostitute. In doing so he neglected to consider the specific sexual exploitation and oppression experienced by women. Feminist theorists have also likened prostitution to marriage. Millett (1970) maintains that prostitution should be defined as the granting of sexual access on a relatively indiscriminate basis for payment. These approaches, however, fail to account for the particular stigmatization encountered by those women who work as prostitutes.

Traditionally, the sociological study of prostitution has taken place within the context of the sociology of crime and deviance (see CRIMINOLOGY and DEVIANCE). Thus, sociologists have often uncritically accepted that prostitution should be regarded as primarily an example of rule-breaking behavior or female deviancy. More recently, the impact of feminism has led to prostitution being examined within the context of wider gender relations and the socioeconomic position of women, particularly working-class and minority women. Sociologists have increasingly acknowledged accounts of prostitution given by prostitutes themselves, particularly those that present prostitution as part of the sex trade or sex industry. Arguably, it may therefore be as useful to examine prostitution in the context of the SOCIOLOGY OF WORK and occupations rather than in the context of deviant behavior.

Protestant ethic a code of conduct derived from the redirection of Christian ASCETICISM by Puritan elements within Protestantism. Asceticism arose in Christianity because zealous believers realized that methodical life planning, self-control, and self-denial were the best defenses against the ethical inconsistency that offended God and so jeopardized achievement of their ultimate end, salvation. In Catholicism, however, asceticism was confined to the monasteries; it did not penetrate the lives of ordinary believers who remained trapped in the ethically inconsistent cycle of sin, repentance, and renewed sin made possible by confession and indulgences. The Protestant ethic rested on a rejection of this dual morality and on an interpretation of monasticism as a selfish evasion of worldly responsibilities. Accordingly it demanded: (a) that all believers maintain ethical consistency by means of ascetic regulation; (b) that they do so, not in the monasteries, but in the faithful discharge of their worldly duties.

Principal among these duties were those associated with the believers' occupations (callings, vocations). It was this emphasis that provided WEBER with the grounds for the conclusion he reached in *The Protestant Ethic and the Spirit of Capitalism* (1930): insofar as it influenced human conduct, the Protestant ethic had a major impact on post-Reformation capitalism. According to Weber, capitalistic conduct was based on individualistic profit-seeking. More analysis, however, disclosed that individual capitalists were animated by a feeling of moral responsibility toward their resources, to increase them without limit by hard work, moderate consumption, and saving for investment. All the elements of asceticism were present in the resultant conduct: it was methodically planned, self-controlled, self-denying—with reference to consumption and leisure—and single-mindedly directed toward achievement of an ultimate end—economic acquisition and expansion.

Conduct like this seemed to Weber to be the result of a fundamental transformation in human character and values. Human beings were not *by nature* ascetic; they were easygoing and inconsistent, preferred leisure to disciplined work, and regarded single-minded devotion to economic acquisition as antisocial and immoral. Since the profit motive and capitalist institutions existed outside the post-Reformation West, without giving rise to ethically legitimated ascetic acquisitiveness, Weber did not think that economic interests provided sufficient incentive for human beings to break the mold of nature and impose ascetic regulation on themselves.

So what did? Weber thought that religion did, and he cited the example of Catholic monasticism to prove it. Once Puritanism redirected this asceticism the achievement of the zealous believers' ultimate end—the assurance of salvation—became linked to the discharge of their vocational obligations. God called Christians to serve Him by vocational activity. For this He gave them gifts of time, talent, and resources and called them to work and save those resources so that His glory might be manifest in their use and increase. Idleness and thriftlessness, therefore, became the deadliest of sins, while the fruits of ascetically regulated diligence and thrift—growing profits and economic expansion—became valued as signs of God's blessing and thus provided believers with an assurance of salvation.

It was this need for assurance that forced people to undertake ascetic regulation. It arose because Puritan teachings about salvation caused anxiety. Puritans held that God granted salvation as a gift, either through pre-destination of a minority—as in Calvinism—or in an offer made directly to individuals—as in other traditions. Either way believers became anxious to assure themselves that they were among the saved. Since God dealt direct-ly with individuals, proof could not be established through the mediation or sacramental ministry of the churches. It had to come through individual conviction developed by faith and a demonstration that God's grace had transformed an individual from the state of nature, indicated by ethical inconsistency, to the state of grace, proved through ascetic vocational con-duct. Human character was thus changed; fear broke the mold of nature and forced people to become ruthless ascetics dedicated to work, saving, and expansion.

Puritanism, therefore, provided capitalism with some signal services: (a) it molded a type of character ideally suited to expanding the system; (b) it legitimated individualistic profit-seeking by making it a duty willed by God; (c) it legitimated the division of labor by making specialist occupational activity a duty; (d) it legitimated capitalist exploitation and work discipline by making conscientious labor a duty; (e) it created a cultural climate in which poverty could be seen as a result of individual moral failings, that is, idleness and thriftlessness, and so freed the successful and the system from responsibility for poverty. Capitalism, nevertheless, soon outgrew the reli-gious origins of its spirit. In its developed form it rests on its own founda-tions; those who refuse to engage in capitalistically appropriate conduct will perish in the struggle for survival.

Weber's thesis generated a great unresolved conflict in which economic historians, church historians, theologians, and other nonsociologists have taken part. Among other things, he has been accused of: (a) failing to see that ethically uninhibited acquisitiveness and economic individualism were older than the Reformation (Robertson, 1933; Tawney, 1926); (b) ignoring Protestant ethical reservations about acquisition (George and George, 1958; Hudson, 1949); (c) ignoring Catholic and lay vocational teachings that were similar in purpose and content to those of the Puritans (Robertson, 1933; Samuelson, 1961). Much of this criticism is, however, based on misunderstandings. Weber was not trying to explain ethically uninhibited acquisitiveness or economic individualism, only the ascetic spirit that developed in capitalism after the Reformation. Nor did he ignore Puritan ethical reservations about acquisition; he admitted them but claimed that they were not directed against wealth as such, only its misuse in idleness and consumption. Weber was also aware of the non-Puritan teachings about vocational diligence. However, he doubted their effective-ness because they were not supported by psychological sanctions of the sort that derived from the Puritan anxiety about salvation. For all this, Weber's thesis remains open to attack; some writers, for example, doubt that Puritanism generated psychological sanctions derived from anxiety

(Keating, 1985; McKinnon, 1988); Puritan writings on economic acquisition are ambiguous enough to sustain both pro- and anti-Weberian interpretations. When it is finally remembered that it is hard to establish unambiguously the direction of influence-holding between religion and economic life—Marxists, for example, would argue for causation in the opposite direction—it is easy to see why Weber's thesis retains an aura of plausibility, while at the same time attracting doubt. It is likely, therefore, to remain controversial so long as social scientists retain an interest in the problem to which it speaks.

psephology the study and analysis of voting and VOTING BEHAVIOR (see ELECTORAL SOCIOLOGY). The term is derived from the Greek practice of voting by writing names on fragments of pottery or stones (Greek *psephos*, pebble). It is mainly in use in POLITICAL SCIENCE.

psychiatry the treatment of the mentally ill by medically trained practitioners. Psychiatry is a branch of general medicine, using drug treatment as a clinical resource, but also other physical methods such as surgery and ECT (electroconvulsive therapy). Thus, on the orthodox medical model, the patient is seen as having a specific dysfunction, and specific physical intervention is used to effect improvement. However, though physical intervention may be a first resort, the influence of PSYCHOANALYSIS, BEHAVIOR THERAPY, and COUNSELING and other nonphysical approaches to treating mental illness have considerably altered this interventionist approach. Though the management of the PSYCHOSES is still dependent on drug treatment, a variety of other techniques are used that emphasize the importance of the patient's perception and experience and the patient's role in their own treatment, and the appropriateness of behavioral techniques for changing behavior is widely acknowledged in the profession. These methods are accepted as being of particular value for the neurotic patient, and this, together with the evidence for severe problems of addiction arising from the prolonged use of tranquilizers, has led to a swing from drug treatment to these so-called softer methods for the neurotic patient beginning in the 1980s. See also ANTIPSYCHIATRY.

psychoanalysis the method of treating mental illness by investigating the *unconscious* and understanding the dynamics of the personality. It was originally developed by FREUD at the end of the 19th century, working particularly with patients with emotional disorders, such as hysteria. FREUD particularly used the techniques of free association and dream interpretation to explore the unconscious.

Psychoanalysis is a lengthy process, often taking several years, and practitioners have to undergo a course of psychoanalysis themselves before being considered qualified to practice. The aim is to gain a full understanding of how one's current behavior was developed as a result of past experiences, especially those of early childhood. These early experiences have to be brought to consciousness and confronted, leading to catharsis, or a release of energy, with the result that the personality becomes freer, less restricted by having to control the energies of the ID, or operate under overly strict demands of the SUPEREGO.

In psychiatric practice, 100 years after its original development, the method is found to be most useful for neurotic disorders in patients who are highly motivated to recover and of good educational background, as self-insight and an interest in the theoretical basis appear to be involved in a positive outcome. However, it is much criticized as having no better record for recovery than time alone (Eysenck, 1961), and it is lengthy and expensive.

psychodrama see MORENO.

psychologism the use of a psychological perspective to the exclusion of all others. Since PSYCHOLOGY's reference point is the individual, and SOCIOLOGY's is society, sociologists typically use psychologism as a term of abuse when explanation appears to be at an inappropriate individualistic level.

psychology the scientific study of behavior. This includes human and animal behavior (see also ETHOLOGY), but its particular concern is with mental events as revealed through behavior, including introspection. As a separate discipline it has only existed since the late 19th century, but in this time has encompassed several influential schools of thought, including PSYCHO-ANALYSIS, behaviorism, the mental testing movement, and the HUMANISTIC MOVEMENT, their differences resting on ideological as well as theoretical and methodological predilictions. For all this, mainstream psychology is a more homogeneous, more professionalized discipline than sociology, with a relatively high degree of agreement on the importance of experimental and statistical methods, reflecting its different subject matter. Nevertheless, in a discipline that straddles physical and social science and has relations with many other disciplines, there is an acceptance of the appropriateness of different approaches and methods for different areas of the subject. Major topic areas within the discipline include comparative psychology (comparisons of human and animal behavior), developmental psychology, cognitive psychology (including a central concern with perception, memory, language, and problem-solving), abnormal psychology, and SOCIAL PSYCHOLOGY. As well as these, numerous special applied psychologies exist, for example, clinical psychology, educational psychology, industrial psychology. Overlaps with sociology occur in a number of areas, especially in social psychology, which exists as a subfield of both disciplines. Overlaps are greatest in those areas where the focus is on actor's meanings and naturally occurring situations. Compare PSYCHOTHERAPY, PSYCHIATRY.

psychosis severe mental illness in which the chief symptom is a distorted perception of reality. These distortions may include delusions and hallucinations, speech may be incoherent or inappropriate, and there may be hyperactivity or complete social withdrawal. A wide variety of manifestations are evident but these are grouped generally under the terms *schizophrenia* and *manic depression*.

PSYCHOTHERAPY

psychotherapy the clinical practice of healing the mind. Help for people with mental or psychological problems can come from many sources—friends, family, voluntary workers, counselors, clinical psychologists, psychotherapists, and psychiatrists. Psychotherapists are generally trained, often intensively and extensively trained, as Jungian or Freudian psychotherapists may be, but are not generally medically qualified. It is this that primarily distinguishes them from psychiatrists (see PSYCHIATRY). Psychotherapy aims to help the person in mental distress by a talking cure, examining past and present concerns and encouraging the client to understand themselves better. See also FREUD, JUNG.

public *(adj.)* open to view or open to access, for example, the published text; *(n.)* the general body of persons within a society able to engage freely in political participation and public discourse.

The expansion of the public domain is a feature of modern societies compared with most preindustrial societies, where involvement in public life and public discourse was usually restricted by law to certain classes, as well as by limited technology and cultural attitudes. In the terminology used by Almond and Verba (1965), preindustrial POLITICAL CULTURES were mainly "subject cultures" rather than "participatory cultures." According to GOULDNER (1976), the expansion and multiplication of distinct and overlapping public realms and the development of the mass media of communication can be seen as "mutually constitutive" developments. See also PRIVATE AND PUBLIC SPHERES.

public goods or **collective goods** (ECONOMICS) commodities or services—for example, defense, public parks, or urban clean air—which when supplied to one person are available to all. The contrast is with *individual or private goods,* which in theory at least are consumed privately.

According to Hirsch (1979), "the central issue" involved in a consideration of the provision of private and public goods "is an adding-up problem": what some individuals individually can obtain, all individuals and society cannot always get; and some things that societies might obtain cannot be obtained except by collective action. Thus, society has to find some means of determining how such different sets of outcomes should be reconciled. If private decision-making provides no automatic best answer to such questions, nor necessarily do centrally controlled economies. Problems of overall coordination, and a lack of consideration for both true productivity and the external social costs of production, have beset both decentralized and centrally controlled economies. See also GALBRAITH, AFFLUENT SOCIETY, PARETO OPTIMALITY, SUBOPTIMALITY, POSITIONAL GOODS AND POSITIONALITY.

public opinion and **opinion polls** expressions of attitudes on political issues or current affairs by members of the general public. Since the advent of *opinion polls*, the term has referred especially to statements of opinion collected in sample surveys. Compare MASS OBSERVATION.

public ownership the state ownership of some or all of the means of production. While the term can be used to apply to state ownership within COMMAND ECONOMIES, its main application has been to sectors of the economy within MIXED ECONOMIES that are state owned. An alternative term for the process in which industries are brought under state ownership is *nationalization*. In Britain the 1945 Labor government undertook an extensive program of nationalization, including coal and gas, iron and steel, electricity, and civil aviation. Subsequently, the process has been reversed as the result of the radical program of PRIVATIZATION under Conservative governments. Justifications for public ownership include the arguments that *public utilities,* especially so-called natural monopolies, require public control, and the more general arguments that socialism and communism are necessary to remove exploitation. Arguments against are that state ownership requires extensive bureaucratic controls, achieves less efficiency, and tends to reduce individual initiative and human freedoms. Between the pro or anti arguments, there also exist arguments for a balance between private and public ownership. While the command economies of Eastern Europe proved inefficient, it has not been established that public ownership and *state planning* are inherently inefficient. Empirical studies have discovered no simple pattern in differences between private and public corporations. External diseconomies, such as pollution and shortages of natural resources may also require public controls—notwithstanding that governments have often failed to take into account environmental issues.

pure type see IDEAL TYPE.

purpose explanation an explanation of an occurrence as the outcome of an actor's own purposes and the purposive acts that follow from these purposes. Debate in philosophy and in sociology exists as to whether or not such explanations should be regarded as a species of causal explanation, explaining events that the actor makes happen. For some theorists "reasons are causes," and "purposive explanations" are "causal explanations," but for others they are not. Either way, however, purposive explanations are not causal explanation in the Humean sense of "universal" empirical regularities involving "casual laws," insofar as they imply that actors could have acted differently. A crucial issue is whether purposive social action can be further explained, for example, in structural terms and/or in lawlike ways. See also ACTION, TELEOLOGY, FREE WILL, EXPLANATION.

Q

qualitative research techniques any research in which sociologists rely on their skills as empathic interviewer or observer to collect unique data about the problem they are investigating. Researchers may have a list of topics they will discuss with their informants in an unstructured way (a focused interview schedule or *aide-mémoire*) or may seek to uncover the informant's own "narrative" or experience with the topic. Similarly, observation techniques may be more or less qualitative, the most qualitative being full PARTICIPANT OBSERVATION. These methods contrast with QUANTITATIVE RESEARCH TECHNIQUES, in which reliance is placed on the research instrument through which measurement is made, that is, the structured questionnaire, the structured observation, or the experiment.

There is a strong emphasis on qualitative methods in ETHNOMETHODOLOGY and ETHNOGRAPHY. The data produced are considered to be rich in detail and closer to the informant's perceived world, while quantitative methods may lead to an impoverishment of data. Any classification of qualitative data can only be at the nominal level (see CRITERIA AND LEVELS OF MEASUREMENT). However, even among research teams fully committed to structured quantitative methods, qualitative methods are often used in the initial stages of an investigation when all aspects of survey design need to be assessed, and information gained qualitatively is then used to produce the structured research instrument.

quality and performance see PATTERN VARIABLES.

quality of working life (QWL) an approach to organizational and work design that advocates the merit of considering the well-being of employees, their participation in work-related decisions and, relatedly, organizational effectiveness. The term originated in the United States in the 1960s, but the underlying theoretical impetus derives from earlier European SOCIOTECHNICAL SYSTEMS writings and experiments, and QWL programs have occurred in various countries. The QWL movement has been concerned with employee health, safety, and job satisfaction and has been associated with attempts to develop techniques and methods for improving the experience of work. These include JOB REDESIGN, autonomous work groups, and labor-management committees (Huse and Cummings, 1985). Critics of such programs suggest that managers are the main beneficiaries. Autonomous work groups, it is argued, help to resolve management problems of control that typically arise from a Taylorian approach to work design (see SCIENTIFIC MANAGEMENT), and do so in ways that involve insignificant adjustment to managerial prerogative. Moreover, traditional work design is seen to be less suited to conditions of tight labor markets and turbulent environments. This kind of reasoning underpins some of the more critical assessments of QWL programs, the popularity of which appears to have waned since the 1970s (Hill, 1981). Such views have to be placed alongside those of theorists and practitioners who suggest that employees also derive considerable benefit from participation in the redesign of work (Mumford, 1980).

quantification the transformation of observations into numerical data to assist analysis and comparison.

quantitative research techniques any research method that results in the data being expressed in numerical form.

There may be some dispute over the inclusion of *ordinal data,* since this describes the situation in which categories of observations are assigned numbers because one category can be ordered. Such data are generally considered to be quantitative even though the numbers have no real value or equal distance between them (see CRITERIA AND LEVELS OF MEASURE-MENT). There is no dispute over the status of *interval* and *ratio data* within quantitative methods. See also RESEARCH METHODS.

quasi-experimental method see COMPARATIVE METHOD.

questionnaire a form containing questions to be administered to a number of people in order to obtain information, record opinions, etc.

Social scientists use questionnaires to: (a) examine the general characteristics of a population (age, sex, occupation, income, etc.); (b) examine attitudes; (c) establish the relationship between two variables (e.g., occupation and voting behavior); and (d) test theories.

A number of problems exist in writing questions for questionnaires. First, in wording the questions, care must be taken to try to ensure that the meaning each respondent attaches to each question is the same. This means that when the questions are being written, this should be done in relation to the target groups under study (see also PILOT STUDY). For example, in undertaking research with children, the words used should be kept as simple as possible and long words avoided (for example, "job" rather than "occupation," "dad" rather than "father"). A second problem is that of whether to use *unstructured* (open-ended) or *structured* (closed, or pre-coded) questions (see UNSTRUCTURED DATA and STRUCTURED CODING). The choice of which of these types of questions to use depends on the nature of the research topic and the means of administration. Where a relatively unexplored topic is being examined, open-ended questions might be preferred, since the researcher may have little idea as to the range of possible replies. The same is often true where the questionnaire is being administered orally, since this enables the researcher to probe the replies given by respondents. Conversely, where postal or mail questionnaires are being used, precoded questions are generally preferred as this simplifies completion. A third problem concerns the sequence of questions on the questionnaire. Generally, the questions should follow logically from one to the next and they should be arranged in such a way that the order of the questions has as little effect as possible on how respondents answer subsequent questions. For example, when examining people's attitudes toward abortion, a general question on whether abortion should be prohibited might be best placed before questions on possible reform of the abortion law. Finally, personal questions about age, sex, occupation and income, and possibly embarrassing questions should be placed at the end of the questionnaire.

Questionnaires can be administered in a number of ways: (a) orally, by the research to the respondents in an interview situation; (b) self-administered where, for example, a teacher might give students questionnaires to be completed in the classroom; (c) printed questionnaires, where they are sent to respondents through the mail. The choice of how to administer a questionnaire depends on a number of factors, of which the nature of the research problems, complexity of the questions, and cost are most important. Where a relatively unexplored topic is being examined and many of the questions are open-ended, then interviews are preferred. Conversely, where a large number of people are being researched and the questionnaire has many precoded questions, mail questionnaires are preferred. Finally, it should be mentioned that although postal questionnaires are relatively cheap to administer, they have the disadvantage of a high nonresponse rate (see NONRESPONSE).

Quetelet, Adolphe (1796–1874) Belgian scientist and pioneering social statistician and social reformer. Quetelet's approach was distinguished by the collection and analysis of large quantities of data, first to establish statistical regularities, and then to seek the underlying causes of social phenomena. His discovery of persistent regularities (for example, associated with births and deaths, or crime) led him to expect that a social science could be established that would be on a par with the physical sciences. Thus he coined the term "social physics" to describe his work. His major influence was on the development of social statistics.

quota sample a population SAMPLE selected by quotas from each defined portion of the population. The method of quota sampling does not fulfill the normal requirements of RANDOM SAMPLING. It involves breaking down the parent populations into strata (see STRATIFIED SAMPLING) according to relevant features (for example, sex, age, social class, place of residence) and calculating how many individuals to include in each of these categories to reflect the parent population structure. At this stage randomness can be achieved, but once the size of each of these cells (that is, the number of people of a certain sex, age, and class living within a certain location) is decided, no attempt at randomness is made. Instead, the interviewers are instructed to achieve appropriate selections (quotas) to fulfill the requirements within each cell.

This lack of randomness in selection of respondents means that though the interviewers achieve the correct proportion of the sexes, of age groups, of social class, etc., there is likely to be BIAS introduced on other VARIABLES, since each member of the parent population has not had an equal chance of being chosen as a member of the sample (the criterion of randomness). Market research and opinion polls commonly use this method for its cheapness and speed, but selecting a sample from individuals walking in downtown areas during daylight hours obviously risks biasing the sample on other variables than those specifically selected for.

R

race a scientifically discredited term formerly used to describe biologically distinct groups of persons who were alleged to have characteristics of an unalterable nature. The concept has been used in the English language since the 16th century. Its meaning has altered several times over the last 400 years in line with changing concepts about the nature of physical and cultural differences and, more importantly, the ideological uses of the concept to justify relationships of superiority and exploitation. Banton, in *Racial Theories* (1987), provides a comprehensive account of the different uses of the concept of race.

Social scientists now recognize that race is exclusively a socially constructed categorization that specifies rules for identification of a given group. Many writers will not use the term except in quotation marks to distance the use of the word from its historical and biological connotations. It is preferable to refer to ETHNICITY or ETHNIC GROUPS. Despite the discredited nature of the concept of race, the idea still exerts a powerful influence in everyday language and ideology. See also RACE RELATIONS, RACISM.

race relations 1. the social relations between ethnic or racial groups. **2.** the academic study of these social relations.

In sociology, race relations has focused on the effects of DISCRIMINATION and RACISM on groups that have been singled out for such treatment, and also on the political struggle against racism. However, the use of the term "race relations" is controversial on two main grounds. First, some sociologists argue that the term lends credence to the biological conception of race, which has no clear scientific foundation. Secondly, it can be argued that race relations are not a distinctive area of social relations but can only be understood within the wider context of political and ideological processes and social relations in general.

racism or **racialism** a set of beliefs, ideologies, and social processes that discriminate against others on the basis of their supposed membership in a so-called racial group (see RACE, ETHNICITY). The term has been used in a variety of ways to describe both systems of thought and doctrines that justify the supposed biological superiority of one social group over another, through to descriptions of practices and attitudes that produce racial DISCRIMINATION and disadvantage. The concept of racism is thoroughly reviewed by Robert Miles (*Racism*, 1989).

Writers such as Michael Banton (*The Idea of Race,* 1977) suggest that racism is a doctrine that asserts stable biological differences between groups standing in relationships of superiority and inferiority. Other writers, such as John Rex (*Race and Ethnicity,* 1986), Martin Barker (*The New Racism,* 1981), and Robert Miles (op. cit.), have variously argued that the essence of racism is the belief that there is a relationship between the membership of a socially created category and the possession of specific characteristics. The underlying explanation of these differences may be, for example, cultural, religious, or historical and need not be biological or pseudobiological.

In Europe, varieties of racist ideology have been used to justify colonial exploitation, aggression against nations, and oppression of minority groups. Most of these ideologies, according to Banton, share assumptions that:

(a) variations in the behavior and constitution of individuals are to be explained as the expression of different underlying biological types of a permanent kind;

(b) differences between these types explain variations in the cultures of human populations;

(c) the distinctive nature of these types explain the superiority of Europeans in general and Nordics in particular;

(d) the friction between nations and individuals of different types arise from these innate characteristics.

Racism played a key part in the rise and dominance of German fascism. The German nation as a supposedly pure RACE was alleged to require elimination of biologically distinct and inferior Jews if it were to survive. This virulent and crude racism led to the death of some six million Jews.

Miles argues that "the concept of racism should be used to refer to what can broadly be called an ideology ... racism works by attributing meanings to certain phenotypical and/or genetic characteristics of human beings in such a way as to create a system of categorization, and by attributing additional (negatively evaluated) characteristics to the people sorted into these categories. This process of signification is therefore the basis for the creation of a hierarchy of groups, and for establishing criteria by which to include and exclude groups of people in the process of allocating resorces and services."

Radcliffe-Brown, Alfred (1881–1955) British structural functionalist anthropologist. His major work is *Structure and Function in Primitive Society,* (1952). With MALINOWSKI he shaped British anthropology's preference for analyzing social structure over culture. Much influenced by COMTE and DURKHEIM, he advocated a version of anthropology he called "comparative sociology." His fieldwork was carried out in the Andaman Islands and Australia, and his research made substantial contributions to the study of KINSHIP. While his POSITIVISM and FUNCTIONALISM are now regarded as dated, his influence on a generation of British anthropologists, teaching at numerous institutions, was immense.

radical social work a term denoting attempts in the 1970s to achieve a fundamental reorientation of SOCIAL WORK practice. ("Radical" denotes a concerted attempt to change the *status quo*.) The 1970s saw a loose movement known as radical social work, with its roots in an undifferentiated political left. Its main contention was that social problems, including those habitually addressed by social workers, had their roots in structural inequality, principally social CLASS, and not in personal inadequacy as earlier theory seemed to imply.

Key ingredients to radical social work as a method were *conscientization* (in Paolo Freire's sense), the *empowerment* of clients, the opening up of social work processes to public and client participation, and attempts to make broad political alliances of so-called progressive forces (community groups, client groups, labor unions, and political parties). In general, radical social workers perceived ambiguity in the state apparatus to the point that real gains were held to be achievable for the working classes.

Currently, a radical right has emerged in social work, stressing individual, family, and to a lesser extent community responsibility for social problems. This has been associated with policy shifts in government, leading to the closing of large institutions for the mentally ill and handicapped, the growth of a private welfare sector, and the recent emphasis on COMMUNITY CARE in welfare provision. Faced with these changes, the tendency has been for the radical left in social work to fragment, focusing on narrower, albeit significant, issues such as RACISM, sexism, and other aspects of inequality.

random sample a SAMPLE from a parent population selected by ensuring that each member of that population has an equal chance of being selected. When this is observed, the sample should have the same profile of features as the parent population, that is, it should be a valid representation of it. Data collected by random sampling (assuming the sample is large enough) should reflect the parent population, but methods that are not random (for example, QUOTA SAMPLING) cannot be relied on to do so. However, it is recognized that samples are not entirely accurate, so account must be taken of SAMPLING ERROR.

The methods used to achieve random selection may be based on random number tables or, more usually in social surveys, on *systematic sampling*, that is, selecting individuals, households, etc. according to their position on a list, when a sample of every name at a fixed interval, say the tenth on the list, is made. See also PROBABILITY.

range see MEASURES OF DISPERSION.

rank a position in a SOCIAL STATUS hierarchy.

Rastafarian (*n.* and *adj.*) a movement dating from the 1930s in Jamaica, but influential worldwide in the 1970s and 1980s, involving the deliverance of black people to a new, free, and sacred homeland in Africa. "Rastafarian" is derived from Ras Tafari, the name of Haile Selassie I (Emperor of Ethiopia from 1930 to 1975) before he assumed his official title.

Rastafarian beliefs have their origins in the teaching and philosophy of Marcus Garvey (1887–1940), who organized the Universal Negro Improvement Association in the United States at the beginning of the 20th century. He believed that integration with whites in the United States was impossible and the foundation of a black homeland in Africa was necessary to retore the dignity and culture of black peoples.

Garvey's teachings were influential in the United States and the West Indies. His prophecies about a glorious kingdom and the return to Africa created interest in the crowning of Ras Tafari as the Emperor of Ethiopia. Followers of Garvey in Jamaica, though not Garvey himself, made connections between the prophecy of a black king (taken to be Haile Selassie) and the day of deliverance to a promised land (Ethiopia). They believed that Selassie was a Messiah who would organize the black exodus to Africa and end the domination of Western imperial powers. As such, the Rastafarian movement is often identified by sociologists as CULT-like, involving many of the features of millennial movements.

By the middle of the 1970s Rastafarianism had become a potent cultural force in the West Indies and the beliefs became more internationalized, especially in parts of the United States, Britain, and Australia.

rational capitalism WEBER'S IDEAL TYPE of Western capitalism, involving the systematic rational calculation of profit and loss (for example, accountancy), in contrast with less rational, non-Western, preindustrial forms of capitalism.

rational choice theory a relatively formal approach to sociological and social science theorizing (for example, drawing on the THEORY OF GAMES, the notion of STRATEGIC INTERACTION and economics), in that it is maintained that social life is principally capable of explanation as the outcome of the rational choices of individual actors.

"When faced with several courses of action, people usually do what they believe is likely to have the best overall outcome. This deceptively simple sentence summarizes the theory of rational choice" (Elster, 1989). It is a form of theorizing characterized by the use of technically rigorous models of social behavior, which seek to derive robust conclusions from a relatively small number of initial theoretical assumptions about rational behavior.

Rational choice theories have been in vogue over the last two decades, prompted by dissatisfaction with macroscopic and structural models in some circles but also by an increased centrality for the rhetoric of individual rational choice in many areas in economic and political life. Despite its often impressive formal architecture, and its undoubted value in illuminating some areas of social reality, two important limitations of rational choice theory can be noted (see Hollis, 1987):

(a) its relative lack of success in overcoming numerous technical difficulties (for example, a regression in actors' expectations concerning the actions of others), which limit its formal rigor and undermine the direct applicability of its models;

(b) an association with positivist and pragmatist epistemologies, which has limited its attention to analysis of action located in norm-guided, rule-following, and rule-changing social behavior. See also EXCHANGE THEORY.

RATIONALISM

rationalism 1. a general confidence in the power of knowledge, both general principles and inductive or empirical knowledge, to describe and explain the world and to solve problems. Such a view was characteristic, for example, of the so-called age of reason (see AGE OF ENLIGHTENMENT). **2.** (philosophy) any epistemological position that emphasizes the A PRIORI basis of knowledge and deductive theories (compare EMPIRICISM). **3.** the doctrines associated with 17th and 18th century philosophers, including Descartes, Spinoza (1632–1677), and Leibniz (1646–1716), that, using deductive methods, a unified knowledge can be attained by "Reason" alone. **4.** the epistemological position of KANT, which succeeded **3.**, that while assured knowledge of the real world, the world of "things-in-themselves," or *noumena,* could not be achieved, it was possible to gain secure knowledge of the *phenomenal* world—the world as known to us. This was possible, according to Kant, given that the phenomenal world was conceptualized and perceived within a fixed frame provided by the human mind, for example, in the fixed *forms* of perception, that is, space and time. **5.** the Hegelian view (see HEGEL), that "the cunning of reason" operates not only in individual thought but is a general and progressive process in history, a rational historical design fully revealed only as history unfolds but ultimately guaranteed. In what was intended to be a "demystified form," this conception of reason, or rationalism, also influenced MARX.

In the 19th century, rationalism in any of these senses often gave way to *irrationalism,* for example, in NIETZSCHE a declining confidence in PROGRESS, endangered by world events as well as by skeptical movements in philosophy. However, rationalism in the sense of a belief in progress survives in a modified form in many areas of sociology and philosophy (for example, see HABERMAS, EVOLUTIONARY THEORY). A further view is that it is a mistake to polarize rationalism and empiricism, since both play a role in human knowledge, which always involves both conception (rationalism) and perception (empiricism), for example, see FEYERABEND.

rationality 1. action that is effective in achieving the purposes it is intended to achieve, that is, the means are appropriate to the ends. In such a definition of *instrumental rationality,* no attempt need be made to appraise the rationality of the ends themselves. This conception of rationality—economic actors are assumed to seek to maximize their own economic returns—is often the basis of theorizing in ECONOMICS, much of this operating by the construction of idealized models (see IDEAL TYPES). For further conceptions of rational action, and questions about these, see FORMAL AND SUBSTANTIVE RATIONALITY, TYPES OF SOCIAL ACTION. **2.** knowledge of beliefs that have been established scientifically, or on some other basis considered rational. Such beliefs are implied in **1.**, but the rationality of knowledge and beliefs raises wider issues than the instrumental effectiveness of knowledge or beliefs, for example, extensive philosophical debates (see EPISTEMOLOGY, ONTOLOGY, RATIONALISM).

Other important debates concern the rationality or otherwise of so-called *primitive mentality*. Lévy-Bruhl (1923) argued that although MYTHOLOGIES and beliefs in preindustrial, prescientific societies may have a cognitive value, they reflect levels of mentality that are prelogical. An alternative view is that the myths and beliefs in such societies are rational in the context in which they occur. (See WINCH, MAGIC, RELATIVISM.)

A rather different point is that many activities that at first sight appear irrational, on closer examination may be found to possess "latent functions" (see LATENT AND MANIFEST FUNCTIONS), for example, the conservatism of many people in Third World societies, who may benefit economically, especially in old age, from having more children. In wider terms, nonrational beliefs, notably RELIGION, may perform general social functions, for example, providing social integration (see also FUNCTIONALIST THEORY OF RELIGION). Such beliefs are sometimes regarded as encapsulating an accumulated institutional rationality, perhaps linked to survival. Conversely, actions that appear rational from the narrow perspective of immediate instrumental rationality (for example, cutting down the Brazilian rain forest) may be seen as nonrational, taking a wider view.

What all these considerations show is that the idea of rationality is often difficult to define. While rationality in its simplest sense, 1., can sometimes be established without undue difficulty, only rarely can the means to an end be fully ordered (for example, in terms of cost, availability, etc.), and actors often lack other salient information, even when this is potentially available (see THEORY OF GAMES, RATIONAL CHOICE THEORY, BOUNDED RATIONALITY).

rationalization 1. the general tendency within modern capitalist societies for all institutions and most areas of life to be transformed by the application of RATIONALITY. As seen by WEBER, for example, such a process of rationalization is the master process that underlies transformation of the economic, political, and legal institutions of Western societies, notably in the spread of BUREAUCRACY and of systematic forms of accountancy and law. Furthermore, the effects of this process are also evident in other sectors of society, for example, the bureaucratization of science and learning, and developments in music and in religious organization.

Weber had major reservations about the implications of the operation of so seemingly inexorable a process, that he sometimes referred to as creating an "iron cage" that would increasingly restrict individuality. He recognized that a narrow calculation of "instrumental rationality" was likely to conflict with "substantive rationality," that is, the rationality of outcomes appraised in terms of wider human objectives. At the same time, however, in a world disenchanted by rationality, he did not believe that a strictly scientific basis existed for a generalized conception of human interests or human needs. Human beings have freedom of action and must therefore ultimately make their own choices (see also VALUE FREEDOM AND VALUE NEUTRALITY).

Other theorists have taken a more optimistic view of the outcome of the rationalization process. HABERMAS, for example, has suggested that "human interests" will be identifiable in a context in which a truly democratic critical discourse exists (see also CRITICAL CULTURAL DISCOURSE). In general, however, sociologists have remained more agnostic on such issues (see also FORMAL AND SUBSTANTIVE RATIONALITY). **2.** any after-the-act justification of an action that seeks to present this action in a favorable light, as having a coherent rationale. In circumstances where such a rational reconstruction lacks plausibility.

PARETO regarded many social accounts, including most sociological and political theorizing, as involving rationalization in this general sense, as lacking a truly objective basis (see RESIDUES AND DERIVATIONS). Although emphasizing the importance of distinguishing rationality from nonrationality, Pareto had no illusions that rationality could ever become the guiding principle in social and political life; on the contrary, he is usually seen as a key figure in the pessimism about progress that typified much thinking in POLITICAL SOCIOLOGY at the turn of the 19th century (see ELITE THEORY, NEO-MACHIAVELLIANS).

realism 1. (philosophy) the ontological assertion that the objects in the world have an existence independently of our conception or perception of them. In this form realism is opposed to philosophical NOMINALISM, SKEPTICISM (for example, HUME), PHENOMENALISM, neutral monism, OPERATIONISM, INSTRUMENTALISM, and also KANTIAN philosophy. **2.** (realist forms of idealist philosophy) the assertion of the existence outside time and space of abstract forms or universals that determine objects in the world. This includes the notion that the objects in the world are as we observe them (see IDEALISM). **3.** (*sociological realism*) the assertion that social reality, social structures, social currents, etc. have an existence over and above the existence of individual actors (for example, DURKHEIM's social reality *sui generis,* his conception of "social facts as things"); compare METHODOLOGICAL INDIVIDUALISM.

reciprocity a state or relationship between two parties or things in that there is mutual action, giving and taking. Sociological and anthropological interest in reciprocity developed from the study *The Gift*, by Mauss (1925). He argued that gifts, often considered as voluntary and disinterested, are in fact obligatory, owing to the social RITUAL involved in giving and taking in all societies. See also GIFT EXCHANGE AND GIFT RELATIONSHIP.

Redfield, Robert (1897–1958) US social anthropologist whose studies of Mexican peasant communities led him to formulate influential conceptions of FOLK SOCIETY and the folk-urban continuum. Main works by Redfield are *The Folk Culture of Yucatan* (1941) and *Peasant Society and Culture* (1956).

redistributive chiefdom a type of economy and political system in a relatively complex form of TRIBAL SOCIETY in which control of a central storehouse for a pool of communal goods is in the hands of a "big man" or chief. According to some theories, such a form of political system can be seen as the forerunner of state formation proper (see Sahlins, 1972; Harris, 1978). Such redistributive systems allow the center to accumulate goods and to use them for the enhancement of rank, and for the employment of specialist personnel such as priests, soldiers, and craftsmen, and for the enhancement of the power and rank of the chief.

reduction an account of the propositions of one science in terms of the propositions of another. See also REDUCTIONISM.

reductionism the doctrine that, either in practice or in principle, the propositions of one science can be explained in terms of the propositions of another, for example, the reduction of chemistry to physics, or the reduction of sociology to psychology.

The contrasting doctrine is that particular sciences may be irreducible to other sciences. For Durkheim, for example, social reality is an emergent reality, a reality *sui generis* irreducible to other sciences such as psychology. Similarly, those sociologists who emphasize human meanings as the basis of social explanations also see this level of analysis as irreducible. In practice, the relationships between the sciences are complex, with no pattern or view of the pattern of these relationships being in the ascendancy. Sometimes the subject matter of one science can be illuminated by analogies with, or reduction to, another; at other times attempted reductions of analogies will be misplaced or misleading.

reference group the actual (or notional) groups or social categories with which SOCIAL ACTORS identify and make comparisons in guiding their personal behavior and social ATTITUDES, for example, the identification of young people with rock stars or sports stars. The term was introduced by the social psychologist Muztafer Sherif in 1948. Reference groups may or may not be synonymous with a social actor's membership groups. Negative as well as positive reference groups may be involved. See also ANTICIPATORY SOCIALIZATION, RELATIVE DEPRIVATION.

reflexivity 1. the capacity possessed by an account or theory when it refers to itself, for example, the sociology of knowledge and the sociology of sociology. **2.** (particularly in ETHNOMETHODOLOGY and SYMBOLIC INTERACTIONISM) the idea that our everyday practical accounts are not only reflexive and self-referring but also socially constitutive of the situations to which they refer. On this view reflexivity is also a capacity possessed by social actors that is decisive in distinguishing human actors from animals.

It is a feature of reflexive social accounts and theories of all types that these accounts may also act to reproduce or transform those social situations to which they refer. Sociologists of all types have given much attention to the implications of this for sociological analysis.

regionalization of action (GIDDENS, 1984) "the temporal, spatial or timespace differentiation of regions" within or between different social *locales*.

Regionalization is seen by theorists such as Balibar and ALTHUSSER, and Giddens, as a counterbalance to the assumption that SOCIETIES always consist of unified social systems.

regression and regression analysis a technique for analyzing the relationship between two or more interval level VARIABLES (see CRITERIA AND LEVELS OF MEASUREMENT) in order to predict the value of one from the other or others. For example, given a regression equation describing the relationship between income and years of education, income can be predicted once the years of education are known.

Multiple linear regression analysis is used when there are several independent interval level variables. For example, a linear equation could be derived that related income to years of education, age, and years of job experience.

In many situations the researcher does not know which or how many independent variables will provide a satisfactory model. There is a choice of methods for adding more independent variables to the model. See also CORRELATION, ANALYSIS OF VARIANCE, CAUSAL MODELING, PATH ANALYSIS.

reification the interpretation of an abstract general concept as real, especially when this is considered to be done illegitimately or misleadingly. Thus, METHODOLOGICAL INDIVIDUALISTS may take the view that others, for example, functionalists, reify general concepts such as society or structure.

Use of the term originated within Marxism to refer to the tendency of many non-Marxists, as well as some Marxists, to attribute a rigid thing-like status to what should more properly be seen as a complex and changing set of social relationships. However, one sociologist's unacceptable reification may be perfectly acceptable to another. If all general concepts are considered abstract but with a potentially real reference, any hard and fast distinction between legitimate and illegitimate reification collapses. Thus, there is no standard line in sociology on what constitutes acceptable and unacceptable forms of reification.

relative deprivation the feelings felt and the judgments reached when an individual or members of a group compare themselves, and especially their social situation, adversely with some other individual within their group or with another group, for example, the less affluent members of an occupational group with the more affluent. The notion is that it is not absolute standards that are important making such judgments, but the relative standards, or frame of reference, in terms of which people make judgments.

As indicated by Stouffer et al. (1949), relative deprivation, somewhat paradoxically, is more often felt when people compare their lot adversely with actual or imaginary others in situations with some similarity but not identical to their own, rather than those who occupy markedly different positions. Feelings of relative deprivation may be strongest in relation to others seen to be in a potentially competitive situation. As suggested by MERTON (1949), the bench mark group or groups with which comparisons are made constitute the REFERENCE GROUP(S) of the individuals or groups experiencing feelings and making judgments of relative deprivation. Thus, Runciman, in *Relative Deprivation and Social Justice* (1966), was able to demonstrate that political opinions and the meanings attached to class membership (see SUBJECTIVE AND OBJECTIVE CLASS) were a function of reference groups and the associated feelings, possibly of relative deprivation. The pronounced attitudinal changes that can be brought about by changes in the relative positions of social groups have been shown to be a potent source of political upheaval and revolutionary change (see Urry, 1973).

relativism an emphasis on the variety and differences of cultures, bodies of knowledge, conceptual schemes, theories, values, etc. The term covers a variety of sociological and philosophical positions, ranging from so-called weak forms to strong forms. At the weak end, the recognition of variety and difference appears to be little more than sociological common sense. However, strong versions of relativism, which can have powerful support, are the subject of much controversy. For example, to claim strongly that "morals are relative"—*moral relativism*—is to claim that what is right is solely a local matter, to be judged so only within particular communities at particular times. This rules out attempts to judge between different moral schemes. Thus, there would be no general basis for rejecting Nazi policies toward non-German racial groups.

Similarly, strong *cognitive relativism* suggests that science and other ways of knowing, for example, MAGIC, are simply different, involving truth claims from different standpoints, so that there are no overarching rules or procedures for deciding between such different belief systems. There may be no scientific grounds for saying "X is a witch," but there can be entirely adequate grounds within witchcraft, or witchhunting, for saying that "X is a witch," so that within such practices this is considered true without rational ground for privileging scientific truth.

In contemporary sociology, some ETHNOMETHODOLOGISTS have argued that the meaning(s) of any categorization are essentially local achievements, unconstrained by any general definition, where any use does not bind future use.

To extreme critical relativists it is customary to reply: "Your theory that all theories are relative is self-defeating." Enthusiastic relativists, however, embrace this response, suggesting that we must take responsibility for our decisions and choices, our own closures. In this, rationality tends to fade into rhetoric, which relativists always assumed was so. See also TRUTH, OBJECTIVITY, PARADIGM, FORM(S) OF LIFE, SAPIR-WHORF HYPOTHESIS, WITTGENSTEIN, FEYERABEND, VALUE RELEVANCE.

reliability the dependability of data collected, or of the test or measurement used to collect it. A reliable measure is one that gives the same results if the same individuals are measured on more than one occasion.

Reliability describes consistency, and this is commonly calculated by a CORRELATION COEFFICIENT. This may be done when social survey data are collected from two samples taken from the same population at the same time, or when the same test is completed by the same people on two different occasions *(test-retest reliability)*, or when two different forms of a test are used *(alternate form reliability)*, or when the similarity between the two halves of a test is calculated *(split-half reliability)*. Compare VALIDITY.

religion 1. the "belief in spiritual beings" (Tylor, 1871) and the institutions and practices associated with these beliefs. **2.** "a unified system of beliefs and practices relative to sacred things," things set apart and held in awe, that unites the believers into a moral community or church (DURKHEIM, 1912). In this definition, in terms of social FUNCTIONS, there is no ultimate distinction between religions that involve beliefs in spiritual beings or other supernatural phenomena and many other kinds of socially unifying ideas, such as nationalism. The latter can be seen as FUNCTIONAL ALTERNATIVES OR FUNCTIONAL EQUIVALENTS of religion in the more conventional sense. Furthermore, even some beliefs and practices conventionally thought of as religions, do not readily correspond to narrower standard dictionary definitions of religion that emphasize the worship of gods and spirits, nor is a distinction between the supernatural and the empirical easy to draw uncontentiously. **3.** any set of doctrines, "theories in a hurry," according to GELLNER, providing overall answers to ultimate and existential questions for which there are no empirical answers. In comparison with definition **2.**, this definition leaves open for empirical analysis the social effects or social functions of religion.

The virtue of either definition **2.** or **3.** is that neither depends on contentious distinctions between the natural and the supernatural that may not be shared by religious believers. The problem with either of the definitions, however, is that they no longer provide any effective distinction between traditional forms of religious phenomena and other forms of belief systems or other forms of ritual behavior, making it difficult, for example, to conceptualize phenomena such as secularization. Under these circumstances, some sociologists have continued to operate with definitions that remain closer to definition **1.**, despite the difficulties associated with it. See also SOCIOLOGY OF RELIGION.

repertory grid technique see PERSONAL CONSTRUCT THEORY.

replication the collection of data under the same conditions established in a previous study. This is often done to test the VALIDITY of the conclusions drawn, since faults in design or analysis may thereby be discovered.

representative sample a SAMPLE that is, or is assumed to be, a true reflection of the parent population, that is, has the same profile of attributes, for example, age structure, class structure, and educational background. A representative sample is achieved by ensuring that its selection is entirely random (see RANDOM SAMPLE). It is essential that a sample be representative in order that the conclusions drawn from its study can be accepted as valid information about the parent population.

research methods the investigative techniques employed within an academic discipline. In sociology, the range of methods is very wide, including many research methods also employed in other disciplines. For example, sociologists have used the critical techniques of the humanities in order to study TEXTS, paintings, buildings, etc.; ethnographic techniques borrowed from anthropology and applied to modern societies (see also ETHNOGRAPHY); and historical methods to understand the genesis of social forms.

Some of the most powerful techniques employed by sociologists are those the discipline shares with central and local government agencies, social survey methods based on SAMPLING, but the popular image of sociology as exclusively based on such methods is plainly erroneous. Among the array of further quantitative and qualitative research methods widely used in sociology are PARTICIPANT OBSERVATION and other forms of direct observation, in-depth INTERVIEWS, ATTITUDE SCALING, CONTENT ANALYSIS, documentary analysis, and SECONDARY ANALYSIS, including reanalysis of OFFICIAL STATISTICS.

In a particular study, the methods chosen will depend on a variety of considerations, including the following:

(a) the nature of the problem addressed (for example, while a study of the incidence of poor health among the elderly might be effective using questionnaires or medical records, study of deviant behavior is likely to require participant observation);

(b) the theoretical stance and the preferred methods of the researcher or research team (for example, symbolic interactionists are likely to prefer direct observation, less likely to operate with standardized variables);

(c) the time and money available (for example, postal questionnaires are cheaper than face-to-face interviews; secondary data analysis is cheaper than conducting new surveys);

(d) the type of research and evidence likely to carry conviction with the sponsors of the research and the audience for the research (for example, the sponsors of research have often been regarded as preferring research that uses quantitative rather than qualitative data).

Of these, (b) is often most important, also influencing the kind of research problem that is chosen. Thus (a) and (b) are often closely interrelated. However, (c) and (d) operate as strong constraints on the choice of research methods.

Debates on the merits of quantitative and qualitative approaches can be fierce. Some researchers committed to quantitative survey methods refuse to acknowledge the strengths and validity of other methods, while others, whose preference is for direct observation, refuse to countenance quantitative techniques. However, a simple polarization of the two sets of techniques is unjustified. Denzin (1970) has suggested that, whenever possible, social research should seek to triangulate different research methods (see TRIANGULATION OF APPROACHES). See also STATISTICS AND STATISTICAL ANALYSIS, METHODOLOGY, MATHEMATICAL SOCIOLOGY.

residues and derivations a distinction drawn by PARETO, as part of his discussion of nonlogical (or irrational) forms of action, in that *residues* are the uniform psychological bases underlying social action, and *derivations* are the rationalizations or so-called theories advanced by social participants as justifications for their social actions. As Pareto saw it, many sociological theories are themselves derivations. He regarded his own theories, in replacing these, as establishing sociology on a new scientific footing (see Fig. 21).

Six main categories of residues were identified by Pareto, but only two of these—*the instinct for combinations* (class I residues) and *the persistence of aggregates* (class II residues)—are critical to an understanding of his approach. These play a central part in his theory of elites (see CIRCULATION OF ELITES).

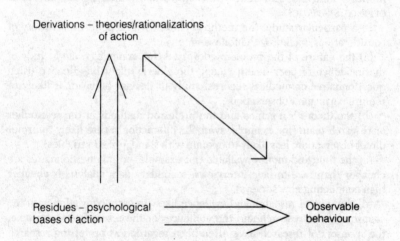

Fig. 21. **Residues and derivations.** As formulated by Pareto, the main causal origins of social action are located in the underlying psychological bases of this action. These bases explain both the action involved and the theories of this action advanced by social actors. Thus, these theories are seen by Pareto as *derivations* from the underlying psychological bases. *Residues* are the universal elements in social action left over once the more ephemeral derivations have been abstracted. For Pareto, they are the true basis of sociological explanations on which scientific sociological theory should be based. In comparison with the influence exerted by residues on derivations and on actions, the causal influnce of derivations on action, or vice versa, is much more limited.

resistance through ritual any ritualized styles of working-class youth culture and leisure behavior—for example, skinheads—that can be interpreted as aimed at resistance to structural and cultural changes. The phrase gained currency after its use as the title of a collection of articles written by British researchers at the Center for Contemporary Cultural Studies (CCCS) in the mid-1970s. The title is indicative of the approach to the study of SUBCULTURES adopted by the CCCS and has been influential subsequently in studies of youth cultures, education, and deviance. Youth subcultures have been studied in this way (M. Brake, 1985). These youth subcultures arise at times of social upheaval—the collapse of community, whether associated with relative affluence or unemployment—and are thought to reflect negotiated responses to these circumstance. In this process the products of mass culture are not simply accepted but richly interpreted, so as to express subcultural concerns.

response rate the proportion of individuals invited to participate in a study who actually do participate. In social surveys using SAMPLING, the response rate is unlikely to be 100%; 90% or over would be considered very good, and over 70% is normally acceptable. The method of collecting data inevitably affects the response rate. POSTAL QUESTIONNAIRES generally have a low rate, while personal INTERVIEWS achieve a higher rate. Reasons for NONRESPONSE include death, change of residence, unwillingness to cooperate, not being available when the interviewer calls, etc. Because of this almost inevitable failure to achieve the selected sample, systematic error or BIAS is introduced, and an assessment of the VALIDITY of extrapolating from the sample to the parent population has to be made. There are various statistical techniques used to strengthen the level of confidence that is put on sample data.

reverse discrimination see POSITIVE DISCRIMINATION.

revisionism any attempts by socialist thinkers to reappraise and revise the revolutionary ideas of MARX in light of changed economic and social conditions. The most famous of all revisionists was the German Social Democrat Eduard Bernstein. In the late 1890s he argued that most of Marx's economic theory and predictions for the future had been disproved by new developments in the capitalist system. As a result, "Peasants do not sink; the middle class does not disappear; crises do not grow even larger; misery and serfdom do not increase." Bernstein concluded that the final aim of the labor movement was unimportant. What was really crucial were the day-to-day battles to win improvements for workers living under capitalism. Socialism could only be achieved through a process of gradual and peaceful evolution entailing legislative reforms rather than violent working class revolution. In the 1960s, there was an upsurge of revisionist ideas in many Western European Communist parties.

Rex, John (1925–) South-African born social theorist and social researcher (especially on race), who for an important part of his career was the

417

Director of the Social Science Research Council (later ESRC) research unit on ethnic relations based first at Aston University and more later at the University of Warwick. His contributions to British sociology have been wide-ranging. In his first and influential book, *Key Problems of Sociological Theory* (1961), he offered a synthesis of classical approaches in sociology that emphasized the role of conflict alongside values and norms in human societies (see also CONFLICT THEORY). He continued to stress the importance of a broad approach to theory in sociology and became impatient when the revival of theory in British sociology, which he had urged, and in which his own work had been greatly instrumental, led in his view to too great a willingness to jettison classical ideas and follow current fashions, and also to a one-sided emphasis on MARX. In the study of race his work has been consistently innovative, as well as radical, and has mixed theory with empirical research in a way that is comparatively rare in British sociology, introducing in particular the idea of HOUSING CLASSES. Examples of these studies are his *Race, Community and Conflict* (1967) and *Colonial Immigrants in a British City* (1973) (with Sally Tomlinson). Other works by John Rex include *Sociology and the Demystification of the World* (1974), *Race, Colonalism and the City* (1970), and the influential collection of invited essays *Discovering Sociology* (1973).

Rickert, Heinrich (1863–1936) German NEO-KANTIAN social philosopher, whose ideas influenced WEBER. His major works include *Science and History* (1899) and *The Limits of Natural Scientific Conceptualization* (1902). He argued that DILTHEY and WINDELBAND's separation of cultural and natural sciences made polar opposites out of a continuum. Like Windelband, Rickert argued that sociological and cultural studies could employ both IDIOGRAPHIC AND NOMOTHETIC methods. The complexity of social phenomena meant that all forms of knowledge involved simplification, that is, relied on generalization or an accounts of phenomena in the light of their relevance for value. He accepted that at base all sociological knowledge was historical, but argued that it was possible to achieve greater objectivity than suggested by Dilthey. His proposal was a science of culture that sought to lay bare its essential components: "constellations of meaning and value." Rickert can be seen as the least subjectivist of the neo-Kantian school.

Riesman, David (1909–) US sociologist and journalist whose work, especially the *The Lonely Crowd* (written in 1950 with N. Glazer and R. Denney), was in vogue in the 1950s and early 1960s. The hypothesis of the study was that the basic character type within US society was changing from an *inner-directed* to an *other-directed* type (see OTHER-DIRECTEDNESS), in that character is increasingly formed by the example of peers and contemporaries rather than as previously by "internalized adult authority." The work raised themes about modern society that were taken up subsequently by many theorists.

riot 1. (in law) the use of unlawful violence on the part of at least twelve persons, in a way that would make "a person of reasonable firmness" fear for his safety. **2.** (in sociology) large-scale public disorder involving violence to property and violent confrontation with the police.

Many sociological studies have been published in Britain in recent years, following urban unrest in St. Paul's, Bristol, in 1980 and in many other towns and cities in the spring and summer of 1981 and autumn of 1985. No single cause has been accepted as the key to understanding why the unrest occurred, but a number of issues have been identified as important. One of these is the term "riot" itself. Many commentators have argued that the term is so loaded, morally and politically—involving only the viewpoint of the authorities—that it is specifically useless. Thus, many have preferred to use more neutral phrases, like "urban unrest," "popular protest," and "public disorder."

The first type of explanation of riots tends to be that of conspiracy, or the influence of outside agitators. So, in the Brixton and other disorders of 1981 in Britain, political agitators were blamed; in the case of Handsworth in 1985, the police argued that the disorders were organized by drug dealers in order to protect their profits. These types of explanation have a history as long as the history of popular protest. Social historians have given accounts of magistrates and police responses to riots in the 18th and 19th centuries that bear an uncanny resemblance to official and media views of those in the 1980s. Sociologically, these explanations are interesting as ideological constructs. They are rarely proven, but usually serve to deflect attention from underlying social problems and tend to absolve the authorities from any responsibility for the occurrences.

Turning to sociological and related explanations of riots in Britain (except for policing strategies, Northern Ireland must be seen as a separate case), there have been a number of influences on theorizing of which perhaps the most important have been social historians' accounts of British riots in previous centuries and American sociologists' explanations of unrest in United States cities in the 1960s. Most explanations have also involved some kind of dialogue with the Scarman Report (1981) in Britain. Scarman's main arguments about the causes of the 1981 unrest concerned material conditions in the areas involved: unemployment, housing, work and other opportunities, together with heavy-handed and confrontational policing, exemplified in a "stop and search" operation, "Operation Swamp '81", which immediately preceded the unrest. His arguments are in line with sociological work on a number of counts, particularly in his rejection of conspiratorial ideas and emphasis on the reality of the problems faced by the rioters. A number of strands have been variously emphasized by sociological researchers. These can be listed under four main headings:

(a) material conditions—all the major outbreaks of disorder occurred in localities with much higher rates of DEPRIVATION than average;

(b) POLICING—in virtually every case the first target of unrest was the police. Disorders often followed a specific police operation (for example, in Bristol 1980, Brixton 1981, and Handsworth 1985) or were associated with high levels of policing. This situation was further complicated by:

(c) RACE—initially several police representatives and politicians gave racist accounts, making arguments about alien cultures, etc. Sociologists have tended to emphasize the importance of the ethnic dimension in different terms. It has long been argued that black people have been subjected to a process of *criminalization* (see Hall et al., 1978) and that institutionalized RACISM is a persistent and inflammatory problem (Policy Studies Institute, 1983). See also ETHNICITY;

(d) marginalization and ALIENATION—in some respects the existence of these is seen as particularly relevant to black British people, but their implication is wider (see Lea and Young, 1983; Hall, in Benyon and Solomos, 1987). The basic argument is that where people are effectively excluded from processes of political and cultural representation, where effective channels for expressing grievances are closed to them and they perceive a general indifference and even hostility to their situation, they may engage in violent unrest as the only means of expressing their anger and making their situation known, even when this may be likely to prove counterproductive. See also MARGINALITY.

All sociological explanations reject the view that unrest is simply irrational or inspired by criminal or political conspirators. They also tend to play down arguments about the so-called copycat effect, which would reduce explanations to the role of the MASS MEDIA in publicizing and amplifying riots (see AMPLIFICATION OF DEVIANCE). They emphasize that there are identifiable causes, found in the living conditions of the people involved and understandable in rational terms as responses to those conditions. Compare COLLECTIVE BEHAVIOR.

ritual 1. any formal action that is set apart from profane action and expresses sacred and religious meaning (see DURKHEIM; DOUGLAS). This use of the term occurs in both anthropology and the sociology of religion. **2.** "bodily action in relation to symbols" (Bocock, 1974). **3.** any everyday practice that is characterized by its routine nature and by its significance to mundane social interaction. The term has been used by GOFFMAN (1972) to denote the routine practices of everyday life.

Ritual action may therefore be regarded as occurring in both the SACRED AND PROFANE domains of social life. In both cases it is the symbolic quality of the action that is its defining characteristic.

A distinction can be made between ritual or ritualistic behavior and ritual action. *Ritual behavior* is behavior devoid of meaning, rigid, and stereotypical. Ethologists may use the term to denote the routine and repetitive behaviors of animals during courtship and defense of territory. By contrast, *ritual action* is imbued with shared social meanings that are culturally transmitted through custom and tradition. *Ritual occasions* may be regarded as social situations that are separate and ceremonial. They are not necessarily characterized by rigidity and repetition, although these might be a feature of many rituals. Rituals may function as a conservative and cohesive force within a society, but they may also be the means for demonstrating social, political, and cultural resistance (see Hall and Jefferson, 1976). See also RESISTANCE THROUGH RITUAL.

While it has been common to study ritual action from perspectives within the SOCIOLOGY OF RELIGION, it is possible to suggest that ritual action is present in secular society. Bocock has argued that "the category of ritual action is not well established within sociology," but he suggests that the term can be usefully employed to cover civic, aesthetic, and political aspects of social life as well as rituals associated with the life cycle. Secularization does not necessarily lead to a decline in ritual action. Such action may be present in the performing arts (for example, mime and dance) and civic ceremonies (for example, state funerals and graduation ceremonies)—see also CIVIC RELIGION.

Life-cycle rituals (rites of passage) continue to have significance in both simple and complex societies. The growth and decay of the human body is a feature of all human societies and consequently necessitates social control and management. Life-cycle rituals are key areas enabling biological change to be made socially meaningful and significant. Life-cycle rituals can be used both to integrate a newly born child into the group and to affirm the continued existence of a group in the event of the death of one of its members. Van Gennep has suggested that rites of passage mark both biological changes and changes in social position. Rites of passage may be seen as characterized by a common structure involving:

(a) separation of the individual from the old order or previous social condition;

(b) a marginal or transitional phase that is highly sacred;

(c) a final stage that incorporates the individual into the new social order or status.

Ritual action may be seen to be present in all areas of social life and is one of the key means whereby individuals and groups resolve problems encountered in the sacred and profane aspects of social existence.

Rogers, Carl (1902–1987) PHENOMENOLOGICAL psychologist within the HUMANISTIC MOVEMENT, known best for the development of client-centered or PERSON-CENTERED COUNSELING (1951). His influence has been so extensive in the area of personal counseling that the methodology is often termed "Rogerian."

Central to Rogers' theory of personality, and to the humanistic movement generally, is the emphasis on a tendency toward "personal growth." He regards this as an "innate organismic tendency," but problems in this developmental process may occur due to environmental constraints.

Particularly, the person has a need for "unconditional positive regard" from others if he or she is to develop positive self-regard. Parents particularly have a responsibility to provide unconditional positive regard and not to impose unrealistic "conditions of worth." If the person has undergone damaging experiences and lost, or not developed, a sense of self-worth, then counseling/therapy may be necessary to generate it.

Phenomenological psychology sees the person as unique, with a unique personal perception of the world. Client-centered therapy therefore aims to facilitate clients in understanding their situations by allowing them to talk, and by reflecting back the content of what is said without further analysis or direction. This is done in a setting of empathy, genuine warmth, and unconditional positive regard, the intention being to enhance positive self-regard and reduce the limiting conditions of worth. This technique has been developed in work with neurotics, and it is within this group, particularly those who are verbal and highly motivated to get well, that it is most successful.

Rogers did not limit himself to individual psychotherapeutic counseling but, as a humanistic psychologist, was interested in assisting everyone toward "self-actualization." He was active in developing group techniques (1970) and also in applying his ideas within education (1969).

role 1. any relatively standardized social position, involving specific rights and obligations, which an individual is expected or encouraged to perform, for example, the parental role. **2.** "the dynamic aspect of STATUS," where "status" refers to the position and "role" to its performance (R. Linton, 1936); it is more usual, however, for the term "role" to apply to both position and performance, with "status" also used as an alternative term for "position." Roles may be *specific* or *diffuse, ascribed* or *achieved*—see PATTERN VARIABLES. In SYMBOLIC INTERACTIONISM the term "role" is used differently. In this perspective social identities and social action are analyzed as the outcome of "taking the role of the other," rather than from adopting ready-made roles. *Role-playing,* a form of social training in which people take part in group exercises calling for acting out a range of social roles, has a similar basis. The expectation is that acting out social roles, including those with which one initially lacks sympathy, will bring greater social understanding.

In FUNCTIONALISM, the theory of role stresses the normative expectations attached to particular positions and the way in which roles are associated with INSTITUTIONS. The emphasis is on the acquisition and enacting of behavior patterns determined by NORMS and rules. MERTON (1949) suggested the further notion of *role-set,* to refer to the range of role relationships associated with a given status. It is recognized that the individual is likely to encounter tensions (*role conflict*) in coping with the requirements of incompatible roles, for example, the roles of worker and mother, or lecturer and researcher. The functional theory of role has been criticized, however, for sometimes implying an unchanging conception of social action.

The earlier, symbolic interactionist approach to role, associated with G.H. MEAD, contrasts with that of functionalism, in that for Mead role-taking is mainly of interest as an essential process in the development of the SELF. Both adults and children establish conceptions of self by imagining themselves in the positions of others (see also LOOKING-GLASS SELF), but there is no conception of fixed roles in the way central in functionalism, and the continually renegotiated character of social action is emphasized.

The writings of GOFFMAN provided other examples of role analysis, for example, the concept of ROLE DISTANCE, in which the performer of a role adopts a subjective detachment from the role.

role conflict see ROLE.

role distance the subjective detachment displayed by a SOCIAL ACTOR while playing a ROLE, for example, a waiter who may indicate to a customer that he is not *only* a waiter.

role-playing see ROLE.

role reversal any situation in which people exchange roles so that one plays the role of the other, for example, master and servant, adult and child, male and female roles. In any societies institutionalized provision exists (for example, Roman *saturnalia*, that is, periods of feasting and social laxity) for such reversals to occur, which are seen as having the function of releasing the social tensions created by the constraints of ROLE. Today, office parties have been suggested as having a similar function.

role-set see ROLE.

role theory any approaches in sociology that emphasize the importance of roles and role-taking in shaping and maintaining social order and social organization. See ROLE.

Rorschach Inkblot Test a device designed by Rorschach (1921) to allow a person to *project* his/her personality so that problems may be uncovered and resolved. This is therefore a PROJECTIVE TEST and is based on a holistic, phenomenological approach to understanding personality dynamics.

In practice, the client/patient is shown a series of inkblot patterns that are regarded as ambiguous stimuli. The ambiguity allows a variety of different interpretations to be put on them, and features selected from them. The client/patient is encouraged to talk about what he or she sees in the patterns, and the therapist uses these responses as clues to unconscious or difficult-to-voice concerns, which can then be explored. A scoring system has been developed through observations made on various clinical and normal groups, but scoring is still necessarily subjective and interpretation of the responses is regarded as a skilled activity, requiring much experience.

routinization 1. any social situation in which social action is repetitive and can be performed with a degree of motivational detachment and lack of involvement (see also ANOMIE). **2.** (as employed by SCHUTZ, the ETHNOMETHODOLOGISTS, and GIDDENS) the "taken-for-granted" habitual character of most of the activities of everyday social life: *routine.*

Rowntree, Benjamin Seebohm (1871–1954) philanthropist and social reformer who had a significant influence on the development of the British WELFARE STATE as a result of his demonstration that the causes of poverty are located in structural features of society, such as the unequal distribution of income and wealth, rather than being explained by the personal lifestyles of the poor. Born into a rich Quaker family, he emulated the poverty surveys of Charles BOOTH. In his three surveys of York, England, in 1898, 1936, and 1950, Rowntree sought to discover the causes of poverty as well as to describe its incidence. In order to make valid claims for state intervention, he distinguished between primary and secondary poverty. Primary poverty, he argued, was the condition of an individual who receives only subsistence to satisfy solely physiological needs; secondary poverty refers to the condition when the satisfaction of basic psychological and social needs, such as the ability to participate in the community and enjoy a social life, has been met. Rowntree also developed the notion of a CYCLE OF DEPRIVATION in which one's chances of being poor may be influenced by one's position in the LIFE COURSE and one's family and social background. Rowntree's work was influential in the development of the first insurance based social security policies and the Beveridge Report. At the direction of Lloyd George, Rowntree was responsible for overseeing the welfare of munitions workers during World War I, and he helped to plan postwar housing policy. In subsequent years, Rowntree's notion of primary poverty has been criticized as being too restricted. However, he never intended that the provision of social security should be directed only at combatting primary poverty.

rules and **rule-following** the specification of a regularity in social behavior where this regularity derives (a) either directly from a SOCIAL ACTOR's attention to the specification, or (b) can be seen as deriving from the operation of such a rule without the actor's direct awareness of the rule.

The term is sometimes loosely used, becoming equivalent to "a regularity in behavior." In a more interesting and narrower sense, rule-following is the production of a regularity by persons who can in principle decide to do otherwise, that is, not to build their behavior by reference to the specification, and are in this sense free (see also FREE WILL). Such freedom remains the case, even where in a second sense a rule restricts an actor's freedom, by being someone else's rule, and where this rule leads to sanctions for not following it. In this sense, rules can still represent an enlargement of freedom, for example, as the basis of social INSTITUTIONS, in bringing predictability in social outcomes that ease social behavior. Such a constitutive aspect of rules may be contrasted with their more mundanely regulative aspect in that they merely control actions within institutions.

Many approaches in sociology have taken social rules, in all their complexity, as their subject matter. Only sometimes has it been assumed that social rules can be rendered equivalent to a law in the sense of this term in empiricist versions of social science. Thus, for example, PARSONS' conception of a rule, or norm, has been criticized as scientistic.

While the narrower sense of rule tends to be associated with humanist and semiotic commitments in social science, some critics have insisted that a rule in itself, as specified in language of some kind, is never enough to allow rule-following. Any rule needs embedding in a context of practice and material circumstances. On the other hand, rule specifications are inherently open, that is, behavior in particular circumstances is only defeasibly construable as in accord with a rule. These aspects together make sociology's rules very different from any empiricist notion of social science.

ruling class or **dominant class 1.** (Marxism) within any society or social formation, the class that enjoys cultural, political, and economic ascendancy (*class domination*) by virtue of its ownership and control over the means of production. **2.** (non-Marxist POLITICAL SOCIOLOGY) *ruling class*, the minority that in any society always forms the political governing class, MOSCA *The Ruling Class* (1896). See also ELITE and ELITE THEORY.

In most Marxist uses but not all, "ruling class" and "dominant class" are virtually synonymous. In *The Communist Manifesto* Marx and Engels did write that in the modern representative state "the bourgeoisie" will often hold "exclusive political sway," that the state would be "the executive committee of the bourgeoisie." For most Marxists, however, even where such a ruling or dominant class does not govern directly (for example, where, as in modern liberal democracies, government is in the hands of persons drawn from several different classes), this does not mean that the economically dominant class is not the ruling class, since it may still rule by virtue of its control over IDEOLOGIES, over dominant ideas, etc. stemming from its economic influence. As Marx and Engels wrote in *The German Ideology:* "The ideas of the ruling class are, in every age, the ruling ideas; that is, the class that is the *dominant* material force in society is at the same time its *dominant* intellectual force." Thus, in this sense a ruling or dominant class may rule even though it does not govern. In some political circumstances, it is argued that it is to the clear advantage of an economically dominant class that it does not rule or govern directly, for example, when a sharing of central political power with other groups allows control to be exerted over diverse forces that are seen as "condensed" at the political center. In such circumstances, however, it can also be argued that the lack of class capacity preventing any one class to rule directly can reflect a state of affairs in which there exists no economically and politically dominant class.

There are today many Marxists (for example, see Poulantzas, 1973) who also emphasize that a tendency always exists for the state to possess a relative autonomy, or even on occasion an absolute autonomy, from underlying economic forces. In this context, a distinction between the political ruling ELITEs and the economically dominant class is one that usually needs to be made. A final problem for Marxism is that *empirically* there often exist many difficulties in any actual identification of the ruling or the dominant class, especially in the study of historical forms of society, for example, in ABSOLUTISM or ASIATIC MODE OF PRODUCTION OR ASIATIC SOCIETY.

For the users of the term "ruling class" in sense **2.**, the predominant concern has been different from that of most Marxists. Their goal has been to expose the pretentions of most modern claims to democracy, including the claims of Marxists that true democracy might one day be achieved. According to Mosca the rulers will always be drawn from an organized minority. Using abstract political justifications, which Mosca called *political formulae*, rulers everywhere seek to legitimize their political rule. In some cases the principles that operate in the selection of political leaders and the social origins of such leaders may merit the empirical use of such terms as "representative democracy." But even in these circumstances the ruling class will always consist of, and be drawn from, a cultural and psychological minority of the population equipped to rule. See also PARETO; MILLS; POWER ELITE; GRAMSCI; HEGEMONY; DOMINANT IDEOLOGY THESIS.

Runciman, Walter (W.G.) (1934–) British sociologist and industrialist, who as an independent scholar and fellow of Trinity College Cambridge has produced a succession of commentaries, research monographs, and theoretical works, especially in the areas of political sociology, class analysis, historical and comparative sociology, and sociological theory. His first book, *Social Science and Political Theory* (1963), was a plea for Anglo-American political theory to give greater attention to European political sociology, especially the work of WEBER and Joseph Schumpeter. In *Relative Deprivation and Social Justice* (1966), he employed historical analysis and social survey data to show that actors' conceptions of social deprivation and class consciousness are relative rather than absolute, varying according to the social comparisons actually made by social actors (see RELATIVE DEPRIVATION, CLASS IMAGERY). Runciman argues that the conception of a "just society" is valid and should embrace notions such as equal provision for need, greater equality of educational opportunity, and increased opportunities for democratic political participation. However, he finds no indication that an automatic development of class consciousness and class action will occur that will lead to this outcome. Runciman's *magnum opus* is a trilogy of volumes on sociological theory, of which two have been completed. The first of these, *A Treatise on Social Theory*, Vol. 1, *The Methodology of the Social Sciences* (1983), identifies three main methods that have a legitimate place within sociology: (a) theory-neutral reportage of empirical facts about the social order, (b) theoretical explanation of overarching social structure, (c) phenomenological description of the "lived textures" of social lives. While the first and second of these are seen as broadly positivistic, the third is not. It is dependent on a coherence' rather than a correspondence view of reality. Runciman's second volume of the trilogy, *Substantive Social Theory* (1989), consists of a wide-ranging comparative analysis and an evolutionary theory of social development in which the struggle between different bases of social power, analogous to Darwinian natural selection, is central (see also EVOLUTIONARY SOCIOLOGY). The trilogy is to be concluded with a volume applying the concepts of volumes 1 and 2 to British social history. In all of this, Runciman regards the role of the sociologist as, ideally, that of the impartial benevolent observer. Runciman's "evolutionism" has been subject to the standard criticisms directed at EVOLUTIONARY THEORY in modern sociology. The distinction he draws between his third and the first and second method has been criticized as overly polarized. But the breadth and the power of his sociological analysis, especially his historical comparative analysis, has been much admired. See also SYSTACT.

rural sociology a branch of sociology concerned with the study of rural communities and agriculture. Rural sociology has existed as a clearly identified subdiscipline only in the United States, where it was encouraged by government policies. Elsewhere the study of rural communities and agriculture has more often been subsumed within other areas of inquiry, including economic anthropology, peasant studies, and development studies. See also ECOLOGY, GREEN MOVEMENT.

S

sacred and profane a distinction particularly employed in sociology by DURKHEIM in that the *sacred,* which includes all phenomena that are set apart and revered, is distinguished from all other phenomena, the *profane.* For Durkheim, beliefs and practices in relation to the sacred are the defining feature of any RELIGION.

Saint-Simon, Comte Henri de (1760–1825) French evolutionary and positivist social theorist who exercized a commanding influence on the development of sociology as a discipline (see EVOLUTIONARY THEORY, POSITIVISM). Saint-Simon's career was as iconoclastic as his sociology. An aristocrat of impeccable lineage, he fought in the American Revolution and found himself imprisoned in the French Revolution. He subsequently amassed large profits from speculation in land, established a famous salon that attracted France's intellectual elite, squandered his money, and from 1804 to the end of his life lived close to poverty. This period was his most productive in an intellectual sense and saw, toward its close, collaboration with Auguste COMTE.

The ideas of the Enlightenment, and especially those of MONTESQUIEU and CONDORCET, were influential in the formation of Saint-Simon's sociology. His own ideas were subsequently to inform those of Comte, and thus DURKHEIM, as well as MARX. These theorists point to the main ingredients of Saint-Simon's work: his positivism and evolutionism on the one hand, and his socialism on the other.

Saint-Simon's evolutionary law argued that society passed through three stages, each characterized by different types of knowledge: the theological, the metaphysical and the positive (see LAW OF THREE STAGES). The positive stage coincided with the emergence of INDUSTRIAL SOCIETY, a term first coined by Saint-Simon himself. For Saint-Simon, industrial society was distinct from previous stages in three ways: the emergence of a single, albeit multilayered class (that is, all those involved in industrial production); its technology, which completed society's struggle to dominate nature; and its potential for the transformation of the state from an instrument of domination to one of enlightened welfare and reform managed on behalf of the new industrial class by an intellectual elite informed by positive sociological knowledge.

Before this benevolent, elitist version of socialism could emerge, however, a transitional period of social dislocation and deregulation would inevitably occur, as the epistemological cement of social order characteristic of previous eras (religion), weakened under the impact of industrial society's secularism. Positive, scientific sociology or *social physics* as Saint-Simon put it, could help hasten and smooth the transition to the new positive stage, and provide the basis of a new secular moral order.

Saint-Simon's ideas continue to reverberate through sociological work. Apart from his enormous influence on the contours of classical theory, Saint-Simon's concepts (of the centrality of knowledge to industrial society, and of the necessity for compatibility between its technologies and forms of social organization) have reemerged in recent theory in terms of the ideas of CONVERGENCE and postindustrialism (see POSTINDUSTRIAL SOCIETY).

sample or **sampling** a selection of individuals made from a larger population (the parent population) and intended to reflect this population's characteristics in all significant respects. The purpose of taking a sample is to investigate features of the population in greater detail than could be done if the total population were used, and to draw inferences about this population. For these inferences to be valid (see VALIDITY) the sample must be truly representative, the only way to ensure this being to take a RANDOM SAMPLE. This involves using either *random numbers* or *systematic sampling*. Random numbers are used to ensure that every individual in the sampling frame (for example, an electoral register or mailing list) has an equal chance of being selected as a member of the sample. Systematic sampling involves randomly selecting the first individual from the list, then subsequently individuals at every fixed interval, for example, every tenth person if a 10% sample is desired.

When the population to be studied is large and the sample relatively small, it may be efficient to use STRATIFIED SAMPLING. This technique involves dividing the population into strata, for example, age groups or social classes, and drawing a random sample from each. This can improve the representativeness of the sample, since the size of the sample from each stratum is made proportionate to the size of the strata in the total population. See also SAMPLING ERROR, CLUSTER SAMPLING, QUOTA SAMPLING, SNOWBALL SAMPLING, PROBABILITY.

sampling error the difference between the true value of a characteristic within a population and the value estimated from a sample of that population. Error occurs because no SAMPLE can be expected to exactly represent the parent population from which it was drawn. To minimize, and to be able to estimate, sampling error, it is necessary to ensure that the selection of the sample is RANDOM, and this is normally done by random numbers or systematic sampling. Sampling error is not the same as BIAS or systematic error, which may occur due to the process of data collection, but has nothing to do with the sample selection.

sanction any means by which a moral code or social norm is enforced, either positively in the form of rewards or negatively by means of punishment. Sanctions may also be formal (for example, legal penalties) or informal (for example, ostracism). The operation of social sanctions is an all-pervasive factor in social relations.

Sapir-Whorf hypothesis the thesis that linguistic categories structure perceptual and cognitive ones. Two United States anthropologists, Edward Sapir (1884–1934) and his student Benjamin Lee Whorf (1897–1941), are credited with this theory of *linguistic relativism*. Essentially, the position states that our language structures our perception of the world. Whorf demonstrates this with his work on Hopi Indians, who appeared to have different concepts of space, time, and matter than so-called standard average European language speakers. Another common example is the plurality of Inuit (Eskimo) words for "snow," supposedly illustrating that they are attuned to elements of their environment that a non-Inuit would be unable to recognize. The strong version of the hypothesis is now rarely accepted, but debate still continues as to where language ends and material culture and social structure begin. See also RELATIVISM, FORM OF LIFE.

Sartre, Jean-Paul (1905–1980) French existentialist philosopher and novelist, whose work blends existentialism with Marxism. Sartre's method was influenced by HUSSERL'S PHENOMENOLOGY, but the central notions of his philosophy derive from HEIDEGGER. This is that although we cannot escape the givens of our initial situation (its "facticity") we are free to act to change it. Sartre draws a distinction between being-in-itself (unconscious, thingness) and being-for-itself (conscious, no-thingness and action). Politicized by World War II and his association with the French Communist Party, his aim of overcoming the economic and social structures of choice that restrict options, linked existentialism with Marxism. His *magnum opus* is *Being and Nothingess* (1956), and his main contribution to Marxism is *Critique of Dialectical Reason* (1960).

Saussure, Ferdinand de (1857–1913) Swiss theorist who is generally regarded as the founder of modern structural linguistics. He was also a major influence on the wider intellectual movement known as STRUCTURALISM. His seminal work, *Cours de linguistique générale* (1916), was published posthumously, compiled from notes taken by his students. In this, SEMIOLOGY, the general study of all sign systems, is first distinguished from the more specific study of language. A number of interrelated distinctions are then introduced that have become central in theoretical linguistics and are often the taking-off points in structuralism:

(a) the distinction between LANGUE AND PAROLE, that is, between the rules of language and actual instances of produced speech;

(b) the distinction between SYNCHRONY AND DIACHRONY, that is, between the study of language without reference to the past, only as an existing system of relationships, and the study of changes in language;

(c) the distinction between *syntagmatic* and *paradigmatic* (earlier called *associative*) relationships, that is, between the combination of words in a particular chain of speech and the relationships of any particular term with related absent terms within the language;

(d) the distinction between signifier and signified, that is, between the term (its acoustical or written form) and the concept (the idea) signified by the term.

Other important notions in Saussure's linguistics are an emphasis on the arbitrary character of the relationship between the signifier and the signified, and the idea that the status or meaning or value of each linguistic unit is established only in relation to all other units, that is, is internal to the language, rather than in terms of an inherently determining phenomenon external to the language. Thus, in Saussure's well-known dictum, in languages "there are only differences."

The importance of Saussure's approach in launching theoretical linguistics on its modern course is undeniable, although the absence of any systematic treatment of syntax or PRAGMATICS in his work left gaps to be repaired by later theorists such as Chomsky. Because the emphasis in Saussure's work is on *langue* rather than *parole,* it is not surprising that this has been seen as leading to a one-sided account of language. When employed analogically, as in structuralism, this conception of language may also give rise to a one-sided account of social structures. Finally, while an emphasis on internal relations within sign systems is consonant with an emphasis on the importance of understanding particular frames of reference (for example, the study of particular scientific PARADIGMS, PROBLEMATIQUES, FORMS OF LIFE), it has been criticized for sometimes encouraging RELATIVISM (see also INCOMMENSURABILITY), and for undervaluing individual agency (see also STRUCTURE AND AGENCY; ALTHUSSER).

savagery one of the stages of development identified in early theories of SOCIAL EVOLUTION. MONTESQUIEU (1689–1755) proposed that the three main stages of social development were (a) hunting or savagery, (b) herding or BARBARISM, and (c) CIVILIZATION.

The concept gained currency in the 19th century through the distinction made between simple-primitive and complex-modern societies in EVOLUTIONARY THEORY. The term was inevitably pejorative, since evolutionary theory saw social development as also involving a civilizing process. Thus "savagery" was meant to convey a condition of brutal backwardness, the opposite of the civilized manners, morals, intellect, and taste of Europe's privileged classes.

Apart from its pejorative connotation, it was also inaccurate. Simple societies were not savage in the way in that Europeans understood the term. The concept had its political uses in an age of expanding colonialism, but its adequacy as a description of non-European preindustrial societies could hardly survive events such as World War I.

scaling a method of measurement in the social sciences, which is applied particularly to the measurement of personality traits and of ATTITUDES. Central is the concept of a *continuum*. This means that personality types, for example, can be arranged or ordered in terms of dichotomous schemes (such as EXTRAVERSION AND INTROVERSION), and attitudes vary on a scale going from one extreme, through neutral, to the other extreme.

There are a number of ways of constructing such scales, but all rely on the assumption that personality traits or attitudes can be assessed from the responses given to statements or questions (see LIKERT SCALE). It is important that an equal number of positively and negatively loaded statements are used, and that only one dimension is tapped. Various statistical techniques are used to check the internal consistency of scales as they are developed.

Schutz, Alfred (1899–1959) Austrian-born sociologist and philosopher, a major architect of SOCIAL PHENOMENOLOGY who, after his move to New York in 1935, worked as a banker. Schutz's main work, for example, *The Phenomenology of the Social World* (1967—Ger. 1932), involved application of Edmund HUSSERL's PHENOMENOLOGY to social phenomena, especially the phenomena of everyday life. This also involved Schutz in a critique of WEBER. According to Schutz, Weber "does not ask how an actor's meaning is constituted or … try to identify the unique and fundamental relations existing between the self and the other." The basic thesis of Schutz's social phenomenology is that sociology must work to uncover the concepts or TYPIFICATIONS by which actors, in intersubjective ways, organize their everyday actions and construct common-sense knowledge. As he saw it, everyday knowledge, unlike scientific knowledge, cannot be studied by abstract methods. Rather, the careful inspection of everyday social life reveals that social actors operate with taken-for-granted assumptions and stock knowledge and achieve a "reciprocity of perspective," a "natural attitude" that must be seen as paramount in social knowledge. Schutz's conception is that social order arises from the general presumption of a common world, but without this presumption being in any way a matter of normative consensus of the kind assumed by functionalism. (See also PRACTICAL KNOWLEDGE, LIFE-WORLD.)

The paradox arising from Schutz's social phenomenology is that although a generalized account of the actor's constitution of social life is reached, this account suggests that there may be limits on the extent to which the macroscopic generalizations about social structures and social change that conventional sociologies have sought can ever by achieved. Schutz's ideas have been taken up by ETHNOMETHODOLOGY. The issue arising is whether scientific and everyday common-sense knowledge are as sharply differentiated as Schutz and the ethnomethodologists suggest, and whether general social structural accounts may still be possible, despite the undoubted elements of INDEXICALITY and REFLEXIVITY of everyday social accounts.

scientific management a set of principles governing the design of jobs that entail the separation of mental from manual labor, subdivision of tasks, deskilling, close managerial control of work effort, and incentive wage payments.

The scientific management movement originated in the United States in the 1890s, F.W. Taylor being its main proponent, hence the terms "Taylorism" and "scientific management" are often used interchangeably. Taylor was trained as an engineer and his principles of management were based on the philosophy that work design is capable of objective measurement by which work can be broken down into its constituent parts as various physical motions that can be precisely timed (thus, *time and motion study*) with a view to reorganizing jobs to achieve the most efficient use of effort to raise productivity. In this sense management would become scientific rather than intuitive, discovering the laws governing work activity as a basis for a set of universal principles defining the best way to organize work. Taylor's philosophy was also based on ideas from classical economics and a psychology that assumed that individuals were naturally lazy and instrumental in their attitude to work. Each individual would be paid in relation to his or her effort and motivated by economic reward. With scientific management labor unions would be obsolete, cooperation in the workplace would be ensured through application of scientific principles, and each worker would pursue his or her individual self-interest.

Scientific management advocated:

(a) fragmentation of work into simple, routine operations.

(b) standardization of each operation to eliminate idle times.

(c) separation of conception from execution, the design and control of work being a management task.

Taylor's principles were primarily directed at the workplace but his methods also implied the functional division of management, including management's separation from owners, which was elaborated by the early proponents of management science into a formal blueprint for organizations, defining lines of authority and spans of control (see also ORGANIZATION THEORY).

Taylor's ideas were also an extension of earlier 19th-century approaches to factory organization and mechanization, notably the work of Andrew Ure and Charles Babbage. The so-called Babbage Principle (1832) asserted that skilled tasks should be fragmented into a skilled component and various deskilled associated tasks, which allow each task to be paid at the lowest possible rate and workers perform only operations commensurate with their skill and training.

Sociological analysis of scientific management has focused on two issues: first, its significance as a management ideology legitimating management control, and secondly, the extent to which scientific management was applied in practice in capitalist societies at various stages of their development. As an ideology, scientific management has had a pervasive influence on work organization and managerial thought up to the present day despite initial opposition from both labor unions and employers. As an ideology it contrasted strongly with earlier employers' attitudes of paternalism and welfarism and was the object of considerable criticism from later HUMAN RELATIONS approaches to management that rejected its individualistic, economistic assumptions about human motivation and advocated instead task variety, group working, and self-fulfillment through work.

scientism any doctrine or approach held to involve oversimplified conceptions and unreal expectations of science, and to misapply methods of natural science to the social sciences, including overconfidence in the capacity of science to solve social problems. Thus the term is mainly a pejorative one.

The notion that the success of the physical sciences could be readily repeated in the social sciences became well established in the 16th and 17th centuries and is seen later in COMTE's POSITIVISM. Claims to a scientific basis have been a feature of many other approaches in sociology, including Marxism. Whether or not such approaches are held to be scientistic, however, is not a straightforward matter, since it depends on what one regards as proper or appropriate science—both in general and in the context of social studies—and this itself is controversial. Thus, at one extreme, accusations of scientism have been associated with wholesale dismissals of natural science as a model for social science, while on other occasions they merely involve a repudiation of obvious excesses.

screening the use of academic qualifications as a means of selecting among candidates for employment, where it is the general level of academic qualification that is decisive rather than the particular content of the education. In this process, the use of educational qualifications, or sometimes also the type of institution attended, may be used as a proxy for general intelligence, perseverance and motivation, or other social background, rather than an employer being interested in the specific content of the education received. See also CULTURAL CAPITAL.

According to the *screening hypothesis,* it is this screening process rather than any direct economic return on education that explains part of the correlation between level of education and level of income. This hypothesis provides an account of the effects of education that is substantially at odds with other hypotheses (compare HUMAN CAPITAL). Screening theorists also suggest that while increased education is sometimes associated with an individual return, and the screening function performed by higher and post-school education also performs a useful function for individual firms, this does not mean that education results in an overall social return or a return for all individuals. The reason for this is that educational expansion brings an increasing competition for jobs in that education becomes ever more necessary for the individual, but no longer sufficient to ensure high status employment; a means of selection and allocation to jobs rather than guaranteeing high status employment. See also CREDENTIALISM, CULTURAL CAPITAL.

secondary analysis any inquiry based on the reanalysis of previously analyzed research data, for example, publicly available data such as CENSUS data, or data available from data banks. The advantages of using such data are its relative cheapness, since the data do not have to be collected, and the opportunity the data can offer for longitudinal historical or cross-cultural analysis. The main disadvantage is that the researcher has far less control over the construction of variables and often has only limited knowledge of the manner and circumstances in which the data were collected. See also OFFICIAL STATISTICS.

secondary deviance or **secondary deviation** the process whereby after an act of PRIMARY DEVIANCE an individual adopts a DEVIANT IDENTITY (Lemert, 1961). This involves a reconstruction of SELF in terms of attitudes, feelings, and cultural or SUBCULTURAL affiliation. In common with the LABELING perspective, Lemert sees this adaptation as identified with, and even produced by, SOCIETAL REACTION. See also DEVIANT CAREER.

second order constructs theories about theories. Since all SOCIAL ACTORS themselves possess so-called theories about their own activities, *all* sociological theories can be seen as second order constructs, which must first of all grasp the social actor's first order constructs. See also DOUBLE HERMENEUTIC.

sect a religious, or sometimes a secular, social movement characterized by its opposition to and rejection of orthodox religious and/or secular institutions, doctrines, and practices, for example, the Shakers, Quakers, and Amish Mennonites.

Sociologists have identified sectarianism with a relatively low level of institutionalization and with a tendency toward doctrinal heresy. Ernst Troeltsch (1912) distinguished between churches and sects (see also CHURCH-SECT TYPOLOGY). Churches were characterized as conservative, orthodox, hierarchic, tradition- and ritual-bound, and having a high degree of organization and institutionalization. By contrast, sects were perfectionist, radical, egalitarian, and manifesting a low degree of organization and institutionalization. Sectarians valued spontaneous action over ritual practice. Troeltsch regarded sect and church as polar opposites. Troeltsch's work was concerned with sectarian movements within Christianity and is consequently difficult to apply outside this context. This is particularly the case where many Third World sectarian movements are concerned.

More recently, Bryan Wilson (1973) has suggested that sects may be regarded as "self-distinguishing protest movements." The protest may not necessarily be directed at orthodox churches but against state and other secular institutions within society. Wilson rejects Troeltsch's dichotomous model and suggests that it is useful to examine sectarian movements by reference to the relation between the following social factors: doctrine, degree of organization, form of association, and social orientation and action. Wilson further suggests that sects may be typified according to their "responses to the world." Many sectarian movements display some degree of conflict and tension with both the religious and secular social world.

SECTORAL CLEAVAGES

Consequently, sectarians are often characterized by a desire to seek both deliverance and salvation from orthodox cultural forms, traditions, and institutions. Wilson suggests that there are at least seven possible responses to the world and to the problem of evil within it. He calls these the "conversionist," "revolutionist," "introversionist," "manipulationist," "thaumaturgical," "reformist," and "utopian" responses.

By going beyond the concern with degree of organization and doctrinal heresy, it is possible to examine sectarian movements that have arisen outside Christian culture. See also CULT, MILLENARIANISM AND MILLENNIAL MOVEMENT, CARGO CULTS, RELIGION, MAGIC, SOCIOLOGY OF RELIGION.

sectoral cleavages the bases of political interests and political action that, to some extent, cut across the basic left-right CLASS CLEAVAGE that has usually been regarded as central in politics (see Dunleavy, 1980). Significant sectoral cleavages include:

(a) private and public-sector employment;

(b) private and collective consumption sectors (for example, interests arising from the existence of public and private sectors in housing, transport, and the provision of welfare).

segregated conjugal-role relationship a division of labor within a household that involves separate tasks for each partner. The term was first used by Elizabeth Bott (1957), who suggested that such relationships were most often found in communities with close networks of family and friends that supported separate areas of activity for women and men. It is often suggested that this kind of role relationship is being replaced by the JOINT CONJUGAL-ROLE RELATIONSHIP, but there is much evidence to suggest that household tasks are still highly gender-segregated. Ironing and automobile maintenance are the most often cited examples. See also SYMMETRICAL FAMILY.

segregation the spatial separation of a RACE, CLASS, or ETHNIC GROUP by discriminatory means. Racial segregation can be enforced by law, as in the South in the United States until the 1950s, or in the system of apartheid in South Africa. Such segregation can take the form of separate facilities (schools, beaches, transport, etc.) or the establishment of racially homogeneous territories (as in the "Bantustan" policy in South Africa). In many countries, residential or educational segregation exists that does not have the force of law but results from economic and social DISCRIMINATION. See also GHETTO.

self a mental construction of the person by the person. It is inevitably formed from social experience—the person sees himself or herself reflected by others, in their reactions, and these are interpreted through the lattice of self-perception. G.H. MEAD (1934) is particularly associated with this idea of the self as being a social construction. Self cannot exist without society. The self is where knowledge resides, but the knowledge is about society, which surrounds it.

self-fulfilling and self-destroying prophecy two ever-present possibilities that accompany any attempts at sociological generalization and prediction. These may either be (a) spuriously confirmed merely as the outcome of their pronouncement, for example, a stock exchange crash brought about by its expectation, or (b) undermined, because when knowledge of these becomes available, people take action to prevent the outcome in question, for example, uncongested roads at a predicted time of congestion during a transit strike because people travel at other times to avoid the rush.

The occurrence of self-fulfilling and self-destroying predictions is an indication of voluntarism and choice in social behavior (that is, it involves purposive social action, in which events get monitored, is capable of reacting to feedback, etc.). Sometimes the fact that this happens is elevated to the status of a general principle that significant sociological generalizations, sociological laws, etc. are not possible in sociology or the social sciences. However, because social participants often have the capacity to change their actions does not mean they always have this capacity, for example, social structural forces may intervene, (see also STRUCTURE AND AGENCY). Thus, all possibility of successful, nonspurious sociological generalizations is not ruled out by the existence of self-fulfilling and self-destroying hypotheses.

self-help groups groups of people, often in some distress, set up for mutual support and assistance toward renewed psychological health. Self-help groups are part of the general group therapy movement, and though not regarding a group leader, or facilitator, as obligatory it is usual to have one. The emphasis is on sharing a common experience and current emotions, and it is through this sharing and the deeper understanding of SELF and others it brings that the healing process takes place. Such groups are commonly found in work with the bereaved, and with people suffering from eating disorders and alcoholism.

semantics the subdivision of linguistics concerned with meaning. Semantics attempts systematic study of the assignment of meanings to minimal meaning-bearing elements and the combination of these in producing more complex meaningful expressions. A variety of theories seek to account for semantic relations, ranging from behaviorist psychology, COMPONENTIAL ANALYSIS, and theories based on modern logics, to sociological accounts taking meaning to be unavoidably a local achievement of interactive negotiation. In logical semantics the current search is for an integrated syntax and semantics. In this, syntax is framed as a structural vehicle for meanings, that moves from "possible worlds" to "truth values." The project amounts to a technical reworking of the verification principle that meaning is to be equated with a set of truth conditions. If the program were to be successful it would have important implications for sociology.

semiology or **semiotics** the science that studies the system of signs, whether these signs appear in language, literature, or the world of artifacts in general. As an aspect of STRUCTURALISM, semiology evolved from the linguistic studies of SAUSSURE. Its leading exponent is Roland BARTHES.

Although the idea of a general science of signs first appeared at the turn of the century in the work of Saussure, it was not until the 1960s, and in the fields of MASS MEDIA research and CULTURAL STUDIES, that the idea was developed. In the realm of cultural studies semiology has involved study of areas ignored by other disciplines (for example, eating habits) and opened up the question of the relationships between cultural codes and power relationships. Its key concepts are the *signifier* (a thing, word, or picture) and the *signified* (the mental picture or meaning indicated by the signifier), and the sign is the association or relationship established between them. Some relationships may be fairly direct (*iconic*), and others may involve considerable mediation because of their arbitrariness. Semiology draws attention to the layers of meaning that may be embodied in a simple set of representations (for example, the representations of Christmas on greetings cards: Santa Claus, Virgin and Child, Christmas trees, and so on). Barthes said that signs communicate latent as well as manifest meanings. They can signify moral values, and they can generate feelings or attitudes in the viewer (for example, a photograph of a Rottweiler = dog = power, a fighting dog = threat to children). Thus, signs may be collected and organized into complex codes of communication. See also BRICOLAGE.

sensitizing concept any sociological concept that, in contrast with fully operationalized or definitive concepts, "merely suggests directions along which to look" (BLUMER, 1954). Whereas definitive concepts have specified empirical referents that can be readily operationalized, for example, "social class" operationalized in terms of income level or years of schooling, sensitizing concepts are less precise. They alert sociologists to certain aspects of social phenomena, for example, GOFFMAN's concept of MORAL CAREER. However, no firm distinction exists between the two kinds of concepts.

sexual division of labor a specific expression of the DIVISION OF LABOR where workers are divided according to certain assumptions about "men's work" and "women's work." The sexual division of labor is based on gender divisions that, although socially constructed, are frequently believed to be the outcome of so-called natural attributes and aptitudes of the sexes. Some form of sexual division of labor is apparent in most known societies, but its particular manifestations and degrees of differentiation are socially and historically relative. It is particularly marked in industrial societies, where it is accompanied by a distinction between unpaid DOMESTIC LABOR and WAGE LABOR, between the PRIVATE AND PUBLIC SPHERES. While these spheres are gendered (the private sphere being associated with women, the public sphere with men) such divisions are more ideological than empirical. Preindustrial societies and, particularly, many stateless societies are characterized by a less defined division between the public and the private spheres, and stateless societies generally have a less pronounced sexual division of labor.

In contemporary capitalist societies, women are concentrated in particular industries, services, and caring professions. Women's experience of paid work is predominantly one of poorer working conditions, lower levels of pay, and under-unionization relative to men. Despite the passing of the *Equal Pay Act 1970* and the *Sex Discrimination Act 1975*, women in Britain continue to earn only approximately 75% of the average male hourly wage. Women are also more likely than men to engage in poorly paid home work and part-time work, and they experience insecure employment. Barrett (1988) has suggested that both a *vertical division of labor* and a *horizontal division of labor* characterize men's work and women's work: men are advantaged with respect to pay and conditions of work, and women are found to be concentrated in a limited number of occupations that both reflect and reinforce social expectations about femininity and domesticity. Coulson et al. (1975) have suggested that the difference between men's work and women's work and the segregation of jobs according to gender amounts to "industrial apartheid."

It is important to recognize that such divisions must be understood by reference to a complex interaction between economic factors and the social order as a whole. Barron and Norris (1976) have argued that the labor market in capitalist societies is characterized by a division between the "primary sector" (highly paid, secure, skills recognized) and the "secondary sector" (low paid, insecure, and deskilled). Men occupy most of the places in the primary sector, and women are consigned to the secondary sector. Such an approach fails, however, to explain why it is women who occupy the secondary sector. (See also DUAL LABOR MARKET.)

The concept of the so-called reserve army of labor has been used to explain the sexual division of labor in capitalist societies by reference to a Marxist theory of capital wage labor. It emphasizes the interests of the employer in ensuring a dispensable work force that can be returned to the domestic sphere during periods of economic recession. Married women's paid labor is seen as similar to migrant labor, in that it too provides capital with an industrial reserve army. However, there is no perfect comparison between married women's work and that of migrant labor. The concentration of women in certain sectors makes it difficult for employers to find substitutes for them, and their lower rates of pay may protect them against layoffs.

The failure of Marxist theory to explain why women occupy the positions they do in the labor market has prompted a concern with the issue of domestic labor in the family and women's responsibility for it (see DOMESTIC LABOR DEBATE). The relationship between women's position in wage labor and their role in domestic work and child care has been stressed by many feminist sociologists. Barrett (1988) has argued that women's position as paid workers is strongly influenced by the structure of the family, women's role in reproduction, and the "ideology of domesticity." Furthermore, the ideology of the "family wage," in which men are regarded as the primary breadwinners has functioned to keep women's wages lower than men's.

shudra (sudra) see CASTE.

sick role or **patient role** sickness viewed as a special status and as the basis of social identity, and distinguished from illness as a biomedical category.

The concept originated from PARSONS' (1951) discussion of the role of medicine in industrial societies and describes a form of socially sanctioned deviance having the following characteristics:

(a) the sick person is exempted from normal social responsibilities;
(b) the sick person cannot be expected to look after himself or herself;
(c) the sick person is expected to desire a return to good health;
(d) the sick person is expected to seek competent professional help.

According to Parsons, being sick interferes with normal social responsibilities and permits exemption from them. Consequently, it may sometimes also be a status desired by those unwilling to meet their social obligations. Medicine, therefore, can be seen as having the function of social control in addition to a therapeutic role. It deters malingerers and promotes an awareness of social obligation among the sick.

Parson's formulation has been subjected to much criticism on empirical and theoretical grounds. Nevertheless, the sick role continues to be used as a sensitizing and organizing concept for empirical studies of interaction in clinical settings by the SOCIOLOGY OF HEALTH AND MEDICINE. See also SYMPTOM ICEBERG, TRIVIAL CONSULTATION.

significance test (STATISTICS) a test designed to assess whether an observed (numerical) result can have occurred by chance. The result of the test is expressed as a statistic (for example, t-ratio, F-ratio) that can be assessed against different levels of probability. It is usual to accept a level of probability of 0.05, that is, that there is only a 5% probability of the result having occurred by chance.

Examples of significance tests are the t-test (parametric) and the Wilcoxon (nonparametric) (see STATISTICS AND STATISTICAL ANALYSIS). These tests are designed to test for the significance of the observed difference between two groups of data. For example, in social survey work two samples may be taken, perhaps racial attitudes in cities with and without ethnic minority problems. There may be an apparent difference (numerical) between these groups, but the groups were samples and therefore the data are subject to SAMPLING ERROR. The difference between them must therefore be tested to see whether there is a statistically significant difference between them. Significance tests are designed to set up a NULL HYPOTHESIS, stating "no difference," and the test result either confirms or negates this.

significant other (sociology) any SOCIAL ACTOR adopted as a role model by another social actor.

Simmel, Georg (1858–1918) German sociologist and philosopher whose extensive and stylish writings and brilliant lectures have ensured his place as one of the influential classical sociologists within the discipline, although not having the extent of influence of MARX, WEBER, or DURKHEIM.

Simmel presented society as a "web of interactions" (see SOCIATION). He is particularly remembered as the founder of FORMAL SOCIOLOGY, based on drawing a distinction between FORM AND CONTENT in social analysis, in that formal sociology deals with the universal recurring (abstract and *a priori*) forms of social interaction, examining the specifics of social interaction, that is, its content, only in light of these forms (see DYAD AND TRIAD, STRANGER, SOCIABILITY). For all this, there remain strong functionalist and evolutionary overtones in his work. For example, he regarded social differentiation as bringing "adaptation" (although also sometimes disorganization). For the most part, however, Simmel regarded claims for a fully unified sociological theory as, at the very least, premature.

Simmel's Jewish background meant that he never achieved the high academic positions his work undoubtedly merited. However, his work was highly influential. After his death, it was promoted in the United States by the Chicago sociologists PARK and Burgess, where it influenced the tenor of the work of the CHICAGO SCHOOL. Simmel's influence is also strongly in evidence in the work of GOFFMAN, with whom there are similarities of presentational style as well as method, and in the CONFLICT THEORY of L. Coser (Coser, 1956, 1965). Coser's work on the "*functions* of social conflict" also underlines an abiding feature of Simmel's sociology, an emphasis on the duality involved in many social forms.

Simmel wrote more than 30 books. As well as the several collections of his numerous essays and fragments from his work, especially *The Sociology of Georg Simmel* (Wolff, 1950) and *Conflict and the Web of Group Affiliations* (Simmel, 1955), the most important in recent discussions of his work have been his extended discussion of MONEY, *The Philosophy of Money* (1978). A recent general discussion of Simmel's work is provided by Frisby, *Sociological Impressionism: a Reassessment of Georg Simmel's Social Theory* (1981).

simple society the least internally differentiated and earliest form(s) of human societies. Along with PRIMITIVE SOCIETY, one of a number of terms used to refer to such societies, and less pejorative than alternatives, its use reflects an evolutionary view of human societies. The contrast drawn is with more internally differentiated, complex societies, and within such a perspective social development may be seen as progressing from simple to complex forms (for example, Sahlins, 1971). In some respects, however, the term "simple society" is undoubtedly a misnomer, as can be seen for example in the frequently complex patterns of KINSHIP within these societies.

situational analysis and situational logic a methodological ideal, most closely associated with METHODOLOGICAL INDIVIDUALISM and the work of

SKEWED DISTRIBUTION

POPPER, in that it is proposed that social situations be analyzed in terms of the motivations and goals of social actors and the logical implications of these, without recourse to either "psychologism" or "sociologism."

skewed distribution a distribution of data obtained from a sample or population that does not show the NORMAL DISTRIBUTION of a bell-shaped curve. In a normal distribution the MEAN, MEDIAN, and MODE fall in the same place—the curve is symmetrical. In a positively skewed distribution (Fig. 22a), the mode and median are less than the mean, while in a negatively skewed distribution (Fig. 22b), the mean is less than the median and mode. Some population characteristics have a normal distribution, for example, height, and others may be skewed, for example, social class among students in higher education.

skill 1. (applied to a job or occupation) qualities required of a particular job in terms of the range and technical complexity of the tasks involved, level of discretion and control over how the work is performed, time needed to learn the job, and the level of knowledge and training necessary. **2.** (applied to a person) capabilities acquired by a person in school and working life, which may include one or more of the following: cognitive abilities (capacity for abstract thought, memory, concentration), manual dexterity, knowledge, and interpersonal abilities (ability to communicate, cooperate, empathize with others, leadership). **3.** (social construct) a label attached to certain types of work or occupation as a result of custom and practice, union negotiation and job regulation that attract differential rates of pay and status, and which are normally reflected in official classifications of occupations as "skilled," "semiskilled," or "unskilled" in the division of labor.

Skill is an ambiguous concept in that its various meanings are often confused or inadequately defined. Different theoretical approaches to changes in skill levels and the empirical research supporting them depend critically on the way skill is defined. For example, theories of DESKILLING often use a so-called objective or technical definition of skill (**1.** above), whereas arguments for upskilling define skill in terms of formal qualifications or official classifications of different occupations. Skill is most frequently defined in

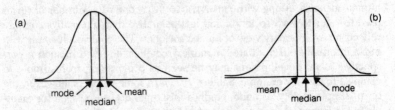

Fig. 22. **Skewed distribution.** (a) Positively skewed distribution. (b) Negatively skewed distribution.

sociology in the first sense, that is, as the objective requirements for a job, using the historical example of craft workers as the benchmark for analysis of changing skill levels.

The definition of skill in the second sense, as the qualities a person brings to a job, derives from industrial psychology, but also informs discussion of the marketability and substitutability of skills in the labor market (see DUAL LABOR MARKET). Skills acquired in this sense may depend partly on natural aptitudes, although sociologists generally argue that most skills are learned. Discussion of changes in the nature and level of skills has included analysis of the rise and decline of skills that are highly specialized and of transferable skills that are more indeterminate and less job-specific and that may, therefore, command higher pay and status. The concept of skill as residing in the person is also important in the analysis of *tacit skills*, which refer to the often unconscious and habitual skills learned in the workplace through close familiarity with machines or work practices. Such tacit skills are frequently job-specific and unrecognized in formal job status, but are nevertheless critical to employers for the day-to-day operation of production or the provision of services.

The definition of skill as a social construct draws attention to the point that the three definitions of skill above may not correspond in practice. Certain types of work may involve high levels of skill in the technical or objective sense but go unrewarded in the labor market, women's work being a notable example (see SEXUAL DIVISION OF LABOR). Conversely, work may attract high pay and status via union negotiation or employers' strategies to divide and rule their work force so that job gradings bear little resemblance to actual differences in skill (see also INTERNAL LABOR MARKET). Similarly, the profusion of semiskilled job titles may refer to jobs that require little or no training—hence the observation that "most workers demonstrate higher skills driving to work than they need to perform their tasks."

Small, Albion (1854–1926) US sociologist who at the University of Chicago in 1892 became chairman of the first graduate school in sociology, and in 1894 (with George Vincent) author of the first textbook in sociology. In 1895 he also founded the *American Journal of Sociology*. In Small's view, sociology implemented a program of analysis that begun with Adam SMITH, and in his own work he sought to detach sociology from too close an identification with the approach of COMTE. Small wrote several books, including *General Sociology* (1905) and *The Origins of Sociology* (1924), but they are rarely read today.

Smith, Adam (1723–1790) Scottish moral philosopher, remembered best for his *An Inquiry into the Nature and Causes of the Wealth of Nations* (1776) in which, after a seminal account of the DIVISION OF LABOR, he proposed that the individual pursuit of self-interest and the unimpeded operation of the market acted as an "invisible hand" resulting in achievement of the "common good." A leading member of the Scottish Enlightenment and a visitor to France, where he met with leading French social and economic thinkers, Smith wrote on many topics apart from economic issues: morality, politics, law, and language. In *The Theory of Moral Sentiments* (1779) he suggested that ethical judgments depend on persons imagining themselves in the position of others and can also be illuminated by considering how an ideal impartial observer might judge right and wrong. Although widely associated with advocacy of the doctrine of laissez-faire, Smith was not blind to the adverse implications of the division of labor, noting its potentially stultifying and dehumanizing effect on workers. He allowed that people might well wish to seek to limit such effects, but he believed that in reality governments were likely to be driven by narrow interests.

snowball sampling a method of selecting a SAMPLE by starting with a small selected group of respondents and asking them for further contacts. This is not therefore a RANDOM SAMPLE, and no inferences about the characteristics of the parent population can be made from such a study. Its use is primarily in the collection of in-depth, qualitative data, perhaps on sensitive topics, where an obvious sampling frame does not exist and the best method of selection is through personal contacts. Such a method might be used in an investigation of sexual habits or bereavement experiences.

sociability any social interaction that exists primarily "for its own sake and for the fascination that in its own liberation from [social] ties, it diffuses" (Wolff, 1950). Simmel refers to this as the "play form" of interaction (see also FORM AND CONTENT). It need have "no extrinsic results," and "entirely depends on the personalities among whom it occurs." However, Simmel sees in sociability a capacity for transferring the "seriousness and tragic to a symbolic and shadowy play-form," which can reveal reality obliquely. Thus, although much social interaction involves elements of sociability, the purer play-forms of sociability, for example, parties or picnics, or mere talk, can be seen as possessing their own specific importance in social life. Although apparently and necessarily undirected and unserious, they perform a definite role, first in providing relaxation, distraction, etc., but also in throwing a fresh light on serious endeavors.

social 1. (of certain species of insects and some animal species, including humankind) living together in organized colonies or groups. **2.** pertaining to human society and/or to human interaction in organizations and groups. **3.** concerned with or responsible for the mutual relations and welfare of individuals (for example, social worker).

social actor any person who undertakes social ACTION. The term is used for the most part without any assumption that social actors always consciously stage-manage their actions. However, as the use of concepts such as ROLE in sociology indicates, social action does often involve actors playing a part, although usually not without the possibility of actors interpreting and reshaping this. That much social action can profitably be understood by viewing it in *specifically* dramaturgical terms is a view taken by some sociologists (see DRAMATURGY, GOFFMAN). Other sociologists (see ETHNOMETHODOLOGY) decline to use the term "social actor" because of its dramaturgical connotations, preferring to use the term "member" instead.

social anthropology the study (by Western investigators) of small-scale, relatively simple, nonindustrial cultures and societies (see also SOCIAL ANTHROPOLOGY). While social anthropology is often indistinguishable from sociology in many of its theoretical orientations and its methodologies, its problem area has conventionally distinguished social anthropology as a separate discipline, since most sociological work has tended to focus on urban, industrialized societies. Even so, there has been reciprocal influence between the two specialities.

As a specialty, social anthropology developed in the 19th century as a scholastic offshoot of imperialist expansion, informed by and engaging in the scientific and pseudoscientific debates of the time. E. Leach (1982) distinguishes a number of tendencies among the founding fathers in the period around 1840, united only in their preoccupation with exotic cultures and, at times, their ETHNOCENTRICITY and arrogance.

The first major theoretical perspective to emerge was that of EVOLUTIONISM. In its time, the variety of evolutionism that became predominant was progressive in the sense that it accepted that the people concerned were "our fellow creatures," as a book of 1843 argued (quoted in Lienhardt, 1964). On the other hand, this evolutionary perspective was based on the racist assumption that the cultures of so-called primitive people belonged to an earlier and inferior stage of human history and that contemporary European observers could see in those cultures the savage origins of their own societies. Henry MAINE (1861) provides a good example: "As societies do not advance concurrently, but at different rates of progress, there have been epochs at which men trained to habits of methodical observation have really been in a position to watch and describe the infancy of mankind." These "habits of methodical observation" and description were a prominent aspect of the development of the subject. In French, German, British, and American studies, intensive field research into single societies became increasingly common and researchers qualified, criticized, and in many cases dismissed earlier assumptions about the supposed irrationality and barbarity of primitive cultures.

In the period after World War I, MALINOWSKI and RADCLIFFE-BROWN were instrumental in advancing the discussion of fieldwork and in establishing STRUCTURAL-FUNCTIONALISM as the dominant perspective in British social anthropology. Influenced by the theoretical work of DURKHEIM, and emphasizing the importance of direct observation in the field, the anthropologists of this period published a great many studies of different cultures, tending to focus on the analysis of INSTITUTIONS. Thus patterns of KINSHIP, religious belief-systems, magic, political systems, etc. were studied in great detail. As in other social sciences, different emphases and schools emerged, and new theoretical debates and issues became important. STRUCTURALISM, particularly as developed in the work of LEVI-STRAUSS, has been especially influential on sociological theories.

In recent years, social anthropologists have also directed their attention to the study of their own and other urban, industrial societies, using the techniques and research practices developed in studying other cultures. This trend has made the discipline even harder to distinguish from sociology in many respects, other than by departmental boundaries or the self-definitions of practitioners. See also CULTURE, ETHNOGRAPHY.

social change the difference between the current and antecedent condition of any selected aspect of social organization or structure, for example, the family, voting patterns, religious attitudes, and economic activity.

The study of social change involves as a logical minimum the identification of the phenomenon to be studied, and the use of a historical perspective in order to identify the changes it has undergone. In practice, this descriptive task is usually linked to the more difficult one of explanation, that is, an attempt to specify the factor(s) that produced or caused the identified changes in the phenomenon studied. More simply, the objective is to show why change occurred in one way rather than another.

Social change is central to much sociological study and research, since neither societies nor their constituent parts are ever static. The whole range of theoretical perspectives and research methods available within sociology can be used in the study of social change. Clearly, a study of the SOCIALIZATION of, say, new recruits to the armed forces or police would require a different research strategy (participant or nonparticipant observation, for example) to one that examined changing patterns of social mobility within the class structures of contemporary industrial societies (sampling and questionnaire). A study of changing conditions of land tenure among 14th-century European peasants would, in turn, necessitate an approach based on the evidence of historical documents.

If it is true that sociology is always, in one way or another, examining social change, it is also true to say that sociology itself was a child of social change. It is no coincidence that sociology emerged as a discipline when theorists attempted to understand the nature of the dramatic social, economic, and political upheavals associated with the industrial revolution of the 18th and 19th centuries in European societies. The seminal work of the three most important figures in early sociological thought—MARX, WEBER, and DURKHEIM—can only really be understood in these terms.

While these three theorists were interested in studying the nature and origins of industrial capitalist societies, they were by no means the only early sociological figures interested in social change. Indeed, a characteristic feature of late 18th- and 19th-century writing was its preoccupation with the topic. COMTE, drawing on the work of SAINT-SIMON, proposed a LAW OF THREE STAGES in the intellectual and social development of societies. This law was, in effect, an EVOLUTIONARY THEORY of human society, and this grandiose concern to see history in terms of progress, direction, and stages of development (see ECONOMIC AND SOCIAL DEVELOPMENT) was shared by many other theorists, for example, CONDORCET, Herbert SPENCER, Lewis MORGAN, Edward TYLOR, and Leonard T. HOBHOUSE.

Though these early models were problematic at a number of levels, interest in evolutionary approaches to social change has not been entirely abandoned by more recent thinkers. Talcott PARSONS (1966), the economist Walt Rostow (1960), and the anthropologists M.D. Sahlins and R.E. Service (1960) have produced new work, more or less successful in remedying the deficiencies of earlier theorists.

Fundamental problems remain, however. Karl POPPER (1957), for example, has argued from a philosophical perspective that social development is inherently unpredictable (because it is affected by the growth of knowledge, which in itself is unpredictable) and moreover that development is a unique historical process. Though it may be possible to describe this in various ways, it cannot be explained in terms of any universal law, because a law explains the recurrence of identical events and cannot therefore be tested against, or explain, those that are unique (see also HISTORICISM). E. GELLNER (1968) has also argued that the temporal ordering of stages of social development given by evolutionary theory is either redundant (if the mechanisms, sources, or causes of change are identified) or insufficient (placing anything in a sequence does not, by itself, explain it).

Both Parsons and Rostow meant their work to have specific implications for development policy in the Third World. Their insufficiency in this respect is highlighted by Popper's arguments. In particular, it is clear that the development of any society alters the context in which any other society can develop. No society can therefore repeat the developmental process of any other. This point has been made trenchantly by Gunder FRANK (1969), who argued that development of the advanced industrial societies involved underdevelopment of others.

At a less ambitious level, sociologists have also attempted to hypothesize about the general causes of social change within societies, rather than bring their historical development under an evolutionary law. Here social change has been variously connected to:

(a) technological development;

(b) social CONFLICT (between races, religions, classes, for example);

(c) malintegration (see INTEGRATION) of the parts of social structure or culture of a society, such as, in Hinduism, caste and capitalism;

(d) the need for ADAPTATION within social systems so that, for example, the development of efficient bureaucracies is an adaptive response of firms to a competitive economic environment;

(e) the impact of ideas (see IDEALISM) and belief systems on social action, most obviously, Weber's hypothesis of a connection between "The Protestant Ethic and the Spirit of Capitalism";

(f) Marx's idea of class conflict generated by contradictions between the forces and relations of production in societies.

Such approaches are less ambitious than evolutionary theory. After all, they attempt, with the partial exception of Marx, to say what it is that produces social change, rather than make predictions about the course of human history. At best, they provide more or less useful suggestions as to where the cause of change may lie when any particular social process is examined. Clearly, however, to argue that all social change in human groups, communities, institutions, organizations, or societies in general is a result of conflict, or ideas, or adaptation, or whatever, is to overstate the case. Inevitably, the more ambitious the theoretical project, the more vulnerable it becomes. In one sense this hardly matters, for theories can remain heuristically useful, and a perfected general theory of social change is not a necessary preliminary to the normal business of sociological research.

social closure the process by which groups seek to increase the advantages of their situation by monopolizing resources and restricting recruitment and access to their group. Examples of this are found in all privileged groups, for example, marital eligibility in European aristocracies; the system of apprenticeship for skilled manual labors; and systems of accreditation and formal membership of professional associations for doctors and lawyers.

The term was first used by WEBER, and, in recent sociology, is particularly associated with the work of Frank Parkin (1979). Following Weber in the critique of Marxism, Parkin argues that property is only one basis for power, and only one form of social closure. The characteristics associated with different STATUS GROUPS, for example, ethnicity, gender, skill level, and religion, can all be bases for closure strategies.

Parkin describes two types of closure strategy or process: *exclusion* and *usurpation*. Exclusion refers to practices that separate the group from outsiders. The examples above, of aristocracy, professions, and skilled artisans, are cases in point. Usurpation is a strategy adopted by low-status or less privileged groups to gain advantages or resources that others are monopolizing. Civil rights movements illustrate this, or, in the Indian CASTE system, the process of SANSKRITIZATION.

The two strategies should not always be regarded as alternatives, or as mutually exclusive. Protestant workers in Northern Ireland in the 1970s, for example, formed the Loyalist Association of Workers essentially to retain their privileges, that is, they adopted an exclusion strategy with regard to Catholics. At the same time they continued normal processes of collective bargaining, involving occasional conflicts with employers; that is, they attempted to increase their share of companies' profits (the usurpation of employers' and shareholders' privilege). Parkin calls this type of joint strategy a process of *dual closure*. It is particularly associated with intermediate groups in the class or status systems.

social cohesion the integration of group behavior as a result of social bonds, attractions, or other forces that hold members of a group in interaction over a period of time. See also SOCIAL SOLIDARITY.

social contract theory a theory of the origins and/or present basis of the STATE that in its simplest form holds that the state arises from a "contract." in that each member gives up his own "natural rights" (see NATURAL RIGHTS AND NATURAL LAW) in return for new rights under the law (see also LOCKE). Social contract theory does not apply to most historical cases of state formation, though it does apply to the foundation of new constitutions, such as that of the United States in 1787, which in part at least have been explicitly enacted under the guidance of social contract theory. Rather than as a straightforwardly explanatory or sociological theory, the historical role of contract theory is as an ethical or logical theory, advanced to provide moral evaluation and reconstruction of existing constitutions, to justify revolutions, etc. See also JUSTICE.

social control practices developed by social groups of all kinds that enforce or encourage CONFORMITY and deal with behavior that violates accepted norms.

Sociologists distinguish two basic processes of social control:

(a) INTERNALIZATION of norms and values. The process of SOCIALIZATION is much concerned with learning acceptable ways of acting as taken-for-granted, unquestioned imperatives or as social routines (see also ETHNOMETHODOLOGY);

(b) the use of sanctions with regard to rule-breakers and nonconforming acts. Sanctions may be positive, rewarding conforming conduct, or they may be negative, punishing nonconformity to norms by processes ranging from informal sanctions like upbraiding, ridiculing, or ostracism, to formal sanctions like a parking ticket, a prison sentence, or execution. See also DEVIANCE.

Social Darwinism a term for social theories that apply Darwinian principles of natural selection to societies (see also DARWIN). The best-known proponents of this position were SPENCER (1820–1903) in Britain, and W.G. Sumner (1840–1910) in the United States, both of whom argued forcefully that society should be viewed as if it were an adaptive organism. It is important to distinguish this from more generally evolutionist social perspectives that may not share the hard FUNCTIONALISM inherent in this approach, but simply a belief in some kind of directed social transformation (see EVOLUTIONARY SOCIOLOGY, SOCIOCULTURAL EVOLUTIONISM). The term is now almost always used pejoratively by social theorists who object to using the biological analogy in the study of human social life. It is also regarded as politically problematic since, if individuals and societies are subject to the survival of the fittest, then the status quo is always seen as justifiable. Social Darwinist ideas are now sometimes presented as SOCIOBI-OLOGY.

social differentiation the process whereby an institutional activity becomes divided and more specialized in two or more separate institutional activities. Differentiation is a term derived from biology to describe the specialization of functions in society in a process of social evolution. For example, the separation and specialization of the economic function of production from the institution of the family, which retains the functions of reproduction and infant socialization. In PARSONS' (1977) model of the social system this process is described in more abstract terms such as the differentiation of the polity from the societal community. Social differentiation is also referred to as *structural differentiation* in functionalist theories of SOCIAL CHANGE (see FUNCTIONALISM).

Nineteenth-century evolutionary theories of social change (for example, SPENCER) saw differentiation as a fundamental principle of social development in biology and sociology whereby societies increase in size and complexity in adapting to the environment (see EVOLUTIONARY THEORY). Differentiation was accompanied by the functional need for increased integration and interdependence in more complex societies. In the writings of DURKHEIM, social differentiation is identical with the social DIVISION OF LABOR. Contemporary theories of social evolution retain the concept of differentiation as central to the general development of adaptive capacity in industrial societies (Sahlins and Service, 1960) and, in the case of Parsons' later work, to analysis of the interdependence between the functional subsystems of modern society. See also MODERNIZATION.

social distance feelings or relations of aloofness and unapproachability, especially between members of different social strata. Conceptions of social distance are formally institutionalized in extreme systems of SOCIAL STRATIFICATION, such as apartheid and CASTE, but informally they exist in all societies. The term was introduced by PARK and Burgess (1924) and popularized by Bogardus (1933), who also formulated a *social-distance* (or *Bogardus*) *scale,* designed to define the extent of tolerance or intolerance between social groups.

social equilibrium a state of persistence or balance between parts within a social system and/or in relation to its external environment. According to PARETO (1935), a social system is in equilibrium if when it is subjected to some modification a reaction takes place tending to restore it to its previous, normal state. Pareto's definition and his general approach to the study of social systems modeled on change in mechanical systems and on approaches in economics influenced a number of theorists, notably Henderson, HOMANS, PARSONS, and Dickson and Roeslisberger (1939). In the work of Parsons in particular, the assumption was made that, even if never fully equilibrated, social systems tend toward a state of equilibrium and can be analyzed as functioning systems with self-equilibrating properties.

social facts as things "a category of facts" with distinctive characteristics, "consisting of ways of acting, thinking and feeling, external to the individual and endowed with a power of coercion by means of which they control him" (DURKHEIM, *The Rules of Sociological Method*, 1895). Durkheim formulated his sociology as resting "wholly on the basic principle that social facts must be studied as things." Durkheim recognized that "there is no principle for which he had received more criticism" but argued that "none is more fundamental" (DURKHEIM, 1897).

Sociologists remain divided between those who stress the externality and the independence of social facts from individuals, and those who emphasize that individuals participate fully in construction of their own social lives (see also METHODOLOGICAL INDIVIDUALISM, STRUCTURE AND AGENCY). Durkheim's aim, however, was not so much to deny all possibility of individual construction of aspects of social reality as to maintain that social facts were in large measure external to particular individuals, and thus could be studied relatively objectively, for example, as external "social currents," such as patterns of law or variations between societies in rates of SUICIDE. Where Durkheim perhaps erred was in sometimes suggesting that this meant sociologists could disregard the subjective ideas of individual actors. Instead it is clear that social phenomena such as SUICIDE can only be studied effectively if the variable meanings that individuals attach to social actions are fully investigated. In addition, the artificial and constructed nature of many sociological data must also be noted (for example, see MEASUREMENT BY FIAT). Thus, the proposal to treat "social facts as things," (Durkheim's conception of a social reality *sui generis*), although undoubtedly useful in avoiding outright subjectivism and individualism in social analysis, is usually regarded as providing a misleading rendering of the so-called facticity of social phenomena.

social history any form of historiography and historical analysis that concentrates attention on changes in overall patterns of social life in societies, rather than merely on political events.

social indicators any regularly collected social statistics that can be used to provide indication of changes in the general state of society, for example, crime rates and health and mortality statistics. Parallels exist with well established *economic indicators,* for example, the retail price index. However, there is far less agreement on the measurement and standardization of social indicators than on the most significant economic indicators. See also OFFICIAL STATISTICS.

social integration and system integration the distinction (LOCKWOOD, 1964) between INTEGRATION into society that arises from SOCIALIZATION and from agreement on values, *social integration*, and integration that

SOCIALIZATION

occurs as the result of the operation of the social substratum, for example, as unintended consequences of economic relations or structures of power, *system integration*. What Lockwood wished to stress was that the two forms of integration are not the same, and that any analysis of society must distinguish carefully between them, something he accused some forms of FUNCTIONALISM as failing to do.

As elaborated by GIDDENS (1984) (see Fig. 23), while social integration can be seen as arising particularly from the face-to-face interaction of individual social actors, system integration is far more a matter of interaction at a distance, and involves so-called reproduced practices, which arise from the interrelation of groups and collectivities and the operation of institutions. These practices tend to occur behind the backs of the individuals involved.

socialization 1. (also called ENCULTURATION) the process in which the CULTURE of a society is transmitted to children; the modification from infancy

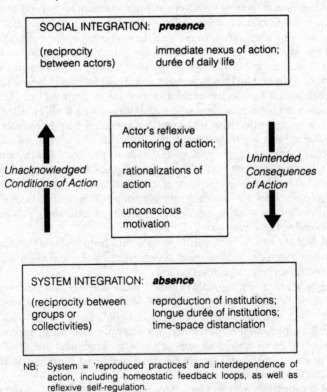

SOCIAL INTEGRATION: *presence*

(reciprocity between actors)   immediate nexus of action; durée of daily life

Actor's reflexive monitoring of action;

Unacknowledged Conditions of Action

rationalizations of action

Unintended Consequences of Action

unconscious motivation

SYSTEM INTEGRATION: *absence*

(reciprocity between groups or collectivities)   reproduction of institutions; longue durée of institutions; time-space distanciation

NB: System = 'reproduced practices' and interdependence of action, including homeostatic feedback loops, as well as reflexive self-regulation.

Fig. 23. Social and system integration. See main entry.

of an individual's behavior to conform with the demands of social life (see ACCULTURATION). In this sense, socialization is a FUNCTIONAL PREREQUISITE for any society, essential to any social life, as well as to the cultural and SOCIAL REPRODUCTION of both general and particular social forms. As emphasized by PARSONS and Bales (1955), socialization undertaken in the FAMILY and elsewhere involves both integration into society (ROLES, INSTITUTIONS, etc.) and the differentiation of one individual from another. **2.** the replacement of private ownership of the means of production by PUBLIC OWNERSHIP. **3.** (Marxism) the tendency of capitalist production to depend increasingly on collective organization, for example, the interrelation of many different processes. This is one important reason why MARX expected a transition to socialism and common ownership of the means of production ultimately to occur.

Of the three conceptions, **1.** is the most important sociological and anthropological use.

Because it is concerned with relationships between the individual and society, it is clear that socialization in this sense is a concept that bridges the disciplines of sociology and PSYCHOLOGY. Theories of socialization have concentrated on:

(a) cognitive development, for example, PIAGET;

(b) acquisition of moral and personal identity through family relationships, for example, FREUD;

(c) the acquisition of the SELF concept and social identity, for example, G.H. MEAD;

(d) internalization of the moral categories and values of the group, for example, DURKHEIM;

(e) the development of social skills that sustain interaction in all settings, chief of which is linguistic communication, through which the social and physical environment are appropriated and interpreted, for example, B. BERNSTEIN.

A distinction is also sometimes drawn between two forms of socialization: (a) the process involved in becoming an adult social being, with the focus largely on childhood, *primary socialization,* and (b) the more general processes through which culture is transmitted, for example, adult peers, media of communication, etc., *secondary socialization.*

According to D. Wrong (1961), it is useful to distinguish between these two forms of socialization **1.**, but it is essential that the active, purposeful, and reflexive dimensions of socialization, of relations between self and others, should be acknowledged for *both* forms of socialization (see OVERSOCIALIZED CONCEPTION OF MAN). See also NATURE-NURTURE DEBATE, DEVELOPMENT **2.** LOOKING-GLASS SELF.

social marginality see MARGINALITY.

social mobility the movement of individuals, sometimes groups, between different positions in the hierarchy of SOCIAL STRATIFICATION within any society. Within modern societies, CLASS positions within the OCCUPATIONAL STRUCTURE are usually of prime interest in studies of social mobility. Social mobility may involve movement up a class or status hierarchy, *upward mobility*, or down, *downward mobility*. It may take place from one generation to another, *intergenerational mobility*, where the focus of interest for sociology is on differences between the socioeconomic class or status of a person's family of origin compared with his or her achieved class or status position, or it may be more short-term, for example, the ups and downs of an individual CAREER, *intragenerational mobility*. In sociology the main focus of study has been on differences in the amount and character of intergenerational mobility within different societies. Interest has been greatest in levels of movement between manual and nonmanual socioeconomic status positions, and movement into and out of ELITE positions and the service class. It is usually accepted that, in general, modern societies allow more mobility than earlier types of society, that is, in comparative terms of *open-class societies*.

Systematic study of social mobility was pioneered by SOROKIN, who saw all societies as possessing "selection agencies," which varied in form between different societies. As have sociologists in general, Sorokin conceived of social mobility, whatever its particular form, as performing vital social functions, for example, promoting talent and acting as a safety valve. Study of social mobility in industrial societies began in earnest with the undertaking of large social surveys designed to establish overall levels of intergenerational social mobility (for example, Glass, 1954; LIPSET and BENDIX, 1959). These studies seemed to suggest that levels of upward intergenerational social mobility, especially between manual and nonmanual occupations, were substantially the same in all industrial societies, despite differences in patterns of industrialization, educational structure, etc. Subsequent studies (see Miller, 1960) have refined this finding, pointing to considerable differences in the more detailed patterns of social mobility. For example, Germany, Italy, and Spain are less open than the United States and Britain, and socialist countries have generally had higher levels of social mobility than nonsocialist countries, for example, Eastern bloc countries and social democratic societies such as Sweden see Heath, 1981).

A further important distinction in studies of social mobility is between *structural* and *nonstructural social mobility*, the former referring to movements made possible by fundamental changes in the form of the occupational structure (for example, in the relative size of particular classes, status groups, etc.) within a particular society, the latter to any movements that do not involve such changes. As indicated in Fig. 24, one main assumption that can be stated in terms of this distinction is that occupational structures are often more fundamental in determining the form and amount of social mobility within a particular society or historical period'—that is, produce "structural mobility"—than are differences in educational institutions, individual motivation, etc.—that is, nonstructural sources of mobility. However, although the capacity of the latter to affect levels of mobility may be limited, nonstructural factors such as education do make a difference, not least where they act to induce changes in occupational structures, for example, in encouraging occupational upgrading or *occupational transition,* involving the substitution of college graduates for nongraduates, or the more general upgrading in the status and content of particular jobs (compare CREDENTIALISM).

While some researchers have concluded that rates of social mobility in Britain have remained relatively stable and have not increased since World War II, studies by GOLDTHORPE et al. (1980) have suggested that overall levels of upward mobility (including entry into the service class) may be higher than assumed. Goldthorpe's suggestion is that most of this increase can be accounted for by structural mobility.

Where EQUALITY OF OPPORTUNITY between social classes is the focus of attention, Glass (1954) argued that it is the extent of mobility *once* changes in the occupational distribution have been taken into account that is mainly of interest, and structural mobility should be discounted. Payne (1989), however, has argued against any automatic assumption: that "the relative chance of mobility ... *without* the artificial removal of structural change" is also of relevance. Thus, comparing studies across time (including Goldthorpe's study, conducted in 1972, with the 1984 Essex study, Marshall et al., 1988), we find that while "the service class's success in retaining class positions does not diminish, the disadvantage experienced by those with working class origins is ameliorated" (Payne, 1989).

Complex methodological problems attend all studies of social mobility,

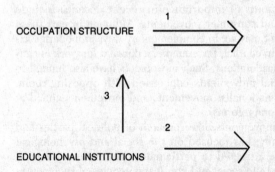

Fig. 24. **Social mobility.** While changes in the occupational structure can be seen as the main determinant of the extent of opportunities for social mobility (1), and educational institutions act mainly as an avenue of social mobility which is particularly important in modern societies and can also influence who becomes mobile (2), educational institutions (3) also induce changes in the occupational structure.

including problems of occupational classification (see also OCCUPATIONAL SCALES), reliance on respondents' memories, and the comparison of older generations with completed careers with younger generations whose careers are incomplete. In the most advanced studies, highly sophisticated statistical and mathematical techniques may be employed, in that some have suggested techniques and measurement run ahead of sociological clarity or relevance. A final problem of major significance is that most studies of social mobility have focused only on men. See also CONTEST AND SPONSORED MOBILITY.

social movement any broad social alliance of people who are associated in seeking to effect or to block an aspect of SOCIAL CHANGE within a society. Unlike political parties or some more highly organized interest or PRESSURE GROUPS, such movements may be only informally organized, although they may have links with political parties and more institutionalized groups, and in time they may lead to formation of political parties.

Four distinct areas in which social movements operate in modern societies have been identified by GIDDENS (1985):

(a) democratic movements, concerned with establishing or maintaining political rights;

(b) labor movements, concerned with defensive control of the workplace and with contesting and transforming the more general distribution of economic power;

(c) ecological movements, concerned with limiting environmental and social damage resulting from transformation of the natural world by social action;

(d) peace movements, concerned with challenging the pervasive influence of military power and aggressive forms of nationalism.

Other social movements of importance in recent decades include women's movements and consumer movements. Although in part these types of social movement may act in complementary ways in modern societies, they may also be in conflict, for example, a demand for work in conflict with ecological considerations. Such movements have also tended to generate contrary social movements concerned with opposing them, including conservative nationalist movements and movements aimed at blocking or reversing moral reforms.

Research on social movements, like research of political parties and interest groups generally, has focused on the social and psychological characteristics of those attracted to participate, the relations between leaders and the led, and the social and political outcomes of such activity. One thing is clear: social movements are a fluid element within political and social systems, from which more formal political organizations arise and may bring radical change. See also COLLECTIVE BEHAVIOR, ANOMIE, PEACE MOVEMENT.

social order the stable patterns of social expectations and social structure that exist in any society; the maintenance of these patterns. As such, the term has a general rather than a specific reference. The problem of what makes societies cohere is sometimes referred to as the *problem of order* (see also PARSONS).

social organization any relatively stable pattern or structure within a society, and the process by which such a structure is created or maintained. As such, the term is a highly general one overlapping with such terms as SOCIAL STRUCTURE, SOCIAL ORDER, etc. See also ORGANIZATION.

social pathology (by analogy with health and sickness in organisms) any condition of society regarded as unhealthy. With biological analogies currently being looked on with suspicion, the term is now relatively little used, but was used by functionalist sociologists, including DURKHEIM (1895). Durkheim drew a distinction between so-called normal and abnormal states of society. He assumed that the average condition in a particular type of society also represented the "normal" and "functional" condition for that type of society. On this basis pathological conditions could in principle also be identified. Thus, while crime, for example, must be regarded as a normal feature of societies, an excessive incidence of crime could be seen as pathological. See also SOCIAL PROBLEMS, ABNORMAL.

social phenomenology a sociological approach, especially associated with the Austrian-American social philosopher and sociologist Alfred SCHUTZ, that investigates the taken-for-granted assumptions of, and the processes involved in, the constitution of social knowledge and social life (see also PHENOMENOLOGY). While a number of sociologists, notably BERGER and Luckmann (1967), have developed Schutz's ideas as a distinctive approach to the SOCIOLOGY OF KNOWLEDGE, these ideas have been especially influential in the development of ETHNOMETHODOLOGY, in that social phenomenology's concerns with the constitution of everyday life have received elaboration as a relatively self-contained theoretical approach, or paradigm, that is highly critical of so-called orthodox sociology. See also PHENOMENOLOGICAL SOCIOLOGY.

social philosophy any philosophical discussion presented as having implications either for (a) social life or (b) social science methodologies. The term is a general one, with no very specific reference.

social policy a field of study that entails economic, political, sociolegal, and sociological examination of the ways in which central and local governmental policies affect the lives of individuals and communities. Social policy is notoriously difficult to define, and its use varies between authors. The term is often, though mistakenly, used in the context of SOCIAL ADMINISTRATION to refer to the institutionalized services provided by the WELFARE STATE, namely, housing, health, education, social security, personal social services and, in some cases, law. This approach to the study of social policy probably has its origins in the social policy courses introduced to train social workers. Authors who use this version of social policy do so to refer to the ways in which the state has assumed some social responsibility by intervening in a market economy to promote individual welfare. This type of discussion has led to inquiries about the distribution of goods and services and has, falsely, distinguished sharply between social policy and economic policy.

There are a number of criticisms of this use of the term:

(a) it lacks any theoretical analysis, which precludes sociological discussion of why policies are introduced and the unintended effects of their introduction;

(b) it leads to a conflation of social policy with the welfare state, yet social policies occur outside the welfare state. As Titmuss argued, apartheid in South Africa is a social policy. Similarly, aspects of welfare lie outside the welfare state. Titmuss demonstrated, for example, that there are occupational welfare benefits such as pension schemes, help with housing and health costs, and so on, that some individuals receive from their employment;

(c) it often leads to a parochial concern with a "history of legislations" in a particular country and precludes the possibility of comparative analysis.

In the 1970s, a more critical approach to social policy developed that was informed by accompanying developments in sociological theory. In particular, Marxist and feminist sociologists developed new accounts of the relationship between social policies and the social structure.

Some authors have argued that the early sociologists had no interest in social policy. However, others have argued that a concern with social policy is implicit in the works of Durkheim, Marx, and Weber.

Following the import of new and critical ideas about social policy, its scope has been widened to include comparative study of social policies in different societies. There has also been a renewed interest in philosophical issues within the study of social policy, such as the nature of JUSTICE, citizenship, and NEEDS. See also SOCIAL REFORM, SOCIAL PROBLEMS.

social problems aspects of social life seen to warrant concern and intervention, for example, CRIME, domestic violence, child abuse, poverty, and drug abuse. The identification of a social problem is the outcome of social processes including a moral evaluation of people's behavior. In analyzing social problems, it is important to identify the group of people for whom the behavior is a problem. For example, some authors have suggested that social policies dealing with poverty have been implemented to support the interests of landowners and owners of capital rather than to eliminate poverty out of humanitarian concern for the poor.

Some authors have also argued that the founders of sociology were motivated to explain the nature and development of industrial, capitalist societies because of their concern about the growth in social problems that are an apparent concomitant of industrialization and urbanization, for example, Durkheim's analysis of SUICIDE.

Identification of a social problem suggests that there ought to be some form of social intervention through SOCIAL POLICIES, new laws, and new forms of social and COMMUNITY WORK, and some authors have suggested that there is a relationship between social problems, social policy, and SOCIAL CONTROL. More extremely, it may be suggested that "social problems" are euphemisms for "political problems," which will only be fully resolved by political solutions. See also HIERARCHY OF CREDIBILITY.

social psychology a subfield of both PSYCHOLOGY and sociology, which, according to ALLPORT, is concerned with the ways in which an individual's "thought, feeling, and behavior" are affected by the existence of others, for example, by social interactions, by groups, etc. Social psychology involves a variey of approaches, partly reflecting its multidisciplinary location. A further complication is that much work within sociology that might be labeled "social psychology" (for example, SYMBOLIC INTERACTIONISM) is not always labeled as such; rather it is often referred to as "microsociology." One of the first writers to use the term "social psychology" was W. McDougall, who published *Introduction to Social Psychology* in 1908. Since the 1920s, social psychology has developed into a more fully fledged field of study, also having wide-ranging applications, especially in education, social policy, work, and mental health.

Despite its broad spectrum of approaches, social psychology can be seen as having a central interest in bridging individual and social theories of human behavior. Following Armistead (1974), two main traditions can be identified: (a) *psychological social psychology,* characterized by its connections with general psychology, including an emphasis on experimentation; and (b) *sociological social psychology,* influenced by the work of symbolic interactionists and laying stress on the social processes involved in development of SELF-identity and on the role of LANGUAGE, and employing qualitative research methods, such as PARTICIPANT OBSERVATION.

An indication of the kinds of topics included as part of the subject matter of social psychology can be had by noting the main topics covered in Roger Brown's popular text *Social Psychology* (1965): SOCIALIZATION, including the acquisition of language; ROLES and STEREOTYPES; ACHIEVEMENT MOTIVATION; the AUTHORITARIAN PERSONALITY; ATTITUDES and attitude change; GROUP DYNAMICS; COLLECTIVE BEHAVIOR. Some commentators (for example, Murphy, John, and Brown, 1984) have suggested that social psychology faced a crisis in the late 1960s and 1970s, centered on the question of whether or not it should be a "socially relevant" subject aimed at solving social problems. Influenced by the wider sociopolitical climate of the 1960s and 1970s, radical social psychologists have argued for the necessity of uniting the "personal" and the "political" within the subfield. Writers such as Baker-Miller (1976) have also challenged what they see as the "gender blind" nature of much mainstream social psychology. However, there continue to be many who argue that social psychology should have as its main aim the development of theory and knowledge about the individual in society. See also MORENO, SCALING, CONFORMITY, COGNITIVE DISSONANCE, PREJUDICE.

social reform political and social policies implemented with the aim of eliminating SOCIAL PROBLEMS. Social reform movements, and the bureaucratic administrative structures set up to implement such reforms, can be seen as a major feature differentiating modern industrial societies from earlier societies. A contrast is often made between social reform, which is incremental and gradualist, and social revolution. Fabians, such as Sidney and Beatrice WEBB, for example, viewed social reform as a method of "social engineering" entailing the gradual improvement of provision of services and materials goods, and rejecting revolutionary change. Some critics have argued that many social reforms are palliatives disguising fundamental social inequalities and problems rather than eliminating them. In Britain, the reform of the National Health Service in 1974 was intended to improve the delivery of health services, but did little to address the causes of ill health to be found in the social structure of society. Analysis of social reform also raises questions about the relationship between social science and value judgments.

social reproduction 1. the process (including biological reproduction and SOCIALIZATION) by which societies reproduce their social institutions and social structure. It is usually assumed, especially of modern societies, that this process is accompanied by elements of social transformation as well as social reproduction. **2.** (Marxism) the maintenance of an existing mode of production and pattern of social relations within a particular society. Within capitalism, this is seen as the outcome of the continual reproduction and extended reproduction of capital and the associated maintenance of existing economic and social relations by recourse to IDEOLOGY. See also CULTURAL REPRODUCTION, ACCUMULATION OF CAPITAL.

social science the entirety of those disciplines, or any particular discipline, concerned with the systematic study of social phenomena. No single conception of science is implied by this usage, although there are sociologists who reject the notion that social studies should be seen as scientific in any sense based on the physical sciences.

A central issue that arises concerning the scientific status of social studies is how far the existence of meaningful purposive ACTION and choice in social life removes any possible basis for explanation involving general scientific laws. In addition to questions about the effectiveness of explanation based on scientific laws, questions also arise as to the appropriate ethical posture to be adopted toward the human social actor.

For some sociologists, the essential features of social action mean that sociology can only explain satisfactorily using MEANINGFUL UNDERSTANDING AND EXPLANATION and that scientific laws can play no part. However, whereas most sociologists recognize that important differences exist between the social and the physical sciences, they usually reject any suggestion that these differences mean that sociology must be seen as nonscience because of this. The more usual position is to see the use of the term "social science" as justified by the existence in sociology of systematic RESEARCH METHODS as well as meaningful explanation and a variety of more general forms of sociological EXPLANATION. Thus, although there are important exceptions, sociologists will usually be found to regard sociology as scientific in one or more of the several senses in which the term "science" is used. Sociologists and philosophers who reject the term "social science" (for example, Winch, 1958) usually do so on the basis of restrictive conceptions of science, when in reality conceptions of both physical and social science are more open and more variegated than this.

social security in the United States, a program of old-age, unemployment, health, disability, and survivors insurance maintained through compulsory payements by employer and employee groups; in Britain, a system of income maintenance provided by the state. Most systems have two components: a contributory system, in Britain labeled *National Insurance* (a system that underwrites benefits associated with unemployment, retirement, and sickness), and a noncontributory so-called safety net that usually has some connection with conceptions of a poverty line. National Insurance owes much to the thinking of Beveridge, the safety net has its historical roots in British Poor Law provision.

Sociologists of welfare have concerned themselves with a variety of related issues, such as the relationship between ideology and social security systems taken as a whole, images of claimants, the notion of redistribution, and the relationship between social security and poverty. See also WELFARE STATE.

social services 1. any state-provided services that have a bearing on the quality of life of all citizens. **2.** more narrowly, the organization and delivery of local authority SOCIAL WORK services in relation to children, the elderly, the disabled, and the mentally ill. In Britain, in addition to state provision, Councils of Social Services are to be found within most localities. They are umbrella organizations to assist and coordinate voluntary social welfare provision. Both voluntary and statutory services are to be distinguished from the recent new and growing private sector.

Sociologists have interested themselves in the relationship between IDEOLOGY and the notions of social responsibility expressed in varying formulations of social policy. Thus, the political right stresses ideas of individual and familial responsibility, the political left the obligations of the state to individuals in guaranteeing some form of social minimums. Marxists and others have recognized and studied the struggles within the state apparatus, both local and national, for the social wage. The recent emergence of the private sector has added another dimension to the voluntarism-statism debates.

SOCIAL SETTINGS

The study of sociology has featured as a significant part of the education and training of professionals and others who work within the social services. See also WELFARE STATE.

social settings the varying kinds of socially created locales or regions in time and space that provide the contexts of different types of social interaction, for example, a courtroom or a school. Thus, social setting refers to more than physical places, but rather to, what GIDDENS (1984), drawing on GOFFMAN, refers to as a "zoning" of social practices.

social solidarity the integration, and degree or type of integration, manifest by a society or group. The basis of social solidarity differs between simple societies and more complex societies. In simple societies it is often based on relations of KINSHIP, and direct mutual relations and shared values. In relations between non-kin, and in more complex societies, social solidarity has various bases, for example, see MECHANICAL AND ORGANIC SOLIDARITY. Whether in more complex societies social solidarity requires shared values, integrative RITUAL, etc. is debated (see CONSENSUS, DOMINANT IDEOLOGY THESIS, RELIGION, CIVIL RELIGION).

social statistics quantitative social data, such as crime statistics, details of marriage and family composition, housing, etc. The acquisition of such data is a fundamental concern in sociology. The term may also be used to refer to the methods used in this acquisition, including the SOCIAL SURVEY, INTERVIEWING, and SAMPLING. See also CENSUS, OFFICIAL STATISTICS, QUANTITATIVE RESEARCH TECHNIQUES, QUETELET.

social status see STATUS.

social stratification the hierarchically organized structures of social inequality (ranks, status groups, etc.) that exist in any society (compare CLASS, especially **1–5**). As in geology, the term refers to a layered structuring or strata, but in sociology the layers consist of social groups, and the emphasis is on the ways in which inequalities between groups are structured and persist over time.

The term provides a focus in which distinctions can be made between the different forms of social ranking and inequality characterizing different societies or found within one society. In historical and comparative perspective, for example, one finds distinctions between slave, CASTE, ESTATE, and modern open-class societies. Also, one finds similar social characteristics structuring inequalities in different societies. Gender, ethnicity, and age, for example, have in various ways been important in relations of domination and subordination in different historical periods and cultures. Access to or command over particular social resources has also been important in producing and sustaining inequalities. Examples here might include literacy (ancient China), religion (Mesopotamia or Incan and Aztec societies), and military resources (in imperial territories throughout history). In addition, bureaucratic elites are extremely important in some societies—Eastern Europe and many Third World societies, for example.

Gender divisions form a basis for social differentiation in all societies and, equally, relate to relations of domination and subordination. Similarly, ethnicity is a major factor in structuring inequalities in many societies.

Since there are many bases on which human inequalities may be understood and on which exploitation and oppression may be produced and reproduced, it is important to recognize that these variables are not mutually exclusive; for example, in the preindustrial world religious and military strata often coexisted along with strata based on gender and ethnicity.

In addition to the different bases of social stratification, different shapes or structural profiles (for example, steepness of hierarchy, number of steps in this hierarchy) of different systems can also be contrasted. See Fig. 25.

The usefulness of the term "stratification" in allowing discussion of different bases and forms of inequality has been largely instrumental in bringing the concept back into the mainstream of sociological debate in recent years. The term had become unfashionable with the revival of Marxian class analysis in the 1960s and 1970s. Feminist critique of conventional class analysis, for example, has demonstrated the independent significance

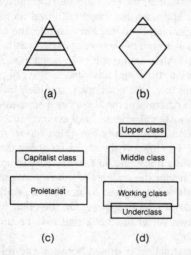

Fig. 25. **Social stratification.** One way of representing alternative patterns of social stratification is diagrammatically. Thus, if some societies, including many traditional agrarian civilizations, exhibit (a) steep pyramid structure, modern western societies can be represented as having a diamond shaped structure (b). In a similiar way, in class analysis, the conflict potential of class structures can be represented diagrammatically. For example, (c) the two-class structure of ideal type Marxian conceptions of capitalist society, or (d) the more complex three (or more) class structure which is sometimes seen as better representing the class structure of modern Western societies.

of gender, cutting across class differences between women (see GENDER STRATIFICATION). In the same way, ethnic divisions cannot be simply reduced to conventional class divisions, and debates about ethnic inequalities have demonstrated the complexity of power and opportunity structures.

In addition to the emphases discussed above, FUNCTIONALISM has also stressed the historical and contemporary functional significance of systems of stratification. The best-known text in this tradition is Davis and Moore (1945). These authors argue that stratification is a FUNCTIONAL PREREQUISITE for *all* societies (see also FUNCTIONAL(IST) THEORY OF SOCIAL STRATIFICATION.) Stratification is universally necessary due to the requirement of any society to motivate individuals to fill important social positions. Unequal rewards, including income and status, are seen as means whereby scarce talents are allocated to important positions. Davis and Moore describe social inequality as "an unconsciously evolved device by which societies ensure that the most important positions are conscientiously filled by the most qualified persons." They identify these positions historically as religious office, government, the economy and technical knowledge.

The functionalist approach has been criticized on numerous grounds, including its ideological implications. For example, the notion of "functional importance" is challengeable—how can we demonstrate this without circularity of argument? Also, opportunities to develop skills are not equal in systems of stratification. Birth and inheritance of social position are important, and recruitment into elite positions is routinely influenced by factors other than talent. Furthermore, the theory makes assumptions about individuals' motivations without evidence, and assumes that a period in higher education, for example, is a penalty for which future rewards have to be guaranteed. Finally, its views of society as an entity that has unequivocal requirements involves a questionable REIFICATION. In one view, particularly in its failure to consider the realities of power relations, the functionalist approach can be considered more as an ideological justification of inequalities than a satisfactory analysis of these. On the other hand, the view that stratification performs social functions that may be universal, cannot be ruled out in principle.

Sometimes the distinction is drawn between the relatively descriptive approach of theorists who use the term "social stratification," and the more analytical approach of those involved in so-called class analysis. As shown from the above, this is an oversimplification. Rather than representing two diametrically opposed forms of analysis, a concern with "stratification" and a concern with "class" in reality involve two closely interrelated sets of terminology for the analysis of structured inequalities (see Westergaard and Restler, 1975, and SOCIAL MOBILITY).

social stratum 1. any identifiable layer within a hierarchical system of SOCIAL STRATIFICATION, social STATUS positions, etc. (compare CLASS). **2.**

(formerly, in Eastern Europe) an identifiable grouping or category within a "nonantagonistic" system of social stratification or social class. Such groupings or classes have been termed *social strata* and/or "nonantagonistic" or acknowledge the claim that all such groups share in a common relation to the means of production. They remain identifiable and socially significant strata, however, since their different levels of education, culture, consciousness, etc. continue to set them apart. See also INTELLIGENTSIA.

social structure 1. any relatively enduring pattern or interrelationship of social elements, for example, the CLASS structure. **2.** the more or less enduring pattern of social arrangements within a particular society, group, or social organization, for example, the social structure of Great Britain.

No single agreed concept of social structure exists in sociology, despite its widespread usage. The definition employed depends on the theoretical perspective within which the concept is used. For example, Herbert SPENCER was interested in showing how social structure, conceived as analogous with, if not identical to, a biological organism, became increasingly differentiated and more specialized as the result of "social evolution." MARX, on the other hand, stressed the overriding importance of the basis (or *infrastructure*) and the more or less dependent *superstructure,* as the two main components of social structure.

In general, disagreement exists as to whether the most decisive elements of social structure consist of the surface rules, roles, and social institutions (for example, PARSONS, 1951, or Nadel, 1957), or whether these arise from mechanisms and processes hidden from view but which underpin social life, as for MARX or for LÉVI-STRAUSS (see also STRUCTURE, STRUCTURALISM).

While a focus on the interrelation of social parts—and hence structural thinking—can be seen as one of the defining features of sociology, numerous reservations exist about the uses to which the concept of social structure is put.

Disagreement and debate about the role of structural thinking in sociology derive from the differences of degree, if not of kind, that would seem to exist between the types of structures in the physical and the biological world and social structures. Reservations exist particularly about the appropriateness of mechanical and biological analogies and the use of conceptions of HOMEOSTASIS, FUNCTION, and SOCIAL SYSTEM as well as conceptions of TELEOLOGY in sociology (see FUNCTIONALISM).

The fact is that social structures do not have the relatively clear-cut boundaries in time and space of many physical and most biological structures, nor do they have the precisely identifiable tendencies to homeostasis possessed by organic structures.

Reservations about structural thinking exist particularly in connection with functionalist thinking, but the identification of the essential, or central, features of particular social structures or types of social structure is often controversial whether or not functional thinking is involved.

social studies of science the interdisciplinary study of the social context in the production of science. As such the approach overlaps with both the SOCIOLOGY OF SCIENCE and the SOCIOLOGY OF KNOWLEDGE, as well as the history and the philosophy of science, although those most associated with the approach have increasingly sought to distance themselves from the latter, above all wishing to instate the primacy of an empirical approach in social studies of science. Adopting the doctrine of the so-called *strong version of the sociology of science* (that is, science has to be explained by the same route as other forms of knowledge of belief, and can have no privileged status as truth or be exempt from social explanation) has sometimes led those associated with the approach to be accused of relativism. However, their intention is simply to place a study of science on the same basis as any other social phenomenon. Advocates of the approach are no more concerned with establishing philosophical RELATIVISM than they have been with preserving traditional EPISTEMOLOGY.

social survey a comprehensive collection of data and information about people living in a specific area or administrative unit.

Social surveys aim to collect a great deal of data about individuals and their lifestyles by means of QUESTIONNAIRES and other QUANTITATIVE RESEARCH TECHNIQUES. They are undertaken for administrative as well as sociological purposes. Although social surveys are often not explicitly sociological in orientation, they provide the sociologist with a rich source of secondary data for analysis of many sociological questions.

social system 1. any, especially a relatively persistent, "patterning of social relations across 'time-space,' understood as reproduced practices" (GIDDENS, 1984). Thus, in this general sense, a SOCIETY or any ORGANIZATION or GROUP constitutes a social system. For Giddens, however, social systems are highly variable to the degree that they exhibit a systematic pattern. They "rarely have the sort of internal unity" true of biological systems, or of the kind usually assumed by FUNCTIONALISM (see also SYSTEM, SYSTEMS THEORY). Compare also SOCIAL STRUCTURE, STRUCTURE. **2.** (more specifically, as in FUNCTIONALISM) any persistent system of interaction between two or more social actors up to and including a unitary SOCIETY, especially where this is associated with a tendency of the system to *boundary maintenance*, that is, to preserve its position *vis-à-vis* its external environment, whether this be other social systems or the physical world. In PARSONS' thinking (1951) and in most modern forms of functionalist and STRUCTURAL-FUNCTIONALIST sociology, such a conception of social system has been particularly associated with conceptions of FUNCTIONAL PREREQUISITES of societies and of societies as self-maintaining systems, etc. (see also SYSTEMS THEORY and SUBSYSTEMS MODEL).

social welfare the general state of health, well-being, and happiness of individuals or a society. The extent to which provision for this should be the responsibility of the STATE or the individual is a central issue running through many debates in modern society. See also WELFARE STATE, JUSTICE.

social work the organized provision of personal welfare services to people in need, including the poor, the physically and mentally disabled, the aged, and needy children. Social work also includes work with delinquents and criminals, for example, the probation service, which is as much an adjunct of policing as concerned simply with the provision of welfare. The twin goals of social welfare and social control can be seen as concerns present in most types of social work. Arising from the new urban conditions that accompanied rapid industrialization in the 19th century, social work at first was provided by private individuals or voluntary bodies. In modern industrial societies, social work has become increasingly professionalized and is now mainly provided by statutory agencies. Training in social work has usually included a major emphasis on sociology. Psychoanalytic perspectives, and more recently a knowledge of law, have also figured strongly. Reflecting in part these disciplinary differences, orientations to social work have sometimes emphasized attitudinal or personality changes at the individual level as the key to effective intervention, while at other times, for example, radical or Marxist orientations to social work, directing attention to the underlying socioeconomic causes of individual problems has been seen as part of the role of the social worker. See also RADICAL SOCIAL WORK.

sociation Kurt Wolff's rendering of SIMMEL's general term (*Vergesellschaftung*) referring to the conscious association of human beings (K. Wolff, 1950). A central concern of Simmel's sociology was to establish the general forms of sociation (see FORMAL SOCIOLOGY).

societal reaction the idea that the social response to an act seen as deviant can be crucial in its consequences, particularly in creating or encouraging a deviant lifestyle or identity, or a DEVIANT CAREER. The term was first used in this special sense by Edwin Lemert (1951), who argued that the effects of actions of social control agencies (for example, the police, courts) were most significant in defining, changing, or confirming deviance and the deviant actor. This is central to the distinction Lemert makes between PRIMARY DEVIANCE and SECONDARY DEVIANCE. The focus on the reactions of others has meant that the term is often associated with LABELING THEORY, or with theories of SOCIAL CONTROL.

society 1. the totality of human relationships. **2.** any self-perpetuating human grouping occupying a relatively bounded territory, having its own more or less distinctive CULTURE and INSTITUTIONS, for example, a particular people such as the Nuer or a long- or well-established NATION-STATE, such as the United States or Britain.

Although one of the most basic concepts in sociology, a number of difficulties and disputes surround the use of the concept, especially in the second sense. If the concept of society in the second sense is usually fairly readily applied in the case of well-established nation-states, which have their own familial, economic, and political institutions and clear borders, the identification of the boundaries of a society is nowhere near as easy in the case of, say, ancient empires, which usually consisted of relatively loose assemblies of different peoples, peasant communities, etc., with no conception of shared nationhood. As indicated by RUNCIMAN (1989), the range of actual societal membership can be highly variable: a "member of a local tribal group inhabiting an area on a boundary between zones of patrilineal and matrilineal inheritance; the member of a separate ethnic and religious community in a country ruled by a colonial power; the member of a separatist commune set up within a state"; and so on. The point at which historically a changing society should or should not be treated as the same society is a further issue that can present difficulties. Ultimately, the capacity of members to interact with each other, the extent of this interaction, and historically the extent of cultural and institutional continuity, is the test of whether the concept of a single society applies. This said, in even the apparently most clearly defined societies, such as nation-states or a geographically and socially isolated simple society, there will be connections with other societies. Given the increasing globalization of modern social relations, some theorists (for example, GIDDENS) have argued that the ever-present risk attached to an overemphasis on the concept of unitary societies in sociology is a failure to give sufficient attention to the major importance of intersocietal connections, multinational organizations, etc.

For DURKHEIM and for some functionalists, society also exists in a third sense. Durkheim promoted sociology as the "science of society" and treated society as a distinct object, with a reality *sui generis*. As an object of study it was distinct from and greater than the sum of its individual component parts. Its reality was a "moral power" external to and constraining human individuals (see SOCIAL FACTS AS THINGS). The issues raised by such further uses of the term have been some of the most contentious of all in sociology. In contrast with classical sociological theory, it can be said that contemporary sociology has been increasingly reluctant to theorize about society in this way (see HOLISM, METHODOLOGICAL, INDIVIDUALISM, STRUCTURE AND AGENCY). See also SOCIAL SYSTEM, FUNCTIONAL REQUISITES.

sociobiology theory and research within the field of evolutionary biology that seeks to provide biological explanations for the evolution of social behavior and organization in animals and man. Proponents of sociobiological theories (for example, E.O. Wilson, 1975) regard the problem of the evolution of altruism as a major challenge, since altruism implies a sacrifice of individual fitness incompatible with classical evolutionary theory. Altruistic behavior to neighbors can evolve, however, when genes are shared among kin or other demographic groups, since in this case that behavior still increases the likelihood of the helping individual's genes persisting into future generations. The goals of sociobiology, that is, to predict features of social organization from knowledge of demographic parameters (for example, rate of population growth) and the genetic structure of populations, also require environmental/ecological pressures, such as defense and foraging needs, to be taken into account. See also ETHOLOGY, TERRITORIAL IMPERATIVE.

sociocultural evolution "the process of change and development in human societies that results from cumulative change in their stores of cultural information available" (Lenski and Lenski, 1970). For Lenski and Lenski, sociocultural evolution occurs on two levels: (a) within individual societies and (b) within the "world-system of societies" in general as part of a process of *intersocietal selection*. Theorists such as Lenski and Lenski regard symbols as playing an analogous role (the transmission of information) within sociocultural systems and sociocultural evolution to that played by genes and natural selection in biological systems and biological evolution: in both processes, continuity and change, variation and extinction, and innovation and selection are evident—see also EVOLUTIONARY THEORY. Important differences between the two processes are recognized:

(a) while biological evolution is characterized by continuous differentiation and diversification (like the branching of a tree), it is characteristic of sociocultural evolution that societies merge or are eliminated, resulting in fewer rather than more societal types (differentiation, however, is an increasing feature within complex societies);

(b) in biological evolution simple species are not eliminated, but in sociocultural evolution they tend to be;

(c) in sociocultural evolution, heritability involves transmission between generations that preserves useful learned behavior, but in biological evolution such *acquired characteristics* are not transmitted (see also LAMARCK); as a consequence, in comparison with biological evolution, sociocultural evolution is rapid, and the potential exists for this to be brought under rational control.

The debate in sociology about evolutionary theory centers not so much on differences between social and biological evolution—there is broad agreement on this. Rather, debate centers on whether similarities or dissimilarities between biological and sociocultural change are regarded as uppermost. For sociocultural evolutionary theorists such as Lenski and Lenski, and some functionalist sociologists (for example, see PARSONS, EVOLUTIONARY UNIVERSALS, NEOEVOLUTIONISM), similarities between the two mean that the term "evolution" and evolutionary theory continue to have an important place in discussions of social change. For other sociologists, however, the differences between the two kinds of change are so great that continued talk of social evolution is not helpful and should be ended. See also EVOLUTIONARY SOCIOLOGY.

sociodrama see MORENO.

socioeconomic group see CLASS, SOCIAL STRATIFICATION.

socioeconomic status a person's overall standing within a social stratification system (LAZARSFELD et al., 1944; GOLDTHORPE AND HOPE, 1974). Imprecisions and uncertainties as to what such general notions refer to, compared with more analytically focused notions of CLASS and STATUS, have meant that the concept has attracted criticism (see MILLS, 1959). See also SOCIAL STRATIFICATION.

sociogram see SOCIOMETRY.

sociolegal studies see SOCIOLOGY OF LAW.

sociolinguistics a field of study, informed by both sociology and psychology, concerned with the social and cultural aspects and functions of LANGUAGE. Although sometimes narrowly identified with somewhat disparate, albeit important, topics such as language and social class (for example, the work of Basil BERNSTEIN), language and ethnicity (for example, Labov, 1967), language and gender, and the like—potentially at least—sociolinguistics, has a much wider brief, including most aspects of language. One general area of major significance, for example, has been an emphasis on the importance of a sociological view of linguistic competence and the inadequacy of a merely physiological and psychological view (for example, Halliday's or HABERMAS's critique of Chomsky's theory of linguistic competence). Among further main areas of sociolinguistic concern are PRAGMATICS and SEMIOTICS. Accordingly, the argument can be advanced that sociolinguistics should be regarded as having an utterly central rather than a peripheral role within the general study of linguistics. See also MULTICULTURALISM.

sociological theory the range of abstract, general approaches and competing and complementary schools of thought that exist in sociology.

While sociological theory in this sense includes some theories that are formalized or mathematical in form (see THEORY, MATHEMATICAL SOCIOLOGY), more usually theory in sociology is looser in form, referring to the main approaches, intellectual paradigms, conceptual schemes, etc. that exist within the discipline.

The following are among the main general theoretical approaches usually identified within sociology:

(a) FUNCTIONALISM, sometimes but not always including EVOLUTIONARY SOCIOLOGY;

(b) SYMBOLIC INTERACTIONISM and INTERPRETIVE SOCIOLOGY, including ACTION THEORY;

(c) MARXIST SOCIOLOGY and CONFLICT THEORY;

(d) FORMAL SOCIOLOGY;

(e) SOCIAL PHENOMENOLOGY and ETHNOMETHODOLOGY;

(f) STRUCTURALISM and POSTSTRUCTURALISM.

In addition to these general approaches, the importance of which would usually be recognized by most sociologists, numerous theoretical approaches of lesser influence can also be identified (for example, EXCHANGE THEO-

RY and STRUCTURATION THEORY). In part all such general approaches can be seen as complementary, emphasizing different aspects of social reality (for example, a complementarity between micro and macro approaches, or between theories of agency and theories of structure). Equally, however, they are also often presented as competing approaches.

Some sociologists, notably MERTON, calling for what he referred to as THEORIES OF THE MIDDLE RANGE, have sought to escape from the emphasis on competition between such general theoretical frameworks, placing a far greater emphasis on working, explanatory, theories and SENSITIZING CONCEPTS that arise from research and interpret findings (see also GROUNDED THEORY, ANALYTICAL INDUCTION).

Other general distinctions between types of theoretical approach relate to:

(a) issues of EPISTEMOLOGY and ONTOLOGY, for example, POSITIVISM versus CONVENTIONALISM or REALISM;

(b) distinctions between surface and deep STRUCTURE (see also SOCIAL STRUCTURE).

sociology (a term coined by COMTE) the scientific and, more particularly, the positivistic study of SOCIETY (see POSITIVISM). Since then, however, the term has gained far wider currency in referring to the systematic study of the functioning, organization, development, and types of human societies, without this implying any particular model of science. In some uses, the term can also encompass approaches that explicitly repudiate the relevance of a physical science orientation to social study.

One problem immediately emerges about such a definition:

(a) it fails to distinguish sociology from SOCIAL SCIENCE in general;

(b) it fails to distinguish sociology from other, less generalist social sciences.

Since no aspect of society is excluded from consideration by sociology, no simple distinction can be drawn between sociology and social science; in some uses the two terms are simply synonymous. More usually, however, whereas sociology necessarily overlaps with the subject matter of more specialized social sciences (for example, economics, POLITICAL SCIENCE), the discipline is conceived of by its practitioners as distinguished from these more focused social science disciplines by an avowedly holistic perspective in social analysis, a commitment to analysis that studies the interrelation of social parts. This said, however, it has to be noted that sociology does not exist as a tightly integrated discipline; not only does the subject encompass many competing paradigms and approaches, it has also remained uniquely open to ideas imported from other disciplines.

A further implication of such a view of sociology is that it does not begin with the work of Comte, but can also be regarded as embracing earlier systematic study of societies, including the plainly sociological thinking, (although not so-called) of major classical philosophers such as Plato or

Aristotle or, closer to modern times, Scottish Enlightenment thinkers such as SMITH or FERGUSON. There is a viewpoint in sociology that sociology's concern as a discipline is with the distinctive problems of modern INDUSTRIAL SOCIETIES (GIDDENS, 1981). However, though this draws attention to an undoubted central emphasis within modern sociology, seen not least in the classical works of the giants of the discipline, such as MARX, WEBER, and DURKHEIM, it understates the range of the subject, which is a concern with all aspects and all types of society.

sociology of art an area of sociological analysis that includes within its compass a concern with exploring the visual arts and sometimes also music, theater, film, and literature. As such, the potential range of concepts and theories is diverse. Influential theoretical approaches have included Marxist and neo-Marxist, including STRUCTURALISM, as well as more conventionally sociological perspectives.

In the United States, mainstream sociologists such as Coser (1978) and BECKER (1982) have focused on organizational and institutional analysis of the agencies involved in artistic and cultural production and their relations with audiences.

Whereas at one time Marxist approaches sought to analyze artistic products reductionistically, in terms of the metaphor of base and superstructure, Marxists are today at the forefront of an emphasis on the importance of analysis of internal features of the artistic object or the text (see also HERMENEUTICS). Structuralist approaches, including SEMIOTIC analysis, exploring the complex codes involved in artistic products, have also been widely employed in recent years. Ultimately, however, it is a combination of an understanding of artistic production in its own terms and an account of its wider socioeconomic location and implications that continues to demarcate the sociology of art from more conventional nonsociological approaches to its analysis, such as literary criticism or art history. This said, it must also be recognized that much seminal work in the sociology of art has been interdisciplinary rather than narrowly sociological. See also AESTHETICS, SOCIOLOGY OF MASS COMMUNICATIONS, LEISURE, CULTURAL STUDIES, BENJAMIN.

sociology of crime and deviance see CRIMINOLOGY, DEVIANCE.

sociology of development that branch of sociology concerned with the examination of social change from agrarian to industrial societies and particularly applied to study of the Third World. More narrowly, the term is sometimes used to refer to those theories of social change associated with MODERNIZATION theory and neo-evolutionary approaches (see NEO-EVOLUTIONISM). This latter use is now less common than in the 1970s, when the sociology of development was contrasted with underdevelopment or DEPENDENCY THEORY.

sociology of education the application of sociological theories, perspectives, and research methods to analysis of educational processes and practices. It is characteristic of industrial societies that, compared with previous societies, education is provided by specialized institutions. It is the performance of these institutions that is the central object of study in the sociology of education.

Although the emergence of the sociology of education as a distinct field of inquiry is of fairly recent origin, it has its roots in the early development of sociology, especially the FUNCTIONALISM of DURKHEIM. For Durkheim (1922), the process of education was to be understood in terms of its contribution to the promotion and maintenance of the social order. A related viewpoint (for example, MANNHEIM) was to regard education as a means of solving problems and removing social antagonisms.

Until the 1950s, the sociology of education remained strongly influenced by such perspectives, although development of the discipline owed much to the role of sociology in teacher training, especially in the Unites States, as well as to the tradition of "political arithmetic" in Britain. The latter tradition led to a range of surveys and statistical studies exploring the social influences on educational attainment, and on educational and occupational selection and SOCIAL MOBILITY (for example, Floud, HALSEY, and Martin, 1957). Although these studies revealed the persistence of class and gender inequalities in educational opportunity, the assumption remained that education could become a means of social transformation in the long run

During the 1960s, a breakdown of the functionalist hegemony in sociology and an increasing pessimism about reformist policies in education, especially in the United States, led to the emergence of a sociology of education markedly different in tenor. Sources of inequality lying outside the school were seen as intractable, and fundamental questions were raised about the traditional sociology of education and the assumed relationship between education and social reform. One aspect of this new phase in the sociology of education was to direct attention to features of schooling such as classroom interaction and curriculum organization, work that derived from the application of standard interactionist approaches. Other work was more radical (for example, Young's work on the curriculum, and Bowles and Gintis's *Schooling in Capitalist America*, 1976), suggesting that schools function above all as agencies that necessarily reproduce the social relations of capitalist production. Part of the inspiration behind analysis of this type was Marxist (for example, drawing on the conceptions of GRAMSCI and ALTHUSSER). Other sociologists, however, combined the thinking of Marx, Durkheim, and Weber to achieve much the same outcome, for example, BOURDIEU's arguments about the dependence of education on CULTURAL CAPITAL.

It would be wrong to imagine that later perspectives in the sociology of education have entirely replaced earlier ones. Nor should it be assumed that all attempts to expand educational opportunity have been to no avail. For example, in Britain the percentage of men and women entering higher education is now approaching parity, the overall proportion of school children entering higher education has substantially increased since the 1950s, and the number of entrants from working-class homes has also greatly increased. On the other hand, class differences in educational achievement remain striking, and the role of educational systems in sustaining a class society is equally apparent. See also BERNSTEIN, HIDDEN CURRICULUM, INTELLIGENCE, MERITOCRACY, CONTEST AND SPONSORED MOBILITY.

sociology of health and medicine the application of sociological approaches to the understanding of the experience, distribution, and treatment of illness. This subarea of the discipline has been a major growth area in terms of research and teaching, and in terms of membership it probably represents the largest section of both the British and American national sociological associations. The reasons for this expansion are perhaps twofold. The first has been the relatively greater access of workers in this area to research funds: both governments and medical sources have been eager to promote research that could improve health policy and patient care. Secondly, it has become manifest that the profile of morbidity and mortality in the industrialized world is now dominated by so-called lifestyle diseases (such as stroke, cancer, and heart disease). As the name implies, the management of these problems often involves an adjustment to ways of living rather than subjection to a regime of drug therapy. Medicine has no magic bullets to destroy these diseases (as antibiotics could with many infectious diseases), or immunization programs to give prophylactic protection. Moreover, lifestyle diseases show a clear social class gradient, generally becoming less frequent as class position improves. There is also, then, a socially structured pattern of opportunity for healthy living. Sociology has an obvious input to make in providing a fuller understanding of these chances for life.

The expansion of health and medicine as an area of sociological concern can be dated from the seminal contribution made by PARSONS' analysis of the SICK ROLE. Parsons' interest, in fact, was part of a much larger theoretical project (1951) on the development of a complex functional model of society, but his contribution served to establish the area of medicine as an institution whose sociological study could enhance the theoretical development of the discipline itself. Herein lies a long-established (if, in the end, overdrawn) distinction between two sociologies of medicine: one, a sociology *in* medicine, whose research agenda is set by governments, policy makers, and clinicians; the other, a sociology *of* medicine, whose questions are determined much more *by* sociologists and *for* sociology.

Parsons' concept of the sick role was subjected to criticism and amendment (see, for example, Morgan et al., 1985, for a recent overview of the major contributions here). Other topics of particular importance in the early expansion of the discipline were medical education and socialization (MERTON et al., 1957, BECKER et al., 1961); the social organization of death

(Glasser and Strauss, 1965, 1968); mental illness (GOFFMAN, 1961a, Scheff, 1966); and the analysis of medicine as a profession (Freidson, 1970a, 1970b). FUNCTIONALISM and SYMBOLIC INTERACTIONISM were the major theoretical traditions that informed much of this early work.

As the sociology of health and medicine has grown both in terms of maturity and in the number and theoretical predilections of its practitioners, research has been extended further. There can now be hardly any substantive area in the field in which work still remains to be initiated. Among the topics that have been, and continue to be, of interest to contemporary researchers are the relationship between medicine and capitalism; medicine as an instrument of social control (medicine and patriarchy and the medicalization of life have been two prominent themes here); gender and health, with particular reference to the role of women as paid and unpaid health workers; eating disorders; inequalities in health and health provision, including those of race and gender as well as class; the social construction of medical knowledge; doctor-patient communication and interaction; patterns of help-seeking and compliance among patients; the holistic health movement and complementary therapies; and, most recently, the study of sexual behavior, with special reference to sexually transmitted diseases and AIDS.

sociology of housing a subject area in sociology that studies and seeks explanations for different patterns of housing provision and housing tenure, both historically and comparatively, as well as within societies. Its subject matter is related to URBAN SOCIOLOGY and the sociology of welfare.

Within Britain, for example, housing tenure has changed greatly since World War I, when most dwellings were privately owned, rented accommodation. By the 1980s, owner occupation had increased to nearly 60 per cent, with public housing 30 per cent, and privately rented accommodation making up the remainder.

In Britain, the right to a home has not generally been recognized for those without children, with many young workers, and especially the young unemployed, unable to afford independent accommodation (see HOME-LESSNESS).

Housing has never quite achieved the status of a social service within Britain despite substantial council housing (public housing) provision and attempts to control the behavior of private landlords. Sociologists have attributed this ideological ambiguity to the way in which housing is simultaneously consumption and capital.

REX and Moore (1967) have suggested that differences in housing can be analyzed profitably using the concept of "housing classes," although the generation of such typologies would appear potentially endless. Others have argued that tenure, the basis of Rex and Moore's housing classes, is not the cause of social status but rather its effect. In a further development, critics of the CHICAGO SCHOOL have argued that cities and areas or zones within them must be seen in the context of the societies of which they are a part (see Castells, 1977). In this view, in capitalist societies, space becomes commodified and subject to market forces, and eligibility for public housing and for mortgages for private house purchase can be seen as features of a struggle for scarce resources.

sociology of knowledge the branch of sociology that studies the social processes involved in production of knowledge. It is concerned with understanding and explaining knowledge in particular cases, and with the relations between the general form(s) of knowledge and social structure, including the effects of knowledge and any social forces that condition either the form or the content of knowledge.

In a general sense, the sociology of knowledge (which may include in its subject matter all ideas and beliefs, as well as knowledge in a more exact sense, for example, scientific, or true, knowledge) is an integral part of many general theories in sociology, for example, Comte's LAW OF THREE STAGES in the intellectual and social development of society. As such, the boundaries of the sociology of knowledge are not tight. It either includes or overlaps related branches of sociological study, such as the SOCIOLOGY OF SCIENCE, the SOCIOLOGY OF RELIGION, the SOCIOLOGY OF ART, and literature.

A further distinction is often made between the sociology of knowledge and EPISTEMOLOGY, the theory of theories of knowledge in philosophy. As illustrated by Comte's POSITIVISM, this boundary has not always been accepted in sociology. Durkheim's contribution was to suggest that a basic analogy exists between our fundamental modes of thought, for example, our concepts of space and time, and our basic forms of social organization, especially our concepts of society. In recent years there has also been a strong movement within philosophy itself to approach epistemological questions in sociological ways, for example, the work of KUHN on science.

Early approaches in the sociology of knowledge tended to be dominated by issues raised by Marxism. According to Marx and Engels, knowledge is often distorted by class interests. Thus, the sociology of knowledge as initiated by Marxism focused mainly on the economic determination of leading ideas in a particular epoch or social formation. This approach was both challenged and built upon by Karl MANNHEIM, who argued that group membership and social location of many kinds, not just class and economic interests, act in ways that condition the formation and outcome of knowledge. Marxism itself was also seen as no exception to this rule. One important distinction made by Mannheim was between realistic, ideological, and utopian forms of knowledge. The social conditions conducive to each of these were also identified. Mannheim also wanted to overcome the tendency to RELATIVISM in the sociology of knowledge. His suggestion was that the knowledge accepted by socially unlocated, free-floating intellectuals might provide the answer.

Mannheim was not alone in thinking that the sociology of knowledge must not confine itself to uncovering the social basis of false claims to knowledge, but should try to contribute also to our identification of the social basis of true knowledge. The work of Comte or Marx also stands foursquare with Mannheim in taking this no longer accepted view. The same objective is also uppermost in major attempts at synthesis in modern sociology, such as HABERMAS's model of three types of "knowledge interests," or in modern sociological forms of scientific REALISM. If it cannot be said that sociology has solved such problems of knowledge once and for all, neither is it the case that it has conceded the ground to outright relativism (see also POSTMODERNISM).

Today the sociology of knowledge is pursued at many levels, in particular in studies in the sociology of science, and in studies of the social construction of everyday knowledge (see SOCIAL PHENOMENOLOGY, ETHNOMETHODOLOGY).

sociology of law the sociological study of the social context, development, and operation of *law:* the system of rules and sanctions, the specialist institutions and specialist personnel, and the several types of law (for example, constitutional, civil, criminal) that constitute the legal system in complex societies.

In the development of this area of study, the works of DURKHEIM and WEBER have been as important as in other areas of sociology, but the development of the sociology of law is complicated by academic approaches overlapping with sociology, notably JURISPRUDENCE and, later, the development of *sociolegal studies.* The latter now exists as a strand of social science thinking and research (including psychology and economic analysis as well as inputs from sociology) and stands in critical relation with traditional orthodoxies in legal theory. CRIMINOLOGY and the wider study of DEVIANCE are further related areas of specialist study.

In the sociology of law and in sociolegal studies, utilitarian, individualistic, and positivist views have been challenged by an interest in exploring the complexities of morality and mechanisms of social control. From Durkheim came the emphasis on the formal expression of what is preeminently social, namely, morality. This was explored in his discussion of the shift from MECHANICAL to ORGANIC SOLIDARITY, which included the distinction between repressive and restitutive law. From Weber's work has come an emphasis on the role of the development of rational and calculable law, legal rationalism, as a precondition for modern political developments and for capitalism. MARX's work, although less concerned with detailed study of legal forms, has also influenced the study of law in a number of ways, ranging from studies of the role of class interests in the content of law, to debates about the overall form of so-called bourgeois legality, an interest inspired by rediscovery of the work of Evgeny Pashukanis (1891–1937).

In addition to such general theoretical bases, lower level empirical studies of the operation of legal institutions have been increasingly important, especially studies of the working of the criminal justice system, including operation of courts, police, etc., and PENOLOGY. See also NATURAL RIGHTS AND NATURAL LAW, COMMON LAW.

sociology of leisure see LEISURE.

sociology of mass communications the subfield of sociology concerned with study of the mass media of communications. In practice it has involved people from a variety of disciplines bringing a multiplicity of theoretical perspectives. The central theoretical problem is the conceptualization of the relationship between the mass media and society, and this has been undertaken through research into mass communication and power and influence, as well as the study of the mass media as institutions, the occupational cultures and practices of media workers, the audiences for mass communications, and the role of the mass media in the overall reproduction of culture. Three general perspectives have guided study: the first has been informed especially by SOCIAL PSYCHOLOGY and has focused on the processes and effects of mass communications (for example, see ADVERTISING); the second, has focused on mass communications institutions as ORGANIZATIONS and their broad social context; the third has been influenced by the structuralist perspective developed in the 1960s in which the focus is on analysis of the messages, images, and meanings conveyed by the mass media (see SEMIOLOGY). See also MASS SOCIETY.

sociology of religion the branch of sociology that deals with religious phenomena (see also RELIGION). Historically, the sociological analysis of religion was central in the analysis of most of the leading classical sociologists, notably WEBER and DURKHEIM. The ideas of these two theorists still constitute the core of the sociology of religion. Durkheim's work was concerned with the role of religion as a functional universal contributing to the integration of society. This remains the foundation of the FUNCTIONALIST THEORY OF RELIGION. Weber's concern was with the comparative analysis of the varying forms of religious beliefs and religious organizations, and the implications of these for development of rationality and for social change. Prior to the work of Weber and Durkheim, the sociology of religion had viewed religion simply as error (as for COMTE, or for MARX, for example, the latter's conception of religion as the "opiate of the masses"), or it had speculated about the origins of religion and the stages of its evolutionary development (see TYLOR, SPENCER).

More recently, the sociology of religion has concentrated its attention on the process of secularization occurring in Western societies. There have also been many studies of religious organizations (for example, B. Wilson, 1967), especially fringe religions and CULTS and SECTS (for example, Scientology or the so-called Moonies). In SOCIAL ANTHROPOLOGY, in HISTORICAL SOCIOLOGY, and in the study of contemporary non-European societies, comparative study of religion as a major social institution continues to occupy a central place in sociological analysis.

sociology of science the branch of sociology concerned with study of the social processes involved in producing scientific knowledge as well as the social implications of this knowledge, including TECHNOLOGY (see also SOCIOLOGY OF KNOWLEDGE, SOCIAL STUDIES OF SCIENCE).

The pioneering work on the sociology of science was by done by Robert MERTON (1938), whose determinedly sociological work on 17th-century British science (especially the Royal Society) emphasized the mix of economic and military concerns, and interests and religious beliefs (notably Protestantism) in the motives of early scientists. In his later work Merton also identified central social characteristics of science (for example, the "norm of universality," which is that, at least in principle, anyone ought to be able to check for themselves the validity of any scientific finding).

If Merton's later work identified ideal types of scientific activity, subsequent work in the sociology of science has tended to break down any sharp distinction between science and other forms of knowledge. In recent years, sociologists have distinguished strong and weak versions of the sociology of science. If earlier weak approaches were based largely on the need to explain the social basis of false claims to knowledge (scientific errors, para-sciences such as astrology, etc.), leaving the basis of true knowledge a matter for the philosophy of science, the more recent strong approach has seen as its role the study and explanation of *all* forms of scientific knowledge (see also EPISTEMOLOGY).

One thing to emerge from this more evenhanded treatment of true and false knowledge is that both forms share a common basis in everyday constructions of social reality, and problems in escaping INDEXICALITY and in establishing warrantability. Understanding of both kinds of knowledge is held to benefit from the study of the social impetus to new scientific ideas provided by economic and social interests, including the disciplinary and personal interests of the scientists.

Examples of recent detailed study in this expanded vein are:

(a) studies of the role of interests, fashions, etc. in particular disciplines or movements in science, for example, the rise and fall of EUGENICS (Harwood, 1977), studies of IQ testing, and even the history of mathematics;

(b) studies of the DIFFUSION of scientific ideas;

(c) studies of so-called scientific revolutions (for example, KUHN, 1962);

(d) ethnographic and related forms of close-up empirical analysis of the everyday social construction of scientific knowledge, for example, in laboratories, presentational arguments, graphic representations, etc. used by science, for example, B. Lator and S. Woolgar, *Laboratory Life* (1979).

sociology of sport a subdiscipline of sociology that focuses on the relationship between sport and society. The sociology of sport is concerned with the relationship between sport and other social institutions (family, education, politics, and the economy), the social organization, social relations and group behavior associated with different types of sport (for example, elite or mass, amateur and professional, the class, gender, or race relations that sport involves), and the social processes (such as ideological incorporation) that occur in conjunction with sport. While once isolated from mainstream sociology, in recent years it has become more fully integrated. Most research has been conducted in North America, but a sociology of sport also exists in Eastern and Western Europe, in Australia and New Zealand and Britain, as well as in Japan. Leading British exponents have included Norbert ELIAS and Eric Dunning (see Elias & Dunning, 1986), and John Hargreaves (1986). See also LEISURE.

sociology of the built environment a recent emphasis in sociology that, according to some theorists, can be the umbrella to bring together a number of special studies previously handled separately, for example, the SOCIOLOGY OF HOUSING, URBAN SOCIOLOGY, sociological analysis of movements in architecture, and town planning. As both material artifacts and expressions of cultural values, the forms taken by individual buildings and by towns and cities are of interest at a number of levels, including:

(a) their relationship with the commodification of space and resistances to such commodification;

(b) the way in which design and planning of buildings and cities reflect cultural goals and cultural movements (for example, the movement from the architectural modernism of Le Corbusier or the Bauhaus school, with its principles of functionalism and fidelity to materials, to postmodernism, which has replaced the "author" and consistent principles with pastiche);

(c) the way in which (a) and (b) are related, for example, the view that architectural postmodernism comes in two forms: one a renewed subservience to commercial values, the other more oppositional and seeking a revival of communal values (Lash, 1989).

sociology of the family sociological inquiry directed at describing and explaining patterns of FAMILY life and variations in family structure. As such, the study of the family overlaps closely with the study of KINSHIP.

One continuing strand of inquiry, which can be traced to social anthropology, has been concerned with the comparative analysis of family and kinship structures. In association with this, evolutionary and developmental accounts of the transformation of family structures have also been important.

A second strand, which dominated much sociological discussion and research up until the 1960s, was the functionalist theory of the family, interested mainly in the universal functions served by the family and the distinctive geographically mobile, *neolocal nuclear family* forms that emerge to meet the particular functional requirements of industrial societies.

A more critical examination of family structures emerged in the 1960s, especially under the influence of new feminist sociologies and feminist critiques of social science (for example, Morgan, 1975).

A final strand of sociological thinking, which has a long ancestry, is Marxist critiques of the family, in which an interest in the association between property relations and family structures has been central.

The functionalist theory of the family portrayed the elementary family unit, whether or not it is embedded in wider social relationships, as performing central social functions, such as:

(a) regulation of sexual activity;

(b) procreation of children, and the determination of relations within the family;

(c) primary socialization of children;

(d) provision of mutual emotional support for the couple.

These may be considered the core functions, but the family usually also performs ancillary functions, although it may increasingly share these with other agencies (an erosion of functions). These include:

(e) provision of housing, domestic services, and general economic support for the family group;

(f) provision of health care and welfare;

(g) support through the long period of education in modern societies.

Talcott PARSONS, a leading exponent of functionalist analysis, also argued that within the family unit, while the male performed instrumental roles, the role of the woman was usually to perform so-called expressive roles.

Criticism of the functionalist view and alternative sociological accounts of modern family structure have made a number of central points and raised a number of general issues:

(a) the existence of a great variety of family forms in modern as well as traditional societies;

(b) the historical oversimplification of the extended/nuclear distinction as applied to preindustrial and industrial society, given that the nuclear family would appear to have preceded industrialism, and the continued importance of extended kin in industrial society (as shown by Young and Wilmott, 1957);

(c) the emotional and intimate ties of family conceal a high degree of conflict and in many cases actual violence, so that the study of the family can also be located within the study of social problems (see also WIFE BATTERING, RADICAL SOCIAL WORK);

(d) the importance of analysis of the family and of households in terms of power and authority relations, and also economic relations;

(e) that, at best, the functionalist's "family [especially functions a and b] is not the name of an entity that is universally found but a concept that has a universal application" (Harris, 1985);

(f) the difficulty of even identifying the family group in preindustrial simple societies. It is for this reason that the term "family" has been relatively little used in social anthropology. See also MARRIAGE, DIVORCE AND SEPARATION.

sociology of work the sociological analysis of work and its organization, especially but not solely in terms of paid work. The general subject matter is analyzed within its wider social, comparative context, in particular its interrelations with social, economic, and political institutions. Work ideologies are also a principal concern in relation to occupational specialization (for example, professionalism). The central unifying theme is the DIVISION OF LABOR. The subdiscipline has been the focus for debates concerning labor process theory and LABOR MARKET analysis within sociology.

The term "sociology of work" became the generally accepted term for this subdiscipline partly as a consequence of the influence of the Open University course *People and Organizations* (cf. Esland and Salaman, 1975). This development was a reaction to the limitations sociologists found in INDUSTRIAL SOCIOLOGY. In particular it had a preoccupation with manufacturing industry within industrial societies in consequence of which industrial sociologists were limited in their ability to fully analyze many aspects of work. Examples of these, now studied in the sociology of work, include the dynamics of work relations and ideologies in relation to gender and race, the organization of domestic labor within society (see SEXUAL DIVISION OF LABOR), and the effects of underemployment and unemployment. See also EMPLOYMENT.

sociometry a widely used method of measurement of social attractiveness within groups, invented by Jacob MORENO. The technique involves administration of a questionnaire in which respondents rank order the attractiveness and unattractiveness of fellow group members as coparticipants or colleagues, either generally or in particular activities. The results of these interpersonal choices are then plotted on a diagram, termed a *sociogram*, the configuration revealing sociometric "stars" and "rejectees," and cliques of mutual positive appraisal and social isolates.

sociotechnical systems approach a prescriptive approach to organizational design that, utilizing SYSTEMS THEORY, emphasizes the need to consider the relationships between social and technical systems.

The approach was developed by the Tavistock Institute of Human Relations largely as a critique both of classical approaches, which sought to establish universal principles of organizational design, and of the common practice of designing plant layout solely according to technical criteria (social and psychological considerations being an afterthought). In contrast, the sociotechnical systems approach questioned the universalist assumption of "one best way" and emphasized the possibility of organizational choice. Technology, for example, is seen as a limiting rather than a determining factor. This makes possible the consideration of alternative technical and social systems. Sociotechnical systems theory aims at systematizing the consideration of alternatives in order to facilitate the best choice. This would allow systems to meet their primary task by optimizing the relationship between technical efficiency and human satisfaction through diagnosing the best fit. The classic illustration of this approach involved analysis of technical change in postwar British coal mines (Trist et al., 1963).

While some theorists and practitioners find much of value in the anti-universalist and humanistic stance of this approach, there are critics and skeptics. At a conceptual level the perspective can be seen to suffer from (a) assumptions associated with systems theory (for example, reification and system goals); (b) the possibility of a reductionist confusion of psychological and structural levels of understanding; (c) the charge of consultant-based managerial sociology (Brown, 1967; Silverman 1970). Thus, some theorists, having contrasted direct and indirect management control systems, point out that control and participation are limited to certain organizational issues and that consideration needs to be given, for example, to the distribution of the benefits of increased productivity. In addition, Mumford's case studies in participative sociotechnical systems design reveal some of the problems of resistance to designing from the bottom up, both from management and higher grade employees, and in the difficulties employees have in participating in design (Mumford, 1980).

Socrates (470–399 BC) Greek philosopher known mainly from his appearance in Plato's Dialogues, who was executed in Athens for refusing to recant when accused of corrupting the young. Socrates appears to have been concerned mainly with ETHICS, which he concluded should not be a matter of custom or habit, but based on rational, deductive inquiry. Socrates' method of instruction, the *Socratic method*, was to initiate a series of questions and answers designed to lead those involved to a reexamination of their fundamental beliefs.

solidarity see SOCIAL SOLIDARITY and MECHANICAL and ORGANIC SOLIDARITY.

solipsism (philosophy) the doctrine that the self, myself, is all that can be known to exist and that "world" outside exists only as the content of individual consciousness. The doctrine arises from a recognition that the objects of our sense experience are mind-dependent. However, solipsism is nowadays thought incoherent. For example, WITTGENSTEIN argued that it is incompatible with the existence of the language in which the theory is expressed. The alternative view is REALISM, that the world outside can be known, although the limits of such knowledge of the world remains an issue. Compare RELATIVISM.

Sorel, Georges (1847–1922) French philosopher, social theorist, best known for his espousal of the roles of myth and VIOLENCE in social affairs. His best-known work is *Reflections on Violence* (1908). Sorel believed in the overthrow of bourgeois society through class struggle, but came to the conclusion that orthodox Marxist accounts of the process were flawed by a tendency to interpret reality through the use of abstract concepts, predicated on the view that human beings were rational and so produced an ordered, regular society, open to scientific analysis and the discovery of laws from which predictions about future utopias could be derived. In Sorel's view, there were no social laws; reality was chaotic and disordered; and any order it exhibited was tenuous and derived from the imposition of human will, rooted not in rationality but in instinct. No revolution could be predicted. It could happen, but only as a result of spontaneous, willed action by the workers, which required solidarity. Two historical developments, however, militated against solidarity: the philosophies of trade and consumerism. Together, these stimulated competition, mistrust, envy, bargaining, and compromise that weakened both the bourgeoisie and the proletariat—the bourgeoisie was weakened by making concessions to the proletariat, which in turn was weakened by allowing itself to be bought off by the concessions. Revolutionary proletarians had, therefore, to eschew intellectualism, political parties, and compromise. Instead, they must develop their own ideas and seek to make the revolution at the point of production through direct action culminating in a general strike.

Sorel's thinking on myth and violence has been widely misunderstood. What he was mainly trying to do was expose rationalist and bourgeois shallowness and hypocrisy. Myth consisted in ideas whose utility lay not in their cognitive value, but in their power to evoke loyalty and to inspire action. All societies had myths that served these purposes. Likewise, all societies employed violence, though usually for repressive and/or predatory purposes. The great myth of the workers was the *general strike;* it inspired them to revolutionary action, the violence of which promoted their solidarity by making them rely on each other as brothers and sisters in the struggle. Likewise with violence. Provided it was neither repressive nor predatory, violence was liberating; its employment weeded out weaklings and compromisers, and so promoted a strong, committed workers' movement capable of overthrowing decadent bourgeois society.

Sorel's ideas had some impact in France and Italy in the early 20th century. Subsequently, however, his thought had relatively little influence, and his ideas are significant today as one important expression of the nonrationalist turn taken by political sociological thought in the early 20th century (see also NEO-MACHIAVELLIANS).

Sorokin, Pitirim (1889–1968) Russian-born US sociologist. Secretary to prime minister Kerensky in the provisional Russian government in 1917 and exiled from Russia in 1922, Sorokin settled in the United States in 1924. His earliest sociological writing in English, *Sociology of Revolutions* (1925), drew on his experience of the Russian Revolution. A pathbreaking study, *Social Mobility* (1927), emphasized the disruptive as well as the creative effects of social mobility. Sorokin's work subsequently was usually on a grand scale, as seen particularly in his studies of macrohistorical change, for example, *Social and Cultural Dynamics,* 4 vols. (1937–1941), and his irreverent and provocative surveys of types of sociological theory, notably *Contemporary Sociological Theory* (1928) and *Sociological Theories of*

Today (1966). Rather than accepting prevailing evolutionary or developmental models, Sorokin regarded societies as better understood as subject to cyclical, though irregular, patterns of change. In the latter part of his career Sorokin's role in sociology was increasingly on the margins as a somewhat eccentric critic of both American sociology and American society. Social disintegration and cultural crisis could only be overcome, he suggested, by a new altruism.

Spearman rank correlation coefficient a NONPARAMETRIC statistical test used for ordinal data (see CRITERIA AND LEVELS OF MEASUREMENT) when a CORRELATION between two VARIABLES is to be measured.

This test uses a ranking procedure to assess the degree of correlation. For example, if it is hypothesized that suicide rates in different countries vary with levels of church attendance, the suicide rates are put in rank order in one column, and the levels of church attendance are separately ranked in another. The correlation coefficient is calculated by a formula that uses the differences between the rankings.

speech act any social act accomplished by virtue of an utterance (for example, promising, cursing). Associated especially with the philosophers J. Austin and J. Searle, the analysis of such illucutionary acts (and *perlocutionary acts*, what is accomplished by words), is a central part of the subject matter of ORDINARY LANGUAGE PHILOSOPHY.

The analytical study of speech acts has affinities with a number of approaches in sociology, including the FORMAL SOCIOLOGY of SIMMEL, the work of GOFFMAN, and CONVERSATION ANALYSIS. The last-mentioned in particular is directly influenced by ordinary language philosophy (see also DEGRADATION CEREMONY). A further example of an approach influenced by the concept of speech act is the ethogenic social psychology of Rom Harré (*Social Being*, 1979), which advances the idea of a possible grammar of social encounters, one however that would be far more complex than is implied in philosophical conceptions of speech acts.

Spencer, Herbert (1820–1903) British social theorist, chiefly remembered for his contribution to the study of SOCIAL CHANGE from an EVOLUTIONARY perspective.

After an unconventional schooling, Spencer to work as a railway engineer, but soon moved into journalism and later became an independent scholar.

His first major work, *Social Statics* (1850), revealed his firm commitment to economic individualism and the free market, a commitment that continued throughout his work and is one of the main reasons for the great popularity of his sociology in the United States.

Spencer's early interest in geology had led him into the field of biology, and from there to the evolutionary theories of LAMARCK. These ideas became the informing principle of his social theory. As early as 1852, in a paper entitled "A Theory of Population," Spencer had argued that the process of social DEVELOPMENT was decisively influenced by "struggle" (for existence) and "fitness" (for survival). Thus he anticipated by some six years aspects of the theory of natural selection that Darwin and Wallace were to apply with such success to the organic world, but he did this while continuing to include Lamarckian assumptions. In *The Principles of Psychology* (1855), Spencer attempts to show how the evolutionary hypothesis could also illuminate mental development.

"Progress: its Law and Cause," an essay written in 1857, found Spencer arguing that the evolutionary principle was a law of universal applicability, defining development in the physical, organic, and social spheres. Evolutionary theory thus provided a basis for the unification of the sciences. Whatever trajectory of development was studied, the movement was always toward increasing DIFFERENTIATION and INTEGRATION of structure. Systems, be they solar, biological, or social, always manifested a tendency to move from a state where their constituent parts were homogeneous and loosely cohering, to one where they were increasingly heterogeneous and integrated.

Spencer's later work, widely read and high influential at the time, was concerned primarily with justifying this position. His *Synthetic Philosophy*, a multivolume project covering sociology, psychology, biology, and ethics, was one outcome. Thus, Spencer's sociology (for example, his *Principles of Sociology*, 1876–96), should properly be seen as one subfield in which he sought the wider objective of securing consent for the universality of the evolutionary process.

Some of Spencer's concepts, such as those of "differentiation" and "integration," have retained their currency as sociological tools, especially within the SOCIAL SYSTEMS perspective and NEO-EVOLUTIONARY work of Talcott Parsons. But Spencer's sociology is deeply compromised by his enthusiasm for unifying it with biology, and for his sometimes uncritical assumption that biological science could provide the appropriate concepts for studying society. If struggle motivated organic evolution, so warfare was important in social development, promoting both internal social cohesion and the development of powerful, specialized industrial economies; if the development of sophisticated nervous systems in the animal world enhanced the survival capacity of certain species, the same was true of telecommunications systems in society, and so on. The connection between these views and Spencer's politics is obvious: if social conflict was an evolutionary positive, the market should be unregulated, and the state minimalist (*The Man Versus the State*, 1884).

Whatever the judgment made about these economic and political prescriptions for social well-being, the sociology from which Spencer derived them is not acceptable. Social systems are not biological systems. People create and transform the environment in which they live. They are moral beings, and "the survival of the fittest" is also a moral judgment (see SOCIAL

DARWINISM). Competition may often be productive but only in a context with a preexisting framework of order and regulation rather than one of anarchy (compare DURKHEIM). The universality of the evolutionary process in the social sphere is also questionable. Developmental patterns cannot be consistent, since the development of some societies alters the possibilities of change for others (see also DIFFUSION, MULTILINEAR EVOLUTION). The most compromising problem with Spencer's work, however, is the circularity of the logic he employs in its execution. It was small wonder that Spencer felt he had proved his evolutionary hypothesis in the social world, since the evidence he used, the classification of different kinds of institutions and types of societies, was a classification derived from the very principles that the examples were supposed to prove. Spencer's legacy to sociology nevertheless remains important. He was a systems theorist and was the first to make systematic use of STRUCTURAL-FUNCTIONAL analysis, still a mainstay of sociological explanation.

sponsored mobility see CONTEST AND SPONSORED MOBILITY.

SPSS see STATISTICAL PACKAGE FOR THE SOCIAL SCIENCES (SPSS).

spurious correlation see MULTIVARIATE ANALYSIS.

stable democracy and **unstable democracy** a distinction drawn by LIPSET (1960) between *stable democracies,* defined as those polities that have enjoyed an "uninterrupted continuation of political democracy since World War I and the absence of a major party opposed to the 'rules of the game,' " and *unstable democracies,* which fail to fulfill these conditions. For non-European/non-English-speaking nations, Lipset also distinguished between "democracies" and "unstable dictatorships" on the one hand and "stable dictatorships."

The factors sustaining stable democracy according to Lipset are:

(a) political cleavage between main competing political parties, institutionalizing broad class conflict between nonmanual "middle-class" and manual "working class";

(b) the historical replacement of previous main bases of political cleavage (for example, religious, rural-urban, center-periphery);

(c) broad consensus on the fundamental legitimacy of prevailing political institutions, a secular politics ("end of ideology"), and the absence of major parties of integration opposing the rules of the political game;

(d) a socioeconomic system that is economically effective and delivers high levels of literacy, welfare, etc.;

(e) a fluid, open class structure and class mixing, which produce CROSS-CUTTING TIES and cross-pressures acting on the individual that help to moderate class conflict and competition between parties;

(f) a "participatory political culture," including extensive participation in voluntary associations and a general strength of groups of all kinds that functions as a protective screen against MASS SOCIETY (see also TWO-STEP FLOW OF MASS COMMUNICATIONS);

STAGES OF DEVELOPMENT

Reworking ideas drawn from classical POLITICAL SOCIOLOGY (especially TOCQUEVILLE and WEBER), Lipset also suggested that stable democracy depends on an elite-mass structure in which representative elites (see PLURAL ELITISM) are central to the working of the system, and can also be seen as safeguarding central democratic values. For Lipset, stable democracy is not just another political system, it is "the good society in action." The theory of stable democracy in these general terms arose as a synthesis of behavioralist and structural-functional and systems-theoretic approaches in US POLITICAL SCIENCE and political sociology. It has been influential, although also widely criticized, not only in discussions of Western democracies but also in discussion of POLITICAL MODERNIZATION and nation-building in developing and Third World nations. See also ELITE, ELITE THEORY, MOSCA, MICHELS, VOTING BEHAVIOR, END OF IDEOLOGY THESIS; compare LEGITIMATION CRISIS.

stages of development specific economic, cultural, social, or political forms that societies are thought to have to pass through to achieve a given destination. The concept is commonly used in EVOLUTIONARY and NEO-EVOLUTIONARY approaches to SOCIAL CHANGE. In understanding economic change, Walt Rostow's approach rests on the delineation of stages. The concept has been much criticized because:

(a) stages are difficult to identify, and there are as many different classifications of stages as there are authors;

(b) it tends to be associated with mechanistic and deterministic approaches to social change;

(c) European history is generally used to construct various stages that then are seen as necessary for other societies to pass through (see MODERNIZATION);

(d) diffusion from one society to another will affect stages in differing societies;

(e) it is difficult to show that any one stage is a necessary prerequisite for the next.

There is, however, some validity in the argument that there are general stages that societies have to pass through, for example, that an AGRARIAN SOCIETY has to exist before there can be an INDUSTRIAL SOCIETY, but there can be various forms contained within those categories. The history of the 20th century in particular has shown that there is a variety of forms of agrarian society that experience transformations to industrial societies in a variety of ways. The fact that the variations seem to be finite does not necessarily justify strong use of the concept of stages of development. See also INDUSTRIALIZATION, EVOLUTIONARY UNIVERSALS.

standard deviation see MEASURES OF DISPERSION.

standard error see MEASURES OF DISPERSION.

standard of living the level of material welfare, for example, real purchasing power, of a person or household. As an average of all incomes, the standard of living of a nation may also be talked of as rising or falling. There are many difficulties with the concept. Obviously, the same level of purchasing power will produce different standards of living in households with different numbers of dependents. In any case, the compilation of appropriate indices of purchasing power is far from straightforward, and comparisons between societies and across time are fraught with difficulties (for example, well-known debate over whether living standards rose or fell in the early decades of the industrial revolution). Issues also rise as to the relationship between the standard of living in such a relatively mechanical sense, and the so-called quality of life, an even more subjective, but not less important, dimension.

Stanford-Binet Test a widely used INTELLIGENCE TEST for children. The original Binet Test was designed by Binet and Simon (published 1905) to select those French children who would not benefit from the normal schooling available, but needed special education. Its revisions in 1908 and 1911 were designed as a series of tests relevant to each yearly age group, which the average child of that age was able to pass. So in fact Binet defined what the average child of each age could do in terms of simple verbal and performance skills; that is, standards or NORMS for each age were set (the concept of "mental age" had appeared). The design was later adapted by Terman of Stanford University to form the Stanford-Binet (1916), and it was Terman who introduced the concept of INTELLIGENCE QUOTIENT. This transformed the test scores into a quotient, making it possible to compare children in different age bands, or to compare the same child as he or she grew older.

The Stanford-Binet tests are individual, in that they have to be administered on a one-to-one basis. They are, therefore, essentially diagnostic and require skilled administration. There have been two further revisions (1937, 1960). Revisions are necessary as its tests become obsolete, for example, a picture of a buttoned shoe would need to be replaced by a picture of a sandal, or, today, a sneaker. A test loses its VALIDITY if the items are no longer relevant to normal experience. The extensive and prolonged use of the Stanford-Binet has made it particularly valuable, since each use provides further data, thus aiding diagnosis. However, new tests have appeared in recent years, the British Intelligence Scale (1977) having been designed to provide a replacement test for use in British schools.

state 1. the apparatus of rule or government within a particular territory. **2.** the overall territory and social system that is subject to a particular rule or domination. In this second sense the terms "state" and "SOCIETY" may sometimes be used interchangeably.

For WEBER, the crucial defining feature of any state is that it successfully upholds a claim "to the monopoly of legitimate use of violence within its territory." It should be stressed, however, that only in extreme circumstances do states depend mainly or entirely on the actual use of violence or physical coercion. These are normally used only in the last resort. The claims to political legitimacy made by rulers usually provide a far more potent and effective basis for trouble-free political rule (see LEGITIMATE AUTHORITY). But the threat of force always remains in the background in the government of states, and compared with theories (for example, NORMATIVE FUNCTIONALISM) that perhaps overemphasize the normative basis of state power, the importance of the threat of violence as an ever-present factor in internal state power must not be neglected. Internationally, as a defensive and an offensive machine, sometimes resorting to WARFARE, the role of violence is again clearly evident.

The first states (see also PRISTINE STATES) appeared about 5,000 years ago, in the Middle East and elsewhere, probably as the outcome of the activity of REDISTRIBUTIVE CHIEFDOMS, or of warfare that led to conquest and class domination. Whatever their precise origins, however, there is agreement that the central appropriation of an economic surplus and SOCIAL STRATIFICATION are both an essential requirement and a consequence of the subsequent development of states.

Prior to the first states (see STATELESS SOCIETIES), the government of societies existed only as a set of functions diffused within the wider society among a number of institutions or organizations playing political roles, for example, lineage groups, age groups, or general meetings. In contrast, modern states usually have a set of clearly differentiated political institutions, for example, an executive, a legislature, a judiciary, armed forces, and police. In comparison with modern NATION STATES, many earlier forms of the state (for example, preindustrial empires), while possessing a differentiated state structure, can be characterized as having a far more fragmentary and contested domination over their territories.

A further feature of modern states is that, whereas most forms of premodern states had only SUBJECTS, modern states have citizens (that is, full members of political communities increasingly enjoying the right to vote, the right to stand for office, freedom of expression, welfare rights; see civil rights, WELFARE STATE). A related distinction is that between state and civil society. This is an important distinction, especially in Marxism, where it provides a vocabulary to distinguish between state and society, or state and individual citizens or groups of citizens.

state capitalism and state monopoly capitalism (Marxism) an interpretation of Soviet society and similar planned or COMMAND ECONOMIES, in which the state elite is seen as acting as a surrogate capitalist class. This class is seen as continuing the historical role of the capitalist class in the accumulation of capital in a situation where the bourgeois class has been overthrown but where the development of the means of production is insufficient as the basis for full transition to socialism. Analogously, these terms may also be used to refer to Western forms of ADVANCED CAPITAL-

ISM, in which monopolistic concentrations of capital and overall state direction of the economy has occurred.

state expenditures the several different kinds of expenditure undertaken by the STATE. On the assumption that the state in capitalist society has two contradictory functions, accumulation and legitimization, O'Connor (1973) and Gough (1979) identify three main categories of expenditure:

(a) *social investment,* "projects and services that increase the productivity of labor";

(b) *social consumption,* "projects and services that lower the reproduction costs of labor";

(c) *social expenses,* projects and services required to maintain social harmony.

It is evident that the load on the state from state expenditures has increased historically, imposing, according to both O'Connor and Gough, "new economic strains on the system" and "simultaneously threatening both capitalist accumulation and political freedoms." It is for this reason that the WELFARE STATE and state expenditures in general have been a source of central social and political conflict in recent decades.

stateless societies various forms of society that lack a clearly identifiable STATE. Two main senses in which societies may be said to be stateless can be noted:

(a) all forms of society that existed prior to formation of the first central states (see PRISTINE OR PRIMAL STATES);

(b) those forms of society that as well as lacking clearly identified machinery of statehood (for example, administrative and military support for the leader) also seem to lack all formalized provision for stable leadership and thus are termed ACEPHALOUS (literally, "headless") societies. These forms of society can achieve coherence, sustain existence, even conduct warfare without clearly differentiated state forms, either because they are small enough to require no differentiated machinery or because they possess a complex segmentary structure.

state socialist societies the centrally directed socialist societies that emerged in the 20th century after revolutions or movements led by political parties adhering to communist or socialist political thought. The societies covered are diverse and include the USSR from 1918 to the present; most Eastern European societies from 1948 until 1989; contemporary People's Republic of China, Cuba, Vietnam, Angola, Mozambique, Ethiopia, North Korea, and Mongolia. Many of these societies are currently experiencing rapid change, so precise characterization and labeling are increasingly difficult.

There is much debate about the character of these societies, which are more generally known as communist, and this term is probably the most neutral, encompassing the variety of such societies and over which there can be most agreement. Some observers claim a more accurate characterization is totalitarianism, since these societies share features with nonsocialist societies without parliamentary democratic practices and institutions such as fascist states. However, this tends to deny any distinguishing role for socialism in the formation and operation of these states.

Those commentators who see the commitment to socialism—principally, abolition or severe curtailment of private productive property—as a differentiating feature of these states have found difficulty in reaching any clear agreement as to their precise nature. Some, following Trotsky, argue that they fall well short of the ideals of a communist society, through their overcentralized and undemocratic political systems, their nationalistic rather than internationalistic policies, the privileges and often personal wealth of their political leaders, and the stagnation of their economies. This has led to various terms, such as *state capitalism, degenerate workers' states,* and *bureaucratic socialism* (see Fig. 26), which deny their claim to being socialist. Others claim that they are forms of society *sui generis* that can be located neither within any Marxism scheme of classification (capitalist, socialist, communist, or transitional between any of these) nor within any existing non-Marxian typology of societies, such as democratic versus totalitarian. Nevertheless, their centralized state systems, their ideological commitment to some variant of communism or socialism, and the curtailments of private productive property all point to some justification of the term "state socialism" or "state socialist societies" as a general term (see Post and Wright, 1989).

Statistical Package for the Social Science (SPSS) a package of statistical computer programs originally written over twenty years ago for the analysis

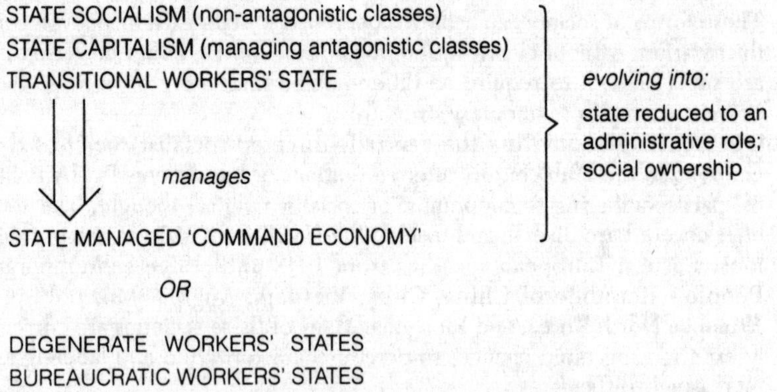

Fig. 26. **State socialist societies.** Official and other Marxian conceptions of socialist societies, which have regarded this form of society as either an evolving or as a degenerative form.

of social science data. The statistical procedures range from simple frequencies to sophisticated multivariate techniques. It is particularly suitable for the analysis of survey data because it has extensive labeling, data modification, and transformation facilities. The package is very flexible and includes procedures for producing tailor-made tables and reports. It is also widely used for analysis of experimental data, time series data, secondary analysis, and database management. The latest mainframe version, SPSS-X, has now been joined by SPSSPC+, which runs on systems compatible with IBM PC/XT or IBM PC/AT microcomputers.

statistics and statistical analysis the assembly and mathematical analysis of numerical data (for example, CENSUS or survey data), which at its simplest involves:

(a) the reporting and summary of data, including graphical representations of data (for example, HISTOGRAMS and pie charts), but in its more sophisticated forms includes

(b) the use of measures of the association between variables (for example, CORRELATION and REGRESSION), and

(c) inferential statistics, in which on the basis of PROBABILITY theory and using random sampling (see RANDOM SAMPLE) permits inferences from a sample to a larger population (see SIGNIFICANCE TESTS). The fundamental idea involved in statistical analysis of this third type is that repeatable phenomena (for example, tossing a coin) can be assumed to conform to an underlying probabilistic model.

Modern statistical analysis has its roots in the work of 18th-century theorists such as Laplace, Poisson, and Gauss, and in the work of early 19th century social statisticians such as QUETELET. However, the modern discipline stems especially from the work of Francis Galton (1822–1911), who formulated the concept of the NORMAL DISTRIBUTION and also popularized the correlation coefficient. Karl Pearson (1859–1936), a student of Galton's, added notions of "goodness of fit" (see CHI SQUARE), and W.S. Gossett (1876–1937) developed NONPARAMETRIC STATISTICS for situations in which ratio or interval levels of measurement (see also CRITERIA AND LEVELS OF MEASUREMENT) cannot be assumed for small samples. Significance tests were added to the armory of techniques by Ronald Fisher (1890–1962).

An important advance in recent decades has been the advent of high-speed and now widely available computer technology, which has removed much of the hard work previously associated with the use of statistics (see STATISTICAL PACKAGE FOR THE SOCIAL SCIENCES (SPSS) and MINITAB). However, while there are many advantages of this development, one disadvantage is that it has sometimes encouraged the use of statistical techniques that are only half understood, thus leading to unwarranted inferences.

While statistical analysis is well established and has become an important adjunct to many disciplines, including most of the social sciences, it has been subjected to a number of criticisms, especially (Selvin, 1958) that the requirements for satisfactory use of significance tests are rarely met in the social sciences. There also exist notable divisions within the discipline of statistics, for example, that between orthodox and Bayesian statistics. Compare MATHEMATICAL SOCIOLOGY.

status 1. any stable position within a social system associated with specific expectations, rights, and duties. Status in this sense is equivalent to ROLE, although it is the latter term that has the wider currency. **2.** the positive or negative honor, prestige, power, etc. attaching to a position or an individual person within a system of SOCIAL STRATIFICATION (often referred to as *social status*). Both conceptions derive from forms of society in which individual social locations were relatively fixed (see ASCRIBED STATUS, MAINE), for example, by religion or by law (see CASTE, ESTATE). In modern societies status positions tend to be more fluid.

status conflict the competition and vying for position and esteem that occur within systems of SOCIAL STRATIFICATION based on STATUS **2.** (see also STATUS GROUP). Status conflicts can be greatest between groups that stand in adjacent positions within a status hierarchy, and are thus direct competitors (see also RELATIVE DEPRIVATION, SOCIAL CLOSURE). This explains why a diminution of distinctions of CLASS and rank, as in some modern societies, may be associated with heightening status tensions and status conflicts, since there is greater scope for competition around subtler distinctions of status (see also STATUS SYMBOL, RIESMAN, GOFFMAN). However, competition and conflict between status groups also exist in preindustrial and traditional societies (see SANSKRITIZATION, CASTE, ESTATE). See also STATUS CONSISTENCY AND INCONSISTENCY.

status consistency and inconsistency the situation of either being ranked consistently across a range of status criteria (*status consistency* or *status congruence*), or being ranked inconsistently (*status inconsistency* or *status incongruence*), for example, blacks or Hispanics in high-status occupations. Sometimes the term *status crystallization* is also used.

Since modern societies usually involve coexistence of parallel hierarchies of CLASS and STATUS (see also CLASS, STATUS AND PARTY; MULTI-DIMENSIONAL ANALYSIS OF SOCIAL STRATIFICATION), Lenski (1966) has suggested that discrepancies in status, especially when acute, are associated with political radicalism. More generally, however, the empirical correlates of status inconsistency have themselves been inconsistent; as one skeptical comment expresses it, in the study of voting behavior "status inconsistency puts greater stress on theorists than voters" (Harrop and Miller, 1987).

status group any group that can be identified in terms of a specific, "positive or negative, social estimation of honor" (WEBER, 1922) within a system of SOCIAL STRATIFICATION. The classical period of relatively clear-cut distinctions between status groups is the era of preindustrial empires. Clear

STATUS hierarchies existed, for example, in India and China, as well as in preindustrial societies for Europe (see also CASTE, ESTATE). However, status groupings and distinctions in status, even when loosely associated with status groups, continue as a significant dimension of social stratification in modern societies (see also CLASS, STATUS AND PARTY; MULTIDIMENSIONAL ANALYSIS OF SOCIAL STRATIFICATION).

status situation the prestige or social honor associated with a particular occupation or position within a community—one of three main dimensions of social stratification identified by Lockwood (1958 and 1966) and Goldthorpe and Lockwood (1968a & b, 1969). Rather than market forces or ownership or nonownership of the means of production alone being decisive in determining a person's overall position within the stratification system, three interrelated dimensions of social stratification are seen as significant: status situation, as well as work situation, and MARKET SITUATION. For example, an Anglican clergyman may enjoy relatively high status within a community, but his income and market situation may be low. See also MULTIDIMENSIONAL ANALYSIS OF SOCIAL STRATIFICATION; CLASS, STATUS AND PARTY; OCCUPATIONAL PRESTIGE; CLASS IMAGERY.

status symbol any commodity or service that is acquired as much or more for the favorable social evaluations it brings from others, and in terms of its enhancement of the acquirer's own self-perceptions. An early journalistic account of status symbols was provided by Packard (1959). A more sociologically sophisticated analysis—although it does not specifically use the term "status symbol"—is BOURDIEU's *Distinction* (1979). For Bourdieu, matters of taste above all involve status claims. Thus the educated may read or go to the theater rather than watch TV. One problem with the concept of status symbol is that analysis of cultural products in terms of their status loadings tends to ignore other dimensions of preference. See also ADVERTISING, CONSUMER CULTURE, POSTMODERNISM AND POSTMODERNITY.

stereotype a set of inaccurate, simplistic generalizations about a group of individuals that enables others to categorize members of the group and treat them routinely according to these expectations. Thus, stereotypes of RACIAL, SOCIAL CLASS, and gender groups are commonly held and lead to perception and treatment of individuals according to unjustified preconceptions. See also PREJUDICE.

stigma any physical or social attribute or sign (for example, physical deformity or a criminal record) that so devalues an actor's social identity as to "disqualify from full social acceptance" (GOFFMAN, 1964). Different implications follow for the stigmatized person according to whether the stigma is visible (the individual is obviously discredited), or hidden (the individual is potentially discreditable). The latter allows a greater number of options to the stigmatized person to manage his or her stigma. But in both cases the actor's problems lie in finding a means of limiting, or even turning to some advantage, the damaging effects of the stigma. In addition to being of interest in its own right, the study of stigmatized identities also throws light on the social construction of normal identities (see DEVIANCE).

stranger any person who is within a group or society but not entirely of that group of society. SIMMEL (Wolff, 1950) suggests three aspects of the social position of the stranger that define it in sociological terms:

(a) the position of the individual on the margin, partly inside and partly outside the group (see also MARGINALITY);

(b) a particular combination of remoteness and proximity (or SOCIAL DISTANCE) between the stranger and group members;

(c) various further implications of the ROLE of the stranger and his or her interactions with the group that make this position of particular sociological interest.

A key feature of the role of the stranger identified by Simmel is the relative detachment and objectivity he or she may bring, for example, in settling disputes. This arises, according to Simmel, because the stranger "imports qualities into the group which do not stem from the group." This explains why the stranger also often meets with surprising openness and confidences. All of this applies, notwithstanding that strangers who arrive in large numbers, with their own cultures and groups, will often be mistrusted and may become persecuted members of the societies they enter. However, even the individual stranger may become mistrusted and be seen as a possible threat to group beliefs, for example, where his or her own vested interest may be involved (see Schermer, 1988).

strategic interaction interaction occurring in situations where one party's gain is the other party's loss, and thus the winning is defined by the losing and *vice versa*. Decision-making in strategic situations may be quite complex, involving not only assessment of the other's knowledge state but also what the other party knows of the first party's knowledge state and likely strategy. GOFFMAN (1969) suggests that strategic interaction is a more commonplace feature of everyday life than is often acknowledged. The concept of social interaction may be effectively described in terms of strategies adopted by parties to the interaction, individual or collective. It avoids the view that interaction is the straightforward outcome of laws or of rules, both of which tend to miss the openness of interaction. It also avoids the view that interaction is entirely a local accomplishment, and that any characterization of it in general terms is an arbitrary closure. If members can adopt and adapt goals and outline paths to those goals without being bound to them, of if others can in turn recognize these and similarly adopt and adapt existing strategies, then the sociologist can do simultaneous justice to choice, creativity and freedom, and also on the other hand to cultural patterning. Some of these patterns are obvious but unrecognized, but may be rendered strikingly explicit, as in the work of Goffman. They may also be formalized, as in the application of the THEORY OF GAMES.

strategic theory (international relations) theoretical analysis of the military and associated political strategies pursued by NATION-STATES in advancing their own interests. Among the social science theories applied in this area have been decision theory and the THEORY OF GAMES.

strategies of independence the ways that individuals find to maintain a measure of functional autonomy within the organizations in which they work, creating social spaces for themselves (GOULDNER, 1959). Gouldner uses the example of strategies of independence borrowed from E.C. Hughes as part of his argument against making too strong assumptions about functional interdependence.

stratificational model of social action and consciousness an interpretation of the human social actor (for example, GIDDENS 1984) that emphasizes the existence of three layers of cognition and motivation:

(a) DISCURSIVE CONSCIOUSNESS, that is, what actors are able to say about social situations, including the conditions of their own action;

(b) practical consciousness, what actors know or believe about social situations, including the conditions of their own interaction, *but are unable to express*, that is, tacit skills or PRACTICAL KNOWLEDGE (compare PRACTICAL REASONING);

(c) the *unconscious*.

The second of these areas of actors' knowledgeability is seen by GIDDENS as neglected in sociological analysis, a neglect that, in Giddens' view, SCHUTZ's SOCIAL PHENOMENOLOGY, and ETHNOMETHODOLOGY have drawn attention to and done much to remedy.

stratified sample a SAMPLE selected by first stratifying the parent population. The procedure involves dividing the population into strata relevant to the study to be undertaken. For example, for a study of voting intention, social class and age may be relevant, and for a study of attitudes toward the benefit system, income level and employment status would be relevant. When the strata have been identified, RANDOM SAMPLES are taken from each. As long as these samples are of sizes proportionate to the size of each stratum within the parent population (proportionate stratification), this method affords improved precision, particularly if a sample is being taken from a relatively large population, since it introduces some controlled restrictions on selection. However, disproportionate stratification may be used if a stratum is too small to yield a sufficiently large sample for analysis if the criterion for selection used in other strata is adopted.

stress a state of tension produced by pressures or conflicting demands with which the person cannot adequately cope. This is therefore subjective in that different people experience the same event differently, and what is experienced as stress by one may not be by another.

Stress, induced by life events, for example, is relevant in a consideration of psychological disorders, sociological studies of social phenomena (for example, SUICIDE), and in physical illness (for example, heart disease). The holistic approach of PERSON-CENTERED COUNSELING and much of alternative medicine aims to treat the person within the context of the life experience and current problems. To use the mechanical analogy, the aim would be to strengthen the person in order to enable him or her to resist damage from life's pressures.

structural anthropology the perspective that stresses the priority of cognitive structures in ordering experience. It is primarily associated with LÉVI-STRAUSS, who took his lead from the linguist F. de SAUSSURE. Studies of KINSHIP and SYMBOLISM by Lévi-Strauss were attempts to demonstrate that a simple set of logical principles underlay sociocultural systems. Myths, for example, could be understood as linguistic transformations of essentially binary oppositions, such as male-female, raw-cooked, and so on, which are constitutive of human thought. Structural anthropology treats cultural phenomena as if they were a language and then attempts to discover the grammar, or what Chomsky has called the "deep structure." While "high structuralism" has been much criticized for its formalism, its methods have found general application in many areas of anthropology (E. Leach), sociology (ALTHUSSER, FOUCAULT), literary criticism, and SEMIOLOGY.

structural-functionalism 1. theoretical approaches in which societies are conceptualized as SOCIAL SYSTEMS, and particular features of SOCIAL STRUCTURES are explained in terms of their contribution to the maintenance of these systems, for example, religious ritual explained in terms of the contribution it makes to social integration. As such, structural-functionalism can be seen as an alternative general term for FUNCTIONALISM. See also FUNCTION, FUNCTIONAL(IST) EXPLANATION. **2.** the particular form of functional analysis associated with Talcott PARSONS, often distinguished from functionalism in general, as structural-functionalism. Sometimes the work of the modern functionalist school in SOCIAL ANTHROPOLOGY, including RADCLIFFE-BROWN and MALINOWSKI, is also referred to by this term.

structuralism 1. any sociological analysis in terms of SOCIAL STRUCTURE. **2.** (more especially) any form of analysis in which structures take priority (ontologically, methodologically, etc.) over human actors. **3.** (in linguistics, for example, SAUSSURE and Chomsky), an approach that concentrates analysis on the structural features of LANGUAGE(s); especially the study of *synchronic* relations between linguistic elements rather than, as previously in linguistics, engaging in *diachronic,* historical, or comparative study (see SYNCHRONIC AND DIACHRONIC). **4.** those methodological and theoretical approaches to cultural and sociological analysis based on the assumption that societies can be analyzed, analogously with language and linguistics (see sense **3.**), as "signifying systems." In these approaches, the emphasis is on the analysis of unobservable but detectable structural relations between conceptual elements in social life (for example, relations of opposition and contrast, or hierarchy). These conceptual elements are seen as the ultimate object of study in social science and the structural determinants of social reality. The view is that essentially the same methods of analysis apply, whether the phenomenon in question be, for example, a text or a society. Structuralism in sociological analysis is seen in the work of the anthropologist Claude LÉVI-STRAUSS, the cultural semiologist Roland BARTHES, and the psychoanalytic theorist Jacques LACAN. In the work of Lévi-Strauss, for example, social myths and, by extension, other social forms are presented as arising from the tendency of the human mind to think in terms of binary opposites (for example, the raw and the cooked, or the marriageable and the unmarriageable). **5.** any doctrine stating that social analysis should be concerned with exploring beneath surface appearances in order to reach the deeper, ultimately more real, structures seen as determining social relations. Symptomatic of this general view is Marx's suggestion that "if essence and appearance coincided there would be no need for science." Although far from always being dependent on linguistic analogies, in recent years structuralism in this sense has gained a new impetus in borrowing some concepts from structuralism sense **4.** (for example, see ALTHUSSERIAN MARXISM). For Lacan, structuralism succeeds by decentering the previously central place of the individual in much social analysis. Likewise, for Foucault, individuals are no longer to be seen as the subjects of history.

Critics of all types of structuralism in sociology argue that sociology must continue to take as central the human actor's involvement in the construction and reconstruction of meaning and the social world: structuralism is accused of an unjustified REIFICATION in its account of social reality. Among other objections to structuralism are a rejection of its ahistorical approach and the speculative and allegedly untestable nature of much of its theorizing.

A halfway position between theories of structure and theories of individual agency has often been attempted. BERGER and Pullberg (1966), for example, propose a dialectical theory of "the social construction of reality," in which "social structure is not characterizable as a thing able to stand on its own, apart from human activity that produced it," but, once created, "is encountered by the individual (both) as an alien facticity (and) … a coercive instrumentality." More recently, GIDDENS has proposed a notion of DUALITY OF STRUCTURE involving both structure and individual agency. For Giddens, to inquire into the "structuration" of social practices "is to seek to explain how it comes about that structures are constituted through actions, and, reciprocally, how action is constituted structurally" (see also STRUCTURATION THEORY).

The debate over agency and structure in sociology can be seen as fundamental to the discipline and unlikely ever to be resolved. The debate revolves around the issue of whether there are underlying causes and UNANTICIPATED CONSEQUENCES (OF SOCIAL ACTION), and if so, how sociologists are able to investigate these. Whatever the reservations about structuralism, it is clear that conceptions of structuralism in all the above senses must be acknowledged as raising central questions in sociological analysis that have been valuable in combatting a one-sided individualism. Structuralism in senses **3.**, **4.**, and **5.** enjoyed a period as a vogue perspective in the 1960s and 1970s, justifiably so because it gave a new impetus to theoretical sociology in a number of areas (for example, see SEMIOTICS). Equally, however, structuralism is often seen as itself unjustifiably one-sided (see STRUCTURE AND AGENCY), even by some of its own previous leading proponents (see POSTSTRUCTURALISM).

structuration "the structuring of social relations across time and space" (Giddens, 1984) as the result of the operation of both preexisting structures and individual agency, but without these structures or agency ever possessing an entirely separate existence. See DUALITY OF STRUCTURE, STRUCTURATION THEORY, STRUCTURE AND AGENCY.

structuration theory the approach to sociological theory adopted by Anthony GIDDENS, in which social relations are seen as structured in time and space as the outcome of the operation of a DUALITY OF STRUCTURE. In this approach the intention is that neither agency nor structure is accorded primacy in sociological explanations. However, opinion is divided as to how far Giddens has been successful in achieving his objective or whether his own work continues to exhibit a bias toward individual agency (see Bryant and Jary, 1990). See STRUCTURE AND AGENCY.

structure 1. any arrangement of elements into a definite pattern, for example, any institutionalized social arrangements (ROLES, ORGANIZATIONS, etc.) for example, the "educational" or "occupational structure" (see also SOCIAL STRUCTURE, STRUCTURAL-FUNCTIONALISM). **2.** the rules (or deep structure) underlying and responsible for the production of a surface structure (especially structures analogous to grammar (see also LÉVI-STRAUSS). For GIDDENS (1984), for example, structure in this latter sense refers to "rules and resources, implicated in the reproduction of social systems" (see also STRUCTURATION, STRUCTURATION THEORY). The distinction (senses **1.** and **2.**) drawn between surface and deep structures is also an important one in STRUCTURALISM senses **3.** and **5.**

Major criticisms are made by theorists of the SYMBOLIC INTERACTION, SOCIAL PHENOMENOLOGY and HERMENEUTIC traditions, who argue that sociology must make central human actors' involvement in the creation and recreation of the social world through symbolic meaning as central. People, not structures, can be seen as creating social order. If structures are treated as rules, then rules also are created by people.

A compromise between theories of structure and theories of meaning has often been attempted by social theorists. In the 1960s, P.L. Berger and associates proposed a dialectical theory of the "social construction of reality," in which "social structure is not characterizable as a thing able to stand on its own, apart from the human activity that produced it" but, once created, "is encountered by the individual (both) as an alien facticity (and) ... as a coercive instrumentality" (Berger and Pullberg, 1966). A humanly constructed reality comes to take on the appearance of having been constructed by some external, nonhuman, force. More recently, Giddens has proposed a theory of STRUCTURATION in which structures are treated as relatively enduring patterns of social action. It is suggested that there is a "duality of structure," both constraining and enabling: "Structures can always in principle be examined in terms of their *structuration* as a series of reproduced practices. To enquire into the structuration of social practices is to seek to explain how it comes about that structures are constituted through action, and reciprocally how action is constituted structurally" (GIDDENS, 1976b). It is doubtful if such formulations can overcome the criticisms of either interpretive sociologies of structuralism, or vice versa. The debate over agency and structure in sociology might be seen as an essential part of the discipline. It boils down to the issue of whether there are UNINTENDED CONSEQUENCES of action and, if so, how sociologists are able to investigate them. It might be noted, however, that some concept of "social structure," as with "society," has to be entailed for a theory to be properly called sociological. See also STRUCTURE AND AGENCY.

structure and agency the two main determinants of social outcomes that are recognized in sociology, but whose relative importance is much debated as a central issue in sociological theory. Three main general positions can be identified:

(a) doctrines (for example, STRUCTURALISM, some forms of FUNCTIONALISM, ALTHUSSERIAN MARXISM) stressing that social life is largely determined by social structure, and that individual agency can be explained mostly as the outcome of structure;

(b) doctrines (for example, METHODOLOGICAL INDIVIDUALISM, SOCIAL PHENOMENONOLOGY, ETHNOMETHODOLOGY) that reverse the emphasis, stressing instead the capacity of individuals—individual agents—to construct and reconstruct their worlds and the necessity of explanations in the actors' terms;

(c) approaches that, variously, emphasize the complementary of the two processes, that is, structural influences on human action and individual agency capable of changing social structure.

Despite many suggestions to the contrary (and notwithstanding that many difficulties and disagreements exist in defining STRUCTURE), most forms of sociological theory can be located in category (c), as recognizing the importance of both structural determinacy and individual agency. Crucial issues arise, however, in conceptualizing the relationship between the two, and it is here that a number of interesting formulations have emerged in recent years, especially those of BERGER and Pullberg (1966), Bhaskar (1979), and GIDDENS (1984) (see also BOURDIEU).

For Berger and Luckman the relation between structure and agency is one in which society forms the individuals who create society in a continuous dialectic. For Bhaskar, a "relational" and a "transformational" view of the individual and society requires a stronger emphasis: "Society is both the ever-present *condition* and the continually reproduced *outcome* of human agency." Finally, Giddens, in perhaps the most sophisticated attempt to break free of the conception of a dualism of structure and agency, argues for a conception of DUALITY OF STRUCTURE in that: (a) "structure is both the medium and the outcome of the conduct it recursively organizes"; (b) "structure" is defined as "rules and resources," which do not exist outside of the actions but continuously impact on its production and reproduction; and (c) analogies with physical structures, of the sort common in functionalism, are regarded as wholly illegitimate. In Giddens' formulation structure must also be seen as both enabling and constraining.

Reformulations of relations between structure and agency have not ended debate about the appropriate conceptualization of relations between the two, or indeed about the prior, or interrelated, question of how "agency" and "structure" should be defined in the first place. Thus, Layder (1981), for example, regards Giddens' conception of structure as depriving this concept of *any* "autonomous properties or pre-given facticity," and commentators have detected in Giddens' formulation a persistent bias toward agency. Moreover, whatever sophistication general formulations of the structure-agency relations may achieve, disputes are likely to persist in particular application of such notions to concrete historical cases. See also STRUCTURATION THEORY, AUTONOMOUS MAN AND PLASTIC MAN, BOURDIEU.

structured coding in QUESTIONNAIRE design, analysis is assisted by the questions being structured, thus constraining response. Structured questions can be either *open-ended* or *closed*. For closed questions, respondents are presented with a list of options and asked to indicate their answers by ticking a box or circling a number. For open-ended questions, respondents are asked to write down their replies, which are then coded according to a precoded schema. The choice between which of these two types of question to use depends generally on the number of possible answers to a question. Where it is less than 10, closed questions are generally preferred.

When using structured questions, several important points must be borne in mind. First, care must be taken that the questions asked refer to only one dimension. For example, religion has at least two distinct dimensions, the strength of each person's religious conviction and the person's nominal religion, the one into which the person was initiated. Secondly, care should be taken to indicate that the answers are mutually exclusive.

Another problem is the purely practical one of including every possible reply in the coding schedule. The use of catchall ("other") categories should be avoided as far as possible at the coding stage, since such a category may contain many different replies.

To assign numerical codes to the data, the researcher should make use where possible of coding schemas that have been professionally designed by experts in the field of study. Not only does this procedure simplify the researcher's task, but it also leads to the accumulation of data that are readily comparable. For example, in undertaking occupational research, the researcher is generally advised to make use of the classification devised for analysis of the appropriate CENSUS material.

Generally, however, researchers are forced to develop their coding schemas. This involves first taking account of the level of measurement (see CRITERIA AND LEVELS OF MEASUREMENT) that is being employed— nominal, ordinal, fixed-interval, ratio-interval. Where interval variables are being employed researchers are advised not to precode data into a series of numerical bands. This means, for example, that if a research worker is interested in age or income, these details should be specifically asked for, rather than representing them with a series of precoded categories. A pre-coded question might result in clustering within one band. Where a variable has ordinal properties, it is generally best to code it as such, as this will increase the number of statistical tests that are acceptable to use. When coding nominal data, attention should be given to whether it is possible to group the data into a more convenient structure at a later stage of the research program.

subculture any system of beliefs, values, and norms shared and actively participated in by an appreciable minority of people within a particular culture. The relationship of the subculture to the so-called dominant culture has been identified as one of subordination and relative powerlessness. Power relations are therefore an important dimension of any sociological consideration of subculture.

Subcultures have been examined in terms of ETHNICITY, CLASS, DEVIANCE, and YOUTH CULTURE. R. MERTON constructed a typology of possible responses to a disjunction between means and goals. These responses might give rise to a number of different subcultures. S. Cohen (1971) has noted the emergence of a succession of youth subcultures in the post-World War II era, for example, in Britain, so-called Teds, Mods, Rockers, and Punks. It has been suggested that such subcultures serve as magical solutions to the problems created for young working-class people in contemporary Western societies (Brake 1980). They serve to provide a means of establishing both individual and group identity, and they are discernible largely through stylistic expression, particularly language, demeanor, music, dress, and dance.

Subcultures, like culture generally, are the result of collective creativity and are therefore subject to historical change and transformation. Feminist theorists such as McRobbie and Garber (1976) have noted that gender is rarely considered in the study of subcultures. They have raised important questions concerning the relationship of young women to youth subcul-

tures. See also CULTURAL STUDIES, CULTURAL CAPITAL, CULTURAL DEPRIVA-
TION, CULTURAL LAG, CULTURAL (AND LINGUISTIC) RELATIVISM.

subject and object (philosophy) twin concepts, *subject* (person, mind, theorist, etc.) and *object* (external world), which have been central in much
philosophical and also sociological discussion, especially EPISTEMOLOGY.
The central issues have been: how the subject can come to know the
object, and how each is constituted (ONTOLOGY). Thus, an empiricist (see
EMPIRICISM) may claim that the world is made up of things, and that the
mind consists of ideas, and that the latter picture or represent the former.
Alternatively in IDEALISM, ideas may be claimed to structure our perception of objects.

Recent movements in philosophy, (for example, POSTSTRUCTURALISM,
POSTEMPIRICISM) have sought to break away from traditional conceptions of
subject and object (see DECONSTRUCTION, DECENTERED SELF), and to move
away from rigid conceptions of epistemology or ontology. In some forms,
such a movement away from traditional conceptions of the foundations of
knowledge has been associated with RELATIVISM (see also INCOMMENSURA-
BILITY), but another view is that it can be presented as a move beyond
objectivism *or* relativism (see FEYERABEND).

subjective and objective class a person's perception of his or her own
class position, that is, *subjective class* (or *class identity*), in contradistinction to that assessed in terms of either observable, or theoretically important, external elements of the person's CLASS position, that is *objective
class*. No assumption need be made that insofar as the former differs from
the latter, the subjective position is false, although this assumption may
sometimes be made.

Discrepancies between subjective and objective class have often been
regarded as significant in research into class and voting, for example, proposed explanations of class-deviant patterns of working-class voting behavior
in terms of subjective middle-class identity (see also EMBOURGEOISEMENT
THESIS, WORKING-CLASS CONSERVATISM). Butler and Stokes (1969) used the
following question to elicit subjective social class: "There's quite a bit of talk
these days about different social classes. Most people say that they belong
to either the middle class or the working class. Do you ever think of yorself
as being in one of these classes?" However, fewer than 50 per cent of
respondents volunteer a "subjective class" without further prompting.
RUNCIMAN (1966) and GOLDTHORPE et al. (1989), among others, have
exposed the equivocal meanings associated with, for example, subjective
middle-class identity, many of them incompatible with any simple hypothesis of EMBOURGEOISEMENT.

subjectivity the perspective of the person (subject); lack of objectivity. The
range of attitudes toward this term indicates its essentially contentious
nature. It is often used pejoratively within positivist sociology to derogate
biased observation or methodology. At the other extreme, it is celebrated

by HERMENEUTICS as the only possible way to locate any attempts to theorize about the social. Any answer to the question of whether subjectivity is inescapable or undesirable relies on ontological and epistemological assumptions about the nature of human beings' relationship to the concrete world. In practice the two terms are used as if they occupied ends of a continuum, greater or lesser degrees of subjectivity being claimed by various authors. Various attempts have been made to illustrate the way in which subjectivities are objectively constructed and vice versa (see PARSONS, ALTHUSSER, GIDDENS, for example), but the dichotomy stubbornly has refused to evaporate.

suboptimality (THEORY OF GAMES) any situation in which an "optimal"—or best overall—outcome (for example, income or benefit) from the point of view of a plurality of consumers and producers cannot be determined.

substantive rationality see FORMAL AND SUBSTANTIVE RATIONALITY.

subsystems model (of action systems and social systems) the fourfold set of functional problems identified by PARSONS (1953), and deriving from Bales (1950), in which any system of action and all social systems and societies are seen as required to cope with the following (see Fig. 27).

(a) the problem of adapting to the external environment of the system ("*adaptation*" in Parson's schema, and in concrete terms "the economy");

(b) the problem of achieving system goals ("*goal attainment*"—in concrete terms, the polity or government);

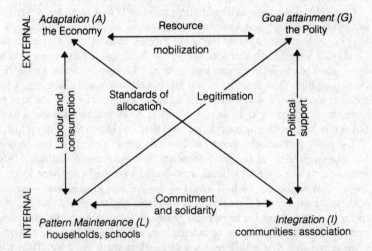

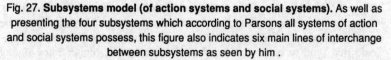

Fig. 27. **Subsystems model (of action systems and social systems).** As well as presenting the four subsystems which according to Parsons all systems of action and social systems possess, this figure also indicates six main lines of interchange between subsystems as seen by him .

(c) the problem of integrating the system (*"integration"*—in concrete terms, communities, associations, and organizations);

(d) the problem of maintaining commitment to values (*"pattern maintenance"*—in concrete terms, the family, households, and schools).

The working-out (often in intricate detail) of the relations between these analytical divisions formed a major part of the "systems theoretic" phase in Parson's FUNCTIONALISM. See also FUNCTIONAL PREREQUISITES, SYSTEM, SYSTEMS THEORY, STRUCTURAL FUNCTIONALISM, SOCIAL SYSTEM.

suicide "all cases of death resulting directly or indirectly from a positive or negative act of the victim himself, that he knows will produce this result" (DURKHEIM, 1897). ATTEMPTED SUICIDE AND PARASUICIDE are different phenomena, requiring separate inquiry. Persons who have attempted suicide or feigned suicide cannot necessarily be studied as a guide to the behavior of successful suicides.

DURKHEIM's analysis of suicide has been highly influential within sociology. His argument was that rates of suicide are related to the type and level of SOCIAL INTEGRATION within a society. Thus, an explanation of these different rates required a distinctively sociological explanation. Using available published statistics, Durkheim first eliminated various environmental and psychological variables previously proposed as explaining suicide, before proposing that four distinctive types of suicide can be identified: EGOISTIC SUICIDE, ALTRUISTIC SUICIDE, ANOMIC SUICIDE, and FATALISTIC SUICIDE, each corresponding to a particular condition of society.

One central problem in Durkheim's account is that OFFICIAL STATISTICS undoubtedly distort and understate the overall incidence of suicide. It is also likely they do so more for some groups than others. For example, Durkheim found Catholics less likely than Protestants to commit suicide, but Catholics may have greater reason to conceal suicide. Some sociologists (for example, J. Douglas, *The Social Meaning of Suicide,* 1976) suggest that social research on suicide must first establish empirically how suicides are designated, for example, by police, coroners, et al. before such social statistics can be used with any confidence, and that Durkheim failed to do this.

Despite reservations about Durkheim's work, aspects of his account have been confirmed by other theorists. For example, Sainsbury (1955) found that suicide rates in London boroughs were highest where levels of social disorganization, such as levels of divorce and illegitimacy, were also highest. Sainsbury and Baraclough (1968) have also suggested that the rank order of suicide rates for immigrant groups to the United States correlated closely with the rank order of suicide rates for their countries of origin, despite the fact that a different set of labelers were involved. Thus they suggest that, though official suicide statistics must be used with caution, they may be less unreliable than sometimes suggested. This view might be seen as gaining further support from regularities in the incidence of suicide that tend to recur across cultures, for example, higher rates among men than women, among the widowed and the divorced, among the unmarried and the childless, among the old compared with the young. Most of these findings are consistent with what Durkheim found.

Sumner, William (1840–1910) early US sociologist, As an evolutionary theorist, influenced particularly by Herbert SPENCER, Sumner produced work that today is relatively little discussed. However, his best-known work, *Folkways* (1906), bequeathed a number of terms that have retained currency. See MORES, FOLKWAYS, ETHNOCENTRICISM, SOCIAL DARWINISM.

superego one of the three elements of the personality in FREUD's theory. The superego is the part of the personality that operates as the conscience, aiming for perfection, and controlling the function of the EGO by placing moral constraints on it.

Like the ego, the superego is said by Freud to develop from the ID in the first few years of life. He proposed that it was formed by the child internalizing the parent's perceived standards and indirectly, therefore, society's standards. This came about through identification with the same sex parent as resolution of the Oedipus complex. Freud's theory thus explained the development of a conscience in boys much better than in girls, and he has been much criticized for the implied inferiority of women as a result. Feminist theorists such as Juliet Mitchell (1974) have explored this aspect of his theory.

superorganic (of human *social evolution*) superimposed on and surpassing merely organic evolution. The term was introduced by Herbert SPENCER, and his choice of this term reflects his view that evolution must be viewed as a transformation that has taken place in three realms: the inorganic, organic, and superorganic. For Spencer, the superorganic is not a feature only of human evolution; it applies also to some social insects as well as many animals. But superorganic evolution is a central aspect particularly in human evolution.

Use of the term "superorganic" (rather than the terms "cultural" or CULTURE) reflects a commitment by Spencer that human social development can only be understood in evolutionary terms, in that, while different from biological evolution, human social evolution retains a basic continuity with biological evolution.

This leaves open the question of *how different* is social evolution. While for Spencer there were definite continuities between the three types of evolution—inorganic, organic, superorganic—other sociologists have not always agreed and have tended instead to emphasize a sharp break between human culture and all previous forms of evolution. See also EVOLUTIONARY SOCIOLOGY, SOCIOCULTURAL EVOLUTION.

surveillance the monitoring, and the associated direct or indirect forms of supervision and superintendence by the modern STATE, of the activities of its citizens. The capacity for surveillance possessed by modern NATION-STATES has increased compared with those available to earlier forms of governments, as the result of spectacular improvements in techniques for collection and storage of information and equally striking improvements in transport and communications.

For FOUCAULT, in *Discipline and Punish* (1975), the "disciplinary power" of modern societies is an all-pervasive feature of these societies and a predominant feature of administrative power within them. Remedial and CARCERAL ORGANIZATIONS, which remove human liberty, are no more than extreme forms of a generalized tendency to heightened surveillance within these societies.

Foucault's emphasis is disputed by many. Our heightened awareness of, and concern about, situations in which some individuals are subject to loss of liberty reflects the new importance of a concern for liberty within modern societies and the many areas of life in which liberties have increased. Nonetheless, few dispute that, for good and for ill, surveillance and control are an important characteristic of modern societies and the modern state. Compare ABSOLUTISM.

survey method a social science research technique using QUESTIONNAIRES and their analysis using various QUANTITATIVE and statistical techniques (see also SOCIAL SURVEY). In sociology the survey method is used for two main reasons: (a) to describe a population and examine its principal characteristics, for example, age, sex occupation, and attitudes; and (b) to test HYPOTHESES and examine the relationship between VARIABLES.

The main problems with the survey method include:

(a) the technique is nonexperimental, that is, the researcher cannot usually control the conditions under which the research is conducted;

(b) researchers have to rely on what respondents tell them, and they are rarely able to verify their findings with direct observations;

(c) the technique is atomistic, that is, it examines individuals rather than entire communities;

(d) it cannot be used to study the dead and past society.

Nevertheless, the survey method does have much to recommend it. It provides a cheap and relatively easy way to obtain a considerable amount of simply quantified data, which can be used to test and verify sociological theory and identify further areas of research.

symbol 1. a sign in which the connection between the meaning and the sign is conventional rather than natural. **2.** an indirect representation of an underlying meaning, syndrome, etc. as, for example, in religious symbolism and RITUAL, or PSYCHOANALYSIS (see also LÉVI-STRAUSS).

Apart from the utterly central role of LANGUAGE in social life, symbolic communication occurs in a variety of further ways (see SEMIOLOGY (AND SEMIOTICS), BODY LANGUAGE).

symbolic interactionism a theoretical approach in United States sociology that seeks to explain action and interaction as the outcome of the meanings actors attach to things and to social action.

For symbolic interactionists, meanings "do not reside in the object" but emerge from social processes. Emphasis is placed on the active, interpretive, and constructive capacities or competence possessed by human actors, as against the determining influence of social structures suggested by theoretical approaches such as FUNCTIONALISM.

The term was coined in 1937 by H. BLUMER, who summarizes the main principles of the approach in terms of three propositions (Blumer, 1969):

(a) "human beings act towards things on the basis of the meanings that things have for them";

(b) these meanings "arise out of social interaction";

(c) social action results from a "fitting together of individual lines of action."

Theorists whose work stands predominantly within this tradition include George Herbert MEAD, Charles COOLEY, and Howard S. BECKER. An important sociologist whose work stands close to the symbolic interactionist tradition is Erving GOFFMAN.

Symbolic interactionism is sometimes seen as a sociologically oriented SOCIAL PSYCHOLOGY. Indeed, it has been described as the first properly social social psychology of any kind. Thus, symbolic interactionism stands opposed to approaches in social psychology such as BEHAVIORISM or ETHOLOGY. As Cooley put it, "Society is not a chicken yard." Human action is seen as distinguished from animal behavior above all by language and by the huge importance of symbolic communication of various kinds.

As well as being the main alternative theoretical approach to functionalism within modern American sociology, symbolic interactionism also provides the main alternative approach in social research to conventional SOCIAL SURVEY using fixed choice QUESTIONNAIRES and standardized VARIABLES. In place of these approaches, its preferred methods include PARTICIPANT OBSERVATION of actors in natural settings and intensive INTERVIEWS.

Although rejecting approaches in psychology and sociology that seek deterministic universal laws or discovery of overarching structural-functional regularities, symbolic interactionists see a place for generalizations within sociology. Thus, BECKER (1953) in his famous study of marijuana use for pleasure claims that his "final generalization is a statement of the sequences of changes in attitude that occurred in every case ... and may be considered as an explanation of all cases." Rather than a root-and-branch objection to generalization in sociology, symbolic interactionism calls for these to be appropriate to the particular subject matter of sociology (see ANALYTICAL INDUCTION, GROUNDED THEORY, DRUG-TAKING FOR PLEASURE).

A further feature of the approach is that it has often adopted a more socially radical posture than either functionalist or conventional social survey research, for example, a "reversal of the usual hierarchies of credibility" by exploring the perspective of "the underdog" (BECKER, 1963).

The main criticism of symbolic interactionism is that in focusing exclusively on microsocial processes and subinstitutional phenomena, it understates the importance of macroscopic structures and historical factors, especially economic forces and institutionalized political power. Thus, rather than exclusive perspectives, sociological focuses on structure and action are seen as complementary perspectives by many theorists, for example, GIDDENS (see also DUALITY OF STRUCTURE, STRUCTURATION THEORY).

A further criticism, that symbolic interactionism fails to explore human creative competence in sufficient depth, is more internal to the interpretive and symbolic interactionist tradition (see SOCIAL PHENOMENOLOGY). A new sociological paradigm, ETHNOMETHODOLOGY, resulted from this criticism.

symmetrical family (according to Young and Wilmott, 1973) the emerging form of FAMILY in industrial societies, distinguished by a sharing of domestic duties and a tendency for both husbands and wives to be in paid employment.

symptom iceberg the submerged mountain of medically serious, personally troubling, painful, or even life-threatening conditions that are never referred for professional help. It has been shown that people who show severe symptoms and physical discomfort may nevertheless describe themselves as in good health, and when they describe themselves as in poor health, it does not follow that they act in the way assumed by the BIOMECHANICAL (OR BIOMEDICAL) MODEL OF ILLNESS and seek medical treatment. Definitions of illness and health are framed by the values of social groups, as are the strategies deemed appropriate once a problem has been identified. The decision to go to a doctor for treatment depends to a large degree on the extent to which the troubling condition interferes with normal living patterns and social relationships. Illness behavior and the acceptance of the SICK ROLE are part of a complex of self-referral patterns; systems of lay, folk, and professional healing; and access to and distribution of health services. Even when a problem has been defined as suitable for medical referral, studies show that people may still not visit a doctor because they do not want to trouble the doctor, they are discouraged by the waiting room or appointments system or receptionist, they fear that the doctor will adopt a judgmental attitude, or they hope the problem will go away.

synchrony and **diachrony 1.** (linguistics) the distinction between the study of language as an existing system of relationships and without reference to the past (*synchrony*) and the study of the changes in language over time (*diachrony*). See also SAUSSURE. **2.** (STRUCTURALISM) the distinction, deriving from the above, between an analysis and explanation of any feature of social life carried out with reference to existing structural features of a society or social system without reference to history (*synchrony*), and historical analysis that focuses on change (*diachrony*). **3.** (similarly, but in sociology more generally) the distinction between accounts of social order and accounts of social change. For example, in Harré's account of social evolutionary processes in *Social Being* (1979), he distinguishes between "synchronic replicators" and "diachronic selectors."

In structuralism the distinction has often been associated with the downgrading of the significance of historical explanations, an associated downgrading of the role of the SUBJECT and human agency, and the elevation of structural explanations to supreme status. However, there is no inherent reason why structural explanations and historical explanations should not be combined, or structural explanations combined with explanations in terms of the agency of individual human subjects (see STRUCTURE AND AGENCY, DUALITY OF STRUCTURE, STRUCTURATION THEORY). This is more easily said than done, with some sociologists, whether for convenience or for reasons of principle, preferring to concentrate on one or the other (see also EPOCHE).

syncretism the combination of elements from different religious or different cultural traditions. Syncretism in religious beliefs and practices has been especially associated with contexts, for example, colonialism, in which a major religion is brought into contact with local religions, but it can also be seen as a general feature of the transformation of religions or cultures. See also CULT, CARGO CULT.

systact a group or category of persons in specified ROLES, where these persons have, by virtue of these roles, "a distinguishable and more than transiently similar location, and, on that account, a common interest" (RUNCIMAN, 1989). The term has been proposed by Runciman with the aim of making it "easier to report and compare the institutions of different societies without having to be precommitted to a view on such vexed and theoretical questions," such as the difference between class and rank societies, ruling class and governing elite.

system 1. (in a loose general sense) any area of organized social provision, for example, the educational system or the transport system. **2.** any set or group of interrelated elements or parts where a change in one part would affect some or all of the other parts, for example, the solar system. **3.** any set or group of elements or parts (for example, an organism or a machine) organized for a definite purpose and in relation to an external environment. Such systems may be natural or man-made, and may be taken to include SOCIAL SYSTEMS. Hence, a SOCIETY or a social ORGANIZATION may be deemed a system in this sense.

A system such as the solar system, which is little changed by its external environment, is referred to as a *closed system;* those, such as organisms or societies, which sustain themselves in response to changes in their environment are referred to as *open systems* (see also HOMEOSTASIS).

Although controversial, the concept in sense **3.** has been important in social theory, which has often treated social relations, groups, or societies as a set of interrelated parts that FUNCTION so as to maintain their boundaries with their wider environment. See also FUNCTIONALISM, PARSONS, FUNCTIONALIST EXPLANATION, ORGANIC ANALOGY, TELEOLOGY, SYSTEMS THEORY, CYBERNETICS.

systematic sample see RANDOM SAMPLE.

system integration see SOCIAL INTEGRATION AND SYSTEM INTEGRATION.

systems approach see POLITICAL SYSTEM.

systems theory approaches to the study of SYSTEMS (especially SYSTEMS sense **3.**), that emphasize the general properties of goal-seeking systems. Thus, the term *general systems theory* is also used to refer to this approach (see also CYBERNETICS). These approaches were in vogue especially in the 1950s and 1960s, and in sociology were particularly associated with the work of Talcott PARSONS and with related theorists in POLITICAL SCIENCE.

The view of general systems theorists is that the general concept of a system can be applied to naturally occurring systems of many types, including SOCIAL SYSTEMS as well as biological and mechanical systems. The basic model is of mechanical systems, especially servomechanisms, and of biological systems, which display such features as *negative feedback,* in which information about the current state of the system feeds back to influence adjustment toward HOMEOSTASIS, correcting deviations from its basic goals.

The concept can be wider than this, however. It also incorporates ideas of additional effects spreading through a system, of *entropy* and *negantropy. Entropy* describes the natural state of a closed system in that it tends to use up its energy and run down (even if over a very long period). However, social systems are not closed. They can import energy, and they have a transaction with the external environment and so can avoid entropy. Such open systems can survive to attain new steady states, adapting to changing conditions, achieving *negantropy.* Thus, a crucial feature of general systems theory as applied to social systems is exchange with an environment and ADAPTATION.

In sociology specifically, influenced by the systems thinking of Vilfredo PARETO, Parsons in particular worked with a number of theorists drawn from the physical as well as the social sciences, including L. Henderson. It is on this basis that Parsons produced a model of the "social system" and of "action systems" in general (see SUBSYSTEMS MODEL OF ACTION SYSTEMS AND SOCIAL SYSTEMS), which constituted the core of his STRUCTURAL-FUNCTIONALISM. The further objective was to integrate the study of different social sciences (ANTHROPOLOGY, PSYCHOLOGY, POLITICAL SCIENCE, economics) under the umbrella of general systems theory.

Although hugely influential at the time, the attempt of Parsons and the many theorists associated with his work to found a new general theory of action systems and social systems is now judged a relative failure. The approach has been accused of making conservative assumptions about the integration of social systems (see GOULDNER, LOCKWOOD), of too high levels of abstraction, of propositions at times verging on tautology (see Black, 1961, MILLS, 1956), and a relative neglect of the independent influence of individual actors' agency, reflexivity, etc. (compare SYMBOLIC INTERACTION-ISM, SOCIAL PHENOMENOLOGY, ETHNOMETHODOLOGY).

For all this, general systems theory, and systems thinking in related forms, remains an important influence in sociology and within the social sciences generally (for example, see SOCIOTECHNICAL SYSTEMS APPROACH). Parsons' general approach has also been taken up recently by radical theorists such as C. Offe and Jurgen HABERMAS. For example, in the latter's analysis of the tendency to LEGITIMATION CRISIS in advanced capitalist societies, a model in which the four main tendencies examined correspond to the four subsystems in Parsons' earlier model.

Finally, general systems models remain of central importance in analysis of ecosystems, and of relations between social systems and the physical environment.

Szasz, Thomas Stephen (1920–), American psychiatrist, best known for his influence on the ANTIPSYCHIATRY movement through *The Myth of Mental Illness* (1961). His name is often associated with that of LAING, since both criticized the diagnosis and treatment of schizophrenia (see PSY-CHOSIS) in the 1950s and 1960s. He was most critical of the role of psychiatrists in labeling as insane people who do not conform to society's norms, and using their power to have them locked up. This meant that psychiatrists were primarily agents of social control, while patients were having their human freedoms denied.

T

taboo or **tabu** any ritual prohibition of certain activities. The term originally comes from Captain Cook's description of Polynesian custom. It may involve avoidance of certain people, places, objects, or actions, and the universal incest taboo is a much cited example of the latter. Much work on taboos has been carried out from within anthropology in an attempt to explain why, for instance, different foods are avoided within various cultures. Functionalists prefer explanations of taboo and TOTEMISM in terms of group solidarity, while structuralists such as M. DOUGLAS in *Purity and Danger* (1966) have focused on taboos as a problem in classifying ambiguity.

tacit knowledge any knowledge that the SOCIAL ACTOR has but may not be able to articulate, which enables him or her to perform competently within a general or specific social context.

Tarde, Gabriel (1843–1904) French social psychologist and criminologist whose studies of crime were couched in terms of an opposition to the biologistic reductionism of LOMBROSO. In sociology he is best remembered for *Les Lois de l'imitation* (1890), a work singled out for criticism by DURKHEIM (*Le Suicide*, 1897) as underestimating the constraining external force of social currents.

Tawney, Richard (1880–1962) English economic historian and egalitarian social philosopher, influenced by his early association with the Workers' Educational Association (WEA) and by his life-long Christianity. As an economic historian Tawney can be seen as a forerunner of modern approaches to economic and social history that emphasize working class resistance to capitalist exploitation. As a social philosopher, in works such as *Equality* (1920) and *The Acquisitive Society* (1931), he raised fundamental questions about the morality of 20th century social institutions. In sociology he is best remembered for his *Religion and the Rise of Capitalism* (1926). In this he agreed with WEBER's thesis that the individualism and worldliness associated with Calvinism and Puritanism were the moral engine of capitalist development, although he regarded Weber as failing to give sufficient emphasis to the two-way causal interaction between religion and economics.

taxonomy the theory and practice of CLASSIFICATION. As a scientific procedure, taxonomy has been especially prominent in biology (for example, hierarchical formal classificatory systems such as that by Linnaeus). Some proposed classifications of societies in sociology have used such classificatory systems as models (for example, the work of Herbert SPENCER and W.G. RUNCIMAN). Although argument has raged in biology and elsewhere as to whether taxonomies should be seen as natural or imposed, the only answer that can be given is that taxonomies are theory-relative, that when theories change, taxonomies will also change, as in the move from pre- to post-Darwinian biology.

technological determinism the assumption that technology is both autonomous and has determinate effects on society. Technology is seen as political and as an INDEPENDENT VARIABLE in social change. This assumption is criticized for ignoring social processes and choices that guide use of technology and the variety of possible social arrangements that coexist with different types of technology. Marx's famous phrase, "the handmill gives you society with the feudal lord; the steam-mill, society with the industrial capitalist," is sometimes used (mistakenly) as an example of technological determinism. MARX, however, saw technology as intimately related to the social relations of production. Technological determinism is associated with neo-evolutionary theories that give technology primacy in the analysis of social change (see NEO-EVOLUTIONISM, POSTINDUSTRIAL SOCIETY, CONVERGENCE), and empirical studies in the SOCIOLOGY OF WORK that describe the effects of technology. See also CULTURAL LAG.

technology the practical application of knowledge and use of techniques in productive activities. This definition reflects a sociological concern with technology as a social product that incorporates both the hardware of human artifacts such as tools and machines and the knowledge and ideas involved in different productive activities. Such knowledge need not depend on science as its driving force, for example, the relatively simple forms of mechanization associated with the early industrial revolution. More recent developments in energy production and information technology may, however, depend on innovations derived from organized science (see also NEW TECHNOLOGY.) Sometimes, technology is referred to in the narrow sense as machines, whereas wider definitions include productive systems as a whole and even work organization and the division of labor. The narrow definition tends to treat technology as autonomous and ignore the social processes involved in design and choice of technology; more inclusive definitions make it difficult to distinguish between technology and the social arrangements with which it is related. (See also SOCIOLOGY OF SCIENCE, TECHNOLOGICAL DETERMINISM.)

The role of technology in social change has been a longstanding issue in sociology, from Marx's analysis of the forces and relations of production to theories of INDUSTRIALIZATION, MODERNIZATION, and POSTINDUSTRIAL SOCIETY. These latter theories were developed in the 1960s and were based on neo-evolutionary assumptions. Technology was accorded a key determining role in shaping the social structure of advanced industrial societies. (See CONVERGENCE, CULTURAL LAG.)

In industrial sociology and the sociology of work, technology has also been identified as a key determining factor for work organization and ALIENATION. This has involved classification of different types or levels of technology of which the most important have included:

(a) Blauner's (1964) classification of four types of technology—craft, machine-minding, assembly-line, and process or automation. Blauner's inverted "U" curve of alienation suggests that alienation is low in craft industries, reaches a peak in assembly-line technology, as in the auto industry, and declines again with automation. His work has been criticized empirically and for its TECHNOLOGICAL DETERMINISM, especially by so-called social action theorists (Silverman, 1970, Goldthorpe, 1966).

(b) Woodward's (1970) classification of three types of production system based on degree of technical complexity—small-batch and unit production, large-batch and mass-production, and finally process production. Each type was related to different organizational characteristics: for example, mass-production led to the most bureaucratic form of authority structure. Different types of technology were seen to require appropriate organizational structures for optimum efficiency (see also CONTINGENCY THEORY; compare SOCIOTECHNICAL SYSTEMS APPROACH).

Both Blauner and Woodward suggest an optimistic approach to technological change with the development of automation, reflected in new types of skilled work, less rigid work organization, and increased job satisfaction. However, the debate about automation in the 1960s has now been subject to extensive theoretical and empirical reappraisal on the basis of research into information technologies. In contrast, labor process theory, based on a Marxist framework, has adopted a more critical perspective toward technology. Technical change is analyzed as the product of capitalist control of the labor process rather than a politically neutral, autonomous development. Braverman's (1974) analysis of technology in the labor process was based on Bright's (1958) classification of technology into 17 levels that progressively substitute machines for manual and then mental skills (see also DESKILLING). This critical analysis of technology is also evident in the work of the FRANKFURT SCHOOL and Habermas in particular, in which technology and technical rationality are seen as a form of ideology.

teleological explanation EXPLANATIONS that have the form "A occurs for the sake of B" (A. Woodfield, 1981). Three main forms of teleological explanation can be identified (see also TELEOLOGY):

(a) PURPOSIVE EXPLANATION, which is concerned with the goal-directed behavior of animals, especially human beings, for example, explanations in terms of purposes, motives, reasons, etc.;

(b) FUNCTIONAL(IST) EXPLANATIONS of biological or societal characteristics, explained (i) as the result of a natural or social selection and (ii) in terms of their continuing contribution (see FUNCTION) to the working and persistence of the plant, animal, society, etc. in question (see also SYSTEM, SYSTEMS THEORY, EVOLUTIONARY THEORY);

(c) accounts of the working of machines that relate to the design and purpose of the machine, including machines that behave or function in an animal-like way (see also CYBERNETICS).

Everyone accepts that human beings act purposively. Furthermore, in explaining human social action it is clear that a knowledge of actors' beliefs and values will often do much to explain their actions. The issue that arises is whether teleological explanations in this sense can suffice in sociology (as some sociologists and philosophers suggest, for example, WINCH) or whether further, even wholly different, explanations are required for adequate sociological explanation, including the second type of teleological explanation(s) or causal explanations of other kinds (see SOCIAL FACTS AS THINGS, BEHAVIORISM).

There is little disagreement that functional and evolutionary forms of teleological explanation are appropriately used in explanations of animal behavior and of the biological realm generally. Usually it is argued that teleological functional and evolutionary explanations are no more than one form of causal explanation. Proposed teleological explanations that involve the end states or goals of societies have been far more controversial, for it is often argued that societies have neither aims nor needs apart from the aims and needs of individual human beings (see also METHODOLOGICAL INDIVIDUALISM). Against this, the view that functionalist and evolutionary accounts have a legitimate place in sociology continues strongly supported in many areas of sociology.

teleology 1. (from the Greek *telos*, "purpose") originally, the conception that all things have their own natural purposes, for example, a stone thrown in the air that falls to the ground. **2.** (later) the ultimate purpose of things, the doctrine of so-called final causes, for example, the doctrine that everything is God's design. **3.** (more generally, including its use in sociology) any theory or account suggesting that the phenomena of nature or social phenomena can be explained not only by their prior causes but also by the end states or purposes to which they are directed. As such, teleological accounts and explanations include both PURPOSIVE EXPLANATIONS AND FUNCTIONAL(IST) EXPLANATIONS. Also included are some forms of developmental and EVOLUTIONARY THEORY. **4.** the process or processes by which teleological end states are approached or achieved.

While teleological accounts in senses **1.** or **2.** fall largely outside social science, those in sense **3.** remain widely used in everyday life and in both the physical and the social sciences, although often controversial. A central issue is whether in their acceptable forms teleological explanations are reducible to more conventional causal accounts. Doctrines of historical inevitability, human destiny, etc. have been especially controversial. See also TELEOLOGICAL EXPLANATION.

Tel Quel Group the group of French academics who edited the avant-garde literary journal *Tel Quel*, which was influential in the development of STRUCTURALISM and SEMIOTICS in the 1960s (among them were Roland BARTHES and Julia Kristeva).

territorial imperative the tendency of individuals or groups of individuals to protect their own territories (Ardrey, 1967). While the territorial behavior of some birds and animals is well established (see ETHOLOGY), the notion that some human behavior is closely analogous, that is, instinctive, is treated with much skepticism in sociology, along with other such suggestions made by SOCIOBIOLOGY.

territory the geographical area under formal jurisdiction or control of a recognized political authority. GIDDENS (1985) distinguished between the jurisdiction of modern NATION-STATES, where the *borders* are strictly demarcated and highly administered, and the much more loosely defined and often contested and ill-defined *frontiers* of preindustrial empires. He sees this as an exemplifation of the much greater control over time and space possessed by modern governments (see TIME-SPACE DISTANCIATION).

terrorism a form of politically motivated action combining psychological (fear-inducing) and physical (violent-action) components carried out by individuals or small groups with the aim of inducing communities or states to meet the terrorists' demands. The concept remains notoriously difficult to define with any precision. The major problem is summarized in the adage "One person's terrorist is another person's freedom fighter." The issue is complicated further because some would argue that acts of terrorism do not belong exclusively to the politically motivated but may also be employed by criminals and psychopaths. However, *political terrorism* can be thought of as the use of violence by a group acting either on behalf of, or in opposition to, an established political authority.

In broad terms, it is possible to identify three major types of politically motivated terrorist behavior: (a) revolutionary terrorism, (b) subrevolutionary terrorism, and (c) terrorist action that is essentially repressive in nature. Thus, it is also necessary to differentiate between terrorism that is perpetrated by the state itself and actions that are undertaken by groups in pursuit of political change. Finally, it is possible to identify *international terrorism*, acts of terrorism that transcend the boundaries of one state. The tactics adopted by terrorists have been widespread, including kidnapping, bombs in public places, hijacking of airplanes, attacks on property, extortion of ransom, raids on banks, and state oppression, arrests, and torture.

Rubenstein (1987) suggests that terrorism usually springs from the political alienation of the INTELLIGENTSIA from both the ruling class and the masses. The former engages in repression, and the latter is indifferent. This combination is particularly likely to appear in colonial situations, although it may occur in any country where a social crisis generated by rapid and uneven economic development isolates intellectuals from the masses for whom they wish to act as political spokesmen. The other precondition for terrorism occurs when a reform movement collapses or when it appears that the movement will not succeed in restructuring society. For advocates of terrorism, individual or small-group violence is seen as the only means that can expose the fragility of the ruling class, raise the consciousness of the masses, and attract new members and supporters to the movement. Rubenstein shares the Marxist view that terrorists have rarely gained mass working-class support and have usually been ineffective in making social revolutions. As an instrument of political change, however, terrorism has often been effective, for example, as an adjunct of nationalist movements.

text any written form of signification. Unlike speech, it can have an independent existence beyond the writer and beyond the context of its production. Rather than a mere supplement to speech, written text is seen by structuralists such as DERRIDA as displaying the fundamental character of *langue* (in contrast with *parole*), that is, as a system of differences that does not depend on an initiating individual subject (see LANGUE AND PAROLE, DECENTERED SELF (OR SUBJECT), SUBJECT AND OBJECT).

Thanatos the death instinct in FREUD's theory of personality. Thanatos involves all instincts that are destructive, such as aggression. It is the opposite of EROS, the life instinct.

theodicy theological explanations for the existence of suffering and evil in the world despite divine presence. As used by WEBER, the concept refers to religious doctrines that legitimate social inequalities, or see purpose in evil, or promise compensation for suffering, for example, the Hindu doctrine of kharma (see CASTE).

theories of the middle range "theories that lie between the minor but necessary working hypotheses that evolve in abundance in day-to-day research and the all-inclusive systematic efforts to develop unified theory that will explain all the observed uniformities of social behavior, organization and social change" (MERTON, 1949). As identified by Merton, compared with "general theories" that may be remote from particular classes of social behavior, such middle range theories are "close enough to observed data to be incorporated in propositions that permit empirical testing." The construction of such theories was an important part of Merton's doctrine that in sociology pieces of empirical research were often too much divorced from one another. In the course of his career in sociology, Merton has been responsible for development of important middle range theories in many areas, including contributions to the theory of REFERENCE GROUPS, BUREAUCRACY, and MASS COMMUNICATIONS, many of them represented in his *Social Theory and Social Structure* (1949 and subsequent editions). Compare MILLS, ABSTRACTED EMPIRICISM.

theory 1. (in physical science and in social science) any set of hypotheses or propositions, linked by logical or mathematical arguments, that is advanced to explain an area of empirical reality or type of phenomenon. See also FORMAL THEORY, MODEL. **2.** in a looser sense, any abstract general account of an area of reality, usually including the formulation of general concepts. See also EXPLANATION, SOCIOLOGICAL THEORY.

Even in the physical sciences, the importance of theories in strictly logical or mathematical form is challenged by some philosophers and historians of science (see KUHN, FEYERABEND).

theory-laden (potentially, of any empirical assertion) relative to (that is, presupposing) theoretical (for example, ontological, epistemological, paradigmatic, etc.) assumptions. See also INCOMMENSURABILITY.

theory of games mathematical accounts of the hypothetical decision-making behavior of two or more persons in situations where (a) each has a finite choice between two or more courses of action (strategies), (b) the interests of each may be partly or wholly in conflict, (c) and for each person, numerical values can be attached to the utility of every combination of outcomes. Developed especially by Von Neumann (see Von Neumann and Morgenstern (1944), the theory of games builds on more conventional forms of rational modeling in ECONOMICS. Various real situations (for example, the arms race, military alliances) possess at least some of the properties that enable them to be analyzed in such terms. However, although it has had some influence on the way in which STRATEGIC INTERACTION is discussed in sociology (see also RATIONAL CHOICE THEORY), the abstract mathematical theory of games makes assumptions about the measurement of social utilities and the availability of information to actors, which in the social sciences are only infrequently justified. See also PRISONERS' DILEMMA, ZERO SUM GAME, RATIONALITY.

thick description (anthropology) the provision of "densely textured facts" about a social context, on the basis of which more general assertions about the role of culture in social life can be sustained (C. Geertz *The Interpretation of Cultures*, 1973). Like the ETHNOMETHODOLOGISTS, Geertz in his interpretive anthropology regards a minute attention to the fine details of everyday social life as the only feasible basis for more extended generalizations, but he makes no assumption that any "thick description," however detailed, can ever be complete.

Thomas, William (1863–1947) pioneer American sociologist, founder member of the CHICAGO SCHOOL. His major work (with Znanieck) is *The Polish Peasant in Europe and America* (1918–1920). He is best known for his use of the LIFE HISTORY as a method of reflecting social history in the biographies of individuals. A theme running through his work is the link between culture and personality, explored through a method that places the individual at the center of the analysis. He also formulated the idea of a SOCIAL ACTOR's definition of the situation, explained in his much quoted aphorism, "If men define situations as real, they are real in their consequences."

Tilly, Charles (1926–) influential US historical sociologist, and head of the Center for Research on Social Organizations based at the University of Michigan. Tilly's work is remarkable in that it has interested historians and sociologists alike. His methods, in works such as *From Mobilization to Revolution* (1978) and *Strikes in France, 1830–1968*, with Edward Shorter (1974), has involved assembly of large data sets and testing of hypotheses over time. His historical inquiries have focused especially on the exploration of changes in the patterns of collective action, including violent political action, that are associated with long-term structural transformations of society such as urbanization, industrialization, expansion of the state, and the spread of capitalism. Rejecting those conceptions of collective action that emphasize its basis mainly in social disorganization, Tilly's research findings have emphasized instead the increasingly strategic character of such action. Other major works by Tilly include *The Vendée* (1964), regarded by many as his best book, *The Rebellious Century, 1830–1930*, with Louise and Richard Tilly (1975), and *As Sociology Meets History* (1981).

time the continuous passage of existence. Time may be measured with reference to any stable or periodic physical or social process. In the latter case, time will often be stated with reference to clear physical periodicies that determine the units of social division, as for example, days and years. In many other respects, however, the divisions of time, though still stated partly in terms of physical periodicies, depend on a patterning of social events that is relatively independent of such natural periodicies, as is so for weeks or hours. Various forms of generic social time may also be identified as, for example, in the distinctions drawn by GIDDENS between:

(a) the repeated day-to-day *durée*—or "reversible time"—of everyday social life;

(b) the *longue durée* involved in the persistence, as against the rise and fall, of social institutions and societies;

(c) the "life span" of the individual—"irreversible time."

As well as this, in social life and in sociological and historical accounts, an almost infinite number of more specific "periodizations" can also be noticed, for example, "Victorian times," "the Age of Reason."

Since time always exists as a fourth coordinate of *time-space* in specifying any event, it must obviously be an important component in any sociological account. A number of sociologists recently have suggested that time has been relatively neglected in sociology, in that sociology has often been concerned with static structural models and has tended to neglect the great variety of ways in which social life is both temporally structured and, as the result of social processes occurring in time, socially transformed—see MANN (1986) and GIDDENS (1984). A resurgence of interest in time has been a feature of recent sociology.

time series ideally, any set of data in which "a well-defined quantity is recorded at successive, equally spaced time points over a specific period" (C. Marsh, 1988), for example, the retail price index. Where the data fail to fulfill all these strict criteria, for example, inadequately standardized variables, or gaps in the series, where the recording interval is not equally spaced, one may still speak of a time series if data over time are involved. However, the problems of interpretation of such a series will be much greater. An important sorce of time series data is the CENSUS.

time-space distanciation the stretching of social relations and systems across time and space, resulting from advances in human techniques of transport and communications and hence social control (GIDDENS, 1985).

time-space edges the "connections, whether conflictual or symbiotic," that "exist between societies of different structural types" both *in* space and *across* time (GIDDENS, 1984). All societies are both social systems and at the same time, in part constituted by their intersection with other social systems, both other SOCIETIES and INTERSOCIETAL SYSTEMS. The significance of the notion of time-space edges in Giddens' work is that not only the spatial location but also the temporal location in particular societies is seen as profoundly affecting the outcomes of action in these societies. See also EPISODE, EPISODIC CHARACTERIZATION.

Titmuss, Richard (1907–1973) British sociologist and influential occupant of the chair of social administration at the London School of Economics. As well as writing about social policy, he played a direct role in the formulation of social policy as adviser to the Labor Party and several foreign governments. The central theme of his work is that the provision of social welfare should concern more than ensuring a safety net for the casualties of society. His main works include *Essays on the Welfare State* (1958), *Income Distribution and Social Change* (1962), and *The Gift Relationship* (1970). The last of these works, a study of blood donors, in which he sees the prevalence of donorship as an indicator of "cultural values and the quality of human relationships" in a particular society, sums up much of what Titmuss stood for (see also GIFT RELATIONSHIP.) His view was that social policy should be aimed at fostering altruistic values and genuine community relations as well as overcoming inequalities and social disadvantage.

Tocqueville, Alexis de (1805–1859) French political scientist and member of the Chamber of Deputies, widely considered to be one of the first comparative political and historical sociologists. His analysis of the political experience of America in the 1830s was undertaken in the belief that lessons could be learned that would be applicable to Europe, especially France. In *Democracy in America* (1835–1840) he argued that democracy—the condition of equality—was an irresistible tendency in modern societies, but which, unchecked, held considerable dangers for liberty, by which he meant responsible self-government based on enlightened self-interest. Democracy, because it tended to undermine all hierarchy and to abolish all intermediary bodies between the individual and society, was likely to be accompanied by two further tendencies: individualism and centralization, which together could lead to tyranny. In America, Tocqueville found these tendencies held in check, though not absent, by two factors. First, the American colonies had been accustomed to self-government. Secondly, through the principle of federalism, the United States Constitution after the Revolution remained a fragmented one, providing multiple points of access for individuals to participate. Tocqueville's conclusion was that where democracy came without such prior establishment of liberty it was likely to lead to tyranny. It was this scenario that, in *The Old Regime and the French Revolution* (1856), Tocqueville concluded had been enacted in France. Revolutionary France had lacked the conditions that made democracy compatible with liberty, including the lack of a strong middle class. In his comparative analysis of political arrangements Tocqueville especially emphasized what subsequently came to be called POLITICAL CULTURE. His analysis of the preconditions for, and character of, modern democracy strongly influenced later theorists. See INTERMEDIATE GROUPS, PLURALISM, MASS SOCIETY.

Tönnies, Ferdinand (1855–1936) German sociologist and founder of the German Sociological Association, who is above all remembered for his coining of the terms GEMEINSCHAFT and GESELLSCHAFT, which were based on a distinction between "natural will" (*Wesenwille*), including habitual as well as instinctual action, and "rational will" (*Kurwille*), including INSTRUMENTAL RATIONALITY. Both sets of distinctions were IDEAL TYPES and were used by Tönnies to analyze historical changes in social organization, including social problems created by breakdown of traditional social structures. Tönnies's concepts and aspects of his thesis of a loss of COMMUNITY in modern societies are not dissimilar from those of WEBER or, to a lesser extent, MARX. They form one influence on the work of the CHICAGO SCHOOL. They were also one of the sources of PARSONS' formulation of PATTERN VARIABLES.

total institution or **total organization** any social organization, including prisons, monasteries, long-stay hospitals, boarding schools, and ships on long voyages, in which the members are required to live out their lives in isolation from wider society. In contrast with normal social life, in which people live in their own homes and usually work, sleep, eat, and engage in leisure activities in a number of different locations, it is characteristic of total organizations that social action is confined to a single location. In these organizations there is no possibility of any complete escape from the administrative rules or values that prevail.

Research has concentrated on the sociological and social psychological consequences (for example, INSTITUTIONALIZATION) that can arise from this form of life and exist for those in superordinate as well as subordinate positions. As seen by GOFFMAN (1961a), various "mortifications of the self" (for example, removal of personal possessions) may occur in total institutions (for example, asylums or prisons), resulting in a reconstruction of the person to fit with the demands of the organization to an extent that could never be achieved in more open social contexts. This reconstruction, however, is never complete. There always remains scope for "inmate culture" to exert some control over the formal organizational structure of a total organization.

TOTEM

totem see TOTEMISM.

totemism the practice of symbolically identifying humans with nonhuman objects, usually animals or plants. The classic case of totemism is one in which a clan claims an animal as a mythological ancestor, but the term has also been used to cover a wide range of symbolic practices. Functional anthropologists such as RADCLIFFE-BROWN (under the influence of DURKHEIM) have explained totems as symbols of group solidarity. FREUD, in *Totem and Taboo,* (1913) used the idea of a totem as a mediator between repressed culture and instinctive nature. Later, structural anthropologists, as exemplified by LÉVI-STRAUSS, focused on their capacity to express structures of difference between humans and animals. He argues that totemism, like TABOO, is yet another instance of nature being "good to think," that is to say, certain objects possess qualities that express vital features of human experience and are thus used to construct a mythology of the concrete.

trade union consciousness the limited, sectionalist, less than revolutionary, social-democratic consciousness that, according to Lenin, the working class spontaneously develops from the narrow "conviction that it is necessary to combine in unions, fight employers and strive to compel governments to pass legislation" (LENIN, 1902). Since these ameliorative objectives serve to impede working class unity and ensure subservience to bourgeois ideology, the theoretical and philosophical insights of intellectuals are necessary for the development of class consciousness. This thesis has influenced subsequent debates about TRADE UNIONS in capitalist societies. See also CLASS CONSCIOUSNESS.

trade unions or **labor unions** employee organizations primarily concerned with improving the conditions and rewards of the working lives of their members. Sociological analysis of trade unions has involved: (a) distinguishing them from other forms of employee organizations; (b) explaining their emergence, the forms they have taken, the objectives they have pursued, and the strategies they have adopted; (c) examining trade union government, levels of member involvement, and trade union democracy; (d) consideration of the impact of trade unions on work and wider society.

Internationally, differences in overall patterns of trade union organization (for example, number of unions, degree of centralization, and involvement in government and level of membership) are striking; sociologists have also been interested in the implications of these differences.

Trade unions can be distinguished from PROFESSIONS, which are fully in control of the content of specific areas of work and often also able to control recruitment, and from *staff associations,* that, as largely management sponsored organizations, are often limited to a consultative role.

Explanations for the emergence of, and variations in types and objectives of, trade unions have occasioned considerable debate. Fundamentally, however, trade unions can be regarded as attempts to offset the unequal relationship between employees and employers under capitalism.

Differences in the manner and degree to which different categories of workers were able to enhance their bargaining capacity accounted for historical differences between different kinds of trade union organization, for example, distinctions between craft, general, and industrial unions. More recently, distinctions between different types of trade unions have tended to break down, with the proliferation of new "market-based unions" (that is, accepting single union, single status, flexible working, no-strike agreements), and a debate within the trade union movement between "traditionalists" and "new realists." The problems currently facing unions in Britain, for example, are those arising from the restructuring of the national and international economy, decline in membership (particularly in manufacturing), anti-trade union legislation and reduced union political influence (see also CORPORATISM).

Analysis of the internal dynamics of trade unions has been largely concerned with testing MICHELS' thesis that as political organizations grow larger they become less democratic and more conservative (see also IRON LAW OF OLIGARCHY). Conclusive statements on this issue are difficult, given the various measures of democracy that exist, for example, responsive leadership, institutionalized opposition, active participation, and effective representation of members' interests. It is clear, however, that variations in levels of democracy are related to the characteristics of the membership of a union (for example, social status) and the context in which the union operates (see also LIPSET).

A main strand of sociological debate about the social impact and effectiveness of trade unions has concerned their implications for CLASS CONSCIOUSNESS and whether they constitute any kind of threat to capitalism. Explanations for what are in fact usually seen as relatively limited trade union objectives, at least in Britain, have focused on: (a) the way in which they have segmented the labor movement by organizing around the stratification of occupations; (b) the emergence of institutions through which conflict has become institutionalized and regulated; and (c) union bureaucracy and member apathy. See also INDUSTRIAL RELATIONS, TRADE UNION CONSCIOUSNESS.

traditional action see TYPES OF SOCIAL ACTION.

traditional authority see LEGITIMATE AUTHORITY.

traditional society a nonindustrial, predominantly rural society that is presumed to be static and contrasted with a modern, changing, INDUSTRIAL SOCIETY. The concept is widely used in the social sciences, but over the last few decades has come to be seen as problematic and therefore avoided by many sociologists. The problems involved in its usages are:

(a) it is a term used to describe a wide variety of societies that in fact differ markedly from one another;

(b) while the rates of SOCIAL CHANGE in such societies are slower than in industrial societies, it is erroneous to accept that no change occurs;

(c) the term gained usage within sociology when systematic knowledge of nonindustrial societies was weak, and increased knowledge no longer warrants the usage;

(d) it is associated with MODERNIZATION theory, which has been criticized for delineating an oversimplified contrast between traditional and modern;

(e) the oversimplifications involved in the term lead either to a romanticized or a pejorative view of such societies.

An example of the problematic use of the term is that in which commentators argue that contemporary Japanese society differs from Western European society because of the stronger survival of traditional society within Japan. This ignores the facts that all societies carry features from the past in their present social arrangements, no societies have complete breaks between so-called traditional and modern, and that such features from the past may be striking to Western observers because of their unfamiliarity, thus adding Eurocentrism to the list of problems. Further, in the case of Japan, in the 19th century the state actively decided to promote what were seen as aspects of traditional Japan for political purposes and for the establishment of Japanese national identity. Thus what is seen as traditional is likely to be an invention (see Hobsbawm and Ranger, 1983).

trait theory a theory of personality that describes individual differences in terms of a number of relatively enduring independent *traits*. A trait is a two-dimensional construct (for example, clever-stupid; mean-generous), often represented by a scale on which individuals can be rated. Trait theories vary largely according to the number of independent traits believed to be necessary to provide a complete description of personality. Personality inventories provide a picture or profile of these trait scores, derived from responses to self-report questions. Examples include the Sixteen Personality Factor Questionnaire (16PF) (Cattell, 1963), and the California Psychological Inventory (CPI) (Gough, 1957). Indirect measurement of traits is also possible (see PROJECTIVE TESTS). A complementary view of personality is provided by *type theories*, which characterize individuals by one of a much smaller number of dominant traits or types (see EXTROVERSION-INTROVERSION).

transcendental argument (philosophy) the assertion of "what must be the case" (that is, can be established A PRIORI) on the supposition that we do have knowledge of the world. Thus, KANT claimed to have established the concepts and principles that organize all our experience and are logically prior to this experience. Similarly, Bhaskar (1989) argues for his version of scientific REALISM on the premise that it is possible to state what, ontologically speaking, the world "must be like prior to any scientific investigation of it" for any science, including a social science, to be possible.

transcendental signifier see DECONSTRUCTION.

transformational model of social activity a model of social activity advanced by Bhaskar (1979) based on the Aristotelian view that any productive activity presupposes both an *efficient* cause and a *material* cause. In this model, the social forms preexisting social action constitute the material cause, and social action the means by which this preexisting reality is either reproduced or transformed (see also STRUCTURE AND AGENCY). It is on the basis of this model of "causal powers" that Bhaskar bases his "realist" argument concerning both the possibility and ontological limits of sociological naturalism. See TRANSCENDENTAL ARGUMENT.

transhumance the seasonal movement of human groups in search of pastures, for example, the movement from dry season to wet season pastures undertaken by the Nuer. See also PASTORALISM, NOMADS, HERDING SOCIETY.

transition from feudalism to capitalism the process in Western Europe between the 15th and 18th centuries by which feudal society was succeeded by capitalist society. The term is most often associated with Marxist approaches, but a distinctive Weberian approach can also be identified.

Marxists disagree about the decisive factors involved in the process. MARX identified two main factors: emergence of autonomous craft manufacturing in the feudal towns around which capital developed; and growth of overseas trade, particularly with the emergence of British trade with the Americas in the 16th century and the emergence of merchant capital. The development was limited while laborers were tied to the land. In England the enclosures movement forced the peasantry off the land, thus providing a labor supply for the towns and wage labor on the land. Other European countries were slower in developing this so-called free labor force. Marx also spoke of the feudal aristocracy being replaced by the new bourgeoisie, but more recent analyses have shown that this is an oversimplification, especially in England, where sections of the aristocracy became capitalist landlords and later became involved in industrial capitalism. Subsequent Marxist debates have centered around whether the growth of trade, the transformation of the labor force, or class conflict within feudalism were the most important aspects of this process. See Hilton (ed.), 1976, and Aston and Philipin (eds.), 1985, for two collections of key debates.

The Weberian approach lays great emphasis on the political changes in Western European feudalism, drawing on WEBER's observation that the key contradiction was between the attempts at centralization by the monarchy, and the local and regional powers invested in the feudal lords. Part of that contradiction was also expressed in the growth of towns as administrative and trading centers. Further, WEBER's thesis on the role of the PROTESTANT ETHIC introduces the role of beliefs in explaining social and economic change largely missing from the Marxist debate. Weber, however, in emphasizing such socioeconomic changes as the growth of trade and transformations of labor force, should not be contrasted in any simplistic fashion with Marx.

This proviso is reflected in recent works that examine the process, drawing on both analytical traditions. Thus, Perry ANDERSON (1974a & b) develops a Marxist approach that relies heavily on Weberian insights into the political contradictions and the role of the Christian Church, and Michael MANN (1986) provides an analysis drawing widely on both. See also SOCIAL CHANGE.

translation the transformation of signs and meanings, especially languages, where these are initially unknown or alien, into a known and familiar set of signs and meanings. The question of the extent to which the ideas and language of one society or culture can be expressed adequately in the language of another society or culture has been an especially important one in SOCIAL ANTHROPOLOGY (for example, see SAPIR-WHORF HYPOTHESIS). Issues also arise in sociology, especially where it is assumed that its subject matter is SEMIOTIC and meaningful, that is, made up of signs, so that an unknown society or set of social interactions is like an unknown language, and the main task is one of translation. Quine (1960) has argued that any translation is in principle "indeterminate," that is, any set of signs can equally well be translated by an indefinite list of alternative possibilities. Davidson (1984) suggests that this leaves no alternative other than a "principle of charity," which assumed that others and their signs will resemble us and our own signs. However, the effect of questions raised about the indeterminacy of translation is to puncture any simple assumptions about ready translation or objectivity in social science. See also RELATIVISM, INCOMMENSURABILITY, FORMS OF LIFE, WITTGENSTEIN.

triad see DYAD AND TRIAD.

triangulation of approaches the employment of a number of different research techniques (see RESEARCH METHODS) in the belief that a variety of approaches offers the best chance of achieving VALIDITY.

tribe and **tribal society 1.** (usually) a pastoral or horticultural society whose members share cultural or linguistic characteristics and are bound together by reciprocal social rights and obligations. Such a society has weak or nonexistent political centralization but strong lineage structures, important for social cohesion and interaction. **2.** a concept developed by anthropologists from the 19th century onward that attempted to categorize one type of stateless society, generally on an evolutionary scale (for example, the sequence: BAND, tribe, CHIEFDOM) but is now often seen as, at the worst, a European-imposed category that related inadequately to empirical reality, and, at best, a term around which no consensus exists.

Definition **1.** is thus only an approximation of some of the concept's usage by some anthropologists, and definition **2.** reflects the work of others, especially over the last two decades, who reject usage of the concept, prefer no narrow classification of such societies, and would substitute the term ETHNIC GROUP. The debate is still current in anthropology. The concept has a general usage to refer to all stateless societies and is sometimes used as a synonym for PRIMITIVE or SIMPLE SOCIETIES.

trivial consultation a form of inappropriate conduct in which patients seek medical advice for problems that are neither medically relevant nor life-threatening. However salient the problems are for patients, they may be dismissed by doctors because they involve factors beyond medical competence (domestic, financial, social, or emotional) and because they cast the doctor in the role of general counselor/advisor. They are a significant element in doctors' lack of job satisfaction, because they are viewed as time-wasting.

truth that which corresponds to the facts, for example, in philosophy, the *correspondence theory of truth*. Strictly interpreted, in that true propositions or ideas picture or represent the world, this is an empiricist notion (see EMPIRICISM). However, this conception of truth has been challenged recently, for example, by postempiricist conceptions of science (see KUHN, FEYERABEND, POSTEMPIRICISM, POSTSTRUCTURALISM). Since both hypotheses and the facts that test these are theory-relative, truth cannot be established simply by recourse to empiricist procedures.

Alternative bases of truth claims include the *consensus theory of truth*, in which truth is a matter of social (including scientific) agreements on reality, reached in a context of open discourse (see HABERMAS). Questions of correspondence with reality remain central, but cannot be settled in the way that empiricists suggest. See also DECONSTRUCTION, DERRIDA.

turn-taking see CONVERSATION ANALYSIS.

two-step flow in mass communications the idea, contrary to theories of MASS SOCIETY, that in a plural society the flow of mass communications is mediated by the action of OPINION LEADERS (LAZARSFELD, et al., 1944, Katz and Lazarsfeld, 1955). The idea has been significant in the development of theories of mass media of communication.

Tylor, Edward (1832–1917) early anthropologist, whose *Researches into the Early History of Mankind and the Development of Civilization* (1865) did much to establish anthropology as a scientific discipline. He can also take credit for the introduction into English of the German, now standard anthropological and sociological usage of the term CULTURE. Drawing on Darwinism and on discoveries in archaeology suggesting that cultures manifest a serial progression, the persistent theme of Tylor's approach was evolutionism. In *Primitive Culture* (1871) he applied this perspective to the development of RELIGION, which he suggested had developed through three stages: ANIMISM, polytheism, and MONOTHEISM. Tylor's were works of synthesis based on comparative analysis in that he searched for evidence of cultural survivals that could provide clues to sequences of social development. His emphasis on the possession of rich cultural traditions by all peoples meant that his anthropology was relatively little marred by the overtones of racism often present in the work of other 19th-century evolutionary theorists. See also EVOLUTIONARY THEORY.

type any abstract or conceptual class or category that may or may not be seen as capable of straightforward empirical reference. Compare IDEAL TYPE. See also TYPOLOGY, TYPIFICATION.

TYPE GENERALIZATION

type generalization see IDEAL TYPE.

types of compliance "three means—physical, material, and symbolic—employed within organizations to make subjects comply," identified by Amitai Etzioni (*A Comparative Analysis of Complex Organizations*, 1961):

(a) *coercive power*, resting "on the application, or the threat of application, of physical sanctions";

(b) *renumerative power*, based "on control over material resorces and rewards through allocation of salaries, wages," etc.;

(c) *normative power*, resting "on the allocation and manipulation of symbolic rewards and deprivations."

These three modes of compliance are associated with three kinds of involvement: *alienative, calculative,* and *moral.*

types of legitimate authority see LEGITIMATE AUTHORITY.

types of religious organization see CHURCH-SECT TYPOLOGY.

types of social action the four IDEAL TYPES of social action identified by Max WEBER:

(a) *zweckrational* or *instrumental action* (as in models of "rational economic action" developed within economics), in which the actor weights the relative efficiency of different available means to an end, and sometimes also the ends themselves, seeking to maximize benefits;

(b) *wertrational action* or *value rationality,* in which the relative effectiveness of alternative means to an end may be assessed but the ends are accepted as given, perhaps as a moral imperative, as in the PROTESTANT WORK ETHIC;

(c) *affectual action*, in which action is governed by emotion;

(d) *traditional action*, in which action is governed by customary or habitual practice.

Related general typologies of social action include PARETO's distinction between "logical" and "nonlogical" action (see also RESIDUES AND DERIVATIONS).

Weber's idealized typology, which describes other forms of action as departures from the *zweckrational* type, is intended to provide a bench mark for the analysis of concrete actions and for comparing societies, and has been widely used in sociology. In addition to the pure types, Weber also allowed for "mixed types" of action. Nonetheless, the criticism is made that in using his typology Weber failed to give adequate credence to systematization of "substantive rationality" as against the "formal" (that is, "formal calculable") form of rationality, despite his reservations about the narrow operation of the latter (see FORMAL and SUBSTANTIVE RATIONALITY). See also RATIONALITY, BUREAUCRACY.

typification the conceptual process by which sociologists and social actors organize their knowledge of the social world, not in terms of the unique qualities of persons, things, or events, but in terms of the typical features of these (see SCHUTZ, 1962–1966).

Typification in sociology can be seen as no more than an extension of a process that already occurs in the social construction of everyday life by social actors. This fact has considerable significance in the eyes of those sociologists (see ETHNOMETHODOLOGY) who wish to deny that a sharp dividing line exists between the "practical sociology" undertaken by everyday actors and "conventional academic sociology." The latter school of thought is seen as failing to recognize this approach as tending to underestimate the rational capacities and cultural competence of ordinary social actors, and thus failing to see that sociology must be built on, and be compatible with, the rational accomplishments of ordinary social actors.

Whether or not these criticisms of conventional academic sociology are fully accepted, attention to the everyday social and cultural competence and the typifications of social actors can be regarded as an essential element of modern sociological analysis (see GIDDENS, 1976a). Yet, the implications of this for academic sociology remain controversial. There is no general acceptance of the view of ethnomethodologists that a total revolution in sociology is necessary (see GOLDTHORPE, 1973).

typology any classificatory conceptual scheme (for example, church, sect) that may or may not be logically exhaustive within its empirical frame of reference. The role and utility of any typology are relative to the theoretical perspective within which the typology is formulated. See also TYPE, IDEAL TYPE, TYPIFICATION.

U

unanticipated consequences or **unintended consequences (of social action)** any consequences of social action that are unintended and unforeseen by social participants. That social actions have consequences unforeseen by SOCIAL ACTORS is a major part of the drive to undertake sociological analysis. The same impetus was often uppermost in many forms of social thought prior to modern sociology, for example, Adam SMITH's "invisible hand" of market forces, an idea taken and transformed by MARX (see also APPEARANCE AND REALITY).

In modern sociology, discussion of unanticipated consequences has been influenced especially by Robert MERTON's discussion of these (see MANIFEST AND LATENT FUNCTIONS, SELF-FULFILLING AND SELF-DESTROYING PROPHECY). The importance of analysis of unanticipated consequences is not confined to FUNCTIONALISM. Rather, it is central to most forms of sociology and in no way implies adherence to or acceptance of a model of societies as self-maintaining social systems, as assumed by functionalists. Within Marxism and modern STRUCTURALISM, for example, the importance of analysis of underlying realities is obvious, but it is also present as a main objective in many other forms of sociology, including Weberian sociology. For example, Protestants did not intend to establish modern capitalism, but according to Weber, this is one outcome of their religious orientation—see PROTESTANT ETHIC.

Notwithstanding that for some forms of meaningful and interpretive sociology, the understanding and representation of actors' meaning have sometimes been seen as the *primary* task of sociology, for most forms of sociology these are considered simply a first task. This is to acknowledge that social action can only be recognized by the grasping of meaning, but once this has been accomplished, the social implications, including the unanticipated and unintended consequences, must also be sought. Thus, a difference must be drawn between those forms of sociology rightly criticized (for example, by ETHNOMETHODOLOGY) for failing to capture or simply setting aside actors' meanings and members' methods, and those forms of sociology that capture meanings and move beyond them. The latter approaches would seem essential if sociology is to be in any position to offer the fullest scientific or critical grasp of social issues.

Among the many reasons why social participants do not always intend or comprehend the implications of their own actions are:

(a) layers of unconscious and subconscious mind beneath conscious intentions, including various modes of tacit knowledge and human social competence;

(b) long chains of interdependence in and between modern societies that no one is in a position to view, still less to anticipate, in their entirety;

(c) the operation of ideological distortions, cultural HEGEMONY, etc. that hide an accurate view of social relations from some or all social participants.

If many unacknowledged and unanticipated consequences, when revealed, may be found to fulfill functional needs, others do not. Sociological analysis therefore tends to expose unwanted social outcomes, and in this way sociology can be seen as an inherently critical discipline.

As there is nothing about social reality that social participants cannot potentially come to know and act on, any sociology is almost bound to involve a critical intervention in social life. This is the minimal sense in which sociology is an inherently critical discipline. Since sociology can be employed in transforming social action, the opportunity also exists for it to be used in a technological or socially manipulative mode to control social participants. There is also, however, a larger sense in which sociology is a critical discipline, a so-called social emancipatory discipline, in that it reveals the underlying truth about social arrangements, thus enabling reform or social revolution (see also FRANKFURT SCHOOL OF CRITICAL THEORY, HABERMAS).

Complaints that such forms of critical sociology override actors' views (for example, see FALSE CONSCIOUSNESS) can be potentially combatted by adopting a "dialogical model" in the application of sociology. This is to say that social participants likely to be affected by application of sociological knowledge should always be given the opportunity to understand, and to accept or reject, the sociological accounts to be applied. A psychoanalytic model of such a dialogic relation is proposed, for example, by Jurgen HABERMAS (see also COMMUNICATIVE COMPETENCE, INVOLVEMENT AND NEUTRALITY).

underclass occupational and status groups that can be seen as located below, or even outside, the main CLASS and SOCIAL STATUS hierarchies. Included in this category are the long-term unemployed; those in short-term, low-paid, and generally unpleasant forms of employment, including migrant workers, some women, and members of ethnic minority groups—see also DUAL LABOR MARKET. Single-parent families and the elderly on state pensions are sometimes also included. The term is controversial. In one argument the underclass does not constitute a class in any strict sense, since people are often located within it only for short periods, for example, at certain points in the LIFE COURSE or in periods of unemployment. Debate also exists as to whether the DEPRIVATION associated with underclass locations is predominantly individual or social structural in source. However, in two cases at least, gender and race, structural sources appear highly significant. Since the underclass is a minority class within modern societies, its fragmented and socially disorganized nature provides little basis for class solidarity, and the capacity of this class to change its situation by political means tends to be limited. Thus, a division between affluent mainstream society and a deprived underclass may persist as a feature of modern societies. See also LUMPENPROLETARIAT, CYCLE OF DEPRIVATION, CULTURE OF POVERTY, GHETTO.

understanding see MEANINGFUL UNDERSTANDING AND EXPLANATION, VERSTEHEN.

unemployment the state of not being employed in paid work, or self-employed, even though the person is available for such activity. Most discussion and analysis of the subject relate to the general level of unemployment rather than the individual's experience of it (see Sinfield, 1981, for a study of the experience of unemployment). In Britain, for example, the official unemployment rate nearly tripled during the 1970s (2.6% in 1970, 7.4% in 1980), and nearly doubled again by 1984 (13.1%) (Price and Bains, 1988). Moreover, these statistics need to be interpreted against the background knowledge that the postwar consensus in Britain until the 1980s was predicated on the WELFARE STATE, which included full employment. For much of the postwar period, British official statistics recorded all those drawing unemployment benefits. This is not the same as the number seeking employment, for it excluded all those not entitled to draw benefits (school dropouts, recent graduates, newly arrived immigrants, and many married women) (Price and Bains, op. cit.). The extent of underestimation, however, was less than is now the case. Since 1980 the British government has chosen also to preclude all persons covered by so-called special employment measures and the Youth Training Scheme, who would otherwise be unemployed. In addition, since 1983, it is no longer a requirement for those over 60 years old to register for work (ibid.).

The debates surrounding the issue of unemployment have qualitatively changed during the 1980s. While the high level of unemployment remains a politically sensitive issue, the government has attempted to restructure the relationship between the state and citizen away from that involved in the welfare state and toward a new liberalism in the labor markets. This new approach also reflects wider economic and technological realities. Some observers are pessimistic in their prognoses, as is the case of Gill (1985), while others, for example Handy (1984), are far more sanguine, not in terms of the possibilities of reducing the general levels of unemployment, but in its redefinition so that unemployment becomes transmogrified into a range of status enhancing and socially valuable activities.

unilinear of any process of SOCIAL CHANGE or development that always proceeds in a single direction, through the same stages, and with the same results. The concept of unilinearity is actually a redundant one in sociology, for no process of social change is actually (or ever could be) unilinear. However, unilinear assumptions were a prominent feature of much 19th-century social theory. See also EVOLUTIONARY THEORY, DIFFUSION.

unobtrusive measures any methods of collecting data without the knowledge of the subject and without affecting the data. Examples are varied, including covert observation, studies of garbage, wear on carpets, and recording how much coffee is consumed in meetings. What these unobtrusive methods have in common is that they avoid the problem of so-called subject reaction to the study. Hence, they are less likely to distort the observations than are standard ways of collecting data, for example, completion of a questionnaire or an attitude test. In the latter cases the subjects are bound to be aware that they are taking part in research, and this can produce artificial results. Unobtrusive measures are often used within a QUALITATIVE RESEARCH design and can be especially useful in evaluation research to reduce any distorting reaction to the evaluation on the part of the people being evaluated.

unstructured data data that has been collected without reference to how it might eventually be coded. Some questions in survey questionnaires (and particularly in pilot questionnaires) yield data of this nature. Respondents are asked to give a direct verbal answer to a question for which there has been no precoding. Much data collected by qualitative researchers are unstructured, and content analysts studying newspapers and historical sociologists studying old manuscript sources make use of unstructured data, because these sources were not compiled with their needs in mind.

The main problem facing the researcher when dealing with unstructured data is that of imposing a structure on it to make it useful. The best procedure for researchers is to fully familiarize themselves with both the material itself and its historical context. In undertaking a study of a 19th-century election based on an analysis of newspapers and election results, for example, books dealing with the political behavior of the period should be consulted. In making sense of the data, a possible structure emerges and can be imposed. For example, to analyze the major issues of a campaign and the various stances taken by each candidate, a matrix might be constructed showing the number of references made by each candidate to each issue, and their political persuasions could then be estimated by counting the number of negative and positive statements on each issue. See also SCALING, QUALITATIVE RESEARCH, CONTENT ANALYSIS, HISTORICAL SOCIOLOGY. Compare STRUCTURED CODING.

untouchables see CASTE.

upper class the topmost class in any society. In modern British society, fore example, this class can be said to consist of:

(a) a core of about 25,000 individuals who exercise strategic control over the economy (Scott, 1982);

(b) a wider group of individuals and families owning considerable, usually inherited, wealth, and distinguished by a distinctive lifestyle.

Since the numbers of individuals involved is relatively small, networks of relationships (for example, public school education, upper class leisure pursuits) play an important part in sustaining the distinctive lifestyle, high social status, and the economic and political power enjoyed by the upper class. Persons whose family origins are upper class are also prominent in elite professions, such as the administrative class of the civil service, the judiciary, and the upper echelons of the military, positions that may be seen as upper class in their own right.

urbanism as a way of life the prevailing feature of modern society, (in the view of L. Wirth, 1938). Wirth regarded this feature as more salient than industrialism or capitalism, since the development of large cities and towns had created a break with "society's natural situation." The process of URBANIZATION had rendered ties of kinship less important and replaced them with relationships of an instrumental, transitory, and superficial character. Urban settlements are characterized by size, density, and heterogeneity, which in combination provide the basis for a complex division of labor and fundamental changes in the nature of social relationships. See also URBAN SOCIOLOGY.

urbanization 1. the statistical measure of the proportion of a country's population living in cities or settlements of a size defined variously by political, cultural, or administrative criteria. The *rate of urbanization* describes changes in the proportion of urban to rural dwellers over time (the reverse process is described as the *rate of deurbanization*). **2.** the social processes and relationships that are both the cause and consequence of the urban rather than rural way of life (see URBANISM AS A WAY OF LIFE).

G. Hurd et al. (1973) have suggested that historically the process of urbanization had three major stages. The first is identified as extending from the time when people first began to live in towns up until the 18th century. During this stage few urban areas had more than 100,000 people. The second stage is the rapid growth in the size and number of cities, contingent on the process of INDUSTRIALIZATION. Tables drawn up by the United Nations Statistical Office show that between 73% and 85% of the populations in the industrial countries of the West live in cities. The third stage is *metropolitanization*, which involves centralization of people and wealth and of society's political, economic, and cultural institutions (see P. Hall, *The World Cities*, 1977). Other writers would refer to a fourth stage of *deurbanization* via the growth of suburbs, migration to rural areas, alternative communities, and planned "new towns."

In its earliest usage the term "urbanize" meant "make urbane," that is, render something or someone polished or refined. The modern sense of "develop an urban character," or "make into a city," emerged in the second half of the 19th century, when the city became a special object of study for social scientists and others concerned about the social consequences of the growth of industrial cities (see URBAN SOCIOLOGY). The relevance of the older usage is that it influenced the way in which thinkers conceptualized the rural and the urban and gave rise to two contrasting sets of images:

(a) the city as the locus of civilization, refinement, excitement, freedom, and change, in contrast with what Marx described as "rural idiocy";

(b) the country as the home of truth and of sharing in "knowable communities" united by common values, in contrast with the alienation of the city. Raymond Williams examines these traditions in *The Country and the City* (1973), where he also says that in writings about the city from the 16th to the 19th century a number of themes emerge in sequence—money and law, wealth and luxury, the mob and the masses, and finally mobility and isolation. He says that in the past, as now, our real experience is of many different types of organization in the city and the country, yet our imagery is always of two opposed realities, the rural-urban dichotomy.

The dichotomy of two different sociocultural systems, one of which is broken down under the force of industrialization, was a prominent element in the study of preindustrial societies and of industrialization.

Although in Europe urbanization and industrialization did occur generally at the same time, it would be a mistake to see these two processes as necessarily contingent on each other. For example, urbanization preceded industrialization in England in that a high and rising proportion of English people had lived in London from the time of its first phase of growth in the 16th century until the early 1700s, when it was estimated to hold 1/7th of the population. London was a city created by agriculture and mercantile capital within an aristocratic political order that tried to arrest its growth by ordinances preventing erection of buildings. The development of cities as centers of industrial activity came later, primarily in the Midlands and North of England, and parts of central Scotland. Today, in many parts of Africa, Asia, and Latin America, there is rapid urban growth via migration and natural increase without any significant development in the direction of an industrial economy.

urban sociology the study of social relationships and structures in the city. It is a subdiscipline of sociology, whose development has been influenced by debate about the distinctiveness of its subject matter, by the willingness or researchers to adopt cross-disciplinary approaches, and by a social-problem orientation that has fostered research outside the mainstream of intellectual change in sociology.

Early sociological writing about the city located the urban dimension within the broader compass of sociological theorizing. TONNIES, SIMMEL, and WEBER in the 1890s addressed such issues as the characteristic forms of association and social life in urban environments, and the role of urban development in social change. With the establishment of the CHICAGO SCHOOL of sociologists in the 1920s, urban studies emerged as a distinct area of research. Focusing on the issues of social order and organization, members of the Chicago School conducted empirical research into the social characteristics of different areas within the city. For example, research on the ZONE OF TRANSITION, the area bordering the central business district characterized by high levels of migration, social heterogeneity, and poor housing stock, explored the relationships between the incidence of social problems such as crime, mental illness, alcoholism, and social cohesion. Urban sociology demonstrated that (a) socioeconomic factors were more significant than geographical or environmental factors in the genesis of social problems, and that (b) meaning and social order exist in areas of apparent disorganization (see W. Whyte's study of Boston street-corner boys, *Street Corner Society*, 1958).

Although the Chicago School established a rich empirical tradition, its theoretical deficiencies led to a decline in urban sociology between the 1940s and 1960s, with the exception of a number of community studies showing urban neighbourhoods to have forms of association commonly associated with rural communities (Gans, 1962, called them "urban villages"). The theoretical poverty of the rural/urban typologies and the metropolitanization of society left urban sociology indistinguishable from the sociological analysis of advanced, industrial, capitalist societies. However, in the late 1960s urban sociology was revived under the influence of a new generation of (a) Weberian and (b) Marxist scholars:

(a) J. Rex and R. Moore published a study of housing and race relations in Sparkbrook, Birmingham, (*Race, Community and Conflict*, 1967), which combined Burgess's insights into the dynamics of the zone of transition with Weber's ideas about the sociological significance of the meaningful actions of individuals. This work relocated urban sociology within the sociological mainstream and in turn stimulated discussion of Weberian stratification theory through the concept of the *housing class*. Because the housing market is structured around different forms of tenure, it gives rise to new status groups or consumption classes whose interests do not necessarily coincide with economic class interests. Housing is a scarce resource whose distribution is influenced by a political group that Pahl termed *urban managers*. The degree of autonomy they possess vis-à-vis the central state, private capital, and the local consumer of social goods is an empirical question, but according to Pahl their operations give rise to forms of social inequality and political struggle that are independent of the sphere of production.

(b) Marxist work on the city began with a critique of urban sociology as ideology. Lefebvre (1967) argued that urban sociology was an apology for capitalism because it failed to examine the ways in which space is actually produced and distributed in capitalist societies. Space is itself a commodity, a scarce and alienable resource, in this view. The contradictions between profit and need, exchange and use value, and the individual versus the collective are exemplified by the conflicting need of capital to exploit space for profit and the social requirements of the people. Castells, although a Marxist, begins his analysis (*The Urban Question*, 1977) with the conventional interest in spatially significant social phenomena, and he does not regard space as a theoretically important issue. What is significant is the role of the urban system in the mode of production. Castells concentrates on the reproduction of LABOR POWER, which he sees as being increasingly concentrated within particular spatial units where the provision of social goods and services is dependent on the state. Centralization of services results in collectivization of consumption. He sees the city as an important element in the struggle against capitalism, because urban crises cut across class boundaries and give rise to social movements with a specifically urban base that can in turn create the conditions for new political alliances. These ideas stimulated discussion of COLLECTIVE CONSUMPTION, an underdeveloped concept in Marx's work, and the political economy of housing and rents. Marxist critics (Pickvance, 1976; Harvey 1973) have argued that these approaches must not replace class struggle with consumption and accumulation as the main factors in the analysis of capitalism.

utilitarianism a philosophical school of thought holding that utility entails the greatest happiness of the greatest number. It is usually associated with Jeremy BENTHAM (1748–1832) and John Stuart MILL (1806–1873), although some would argue that the earlier philosophical works of HOBBES, HUME, and LOCKE are also utilitarian. This philosophy holds that the realization of utility should be the proper goal in life, but may be hindered by selfish prejudice and ignorance. Behavior that enhances happiness and reduces pain ought to be encouraged and behavior that increases unhappiness ought to be proscribed. Utilitarianism, therefore, implies a model of social action in which individuals rationally pursue their own self-interests, with SOCIETY being no more than the aggregation of individuals brought together in the realization of their individual goals. Bentham applied these principles to economics, SOCIAL POLICY, and LAW. Utilitarianism influenced the creation of many of the 19th-century institutions, many of which still survive, such as the prison and the mental hospital (see PANOPTICON). SPENCER was influenced by utilitarian ideas, although DURKHEIM was critical, arguing that SOCIAL ORDER is the outcome of cultural traditions that are not reducible to individual interests.

utopia (from the Greek for "nowhere") any imaginary society or place, intended to stand as an ethical or theoretical ideal or to provide an illuminating contrast with existing patterns of social organization. Utopia may be based on historically existing societies or located in the future. Well-known examples of utopias are Plato's *Republic* and Sir Thomas More's *Utopia* (1516).

Assessments of the value of utopian thinking vary. By its advocates the use of utopian imagery is justified if it aids critical imagination and extends awareness of alternatives to existing forms of social organization. By its detractors it is seen as liable to mislead and to promote unreal expectations about social change. See also UTOPIANISM. Compare IDEAL TYPE.

utopian communities communities established with the aim of realizing, or moving toward, an ideal form of society, for example, 19th-century socialist communities such as Robert Owen's New Harmony, or recent sectarian religious communities such as Jonestown (Guyana). Such communities have often been short-lived, but as social experiments they have attracted considerable attention in sociology for the indication they may offer on the viability of alternative patterns of social organization. See UTOPIA.

utopianism any form of social or political thinking or social theory that presents an ideal form of society as a realizable model of future society (see UTOPIA).

Such thinking has sometimes been criticized as fostering political objectives or political strategies that may have little empirical or theoretical basis (compare Marx's rejection of UTOPIAN SOCIALISM). For MANNHEIM (*Ideology and Utopia,* 1929), however, utopian ideas can be distinguished from most ideologies in always possessing a potentially "transforming effect upon an existing historical social order." In this sense utopianism may sometimes help bring about at least some aspects of the ideal model of society that it advances (see also FRANKFURT SCHOOL OF CRITICAL THEORY). At the same time, Mannheim did not fail to notice that utopianism was often rooted in irrationalism. See also MILLENARIANISM, COLLECTIVE BEHAVIOR.

utopian socialism early forms of modern socialist thinking (including the ideas of SAINT-SIMON, Fourier, and Owen) criticized by Marx as "utopian" (see UTOPIA, UTOPIAN COMMUNITIES), since they were seen by him as based on an inadequately scientific conception of the dynamics of capitalist society and the necessity of class struggle.

V

validity the extent to which a measure, indicator, or method of data collection has the quality of being sound or true as far as can be judged. For example, if a psychological measure, such as an intelligence test, is considered to be valid, this means it is thought to measure what it sets out to measure. If social survey observations are said to have produced valid data, then they are considered to be a true reflection of the phenomenon being studied in the population being studied (for example, projections of voting behavior), and the survey method can be said to have validity. Compare RELIABILITY.

In practice, in sociology and the social sciences generally, the relation between indicators and measures on the one hand and the underlying concepts they are taken to represent is often contested (see OFFICIAL STATISTICS, MEASUREMENT BY FIAT).

value freedom and **value neutrality 1.** the view that sociology can and should conduct research according to the dictates of science, excluding any influence of the researcher's own values (see VALUES sense **1.**). **2.** the doctrine, particularly associated with Max WEBER (1949)—sometimes expressed as *value neutrality*—that sociologists, if they cannot ever hope to exclude all biases introduced into their work by their own values, can at least make clear what these values are and how they affect their work. **3.** the doctrine of *value freedom* or *value neutrality* or (sometimes) *ethical neutrality,* that, while social science may establish the facts about social reality, in doing so, it cannot settle questions of ultimate VALUE **1.**, since a logical gap always exists between empirical evidence and moral actions, between facts and values (see FACT-VALUE DISTINCTION). **4.** the doctrine, also particularly associated with Weber (and related to his acceptance of value freedom/value neutrality in senses **2.** and **3.**) that the sociologist *qua* sociologist should *not* seek to pronounce on ultimate values, and especially should not seek to use his or her professional position as a teacher of students to seek to advance particular value positions.

The four senses of value freedom/value neutrality all raise problems. The problem with **1.** is that it is difficult to exclude or even control all influence of the researcher's values on the choice and execution of social research, hence Weber's position, sense **2.** Furthermore, it is not apparent that sociological research that starts from the researcher's values must inevitably lose in VALIDITY and OBJECTIVITY—if this were so, then almost all the work of the major classical sociologists, including positivistically inclined sociologists such as DURKHEIM, would be fatally flawed. Moreover, the idea also seems out of gear with what we know about science in general, that is, it can never operate in a presuppositionless way (see also OBJECTIVITY, THEORY-RELATIVITY).

VALUE JUDGMENT

The alternative to sense **1.** provided by Weber's conception of VALUE RELEVANCE, is that sociologists will inevitably be guided by a concern for values, but that so long as this is made clear, it need not compromise the achievement of objectivity *within* the chosen frame of reference. However, the problem with this view, especially when made in conjunction with senses **3.** and **4.**, is that it would appear to support a view of the arbitrariness and ultimate irrationalism of values. For many sociologists, including Durkheim and MARX, such a view is unacceptable, and a more general scientific basis for values remains a goal (see also VALUE JUDGMENT).

A more specific objection to Weber's doctrine of value freedom in sense **4.** is advanced by BECKER (1967; 1970) and GOULDNER (1956; 1973): any acceptance of this doctrine enables sociologists, if they wish, to undertake research for the rich and powerful, who can afford to commission research or can readily set the agenda of social problems seen as requiring attention (see HIERARCHY OF CREDIBILITY). See also ETHICAL INDIFFERENCE, RELATIVISM.

value judgment an ethical or moral evaluation, especially where this leads to a statement of what, on ethical or moral grounds, ought to be done. In Logical Positivism (see POSITIVISM) the assumption is sometimes made that no value judgment can ever be derived from a purely scientific statement (see FACT-VALUE DISTINCTION). However, two other possibilities exist:

(a) that facts and theories, although they can never dictate our values, can inform us about causal connections, etc., thus also indicating how we might go about achieving our ethical goals (this was approximately WEBER's view; see also HYPOTHETICAL IMPERATIVE);

(b) that the notion of an insurmountable divorce between facts and values is false, and that whenever possible we should always seek to ground our ethical and moral positions and our value judgments on firm sociological foundations (the position, for example, of COMTE or DURKHEIM, or the FRANKFURT SCHOOL OF CRITICAL THEORY).

All three positions continue to be held by various sociologists in modern sociology.

value relativity the proposition that all sociological knowledge is relative to particular values, and that these values, in turn, are also relative to social content. See RELATIVISM, VALUE RELEVANCE, OBJECTIVITY.

value relevance the doctrine that sociological research topics will inevitably, and rightly, often be chosen for their ethical interest, but that this need not prevent the researcher from seeking OBJECTIVITY within the particular frame of reference adopted. The doctrine is especially associated with Max WEBER in association with his conception of VALUE FREEDOM and VALUE NEUTRALITY (senses **2.** and **4.**). This means that he identified three stages in the overall relation between values and sociological research: (a) a researcher's values often influence the choice of topic, (b) this need not prevent objective research, for example, research establishing the empiri-

VARIABLE

cal importance of particular values such as the PROTESTANT ETHIC; but (c) the outcome of any research never amounts to outright justification of particular values. See also FACT-VALUE DISTINCTION.

values 1. ethical ideals and beliefs. The term is often used to distinguish scientific knowledge from values, especially where such ethical ideals, "oughts," etc. are held not to be, or as inherently incapable of ever being, scientific. See also FACT-VALUE DISTINCTION, POSITIVISM, VALUE FREEDOM and VALUE NEUTRALITY. **2.** the central beliefs and purposes of an individual or society. In Talcott PARSONS' structural-functionalism, internalized shared values are regarded as playing a decisive role in the social integration of any society (see also CONSENSUS). Criticism of this view is that it overstates the extent to which social integration depends on shared values and understates the importance of political or economic POWER (see also OVERSOCIALIZED CONCEPTION OF MAN; CONFLICT THEORY). Most sociologists recognize that societies can exist even though riven by value divisions, and that an adherence to prevailing beliefs and values is often expedient or pragmatic rather than deeply held (for example, see DEFERENCE). Equally, however, most sociologists also acknowledge that naked economic or political force is rarely the sole basis of social integration (for example, is an unstable basis of political power) and that values usually play an important role.

In a similar way to criticisms of functionalism, Marxist theories that posit a dominant role for IDEOLOGIES in maintaining social power are also criticized for overemphasizing the role of internalized beliefs and values (see DOMINANT IDEOLOGY THESIS).

variable a characteristic that can be measured and may vary along a continuum (for example, height), be more discrete (for example, family size) or be bipolar (for example, sex). The term is commonly used in empirical social research to denote the representation of a social factor such as age, social class, employment status, or years of education, which can be observed to affect other measures, such as income level, which may be influenced by all of those mentioned. Social and psychological research is particularly interested in defining which aspects of society or experience influence other social parameters or behaviors, with the intention of explaining social phenomena. In one view, for this to be managed scientifically, possible influences and possible effects have to be defined and quantified so that methods such as concomitant variation, survey research, or experiment can be set up to test HYPOTHESES. It is these definitions and quantifications that result in the variables used in scientific data analysis. In some traditions in sociology, however, the appropriateness of the concept of the variable in the above sense has been questioned. From the perspective of SYMBOLIC INTERACTIONISM, for example, Herbert BLUMER (1956) has suggested that use of standardized variables in social analysis leads to neglect of the close study required for effective study of social situations and distorted representation of social reality. Similar skepticism is voiced in approaches such as ETHNOMETHODOLOGY (see also MEASUREMENT BY FIAT, OFFICIAL STATISTICS).

Varna see CASTE.

Veblen, Thornstein (1857–1929) US economist, sociologist, and social critic who founded the approach known as *institutional economics*. In *Theory of the Leisure Class* (1899), Veblen presented an uncompromising critique of the lifestyle of emulation and CONSPICUOUS CONSUMPTION of the dominant social groupings in American society. In a further series of works, notably *The Theory of the Business Enterprise* (1904), *The Instinct for Workmanship* (1914), and *The Engineers and the Price System* (1921), he was responsible for an equally trenchant critical analysis of American capitalism, which he regarded as predatory and parasitic. Veblen's hope was that one day the LEISURE CLASS and modern corporate power would be replaced by the rule of engineers and that the human "instinct for workmanship" would prevail. However, he was not surprised that capitalism should have led to world war, the origins of which he traced to Germany's late industrialization and its lack of a democratic political tradition. There is some similarity between Veblen's style of sociology (and the hostile response it often generated) and the later work of another major sociological critic of American society, C. Wright MILLS. However, the critical reception of Veblen's work reflects weakness in his methods as well as undoubted ideological resistance to his critique of US society.

Verstehen the German word for "understanding," which, when used in a sociological context in English-speaking sociology, usually refers to MEANINGFUL UNDERSTANDING, the procedure in which both social actors and sociologists interpret and gain access to the meanings of others.

The German term is especially associated with the work of Max WEBER, who stated as "the specific task of the sciences of action, ... the interpretation of action in terms of its subjective meaning" (Weber, 1922), distinguishing the social sciences from the natural sciences by the presence of such an orientation.

A confusion exists in the literature—illustrating the problems that can arise in any understanding of meanings—as to whether in Weber's use *Verstehen* refers only to a doubtful psychologistic and introspective, empathic understanding, in which the sociologist merely imagines herself or himself in the place of a person or group, or whether—something capable of far more objective evaluation—actors' subjective meanings can be read from the existence of an explicit language of social meanings that can be objectively demonstrated.

In fact, Weber's usage would appear to have involved elements of *both* possibilities, but in the former case he tried to found any existential psychological assumptions involved in "empirical regularities of experience." Nevertheless, there remain some critics who wrongly see Weber's and *any* other use of *Verstehen* as *only* involving a doubtful introspective psychology (for example, Abel, 1977). While others (for example, WINCH, 1958, or Macintyre, 1962) argue that it would have been better if Weber had confined his use of *Verstehen* to meaningful understanding in the second sense, and not sought to merge meaningful understanding and causal explanation.

What Weber meant by "causal explanation" in the context of actors' meanings is another issue: either these could refer (a) to meanings *in themselves* functioning as causes (a use to which some philosophers object; compare WINCH), or (b) *Verstehen* is a way of generating wider causal hypotheses based on universals, which at least to some degree must themselves in turn be verified against experience.

Again Weber does seem to have made reference to causes in *both* these senses. It is in this context that Weber's sociology may be seen as constituting a mid-position between a purely positivistic sociology with no place for actors' meanings, and a purely interpretive sociology with no place for causal analysis. In all of this Weber's view was that sociology should go as far as is appropriate in making sociology a science, and no further. Thus, he insisted that actors' meanings and choices could never be reduced to merely physical or mechanical causation.

violence the infliction of physical harm on the human body, or on human property, by physical force, using the body or weapons. The ability to marshall physical force is often a determining factor in social actions, for example, between husbands and wives (see WIFE BATTERING), or parents and children. In politics, the sustaining of a claim to legitimate monopoly of control over the means of violence within a territory (including defense of the nation), is a defining feature of the STATE. Equally, however, the threat of a recourse to violence against rulers by the ruled acts as a major constraint on the powers of rulers.

vocabularies of motive the verbalizations and terminologies employed by social actors, not only to describe their motives but to persuade others as to the acceptability of their actions. As used by MILLS (1940), such vocabularies of motivation do not refer to the universal psychic structure of the human organism. Rather, they are the typical terms in which, in particular societies, actors justify their actions. It is suggested by Gerth and Mills that these vocabularies become embedded in our individual and collective psychic structure, but in particular, rather than universal, ways.

voodoo or **voodooism** a syncretic religious CULT, probably of African origin, that is pervasive among the peasantry and urban poor in parts of the Caribbean and Central America, most particularly in Haiti. Voodoo practices involve magic and witchcraft, especially the use of charms and spells.

voting behavior the decision-making processes and the social factors influencing patterns of voting.

Studies of voting behavior have been of four main types: constituency studies, nationwide studies, cross-national studies, and studies focused on particular categories of voters or the political implications of particular class locations. The seminal studies that influenced most later work were by LAZARSFELD et al. (1944) and Berelson et al. (1954). These American studies established the importance of socioeconomic variables such as socioeconomic status, religion, age, and gender as determinants of voting behavior. They also made clear the part played by group pressures and OPINION LEADERSHIP as influences on voting behavior. The dominant paradigm that resulted was that most voting behavior could be accounted for in terms of the PARTY IDENTIFICATION of voters, which for most individual voters was assumed to be relatively stable.

This model also informed the important study of the British electorate by Butler and Stokes (1969). These researchers painted a picture of voting behavior in Britain in which, as well as being influenced by CLASS, voters tended to inherit their party identification from their parents, where this had been strong, was shared by both parents, and was for principal parties. With the apparently increased volatility of voting behavior in recent years ("erosion of partisanship") this model of voting behavior is now under review (see also CLASS DEALIGNMENT). Since many focused studies of voting behavior and political attitudes (for example, McKenzie and Silver, 1968, on WORKING CLASS CONSERVATISM, and GOLDTHORPE and LOCKWOOD et al., 1968b, on AFFLUENT WORKERS) have assumed the predominance of class-based voting, seeking to explain departures from this, any overall decline in class voting would also have implications for the interpretation of such cross-class patterns of voting, which would no longer be exceptional. See also PARTY IMAGE, POLITICAL ATTITUDES, STABLE DEMOCRACY.

W

Wallas, Graham (1858–1932) English political scientist who is sometimes regarded as one of the founding fathers of the BEHAVIORAL APPROACH in political analysis. His most influential book was *Human Nature in Politics* (1908), in which he argued for a greater emphasis on the role of nonrational factors in politics, including custom and human psychology. Perhaps his most potent contribution was to coin the term *political image*.

Wallerstein, Immanuel, (1930–) US sociologist and social historian, born in New York and educated at Columbia University. He researched primarily in Africa, between 1955 and 1970. The first volume of his *Modern World-System* appeared in 1974, and since 1976 he has been Distinguished Professor of Sociology at the State University of New York, Binghamton, and Director of the Fernand Braudel Center for the Study of Economies, Historical Systems, and Civilizations. His major contribution has been the development of world systems theory and the coordination of a large body of research that comprises interdisciplinary studies in sociology, economics, politics, and history. The most general statements of his approach are contained in his *The Capitalist World-Economy* (1979), a collection of essays, and *Historical Capitalism* (1983). See also CENTER AND PERIPHERY.

Ward, Lester (1841–1913) US sociologist and evolutionary theorist (see EVOLUTIONARY THEORY). Ward's education and career were informed by self-help and eclecticism. He studied botany and law and went on to work and research in botany and geology, before eventually obtaining a professorship of sociology in 1906. His sociology emphasized the psychological dimension, and his four-stage evolutionary theory reflected this stance. He made the distinction, familiar to much 19th-century social thought, between the study of social dynamics and social statics, more familiarly, between the study of social process and change, and the description of social structure.

Ward, following thinkers like COMTE, was a positivist (see POSITIVISM) in the sense that he was eager to use sociological knowledge for political purposes, though his predilection was to develop the discipline by way of concepts and classification, rather than by quantitative data. Indeed, he argued strongly that social reform should be based on, or at least be in accordance with, the social laws that it was the objective of sociology to identify. Ward's evolutionary and positivist perspective, however, did not lead him, as it easily could have done, to a politics of nonintervention. One of his principal concepts was telesis, roughly the guiding of evolutionary change by purposive selection, and it was on this basis that Ward supported movements aimed at emancipating women and America's industrial working class. He was a critic of social and economic inequality, but the achievement of a less unequal society could not be by imposition from above. The state, however, by acting on the principle of telesis, could produce policies, such as universal education, that would help produce greater egalitarianism.

warfare 1. violent, usually armed, conflict between STATES or peoples. **2.** comparable but not necessarily violent conflicts between classes, etc., but which stop short of war in sense **1.** The first of these uses is by far the most important and is dealt with here.

Warfare and preparation for warfare are often regarded as a nearly universal feature of human societies. This is sometimes explained by presence of innate human aggression as well as by operation of a TERRITORIAL IMPERATIVE in human societies. Against this however, it is also clear that the incidence of warfare is highly variable, and that in some societies there is little recourse to warfare and no tradition of militarism. Plainly, warfare is a culturally influenced rather than biologically determined phenomenon. Nor would there appear to be, in simple or in more developed societies, any straightforward pattern of ecological or territorial pressures that can provide an explanation of variations in the incidence of warfare. In modern societies in particular, warfare requires understanding in politicoeconomic terms.

As the historian TILLY remarks, "The state made war, and war made the state." In particular, as numerous commentators have insisted, the modern European NATION STATE can be seen as having been "built for the battlefield" (ANDERSON, 1974b)—see ABSOLUTISM. In addition, the entire modern NATION STATE SYSTEM remains centered on sovereign nation states in which the threat of war is ever present, and in which, at least until recently, the survival of the world was threatened by the antagonism of superpowers. Under these circumstances, and given that the economic and the political side effects of war have also been extensive (for example, as a stimulus to reform or revolution or to political reaction), it is surprising that the study of warfare has not been more central in sociology. Recently this is being remedied with a much greater attention being given to the subject by sociologists (for example, the work of MANN and GIDDENS). A key general issue is how political and military changes and economic and social changes interact. Whereas classical Marxism and many other areas of social science have in the past tended to explain the former in terms of the latter, now the tendency is to give much greater credence to the reverse relationship.

Webb, Sydney (1859–1947) and **Beatrice,** *née* Potter (1858–1943) English social researchers and social activists, who in partnership played a formative role in the development of labor history (for example, *The History of Trade Unions,* 1894, and *Industrial Democracy,* 1897); founded the London School of Economics and Political Science, in 1895; wrote voluminously on local government (*History of English Local Government*, 9 vols., 1903–29); were responsible for the minority report of the Poor Law Commission (1905–7); founded the *New Statesman* (1913); were influential in the Fabian Society and the British Labor Party; and were advocates in the cause of the USSR (*Soviet Communism: A New Civilization?*, 1935). Besides the twenty or so books written in collaboration, each wrote many more books and pamphlets separately. In *Our Partnership* (1948), describing their life and work, Beatrice Webb wrote that they regarded their concern with "the study of social institutions" as "sociology." Not all modern sociologists would agree, for the Webbs' work often related only relatively obliquely to the most central concerns of sociology as a developing academic discipline. But that the Webbs contributed much to historical understanding, to empirical social investigation in the English tradition, and to the promotion of social welfare is undeniable.

Weber, Max (1864–1920) German economist, historian, and major classical sociologist and, along with MARX and DURKHEIM, usually regarded as one of a trinity of three major classical sociologists. Weber was born in Erfurt, Thuringia, and educated at the Universities of Heidelberg, Berlin, and Göttingen. After initial studies in philosophy and law, his interests gravitated toward economics and history and latterly sociology. As a result, Weber's scholarship cannot be confined within narrow disciplinary boundaries; he taught law in Berlin from 1892 before becoming professor of political economy at Freiburg in 1894 and professor of economics at Heidelberg in 1897, when a depressive illness interrupted his research and precluded further involvement in teaching until he accepted chairs in sociology at Vienna in 1918, and at Munich in the following year. Throughout his life Weber took an active interest in the social and political affairs of Germany; his politics were nationalist in tendency, yet critical, liberal, and antiauthoritarian, especially in his defense of academic freedom against those who sought to make the universities serve the interests of the state.

Weber's scholarly output is formidable in extent and controversial in its content and interpretation. In summary his aims were:

(a) to put the social sciences on a sound methodological footing;

(b) to establish their limits with respect to VALUE RELEVANCE and social policy issues;

(c) to provide a range of generalizations and concepts for application to the study of substantive problems;

(d) to contribute to the study of issues that interested him, especially those associated with the nature and origins of modern industrial society and of the process of rationalization that underpinned it.

In pursuit of these aims he wrote extensively on the methodology and philosophy of the social sciences (especially see Weber, *The Methodology of the Social Sciences* (ed. Finch), 1949), and contributed to the study of ancient society, economic history, the comparative religion and social structures of China, India, and Europe, and *inter alia* to the sociologies of law, politics, and music. The most comprehensive systematization of his sociological thinking is *Wirtschaft and Gesellschaft*, (1922).

For Weber, the aim of sociology was to achieve an interpretive understanding of subjectively meaningful human action, which exposed to view the actors' motives, at one level the causes of ACTIONS. Acting individuals constituted the only social reality, and so he was opposed to the use of collective concepts (the STATE, SOCIETY etc.) unless these were firmly related to the actions of individuals. He also opposed the idea that the social sciences could discover laws, especially development laws, in the manner of the natural sciences, though he thought that social scientists could and should employ lawlike generalizations—statements of tendency—about the nature, course, and consequences of human conduct. These were possible because human behavior tended to follow more or less regular patterns. They were necessary in order to establish the causal adequacy of explanation, and could be given statistical expression provided that the statistics were supported by meaningful interpretation of the conduct to which they referred.

Weber's work abounds in generalizations and in concepts ranging from a basic typology of SOCIAL ACTION to well-known constructs like BUREAUCRACY, charisma, etc., all of which are designed to facilitate analysis of action and to elucidate its causes, consequences, and institutional expressions. Many of these concepts are IDEAL TYPES, that is, logical simplifications of tendencies more or less present in a complex reality, constructed from a one-sided, selective viewpoint by the sociologist. Weber insisted that scientific concepts cannot exhaust reality, which is infinite and too complex for the finite human mind to grasp completely. Concepts, therefore, could never stand as final, exhaustive, definitive accounts, but were heuristic devices against which reality could be compared and measured for the purposes of its further exploration and explanation.

The intimate connection between social sciences and values arose from this need for selectivity; social science was value relevant in that the problems scientists selected for study, and their conceptualization, were determined by the values of the scientists and/or those of their communities (see VALUE RELEVANCE). Yet, social science also had to be value free insofar as values should not be allowed to intrude into the actual investigations and their results (see VALUE FREEDOM), and science could never finally validate value judgments, moral choices, or political preferences. In this sense, the world of science and the world of moral and political choice were seen by Weber as logically disjunct. To assume otherwise would be to abdicate human responsibility for making choices and standing by their consequences.

Weber held these views during the bitter debates about methodology and values that took place in early 20th-century German social science (see also METHODENSTREIT). At the same time he developed his own research interests, which found a major focus in the process of rationalization underpinning modern industrial society. Weber applied the term RATIO-NALIZATION to the West in order to capture a process of disenchantment of the world, in which action was increasingly reduced to prosaic calculation and oriented to the routine administration of a world dominated by large-scale organizations and the specialized division of labor that found their ultimate expression in bureaucracy. Weber felt uneasy about this process, which he saw as destructive of human vitality and freedom; the rule-bound bureaucratic *milieu* compelled people to become narrow specialists; orientation to its values made people into conforming moral cowards who preferred the security of the routine to the exercise of creative imagination and responsibility, which were necessary for preserving human freedom—the highest ideal of the West.

Weber saw this process as uniquely European in origin. In a sweeping comparative analysis of European and Oriental religion and social structures—somewhat misleadingly subsumed under the rubric of the SOCIOLO-GY OF RELIGION—he tries to show how human beings, orienting to different religious, social, and political values, created ideas and structures that inhibited the process in the East and facilitated it in the West. In these studies he tried to indicate how Western religion alone broke the power of MAGIC and thus exercised a decisive influence, independently of economic interests, on the rationalization of economic and social life. Here also he sought to demonstrate how the decentralized Western political structure, together with the legacy of Roman law, created the conditions for development of individual rights and rational administration that capitalism needed and further fostered as it grew. The much discussed, sometimes maligned and much misunderstood PROTESTANT ETHIC thesis is, therefore, but a small fragment of a much larger analysis of Western capitalist society and its origins.

Weber's emphasis on the power of religious interests to influence human conduct makes it tempting to regard him as a thinker opposed to Marx. Yet this judgment may be too simple. Weber regarded MARX and NIETZSCHE as the intellectual giants of his age. Thus, while he rejected the crude economic determinism of vulgar Marxists, it is by no means obvious that he imputed such determinism to Marx himself. Weber, in fact, accepted that economic interests were a prime, often a decisive, mover in shaping human action. More, his concern about modern society's implications for human freedom and creativity has something in common with the concern Marx expressed through his concept of ALIENATION. Nevertheless, Weber's analysis of the structure and dynamics of modern capitalist society differs from Marx's. He does not, for example, see it splitting into two great hostile classes based on property relations. Instead he saw the bases for conflict group formation as being wider, involving:

(a) a larger number of classes, determined by market relationships and thus by credentials and skills as well as property relations;

(b) potentially complicating considerations of status and party that provided possible focuses for conflict independently of class (see also CLASS, STATUS AND PARTY, and MULTIDIMENSIONAL ANALYSIS OF SOCIAL STRATIFICATION).

Above all, however, Weber did not share Marx's optimism about the possibilities for liberation held to inhere in socialism. Insofar as socialism involved centralization of economic and political power, it would extend bureaucratization and thus intensify, rather than alleviate, the problems confronting freedom.

When Weber's work touches the future of Western society, therefore, it is shot through with pathos; it seems ironic to him that a people who established individual freedom should have created conditions that did so much to diminish it. His analysis of modern mass-democratic politics did little to reassure him. Based as they were on mass bureaucratic parties, led by individuals who compromised their ideals in the interest of preserving their organizations and their jobs, these politics tended to be supportive of the *status quo* and provided little scope for critical input from the individual. Weber's longing for great charismatic leaders, for people who by force of their personalities could rouse the masses and challenge the structure of bureaucratic domination, is perhaps understandable in light of this analysis, even if it is a little distasteful in light of a figure like Hitler. Weber, however, was not a proto-Nazi; he clearly believed in political conflict, in which the leaders and their parties competed for, and exchanged, power through the mechanism of elections; he defended academic freedom and the rights of Jewish and Marxist intellectuals against a state that tended to discriminate against them. Nevertheless, his nationalism was undoubted, and this makes it difficult for some people to accept him as a liberal thinker (DAHRENDORF, 1967).

Weber's output has not escaped criticism. Some have suggested that he failed in his aim to provide an adequate foundation for a "meaningful sociology" (SCHUTZ, 1967; WINCH, 1958), and others have suggested that his empirical work is more concerned with elucidating the structural determinants of action than with meanings. His views on ethical neutrality have also come under attack (especially see GOULDNER, 1973), though they also attract considerable support in contemporary sociology. As Boudon and Bourricaud (1989) suggest, however, "the Weberian heritage has furnished a series of continually relevant landmarks to those researchers who have not given up the association of both a wide-ranging historical-comparative perspective with careful institutional analysis and personal commitment with methodological detachment."

welfare state any from of state in which there has been extensive state legislation leading to state provision of support and services intended to improve the quality of people's lives. The term was introduced after World

War II to refer to social legislation, particularly in the areas of health, education, income maintenance, housing, and personal social services. The welfare state intervenes in people's lives at national and local levels. Since 1945, the welfare state has expanded its scope in Britain, and it is now a major concern of government in its cost and operation. Life in all modern Western societies is now affected by welfare concerns, and the idea of a welfare society has a strong ideological appeal.

There are differing sociological explanations of the welfare state:

(a) the citizenship view, most developed in the work of T.H. MARSHALL, which suggests that the state needs to provide minimal welfare support to ensure that an individual can properly participate in a liberal democratic society;

(b) the functionalist view (especially the view of T. PARSONS, that state intervention through social policy is necessary for resolving conflict in complex industrial societies);

(c) the Marxist view, which suggests that the welfare state has an ideological role in legitimating capitalist social relations, and that individuals give support to the state and to a capitalist economic system because they adhere to a belief in the welfare a capitalist state provides.

Marxists have also argued that a welfare state supports the owners of the means of production by reducing the reproduction costs of labor; the welfare state's function is to provide a healthy, educated, well-housed labor force. Further, the conditions under which welfare support is given, that people receive minimal support and have to prove eligibility, are seen to act as a powerful means of social control. However, Marxists have also argued that aspects of the welfare state are genuinely beneficial to the working classes, such as the National Health Service in Britain or rent subsidies. They have argued that these benefits are the result of political pressure coming from the labor movement. Marxists see the welfare state, therefore, as an arena of class conflict that is ambivalent in its operation, partially supporting the owners of the means of production and partially supporting the working classes. More recently, feminist sociologists have argued that explanations of the welfare state have ignored the relationship between women and the welfare state. They argue that many aspects of the welfare state were achieved by women working within the labor movement before 1945, such as the Women's Labor League and the Women's Cooperative Guild. They have also argued that the welfare state has been a powerful regulator of women's lives by sustaining ideas about the roles of women as careers. For example, the Beveridge Report of 1942 specifically excluded married women from being eligible for national insurance benefits; they were to be dependent on their husbands for any social security support. Feminists have also been critical of policies promoting COMMUNITY CARE, arguing that community care is euphemistic for the care women provide for dependent relatives.

Following introduction of monetarist policies and talk of FISCAL CRISIS in a number of Western societies since 1979, the idea of welfare being provided by the state has been questioned. Supporters of this way of thinking have argued that the welfare state is expensive and wasteful and have promoted policies in which welfare services are provided by private organizations, giving people a choice of which services they want to pay for, and whom to get them from.

white-collar worker a nonmanual employee. The term is mainly applied to those who occupy relatively routine posts in the lower sectors of nonmanual employment. A focus on differences in dress between nonmanual and manual workers reflects historical underlying differences in STATUS and work situation, as well as MARKET SITUATION, between the two types of workers.

Whorf, Benjamin Lee see SAPIR-WHORF HYPOTHESIS.

wife battering a colloquial term now also used in sociology to refer to the physical abuse of women by their husbands or sexual partners. Feminist theorists hold such physical abuse explicable, not only as the outcome of the greater physical strength of most males, but as an adjunct of a wider cultural climate that supports male domination. The incidence of wife battering is difficult to determine, but, in Britain, for example, an increased willingness of women to report such actions, and of police and other authorities to take action, has meant its greatly increased visibility.

Winch, Peter (1926–) British philosopher, in the analytic tradition of WITTGENSTEIN, who has written primarily in moral philosophy, and, early in his career, on the philosophy of social science. His early contributions, notably *The Idea of a Social Science* (1958), have been enormously influential. Winch attacked the dominant form of sociology, which was a broadly positivist and functionalist one, arguing that fundamental investigations of social life must be philosophical and ethical rather than aping the natural sciences. For Winch social action is a matter of following and breaking the rules and conventions that underlie the meanings of actions and can be grasped or understood by sociologists (see also RULES AND RULE FOLLOWING). Winch wanted specifically to exclude "causation" (in the sense of "constant conjunction" in David HUME's theory of causality). Social life, he suggested, is more like the unfolding of discourse than of chains of causation. He argued that the heart of philosophy, EPISTEMOLOGY, rests on rules and conventions (Wittgenstein's FORMS OF LIFE) and that philosophical and sociological investigations are therefore inseparable. His insistence on the variety of ways of living, each with a differently based epistemology, also seemed to result in the notion of truth being relativized, leading Winch to be regarded as a social and cognitive relativist.

The refutation of Winch's arguments has been attempted by many. The most successful have challenged his Humean notion of science, arguing that a logical line between causal science and nonscience cannot be drawn, and that "forms of life" cannot finally be circumscribed in the way Winch suggests.

Windelband, Wilhelm (1848–1915) NEO-KANTIAN German philosopher, remembered largely for his distinction between two contrasting focuses of interest in social studies: IDIOGRAPHIC AND NOMOTHETIC, the latter concerned with the discovery of scientific laws and the former the distinctive approach required when dealing with individual historical phenomena. Along with RICKERT, Windelband argued that while economics and sociology, in seeking to establish generalizations, could properly adopt a natural science methodology, it must also be recognized that historical and cultural studies often required use of idiographic methods. One important emphasis in Windelband's work was the significance of values in the selection of problems for study in the cultural realm, a view that influenced WEBER (see VALUE RELEVANCE), although unlike him, Windelband held open the possibility that universally valid ethical norms might be established.

Wittfogel, Karl (1896–) German-born comparative sociologist best known for his work on Chinese society and for his controversial book *Oriental Despotism* (1957). From 1925 until 1933 Wittfogel worked at the Institute for Social Research at Frankfurt (see FRANKFURT SCHOOL OF CRITICAL THEORY). He later moved to the United States.

Wittgenstein, Ludwig (1889–1951) Austrian-born philosopher whose influence on modern philosophy and on certain sectors of sociology has been immense. Wittgenstein is unusual among philosophers in making a major contribution to two divergent major movements within the subject:

(a) In *Tractatus Logico-Philosophicus* (1923), language was presented as "picturing" the world. According to this theory, the truth or falsity of a proposition is ultimately a matter of its correspondence or otherwise with the "atomic facts," that is, the "ultimate simples" that make up the world. This view, connected with Russell's "logical atomism," had a major influence on LOGICAL POSITIVISM.

(b) In *Philosophical Manuscripts* (1953), published posthumously, Wittgenstein, who had previously given up philosophy, believing his task completed with the *Tractatus*, repudiated his "picture theory," advancing instead a theory in which language was seen as providing tools that operate only within particular social contexts or in relation to particular tasks. This is the meaning of Wittgenstein's most influential concept at this stage: language as a FORM OF LIFE (see also LANGUAGE GAMES). Whereas in the *Tractatus* language was the basis of universal truths, a secure basis for science, now there were multiple langauges, and any truth was relative to these. Arguably, Wittgenstein's later philosophy was implicit in his earlier view, for in quitting philosophy at this stage, he had reported himself as leaving unsaid "what cannot be said." In his later philosophy, there is much that can be said, but nothing that can be said independently of particular languages.

It is in its second form, that Wittgenstein's philosophy has exerted a ramifying influence on sociology, especially on SOCIAL PHENOMENOLOGY and ETHNOMETHODOLOGY, partly through its influence on linguistic philosophy and partly more directly, and also through the work of Peter WINCH. It has also had a profound effect on historical and social studies of natural science, seen especially in the work of Thomas KUHN and Paul FEYERABEND. The influence of the later Wittgenstein has been seen as baneful by some sociological commentators, for example, GELLNER (1974), who sees Wittgenstein's influence on Winch as ushering in a "new idealism" and a "new relativism." For others (as for Winch), the MEANINGFUL UNDERSTANDING of social actors' beliefs and values in the particular social contexts in which these are located is of the essence in sociological analysis, and the subject's only goal. There is also a third view, however. For many, Wittgenstein's emphasis on first understanding social actors' beliefs and values before trying to explain them is what is most important and valuable. In such a viewpoint, there are direct parallels between what some sociologists have taken from Wittgenstein, and can also be found in WEBER's conception of accounts of social reality: meaningful and wider causal explanations are combined.

women's liberation movement the multifaceted resurgence of Western FEMINISM from the 1960s. The experience of women activists in the civil rights movement in the United States prompted them to focus on the need to struggle against the subordination of women. In contrast to earlier women's movements, the women's liberation movement stressed that the "personal is political" and saw consciousness-raising as the basis for all theory and practice. The emphasis was therefore on a concrete personal politics that would enable women to analyze the nature of their oppression and struggle to overcome it.

The movement is diverse and nonhierarchical, loosely structured, and without rigid principles. There is no one leader, and a concern with the liberation of women finds expression in many different social contexts. The strands of the movement are, however, united around one major tenet—all women share a common oppression, an oppression not shared by men, who are identified as benefiting from the oppression.

A major concern in the early years of the movement was with the importance of *sisterhood*—a sense of identifying with and belonging to a global community of women. Hooks (1981), among others, has stressed the inauthenticity of this concept in the face of continuing racism within the movement. In the 1980s the *divisions* between women began to be explored alongside the social factors that unite them.

Trivialization of the term WOMEN'S LIBERATION MOVEMENT ("women's lib") by the Western mass media has led many feminists to use "women's movement" in preference. In doing so there is a danger that awareness of the movement's commitment to feminist principles and to the goal of liberation may be eroded. Nevertheless "women's movement" has the advantage of being the more inclusive term and allows connections to be made between women's struggles cross-culturally. See also FEMINIST THEORY.

women's studies a multidisciplinary approach to analysis and understanding of the position and experience of women in patriarchal societies past and present. Emerging alongside the growth of the WOMEN'S LIBERATION MOVEMENT in the late 1960s, women's studies programs have been developed and expanded in higher education establishments in Europe and the United States. Informed essentially by a commitment to feminist theories, methodologies, and practice, women's studies programs seek, via a woman-centered approach to learning, to challenge the misrepresentation of women found in traditional disciplines, including sociology. The content of women's studies courses has been shaped by feminists working within the humanities, natural sciences, and social sciences. It has also been shaped by feminists working in the community, particularly in women's organizations. Thus women's studies programs have emerged out of women's direct experience of and response to sexual exploitation and oppression. An essential aim of women's studies is to render visible women's engagement with society and culture while making explicit the masculine biases underpinning traditional knowledge. Women's studies programs seek to challenge all major forms of discrimination and to question the rigid boundaries demarcating one academic subject from another. As such, they provide a radical critique of established academic knowledge and educational practice. The content of such programs varies, but most courses aim to combine a feminist analysis of women's oppression with the development of practical skills, such as assertiveness training. Traditional methods of teaching and assessment are reevaluated in the light of women's needs, and links are drawn between theoretical concerns and the daily experience of women.

working class 1. manual workers, that is, those who labor primarily with their hands, rather than their brains (nonmanual workers). In this sense, in Britain, for example, the proportion of the population that is working class has declined steadily over the course of the 20th century. However, an issue exists as to whether, for some purposes, routine white-collar workers should also be included as part of the working class (see also PROLETARIAN-IZATION). **2.** members of the PROLETARIAT, that is, all those employed as wage laborers or salaried workers, who neither own nor control the means of production. In this second sense, the working class embraces by far the majority of the working population (but see also INTERMEDIATE CLASSES; CONTRADICTORY CLASS LOCATIONS).

In either sense **1.** or **2.**, divisions and variations in class consciousness within the working class have also been a major interest—see WORKING-CLASS CONSERVATISM, LABOR ARISTOCRACY, CLASS IMAGERY.

WORKING-CLASS CONSERVATISM

working-class conservatism (in Britain) manual working-class voting for the Conservative Party, and the attitudes associated with this. Since this behavior deviates from the working class norm, and is also sometimes seen as at odds with working class interests, a number of explanations have been proposed:

(a) DEFERENCE, that is, acceptance of the middle class and the Conservative Party as the traditional ruling class, especially by older voters;

(b) a particular tendency to working-class conservatism among women, explained in part by their different work locations and less frequent contact with traditional modes of working-class political organization, such as labor unions;

(c) affluence and *embourgeoisement*, seen as occurring especially among voters moving from traditional working localities (see AFFLUENT WORKER, EMBOURGEOISEMENT THESIS);

(d) MEDIATED CLASS LOCATIONS, for example, *middle class connections*, such as a spouse or one or both parents with a nonmanual background, leading to "cross-pressures" on manual working class voters (see GOLD-THORPE et al., 1968a);

(e) a continuing tendency to generalized ideological incorporation of the working class existing in Western capitalist societies, resulting from an over-all CULTURAL HEGEMONY achieved by right-wing values in these societies.

These explanations are sometimes complementary, each explaining only a part of the phenomenon, although not all are accepted by every theorist (for example, see DOMINANT IDEOLOGY THESIS).

For whatever reasons, it is clear that the late 20th century has also witnessed a more general decline in working-class support for the Labor Party and perhaps an overall CLASS DEALIGNMENT in British politics, involving increased working-class support for the Conservative Party but also increased middle-class voting for the Labor Party (see also MIDDLE-CLASS RADICALISM). Some commentators have suggested that this points to a decline in the general salience of class in voting behavior (Crewe, 1977), also shedding doubt on traditional conceptions of working-class interests and any interpretations of working-class conservatism as involving FALSE CONSCIOUSNESS. Whether or not these notions of CLASS DEALIGNMENT are held to be cogent, it is clear that any general increase in levels of cross-class voting means that explanations of working-class conservatism require somewhat different explanations than at a time when such voting was more atypical. See also VOTING BEHAVIOR, PARTY IDENTIFICATION.

wrong level fallacy see ECOLOGICAL FALLACY or WRONG LEVEL FALLACY.

XYZ

xenophobia an exaggerated hostility toward or fear of foreigners. See ETH-NOCENTRICISM.

youth culture the subcultural features that surround youth as a social category. These include:

(a) distinctive fashions and tastes, especially in music and clothing;

(b) social relationships centered on friendship and peer groups rather than families;

(c) a relative centrality of leisure rather than work;

(d) a challenge to adult values, and individual experimentation with lifestyles;

(e) a degree of classlessness in leisure tastes and behavior.

Although divisions between adult and youth are evident, youth culture is far from being completely uniform, but is divided by gender and ethnicity, as well as by class and education, and by a myriad of competing cultural styles.

The rise of distinctive youth cultures in modern societies is associated with the central role of mass media of communications and with increasing affluence. These have created new markets in cultural products aimed primarily at young people. See also ADOLESCENCE, LIFE COURSE, RESISTANCE THROUGH RITUAL, LEISURE.

youth unemployment a specific form of UNEMPLOYMENT associated with the period between leaving school and entry into employment. In the 1970s and 1980s youth unemployment grew steadily in most of the Western world. Its persistence, and public policy measures designed to alleviate it, led to a number of research projects. An emphasis on labor supply factors (demographic change, high cost of labor, and lack of work skills) led to arguments and policies for more vocationalism in education. Sociologists have tended to criticize supply-side arguments as "blaming the victim" for being unemployed. Unemployment is seen by sociologists as a result of structural and institutional factors, rather than the characteristics of the particular social groups affected by it.

Yule's Q a measure of association (CORRELATION) invented by the mathematician G.V. Yule. Q can be used to calculate the association between two VARIABLES that can take only two possible values. For example, in Fig. 28, the variable "class" has the values "nonmanual" and "manual," and the variable "health status" has the values "good" and "poor," that is, it is a two-by-two contingency table.

Like many measures of association, Yule's Q has values along the range of -1 to +1. The value of +0.63 in Fig. 28 suggests a moderate positive asso-

Health Status	Class	
	non-manual	manual
good	57 (a)	30 (b)
poor	20 (c)	47 (d)
The formula to calculate Q is	$Q = \dfrac{ad - bc}{ad + bc} = +0.63$	

Fig. 28. **Yule's Q.** See main entry.

ciation between the nonmanual class and good health. However, the direction, indicated by negative or positive value, depends only on the order of the columns. Reversing the columns changes a negative value to a positive value, that is, a negative association between the manual class and good health.

Zeitgeist (German) the spirit of a particular age. This is a term particularly employed in the study of 19th-century romanticism to denote the essential beliefs and feelings of a particular epoch. See also DILTHEY.

zero-sum game any game or analogous social situation in which what one player or side loses the other gains (Von Neumann and Morgenstein, 1947). See also THEORY OF GAMES, PRISONERS' DILEMMA.

Znaniecki, Florian (1882–1958) Polish-born US sociologist best known for his seminal work *The Polish Peasant in Europe and America* (1918–1920).

zone any area, especially within a town or city, possessing particular functions or characteristics. The occurrence of zones may be planned as well as unplanned, for example, the zoning of school attendance and planning restrictions on industrial or commercial development. See also ZONE OF TRANSITION.

zone of transition an area of the city, according to the perspective of urban ecology, that borders the central business district. Although its socioeconomic makeup is constantly changing due to the processes of urban growth and relocation, it is characterized by high levels of migration (as poorer people and newcomers to the city move into the area and as well-off people move to the so-called better areas of the suburbs), by social heterogeneity, multi-occupation of dwellings, and a high incidence of reported social problems, such as crime, mental illness, and alcoholism. The coincidence of social problems with the decline in housing stock and the spread of slums resulted in the recent past in programs of slum clearance and the building of high-rise accommodation. Although the material fabric of the environment is regarded as important, urban ecology argues that the lack of social ties and sense of community found in these areas are the chief cause of social pathology.

More recently the term has been superseded by INNER CITY to denote the growth of settled communities of people of minority heritage backgrounds. In Britain, for example, people who immigrated to find work during the phase of decolonization, and their descendants who experience discrimination, relative deprivation, and low socioeconomic status can be regarded as an UNDERCLASS in capitalist society. See also URBAN SOCIOLOGY, URBANIZATION.

Zweckrational action see TYPES OF SOCIAL ACTION.

BIBLIOGRAPHY

This bibliography lists many works, most of which are referred to in the text. The major exception is that it does not include many references where the title of the book or article has already been given in the text, either at the point where the reference occurs or listed under a "person" headword. If not listed in the bibliography, a reference such as Raymond ARON (1935) in the text leads to *German Sociology* (1935) within the entry **Aron, Raymond.**

In the text and the bibliography, unless otherwise indicated, the year given for each work is either the year of first publication or, as for some foreign language works, the year of a first English language edition. For works first published in Britain and the United States in different but adjacent years, the year given is not always the earlier of the two. Details of place of publication and publishers given in the bibliography are sometimes those for a more recent, more accessible edition, in which case, the date of this edition is also given.

Abbot, S. and Love, B., 1972, *Sappho Was Right On Woman: a Liberated View of Lesbianism,* New York: Stein and Day.

Abel T. 1977, "The Operation Called *Verstehen,*" in F. Dallmayr and T. McCarthy (eds.), *Understanding and Social Inquiry,* University of Notre Dame Press.

Abercrombie, N., Hill, S., and Turner, B. 1980, *The Dominant Ideology Thesis,* London: Allen and Unwin.

Abercrombie, N., Hill, S., and Turner, B. 1984, *Dictionary of Sociology,* Harmondsworth, England: Penguin.

Abercrombie, N. and Urry, J. 1983, *Capital, Labour and the Middle Classes,* London: Allen and Unwin.

Aberle, D. et al. 1950, "The Functional Requisites of a Society," *Ethics,* 60.

Abrams, M. 1960, "The 'Socialist Commentary Survey'" in M. Abrams and R. Rose (eds.) *Must Labour Lose?* Harmondsworth, England: Penguin.

Abrams, P. 1982, *Historical Sociology,* Shepton Mallet: Open Books.

Adorno, T., Frenkel-Brunswick, E, Levinson, D, and Sanford, R. 1950, *The Authoritarian Personality,* New York: Harper.

Alavi, H. 1965, "Peasants and Revolution," *Socialist Register,* London: Merlin.

Albrow, M. 1970, *Bureaucracy,* London: Macmillan and Pall Mall Press.

Alford, R. 1967, "Class and Voting in the Anglo-American Political Systems," in *Party Systems and Voter Alignments,* S. Lipset and S. Rokkan (eds.), New York: Free Press.

Allport, F. 1924, *Social Psychology,* Boston: Houghton Mifflin.

Allport, G. 1935, "Attitudes," in C. Murchison (ed.) *Handbook of Social Psychology,* Worcester, Mass.: Clark University Press.

Almond, G. 1958, "Comparative Study of Interest Groups and the Political Process," *American Political Science Review*, 52.

Almond, G. and Coleman, J. 1960, *The Politics of the Developing Areas*, Princeton: Princeton University Press.

Almond, G. and Verba, S. 1963, *The Civic Culture: Political Attitudes and Democracy in Five Nations*, Princeton: Princeton Univ. Press.

Althusser, L. 1966, *For Marx*, London: Allen Lane Press.

Althusser, L. 1971, *Lenin and Philosophy and Other Essays*, London: New Left Books.

Althusser, L. and Balibar, E. 1968, *Reading Capital*, London: New Left Books (1970).

Amin, S. 1980, *Class and Nation Historically and in the Current Crisis*, London: Heinemann.

Anderberg, M. 1973, *Cluster Analysis for Applications*, New York: Academic Press.

Anderson, P. 1974a, *Passages from Antiquity to Feudalism*, London: New Left Books.

Anderson, P. 1974b, *Lineages of the Absolutist State*, London: New Left Books.

Anderson, P. 1977, "The Antinomies of Antonio Gramsci," *New Left Review*, 100 (November 1976–January 1977).

Andreski, S. 1954, *Military Organization and Society*, London: Routledge & Kegan Paul.

Andreski, S. (ed.) 1974, *The Essential Comte*, London: Croom Helm.

Archer, M. 1979, *The Social Origins of Educational Systems*, Beverly Hills: Sage (abridged edition, 1984).

Archer, M. (ed.) 1982, *The Sociology of Educational Expansion*, Beverly Hills: Sage.

Ardrey, R. 1967, *The Territorial Imperative*, London: Collins.

Argyle, M. 1967, *The Psychology of Interpersonal Behaviour*, Harmondsworth, England: Penguin.

Argyle, M. 1969, *Social Interaction*, London: Methuen.

Ariès, P. 1962, *Centuries of Childhood*, Harmondsworth, Engalnd: Penguin.

Armistead, N. 1974, *Reconstructing Social Psychology*, Harmondsworth, England: Penguin.

Armstrong, W. 1972, "The Use of Information About Occupations," in E. Wrigley (ed.) 1972, *Nineteenth Century Society: Essays in the Use of Quantitative Methods for the Study of Social Data*, Cambridge, England: Cambridge University Press.

Asch, S. 1952, *Social Psychology*, Englewood Cliffs, New Jersey: Prentice-Hall.

Ashton, D., Maguire, M. and Spilsbury, M. 1987, "Local Labour Markets and Their Impact on the Life Chances of Youths," in R. Coles (ed.) *Young Careers*, Milton Keynes: Open University Press.

Ashton, T. 1954, "The Treatment of Capitalism by Historians," in F. Hayek, *Capitalism and the Historians*, London: Routledge & Kegan Paul.

BIBLIOGRAPHY

Aston, T. and Philipin, C. (eds.) 1985, *The Brenner Debate: Agrarian Class Structure and Economic Development in Pre-Industrial Europe,* Cambridge, England: Cambridge University Press.

Atkinson, P. 1981, *The Clinical Experience: the Construction and Reconstruction of Medical Reality,* Farnborough: Gower.

Austin, J. 1962, *How to Do Things with Words,* London: Oxford University Press.

Bachofen, J. 1861, "Mother Right" in *Myth, Religion and Mother Right* (tr. R. Mannheim), Princeton: Princeton Univ. Press (1967).

Bachrach, P. 1967, *The Theory of Democratic Elitism: A Critique,* London: University of London Press.

Bachrach, P. and Baratz, M. 1962, "The Two Faces of Power," *American Political Science Review,* 56.

Baker-Miller, J. 1976, *Towards a New Psychology of Women,* Boston: Beacon Press.

Bales, R. 1950, *Interaction Process Analysis: A Method for the Study of Small Groups.* Cambridge, Massachusetts: Addison-Wesley.

Ball, M. and Smith G. 1991, *Analyzing Visual Data,* California: Sage.

Bandura, A. 1977, *Social Learning Theory,* Englewood Cliffs, New Jersey: Prentice-Hall.

Banji, J. 1977, "Modes of Production in a Materialist Conception of History," *Capital and Class,* 3.

Baran, P. 1957, *The Political Economy of Growth,* New York: Monthly Review Press, and Harmondsworth, England: Penguin (1973).

Baran, P. and Sweezy, P. 1966, *Monopoly Capital,* Harmondsworth, England: Penguin.

Barber, B. 1969, "Conceptual Foundations of Totalitarianism," in C. Friedrich, et al., *Totalitarianism in Perspective,* London: Pall Mall.

Barbour, F. (ed.) 1969, *The Black Power Revolt,* Boston: Collier-MacMillan.

Barker Lunn, J. 1970, *Streaming in the Primary School,* National Foundation for Educational Research.

Barratt-Brown, M. 1968, "The Controllers of British Industry," in K. Coates (ed.) *Can Workers Run Industry?* London: Sphere.

Barrett, M. 1988. *Women's Oppression Today,* London: Verso.

Barron, R. and Norris, S. 1976, "Sexual Divisions and the Dual Market," in D. Barker and S. Allen (eds.) *Dependence and Exploitation in Work and Marriage,* London: Longman.

Barth, F. 1970, *Ethnic Groups and Boundaries—The Social Organization of Cultural Difference,* London: Allen and Unwin.

Bateson, G. 1936, *Naven,* Cambridge, England: Cambridge University Press.

Baudrillard, J. 1970, *La Société de consommation,* Paris: Gallimard.

Baudrillard, J. 1983, *Simulations,* New York: Semiotext(e).

Beard, C. 1910, *An Economic Interpretation of the Constitution,* New York: Macmillan.

Bechhofer, F. et al. 1974, "The Petite Bourgeoisie in the Class Structure," in F. Parkin (ed.) *The Social Analysis of Class Structure*, London: Tavistock.

Becker, D., Frieden, J., Schtatz, S., and Sklar, R. 1987, *Postimperialism: International Capitalism and Development in the Late Twentieth Century*. Boulder and London: Lynne Rienner.

Becker, Howard, 1950, *Systematic Sociology*, New York: Wiley.

Becker, H.S. 1953, "Becoming a Marijuana User," *The American Journal of Sociology*, 59.

Becker, H.S. 1963, *Outsiders: Studies in the Sociology of Deviance*, Glencoe, Illinois: Free Press.

Becker, H.S. 1967, "Whose Side Are We On?" *Social Problems*, 14.

Becker, H.S. 1970, *Sociological Work: Method and Substance*, Chicago: Chicago University Press.

Becker, H.S. 1982, *Art Worlds*, London: University of California Press.

Becker, H.S., Geer, B., Hughes, E., and Strauss, A. 1961, *Boys in White: Student Culture in Medical School*, Chicago: University of Chicago Press.

Becker, H.S., Geer, B., and Hughes, E. 1968, *Making the Grade: the Academic Side of College*, New York: Wiley.

Bell, D. 1960, *The End of Ideology*, New York: Collins.

Bell, D. (ed.) 1964, *The Radical Right*, (rev. edition) New York: Doubleday.

Bell, D. 1965, "Twelve Modes of Prediction," in J. Gould (ed.) *Penguin Survey of the Social Sciences, 1965*, Harmondsworth, England: Penguin.

Bell, D. 1973, *The Coming of Post-Industrial Society: A Venture in Social Forecasting*, London: Heinemann (1974).

Bell, D. 1976, *The Cultural Contradictions of Capitalism*, New York: Basic Books.

Bell, D. 1980, "The Social Framework of the 'Information Society,'" in T. Forester, (ed.) *The Microelectronics Revolution*, Basil Blackwell: Oxford.

Bendix, R. 1960, *Max Weber: An Intellectual Portrait*, London: Heinemann.

Bendix, R. 1970, "Tradition and Modernity Reconsidered," in *Embattled Reasons*, New York: Oxford University Press.

Bendix, R. 1974, *Work and Authority in Industry*, Berkeley and London: University of California Press (originally 1936).

Berelson, B., Lazarsfeld, P., and McPhee, W. 1954, *Voting*, Chicago: Chicago University Press.

Berg, I. 1970, *Education and Jobs: the Great Training Robbery*, Harmondsworth, England: Penguin (1973).

Berger, P. and Pullberg, S. 1966, "Reification and the Sociological Critique of Consciousness," *New Left Review*, 35.

Berger, P. and Luckmann T. 1967, *The Social Construction of Reality*, London: Allen Lane.

Berle, A. and Means, G. 1932, *The Modern Corporation and Private Property*, New York: Harcourt Brace.

Bernstein, B. 1971, "On the Classification and Framing of Educational

BIBLIOGRAPHY

Knowledge," in M. Young (ed.) *Knowledge and Control,* London: Macmillan.

Bernstein, B. 1971–7, *Class, Codes and Control* (3 volumes), London: Routledge & Kegan Paul.

Bernstein, R. 1976, *The Restructuring of Social and Political Theory,* New York: Harcourt, Brace.

Bernstein, R. 1983, *Beyond Objectivism and Relativism,* Oxford: Blackwell.

Berthoud, R. 1976, *The Disadvantages of Inequality: A Study of Social Deprivation,* MacDonald and Jane.

Bettelheim, B. 1960, *The Informed Heart: Autonomy in a Mass Age,* London: Thames and Hudson (1961).

Bettelheim, B. 1969, *The Children of the Dream,* London: Thames and Hudson.

Beynon, H. 1973, *Working for Ford,* Wakefield: E.P. Publishing.

Beynon, J. and Solomos, J. (eds.) 1987, *The Roots of Urban Unrest,* Oxford: Pergamon.

Bhaskar, R. 1975, *A Realist Theory of Science,* Leeds: Leeds Books.

Bhaskar, R. 1979, *The Possibility of Naturalism,* Brighton: Harvester.

Bhaskar, R. 1986, *Scientific Realism and Human Emancipation,* London: Verso.

Bhaskar, R. 1989, *Reclaiming Reality,* London: Verso.

Black, M. (ed.) 1961, *The Social Theories of Talcott Parsons,* Englewood Cliffs, New Jersey: Prentice Hall.

Blalock, H. 1960, *Social Statistics,* New York: McGraw-Hill.

Blalock, H. 1961, *Causal Inference in Non-Experimental Research,* University of North Carolina Press.

Blau, P. 1955, *The Dynamics of Bureaucracy,* Chicago: Chicago University Press.

Blau, P. 1964, *Exchange and Power in Social Life,* New York: Wiley.

Blau, P. and Duncan, O. 1967, *The American Occupational Structure,* New York: Wiley.

Blau, P. and Scott, W. 1962, *Formal Organizations: A Comparative Approach,* San Francisco: Chandler.

Blauner, R. 1964, *Alienation and Freedom,* Chicago: University of Chicago Press.

Bloch, M. 1961, *Feudal Society,* Vols. 1 and 2, London: Routledge & Kegan Paul.

Blok, R. 1974, *The Mafia of a Sicilian Village 1860–1960,* Oxford: Oxford University Press.

Blumer, H. 1954, "What's Wrong with Social Theory?" *American Sociological Review,* 19.

Blumer, H. 1956, "Sociological Analysis and the Variable," *American Sociological Review,* 21.

Blumer, H. 1969, *Symbolic Interactionism–Perspective or Method,* Englewood Cliffs, New Jersey: Prentice Hall.

Bocock, R. 1974, *Ritual in Industrial Society: a Sociological Analysis of Ritualism*, London: Allen and Unwin.

Boeke, J. 1953, (revised edition) *Economics and Economic Policy of Dual Societies*. New York: Institute of Pacific Relations.

Bogardus, E. 1933, "A Social Distance Scale," *Sociology and Social Research*, 17.

Bott, E. 1957, *Family and Social Network*, London: Tavistock.

Bottomore, T. et al. (eds.) 1983, *A Dictionary of Marxist Thought*, Oxford: Blackwell.

Bourdieu, P. 1977, *Outline of a Theory of Practice*, Cambridge, England: Cambridge University Press.

Bourdieu, P. 1984a, *Distinction: A Social Critique of the Judgment of Taste*. London: Routledge & Kegan Paul.

Bourdieu, P. 1984b, quoted in J. Thompson, *Studies in the Theory of Ideology*, Cambridge, England: Polity Press.

Bourdon, R. and Bourricaud, F. 1989, *A Critical Dictionary of Sociology*, Routledge (original French edition, 1982).

Bowles, S. and Gintis, H. 1976, *Schooling in Capitalist America*, Routledge & Kegan Paul.

Brake, M. 1980, *The Sociology of Youth Culture and Youth Subcultures*, Routledge & Kegan Paul.

Brake, M. 1985, *Comparative Youth Culture: The Sociology of Youth Cultures in America, Britain and Canada*, London: Routledge & Kegan Paul.

Braverman, H. 1974, *Labor and Monopoly Capitalism: The Degradation of Work in the Twentieth Century*, New York: Monthly Review Press.

Brenner, R. 1977 "The Origins of Capitalist Development: A Critique of Neo-Smithian Marxism," *New Left Review*, 104.

Bridgman, P. 1927, *Dimensional Analysis*, New Haven: Yale University Press.

Bright J. 1958, *Automation and Management*, Cambridge, Massachusetts: Harvard Univ. Press.

Brown, R. 1967, "Research and Consultancy in Industrial Enterprises," *Sociology*, 1.

Bruner, J. 1968, *Towards a Theory of Instruction*, New York: Norton.

Bryant, J. and Jary, D. (eds.) 1991, *Giddens' Theory of Structuration: A Critical Appreciation*, London: Routledge.

Budge, I. 1976, *Agreement and Stability in Democracy*, Chicago: Markham.

Bühler, C. 1953, "The Curve of Life as Studied in Biographies," *Journal of Applied Science*, 9.

Bulmer, M. (ed.) 1975, *Working Class Images of Society*, London: Routledge & Kegan Paul.

Burgess, R. (ed.) 1986, *Key Variables in Social Research*, London: Routledge & Kegan Paul.

Burke, E. 1790, *Reflections on the Revolution in France*, (ed. C. O'Brien) Harmondsworth, England: Penguin (1969).

Burnham, J. 1943, *The Managerial Revolution*, London: Putman and Co.

BIBLIOGRAPHY

Burns, T. 1961, "Micro-politics: Mechanisms of Institutional Change" *Administrative Science Quarterly*, 6.

Burns, T. 1962, "The Sociology of Industry," in A. Welford (ed.), *Society: Problems and Methods of Study*, London: Routledge & Kegan Paul.

Burns, T. and Stalker G. 1961, *The Management of Innovation*, London: Tavistock.

Burrell, G. and Morgan G. 1979, *Sociological Paradigms and Organizational Analysis*, London: Heinemann.

Butler, D. and Stokes, D. 1969, *Political Change in Britain*, London: Macmillan.

Byres, T. (ed.) 1983, *Sharecropping and Sharecroppers*. London: Frank Cass.

Carchedi, G. 1977, *On the Economic Identification of Social Classes*, London: Routledge & Kegan Paul.

Cardoso, F. and Faletto, E. 1979, *Dependency and Development in Latin America*, Berkeley: University of California Press.

Carey, A. 1967, "The Hawthorne Studies," *American Sociological Review*, 32.

Carlen, P. and Worrall, A. (eds.) 1987, *Gender, Crime and Justice*. Milton Keynes: Open University.

Carneiro, R. 1970, "A Theory of the Origin of the State," *Science*, 169.

Carrillo, S. 1977, *Eurocommunism and the State*, London: Lawrence and Wishart.

Case, S. 1988, *Feminism and the Theatre*, London: Macmillan.

Castells, M. 1976, "Theory and Ideology in Urban Sociology," in C. Pickvance (ed.), *Urban and Sociology*, London: Tavistock.

Castells, M. 1977, *The Urban Question: A Marxist Approach*, London: Edward Arnold.

Castells, M. 1978, *City, Class and Power*, London: Macmillan.

Castells, M. 1983, *The City and the Grassroots: A Cross-Cultural Theory of Urban Social Movements*, London: Edward Arnold.

Catell, R. 1963, *The Sixteen Personality Factor Questionnaire*, Illinois: Institute for Personality and Ability Testing.

Chatfield, C. and Collins, A. 1980, *Introduction to Multivariate Analysis*, London: Chapman and Hall.

Child, J. 1972, "Organizational Structure, Environment and Performance–the Role of Strategic Choice," *Sociology*, 6.

Child, J. 1985, *Organizations: A Guide to Problems and Practice*, New York: Harper and Row.

Chinoy, E. 1955, *Automobile Workers and the American Dream*, New York: Doubleday.

Chodorow, N. 1978, *The Reproduction of Mothering*, Berkeley: University of California Press.

Chomsky, N. 1962, "Explanatory Models in Linguistics," in Nagel, E., Suppes, P., and Tarski, A. (eds.) *Logic, Methodology and Philosophy of Science*, Stanford University Press.

Chomsky, N. 1965, *Aspects of the Theory of Syntax*, Cambridge, Massachusetts: MIT Press.

Chomsky, N. 1969, *American Power and the New Mandarins*, Harmondsworth, England: Penguin.

Cicourel, A. 1964, *Method and Measurement in Sociology*, New York: Free Press.

Clark, B. 1960a, *The Open Door College: A Case Study*, New York: McGraw-Hill.

Clark, B. 1960b, "The 'Cooling Out' Function in Higher Education," *American Journal of Sociology*, 6.

Clark, B. 1983, *The Higher Education System: Academic Organization in Cross-National Perspective*, Berkeley: University of California Press.

Clarke, J., Critcher C. and Johnson R., 1979, *Working Class Culture*, London: Hutchinson.

Clausewitz, C. von, 1932, *On War*, Harmondsworth, England: Penguin (1968).

Clegg, S. 1960, *A New Approach to Industrial Relations*, Oxford: Blackwell.

Clegg, S. and Dunkerley, D. 1970, *Organization, Class and Control*, London: Routledge & Kegan Paul.

Cloward, R. and Ohlin, L. 1960, *Delinquency and Opportunity*. New York: Collier-Macmillan.

Coates, K. and Topham, T. 1972, *The New Unionism*, London: Owen.

Coch, L. and French. J. 1949, "Overcoming Resistance to Change," *Human Relations*, 1.

Cockburn, C. 1983, *Brothers*, London: Pluto Press.

Cohen, A. 1955, *Delinquent Boys*, Chicago: Free Press.

Cohen, G. 1978, *Karl Marx's Theory of History: A Defence*, Oxford: Clarendon Press.

Cohen, S. (ed.) 1971, *Images of Deviance*, Harmondsworth, England: Penguin.

Cohen, S. 1973, *Folk Devils and Moral Panics*, London: Paladin (revised edition, 1980).

Cohen, S. 1981, "Footprints in the Sand," in M. Fitzgerald, et al. (eds.) *Crime and Society*, Milton Keynes: Open University Press.

Cohen, S. 1988, *Visions of Social Control*, Cambridge, England: Polity Press.

Cohn, N. 1957, *The Pursuit of the Millenium*, London: Palladin.

Collard, A 1988, *Rape of the Wild*, London: The Women's Press.

Comte, A. 1830–42, *Cours de philosophie positive* (6 vols), Paris: Buchelier.

Comte, A. 1875–7, *Système de politique positive* (4 volumes), London: Longmans Green.

Condorcet, A. 1795, *Sketch for a Historical Picture of the Progress of the Human Mind*, tr. Jean Barraclough, New York: Noonday Press.

Cooley, C. 1909, *Social Organization*, New York: Scribner.

Coombes, R. 1978, "Labor and Monopoly Capital," *New Left Review*, 107.

Coombs, R. 1985, "Automation, Management Strategies and Labor Process Change," in D. Knights, et al. (eds.) *Job Redesign*, Aldershot: Gower.

BIBLIOGRAPHY

Coser, L. 1956, *The Functions of Social Conflict,* New York: Free Press.

Coser, L. (ed.) 1965, *Georg Simmel,* Englewood Cliffs, New Jersey: Prentice Hall.

Coser, L. 1978, "The Production of Culture," *Social Research,* 45.

Coulson, M., Magas, B. and Wainwright, H. 1975, "The Housewife and Her Labor Under Capitalism: A Critique," in *New Left Review,* 89.

Coward, R. and Ellis, J. 1977, *Language and Materialism,* London: Routledge & Kegan Paul.

Cowell, D. et al. (eds.) 1982, *Policing the Riots,* Junction Books.

Crensen, M. 1971, *The Un-Politics of Air Pollution,* London and Baltimore: Johns Hopkins Press.

Crewe, I., Alt, J., and Sarlvik, B. 1977, "Partisan Dealignment in Britain," *British Journal of Political Science,* 6.

Croix, de Ste. G. 1981, *The Class Struggle in the Ancient Greek World,* London: Duckworth.

Crompton, R. and Jones, G. 1984, *White-Collar Proletariat: Deskilling and Gender in Clerical Work.* London: Macmillan.

Crossick, G. 1978, *An Artisan Elite in Victorian Society,* Beckenham, England: Croom Helm.

Crouch, C. 1982, *Trade Unions: The Logic of Collective Action,* London: Fontana.

Crow, B., Thomas, A. et al. 1983, *Third World Atlas,* Milton Keynes: Open University Press.

Crow, B., Thorpe M. et al. 1988, *Survival and Change in the Third World,* Cambridge: Polity Press.

Crowther Report, The 1959, *Fifteen to Eighteen—Report of the Central Advisory Committee for Education,* London: HMSO.

Crozier, M. 1964, *The Bureaucratic Phenomenon,* London: Tavistock.

Crutchfield, R. 1955, "Conformity and Character," *American Psychologist,* 10.

Dahl, R. 1956, *A Preface to Democratic Theory,* Chicago University Press.

Dahl, R. 1961, *Who Governs?* New Haven and London: Yale University Press.

Dahl, R. 1985, *Polyarchy,* New Haven: Yale University Press.

Dahrendorf, R. 1959, *Class and Class Conflict in an Industrial Society.* London: Routledge & Kegan Paul.

Dahrendorf, R. 1967, *Society and Democracy in Germany,* London: Weidenfeld & Nicolson.

Dahrendorf, R. 1975, *The New Liberty,* London: Routledge & Kegan Paul.

Dahrendorf, R. 1979, *Life Chances,* London: Weidenfeld & Nicolson.

Dale, A., Arber, S., and Procter, M. 1988, *Doing Secondary Analysis,* London: Unwin Hyman.

Dalla Costa, M. 1972, *The Power of Women and the Subversion of the Community,* Bristol, England: Falling Wall Press.

Daly, M. 1981, *Gyn-Ecology,* Boston: Beacon Press.

Davidoff, R. 1979, "The Separation of Home from Work," in S. Burnham, (ed.)

Fit Work For Women, London: Croom Helm.

Davidoff, L. and Hall, C. 1987, *Family Fortunes: Men and Women of the English Middle Class 1780–1850,* London: Hutchinson.

David, S. and Moore, W. 1945, "Some Principles of Social Stratification," *American Sociological Review,* 10.

Davidson, D. 1984, *Enquiry into Truth and Interpretation,* Oxford: Oxford University Press.

Davis, F. 1964, "Deviance Disavowal: The Management of Strained Interaction by the Visibly Handicapped," in H.S. Becker (ed.) 1967, *The Other Side,* New York: Free Press.

Davis, H. 1979, *Beyond Class Images,* London: Croom Helm.

Davis, K. 1948, *Human Society,* New York: Macmillan.

Davis, K. 1959, "The Myth of Functional Analysis as a Special Method in Sociology and Anthropology," *American Sociological Review,* 24.

Dawe, A. 1971, "The Two Sociologies," in K. Thompson and J. Tunstall (eds.) *Sociological Perspectives,* Harmondsworth, England: Penguin.

Dawkins, R. 1976, *The Selfish Gene,* London: Oxford University Press.

Deal, T. and Kennedy, A. 1988, *Corporate Cultures: The Rites and Rituals of Corporate Life,* Harmondsworth, England: Penguin (originally published in the United States, 1982).

Deem, R. 1986, *All Work and No Play: The Sociology of Women and Leisure,* Milton Keynes: Open University Press.

Delphy, C. 1984, *Close to Home: A Materialist Analysis of Women's Oppression,* London: Hutchinson.

Demerath, H. and Peterson, R. (eds.), 1967, *System, Change and Conflict,* New York: Free Press.

Dennis, N., Henriques, F., and Slaughter, C. 1956, *Coal Is Our Life,* London: Eyre and Spottiswoode.

Denzin, N. (ed.) 1970, *Sociological Methods: A Source Book,* Chicago: Aldine.

Derrida, J. 1978, *Writing and Difference,* Chicago: University of Chicago Press.

Dex, S. 1985, *The Sexual Division of Work: Conceptual Revolutions in the Social Sciences,* Brighton, England: Wheatsheaf.

Djilas, M. 1957, *The New Class,* London: Thames and Hudson.

Dobb, M. 1946, *Studies in the Development of Capitalism,* London: Routledge & Kegan Paul (1963).

Doeringer, P. and Piore, M. 1971, *Internal Labor Markets and Manpower Analysis,* Lexington, Massachusetts: D.C. Heath.

Dohrenwend, B. and Dohrenwend, B. (eds.) 1974, *Stressful Life Events: Their Nature and Effects,* New York: Wiley.

Donnelly, P. 1988 "Sport as a Site for 'Popular' Resistance," in Gruneau, R. (ed.) *Popular Cultures and Political Practices,* Canada: Garamond Press.

Dore R. 1976, *The Diploma Disease,* London: Allen and Unwin.

Douglas, Jack 1967, *The Social Meanings of Suicide,* Princeton: Princeton University Press.

BIBLIOGRAPHY

Douglas, J.B. 1964, *The Home and the School,* London: MacGibbon & Kee.

Douglas, M. 1966, *Purity and Danger,* London: Routledge & Kegan Paul.

Downes, D. 1966, *The Delinquent Solution,* London: Routledge & Kegan Paul.

Dowse, R. and Hughes, J. 1972, *Political Sociology,* London: John Wiley.

Dubin, R. 1955, "'Industrial Workers' Worlds," *Social Problems,* 3.

Duncan, K. and Rutledge, I. (eds.) 1977, *Land and Labour in Latin America,* Cambridge, England: Cambridge University Press.

Dunleavy, P. 1980, "The Political Implications of Sectoral Cleavages," *Political Studies,* 28.

Dunning, E., Murphy, P. and Williams, J. 1988, *The Roots of Football Hooliganism,* Routledge.

Dunning, E. and Sheard, K. 1979, *Barbarians, Gentlemen and Players: A Sociological Study,* London: Martin Robertson.

Duprese, M. 1981, *Family Structure in the Staffordshire Potteries,* unpublished Ph.D. thesis, University of Oxford.

Durkheim, E. 1893, *The Division of Labor,* Glencoe, Illinois: Free Press (1938).

Durkheim, E. 1985, *The Rules of Sociological Method,* Glencoe, Illinois: Free Press (1938).

Durkheim, E. 1897, *Suicide,* London: Routledge & Kegan Paul (1952).

Durkheim, E. 1912, *The Elementary Forms of Religious Life,* London: Allen and Unwin (1954).

Durkheim, E. 1922, *Education and Sociology,* Glencoe, Illinois: Free Press (1956).

Duverger, M. 1964, *Political Parties,* New York: Wiley.

Dworkin, A. 1976, *Our Blood: Prophecies and Discourses on Sexual Politics,* New York: Harper and Row.

Eastlea, B. 1983, *Fathering the Unthinkable,* London: Pluto Press.

Eberhard, W. 1965, *Conquerers and Rulers,* Leiden: Brill.

Eckstein, H. 1960, *Pressure Group Politics,* London: Allen and Unwin.

Edwards, R. 1979, *Contested Terrain,* London: Heinemann.

Ehrenreich, R. and Ehrenreich, J. 1979, "The Professional and Managerial Class," in P. Walker (ed.) *Between Labor and Capital,* New York: Monthly Review Press.

Eichenbaum, L. and Orbach, S. 1982, *Outside In, Inside Out,* Harmondsworth, England: Penguin.

Eisenstadt, S. 1956, *From Generation to Generation,* Chicago: Free Press.

Eldridge, J. 1971, *Sociology and Industrial Life,* London: Nelson.

Eldridge, J. 1980, *Recent British Sociology,* London: Macmillan.

Elias, N. 1939, *The Civilizing Process,* Vol. 1. *The History of Manners* (1978), Vol. 2 *State and Civilization,* (1982), Oxford: Blackwell.

Elias, N. 1969, *The Court Society, Oxford: Blackwell* (translated 1983).

Elias, N. 1970, *What Is Sociology?* London: Hutchinson.

Elias, N. 1982, *The Loneliness of the Dying,* Oxford: Blackwell.

Elias, N. 1986, *Involvement and Detachment*, Oxford: Blackwell.

Elias, N. and Dunning, E. 1986, *Quest for Excitement: Sport and Leisure in the Civilizing Process*, Oxford: Blackwell.

Eliot, T.S. 1948, *Notes Towards the Definition of Culture*, London: Faber.

Elliott, G. 1987, *Althusser: The Detour of Theory*, London: Verso.

Elshtain, J. 1981, *Public Man, Private Woman*, Princeton: Princeton University Press.

Elster, J. 1989, *Nuts and Bolts for the Social Sciences*, Cambridge, England: Cambridge University Press.

Emmanuel, A. 1972, *Unequal Exchange: A Study of the Imperialism of Trade*, London and New York: Monthly Review Press.

Engels, F. 1884, *The Origin of the Family, Private Property and the State*, London: Penguin (1985).

Erikson, E. 1950, *Childhood and Society*, Harmondsworth, England: Penguin (1963).

Esland, G. and Salaman, G. 1975, "Towards a Sociology of Work," in Esland, G, Salaman, J., and Speakman, M. (eds.), *People and Work*, Edinburgh: Holmes-McDougall/The Open University.

Ettore, E. 1978, "Women, Urban Social Movements and the Lesbian Ghetto," *International Journal of Urban and Regional Research*, 2.

Etzioni, A. 1961, *The Comparative Analysis of Complex Organizations*, New York: Free Press.

Evans, P. 1979. *Dependent Development: The Alliance of Multinationals, the State and Local Capital in Brazil*, Princeton: Princeton University Press.

Evans-Pritchard, E. 1937, *Witchcraft, Magic and the Oracles Among the Azande*, Oxford: Clarendon Press.

Evans-Pritchard, E. 1940, *The Nuer*, Oxford: Clarendon Press.

Everitt, B. 1974, *Cluster Analysis*, London: Heinemann.

Eysenck, H. 1953, *The Structure of Human Personality*, London: Methuen

Eysenck, H. 1961, *Handbook of Abnormal Psychology*, London: Pitman.

Eysenck, H. 1967, *The Biological Basis of Personality*, Springfield: Thomas.

Fanon, F. 1967, *The Wretched of the Earth*, Harmondsworth, England: Penguin.

Featherstone, M. 1988, "In Pursuit of the Postmodern," in *Postmodernism*, special double issue of *Theory, Culture and Society*, 5.

Featherstone, M. 1990, "Perspectives on Consumer Culture," *Sociology*, 24.

Feigenbaum, E. and McCordnuck, P. 1984, "Land of the Rising Fifth Generation," in *The Information Technology Revolution*, Oxford: Blackwell.

Ferguson, A. (1767) *An Essay on the History of Civil Society*, Philadelphia: Finley (8th. edition, 1819).

Fernandez, R. 1977, *The I, the Me and the You: an Introduction to Social Psychology*, New York: Praeger.

Festinger, L. 1957, *A Theory of Cognitive Disonance*, Evanston, Illinois: Row, Peterson.

BIBLIOGRAPHY

Feyerabend, P. 1975, *Against Method*, London: New Left Books.

Feyerabend, P. 1978, *Science in a Free Society*, London: New Left Books.

Feyerabend, P. 1981, *Problems of Empiricism*. (2 volumes), Cambridge, England: Cambridge University Press.

Feyerabend, P. 1987, *Farewell to Reason*, London: Verso.

Fidler, J. 1981, *The British Business Elite*, Routledge & Kegan Paul.

Fitzgerald, J. and Muncie J., 1987, *System of Justice*, Oxford: Blackwell.

Flechtheim, O. 1965, *History and Futurology*, Meisenheim am Glan.

Flew, A (ed.) 1979, *A Dictionary of Philosophy*, London: Pan Books.

Flexner, A. 1910, *Report on Medical Education in the United States and Canada*, New York: Carnegie.

Flexner, A. 1962, "Is Social Work a Profession?" in H. Becker, *Education for the Professions: the 61st Yearbook of the National Society for the Study of Education*, University of Chicago Press.

Florescano, E. 1987, "The Hacienda in New Spain," in L. Bethell (ed.), *Colonial Spanish America*, Cambridge, England: Cambridge University Press.

Floud, J., Halsey, A. and Martin F. 1956, *Social Class and Educational Opportunity*, London: Heinemann.

Forester, T. 1987, *High-Tech Society*, Oxford: Basil Blackwell.

Form, W. and Rytinna J. 1969, "Ideological Beliefs in the Distribution of Power in the US," *American Sociological Review*, 34.

Fortes, M. 1969, *Kinship and the Social Order: The Legacy of Lewis Henry Morgan*, London: Routledge & Kegan Paul.

Foster, J. 1974, *Class Struggle and the Industrial Revolution*, London: Methuen.

Foucault, M. 1962, *Madness and Civilization*, New York: Pantheon (1967).

Foucault, M. 1972, *The Archaeology of Knowledge*, London: Tavistock.

Foucault, M. 1975, *Discipline and Punish*, London: Tavistock (1977).

Foucault, M. 1979, *History of Sexuality*, Vol. 1, *An Introduction*, London: Allen Lane.

Fox, A. 1965, "Industrial Sociology and Industrial Relations," Research Paper No. 3, *Royal Commission on Trade Unions and Employers' Associations*, London: HMSO.

Frank, A. 1967a, "Sociology of Development and Underdevelopment of Sociology," *Catalyst*, Summer 1967 (reprinted in Frank, 1969).

Frank, A. 1967b, *Capitalism and Underdevelopment in Latin America*, New York and London: Monthly Review Press.

Frank, A. 1969, *Latin America: Underdevelopment or Revolution*, Harmondsworth, England: Penguin.

Frank, A. 1980, *Crisis in the World Economy*, London: Heinemann.

Freedman, M. 1976, *Labor Markets: Segments and Shelters*. New York: Allanhead, Osman/Universal Books.

Freeman, C. 1982, *Unemployment and Technical Innovation*, London: Frances Pinter.

Freidson, E. 1970a, *Professional Dominance*, Chicago: Aldine.

Freidson, E. 1970b, *Professional of Medicine*, New York: Dodd Mead.

Fried, M. 1960, "On the Evolution of Stratification and the State," in Diamond, S. (ed.) *Culture in History*, New York: Columbia University Press.

Fried, M. 1967, *The Evolution of Political Society*, New York: Random House.

Friedman, A. 1977, *Industry and Labour: Class Struggle at Work and Monopoly Capitalism*, London: Macmillan.

Friedrich, C. 1954, *Totalitarianism*, Cambridge, Massachusetts: Harvard University Press.

Frobel, F., Heinrichs, J., and Kreye, O. 1980, *The New International Division of Labour*, Cambridge, England: Cambridge University Press.

Fromm, E. 1941, *Fear of Freedom*, (US title *Escape from Freedom*), London: Routledge & Kegan Paul (1942).

Fromm, E. 1955, *The Sane Society*, New York: Holt Rinehart.

Furtado, C. 1964, *Development and Underdevelopment*, Los Angeles: University of California Press.

Gadamer, H. 1960, *Truth and Method*, London: Sheed & Ward (English translation 1975).

Galbraith, J. 1952, *American Capitalism, the Concept of Countervailing Power*, London: Hamish Hamilton.

Galbraith, J. 1958, *The Affluent Society*, London: Hamish Hamilton.

Galbraith, J. 1967, *The New Industrial State*, Harmondsworth, England: Penguin.

Gallie, D. 1978, *In Search of the New Working Class*, Cambridge, England: Cambridge University Press.

Gallie, W. 1955, "Essentially Contested Concepts," *Proceedings of the Aristotelian Society*, 56.

Galton, F. 1870, *Hereditary Genius*, New York: Appleton.

Gamble, A. 1985, *Britain in Decline* (second revised edition), London: Macmillan.

Gamble, A. 1988, *The Free Economy and the Strong State: The Politics of Thatcherism*, London: Macmillan.

Gans, H. 1962, *The Urban Villagers: Groups and Class in the Life of Italian-Americans*, (second edition), New York: Free Press.

Garfinkel, H. 1956, "The Conditions of Successful Degradation Ceremonies," *American Journal of Sociology*, 61.

Garfinkel, H. 1967, *Studies in Ethnomethodology*, Englewood Cliffs, New Jersey: Prentice Hall.

Garner, L. 1979, *Your Money or Your Life*, Harmondsworth, England: Penguin.

Garrard, J. et al. 1978, *The Middle Class in Politics*, Farnborough, England: Saxon House.

Geddes, P. 1915, *Cities in Evolution*, London: Williams & Norgate.

Geiger, T. 1949, *Die Stennung der Intelligenz in der Gesellschaft*, Stuttgart.

BIBLIOGRAPHY

Gellner, E. 1959, *Words and Things,* London: Gollancz.

Gellner, E. 1964, *Thought and Change,* London: Weidenfeld and Nicolson.

Gellner, E. 1969, *Saints of the Atlas,* London: Weidenfeld and Nicolson.

Gellner, E. 1974, "The New Idealism–Cause and Meaning in the Social Sciences," reprinted in Giddens, A. (ed.), *Positivism and Sociology,* London: Heinemann.

Gellner, E. 1988, *Plough, Sword and Book,* London: Collins Harvill.

Genovese, E. 1971, *In Red and Black,* London: Allen Lane.

Genovese, E. 1974, *Roll Jordan Roll: The World the Slaveholders Made,* New York: Knopf.

George, C. and George K. 1961, *The Protestant Mind and the English Reformation,* London: Methuen.

Gerth, H. and Mills, C. 1953, *Character and Social Structure,* London: Routledge & Kegan Paul.

Giddens, A. 1973, *The Class Structure of the Advanced Societies,* London: Hutchinson (revised edition 1981).

Giddens, A. 1976a, *New Rules of Sociological Method,* London: Hutchinson.

Giddens, A. 1976b, "Functionalism: Après la Lutte," *Social Research,* 43 (reprinted in Giddens, 1977).

Giddens, A. 1977, *Studies in Social and Political Theory,* London: Hutchinson.

Giddens, A. 1981, *A Contemporary Critique of Historical Materialism,* London: Macmillan.

Giddens, A. 1982, *Profiles and Critiques in Social Theory,* London: Macmillan.

Giddens, A. 1984, *The Constitution of Society,* Cambridge, England: Polity Press.

Giddens, A. 1985, *The Nation-State and Violence,* Cambridge, England: Polity Press.

Giddens, A. 1987, "Structuralism, Poststructuralism," in Giddens and J. Turner (1987) *Social Theory Today,* Cambridge, England: Polity Press.

Giddens, A. 1989, *Sociology,* Cambridge; Polity Press.

Gill, C. 1985, *Work, Unemployment and the New Technology,* Oxford: Blackwell.

Glaser, B. 1968, *A Time for Dying,* Chicago: Aldine.

Glaser, B. and Strauss, A. 1965, *Awareness of Dying,* Chicago: Aldine.

Glaser, B. and Strauss, A. 1968, *The Discovery of Grounded Theory,* London: Weidenfeld & Nicolson.

Glass, D. (ed.) 1954, *Social Mobility in Britain,* London: Routledge & Kegan Paul.

Glazer, N. 1975, *Affirmative Discrimination,* New York: Basic Books.

Gleichman, P. et al., 1977, *Human Figurations,* Amsterdam: *Sociologisch Tijdschift.*

Gluckman, M. 1963, *Order and Rebellion in Tribal Africa,* London: Cohen and West.

Goffman, E. 1959, *The Presentation of Self in Everyday Life,* New York: Doubleday.

Goffman, E. 1961a, *Asylums*, New York: Doubleday, Anchor.

Goffman, E. 1961b, *Encounters: Two Studies in the Sociology of Interaction*, Indianapolis: Bobbs-Merrill.

Goffman, E. 1963, *Behavior in Public Places, Notes on the Organization of Gatherings*, New York: Free Press.

Goffman, E. 1964, *Stigma, Notes on the Management of Identity*, Harmondsworth, England: Penguin.

Goffman, E. 1967, *Interaction Ritual: Essays on Face-To-Face Behavior*, New York: Doubleday.

Goffman, E. 1969, *Strategic Interaction*, Philadelphia: University of Pennsylania Press.

Goffman, E. 1971, *Relations in Public: Microstudies of the Public Order*, London: Allen Lane.

Goffman, E. 1974, *Frame Analysis: an Essay on the Organization of Experience*, Harmondsworth, England: Penguin.

Goffman, E. 1979, *Gender Advertisements*, London: Macmillan.

Goffman, E. 1981, *Forms of Talk*, Oxford: Blackwell.

Golding, P. 1983, "Rethinking Common Sense About Social Policy," in D. Bull and P. Wilding (eds.), *Thatcherism and the Poor*, Child Poverty Action Group.

Goldthorpe, J.E. 1975, *The Sociology of the Third World: Disparity and Involvement*, Cambridge, England: Cambridge University Press (second edition 1984).

Goldthorpe, J.H. 1966, "Attitudes and Behaviour of Car Assembly Workers–a Deviant Case and a Theoretical Critique," *British Journal of Sociology*, 27.

Goldthorpe, J.H. 1974, "Industrial Relations in Great Britain: a Critique of Reformism," reprinted in Clarke, T. and Clements, I., (eds.) *Trades Unions Under Capitalism*, London: Faber.

Goldthorpe, J.H. 1973, "A Revolution in Sociology," *Sociology*, 7.

Goldthorpe, J.H. and Hope, K. 1974, *The Social Grading of Occupations*, Oxford: Clarendon Press.

Goldthorpe, J.H. and Llewellyn, C. 1977, "Class Mobility in Britain: Three Theses Examined," *Sociology*, 11.

Goldthorpe, J.H., Llewellyn, C., and Payne, C. 1980, *Social Mobility and Class Structure in Britain*, Oxford: Clarendon Press.

Goldthorpe, J.H., Lockwood, D., Bechhofer, F., and Platt, J. 1968a, *The Affluent Worker: Industrial Attitudes and Behaviour*, Cambridge, England: Cambridge University Press.

Goldthorpe, J.H., Lockwood, D., Bechhofer, F., and Platt, J. 1968b, *The Affluent Worker: Political Attitudes and Behaviour*, Cambridge, England: Cambridge University Press.

Goldthorpe, J.H., Lockwood, D., Bechhofer, F., and Platt, J. 1969, *The Affluent Worker in the Class Structure*, Cambridge, England: Cambridge University Press.

Goode, W. and Hatt, P. 1952, *Methods in Social Research*, New York: McGraw-Hill.

BIBLIOGRAPHY

Goodman, P. 1956, *Growing Up Absurd*, New York: Vintage Books.

Goody, J. (ed.), *Kinship*, Harmondsworth, England: Penguin.

Gorz, A. 1967, *Strategy for Labor*, Boston: Beacon Press.

Goudsblom, J. 1977, *Sociology in the Balance*, Oxford: Blackwell.

Gough, H. 1957, *California Psychological Inventory*, Palo Alto: Consulting Psychologists Press.

Gough, I. 1979, *The Political Economy of the Welfare State*, London: Macmillan.

Gouldner, A. 1954, *Patterns of Industrial Bureaucracy*, New York: Free Press.

Gouldner, A. 1955a, *Wildcat Strike*, London: Routledge & Kegan Paul.

Gouldner, A. 1955b, "Metaphysical Pathos and the Theory of Bureaucracy," *American Political Science Review*, 49.

Gouldner, A. 1959, "Reciprocity and Autonomy in Functional Theory," in L. Gross (ed.) *Symposium on Sociological Theory*, New York: Harper and Row.

Gouldner, A. 1970, *The Coming Crisis in Sociology*, New York: Basic Books.

Gouldner, A. 1973, *For Sociology*, London: Allen Lane (Penguin edition, 1975).

Gouldner, A. 1976, *The Dialectic of Ideology and Technology*, London: Macmillan.

Gouldner, A. 1979, *The Future of Intellectuals and the Rise of the New Class*, London: Macmillan.

Gramsci, A. 1971, *Selections from Prison Notebooks*, London: New Left Books.

Gray, R. 1976, *The Labour Aristocracy in Victorian Edinburgh*, Oxford: Clarendon Press.

Griffin, K. 1979, *The Political Economy of Agrarian Change: An Essay on the Green Revolution*, (second edition) London: Macmillan.

Griffin, S. 1982, *Made From This Earth*, London: Women's Press.

Gross, K. 1901, *The Play of Man*, New York: Appleton.

Gruneau, R. 1982, "Sport and the Debate on the State," in Cantelon, H. and Gruneau, R. (eds.) *Sport, Culture and the Modern State*, Toronto: University of Toronto Press.

Gruneau, R. 1983, *Class, Sports and Social Development*, University of Massachusetts Press.

Guttman, L. 1950, "The Basis for Scalogram Analysis," in Stouffer, L., Guttman, L., Suchman, E., Lazarsfeld, P., Srar, S., and Clausen, S., *Measurement and Prediction*, Princeton: Princeton University Press.

Haber, R. and Fried, A. 1975, *An Introduction to Psychology*, New York: Holt, Rinehart and Winston.

Habermas, J. 1970a, *Towards a Rational Society*, London, Heinemann (1971).

Habermas, J. 1970b, "On Systematically Distorted Communication," and "Towards a Theory of Communicative Competence," *Inquiry*, 13.

Habermas, J. 1972, *Knowledge and Human Interests*, London: Heinemann, (Germany 1968).

Habermas, J. 1974, *Theory and Practice*, London: Heinemann (abridgment of German edition 1973).

Habermas, J. 1975, *Legitimation Crisis*, London: Heinemann (German edition 1973).

Habermas, J. 1979, *Communication and the Evolution of Society*, London: Heinemann.

Habermas, J. 1984 and 1988, *The Theory of Communicative Competence*, (2 volumes) (German edition 1982).

Hall, G. 1904, *Adolescence*, New York: Appleton.

Hall, J. 1985, *Powers and Liberties*, Oxford: Blackwell.

Hall, S. 1983, in Hall and Jacques, 1983.

Hall, S. et al. 1978, *Policing the Crisis*, London: Macmillan.

Hall, S. and Jacques, M. (eds.) 1983, *The Politics of Thatcherism*, London: Lawrence and Wishart.

Hall, S. and Jefferson, T. 1976, *Resistance Through Rituals–Youth Cultures in Post War Britain*, London: Hutchinson.

Halsey, A. 1978, *Change in British Society*, Oxford: Oxford University Press.

Halsey, A., Floud, J., and Anderson, C. 1961, *Education, Economy and Society: A Reader*, Glencoe, Illinois: Free Press.

Halsey, A., Heath, A., and Ridge, J., 1980, *Origins and Destinations: Family, Class and Education in Britain*, Oxford: Oxford University Press.

Handy, C. 1984, *The Future of Work: A Guide to a Changing Society*, Oxford: Blackwell.

Handy, C. 1985, *Understanding Organizations*, Harmondsworth, England: Penguin, third edition.

Harding, N. 1977, *Lenin's Political Thought*, London: Macmillan.

Hargreaves, D. 1967, *Social Relations in a Secondary School*, London: Routledge & Kegan Paul.

Hargreaves, D. 1982, *The Challenge for the Comprehensive School*, London: Routledge & Kegan Paul.

Hargreaves, J. 1986, *Sport, Power and Culture*, Cambridge, England: Polity Press.

Harré, R. 1970, *The Principles of Scientific Thinking*, London: Macmillan.

Harré, R. 1979, *Social Being*, Oxford: Blackwell.

Harré, R. and Madden, E. 1975, *Causal Powers: A Theory of Natural Necessity*, Oxford: Blackwell.

Harrington, J. 1968, *Soccer Hooliganism*, Bristol: John Wright.

Harris, C. 1989. "The Family," in Kuper, A. and Kuper, J. (1985).

Harris, M. 1978, *Cannibals and Kings: The Origins of Cultures*, London: Fontana.

Harris, M. 1969, *The Rise of Anthropological Theory*, London: Routledge & Kegan Paul.

Harris, N. 1987, *The End of the Third World: Newly Industrializing Countries and the Decline of an Ideology*, Harmondsworth, England: Penguin.

Harris, O. 1981, "Households as Natural Units." in Young, K., Wolkowitz, C., and McCullah, R. (eds.) *Of Marriage and the Market: Women's Subordination in International Perspective* London: CSE Books.

BIBLIOGRAPHY

Harrop, M. and Miller, W. 1987, *Elections and Voters: A Comparative Introduction*, London: Macmillan.

Hartmann, H. 1979, "The Unhappy Marriage of Marxism and Feminism," *Capital and Class*, Summer.

Harvey, D. 1973, *Social Justice and the City*, London: Edward Arnold.

Harvey, D. 1989a, *The Urban Experience*, Oxford: Blackwell.

Harvey, D. 1989b, *The Condition of Post Modernity*, Oxford: Blackwell.

Harwood, J. 1979, "The Race-Intelligence Controversy: A Sociological Approach," *Social Studies of Science*, 6 & 7.

Hayek, F. von 1944, *The Road to Serfdom*, London: Routledge & Kegan Paul.

Heath, A. 1891, *Social Mobility*, London: Fontana.

Hechter, M. 1975, *Internal Colonialism: The Celtic Fringe in British National Development, 1536–1966*, London: Routledge & Kegan Paul.

Held, D. 1980, *Introduction to Critical Theory*, London: Hutchinson.

Hempel, C. 1959, "The Logic of Functional Analysis," in L. Gross (ed.) *Symposium on Sociological Theory*, New York: Harper and Row.

Hepple, L. 1985, "Time-Space Analysis," in Kuper, A. and Kuper, J., 1985.

Herberg, W. 1960, *Protestant, Catholic, Jew*, New York: Doubleday.

Herzberg, F. 1968, *Work and the Nature of Man*, London: Staples Press.

Hesse, M. 1980, *Revolutions and Reconstructions in the Philosophy of Science*, Brighton, England: Harvester Press.

Hill, P. 1986, *Development Economics on Trial: The Anthropological Case for a Prosecution*, Cambridge, England: Cambridge University Press.

Hill, S. 1981, *Competition and Control at Work*, London: Heinemann.

Hilton, R. 1973, *Bond Men Made Free: Medieval Peasant Movements and the English Rising of 1381*, London: Temple Smith.

Hilton, R. (ed.) 1976, *The Transition from Feudalism to Capitalism*, London: New Left Books.

Hindess, B. 1973, *The Use of Official Statistics*, London: Macmillan.

Hindess, B. and Hirst, P. 1975, *Pre-Capitalist Modes of Production*, London: Routledge & Kegan Paul.

Hirsch, F. 1977, *Social Limits to Growth*, London: Routledge & Kegan Paul.

Hobsbawm, E. 1964, "The Labour Aristocracy," in E. Hobsbawn, *Labouring Men*, London: Weidenfeld & Nicolson.

Hobsbawm, E., 1969, *Bandits*, London: Weidenfeld and Nicolson.

Hobsbawm, E. and Ranger, T. (eds.) 1983, *The Invention of Tradition*, Cambridge, England: Cambridge University Press.

Hodges, D. 1961, "The 'Intermediate Classes' in Marxian Theory," *Social Research*, 23.

Hodgson, G. 1982, *Capitalism, Value and Exploitation*, Oxford: Martin Robertson.

Hollis, M. 1977, *Models of Man*, Cambridge, England: Cambridge University Press.

Hollis, M. 1987, *The Cunning of Reason*, Cambridge, England: Cambridge University Press.

Holton, R. 1985, *The Transition from Feudalism to Capitalism,* Basingstoke and London: Macmillan.

Hooks, B. 1981, *Ain't I a Woman?* London: Pluto Press.

Hope, K. and Goldthorpe, J.H. 1974, *The Social Grading of Occupations: A New Approach and Scale,* Oxford: Clarendon Press.

Horkheimer, M. 1947, *Eclipse of Reason,* New York: Oxford University Press.

Horkheimer, M. 1972, *Critical Theory: Selected Essays,* New York: Herder.

Horkheimer, M. and Adorno, T. 1972, *Dialectic of Enlightenment,* New York: Herder (German, 1947).

Hudson, W. 1949, "Puritanism and the Spirit of Capitalism," *Church Times,* 18.

Hughes, E. 1952, *Men and Their Work,* Glencoe, Illinois: Free Press.

Humm, M. 1989, *A Dictionary of Feminist Theory,* London: Harvester/Wheatsheaf.

Hunter, F. 1963, *Community Power Structure,* New York: Anchor Books.

Hurd, G. et al. 1973, *Human Societies–An Introduction to Sociology,* London: Routledge & Kegan Paul.

Huse, E. and Cummings, T. 1985, *Organization, Development and Change,* (third edition).

Hyman, R. 1984, *Strikes,* Glasgow: Fontana (third edition, originally 1972).

Hymes, D. 1966, *On Communicative Competence, Report of Research Planning Conference on Language Development Among Disadvantaged Children,* New York: Yeshiva University.

Illich, I. 1971, *Deschooling Society,* London: Calder and Boyars (1972).

Illich, I. 1975, *Medical Nemesis,* London: Calder and Boyars.

Inglehart, R. 1977, *The Silent Revolution–Changing Values and Political Styles Among Western Mass Publics,* Princeton: Princeton University Press.

Ingold, T. 1989, *BASAPP Newsletter,* 3.

Institute of Race Relations, 1987, *Policing Against Black People,* London: Institute of Race Relations.

Jacobs, P. and Lindau, S. 1966, *The New Radicals,* Harmondsworth, England: Penguin.

Jackson, B. and Marsden, D. 1962, *Education and the Working Class,* London: Routledge & Kegan Paul.

James, C. 1980 (first published 1938), *The Black Jacobins: Toussaint L'Ouverture and the San Domingo Revolution,* London: Allison and Busby.

James, S. 1974, "Sex, Race and Working Class Power," *Race Today,* January.

Jameson, F. 1984, "Postmodernism or the Cultural Logic of Late Capitalism," *New Left Review,* 146.

Jary, D. 1978, "A New Significance for the Middle Class Left?" in Garrard et al., 1978.

Jary, D. 1991, "Society as 'Time-Traveller': Giddens on Historical Change, Historical Materialism and the Nation-State in World Society," in Bryant, C., and Jary, D., 1991.

Jay, M. 1973, *The Dialectical Imagination,* London: Heinemann.

BIBLIOGRAPHY

Jeffrey, P. 1979, *Frogs in a Well: Indian Women in Purdah,* London: Zed Press.

Jenkins, R. 1984, Divisions over the International Division of Labour," *Capital and Class,* 22.

Jenkins, R. 1986, *Transitional Corporations and the Latin American Motor Industry,* London: Macmillan.

Jensen, A. 1969, "How Much Can We Boost IQ and Educational Achievement?" *Harvard Educational Review,* 39.

Jessop, B. et al. 1984, "Authoritarian Populism, Two Nations and Thatcherism," *New Left Review,* 147.

Jessop, B., Bonnet, K., Bromley, S., and Ling, T. 1989, *Thatcherism,* Cambridge, England: Polity Press.

Johnson, T. 1972, *Professions and Power,* London: Macmillan.

Jones, T., Maclean, B., and Young, J. 1986, *The Islington Crime Survey: Crime, Victimization and Policing in Inner-City,* London: Gower.

Jung, C.G. 1928, *Collected Works,* London: Routledge & Kegan Paul.

Karabel, J. and Halsey, A. 1977, *Power and Ideology in Education,* New York: Oxford University Press.

Katz, D. and Kahn, R. 1966, *The Social Psychology of Organizations,* New York: Wiley.

Katz, E. and Lazarsfeld, P. 1955, *Personal Influence,* Glencoe, Illinois: Free Press.

Katz, F. 1968, *Autonomy and Organization: The Limits of Social Control,* New York: Random House.

Keating, P. 1985, *Clerics and Capitalists: A Critique of the Weber Thesis,* Salford Papers in Sociology and Anthropology, 2.

Kelly, G. 1955, *The Psychology of Personal Constructs,* New York: Norton.

Kelly, J 1982, "Early Feminist Theory and the Querelle des Femmes, 1400–1789," *Signs,* 8.

Kendon, A. 1988, "Goffman's Approach to Face-to-Face Interaction," in Dolin, P., and Wootton, A., *Exploring the Interaction Order,* Cambridge, England: Polity Press.

Kerr, C. 1954, "The Balkanization of Labor Markets," in E. Wight Bakke et al. (eds.) *Labor Mobility and Economic Opportunity,* Cambridge, Massachusetts: MIT Press.

Kerr, C. 1982, *The Uses of the University,* Cambridge, Massachusetts: Harvard University Press (third edition).

Kerr, C. 1983, *The Future of Industrial Societies: Convergence or Continuing Diversity,* Cambridge, Massachuetts: Harvard University Press.

Kerr, C. et al. 1962, *Industrialism and Industrial Man,* London: Heineman.

Kershaw, I. 1989, *The Nazi Dictatorship: Problems and Perspectives of Interpretation,* Edward Arnold: London (second edition).

Kinsey, A. et al. 1948, *Sexual Behavior in the Human Male,* Philadelphia: W.B. Saunders.

Kinsey, A. et al. 1953, *Sexual Behavior in the Human Female,* Philadelphia:

W.B. Saunders.

Kinsey, R., Lea, J. and Young, J. 1986, *Losing the Fight Against Crime*, Oxford: Blackwell.

Kitchen, M. 1976, *Fascism*, London: Macmillan.

Kitzinger, C. 1987, *The Social Construction of Lesbianism*, London: Sage.

Kluckhohn, C. 1944, *Navaho Witchcraft*, Boston: Beacon Press.

Konrád, G. and Szelényl, I. 1979, *The Intellectuals on the Road to Class Power*, Brighton, England: Harvester.

Kuhn, T. 1962, *The Structure of Scientific Revolutions*, Chcago: Chicago University Press, (second edition 1970).

Kuhn, T. 1977, *The Essential Tension*, Chicago: Chicago University Press.

Kumari, R. 1989, *Women-headed Households in Rural India*, London: Sangam Books.

Kuper, A. and Kuper, J. 1985, *The Social Science Encyclopedia*, London: Routledge (1989).

Laboriz, S. 1970, "The Assignment of Numbers to Rank Order Categories," *American Sociological Review*, 33.

Labov, W. 1967, *The Social Stratification of English in New York City*, Washington, DC: Center for Applied Linguistics.

Labov, W. 1972, "The Logic of Nonstandard English," in P. Giglioli (ed.) *Language and Social Context*, Penguin.

Lacey, C. 1970, *Hightown Grammar*, Manchester: Manchester University Press.

Laing, R. 1959, *The Divided Self*, London: Tavistock (1960).

Laing, R. 1961, *The Self and Others*, London: Tavistock (1969).

Laing, R. 1967, *The Politics of Experience and the Bird of Paradise*, Harmondsworth, England: Penguin.

Laing, R. and Esterson A. 1964, *Sanity, Madness and the Family*, Harmondsworth: Penguin.

Lakatos, I. 1976, *Proofs and Refutations: The Logic of Mathematical Discovery*, Cambridge, England: Cambridge University Press.

Lakatos, I. and Musgrave, A. (eds.) 1970, *Criticism and the Growth of Knowledge*, Cambridge, England: Cambridge University Press.

Lash, S. 1990, *The Sociology of Postmodernism*, London: Routledge.

Lash, S. and Urry, J. 1987, *The End of Organized Capitalism*, Cambridge, England: Polity Press.

Laslett, P. (ed.) 1972, *Household and Family in Past Time*, Cambridge, England: Cambridge University Press.

Lasswell, H. 1941, "The Garrison State," *American Journal of Sociology*, 46.

Lawrence, P. and Lorsch, J. 1967, *Organization and Environment: Managing Differentiation and Integration*, Cambridge, Massachusetts: Harvard University Press.

Layder, D. 1981, *Structure, Interaction, and Social Theory*, London: Routledge & Kegan Paul.

BIBLIOGRAPHY

Lazarsfeld, P. et al. 1944, *The People's Choice,* New York: Columbia University Press (1948, second edition).

Lazarsfeld, P. and Rosenberg, M. (eds.) *The Language of Social Research,* Glencoe, Illinois: Free Press.

Lea, J. and Young, J. 1983, *What Is to Be Done About Law and Order?* Harmondsworth, England: Penguin.

Leach, E. 1954, *The Political Systems of Highland Burma,* Cambridge.

Leach, E. 1959, "Hydraulic Society in Ceylon," *Past and Present,* 15.

Leach, E. 1970, *Lévi-Strauss,* London: Fontana.

Leach, E. 1982, *Social Anthropology,* London: Fontana.

Le Bon, G. 1895, *The Crowd,* New York: Viking Press (1960).

Lefebvre, H. 1967, "Neighborhoods and neighborhood life," in *Le quartier et la ville,* Cahiers de l'IAAURPA, 7.

Le Grande, J. 1982, *The Strategy of Equality: Redistribution and the Social Services,* London: Allen and Unwin.

Lemert, E. 1951, *Social Pathology: A Systematic Approach to Sociopathic Behavior,* Englewood Cliff, New Jersey: Prentice Hall.

Lemert, E. 1961, *Social Pathology,* New York: McGraw-Hill.

Lenin, V. 1902, "What Is to Be Done?" reprinted in Clarke, T., and Clements, L., (eds.) *Trades Unions Under Capitalism,* (1977).

Lenin, V. 1916, *Imperialism, the Highest Stage of Capitalism,* New York: International Publishers (1939).

Lenk, K. 1982, "Information and Society," in *Microelectronics and Society: For Better or for Worse,* G. Friedrichs and A. Schaff (eds.), Oxford: Pergamon Press.

Lenski, G. 1961, *The Religious Factor,* New York: Doubleday.

Lenski, G. 1966, *Power and Privilege,* New York: McGraw-Hill.

Lenski, G. and Lenski, J. 1970, *Human Societies,* New York: McGraw-Hill (fifth edition 1987).

Le Roy Ladurie, E. 1978, *Montaillou,* London: Scholar Press.

Lévi-Strauss, C. 1963, *Structural Anthropology,* (vol. 1; vol. 2 1976), New York: Basic Books.

Lévi-Strauss, C. 1967, *The Scope of Anthropology,* London: Cape.

Lévi-Strauss, C. 1969, *The Elementary Structure of Kinship,* second edition, Eyre and Spottiswoode.

Lévy-Bruhl, L. 1923, *The Primitive Mentality,* Boston: Beacon Press.

Lewin, K. 1951, *Field Theory in Social Science,* New York: Harper.

Lewis, O. 1961, *The Children of Sanchez,* New York: Random House.

Lewis, O. 1968, *A Study of Slum Culture: Backgrounds for La Vida,* New York: Random House.

Lienhardt, G. 1964, *Social Anthropology,* Oxford: Oxford University Press.

Likert, R. 1932, "A Technique for the Measurement of Attitudes," *Archives of Psychology,* 40.

Linder, S. 1970, *The Harried Leisure Class,* New York: Columbia University Press.

Lindesmith, A.R. 1947, *Opiate Addiction*, Bloomington, Indiana: Principia.

Linton, R. 1936, *The Study of Man*, New York: Appleton-Century.

Lipset, S. 1959, "Political Sociology," in R. Merton et al. (eds.) *Sociology Today*, New York: Basic Books.

Lipset, S. 1960, *Political Man: The Social Bases of Politics*, London: Heinemann.

Lipset, S. and Bendix, R. 1959, *Social Mobility in Industrial Society*, Berkeley: University of California Press.

Littler, C. 1982, *The Development of the Labour Process in Capitalist Societies*, London: Heinemann.

Lockwood, D. 1956, "Some Remarks on the 'Social System.'"27 *British Journal of Sociology*, 7.

Lockwood, D. 1958, *The Black-Coated Worker*, London: Allen and Unwin.

Lockwood, D. 1964, "Social Integration and System Integration," in Zollschan, Z., and Hirsch, W., (eds.) *Explorations in Social Change*, London: Routledge & Kegan Paul.

Lockwood, D. 1966, "Sources of Variation in Working Class Images of Society," *Sociological Review*, 14.

Lomnitz, L. 1977, *Networks and Marginality: Life in a Mexican Shanty-town*, London: Academic Press.

Lorder, A. 1979, "Need," *Heresies*, 2.

Lowe, S. 1986, *Urban Social Movements: The City After Castells*, London: Macmillan.

Löwy, M. 1981, *The Politics of Combined and Uneven Development: The Theory of Permanent Revolution*, London: Verso.

Lukacs, G. 1971, *History and Class Consciousness*, London: Merlin Books (original German edition 1923).

Lukes, S. 1968, "Methodological Individualism Reconsidered," *British Journal of Sociology* (reprinted in Lukes, 1977).

Lukes, S. 1973, *Emile Durkheim: His Life and Work*, London: Allen Lane.

Lukes, S. 1974, *Power: A Radical View*, London: Macmillan.

Lukes, S. 1977, *Essays in Social Theory*, London: Macmillan.

Lyon, D. 1988, *The Information Society: Issues and Illusions*, Cambridge, England: Polity Press.

Lyotard, J. 1984, *The Postmodern Condition*, Manchester, England: Manchester University Press.

Machin, H. (ed.) 1983, *National Communism in Western Europe: A Third Way to Socialism?* London: Methuen.

MacInnes, J. 1987, *Thatcherism at Work*, Oxford: Oxford University Press.

MacIntyre, A. 1962, "A Mistake About Causality in Social Science," in Laslett, P., and Runciman, W., *Philosophy, Politics and Society*, Second Series, Oxford: Blackwell.

MacPherson, C. 1962, *Possessive Individualism*, Oxford: Clarendon Press (1964).

BIBLIOGRAPHY

Madge, C. 1964, *Society in the Mind*, London: Faber & Faber.

Maine, H. 1861, *Ancient Law: Its Connection with the Early History of Society, and Its Relations to Modern Ideas*, New York: Dutton (revised edition 1960).

Malinowski, B. 1926, *Crime and Custom in Savage Society*, London: Kegan Paul.

Malinowski, B. 1944, *A Scientific Theory of Culture and Other Essays*, New York: Oxford University Press.

Malinowski, B. 1948, *Magic, Science and Religion*, Boston: Beacon Press.

Mallet, S. 1975, *Essays on the New Working Class*, St. Louis: Telos Press.

Mandel, E. 1962, *Marxist Economic Theory*, London: Merlin.

Mann, M. 1970, "The Social Cohesion of Liberal Democracy," *American Sociological Review*, 35.

Mann, M. 1973, *Consciousness and Action in the Western Working Class*, London: Macmillan.

Mann, M. 1983, *Student Encyclopedia of Sociology*, London: Macmillan.

Mann, M. 1986, *The Sources of Social Power*, Vol.1, *A History of Power from the Beginning to A.D. 1760*, Cambridge, England: Cambridge University Press.

Mann, M. 1988, *States, War and Capitalism: Studies in Political Sociology*, Oxford: Blackwell.

Mannheim, K. 1936, *Ideology and Utopia*, London: Routledge & Kegan Paul; 1929, English translation and revised edition, *Idéologie and Utopie*, Bonn: S. Cohen.

Mannheim, K. 1953, "Conservative Thought," in *Essays on Sociology and Social Psychology*, London: Routledge.

March, J. and Simon H. 1958, *Organizations*, New York: Wiley.

Marcuse, H. 1964, *One-Dimensional Man*, London: Sphere.

Marcuse, H. 1968, *Negations: Essays in Critical Theory*, London: Allen Lane Press.

Marsden, D. 1971, *Politicians, Comprehensives and Equality*, Fabian Society Tract. London: Gollancz.

Marsh, A. 1977, *Protest and Political Consciousness*, Beverley Hills: Sage.

Marsh, C. 1988, *Exploring Data: An Introduction to Data Analysis for the Social Sciences*, Cambridge, England: Polity Press.

Marsh, P., Rosser, E., and Harré, R. 1978, *The Rules of Disorder*, London: Routledge & Kegan Paul.

Marshall, G., Newby, H., Rose, D., and Vogler, C. 1988, *Social Class in Modern Britain*, London: Hutchinson.

Marshall, T. 1963, *Sociology at the Crossroads*, London: Heinemann.

Martin, D. 1969, *The Religious and the Secular*, London: Routledge & Kegan Paul.

Marwick, M. (ed.) 1970, *Witchcraft and Sorcery*, Harmondsworth, England: Penguin (second edition 1982).

Marx, K. (1857–8), *Grundrisse*, Harmondsworth, England: Penguin (1973).

Marx, K. (1867–94), *Capital*, Volumes 1–3, London: Lawrence and Wishart

(1954).

Matza, D. 1964, *Delinquency and Drift,* New York: Wiley.

Mayo, E. 1949, *The Social Problems of an Industrial Civilization,* London: Routledge & Kegan Paul.

McCarthy, T. 1978, *The Critical Theory of Jurgen Habermas,* London: Heinemann.

McClelland, D. 1961, *The Achieving Society,* Princeton: Van Nostrand.

McKenzie, R. 1963, *British Political Parties,* London: Heinemann, (second edition).

McKenzie, R. and Silver, A. 1968, *Angels in Marble,* London: Heinemann.

McKinnon, C. 1989, "Calvinism and the Infallible Assurance of Grace: The Weber Thesis Reconsidered," *British Journal of Sociology,* 39 (pp. 143–177; see also pp. 178–210).

McLennan, J. 1865, *Primitive Marriage,* Edinburgh: Adam and Charles Black.

McRobbie, A. and Garber, J. 1976, "Girls and Subcultures," in Hall, S. and Jefferson, T., 1976.

Mead, G.H. 1934, *Mind, Self and Society,* Chicago: Chicago University Press.

Mead, L. 1985, *Beyond Entitlements,* New York: Macmillan.

Mead, M. 1935, *Sex and Temperament in Three Primitive Societies,* New York: Morrow.

Mennell, S. 1985, *All Manner of Food: Eating and Taste in England and France,* Oxford: Blackwell.

Merton, R. 1949, *Social Theory and Social Structure,* Glencoe, Illinois: Free Press. (third edition 1968).

Merton, R. 1957, "Bureaucratic Structure and Personality," in Merton, *Social Theory and Social Structure,* revised edition.

Merton, R., Reader, G., and Kendall, P. 1957, *The Student Physician,* Cambridge, Massachusetts: Harvard University Press.

Michels, R. 1911, *Political Parties,* New York: Collier (1962).

Miles, A. 1986, "Economism and Feminism: A Comment on the Domestic Labour Debate," in Hamilton, R., and Barrett, M., *The Politics of Diversity,* London: Verso.

Miliband, R. 1966, *The State in Capitalist Society,* London: Weidenfeld and Nicolson.

Mill, J.S. 1843, *A System of Logic,* London: Longmans (eighth edition).

Mill, J.S. 1859, *On Liberty,* London: Watts.

Millar, S. 1968, *The Psychology of Play,* Harmondsworth, England: Penguin.

Miller, S. 1960, "Comparative Social Mobility: Trend Report and a Bibliography," *Current Sociology,* 9.

Millett, K. 1970, *Sexual Politics,* New York: Doubleday.

Mills, C. 1940, "Situated Actions and Vocabularies of Motive," *American Sociological Review,* 5.

Mills, C. 1956, *The Power Elite,* New York: Oxford University Press.

Mills, C. 1959, *The Sociological Imagination,* New York: Oxford Univ. Press.

BIBLIOGRAPHY

Millward, N. and Stevens, M. 1986, *British Workplace Industrial Relations 1980–84: The DE/ESRC/PSI/ACAS Surveys*, Aldershot, England: Gower.

Mishan, E. 1967, *The Costs of Economic Growth*, London: Staple Press.

Mitchell, J. 1974, *Psychoanalysis and Feminism*, London: Allen Lane.

Montesquieu, Baron C. de, 1748, *The Spirit of the Laws*, New York: Harper.

Moore, B. 1967, *Social Origins of Dictatorship and Democracy: Lord and Peasant in the Making of the Modern World*, London: Allen Lane, The Penguin Press.

Moore, B. 1972, *Reflections on the Causes of Human Misery*, London: Allen Lane.

Moore, B. 1978, *Injustice: The Social Basis of Obedience and Revolt*, London: MacMillan.

Morgan, D. 1975, *Social Theory and the Family*, London: Routledge & Kegan Paul.

Morgan, G. 1986, *Images of Organization*, London: Sage.

Morgan, L. 1870, *Systems of Consanguinity and Affinity of the Human Family*, Washington, DC: Smithsonian Institution.

Morgan, M. 1985, *Sociological Approaches to Health and Medicine*, Beckenham, England: Croom Helm.

Morris, D. 1978, *Manwatching*, St. Albans: Triad/Panther.

Mort, F. 1980, "Sexuality: Regulation and Contestation," in Gay Left Collective (ed.), *Homosexuality: Power and Politics*, London: Allison and Busby.

Mosca, G. 1884, *Elementi di scienza politics* (English translation, *The Ruling Class*, New York: McGraw-Hill (1939).

Mouzelis, N. 1975, *Organization and Bureaucracy*, London: Routledge & Kegan Paul.

Mouzelis, N. 1986, *Politics in the Semi-Periphery: Early Parliamentarism and Late Industrialisation in the Balkans and the Latin America*, London: Macmillan.

Mouzelis, N. 1988, "Sociology of Development: Reflections on the Present Crisis," *Sociology*, 22.

Mulvey, L. 1975, "Visual Pleasure and Narrative Cinema," *Screen*, 16.

Mumford, E. 1980, "The Participative Design of Clerical Information Systems: Two Case Studies," in N. Bjorn-Anderson, *The Human Side of Information Processing*, Holland: IAG.

Mumford, E. and Banks, O. 1967, *The Computer and the Clerk*. London: Routledge & Kegan Paul.

Murdock, G. 1949, *Social Structure*, New York: Macmillan.

Murdock, G. 1967, *Ethnographic Atlas*, Pittsburgh: University of Pittsburgh Press.

Murphy, J., John, M., and Brown, H. 1984, *Dialogues and Debates in Social Psychology*, Milton Keynes: Open University Press.

Myrdal, G. et al. 1944, *An American Dilemma*, New York: Harper and Row.

Nachmias, D. and Nachmias, D. 1976, *Research Methods in Social*

Investigation, London: Edward Arnold.

Nadel, S. 1957, *The Theory of Social Structure,* London: Cohen and West.

Nairn, T. 1977, *The Break-Up of Britain,* London: New Left Books.

Narroll, R. 1964, "Ethnic Unit Classification," *Current Anthropology,* 5.

Nestle, J. 1981, "Butch-fem Relationships: Sexual Courage in the 1950s," *Heresies,* 3.

Neumann, F. 1942, *Behemoth,* New York: Harper Torch (translation 1963).

Neumann, S. 1956, "Toward a Comparative Study of Political Parties," in Neumann S. (ed.) *Modern Political Parties,* Chicago: University of Chicago Press.

Newby, H. 1977, *The Deferential Workers,* London: Allen Lane (Penguin, 1979).

Nichols, T. 1969, *Ownership, Control and Ideology,* London: Allen and Unwin.

Nichols, T. and Armstrong, P. 1976, *Workers Divided,* London: Fontana.

Nichols, T. and Beynon, H. 1977, *Living with Capitalism,* London: Routledge & Kegan Paul.

Nicolaus, M. 1972, "Sociology Liberation Movement," in Pateman, T. (ed.) *Counter Course: A Handbook of Course Criticism,* Harmondsworth, England: Penguin.

Northcott, J. 1988, *The Impact of Micro Electronics in Industry,* London: PSI.

Nozick, R. 1974, *Anarchy, State and Utopia,* New York: Basic Books.

Oakley, A. 1974, *Housewife,* London: Allen Lane.

O'Connor, J. 1973, *The Fiscal Crisis of the State,* New York: St Martin's Press.

Offe, C. 1985, *Disorganized Capitalism,* Cambridge, England: Polity Press.

Ogburn, W. 1964, *On Culture and Social Change: Selected Papers,* Chicago: Chicago University Press.

Okley, J. 1975, "Gypsy Women: Models in Conflict," in S. Ardener, (ed.) *Perceiving Women,* London: Dent.

O'Leary, B. 1989, *The Asiatic Mode of Production,* Oxford: Blackwell.

Ortega y Gasset, J. 1930, *The Revolt of the Masses,* London: Allen & Masses.

Osgood, C., Suci, G., and Tannenbaum, P. 1957, *The Measurement of Meaning,* Urbana, Illinois: University of Illinois Press.

Ouchi, N. 1981, *Theory Z: How American Business Can Meet the Japanese Challenge,* Reading, Massachusetts: Addison-Wesley.

Outhwaite, W. 1985, "Gadamer," in Skinner, Q. (ed.) *The Return of Grand Theory,* Cambridge, England: Cambridge University Press.

Packard, V. 1957, *The Hidden Persuaders,* New York: McKay (Penguin, 1961).

Packard, V. 1959, *The Status Seekers,* New York: McKay (Penguin, 1961).

Pahl, R. 1984, *Divisions of Labour,* Oxford: Basil Blackwell.

Pahl, R. and Gershuny, J. 1979, "Work Outside Employment–Some Preliminary Speculations," *New University Quarterly,* 34.

Pahl, R. and Gershuny, J. 1980, "Britain in the Decade of the Three Economies," *New Society,* January 3rd.

Pahl, R. and Winkler, J. 1974, "The Coming Corporatism," *New Society,* 10.

BIBLIOGRAPHY

Palmer, P. 1989, *Contemporary Women's Fiction,* London: Harvester.

Park, R. 1928, "Human Migration and the Marginal Man," *American Journal of Sociology,* 33.

Park, R. and Burgess, E. 1921 and 1924 (second edition), *Introduction to the Science of Sociology,* Chicago: University of Chicago Press.

Parker, S. 1971, *The Future of Work and Leisure,* London: MacGibbon and Kee.

Parkin, F. 1968, *Middle Class Radicalism,* Manchester: Manchester University Press.

Parkin, F. 1971, *Class Inequality and Political Order,* London: MacGibbon and Kee.

Parkin, F. 1974, "Strategies of Social Closure in Class Formation," in Parkin (ed.) *Social Analysis of the Class Structure,* London: Tavistock.

Parkin, F. 1979, *Marxism and Class Theory: A Bourgeois Critique,* London: Tavistock.

Parry, N. and Parry J. 1976, *The Rise of the Medical Profession,* London: Croom Helm.

Parsons, T. 1937, *The Structure of Social Action,* Glencoe, Illinois: Free Press (1949).

Parsons, T. 1939, "The Professions and Social Structure," *Social Forces,* 17, reprinted in *Essays in Sociological Theory,* Free Press (1954 and 1964, revised edition).

Parsons, T. 1951, *The Social System,* London: Routledge & Kegan Paul.

Parsons, T. 1956, "Suggestions for a Sociological Approach to the Theory of Organizations," *Administrative Science Quarterly,* 1.

Parsons, T. 1959, "The School Class as a Social System," in A. Halsey, et al. (1961) *Education, Economy and Society,* New York: Free Press.

Parsons, T. 1963, "On the Concept of Political Power," *Proceedings of the American Philosophical Society,* 107.

Parsons, T. 1964a, "Evolutionary Universals in Society," *American Sociological Review,* 29.

Parsons, T. 1964b, *Social Structure and Personality,* New York: Free Press.

Parsons, T. 1966, *Societies: Evolutionary and Comparative Perspectives,* Englewood Cliffs, New Jersey: Prentice Hall.

Parsons, T. 1971, *The System of Modern Societies,* Englewood Cliffs, New Jersey: Prentice Hall.

Parsons, T. 1977, *The Evolution of Societies,* Englewood Cliffs, New Jersey: Prentice Hall.

Parsons, T. and Bales, R. 1955, *Family: Socialization and Interaction Process,* London: Routledge (1956).

Parsons, T., Bales, R., and Shils, E. 1963, *Working Papers on the Theory of Action,* Glencoe, Illinois: Free Press.

Parsons, T. and Shils, E. 1951, *Towards a General Theory of Action,* Cambridge, Massachusetts: Harvard University Press.

THE AUTHORS

David Jary, BSc (Econ.) is Professor and Head of Department of Sociology at Staffordshire Polytechnic in England. Previously he was Senior Lecturer in Sociology as the University of Salford, and before that he was subject leader in Sociology at Manchester Polytechnic. His previously edited works include *The Middle Class in Politics* (with J. Garrard, M. Goldsmith and A. Oldfield), *Sport, Leisure and Social Relations* (with J. Horne and A. Tomlinson) and *Giddens' Theory of Structuration* (with C. Bryant).

Julia Jary, BSc (Soc.), BA, MA, PhD is part-time lecturer in Psychology at Staffordshire Polytechnic in England and also teaches general psychology and cognitive psychology for the Open University. Previously she has worked as a lecturer at the Universities of Manchester and Salford.

Wood, S. 1989, *The Transformation of Work,* London: Hutchinson.

Wood, S. and Elliott, R. 1977, "A Critical Evaluation of Fox's Radicalization of Industrial Relations Theory." *Sociology,* 11.

Woodfield, A. 1981 "Teleology," in W. Brynum, E. Brown, and R. Porter, *Dictionary of the History of Science,* London: MacMillan.

Woodward, J. 1965 (new edition 1970), *Industrial Organization: Theory and Practice,* London: Oxford University Press.

Worsley, P. 1968, *The Trumpet Shall Sound,* (revised edition), London: MacGibbon & Kee.

Worsley, P. 1984, *Three Worlds: Culture and World Development,* London: Weidenfeld and Nicolson.

Worsley, P. 1987, *New Introductory Sociology,* (third edition), London: Penguin.

Wright, E. 1978, *Class, Crises and the State,* London: New Left Books.

Wright, E. 1981, "The Value Controversy and Social Research," in T. Steedman, 1981.

Wright, E. 1983, "Giddens' Critique of Marxism," *New Left Review,* 138.

Wright, E. 1985, *Classes,* London: Verso.

Wright, E. 1989, *The Debate on Classes,* London: Verso.

Wrigley, E. (ed.) 1966, *An Introduction to English Historical Demography,* London: Weidenfeld and Nicolson.

Wrong, D. 1961, "The Oversocialized Conception of Man in Modern Sociology," *American Sociological Review,* 26 (reprinted in Demerath & Peterson, 1967).

Young, J. 1971, *The Drugtakers: The Social Meaning of Drug Use,* London: MacGibbon and Key.

Young, J. 1980, "The Development of Criminology in Britain," *British Journal of Criminology,* 28.

Young, M. 1971, *Knowledge and Control,* London: Collier-Macmillan.

Young, M. and Wilmott, P. 1957, *Family and Kinship in East London,* Harmondsworth, England: Penguin (1960).

Young, M. and Wilmott, P. 1973 *The Symmetrical Family,* Harmondsworth, England: Penguin.

Zeitlin, M. 1974, "Corporate Ownership and Control: The Large Corporation and the Capitalist Class," *American Journal of Sociology,* 80.

Zeitlin, M. 1977, *American Society Inc.: Studies of the Social Structure and Political Economy of the United States,* (second edition) Chicago: Rand McNally.

Zetterberg, H. 1965, *On Theory and Verification in Sociology,* (third edition), Totowa, New Jersey: Bedminster Press.

Zweig, F. 1961, *The Worker in an Affluent Society: Family Life and Industry,* London: Heinemann.

Patterson, O. 1982, *Slavery and Social Death: a Comparative Study*, Cambridge, Massachusetts and London: Harvard University Press.

Pavlov, I. 1911, *Conditioned Reflexes*, Oxford: Oxford University Press (1927).

Payne, G. 1989, "Mobility and Bias: A Reply to Saunders," *Network*, 45.

Peach, P. 1981, *Ethnic Segregation in Cities*, London: Croom Helm.

Pearce, R. 1983, "Sharecropping: Towards a Marxist View," in T. Byres (ed.) *Sharecropping and Sharecroppers*, London: Frank Cass.

Pearson, G. 1983, *Hooligan, A History of Respectable Fears*, London: Macmillan.

Perrow, C. 1979, *Complex Organizations: A Critical Essay*, Illinois: Scott Forseman.

Peters, T. and Waterman, R. 1982, *In Search of Excellence*, New York: Harper and Row.

Pettigrew, A. 1973, *The Politics of Organizational Decision-Making*, London: Tavistock.

Phillips, L. 1973, *Bayesian Statistics for Social Scientists*, London: Nelson.

Piaget, J. 1932, *The Moral Judgment of the Child*, London: Routledge & Kegan Paul.

Pickvance, C. 1976, *Urban Sociology*, London: Tavistock.

Pickvance, C. 1984, "Voluntary Associations," in R. Burgess, 1986.

PICT, 1985, "A Report of the Project on Information Technologies," Economic and Social Research Center.

Pike, K. 1967, *Language in Relation to a Unified Theory of the Structure of Human Behavior*, Part 1, Preliminary Edition, Glendale Summer Institute of Linguistics.

Pinker, R. 1971, *Social Theory and Social Policy*, London: Heinemann.

Pinto-Duschinsky, M. 1985, "Corruption," in Kuper, A. and Kuper, J., 1985.

Piore, M. and Sabel, C. 1984, *The Second Industrial Divide*, New York: Basic Books.

Pippin, R., Feenberg, A., and Webel, C. (eds.), 1988, *Marcuse: Critical Theory and the Promise of Utopia*, London: Macmillan.

Policy Studies Institute, 1983, *Police and People in London*, (4 volumes) London: Policy Studies Institute.

Pollart, A. 1981, *Girls, Wives, Factory Lives*, London: Macmillan.

Polsky, N. 1969, *Hustlers, Beats and Others*, Harmondsworth, England: Penguin.

Poole, M. 1966, *Workers' Participation in Industry*, London: Routledge.

Popitz, H. et al. 1957, "The Worker's Image of Society," in T. Burns (ed.) *Industrial Man*, Harmondsworth, England: Penguin.

Popper, K. 1934, *The Logic of Scientific Discovery*, London: Hutchinson (1959).

Popper, K. 1957, *The Poverty of Historicism*, London: Routledge & Kegan Paul.

Post, K. 1972, "'Peasantization' and Rural Political Movements in West Africa," *European Journal of Sociology*, 13.

Post, K. and Wright, P. 1989, *Socialism and Underdevelopment*, London: Routledge.

BIBLIOGRAPHY

Poulantzas, N. 1973, *Political Power and Social Classes,* London: New Left Books.

Poulantzas, N. 1974, *Fascism and Dictatorship,* London: New Left Books.

Pribicevic, B. 1959, *The Shop Stewards' Movement and Workers' Control,* Oxford: Blackwell.

Price, R. and Bains, G. 1988, "The Labour Force," in A. Halsey (ed.) *British Social Trends Since 1990: A Guide to the Changing Social Structure of Britain,* (second edition), London: Macmillan.

Prothro, G. and Grigg, C., 1960, "Fundamental Principles of Democracy," *Journal of Politics,* 22.

Pugh, D. and Hickson, D. 1968, "The Comparative Study of Organizations," in D. Pym (ed.) *Industrial Society,* Harmondsworth, England: Penguin.

Purcell, K. 1986, "Work, Employment and Unemployment," in R. Burgess, 1986.

Quine, W. 1960, *Word and Object,* Cambridge, Massachusetts: MIT Press.

Quine, W. 1987, *Quiddities: an Intermittently Philosophical Dictionary,* Harmondsworth, England: Penguin Books.

Rapoport, A. (ed.) 1968, "Introduction" to *Clausewitz,* Harmondsworth, England: Penguin.

Redclift, M. 1987, *Sustainable Development: Exploring the Contradictions,* London: Methuen.

Redfield, R. 1941, *The Folk Culture of Yucatan,* Chicago: Chicago University Press.

Redfield, R. 1956, *Peasant Society and Culture,* Chicago: Chicago University Press.

Reid, I. 1986, *The Sociology of School and Education,* London: Fontana.

Reimer, E. 1971, *School Is Dead: An Essay on Alternatives in Education,* Harmondsworth, England: Penguin.

Renner, K. 1953, "The Service Class," in T. Bottomore and P. Goode (eds.), *Austro-Marxism,* 1978, Oxford: Oxford University Press.

Rex, J. 1961, *Key Problems of Sociological Theory,* London: Routledge & Kegan Paul.

Rex, J. 1967, *Race, Community and Conflict,* Oxford: Oxford University Press.

Rex, J. 1970, *Race, Colonialism and the City,* London: Routledge & Kegan Paul.

Rex, J. (ed.) 1973, *Discovering Sociology,* London: Routledge & Kegan Paul.

Rex, J. 1974, *Sociology and the Demystification of the World,* London: Routledge & Kegan Paul.

Rex, J. 1986, *Race and Ethnicity,* Milton Keynes: Open University Press.

Rex, J. and Tomlinson, S. 1973, *Colonial Immigrants in a British City,* London: Routledge & Kegan Paul.

Rey, P-P. 1975, "The Lineage Mode of Production," *Critique of Anthropology,* 3.

Rich, A. 1980, "Compulsory Heterosexuality and Lesbian Existence," *Signs,* 5.

Richardson, L. 1960, *Statistics of Deadly Quarrels,* London: Stevens.

Ricoeur, P. 1981, *Hermeneutics and the Human Sciences,* Cambridge, England: Cambridge University Press.

Riley, M. 1963, *Sociological Research: A Case Approach*, Vol.1. New York: Harcourt, Brace and World.

Roberts, B. 1978, *Cities of Peasants*, London: Arnold.

Robertson, H. 1933, *Aspects of the Rise of Economic Individualism*, Cambridge, England: Cambridge University Press.

Robinson, W. 1950, "Ecological Correlation and Behavior of Individuals," *American Sociological Review*, 15.

Robinson, W. 1951, "The Logical Structure of Analytical Induction," *American Sociological Review*, 16.

Robinson, W. et al. 1968, *Measures of Political Attitude*, University of Michigan.

Roemer, J. 1982, *A General Theory of Exploitation and Class*, Cambridge, Massachusetts: Harvard University Press.

Roethlisberger, F. and Dickson, W. 1939, *Management and the Worker*, Cambridge, Massachusetts: Harvard University Press.

Rogers, C. 1951, *Client-Centered Therapy*, New York: Houghton.

Rogers, C. 1969, *Freedom to Learn*, Columbus, Ohio: Charles Merrill.

Rogers, C. 1970, *Encounter Groups*, Harmondsworth, England: Penguin.

Rogers, C. 1970, *Encounter Groups*, New York: Harper and Row.

Rogers, C. 1986, *Freedom to Learn for the Eighties*, Columbus, Ohio: Charles Merrill.

Rogers, C.D. 1983, *The Family Tree Detective*, Manchester, England: Manchester University Press.

Rogers, E. 1983, *Diffusion of Innovations*, third edition, New York: Free Press.

Rokeach, M. 1960, *The Open and Closed Mind*, New York: Basic Books.

Rorschach, H. 1921, *Psychodiagnostics: A Diagnostic Test Based on Perception*, Berne: Huber (translated 1942).

Rose, D. (ed.) 1988, *Social Stratification and Economic Change*, London: Hutchinson.

Rose, H. 1986, "Women's Work: Women's Knowledge," in J. Mitchell and A. Oakley, (eds.) *Essay on Sex Equality*, Chicago: University of Chicago Press.

Rose, M. 1988, *Industrial Behavior*, Harmondsworth, England: Penguin (second edition, first edition 1975).

Rose, R. (ed.) 1960, *Must Labor Lose?* Harmondsworth, England: Penguin.

Rose, S. 1973, *The Conscious Brain*, London: Weidenfeld and Nicolson.

Rostow, W. 1960, *The Stages of Economic Growth, A Non-Communist Manifesto*, Cambridge, England: Cambridge University Press.

Routh, G. 1980, *Occupation and Pay in Great Britain*, London: Macmillan.

Rowbotham, S. 1972, *Women, Resistance and Revolution*, New York: Penguin.

Rowbotham, S. 1973, *Women's Consciousness, Man's World*, Harmondsworth, England: Penguin.

Roxborough, I. 1984, "Unity and Diversity in Latin American History," *Journal of Latin American Studies*, 16.

Rubenstein, R. 1987, *Alchemists of Revolutions: Terrorism in the Modern*

BIBLIOGRAPHY

World, New York: Basic Books.

Rubery, J. 1978, "Structured Labour Markets, Worker Organization and Low Pay," *Cambridge Journal of Economics*, 2.

Runciman, W. 1966, *Relative Deprivation and Social Justice*, London: Routledge & Kegan Paul.

Runciman, W. 1983, *A Treatise on Social Theory*, Vol. 1, Cambridge, England: Cambridge University Press.

Runciman, W. 1989, *A Treatise on Social Theory*, Vol. 2, Cambridge, England: Cambridge University Press.

Rushton, J. and Sorrentino, R. (eds.) 1981, *Altruism and Helping Behavior: Social, Personality and Developmental Perspectives*, Hillsdale, New Jersey.

Sacks, H., Schegloff, E., and Jefferson, G. 1974, "A Simplest Systematics for the Organization of Turn-Taking for Conversation," *Language*, 50.

Sahlins, M. 1971, *Culture and Practical Reason*, Chicago: Aldine.

Sahlins, M. 1972, *Stone Age Economics*, Chicago: Aldine.

Sahlins, M. and Service, E. 1960, *Evolution and Culture*, Ann Arbor, Michigan: University of Michigan Press.

Said, E. 1978, *Orientalism*, Harmondsworth, England: Penguin (1985).

Sainsbury, P. 1955, *Suicide in London: An Ecological Study*, London: Chapman.

Sainsbury, P. and Barraclough, B. 1968, "Differences Between Suicide Rates," *Nature*, 220.

Samuelson, K. 1961, *Religion and Economic Action: A Critique of Max Weber*, New York: Harper.

Sarah, E. 1982, "Towards a Reassessment of Feminist History," *Women's Studies International Forum*, 5.

Sayers, J. et al. (eds.) 1987, *Engels Revisited: New Feminist Essays*, London: Tavistock.

Scarman, Lord 1981, *The Brixton Disorders*, London: HMSO.

Scase, R. and Goffee, R. 1982, *The Entrepreneurial Middle Class*, London: Croom Helm.

Scheff, T. 1966, *Being Mentally Ill*, Chicago: Aldine.

Schermer, H. 1988, *Towards a Sociological Model of the Stranger*, Staffordshire Polytechnic, Department of Sociology Occasional Paper, Number 9.

Schumacher, E. 1973, *Small Is Beautiful*, Harmondsworth, England: Penguin.

Schutz, A. 1962–6, *Collected Papers*, Vol. 1, The Hague: Nijhoff.

Schutz, A. 1967, *The Phenomenology of the Social World*, London: Heinemann, (original German edition 1932).

Schutz, A. and Luckmann, T. 1973, *The Structures of the Life World*, London: Heinemann (1974).

Scocpol, T. 1979, *States and Social Revolutions: A Comparative Analysis of France, Russia and China*, Cambridge, England: Cambridge University Press.

Scott, J. 1979, *Corporations, Classes and Capitalism*, London: Hutchinson.

Scott, J. 1982, *The Upper Class*, London: Macmillan.

Scott, J.C. 1985, *Weapons of the Weak: Everyday Forms of Peasant Resistance*, New Haven and London: Yale University Press.

Scott, R.L. 1977, "Communication as an International Social System," *Human Communication Research*, 3.

Scott, R. and Shore, A. 1979, *Why Sociology Does Not Apply–A Study of the Uses of Sociology in Social Policy*, New York: Elsevier.

Scraton, P. 1982, "Policing and Institutionalized Racism on Merseyside," in D. Cowell et al. 1982.

Scraton, P. 1985, *The State of the Police*, London: Pluto.

Scruton, R. 1986, *Sexual Desires: A Philosophical Investigation*, London: Weidenfeld.

Searle, J. 1969, *Expression and Meaning: Speech Act Theory and Pragmatics*, New York: World.

Searle, J. 1984, *Minds, Brains and Science*, London: Penguin Books.

Sebestyen, A. 1978, in A. Oakley, *Subject Women*, Martin Robertson, 1984.

Sebestyen, A. 1979, "Tendencies in the Women's Liberation Movement," in *Feminist Practice: Notes from the Tenth Year*, London: Radical Feminist Collective.

Secord, P. and Backman, C. 1964, *Social Psychology*, New York: McGraw-Hill.

Selznik, P. 1966, *TVA and the Grass Roots*, New York: Harper Torch Books.

Selvin, H. 1958, "A Critique of Tests of Significance in Survey Research," *American Sociological Review*, 23.

Sen, A. 1981, *Poverty and Famines: An Essay on Entitlement and Deprivation*, Oxford: Clarendon Press.

Seymour-Smith, C. 1986, *Macmillan Dictionary of Anthropology*, London: Macmillan.

Shanin, T. 1982, "Defining Peasants: Conceptualizations and Deconceptualizations," *Sociological Review*, 30.

Shanin, T. (ed.) 1988, *Peasants and Peasant Societies*, Harmondsworth, England: Penguin.

Sharp, R. and Green, A. 1975, *Education and Social Control*, Routledge & Kegan Paul.

Shaw, C. 1930, *The Jack Roller*, Chicago: University of Chicago Press.

Shaw, C. and McKay, H. 1929, *Juvenile Delinquency and Urban Areas*, Chicago: University of Chicago Press.

Shaw, M. 1985, *Marxist Sociology Revisited: Critical Assessments*, London: Macmillan.

Sherif, M. 1935, "A Study of Some Social Factors in Perception," *Archives of Psychology*, 27.

Shils, E. and Young, M. 1953, "The Meaning of the Coronation," *Sociological Review*, 1.

Siltanen, J. and Stanworth, M. 1984, *Women and the Public Sphere*, London: Hutchinson.

BIBLIOGRAPHY

Silverman, D. 1970, *The Theory of Organizations,* London: Heinemann.

Simey, M. 1982, "Police Authorities and Accountability," in D. Cowell et al. 1982.

Simmel, G. 1900, *The Philosophy of Money,* (ed. D. Frisby), London: Routledge & Kegan Paul (1978).

Simmel, G. 1903, "Metropolis and Mental Life," in K. Woolf (ed.) 1950.

Simmel, G. 1955, *Conflict and the Web of Group Affiliations,* Glencoe, Illinois: Free Press (originally chapters 4 & 6 of *Sociologie,* 1908).

Simon, H. 1957a, *Models of Man,* New York: Wiley.

Simon, H. 1957b, *Administrative Behavior,* New York: Macmillan.

Sinfield, A. 1981, *What Unemployment Means,* Oxford: Martin Robertson.

Skinner, B. 1953, *Science and Human Behavior,* New York: Macmillan.

Skinner, B. 1957, *Verbal Behavior,* New York: Appleton-Century-Crofts.

Small, A. 1905, *General Sociology,* Chicago: University of Chicago Press.

Small, A. 1924, *The Origins of Sociology,* Chicago: University of Chicago Press.

Smart, C. 1976, *Women, Crime and Criminology,* London: Routledge & Kegan Paul.

Smelser, N. 1962, *Collective Behavior,* London: Routledge & Kegan Paul.

Smelser, N. 1968, *Essays in Sociological Explanation,* Englewood Cliffs, New Jersey: Prentice Hall.

Smith, A. 1776, *An Inquiry into the Nature and Causes of the Wealth of Nations,* London: Routledge.

Smith, D. 1983, *Barrington Moore Jr: Violence, Morality and Political Change,* London: Macmillan.

Sohn-Rethel, A. 1978, *Intellectual and Manual Labour,* London: Macmillan.

Southall, A. 1954, *Alur Society: a Study of Processes and Types of Domination,* Cambridge, England: Heffer.

Spencer, H. 1881, *Principles of Psychology,* London: Williams and Norgate.

Spencer, H. 1884, *The Man Versus the State,* (ed. D. Macrae), Harmondsworth, England: Penguin (1969).

Spencer, H. 1893, *Principles of Sociology,* (3 volumes, third edition), Williams & Norgate.

Spencer, H. 1971, in K. Thompson and J. Tunstall, *Sociological Perspectives: Selected Readings,* Harmondsworth, England: Penguin.

Spender, D. 1980, *Man-Made Language,* London: Routledge & Kegan Paul.

Spooner, B. 1973, *The Cultural Ecology of Pastoral Nomads.*

Sraffa, P. 1960, *The Production of Commodities by Means of Commodities,* London: Cambridge University Press.

Stacey, M. 1969, "The Myth of Community Studies," *British Journal of Sociology,* 20.

Stanley, L. and Wise, S. 1983, *Breaking Out: Feminist Consciousness and Feminist Research,* London: Routledge & Kegan Paul.

Stanworth, P. and Giddens, A. 1974, "An Economic Elite: A Demographic Profile of Company Chairmen," in P. Stanworth and A. Giddens (eds.) *Elites*

and Power in British Society, Cambridge, England: Cambridge University Press.

Stavenhagen, R. 1975, *Social Classes in Agrarian Societies*, New York: Anchor Press.

Steadman-Jones, G. 1975, "Class Struggle and the Industrial Revolution," in G. Steadman-Jones, *Languages of Class*, Cambridge, England: Cambridge University Press.

Steedman, I. et al. 1981, *The Value Controversy*, London: Verso.

Stevens, S. 1944, "On the Theory of Scales of Measurement," *Science*, 103.

Stevens, S. 1951, "Mathematics, Measurements and Psychophysics," in S. Stevens, (ed.) *Handbook of Experimental Psychology*. New York: Wiley.

Stouffer, S. 1955, *Communism, Conformity and Civil Liberties*, New York: Doubleday.

Stouffer, S. et al. 1949, *The American Soldier*, Princeton: Princeton University Press.

Summer, W. 1906, *Folkways*, New York: Doubleday (1959).

Summers, A. 1979, "A Home from Home–Women's Philanthropic Work in the Nineteenth Century," in S. Burnham, (ed.) *Fit Work for Women*, London: Croom Helm.

Suttles, G. 1970, "Friendship as a Social Institution," in G. McCall et al., *Social Relationships*, Chicago.

Swift, D. 1967, "Social Class, Mobility, Ideology and 11+ Success," *British Journal of Sociology*, 17.

Sykes, G. and Matza, D. 1957, "Techniques of Neutralization," *American Sociological Review*, 22.

Szalai, A. 1972, *The Use of Time*, The Hague: Mouton.

Szasz, T. 1961, *The Myth of Mental Illness*, London: Secker and Warburg.

Szasz, T. 1970, *The Manufacture of Madness*, London: Paladin.

Szasz, T. 1973, *Ideology and Insanity*, New York: Calder and Boyers.

Tawney, 1926, *Religion and the Rise of Capitalism*, Harmondsworth, England: Penguin (1938).

Taylor, I. 1971, "Football Mad," in Dunning, E. (ed.) *The Sociology of Sport*, London: Frank Cass.

Taylor, J. 1979, *From Modernization to Modes of Production: A Critique of the Sociologies of Development and Underdevelopment*, London: Macmillan.

Taylor, I., Walton, P. and Young, J. 1973, *The New Criminology*, London: Routledge & Kegan Paul.

Taylor, L. 1981, *Justice for Victims of Crime*, London: Macmillan.

Taylor, M. 1983, "Ordinal and Interval Scaling," *Journal of the Market Research Society*, 25.

Teichler, U. 1988, *Changing Patterns of the Higher Education System*, London: Jessica Kingsley Publishers.

Terray, E. 1972, *Marxism and "Primitive" Societies*, New York: Monthly Review Press.

BIBLIOGRAPHY

Thomas, W. (with Thomas, D.) 1928, *The Child in America*, New York: Knopf.

Thompson, E. 1967, "Time, Work-Discipline and Industrial Capitalism," *Past and Present*, 38.

Thompson, E. 1978, "The Poverty of Theory," in E. Thompson, *The Poverty of Theory and Other Essays*, London: Merlin.

Thompson, E. 1982, *Zero Option*, London: Merlin.

Thompson, E. 1982, *Beyond the Cold War*, London: Merlin.

Thompson, K. 1976, *Auguste Comte: The Foundations of Sociology*, London: Nelson.

Thompson, P. 1989, *The Nature of Work*, (second edition), London: Macmillan.

Thompson, T. 1981, *Edwardian Childhoods*, London: Routledge & Kegan Paul.

Thorndike, E. 1911, *Animal Intelligence*, New York: Macmillan.

Thorner, D., Ferblay, B., and Smith, R. 1966, *Chayanov on the Theory of Peasant Economy*, Homewood, Illinois: Richard D. Irwin.

Thurstone, L. and Chave, E. 1929, *The Measurement of Attitude*, Chicago: University of Chicago Press.

Toffler, A. 1970, *Future Shock*, London: Bodley Head.

Tönnies, F. 1887, *Gemeinshaft und Gesellschaft* (translated as *Community and Society*), London: Routledge (1955).

Touraine, A. 1971, *The Post-Industrial Society*, New York: Random House.

Trist, E., Higgins, G., Murray, H., and Pollock, A. 1963, *Organizational Choice*, London: Tavistock.

Troeltsch, E. 1912, *The Social Teachings of the Christian Churches*, London: Allen and Unwin (1956).

Trow, M. 1962, "Reflections on the Transition from Elite to Mass Higher Education," *Daedalus*, 90.

Tumin, M. 1953, "Some Principles of Social Stratification: A Critical Analysis," *American Sociological Review*, 18.

Turiel, E. 1983, *The Development of Social Knowledge*, Cambridge, England: Cambridge University Press.

Turner, R. 1960, "Sponsored and Contest Mobility in the School System," *American Sociological Review*, 25.

Tylor, E. 1871, *Primitive Culture*, New York: Harper (1958).

Urry, J. 1973, *Reference Groups and the Theory of Revolution*, London: Routledge & Kegan Paul.

Urry, J. 1981, *The Anatomy of Capitalist Societies*, London: Macmillan.

Von Neumann, J. and Morgenstern, O. 1944, *Theory of Games and Economic Behavior*, Princeton: Princeton University Press.

Von Wright, G. 1971, *Explanation and Understanding*, London: Routledge & Kegan Paul.

Von Wright, G. 1983, *Philosophical Papers, Vol.1: Practical Reason*, Oxford: Basil Blackwell.

Voslensky, M. 1984, *Nomenklatura: Anatomy of the Soviet Ruling Class*, London: Bodley Head.

Walby, S. 1986, *Patriarchy at Work*, Cambridge, England: Polity Press.

Walker, A. 1980, "Coming Apart," in L. Lederer (ed.) *Take Back the Night: Women as Pornography*, New York: Morrow.

Walker, A. 1983, *In Search of Our Mother's Gardens*, New York: Harper and Row.

Wallerstein, I. 1974, *The Modern World System: Capitalist Agriculture and the Origins of the European World-Economy in the Sixteenth Century*, London: Academic Press.

Wallerstein, I. 1979, *The Capitalist World-Economy*, Cambridge, England: Cambridge University Press.

Wallerstein, I. 1980, *The Modern World System: Mercantilism and the Consolidation of the European World-Economy, 1600–1750*. London: Academic Press.

Wallerstein, I. 1983, *Historical Capitalism*, London: Verso.

Walton, J. 1984, *Reluctant Rebels: Comparative Studies of Revolution and Underdevelopment*, New York: Columbia University Press.

Walzer, M. 1966, *The Revolution of the Saints: A Study in the Origins of Radical Politics*, London: Weidenfeld & Nicolson.

Warde, A. 1990, "Introduction to the Sociology of Consumption," *Sociology*, 24.

Warren, B. 1980, *Imperialism: Pioneer of Capitalism*, London: Verso.

Watt, M. 1961, *Islam and the Integration of Society*, London: Routledge & Kegan Paul.

Weber, M. 1912, *The City*, Glencoe, Illinois: Free Press 1958.

Weber, M. 1922, *Wirtschaft und Gesellschaft*, translated as *Economy and Society: An Outline of Interpretive Sociology*, New York: Bedminster Press (1968) (translated by G. Roth and G. Wittich).

Weber, M. 1930, *The Protestant Ethic and the Spirit of Capitalism*, London: Allen and Unwin, (original German edition 1904–5, revised edition 1920).

Weber, M. 1949, *The Methodology of the Social Sciences*, New York: Free Press (original German 1903–17).

Weber, M. 1951, *Religion of China*, Glencoe, Illinois: Free Press (original German 1920–1).

Weber, M. 1952, *Ancient Judaism*, Glencoe, Illinois: Free Press (original German 1920–21).

Weber, M. 1958, *The Religion of India*, New York: Macmillan, (original German 1920–1).

Weber, M. 1963, *The Sociology of Religion*, Boston, Massachusetts: Beacon (original German 1922).

Weeks, J. 1977, *Coming Out: Homosexual Politics in Britain from the Nineteenth Century to the Present*, London: Quartet Books.

Weeks, J. 1985, *Sexuality and Its Discontents*, London: Routledge & Kegan Paul.

BIBLIOGRAPHY

Weiner, N. 1949, *Cybernetics: or Control and Communication in Man and Machine*, Cambridge, Massachusetts: MIT Press.

Weinstein, A. and Gatell, F., 1979, *American Negro Slavery*, Oxford: Oxford University Press (third edition).

Weizenbaum, J. 1984, *Computer Power and Human Reason* Harmondsworth, England: Penguin.

Westergaard, J. and Resler H. 1975, *Class in a Capitalist Society*, London: Heinemann.

White, G. 1983, "Chinese Development Strategy After Mao," in G. White et al. (eds.) 1983, *Revolutionary Socialist Development in the Third World*, Brighton, England: Wheatsheaf Books.

Whitley, R. 1974, "The City and Industry," in P. Stanworth and A. Giddens, (eds.) *Elites and Power in British Society*, Cambridge, England: Cambridge University Press.

Whyte, W. 1955, *Street Corner Society*, Chicago: Chicago University Press.

Whyte, W. 1956, *The Organization Man*, Harmondsworth, England: Penguin.

Wilkins, L. 1965, "Some Sociological Factors in Drug Addiction Control," in B. Rosenberg, I. Bernard, and F. Howlen (eds.), *Mass Society in Crisis*, New York: Free Press.

Wilkins, L. 1975, *Social Deviance*, London: Tavistock.

Williams, R. 1976, *Keywords*, London: Fontana (second edition 1983).

Williams, R. 1973, *The Country and the City*, London: Chatto and Windus.

Williamson, J. 1978, *Decoding Advertisements, Ideology and Meaning in Advertising*, London and New York: Marion Boyars.

Willis, P. 1977, *Learning to Labour*, Farnborough, England: Saxon House.

Wilson, B. 1967, *Patterns of Sectarianism*, London: Heinemann.

Wilson, B. 1970, *Religious Sects*, London: Weidenfield & Nicolson.

Wilson, B. 1973, *Magic and the Millennium*, London: Heinemann.

Wilson, E. 1975, *Sociobiology: The New Synthesis*, Cambridge Massachusetts: Harvard University Press.

Wilson, H. and Herbert, G. 1978, *Parents and Children in the Inner City*, London: Routledge & Kegan Paul.

Winch, P. 1958, *The Idea of Social Science*, London: Routledge & Kegan Paul.

Wirth, L. 1938, "Urbanism as a Way of Life," *American Journal of Sociology*, 44.

Wittfogel, K. 1955, *Oriental Despotism*, New Haven: Yale University Press.

Wolf, E. 1966, *Peasants*, Englewood Cliffs, New Jersey: Prentice Hall.

Wolf, E. 1971, *Peasant Wars of the Twentieth Century*. London: Faber & Faber.

Wolff, K. (ed.) 1950, *The Sociology of Georg Simmel*, New York, Free Press.

Wolpe, H. 1972, "Capitalism and Cheap Labour Power in South Africa: From Segregation to Apartheid," *Economy and Society*, 1.

Womack, jr. J. 1969, *Zapata and the Mexican Revolution*, London: Thames & Hudson.